**Wiley
CMAexcel Learning System
Exam Review 2015**

About IMA® (Institute of Management Accountants)

IMA®, the association of accountants and financial professionals in business, is one of the largest and most respected associations focused exclusively on advancing the management accounting profession. Globally, IMA supports the profession through research, the CMA® (Certified Management Accountant) program, continuing education, networking, and advocacy of the highest ethical business practices. IMA has a global network of more than 65,000 members in 120 countries and 300 local chapter communities. IMA provides localized services through its offices in Montvale, NJ, USA; Zurich, Switzerland; Dubai, UAE; and Beijing, China. For more information about IMA, please visit www.imanet.org.

Wiley CMAexcel Learning System Exam Review 2015

Self-Study Guide

Part 1: Financial Reporting, Planning, Performance, and Control

Cover Design by David Riedy
Cover image: © iStock.com/turtleteeth

Copyright © 2014 by Institute of Management Accountants. All rights reserved.
Published by John Wiley & Sons, Inc., Hoboken, New Jersey.
Published simultaneously in Canada.

These materials are copyrighted and may not be reproduced in any form or used in any way to create derivative works. Any reproduction, reuse, or distribution of CMA Learning System® materials without prior written permission from the Institute of Management Accountants (IMA) is illegal and a material violation of the *IMA Statement of Ethical Professional Practice*.

Any Certified Management Accountant (CMA) or CMA candidate who reproduces, reuses, or distributes CMA Learning System® materials or content in any form without prior authorization from IMA is subject to legal action and will be reported to the Institute of Certified Management Accountants (ICMA) and immediately expelled from the IMA and CMA program.

It is your responsibility to ensure that any CMA exam review materials that you are using have been provided to you through authorized channels or personnel. If you are in doubt about the authenticity of your materials or question the means by which they have been provided to you, contact IMA customer service at (800) 638-4427 in the U.S. or +1 (201) 573-9000.

This material is designed for learning purposes and is distributed with the understanding that the publisher and authors are not offering legal or professional services.

No part of this publication may be reproduced, stored in a retrieval system, or transmitted in any form or by any means, electronic, mechanical, photocopying, recording, scanning, or otherwise, except as permitted under Section 107 or 108 of the 1976 United States Copyright Act, without either the prior written permission of the Publisher, or authorization through payment of the appropriate per-copy fee to the Copyright Clearance Center, Inc., 222 Rosewood Drive, Danvers, MA 01923, (978) 750-8400, fax (978) 646-8600, or on the Web at www.copyright.com. Requests to the Publisher for permission should be addressed to the Permissions Department, John Wiley & Sons, Inc., 111 River Street, Hoboken, NJ 07030, (201) 748-6011, fax (201) 748-6008, or online at www.wiley.com/go/permissions.

Limit of Liability/Disclaimer of Warranty: While the publisher and author have used their best efforts in preparing this book, they make no representations or warranties with respect to the accuracy or completeness of the contents of this book and specifically disclaim any implied warranties of merchantability or fitness for a particular purpose. No warranty may be created or extended by sales representatives or written sales materials. The advice and strategies contained herein may not be suitable for your situation. You should consult with a professional where appropriate. Neither the publisher nor author shall be liable for any loss of profit or any other commercial damages, including but not limited to special, incidental, consequential, or other damages.

For general information on our other products and services or for technical support, please contact our Customer Care Department within the United States at (800) 762-2974, outside the United States at (317) 572-3993 or fax (317) 572-4002.

Wiley also publishes its books in a variety of electronic formats. Some content that appears in print may not be available in electronic books. For more information about Wiley products, visit our web site at www.wiley.com.

Library of Congress Cataloging-in-Publication Data

Wiley CMA exam review learning system.
    v. cm.
    Contents: pt. 1. Financial reporting, planning, performance, and control—pt. 2. Financial decision making.
    Includes bibliographical references and index.
    ISBN 978-1-118-95616-8 (Part 1, 1-year access)
    ISBN 978-1-118-95618-2 (Part 2, 1-year access)
    ISBN 978-1-118-99529-7 (Part 1, 2-year access)
    ISBN 978-1-118-99533-4 (Part 2, 2-year access)
    ISBN 978-1-118-95615-1 (Part 1, no pin)
    ISBN 978-1-118-95617-5 (Part 2, no pin)
    ISBN 978-1-118-95624-3 (Part 1 + OIR, 1-year access)
    ISBN 978-1-118-95625-0 (Part 2 + OIR, 1-year access)
    ISBN 978-1-118-99535-8 (Part 1 + OIR, 2-year access)
    ISBN 978-1-118-99542-6 (Part 2 + OIR, 2-year access)
      1. Accounting—Examinations—Study guides. 2. Accounting—Examinations, questions, etc.
I. Title: Wiley Certified Management Accountant exam review learning system.   II. Title: CMA exam review learning system.
    HF5661.W499 2014
    657.076—dc23

2012022854

Printed in the United States of America

10 9 8 7 6 5 4 3 2 1

Contents

Acknowledgments of Subject Matter Experts	ix
Candidate Study Information	xi
How to Use the Wiley CMAexcel Learning System	xv
Create a Study Plan	xix
Introduction	1

Section A
External Financial Reporting Decisions — 3

Topic 1:	Financial Statements	25
Topic 2:	Recognition, Measurement, Valuation, and Disclosure	45
Practice Questions: External Financial Reporting Decisions		203

Section B
Planning, Budgeting, and Forecasting — 211

Topic 1:	Strategic Planning	233
Topic 2:	Budgeting Concepts	273
Topic 3:	Forecasting Techniques	291
Topic 4:	Budgeting Methodologies	307
Topic 5:	Annual Profit Plan and Supporting Schedules	319
Topic 6:	Top-Level Planning and Analysis	347
Practice Questions: Planning, Budgeting, and Forecasting		365

Section C
Performance Management — 375

Topic 1:	Cost and Variance Measures	391
Topic 2:	Responsibility Centers and Reporting Segments	425
Topic 3:	Performance Measures	437

Practice Questions: Performance Management — 465

Section D
Cost Management — 475

Topic 1:	Measurement Concepts	495
Topic 2:	Costing Systems	521
Topic 3:	Overhead Costs	553
Topic 4:	Supply Chain Management	571
Topic 5:	Business Process Improvement	591

Practice Questions: Cost Management — 609

Section E
Internal Controls — 621

Topic 1:	Governance, Risk, and Compliance	637
Topic 2:	Internal Auditing	661
Topic 3:	Systems Controls and Security Measures	675

Practice Questions: Internal Controls — 697

Essay Exam Support Materials — 703

Essay Exam Study Tips — 707

Examples of Essay Question Answers — 709

Practice Essay Questions and Answers — 719

Answers to Section Practice Questions — 801

Appendix A: ICMA Learning Outcome Statements—Part 1 — 869

Bibliography and References — 885

Index — 889

Acknowledgments of Subject Matter Experts

The Wiley CMAexcel Learning System (WCMALS) content is written to help explain the concepts and calculations from the Certified Management Accountant (CMA) exam Learning Outcome Statements (LOS) published by the Institute of Certified Management Accountants (ICMA).

IMA would like to acknowledge the team of subject matter experts who worked together in conjunction with IMA staff to produce this version of the WCMALS.

Lynn Clements, DBA, CMA, CFM, CPA, Cr. FA, CFE, is a professor of accounting at Florida Southern College in Lakeland, Florida. She earned her Ph.D. in business administration with an accounting concentration from Nova Southeastern University. Clements has been a member of the Institute of Management Accountants since 1990. She has published many research articles and regularly teaches continuing professional education courses to the accounting community.

Saurav Dutta, CMA, is an associate professor and former chair of the Accounting Department at the State University of New York at Albany. Dutta is the author of some 20 research articles published in various academic journals. He received his Ph.D. in accounting from the University of Kansas and is also the recipient of the Robert Beyer Silver Medal for securing the second highest total score in a CMA examination.

Tony Griffin, CMA, is the accounting manager for Dayton Aerospace, Inc., a senior management consulting firm specializing in defense acquisition and logistics support to government and industry customers. Griffin has been actively involved in supporting the IMA and the CMA certification by serving as president of his local IMA chapter and by organizing and leading CMA review courses in the Dayton, Ohio, area.

Karen L. Jett, CMA, is a consultant specializing in values-based organizational development and ethics training. Prior to starting her own business (Jett Excellence), she acquired over two decades of experience working in privately held companies and holds a degree in accounting from Temple University (Philadelphia, PA). Jett is author of *Grow Your People, Grow Your Business* (Mira Digital, 2008) and Questioning Ethics, an innovative ethics training system designed specifically for smaller businesses. She has taught the CMA Review Courses for many years, both as an adjunct professor at Villanova University (Villanova, PA) and directly to corporate clients.

Jan Kooiman, CMA, holds a doctorate in business economics from the University of Amsterdam. He worked for an accounting and audit firm before stepping into the professional world as chief financial officer and board member of an international company. Kooiman is a qualified transactional Six Sigma Black Belt and Trainer and is adjunct professor of finance, business, and accounting at the Webster and Leiden University in the Netherlands, teaching MBA Finance and Management Accounting. He is also the program manager and instructor of the CMA program at the World Trade Center Amsterdam.

Lou Petro, CMA, CPA, CGMA, CIA, CCP, CISA, CFE, CFM, PE, is a senior manager with a major fraud investigation firm and a former consultant and auditor. Petro specializes in fraud deterrence and investigation, corporate governance, bankruptcy, information systems auditing, production and inventory controls, internal controls, and cost and managerial accounting. He has also taught auditing, systems, accounting, and finance courses at colleges and universities in Michigan and Ontario.

Tara Shawver, DBA, CMA, is an associate professor of accounting at King's College (Wilkes-Barre, PA). She earned her Ph.D. in business administration with an accounting concentration from Nova Southeastern University. Shawver has been an active member of the Institute of Management Accountants since 2003. She is an active volunteer with the IMA, serving as president of the Pennsylvania Northeast Chapter. She has published many research articles and frequently presents at IMA's Annual Conference and Exhibition and the American Accounting Association.

Siaw-Peng Wan, CFA, is a professor of finance and the MBA program director at Elmhurst College (Elmhurst, IL). He received his Ph.D. in economics from the University of Illinois at Urbana-Champaign, and he recently became a CFA charter holder. His most recent articles on online investing and banking have appeared in *The Internet Encyclopedia* and *The Handbook of Information Security*. Wan has taught CMA Review Courses at Northern Illinois University since 2004.

Candidate Study Information

CMA Certification from ICMA

The Certified Management Accountant (CMA) certification provides accountants and financial professionals with an objective measure of knowledge and competence in the field of management accounting. The CMA designation is recognized globally as an invaluable credential for professional accountancy advancement inside organizations and for broadening professional skills and perspectives.

The two-part CMA exam is designed to develop and measure critical thinking and decision-making skills and to meet these objectives:

- To establish management accounting and financial management as recognized professions by identifying the role of the professional, the underlying body of knowledge, and a course of study by which such knowledge is acquired.
- To encourage higher educational standards in the management accounting and financial management fields.
- To establish an objective measure of an individual's knowledge and competence in the fields of management accounting and financial management.
- To encourage continued professional development.

Individuals earning the CMA designation benefit by being able to:

- Communicate their broad business competency and strategic financial mastery.
- Obtain contemporary professional knowledge and develop skills and abilities that are valued by successful businesses.
- Convey their commitment to an exemplary standard of excellence that is grounded on a strong ethical foundation and lifelong learning.
- Enhance their career development, salary qualifications, and professional promotion opportunities.

The CMA certification is granted exclusively by the Institute of Certified Management Accountants (ICMA).

CMA Learning Outcome Statements (LOS)

The Certified Management Accountant exam is based on a series of Learning Outcome Statements (LOS) developed by the Institute of Certified Management Accountants (ICMA). The LOS describes the knowledge and skills that make up the CMA body of knowledge, broken down by part, section, and topic. The Wiley CMAexcel Learning System (WCMALS) supports the LOS by addressing the subjects they cover. Candidates should use the LOS to ensure they can address the concepts in different ways or through a variety of question scenarios. Candidates should also be prepared to perform calculations referred to in the LOS in total or by providing missing components of a calculation. The LOS should not be used as proxies for exact exam questions; they should be used as a guide for studying and learning the content that will be covered on the exam.

A copy of the ICMA Learning Outcome Statements is included in Appendix A at the end of this book. Candidates are also encouraged to visit the IMA Web site to find other exam-related information at www.imanet.org.

CMA Exam Format

The content tested on the CMA exams is at an advanced level—which means that the passing standard is set for mastery, not minimum competence. Thus, there will be test questions for all major topics that require the candidate to synthesize information, evaluate a situation, and make recommendations. Other questions will test subject comprehension and analysis. However, compared to previous versions, this CMA exam will have an increased emphasis on the higher-level questions.

The content is based on a series of LOS that define the competencies and capabilities expected of a management accountant.

There are two exams, taken separately: Part 1: Financial Reporting, Planning, Performance, and Control; and Part 2: Financial Decision Making. Each exam is four hours in length and includes multiple-choice and essay questions. One hundred multiple-choice questions are presented first, followed by two essay questions. All of these questions—multiple-choice and essay—can address any of the LOS for the respective exam part. Therefore, your study plan should include learning the content of the part as well as practicing how to answer multiple-choice and essay questions against that content. The study plan tips and the final section of this WCMALS book contain important information to help you learn how to approach the different types of questions.

Note on Candidate Assumed Knowledge

The CMA exam content is based on a set of assumed baseline knowledge that candidates are expected to have. Assumed knowledge includes economics, basic statistics, and financial accounting. Examples of how this assumed knowledge might be tested in the exam include:

- How to calculate marginal revenue and costs as well as understand the relevance of market structures when determining prices
- How to calculate variance when managing financial risk
- How to construct a cash flow statement as part of an analysis of transactions and assess the impact of the transactions on the financial statements

Please note that prior courses in accounting and finance are highly recommended to ensure this knowledge competency when preparing for the exam.

Overall Expectations for the CMA Candidates

Completing the CMA exams requires a high level of commitment and dedication of up to 150 hours of study for each part of the CMA exam. Completing the two-part exam is a serious investment that will reap many rewards, helping you to build a solid foundation for your career, distinguish yourself from other accountants, and enhance your career in ways that will pay dividends for a lifetime.

Your success in completing these exams will rest heavily on your ability to create a solid study plan and to execute that plan. IMA offers many resources, tools, and programs to support you during this process—the exam content specifications, assessment tools to identify the content areas you need to study most, comprehensive study tools such as the Online Test Bank, classroom programs, and online intensive review courses. We encourage you to register as a CMA candidate as soon as you begin the program to maximize your access to these resources and tools and to draw on these benefits with rigor and discipline that best supports your unique study needs. We also suggest candidates seek other sources if further knowledge is needed to augment knowledge and understanding of the ICMA LOS.

For more information about the CMA certification, the CMA exams, or the exam preparation resources offered through IMA, visit www.imanet.org.

Updates and Errata Notification

Please be advised that our materials are designed to provide thorough and accurate content with a high level of attention to quality. From time to time there may be clarifications, corrections, or updates that are captured in an Updates and Errata Notification.

To ensure you are kept abreast of changes, this notification will be available on Wiley's CMA update and errata page. You may review these documents by going to www.wiley.com/go/cmaerrata2015.

How to Use the Wiley CMAexcel Learning System

This product is based on the CMA body of knowledge developed by the Institute of Certified Management Accountants (ICMA). This material is designed for learning purposes and is distributed with the understanding that the publisher and authors are not offering legal or professional services. Although the text is based on the body of knowledge tested by the CMA exam and the published Learning Outcome Statements (LOS) covering the two-part exams, the Wiley CMAexcel Learning System (WCMALS) program developers do not have access to the current bank of exam questions. It is critical that candidates understand all LOS published by the ICMA, learn all concepts and calculations related to those statements, and have a solid grasp of how to approach the multiple-choice and essay exams in the CMA program.

Some exam preparation tools provide an overview of key topics; others are intended to help you practice one specific aspect of the exams such as the questions. The WCMALS is designed as a comprehensive exam preparation tool to help you study the content from the exam LOS, learn how to write the CMA exams, and practice answering exam-type questions.

Study the Book Content

The **table of contents** is set up using the CMA exam content specifications established by ICMA. Each section, topic, and subtopic is named according to the content specifications and the **Learning Outcome Statements (LOS)** written to correspond to these specifications. As you go through each section and major topic, refer to the related LOS found in Appendix A. Then review the WCMALS book content to help learn the concepts and formulas covered in the LOS.

The **Learning Outcome Statements Overviews** provide a quick reference to the LOS as well as key points to remember within them. These sections should not replace the in-depth discussion of the material that is in this book. However, these overviews do serve as a refresher on what has been learned and can be used as a tool to reinforce the knowledge that you have obtained.

The **knowledge checks** are designed to be quick checks to verify that you understand and remember the content just covered by presenting questions and correct answers. The answers refer to the appropriate sections in the book for you to review the content and find the answer yourself.

The **practice questions** are a sampling of the type of exam questions you will encounter on the exam and are considered complex and may involve extensive written and/or calculation responses. Use these questions to begin applying what you have learned, recognizing there is a much larger sample of practice questions available in the Online Test Bank (described in the next section).

The WCMALS also contains a **bibliography and references** in case you need to find more detailed content on an LOS. We encourage you to use published academic sources. While information can be found online, we discourage the use of open-source, unedited sites such as Wikipedia.

Suggested Study Process Using the WCMALS

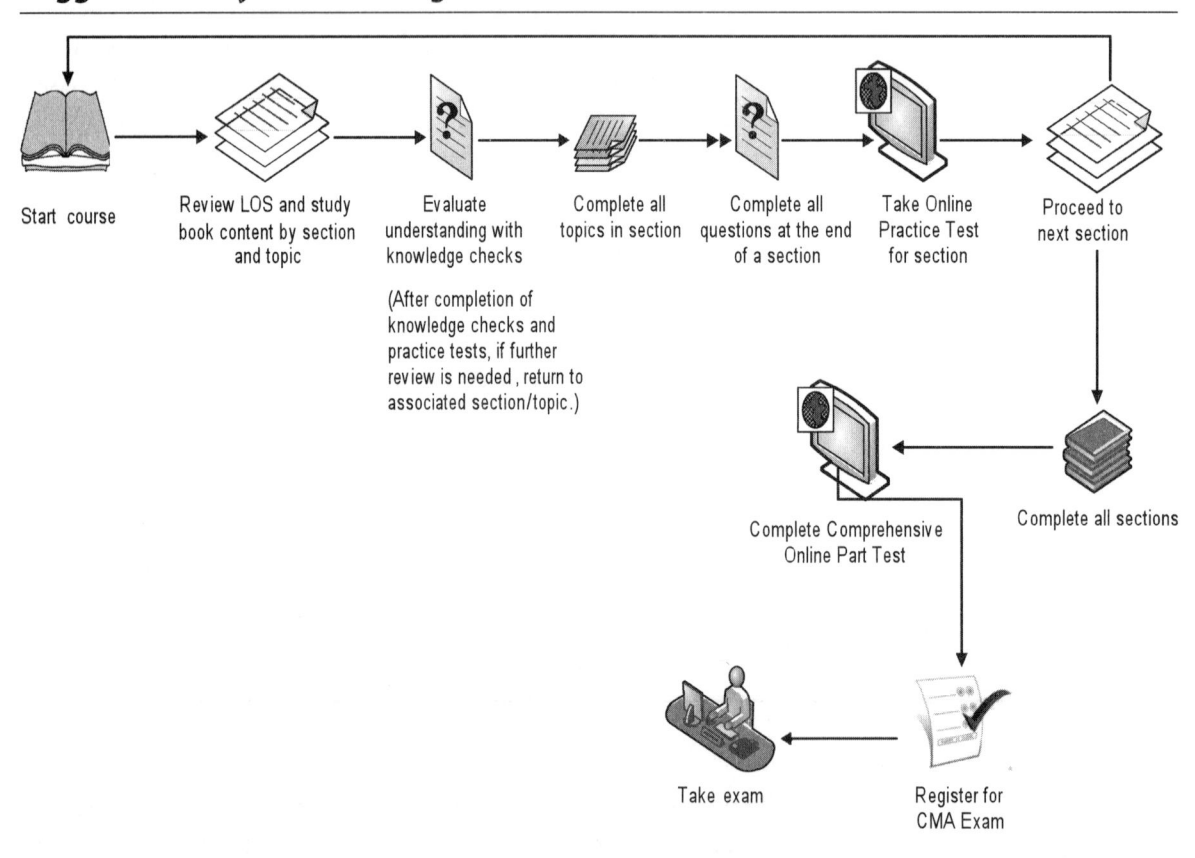

Start course → Review LOS and study book content by section and topic → Evaluate understanding with knowledge checks (After completion of knowledge checks and practice tests, if further review is needed, return to associated section/topic.) → Complete all topics in section → Complete all questions at the end of a section → Take Online Practice Test for section → Proceed to next section

Complete all sections → Complete Comprehensive Online Part Test → Register for CMA Exam → Take exam

WCMALS Book Features

The WCMALS books use a number of features to draw your attention to certain types of content:

Key terms are **bolded** where they appear in the text with their definition, to allow you to quickly scan through and study them.

Key formulas are indicated with this icon. Be sure you understand these formulas and practice applying them.

Knowledge checks at the end of each topic are review questions that let you check your understanding of the content just read. (They are not representative of the type of questions that appear on the exam.)

Study tips offer ideas and strategies for studying and preparing for the exam.

Practice questions are examples of actual exam questions. Presented at the end of each section, these questions help you solidify your learning of that section and apply it to the type of questions that appear on the exam.

Online Test Bank

Included with your purchase of the Wiley CMAexcel Learning System Part 1 book is an Online Test Bank made available to you through www.wileycma.com. This test bank includes **five section-specific tests** that randomize questions from a selected section only. The course also includes **a comprehensive Part 1 test** that emulates the percentage weighting of each section on the actual Part 1 exam. All questions are drawn from a bank of more than 800 questions, so that each time you repeat the test, you will receive a different set of questions covering all the topics in the section. All the multiple-choice questions provide feedback in response to your answers.

It is suggested that you integrate the Online Test Bank throughout your study program instead of leaving them until the end. The section-specific tests are designed for you to practice questions related to the section content—read and learn a section and then practice the online questions related to the section. This also will help you identify whether further study of the section content is required before moving to the next section.

The comprehensive Part 1 test is designed to help you simulate taking the actual CMA exam. Try the comprehensive Part 1 test after you have studied all the Part 1 content. You can take this exam multiple times. Each time you will receive a different combination of questions. It is recommended that you set up your own exam simulation—set aside four hours in a room without interruption, do not have any reference books open, and work through the comprehensive part exam as if you were taking the real exam. This will prepare you for the exam setting and give you a good idea of how ready you are.

In addition, sample essay questions are provided that simulate the testing environment. The correct answer is provided which will enable you to self-score your answer.

You are strongly encouraged to make full use of all online practice and review features as part of your study efforts. Please note that these features are subscription based and available only for a specific number of months from the time of registration.

Learn to Write the CMA Exam

The four-hour CMA exam will test your understanding of each part's content using both multiple-choice and essay questions. This means you must learn to write two types of tests in one sitting. The WCMALS books contain tips, instruction, and examples to help you learn to write an essay exam. Be sure to study the Essay Exam Support Materials section so that in addition to practicing with the Online Test Bank, you also learn to respond to the part content in essay format.

Create a Study Plan

Each part of the two-part CMA exam uses a combination of a multiple-choice format and an essay format to test your understanding of the part concepts, terms, and calculations. Creating a study plan is an essential ingredient to planning a path to success. Managing your plan is critical to achieving success. The next tips and tactics are included to help you prepare and manage your study plan.

Study Tips

There are many ways to study, and the plan you create will depend on things such as your lifestyle (when and how you can schedule study time), your learning style, how familiar you are with the content, and how practiced you are at writing a formal exam. Only you can assess these factors and create a plan that will work for you. Some suggestions that other exam candidates have found helpful follow.

- Schedule regular study times and stay on schedule.
- Avoid cramming by breaking your study times into small segments. For example, you may want to work intensely for 45 minutes with no interruptions, followed by a 15-minute break during which time you do something different. You may want to leave the room, have a conversation, or exercise.
- When reading, highlight key ideas, especially unfamiliar ones. Reread later to ensure comprehension.
- Pay particular attention to the terms and equations highlighted in this book, and be sure to learn the acronyms in the CMA body of knowledge.
- Create personal mnemonics to help you memorize key information. For example, CCIC to remember the four ethical standards: Competence, Confidentiality, Integrity, and Credibility.
- Create study aids such as flash cards.
- Use index cards, and write a question on one side and the answer on the other. This helps reinforce the learning because you are writing the information as well as reading it. Examples: What is ____? List the five parts of ____.
- In particular, make flash cards of topics and issues that are unfamiliar to you, key terms and formulas, and anything you highlighted while reading.
- Keep some cards with you at all times to review when you have time, such as in an elevator, while waiting for an appointment, and so on.

- Use a flash card partner. This person does not need to understand accounting. He or she only needs the patience to sit with you and read the questions off the flash card.
- As test time approaches, start to eliminate the questions you can easily answer from your stack so you can concentrate on the more challenging topics and terms.
- If particular topics are difficult, tap into other resources, such as the Internet, library, accountant colleagues, or professors, to augment your understanding.
- Use your study plan—treat it as a living document and update it as you learn more about what you need to do to prepare for the exam.
- Use the knowledge checks in the book to assess how well you understand the content you just completed.
- Use the Online Test Bank to test your ability to answer multiple-choice practice questions on each section's content as you finish it. After completing the first 40 questions presented, review areas in the book that you were weak on in the practice test. Then try the section test again.
- Be sure to learn how to take a multiple-choice question exam—there are many online resources with tips and guidance that relate to answering multiple-choice exams.
  - Make an attempt to answer all questions. There is no penalty for an incorrect answer—if you don't try, even when you are uncertain, you eliminate the potential of getting a correct answer.
  - Create your own "simulated" multiple-choice trial exam using the full Part 1 Online Practice Test.
- Learn to write an effective essay answer.
  - Use the Essay Exam Support Materials section of this book. This content shows a sample grading guide and includes a sample of a good, a better, and a best answer in addition to some helpful tips for writing an essay answer.
  - Learn how points are awarded for an essay answer so that you can ensure you get the most points possible for your answers, even when you are very challenged by a question.
  - Practice essay responses using the questions in this WCMALS book as well as the Online Test Bank.
- Be sure to access the Online Test Bank and its Essay Questions until you are comfortable with the content.

Ensure you are both well rested and physically prepared for the exam day as each exam is four hours in length with no break for meals. Learning how to answer a multiple-choice and essay exam and being mentally and physically prepared can improve your grade significantly. Know the content and be prepared to deal with challenges with a focused, confident, and flexible attitude.

Introduction

Welcome to Part 1: Financial Reporting, Planning, Performance, and Control of the Wiley CMAexcel Learning System.

This Part 1 textbook is composed of five sections:

Section A: External Financial Reporting Decisions covers the four financial statements (balance sheet, income statement, statement of changes in equity, and statement of cash flows) as well as recognition, measurement, valuation, and disclosure concepts.

Section B: Planning, Budgeting, and Forecasting looks at basic budgeting concepts and forecasting techniques that provide the information a company can use to execute its strategy and pursue its short- and long-term goals.

Section C: Performance Management deals with the methods of comparing actual financial performance to the budget. It also describes tools that incorporate both financial and nonfinancial measures to aid an organization in matching its planning to its overall strategy.

Section D: Cost Management describes various costing systems that can be used to monitor a company's costs and provide management with information it needs to manage the company's operations and performance.

Section E: Internal Controls begins with a discussion of the assessment and management of risk. Understanding risk provides the basis for internal auditing activities and the means of ensuring the security and reliability of the information on which the company bases its decisions.

Many of these subjects, tested in the Part 1 CMA exam, provide a foundation for the concepts and methodologies that will be the subject of the Part 2 exam.

SECTION A

External Financial Reporting Decisions

To perform their duties, management accountants must understand the four external financial statements—the balance sheet, income statement, statement of changes in equity, and statement of cash flows—and the concepts underlying these statements. Concepts underlying the four financial statements include recognition, measurement, valuation, and disclosure as well as an understanding of the key differences between U.S. generally accepted accounting principles (GAAP) and International Financial Reporting Standards (IFRS).

Topics covered in this section include the financial statements themselves, asset and liability valuation, income taxes, lease, equity transactions, revenue and expense recognition, income measurement and determination, and U.S. GAAP and IFRS differences.

Learning Outcome Statements Overview: External Financial Reporting Decisions

Section A.1. Financial Statements

For the balance sheet, income statement, statement of changes in equity, and the statement of cash flows, the candidate should be able to:

A. Identify the users of these financial statements and their needs.
   a. The users of financial statements are the following:
      - Investors
      - Employees
      - Lenders
      - Trade creditors
      - Customers
      - Governments and governmental agencies
      - The public

   Investors require information to help them whether to buy, sell, or hold an interest in a corporation. Shareholders require information regarding the corporation's ability to pay dividends. Employees are interested in the stability, sustainability, and profitability of employer organizations. Lenders need to be able to assess the borrower's ability to pay debts in full and on time. Trade creditors need information enabling them to determine whether they should sell on credit and whether amounts owed them will be paid. Customers require information regarding the organization's continuity and sustainability. Governments and their agencies need information to regulate organizational activities, to determine tax policies, and for national income statistics. The public requires information on an organization's contributions to the local community and its development.

B. Demonstrate an understanding of the purposes and uses of each statement.
   a. The purpose of the balance sheet is to show the financial position (assets and claims on those assets) of an organization at a point in time. The

income statement shows the results of operations (revenues and gains less expenses, losses, and taxes) for an organization for a period of time (fiscal period). The statement of changes in equity shows the changes in capital received and retained earnings for a fiscal period. Changes in capital received include the issuance and repurchase of shares. Changes in retained earnings include net income and dividends for the period. The statement of cash flow presents the change in cash and cash equivalents classified as operations, investing, or financing.

C. Identify the major components and classifications of each statement.
   a. Balance sheet
      i. Current assets—Assets that may be converted into cash, sold, or consumed within a year or operating cycle, whichever is longer.
      ii. Long-term assets—Assets that may not be converted to cash, sold, or consumed within a year or operating cycle, whichever is longer.
      iii. Current liabilities—Debts that are due to be paid within a year or operating cycle, whichever is longer.
      iv. Long-term liabilities—Debts that are to be paid at some date beyond the longer of one year or one operating cycle.
      v. Shareholder's equity—Represents investments from shareholders and retained earnings. Represents shareholders' interest in the net assets of the company.
   b. Income statement
      i. Sales—Total sales (revenues) from the ordinary course of business.
      ii. Cost of goods sold—Direct costs related to the product sold or service rendered.
      iii. Operating expenses—Other necessary and ordinary expenses of a company that are not included in cost of goods sold.
      iv. Other revenues and expenses—Other inflows and outflows not related directly to operations.
      v. Taxes—Tax liability incurred in connection with the reported income.
   c. Statement of cash flows
      i. Operating activities—Cash flows related to normal course of business; cash from customers; cash paid to employees, suppliers, vendors, and interest portion of debt payments.
      ii. Investing activities—Cash flows related to long-term asset accounts; sale and purchase of property, plant, and equipment and investments.
      iii. Financing activities—Cash flows related to long-term liability or equity accounts; inflows from proceeds of debt or issuances of stock, outflows for payment of debt and dividends to shareholders.
   d. Statement of changes in shareholders' equity
      Beginning Equity + New Investments − Dividends = Ending Equity

D. Identify the limitations of each financial statement.
   a. All four of the statements are limited by the use of historical costs, the use of different accounting principles and methods, and estimates and judgments. The balance sheet in particular excludes people and liabilities handled off balance sheet.
E. Identify how various financial transactions affect the elements of each of the financial statements, and determine the proper classification of the transaction.
   a. How various financial transactions affect the elements of each of the financial statements and the proper classification of the various financial transactions is covered in Topic 2: Recognition, Measurement, Valuation, and Disclosure.
F. Identify the basic disclosures related to each of the statements (footnotes, supplementary schedules, etc.).
   a. The footnotes or disclosures to financial statements are used when parenthetical explanations would not suffice to describe situations particular to the entity. Typical disclosures include contingencies, contractual situations, accounting policies, and subsequent events.
G. Demonstrate an understanding of the relationship among the financial statements.
   a. The four financial statements are integrally related. The balance sheet is connected to the income statement (net income) through the change in retained earnings shown in the statement of changes in shareholders' equity. The balance sheet change in cash and other changes in financial position are presented in the statement of cash flow. Changes in capital received in the balance sheet are shown in the statement of changes in shareholders' equity.
H. Prepare a balance sheet, an income statement, a statement of changes in equity, and a statement of cash flows (indirect method).
   a. Balance sheet

Robin Manufacturing Company
Balance Sheet
December 31, Year 1

Assets	
Current assets:	
Cash and short-term investments	$24,628
Trade receivables, net of $30K allowance	552,249
Other receivables	18,941
Note receivable—related party	80,532
Inventory	252,567
Prepaid insurance	7,500
Total current assets	936,417

Fixed assets:		
Property and equipment		209,330
Less: Accumulated depreciation		(75,332)
Net fixed assets		133,998
Total assets		$1,070,415
Liabilities and Equity		
Current liabilities		$175,321
Accounts payable		2,500
Accrued expenses		
Current portion of long-term debt		36,000
Line of credit		145,000
Total current liabilities		358,821
Long-term debt		117,343
Total current and long-term liabilities		476,164
Shareholders' equity:		
Common stock, par		25,680
Additional paid-in capital		360,320
Retained earnings		208,251
Total shareholders' equity		594,251
Total liabilities and shareholders' equity		$1,070,415

b. Income statement

Robin Manufacturing Company
Income Statement For the Year Ended December 31, Year 1 (Y1)

Sales Revenue			
Sales			$2,808,835
Less: Sales discounts		$22,302	
Less: Sales returns and allowances		51,913	74,215
Net sales revenue			2,734,620
Cost of Goods Sold			
Merchandise inventory, Jan. 1, Y1		424,321	
Purchases	$1,830,518		
Less: Purchase discounts	17,728		
Net purchases	1,812,790		
Freight and transportation—in	37,363	1,850,153	
Total merchandise available for sale		2,274,474	
Less: Merchandise inventory, Dec. 31, Y1		450,536	
Cost of goods sold			$1,823,938
Gross profit on sales			910,682
Operating Expenses			
Selling expenses			
Sales salaries and commissions	186,432		
Sales office salaries	54,464		

Travel and entertainment	45,025		
Advertising expense	35,250		
Freight and transportation—out	37,912		
Shipping supplies and expense	22,735		
Postage and stationery	15,445		
Depreciation of sales equipment	8,285		
Telephone and Internet expense	<u>11,238</u>	416,786	
Administrative expenses			
Officers' salaries	171,120		
Office salaries	56,304		
Legal and professional services	21,823		
Utilities expense	21,413		
Insurance expense	15,667		
Building depreciation	16,614		
Office equipment depreciation	14,720		
Stationery, supplies, and postage	2,645		
Miscellaneous office expenses	<u>2,403</u>	<u>322,709</u>	<u>739,495</u>
Income from operations			171,187
Other Revenues and Gains			
Dividend revenue		90,620	
Rental revenue		<u>67,077</u>	<u>157,697</u>
			328,884
Other Expenses and Losses			
Interest on bonds and notes			<u>115,975</u>
Income before income tax			212,909
Income tax			<u>61,579</u>
Net income for the year			$151,330
Earnings per common share			$1.89

c. Statement of cash flows

Statement of Cash Flows—Indirect Method

Operating Activities	
Net income	$151,330
Adjustments to convert net income to a cash basis:	
Depreciation and amortization charges*	75,332
Decrease (increase) in accounts receivable	(31,445)
Increase (decrease) in merchandise inventory	(4,165)
Increase (decrease) in accounts payable	6,740
Increase (decrease) in accrued wages and salaries payable	4,543

	Increase (decrease) in accrued income taxes payable	3,984
	Increase (decrease) in deferred income taxes	(4,950)
	Gain on sale of store**	(1,255)
	Net cash provided by operating activities	200,114
Investing Activities		
	Additions to property, buildings, and equipment	(123,730)
	Proceeds from sale of store	3,980
	Net cash used in investing activities	(119,750)
Financing Activities		
	Increase (decrease) in notes payable	1,100
	Increase (decrease) in additional paid-in capital	14,800
	Increase (decrease) in long-term debt	(50,500)
	Increase (decrease) in common stock	1,000
	Cash dividends paid	(33,330)
	Net cash used in financing activities	(66,930)
	Net increase in cash and cash equivalents	13,434
	Cash and cash equivalents at beginning of year	11,194
	Cash and cash equivalents at end of year	$24,628

d. Statement of changes in equity

Robin Manufacturing Company
Schedule of Changes in Shareholders' Equity
For Year Ended December 31, Year 1 (Y1)

	Common Stock, $1 Par	Additional Paid-In Capital	Retained Earnings	Total
Balance, Jan. 1, Y1	$24,680	$345,520	$90,251	$460,451
Net income			151,330	151,330
Cash dividends paid			(33,330)	(33,330)
Common stock issued	1,000	14,800		15,800
Balance, Dec. 31, Y1	$25,680	$360,320	$208,251	$594,251

Section A.2. Recognition, Measurement, Valuation, and Disclosure

A. Identify issues related to the valuation of accounts receivable, including timing of recognition and estimation of uncollectible accounts.
   a. GAAP requires that accounts receivable be carried on the balance sheet at net realizable value (NRV). NRV is gross accounts receivable less the allowances for uncollectible accounts, returns and allowances, and discounts. Allowances for returns and allowances and discounts are not covered on the CMA examination.
B. Determine the financial statement effect of using the percentage-of-sales (income statement) approach as opposed to the percentage-of-receivables (balance sheet) approach in calculating the allowance for uncollectible accounts.
   a. GAAP allows either approach noted above for the determination of uncollectible expense and the allowance for uncollectible accounts. The percentage-of-sales method calculates the uncollectible expense and credits the allowance to determine the balance in the allowance account. The percentage-of-receivables method calculates the ending balance in the allowance account and "backs" into the uncollectible expense.
C. Distinguish between receivables sold (factoring) on a with-recourse basis and those sold on a without-recourse basis, and determine the effect on the balance sheet.
   a. Factoring without recourse transfers the ownership of the receivable to the factor and removes it from the balance sheet. When factoring with recourse, rights of ownership remain with the original owner of the receivable and are not transferred to the factor. The receivable then remains on the original owner's balance sheet.
D. Identify issues in inventory valuation, including which goods to include, what costs to include, and which cost assumption to use.
   a. All goods available for sale and still owned by the company are included in inventory. This would include goods out on consignment, goods in transit shipped FOB destination (title transfers at the destination) as well as owned goods on hand. Which of the three inventory cost assumptions noted below to use is up to management
E. Identify and compare cost flow assumptions used in accounting for inventories.
   a. The cost flow assumptions used for inventory valuation are FIFO (first in, first out), LIFO (last in, first out), and average cost (weighted average for a periodic inventory moving average for a perpetual inventory). FIFO values the ending inventory at the newest (current) costs and the cost of goods sold at the oldest costs. LIFO values the ending inventory at the oldest costs and cost of goods sold at the newest (current) costs. Weighted average cost values both the ending inventory and cost of goods sold at the weighted average cost of the goods for the period. The moving average method recomputes the average cost of the inventory whenever a shipment

is received and uses the recomputed average to determine the cost of the next sale.

F. Demonstrate an understanding of the lower of cost or market rule for inventories.
   a. GAAP requires that inventories be valued and carried at lower of cost or market (LCM). Cost may be one of the following: FIFO, LIFO, average cost, or specific identification. Market is defined as replacement cost. There is, however, a ceiling and a floor on replacement cost. The ceiling is NRV (replacement cost less costs to complete and dispose of). The floor is NRV reduced by the normal profit margin.

G. Calculate the effect on income and on assets of using different inventory methods.
   a. When inventory costs are consistently rising, FIFO results in the highest net income due to the lowest cost of sales and the highest inventory value on the balance sheet. LIFO results in the lowest net income due to the highest cost of sales and lowest inventory value on the balance sheet. Average cost results would be between FIFO and LIFO. When inventory costs are consistently falling, FIFO and LIFO would be reversed; an average cost would still be in between. The relationships of the three methods would be indeterminable if inventory costs are fluctuating up and down.

H. Analyze the effects of inventory errors.
   a. An error in the end-of-period inventory will affect the cost of sales for the period, net income for the period, ending retained earnings for the period, beginning inventory for the next period, cost of sales for the next period, and net income for the next period. The cost of sales and net income errors in the next period would be in the opposite direction from those in the first period. The retained earnings at the end of the next period would be correct. For example, a dollar overstatement in this period's inventory will understate this period's cost of sales by a dollar, overstate its net income by a dollar, and overstate its retained earnings by a dollar. The error will overstate the next period's beginning inventory by a dollar, overstate its cost of sales by a dollar, understate its net income by a dollar, and restore retained earnings to where it would have been had the error not occurred.

I. Identify advantages and disadvantages of the different inventory methods.
   a. FIFO generates an ending inventory valuation close to current (replacement) cost. It minimizes income taxes when prices are consistently falling. One disadvantage of FIFO is that it matches older costs in cost of sales to revenue in income determination. Second, it results in higher income taxes than either LIFO or average cost when inventory costs are consistently rising.
   b. LIFO matches the most current costs (through cost of sales) to revenue in income determination. It minimizes income taxes when inventory costs are consistently rising. Its main disadvantage is that the inventory valuation on the balance sheet could be many years out of date. Since LIFO become available prior to World War II, the inventory valuation could be

over 70 years old. Last, it is an extremely complex system when used for perpetual inventory valuation.

c. Average costing is an easy-to-use and understand method. It is relatively easily programmed when used for perpetual inventory valuation. It provides little tax advantage when costs are consistently rising or falling.

J. Recommend the inventory method and cost flow assumption that should be used for a firm given a set of facts.

a. LIFO is the recommended system when prices are consistently rising and the inventory level is constant or rising. FIFO would be best when prices are consistently falling or the inventory is being depleted. Average cost is recommended when the inventory level fluctuates materially and/or the prices fluctuate. Average cost is best for commodities and fungible goods.

K. Demonstrate an understanding of the following security types: trading, available for sale, and held to maturity.

a. Trading securities are bought and sold to generate profit on short-term price changes. They consist of debt securities with maturities less than one year as well as equity securities. Typical trading securities are Treasury bills, commercial paper, money market and euro deposits, and short-term certificates of deposit (CDs) purchased with excess short-term cash. Trading securities are carried on the balance sheet at fair market value (marked to market). Holding gains and losses when marking to market are reported directly in the income statement.

b. Available-for-sale securities are those debt and equity securities that are neither trading securities nor held-to-maturity securities (discussed below). They may be short term or long term and are marked to market, as are trading securities. Holding gains and losses are carried in other comprehensive income rather than in net income.

c. Held-to-maturity securities are either debt securities intended to be held to maturity or equity securities purchased with the intent to acquire the issuing corporation. Held-to-maturity debt securities are carried at amortized historical cost. A typical held-to-maturity security would be a corporate bond. Held-to-maturity equity investments are accounted for by the fair value method (same as available-for-sale securities noted above) if they represent less than 20% of the outstanding stock of the issuer or by the equity method if they represent 20% or more.

L. Demonstrate an understanding of the fair value method, equity method, and consolidated method for equity securities.

a. The fair value method is covered under available-for-sale securities.

b. The equity method is used by the investor when ownership of 20% or more of the issuer's voting stock is considered sufficient to influence the issuer's operations. The main features of the equity method are:

- The owners' original investment is recorded at cost in the investment account.
- The owner/investor records its percentage share of the investee/issuer's periodic net income as an increase in the investment account

and as credit to the equity is earnings account. The investor records its share of a periodic investee loss as a decrease in the investment account and a debit to the equity in loss account.
- When the investor receives a cash dividend from the investee, cash is increased and the investment account is decreased the amount of the dividend.

M. Determine the effect on the financial statements of using different depreciation methods.
   a. Depreciation is the systematic, rational allocation of a tangible asset's cost less estimated residual (net salvage) value over the estimated life of the asset. The periodic depreciation is debited to depreciation expense shown on the income statement and credited to the accumulated depreciation account (an offset or contra account to the asset account).
   b. Straight-line depreciation produces a constant amount of depreciation per period calculated as cost less estimated residual divided by the estimated asset life.
   c. Accelerated depreciation produces a declining amount of depreciation per period calculated as the declining balance percentage divided by the estimated life times the net book value of the asset at the beginning of the period. Estimated residual value is ignored in the calculation. The net book value is cost less accumulated depreciation. Care must be taken to depreciate the asset down to its estimated residual value but not below it.
   d. Units of production or activity depreciation produces a varying amount of depreciation per period calculated as the cost less estimated residual value divided by the estimated production or activity level expected over the life of the asset times the amount of actual production or activity for the period.

N. Recommend a depreciation method for a given set of data.
   a. The following is an example of the application of the three methods of depreciation (straight line, declining balance, and production/activity) discussed. The recommendation of a specific method depends on the depreciation pattern preferred by the organization. The following data applies to all three methods:
      - Cost of the asset = $100,000
      - Estimated residual value = $10,000
      - Estimated useful life = 5 years or 200,000 units of production
      - Actual production for the five years = 50,000, 42,000, 36,000, 32,000, and 34,000, respectively
   b. The straight-line depreciation would be $18,000 per year [(100,000 − 10,000)/5 = 90,000/5] for each of the five years.
   c. The double (200%) declining balance method would produce the following annual depreciations:
      1. Year 1 $40,000 (2/5)(100,000).
      2. Year 2 $24,000 (2/5)(100,000 − 40,000) = .4(60,000).
      3. Year 3 $14,400 (2/5)(60,000 − 24,000) = .4(36,000).

4. Year 4 $8,640 (2/5)(36,000 − 14,400) = .4(21,600)
5. Year 5 $2,960. To get the accumulated depreciation to $90,000 (cost of 100,000 less estimated residual of 10,000).
d. The production/activity method utilizes a rate of $.45 per unit [(100,000 − 10,000)/200,000 = 90,000/200,000 = .45] per unit and would produce the following annual depreciations:
1. Year 1 $22,500 .45(50,000).
2. Year 2 $18,900 .45(42,000).
3. Year 3 $15,300 .45(34,000).
4. Year 4 $16,200 .45(36,000).
5. Year 5 $17,100. To get the accumulated depreciation to $90,000 (cost of 100,000 less estimated residual of 10,000).

O. Demonstrate an understanding of the accounting for impairment of long-term assets.
   a. The determination of impairment of a long-term asset involves two steps. The first is a recoverability test, where the carrying (net book) value of the asset is compared with the expected undiscounted cash flows from the asset's use and disposal. If the carrying value exceeds the expected cash flows, an impairment loss calculation is required. The impairment loss is the amount by which the carrying value exceeds the fair value of the asset. The fair value of the asset would be the net proceeds from selling the asset in an orderly market.

P. Demonstrate an understanding of the accounting for impairment of intangible assets, including goodwill.
   a. The impairment of an intangible other than goodwill involves determining if the carrying value of the intangible exceeds its fair value. If it does, an impairment loss equal to the difference has occurred and must be recognized.
   b. The impairment of goodwill involves three steps. First, the company performs a qualitative assessment to determine whether it is likely that the fair value of the reporting unit to which the goodwill is attached is less than its carrying value. Then, if it is, a recoverability test need be performed. The test involves a comparison of the carrying amount of the reporting unit with the fair value of the reporting unit. If the carrying amount exceeds the fair value, an impairment loss equal to that difference has occurred and must be recognized.

Valuation of Liabilities

Q. Identify the classification issues of short-term debt expected to be refinanced.
   a. ASR No. 148 requires that refinanced short-term debt be classified as a current liability unless the refinancing would extend the maturity date beyond one year.
R. Compare the effect on financial statements when using either the expense warranty approach or the sales warranty approach for accounting for warranties.

a. The expense warranty method is the generally accepted method of accounting for warranty expense and liability and should be used whenever the warranty is an integral and inseparable part of the sale that creates a warranty loss contingency. The estimated warranty expense and associated liability are recorded in the year of the sale of the product for which the warranty applies. Actual warranty expenditures when they occur are charged to the estimated liability. The expense method provides for the proper matching of warranty expense to the product revenue through accrual accounting.
b. The sales warranty approach defers a portion of the original sales price (the estimated warranty expense) until the actual warranty costs are incurred. At that time the revenue and expense equal tothe amount deferred are recognized. The result is a type of cash basis accounting that does not provide a proper match of revenue and expense.

S. Define off-balance sheet financing, and identify different forms of this type of borrowing.
   a. Off-balance sheet financing is a form of financing whereby liabilities are kept off the organization's balance sheet. It is often used to keep the organization's debt/equity and equity multiplier (leverage) ratios low to avoid debt covenant violations. Examples of off-balance sheet financing are joint borrowing ventures where each partner has 50% and operating lease obligations.

Income Taxes (Applies to Assets and Liabilities Subtopics)

T. Demonstrate an understanding of interperiod tax allocation/deferred income taxes.
   a. Deferred income tax liabilities or assets are created by the temporary differences between the handling of revenues and expenses for financial purposes (books) as opposed to for income tax purposes. Income tax expense is based on the financial statement handling of revenues and expenses. Income tax payable is calculated based on the Internal Revenue Service (IRS) rules and regulations. The deferred income tax liability or asset is basically the difference between the income tax expense and the income tax payable.

U. Define and analyze temporary differences, operating loss carrybacks, and operating loss carryforwards.
   a. Temporary differences between book and tax are those that will reverse in the future. There are four types of temporary differences. They are:
   1. Revenues or gains taxable after book recognition.
   2. Expenses or losses tax deductible before book recognition.
   3. Revenues or gains taxable before book recognition.
   4. Expenses or losses deductible after book recognition.
       Items 1 and 2 create deferred tax liabilities while items 3 and 4 create deferred tax assets. Examples of each are given later.

b. Operating losses that offer no tax benefit in the year of occurrence may be carried back or carried forward to offset either prior or future tax liabilities. Operating losses may be carried back two years and carried forward 20 years. An operating loss carryback is recognized in the year of the loss since it is realizable and measurable. Operating loss carryforwards create need future tax liabilities to offset against and create a deferred tax asset.

V. Distinguish between deferred tax liabilities and deferred tax assets.
   a. Deferred tax liabilities represent future tax liabilities that ensue from deferring taxes to be paid into the future. Deferred tax assets represent future tax benefits (reductions) that ensue from deferring tax benefits into the future.

W. Differentiate between temporary differences and permanent differences, and identify examples of each.
   a. Examples of temporary differences creating deferred tax liabilities are:
      - Using the cash basis for tax recognition of profit from installment sales.
      - Using the cash basis for recognition of earnings of subsidiaries.
      - Using Modified Accelerated Cost Recovery System (MACRS) depreciation for taxes and straight line for book.
   b. Examples of temporary differences creating deferred tax assets are:
      - Using the cash basis for tax recognition of rental incomes.
      - Using the cash basis for recognition of warranty expenses.
      - Using the direct write-off method for bad debt recognition or tax purposes and the allowance method for books.

X. Indicate the proper income statement and balance sheet presentation of income tax expense and deferred taxes.
   a. Income tax expense is presented on the income statement in two ways. Income tax expense related to continuing operations may be shown as one of the continuing operations expenses deducted from continuing operations revenues to obtain net income, or, preferably, it could be shown as a deduction from continuing operations earnings before taxes. Income taxes related to discontinued operations or extraordinary items are netted with the gain or loss from the discontinued operation or extraordinary item.
   b. Deferred tax assets and deferred tax liabilities are shown on the balance sheet as noted in Y.

Y. Explain the issues involved in determining the amount and classification of tax assets and liabilities.
   a. The amounts of the deferred tax assets and liabilities are calculated using the tax rates enacted at the time of the calculation. Deferred tax assets may be current assets or other long-term assets, depending on when the tax benefit is expected to be realized. Current is one year or less while long term is greater than one year. Similarly, deferred tax liabilities may be current or long-term liabilities, depending on when they are expected to be paid.

Leases (Applies to Assets and Liabilities Subtopics)

Z. Distinguish between an operating lease and a capital lease.
  a. A lessee has an operating lease if the long-term lease does not meet any of the following criteria:
  - Title transfers to the lessee at the end of the lease term.
  - A bargain purchase option is available to the lessee.
  - The lease term is greater than or equal to 75% of the leased asset's useful life.
  - The present value of the lease payments at the lessee's borrowing rate is greater than or equal to 90% of the asset's fair market value (FMV).
  Meeting any one of the criteria makes the lease a capital lease for financial accounting purposes.
  b. In order for the lessor to consider the lease as a capital lease, two additional criteria must be met. They are:
  - The rental collections are reasonably assured.
  - Future costs are reasonably predicable; that is, there are no expected unreimbursed costs.

AA. Explain why an operating lease is a form of off-balance sheet financing.
  a. An operating lease is a form of off-balance sheet financing because the lease creates a liability for the present value of the expected lease payments that is not shown on the balance sheet. The lease payment commitment, however, should be disclosed in the appropriate footnote

BB. Demonstrate an understanding of why lessees may prefer accounting for a lease as an operating lease as opposed to a capital lease.
  a. The lessee would prefer that leases be operating as opposed to capital in order to keep the lease liability of the balance sheet and to show the interest porting of the lease payment. Treating a lease as an operating lease would improve the organization's solvency ratios, such as debt or debt/equity, as well as its interest coverage (number of times interest is earned). The improved solvency ratios make it less likely that the organization will violate debt covenants or restrictions.

CC. Recognize the correct financial statement presentation of operating and capital lease.
  a. Operating lease payments are shown as expenses in the income statement, as dictated by accrual accounting. There is no balance sheet presentation of the lease.
  b. A capital lease creates a liability on the balance sheet equal at the lease's inception to the present value of the future lease payments at the lessee's borrowing rate. The lease payments, therefore, consist of an interest portion and a reduction in the lease liability. The interest portion is equal to the lessee borrowing rate times the amount of lease liability at the beginning of the period covered by the payment. The splitting of the lease payments into interest and liability reduction requires the lessee to set

up a lease amortization table similar to a mortgage amortization table. The lessee treats the leased asset as part of long-term assets and depreciates the asset as appropriate. The depreciation is included with other depreciation on the income statement

Equity Transactions

DD. Identify transactions that affect paid-in capital and those that affect retained earnings.
   a. Paid-in capital or capital received consists of capital stock at par or stated value plus capital received in excess of par or stated value. Transactions affecting paid-in capital include proceeds from the issuance of shares, retirement of repurchased shares, stock splits, stock dividends, and the conversion of debt to equity.
   b. Retained earnings are the "running" record of net incomes minus dividends since the inception of the corporation. In addition to net incomes and dividends, retained earnings are affected by the appropriation of retained earnings or the removal of an appropriation.

EE. Determine the effect on shareholders' equity of large and small stock dividends and stock splits.
   a. Stock dividends occur when the corporation issues shares to existing shareholders on a pro rata basis. A large stock dividend occurs when the number of shares issued exceeds 25% of the outstanding shares. The accounting for a large stock dividend requires the capitalization of retained earnings at the par or stated value of the stock. An amount equal to said value is transferred from retained earnings to common stock par or stated value.
   b. A small stock dividend occurs when the number of shares issued is less than 20% of the outstanding shares. In this case, retained earnings are capitalized at the market value of the stock at the time of the stock dividend issue. An amount equal to that value is transferred from retained earnings to capital received (par or stated value and excess over par or stated value) as appropriate.
   c. A stock split involves the recall and reissue of all shares to reflect a change in the par or stated value caused by the split. For example, a two-for-one stock split would involve halving the par or stated value of the shares and doubling the number of shares authorized, issued, and outstanding and in the treasury.

FF. Identify reasons for the appropriation of retained earnings.
   a. The appropriation (restriction or reservation) of retained earnings puts shareholders on notice that the portion of retained earnings appropriated is no longer available for dividend distribution. Reasons for the appropriation of retained earnings include plant expansion, sinking funds for debt retirement, and treasury stock acquisition.

Revenue Recognition

GG. Apply revenue recognition principles to various types of transactions.
  a. The basic revenue recognition principle states that revenue is recognized when the following criteria are met:
   - The earnings process is compete or virtually complete.
   - A measurable exchange has taken place.
   - The collectibility of cash is reasonably assured.

     In other words, it is earned, measurable, and collectible, and an exchange has taken place. This describes the default point-of-sale method.

HH. Identify issues involved with revenue recognition at point of sale, including sales with buyback agreements, sales when right of return exists, and trade loading (or channel stuffing).
  a. A sale with a buyback agreement may not be recognized as a sale (revenue) until the buyback period expires. The earnings process is not complete. A sale with a right of return may be recorded as a sale (revenue) as long as sales returns and an allowance for returns are presented on the income statement and balance sheet, respectively. Again, the earnings process is not complete.
  b. Trade loading or channel stuffing involves shipping to your customers without a customer order. It is normally done at year-end to inflate revenues. Since there is no customer order, there is no agreement with the customer, and, consequently, a sale should not be recognized. As before, the earnings process is not complete.

II. Identify instances where revenue is recognized before delivery and when it is recognized after delivery.
  a. The recognition of revenue before delivery occurs with either the percentage-of-completion method for recording long-term contracts or the production method for handling the mining of precious metals such as platinum and gold that have a ready market with a determinable price. The production method also applies to diamond mines.
  b. The recognition of revenue after delivery occurs in two cases. The first occurs when there are "strings" attached to the sale, such as a buyback provision or right of return. The second occurs when the collectibility of cash is not reasonably assured. In this second case, revenue is recognized by a cash method called the installment sales method.

JJ. Distinguish between percentage-of-completion and completed-contract methods for recognizing revenue.
  a. Both the percentage-of-completion method and the completed contract method apply to the recognition of revenue and expenses related to long-term construction contracts. The percentage-of-completion method recognizes construction revenue and expenses as the construction project progresses over time. The completed contract recognizes all of the revenue and expenses related to the project at the project's completion.

KK. Compare and contrast the recognition of costs of construction, progress billings, collections, and gross profit under the two long-term contract accounting methods.
   a. When using the completed contract method, the progress billings and collections are recorded in construction receivables on the balance sheet. Costs of construction are carried on the balance sheet in an inventory account called "construction in progress" and are expensed to the income statement when the project is completed and the revenue is recognized.
   b. Under the percentage-of-completion method, the progress billings, collections, and construction in progress are handled in the same fashion as with the completed contract method. Revenue is recognized by the percentage-of-completion of the project in a given period. The credit to revenue is offset by debits to costs of revenue equal to the construction costs incurred and to construction in progress. The debit to construction in progress is equal to the difference between the revenue and costs of revenue. It is the gross profit from the project for the period.

LL. Identify situations in which each of the following revenue recognition methods would be used: installment sales method, cost recovery method, and deposit method.
   a. There are three methods of recognizing revenue after delivery: the installment sales method, the cost recovery method, and the deposit method. The installment sales method is used when the collectibility of cash is spread over a long period of time. This is common for real estate and franchise contracts. The revenue is recognized on a pro rata basis through the gross profit on the contract. The cost recovery method does not recognize revenue until all of the costs related to the sale have been collected. It is used when the collectibility is highly uncertain. The deposit method is used when the seller receives cash before the transfer of ownership occurs. Since the risks and rewards of ownership have not transferred, the deposits are recorded as unearned revue (a performance obligation). Revenue is recognized upon the transfer of ownership.

MM. Discuss issues and concerns that have been identified with respect to revenue recognition practices.
   a. The issues related to revenue recognition were presented in the coverage of the revenue recognition principle in GG. The issues are:
      - Has the revenue been earned?
      - Is the revenue measurable?
      - Has an exchange taken place?
      - Is the collectibility of cash reasonably assured?

NN. Demonstrate an understanding of the matching principle with respect to revenues and expenses, and be able to apply it to a specific situation.
   a. The matching principle states that expenses are either to be matched to the revenues they create, as in matching cost of sales to sales, construction costs of revenue to construction revenue, or gross profits in the installment sales method, or matched to the period to which they pertain.

Matching to the period would include such expenses as advertising, promotion, research and development, interest, and utilities.

Income Measurement

OO. Define gains and losses, and indicate the proper financial statement presentation.
  a. A gain is the excess of revenue over cost from a transaction that is outside the normal course of business. Examples would be the gain from the sale of fixed assets or investments or the gain from early retirement of debt. A loss is the expiration of an asset without creating revenue. It occurs when there is an excess of cost over revenue from a transaction outside the normal course of business. Examples would be a fire loss, loss on sale of fixed assets or investments, or loss on early debt retirement. Gains and losses are preferably shown in other revenues, expenses, gains, and losses shown below operating income on the income statement.

PP. Demonstrate an understanding of the proper accounting for losses on long-term contracts.
  a. Expected losses on long-term contracts are to be recorded in the period in which the loss becomes apparent.

QQ. Demonstrate an understanding of the treatment of gain or loss on the disposal of fixed assets.
  a. The gain or loss on the disposal of a fixed asset should be shown in the income statement as part of other revenue, expenses, gains, and losses below operating income as noted in OO.

RR. Demonstrate an understanding of expense recognition practices.
  a. Expense recognition practices and principles were covered under the matching principle in NN.

SS. Define and calculate comprehensive income.
  a. Comprehensive income includes net income from the income statement and other comprehensive net income. Other comprehensive net income includes, for the most part, unrealized gains and losses on investments, foreign currency translation gains and losses, and unrealized gains and losses on hedging transactions. Other comprehensive income may be appended to the income statement or shown as a separate statement of comprehensive net income. It cannot be buried in the statement of stockholders' equity or retained earnings.

TT. Identify correct treatment of extraordinary items and discontinued operations.
  a. Discontinued operations are shown net of tax in the income statement after the after-tax net income from continuing operations. The net gain or loss from discontinued operations is split between the gain or loss from the operations as it was running and the gain or loss from the disposal of the discontinued operation.

b. Extraordinary items are shown net of tax after discontinued operations (if they exist) in the income statement. For an item to be extraordinary, it must meet three requirements. It has to be unusual, infrequent, and outside management control.

GAAP–IFRS Differences

UU. Identify and describe the following differences between U.S. GAAP and IFRS: (i) revenue recognition with respect to the sale of goods, services, deferred receipts, and construction contracts; (ii) expense recognition with respect to share-based payments and employee benefits; (iii) intangible assets with respect to development costs and revaluation; (iv) inventories with respect to costing methods, valuation, and write-downs (e.g., LIFO); (v) leases with respect to leases of land and buildings; (vi) long-lived assets with respect to revaluation, depreciation, and capitalization of borrowing costs; (vii) impairment of assets with respect to determination, calculation, and reversal of loss; and (viii) financial statement presentation with respect to extraordinary items and changes in equity.

i. IFRS requires revenue recognition based on a contract with the customer. Revenue is recognized as contract milestones are met. IFRS allows only the percentage-of-completion method for the recognition of revenue for long-term or multiyear contracts. U.S. GAAP allows both percentage-of-completion and completed contract methods.

ii. The differences between U.S. GAAP and IFRS treatment of share-based payments and employee benefits are beyond the scope of the CMA examination.

iii. Both IFRS and U.S. GAAP require the expensing of basic research expenditures. U.S. GAAP allows the capitalization of development costs when the project is technically feasible only. IFRS requires the intention to complete the project, the ability to sell the resulting product(s), and the availability of resources to complete the project as well as technical feasibility. IFRS allows the revaluing of intangibles to fair value less accumulated amortization. U.S. GAAP does not.

iv. IFRS does not allow the use of LIFO for inventory valuation while U.S. GAAP does. IFRS does not have the ceiling (net realizable value – NRV) and floor (NRV reduced by the normal profit margin) rules for LCM. It only uses NRV.

v. IFRS requires the disclosure of the net present value (NPV) of operating leases. Operating leases are recorded as liabilities if there are long-term provisions. Under IFRS, when leasing real estate (land and buildings), the land and buildings must be considered separately. U.S. GAAP considers them separately only when the land value at the inception of the lease exceeds 25% of the fair value of the leased real estate. Capital lease treatment in IFRS and in U.S. GAAP is basically the same.

vi. IFRS allows the revaluation of long-lived assets (property, plant, and equipment [PP&E]) to fair value less accumulated depreciation. U.S. GAAP does not. Both IFRS and U.S. GAAP require the capitalization of interest during construction (IDC) when borrowed funds are used in connection with expenditures for self-constructed assets.

vii. Under U.S. GAAP, the amount of impairment loss on long-lived assets is the amount by which its carrying value exceeds its fair value. IFRS calculates the impairment loss as the amount by which the carrying value exceeds the recoverable amount. The recoverable amount is the higher of: (1) fair value less cost to sell and (2) value in use (the present value of the future cash flows in use, including the disposal value). IFRS allows the reversal of impairment losses not to exceed the initial carrying amount of the asset. U.S. GAAP prohibits reversal of any impairment losses. IFRS prohibits reversals for goodwill.

viii. IFRS prohibits the separate presentation of extraordinary items in the income statement. U.S. GAAP allows presentation of extraordinary items. Extraordinary items are those that are unusual, infrequent, and outside management control. All three criteria must be met.

TOPIC 1

Financial Statements

THE FOUR FINANCIAL STATEMENTS DISCUSSED in this topic present a basic picture of an entity, are required by the Securities and Exchange Commission (SEC) for all publicly traded companies, and are a useful tool for any company. They include:

1. The income statement, which shows the results of business activities.
2. The statement of changes in equity, which shows owner investments, distribution of profits to owners, and profits retained by the company.
3. The balance sheet, which shows an entity's ending financial position.
4. The statement of cash flows, which shows an entity's cash receipts, payments, and the cash effects of its operating, investing, and financing activities during the accounting period.

The financial statements shown in this topic are all for a fictitious organization, Robin Manufacturing Company, for a given year, and linkages between the various statements are illustrated with notes and by the amounts themselves. The footnotes to financial statements, which present required disclosures, are also covered.

Most entities provide prior years' financial statement information alongside the current year's information for comparison. For example, income and cash flow statements usually show three years of results. This allows analysts to compare past performance to present performance and make a determination of future success.

This topic ends with a discussion of the needs of external users and how financial statements satisfy some of those needs.

READ the Learning Outcome Statements (LOS) for this topic as found in Appendix A and then study the concepts and calculations presented here to be sure you understand the content you could be tested on in the CMA exam.

Income Statement

The income statement, commonly called a profit and loss (P&L) statement, measures the earnings of an entity's operations over a given time period, such as a quarter or fiscal year. The income statement is used to measure profitability, creditworthiness, and investment value of an entity. Along with the other statements, it helps assess the amounts, timing, and uncertainty of future cash flows.

Income and Other Comprehensive Income

The financial statement elements reported on the income statement are revenues, expenses, gains, and losses. Financial Accounting Standards Board (FASB) Accounting Standards Codification (ASC) Topic 220, *Comprehensive Income* (formerly SFAS No. 130), requires firms to report certain unrealized gains and losses outside of net income as components of other comprehensive income. Comprehensive income is the sum of net income plus (or minus) the items of other comprehensive income.

Firms have the option of presenting the calculation of comprehensive income either as part of an income statement (appended at the end) or as a separate statement of comprenhensive income. Comprehensive income can no longer be presented as a part of the statement of shareholders' equity.

Format of Financial Information

The two most common formats are single-step income statements and multiple-step income statements.

Single-Step Income Statement

A single-step income statement subtracts total expenses and losses from total revenues and gains in a single step. No attempt is made to categorize expenses and revenues or arrive at interim subtotals.

Single-step income statements are simple, and some find the lack of priority of one type of revenue or gain (or expense or loss) over another to be a way to avoid classification problems. However, the multiple-step income statement is currently more popular.

Figure 1A-1 shows a single-step income statement for Robin Manufacturing Company, Year 1. (Year 1 is used to show a consistent time period; do not assume that this is the company's first year in business.)

Figure 1A-1 Single-Step Income Statement

Robin Manufacturing Company Income Statement for the Year Ended December 31, Year 1	
Revenues	
Net sales	$2,734,620
Dividend revenue	90,620
Rental revenue	67,077
Total revenues	2,892,317
Expenses	
Cost of goods sold	1,823,938
Selling expenses	416,786
Administrative expenses	322,709
Interest expense	115,975
Income tax expense	61,579
Total expenses	2,740,987
Net income	$151,330
Earnings per common share	$1.89

→ **To** statement of changes in equity section **(Figure 1A-4)**

Multiple-Step Income Statement

The multiple-step income statement disaggregates information into operating and non-operating categories in an attempt to make the information more useful. The sections in the statement that do not relate to operating cash flows are called "other revenues and gains" and "other expenses and losses." These categories could include gains and losses from the sale of equipment, interest revenue and expense, or dividends received.

The multiple-step income statement has subcategories, such as cost of goods sold (COGS); operating (selling and administrative) expenses; and other revenues, expenses, gains, and losses. These subcategories allow users to compare a company's results over time or with those of a competitor to determine the efficiency with which the entity's scarce resources are used. Such comparisons are especially valuable when several years' income statements are compared.

The multiple-step income statement often reports subtotals for gross profit and income from operations, which are useful for financial statement analysis purposes. For example, gross profit can be used to compare how competitive pressures have affected profit margins.

Figure 1A-2 shows a multiple-step income statement.

Figure 1A-2 Multiple-Step Income Statement

Robin Manufacturing Company
Income Statement for the Year Ended December 31, Year 1 (Y1)

Sales Revenue
Sales			$2,808,835
Less: Sales discounts		$22,302	
Less: Sales returns and allowances		51,913	74,215
Net sales revenue			2,734,620

Cost of Goods Sold
Merchandise inventory, Jan. 1, Y1		424,321	
Purchases	$1,830,518		
Less: Purchase discounts	17,728		
Net purchases	1,812,790		
Freight and transportation—in	37,363	1,850,153	
Total merchandise available for sale		2,274,474	
Less: Merchandise inventory, Dec. 31, Y1		450,536	
Cost of goods sold			$1,823,938
Gross profit on sales			910,682

Operating Expenses
Selling expenses
Sales salaries and commissions	186,432		
Sales office salaries	54,464		
Travel and entertainment	45,025		
Advertising expense	35,250		
Freight and transportation—out	37,912		
Shipping supplies and expense	22,735		
Postage and stationery	15,445		
Depreciation of sales equipment	8,285		
Telephone and Internet expense	11,238	416,786	

Administrative expenses
Officers' salaries	171,120		
Office salaries	56,304		
Legal and professional services	21,823		
Utilities expense	21,413		
Insurance expense	15,667		
Building depreciation	16,614		
Office equipment depreciation	14,720		
Stationery, supplies, and postage	2,645		
Miscellaneous office expenses	2,403	322,709	739,495
Income from operations			171,187

Other Revenues and Gains
Dividend revenue		90,620	
Rental revenue		67,077	157,697
			328,884

Other Expenses and Losses
Interest on bonds and notes			115,975
Income before income tax			212,909
Income tax			61,579
Net income for the year			$151,330
Earnings per common share			$1.89

→ **To** states of change in equity **(Figure 1A-4)**

Additional Income Statement Presentation Items

Occasionally, companies will experience an event that requires separate reporting below income from continuing operations. Additional items that may be located at the end of the income statement include discontinued operations and extraordinary items.

- **Discontinued operations.** When a component of an entity that has clearly distinguishable operations and cash flows is disposed of, the item is recorded in a separate section of the income statement after continuing operations and before extraordinary items. Discontinued operations are shown net of tax.
- **Extraordinary items.** Material items that are both unusual in nature and infrequent in occurrence, such as a government restriction or banning of a product line, require a separate section in the income statement, shown net of tax.

Figure 1A-3 shows how net income is determined when these items are included.

Figure 1A-3 Multistep Income Statement with Additional Income Statement Items

	Net sales
	– Cost of goods sold
	Gross profit on sales
	– Operating expenses
	Operating income
+/–	Other gains and losses
	Earnings before tax
	– Tax expense
	Income from continuing operations
	+/– Discontinued operations
	+/– Extraordinary items
	+/– Changes in accounting principle
	Net income

States of Change in Equity

When a balance sheet is issued, the FASB requires disclosure of the changes in each separate shareholder's equity account. This requirement satisfies the FASB's suggestion that complete financial statements should include investments by and distributions to owners during the period. The required states of change in equity is intended to help external users assess how changes in the company's financial structure may affect its financial flexibility.

Major Components and Classifications

Shareholders' equity includes several components: capital stock (par value of preferred and common shares), additional paid-in capital, retained earnings, and accumulated other comprehensive income. Capital stock is the par value (or face value) for the shares, and additional paid-in capital is the amount paid for the shares in excess of par. Thus, these two categories combine to form contributed capital, also called paid-in capital. Retained earnings can be subdivided into general earnings retained for company use and appropriated earnings set aside for some purpose.

Format of Financial Information

The statement of changes in equity usually lists information in the following order:

- Beginning balance for the period
- Additions
- Deductions
- Ending balance for the period

Figure 1A-4 shows a sample statement of changes in equity. This example shows the statement listed in a columnar format for a company with only common stock outstanding.

Figure 1A-4 Statement of Changes in Equity

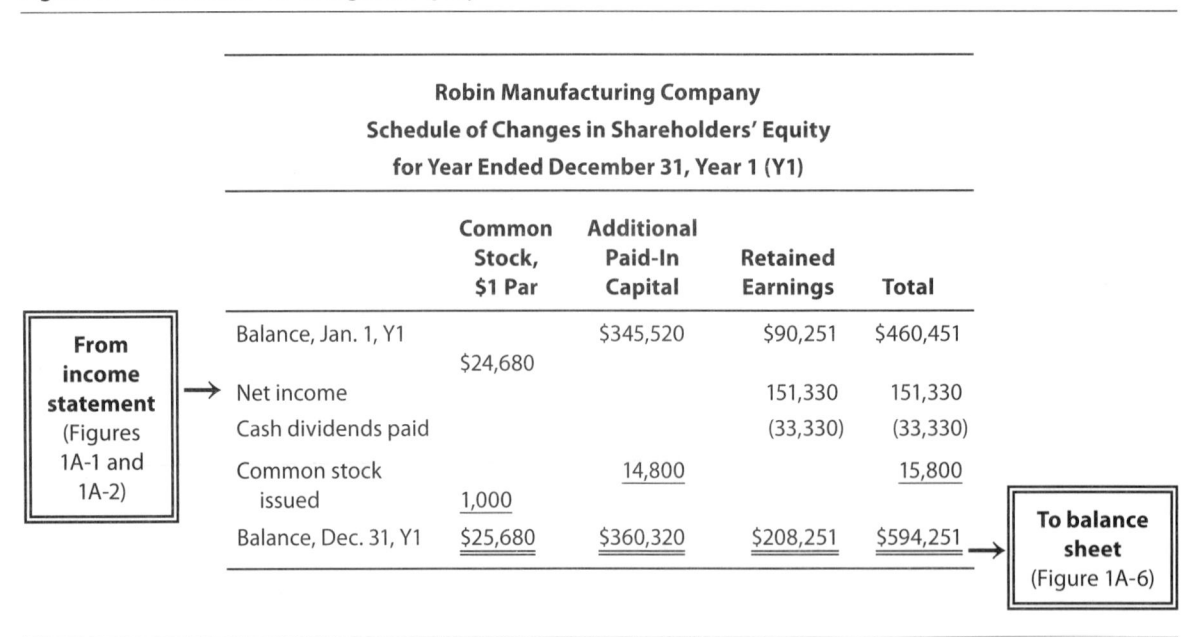

Robin Manufacturing Company
Schedule of Changes in Shareholders' Equity
for Year Ended December 31, Year 1 (Y1)

	Common Stock, $1 Par	Additional Paid-In Capital	Retained Earnings	Total
Balance, Jan. 1, Y1	$24,680	$345,520	$90,251	$460,451
Net income			151,330	151,330
Cash dividends paid			(33,330)	(33,330)
Common stock issued	1,000	14,800		15,800
Balance, Dec. 31, Y1	$25,680	$360,320	$208,251	$594,251

From income statement (Figures 1A-1 and 1A-2) → Net income, Cash dividends paid

To balance sheet (Figure 1A-6)

Balance Sheet

The balance sheet (sometimes called a statement of financial position) is an essential tool in assessing the amounts, timing, and uncertainty of prospective cash flows. It is referred to as the balance sheet because of the balance expressed by the accounting equation:

$$\text{Assets} = \text{Liabilities} + \text{Shareholders's Equity}$$

Alternatively, equity equals assets less liabilities, which is also known as net assets. The balance sheet provides a snapshot of the company's assets and the claims on those assets at a specific point in time.

While the balance sheet does not claim to show the value of the entity, along with the other statements and other information, it should allow external users to make their own estimates of the entity's value.

The balance sheet helps users evaluate the capital structure of the entity and assess the entity's liquidity, solvency, financial flexibility, and operating capability.

The balance sheet is also essential in understanding the income statement. Revenues and expenses reflect changes in assets and liabilities, so an analyst must evaluate both statements together.

Major Components and Classifications

The balance sheet is divided into three sections: assets, liabilities, and shareholders' equity. These classifications are designed to group similar items together so they can be analyzed more easily. Assets are listed with the most liquid items first and the least liquid last. Liabilities are listed in the order in which they become due. In the case of equity, the items that have most claim to the equity are listed before items with less claim. Figure 1A-5 summarizes the general subdivisions of each category.

Figure 1A-5 Balance Sheet Components

Assets	Current assets (cash, accounts receivable [A/R], inventory, etc.)	Intangible assets (patents, goodwill, etc.)
	Long-term investments	Other assets
	Property, plant, and equipment (PP&E)	
Liabilities	Current liabilities (accounts payable [A/P], interest payable, current portion of long-term debt, etc.)	Long-term liabilities (bonds, mortgages, etc.)
		Other liabilities
Shareholders' equity	Capital stock	Accumulated other comprehensive income
	Treasury stock (contra equity)	Retained earnings
	Additional paid-in capital	

The components of assets, liabilities, and equity are more thoroughly discussed in Topic 2 of this section.

Format of Financial Information

The two most common formats for the balance sheet are the account form and the report form. All styles of balance sheets break down the assets, liabilities, and shareholders' equity into the categories listed in Figure 1A-5 (current assets, etc.). The account form lists assets on the left side and liabilities and shareholders' equity on the right side. The report form, shown in Figure 1A-6, lists assets at the top and liabilities and shareholders' equity at the bottom. These two formats follow the accounting equation: The sum of all assets equals the sum of all liabilities and shareholders' equity. Outside the United States, other balance sheet formats are used, such as the financial position form, which deducts current liabilities from current assets to show working capital.

Figure 1A-6 Balance Sheet

Robin Manufacturing Company
Balance Sheet
December 31, Year 1

Assets	
Current assets:	
Cash and short-term investments	$24,628
Trade receivables, net of $30K allowance	552,249
Other receivables	18,941
Note receivable—related party	80,532
Inventory	252,567
Prepaid insurance	7,500
Total current assets	936,417
Fixed assets:	
Property and equipment	209,330
Less: Accumulated depreciation	(75,332)
Net fixed assets	133,998
Total assets	$1,070,415
Liabilities and Equity	
Current liabilities	
Accounts payable	$175,321
Accrued expenses	2,500
Current portion of long-term debt	36,000
Line of credit	145,000
Total current liabilities	358,821
Long-term debt	117,343
Total current and long-term liabilities	476,164
Shareholders' equity:	
Common stock, par	25,680
Additional paid-in capital	360,320
Retained earnings	208,251
Total shareholders' equity	594,251
Total liabilities and shareholders' equity	$1,070,415

From states of change in equity (Figure 1A-4) → Common stock, par; Additional paid-in capital; Retained earnings; Total shareholders' equity

In Figure 1A-6, the assets and liabilities are also categorized by their levels of financial flexibility. For example, current assets are shown separately from fixed assets.

Statement of Cash Flows

Cash is a company's most liquid resource, and therefore it affects liquidity, operating capability, and financial flexibility. FASB ASC Topic 230, *Statement of Cash Flows* (formerly SFAS No. 95), says that a statement of cash flows "must report on a company's cash inflows, cash outflows, and net change in cash from its operating, financing, and investing activities during the accounting period, in a manner that reconciles the beginning and ending cash balances." The statement helps interested parties determine if an entity needs external financing or is generating cash flows, meeting obligations, and paying dividends. Keep in mind that a company could have high income but still have negative cash flow.

Components and Classifications

Cash receipts and cash payments are classified in the statement of cash flows as related to operating, investing, or financing activities.

Operating Activities

Cash flows from operating activities are those related to the normal course of business. Any transaction that does not qualify as an investing or financing activity is included in the operating activity section. Examples of cash inflows include cash receipts from sales of any kind, collection of A/R, collection of interest on loans, and receipts of dividends. Cash outflows include cash paid to employees, suppliers, and the Internal Revenue Service (IRS) and to lenders for interest.

Statements that are compliant with generally accepted accounting principles (GAAP) use accrual accounting, so net income includes noncash revenues (e.g., uncollected credit sales) and noncash expenses (e.g., unpaid expenses). Other items that accrual accounting includes are depreciation, depletion, amortization, and other costs that were incurred in prior periods but are being charged to expenses in the current period. These items reduce net income but do not affect cash flows for the current period. Therefore, these items are added back when determining net cash flow from operating activities.

Examples of noncash expense and revenue items that must be added back to net income include those listed next.

- Depreciation expense and amortization of intangible assets
- Amortization of deferred costs, such as bond issue costs
- Changes in deferred income taxes
- Amortization of a premium or discount on bonds payable
- Income from an equity method investee

To determine operating cash flows, FASB ASC Topic 230, *Statement of Cash Flows*, allows entities to use either the indirect method or the direct method.

Indirect Method

The indirect method, or reconciliation method, is the most popular method of converting net income to net cash flow from operating activities. It starts with net income and then adjusts it by adding back noncash expenses and paper losses and subtracting noncash revenues and paper gains that have no effect on current period operating cash flows. Additional adjustments are made for changes in current asset and liability accounts related to operations by adding or subtracting amounts, as shown in Figure 1A-7. For example, an increase in A/R (a current asset) would be subtracted from net income to arrive at operating cash flows because it means that the amount of cash collected from customers is less than the amount of accrual revenue reported. See Figure 1A-7 for an example of the indirect method.

Figure 1A-7 Cash Flows from Operating Activities—Indirect Method

Net income
+ Noncash expenses (typically depreciation and amortization expenses)
− Gains from investing and financing activities
+ Losses from investing and financing activities
+ Decreases in current assets
− Increases in current assets
+ Increases in current liabilities
− Decreases in current liabilities
+ Amortization of discounts on bonds
− Amortization of premiums on bonds
Operating cash flow

Direct Method

In the direct method, or income statement method, net cash provided by operating activities is calculated by converting revenues and expenses from the accrual basis to the cash basis. Although the FASB encourages the use of the direct method, it is rarely used. Furthermore, if the direct method is used, the FASB requires that the reconciliation of net income to net cash flow from operating activities be disclosed in a separate schedule. Figure 1A-8 shows how a direct method statement is arranged. (The figure includes sample amounts for illustration.)

Investing Activities

Most items in the investing activities section come from changes in long-term asset accounts. Investing cash inflows result from sales of PP&E, sales of investments in another entity's debt or equity securities, or collections of the principal on loans to another entity. (Interest is included in operating cash flows.) Investing cash outflows

Figure 1A-8 Cash Flows from Operating Activities—Direct Method

Cash received from customers	$100,000
Cash paid to suppliers	(40,000)
Cash paid for interest	(5,000)
Cash paid for taxes	(10,000)
Cash paid for operating expenses	(25,000)
Cash provided by operating activities	$20,000

result from purchases of PP&E, purchases of other companies' debt or equity securities, and the granting of loans to other entities.

Financing Activities

Most items in the financing activities section come from changes in long-term liability or equity accounts. Financing cash inflows come from the sale of the entity's equity securities or issuance of debt, such as bonds or notes. Cash outflows consist of payments to stockholders for dividends and payments to reacquire capital stock or redeem a company's outstanding debt. In other words, investing activities involve the purchase or sale of fixed assets and investments in another company's securities, while financing activities involve the issuance and redemption of a company's own equity and debt securities.

Footnotes

The statement of cash flows requires footnote disclosure of any significant noncash investing and financing activities, such as the issuing of stock for fixed assets or the conversion of debt to equity. In addition, when the indirect method for cash flow from operations is used, both interest paid and income taxes paid need to be disclosed.

Example of a Statement of Cash Flows

The statement of cash flows shown in Figure 1A-9 illustrates the more commonly used indirect approach for calculating operating cash flows. Cash flows from each category (operating, investing, and financing) are separately classified and totaled. The sum of cash inflows (or outflows if negative) from these three categories equals the net increase or decrease in cash for the period. This net cash inflow (outflow) is added to (subtracted from) the cash balance at the beginning of the year to obtain the cash balance at the end of the year (highlighted in gray). Thus the cash flow statement explains the net change in the amount of cash and cash equivalents (short-term, highly liquid investments that are close to maturity) from the beginning to the ending balance sheet.

Figure 1A-9 Statement of Cash Flows—Indirect Method

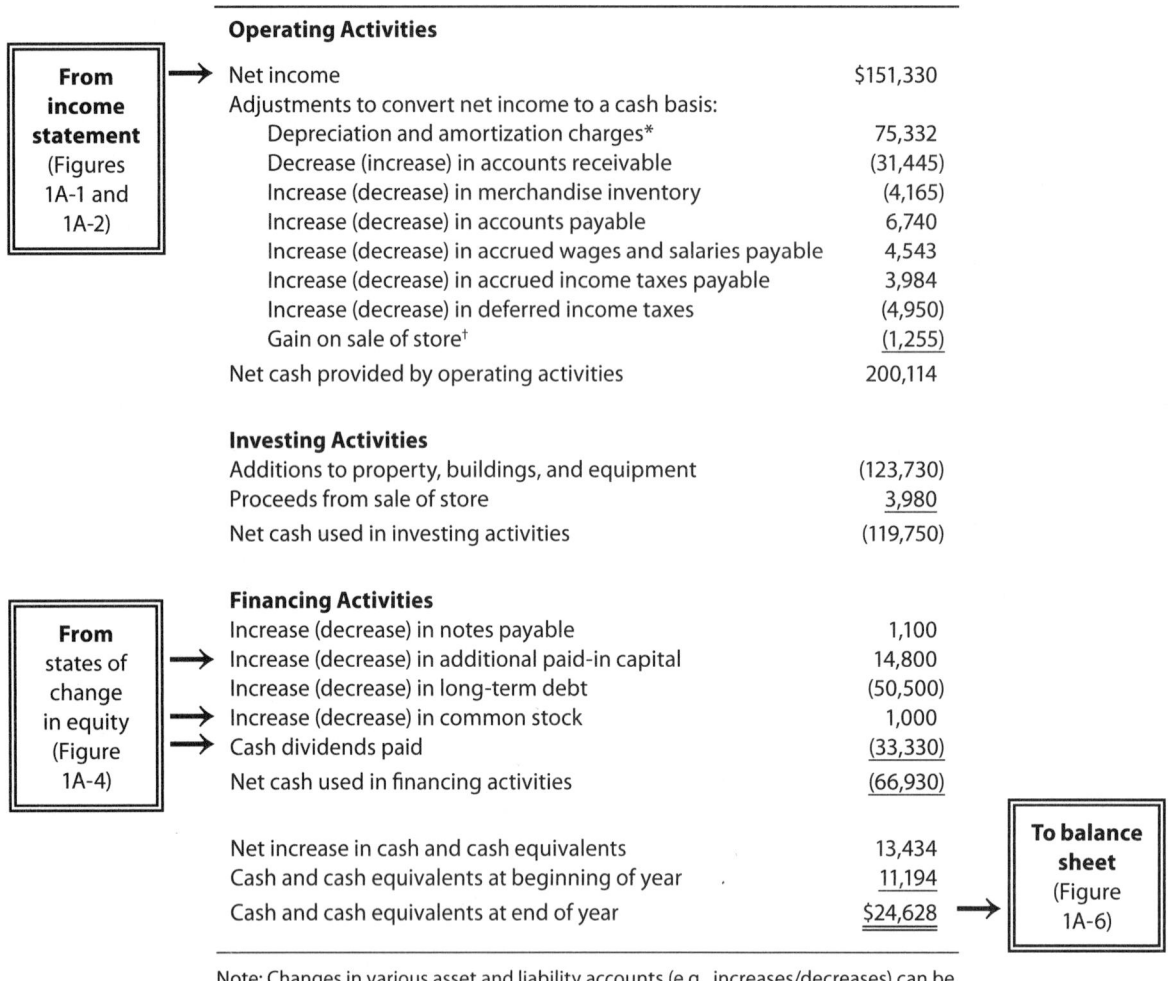

From income statement (Figures 1A-1 and 1A-2) →

Operating Activities	
Net income	$151,330
Adjustments to convert net income to a cash basis:	
Depreciation and amortization charges*	75,332
Decrease (increase) in accounts receivable	(31,445)
Increase (decrease) in merchandise inventory	(4,165)
Increase (decrease) in accounts payable	6,740
Increase (decrease) in accrued wages and salaries payable	4,543
Increase (decrease) in accrued income taxes payable	3,984
Increase (decrease) in deferred income taxes	(4,950)
Gain on sale of store†	(1,255)
Net cash provided by operating activities	200,114
Investing Activities	
Additions to property, buildings, and equipment	(123,730)
Proceeds from sale of store	3,980
Net cash used in investing activities	(119,750)
Financing Activities	
Increase (decrease) in notes payable	1,100
Increase (decrease) in additional paid-in capital	14,800
Increase (decrease) in long-term debt	(50,500)
Increase (decrease) in common stock	1,000
Cash dividends paid	(33,330)
Net cash used in financing activities	(66,930)
Net increase in cash and cash equivalents	13,434
Cash and cash equivalents at beginning of year	11,194
Cash and cash equivalents at end of year	$24,628

From states of change in equity (Figure 1A-4) →

To balance sheet (Figure 1A-6)

Note: Changes in various asset and liability accounts (e.g., increases/decreases) can be obtained by comparing two consecutive years' balance sheets.

* Depreciation and amortization charges are included in the income statement as part of administrative expenses.

† Gain on sale of store is included in the income statement as part of other revenue.

Limitations of the Financial Statements

Limitations of the financial statements are listed next.

- **Historical cost.** Most asset accounts of a nonfinancial nature are reported at historical cost. While historical cost measures are considered reliable because the amounts can be verified, they are also considered less relevant than fair value or current market value measures would be for assessing a firm's current financial position.
- **Different accounting methods.** Employing different accounting methods will yield different net incomes. Each choice of two or more accounting methods

will further change the results reported, making the task of comparing different entities very difficult, even when these methods are disclosed.
- **Omit nonobjective items of value.** Financial statements exclude valuable assets that are of financial importance but cannot be objectively expressed in numbers. For example, the value of human resources, intangibles such as brand recognition and reputation, or the value of the entity's customer base cannot be exactly or reliably estimated, so they are not included on the balance sheet. Therefore, the balance sheet does not purport to measure the value of the company as a whole.
- **Use of estimates and judgments.** Financial statements incorporate the use of numerous estimates and professional judgments. Differences in estimates mean that the income statements for two or more entities may be difficult to compare. Common estimates include the amount of receivables allocated to an allowance for doubtful accounts and the useful life and salvage value of a piece of equipment.
- **Off-balance-sheet information.** Transactions may be recorded in a way that avoids reporting liabilities and assets on the balance sheet, for example, with an operating lease. The Sarbanes-Oxley Act of 2002 (SOX) requires publicly traded firms to disclose off-balance-sheet information in their filings with the SEC.
- **Noncash transactions.** The statement of cash flows omits noncash transactions, such as the exchange of stock for a property, exchanges of nonmonetary assets, conversion of preferred stock or debt to common stock, or issuing equity securities to retire a debt. Disclosure of any noncash transactions that affect assets or liabilities would be reported in a note or a supplemental schedule.

Footnotes/Disclosures to Financial Statements

Footnotes or disclosures to financial statements are used when parenthetical explanations would not suffice to describe situations particular to the entity. Typical disclosures include contingencies, contractual situations, accounting policies, and subsequent events.

Contingencies

Contingencies are material events with an uncertain outcome dependent on the occurrence or nonoccurrence of one or more future events. Contingencies can be either gain contingencies or loss contingencies. To avoid the premature recognition of income before its realization, accounting recognition is not given to gain contingencies. However, loss contingencies must be recognized when it is both probable that a loss has been incurred and the amount of the loss is reasonably estimable. Other material loss contingencies should be disclosed in the footnotes to the financial statements; gain contingencies may also be disclosed.

Loss contingencies result from situations such as pending litigation, warranty and premium costs, environmental liabilities, and self-insurance risks. Gain contingencies result from pending litigation (where the outcome is favorable to the company), possible refunds of disputed tax amounts, and tax loss carryforwards.

Contractual Situations

Contractual agreements, such as pension obligations, lease contracts, and stock option plans, are required to be disclosed in the notes to financial statements. Other significant items should also be included. Contractual situations may require an entity to restrict certain funds, for example, and analysts need to understand how such provisions will affect the entity's financial flexibility.

Accounting Policies

Whenever GAAP or industry-specific regulations allow a choice between two or more accounting methods, the method selected should be disclosed. FASB ASC Topic 235, *Notes to Financial Statements* (formerly Accounting Principles Board (APB) Opinion No. 22), states that "a description of all significant accounting policies of the reporting entity should be included as an integral part of the financial statements."

ASC Topic 235 notes that three types of accounting disclosures related to recognition and asset allocation should be made:

1. Selection between acceptable alternatives
2. Selection of industry-specific methods
3. Unusual or innovative applications of GAAP

Most companies prepare a separate note, "Summary of Significant Accounting Policies," in which they report on the methods used to recognize revenue, calculate depreciation, value inventory, and measure other amounts reported on the financial statements.

Subsequent Events

It may take weeks or even months to issue the annual report after the accounting period has closed, and significant business events and transactions may occur during this period. A *subsequent event* is an event occurring between the balance sheet date and the issuance date of the annual report. If the event provides additional evidence about conditions that existed as of the balance sheet date and alters the estimates used in preparing the financial statements, then the financial statements should be adjusted.

Subsequent events that provide evidence regarding conditions that did not exist on the balance sheet date should be disclosed in a note, supplemental schedule, or pro forma statement.

In addition to the disclosures mentioned already, Figure 1A-10 lists other major areas that require some form of disclosure beyond the information presented in the financial statements.

These disclosures are covered in more detail throughout the rest of this book.

Figure 1A-10 Summary of Required Footnotes/Disclosures

Category	Footnote/Disclosure
Inventories	Valuation basis (net realizable value, cost, lower of cost or market)
	Cost flow assumption (specific identification; average cost; first in, first out [FIFO]; last in, first out [LIFO])
	Inventory classifications (purchases, raw materials, work-in-process accounts, finished goods, supplies); classified separately only if significant
	Product financing arrangements, if any
	FIFO equivalent if the company uses LIFO
Revenue	Policy on revenue recognition
Accounts receivable	Collectibility
	Collection policy
	Determination of bad debt
	Allowance for bad debt
PP&E	Valuation basis
	Depreciation expenses for the period
	Accumulated depreciation at the balance sheet date
	Depreciable asset balances by major class (either by nature or function)
	General description of the depreciation methods used by major class of depreciable asset
Intangibles (e.g., patents)	Description of the nature of the intangible
	Amount of amortization expense for the period
	Method and period of amortization
	Remaining useful life of the intangible
Bonds payable	Par value
	Stated and effective interest rate
	Call provisions
	Maturity date
Preferred stock	Par or stated value
	Changes in the number of shares authorized, issued, and outstanding for the period
	Dividend rate
	Special features of the preferred stock (convertible, cumulative, participating)
	Dividends in arrears
Common stock	Par or stated value
	Changes in the number of shares authorized, issued, and outstanding for the period
	Dividends declared (amount and type)
Other	Amount, nature, duration, and other significant provisions of any restrictions on retained earnings
	Prior period adjustments
	Employee plans, such as an employee stock option plans (ESOPs)

Users of Financial Statements

Financial statements are intended to aid in decision making. The most efficient companies will attract investors or will be granted credit first and will also be more likely to produce a higher return on investment. Moreover, a company becomes efficient partly through the proper allocation of its internal resources to those areas most likely to produce a profit. Financial statements are an integral part of the decision-making process for users both internal to the organization and external to it.

Internal and External Users

Internal Users

Internal users need financial statements (plus other sources of information) for internal decision making. The information is used to plan and control operations on both a short-term and long-term basis. The quality of these decisions will have an impact on how internal resources are allocated, how profitable the organization is, and, ultimately, whether the organization will survive. Internal users of financial statements include executives, managers, management accountants, and other employees (such as those with stock options or investments in the organization). Unlike external users, internal users may request or generate any type of information that is available in their accounting system. The potential of misuse of such information requires an organization to place internal controls on the use and access to such information, but not to the extent that the internal decision makers cannot access the information in a timely manner.

External Users

External users are any interested parties who must rely on the published financial statements and other publicly available information of an entity when making investment decisions. Some external users, such as lending institutions, may be in a position to demand additional information from an entity that is not publicly available. As mentioned earlier, the FASB defines external users as current and potential investors and creditors (and their advisors) who have a reasonable understanding of business and economics and who are willing to study the information with reasonable diligence. Investors, creditors, unions, analysts, financial advisors, competitors, and government agencies are all external users of information. Investors include individuals and other corporations. Creditors include lending institutions and suppliers of raw materials and other goods.

Needs of External Users

Creditors and investors comprise the two main sources of capital for publicly traded entities, so primary focus of financial statements is the needs of these two types of users. According to the FASB, financial reporting should provide information that is useful to external users in making reasoned choices among alternative investment, credit, and similar decisions. Users cannot absorb infinite amounts of data, and too much information may obscure the most relevant measures of the success of a business. Therefore, the goal of accounting is to summarize the vast amount of information into understandable reports and disclosures. The FASB's statements are intended to require a minimum level of disclosure, but it is still up to each entity to make this information user friendly.

Needs of Investors and Creditors

Financial information must be relevant and reliable for it to be useful, and relevance means that it must also be presented in a timely fashion. Investors and lenders are interested in both a return *of* their investment and a return *on* their investment. They receive a return of their investment only if the organization can maintain its capital. They receive a return on their investment through dividends and interest. Investors in the stock market receive a return on their investment if the market perceives that the company is doing well. Actual or potential investors have or are considering a direct ownership stake in an entity, and they need financial information primarily to decide whether to initiate or continue this relationship (i.e., buy, hold, or sell the firm's securities).

Actual or potential creditors are interested in the ability of the entity to comply with debt covenants. The four decisions they are concerned with are to extend credit, maintain credit, deny credit, or revoke credit. Creditors are also interested in financial statements to determine the risk level of their loan. Lending institutions expect a higher return on investment for more risky endeavors and will make low-return investments only when the risk is similarly low. Therefore, the entity's credit rating is of particular importance. The credit rating is based primarily on the entity's liquidity, solvency, and financial flexibility, all of which are determined from the entity's financial statements and other disclosures.

Other users of financial statements include stock exchanges (for rule making, listings, and cancellations), unions (for negotiating wages), and analysts (for advising others).

Knowledge Check: Financial Statements

The next questions are intended to help you check your understanding and recall of the material presented in this topic. They do not represent the type of questions that appear on the CMA exam.

Directions: Answer each question in the space provided. Correct answers and section references appear after the knowledge check questions.

1. On the statement of cash flows, which of the following is included in the operating activities section?
   - ☐ a. Purchase of equipment
   - ☐ b. Purchase of treasury stock
   - ☐ c. Issuing 1,000 shares of common stock
   - ☒ d. Income taxes paid

2. On the balance sheet, which of the following accurately describes the order in which items are listed?
   - ☒ a. Assets are listed from most to least liquid; liabilities are listed in the order in which they become due.
   - ☐ b. Assets and liabilities are listed in the order in which they become due; equity is listed from least to most liquid.
   - ☐ c. Assets are listed from least to most liquid; liabilities are listed in the order in which they become due.
   - ☐ d. Assets and liabilities are listed from most to least liquid; equity is listed in the order in which the items are used.

3. True or false? The balance sheet does not show the value of the entity.
   - ☒ a. True
   - ☐ b. False

4. True or false? The income statement presents the following items net of tax: gains and losses from discontinued operations, and extraordinary items.
   - ☐ a. True
   - ☐ b. False

Knowledge Check Answers: Financial Statements

1. On the statement of cash flows, which of the following is included in the operating activities section? [See **Balance Sheet**.]
   - ☐ a. Purchase of equipment
   - ☐ b. Purchase of treasury stock
   - ☐ c. Issuing 1,000 shares of common stock
   - ☑ d. Income taxes paid

2. On the balance sheet, which of the following accurately describes the order in which items are listed? [See **Multiple-Step Income Statement**.]
   - ☑ a. Assets are listed from most to least liquid; liabilities are listed in the order in which they become due.
   - ☐ b. Assets and liabilities are listed in the order in which they become due; equity is listed from least to most liquid.
   - ☐ c. Assets are listed from least to most liquid; liabilities are listed in the order in which they become due.
   - ☐ d. Assets and liabilities are listed from most to least liquid; equity is listed in the order in which the items are used.

3. True or false? The balance sheet does not show the value of the entity. [See **Multiple-Step Income Statement**.]
   - ☑ a. True
   - ☐ b. False

4. True or false? The income statement presents the following items net of tax: gains and losses from discontinued operations and extraordinary items. [See **Format of Financial Information**.]
   - ☑ a. True
   - ☐ b. False

TOPIC 2

Recognition, Measurement, Valuation, and Disclosure

This topic covers the recognition, measurement, valuation, and disclosure requirements of accounting transactions and specific accounts within a company's financial statements. In that regard, and because of the increasing use of fair value measurement in accounting transactions over the past decade, which have helped promote relevance in financial reporting and, consequently, better and more informed decisions, this topic begins by discussing current fair value accounting standards and the FASB's framework for integrating fair value measurements and disclosures into the financial reporting process as appropriate. The topic concludes with a comparison of International Financial Reporting Standards (IFRS) and U.S. GAAP as those standards relate to key financial statement accounts and transactions.

> **READ** the Learning Outcome Statements (LOS) for this topic as found in Appendix A and then study the concepts and calculations presented here to be sure you understand the content you could be tested on in the CMA exam.

Fair Value Standards and Measurements

Financial Accounting Standards Codification (ASC) Topic 820, *Fair Value Measurements and Disclosures* (formerly FASB Statement) No. 157 defines *fair value* and establishes a framework for measuring fair value uniformly for various accounts and accounting transactions. A fair value measurement assumes that the asset or liability is exchanged in an orderly transaction between market participants on the measurement date. When a principal market exists, the price at that market is the fair value. However, in situations where a principal market does not exist, the price at the "most advantageous" market would be used to determine the fair value if there are multiple markets for the asset or the liability. Additionally, a fair value measurement assumes the highest and best use of the asset by market participants. In broad terms, the phrase *highest and best use* refers to use of an asset that would maximize the value of the asset. Best use is determined based on the use of the asset by market participants even if the intended use is different. For example, if a land in prime residential neighborhood is acquired to build a warehouse, the fair value of the land would be the value if it were used for residential purposes.

In order to determine fair value, three approaches are suggested: **market approach, income approach**, and **cost approach**. The market approach uses prices generated by transactions involving identical or comparable assets. The income approach uses valuation techniques to convert future amounts to a single discounted present amount. The cost approach is based on the replacement value of the asset (i.e., the amount required to replace the asset).

To increase consistency and comparability in fair value measurements, a fair value hierarchy is created to prioritize the inputs to valuation techniques to determine the fair value. This hierarchy gives the highest priority to quoted prices in active markets (Level 1) and lowest priority to unobservable inputs (Level 3). In the intermediate, the input could be determined indirectly from the values of related assets, which have quoted prices in active markets (Level 2). The disclosure in the financial statement has to include the classification of assets into these three categories.

Using fair value in financial reporting, as opposed to cost-based reporting, provides more current information about the valuation of assets in comparison to using historical cost. Many financial institutions and investors rely on fair values to make decisions that involve financial assets and liabilities. In many cases, fair value represents the market's expectations about expected future cash flows that may be derived from such assets or liabilities. Fair value makes it possible to compare financial instruments (assets or liabilities) that embody the same economic characteristics, regardless of when they were issued or purchased, when making decisions to buy, hold, or sell those financial instruments. The disadvantages of using fair value include increased volatility in the value of the asset and uncertainty as to the reliability of estimates related to the flexibility in the estimate of the fair value of those instruments.

In May 2011 the International Accounting Standards Board issued IFRS No. 13, *Fair Value Measurement*, which aligns with ASC Topic 820. This new guidance established a single source framework for fair value measurement and set forth requirements for fair value disclosure smliar to that of U.S. GAAP.

Cash and Marketable Securities

Cash

Cash is any coin, currency, funds available on deposit, money order, certified check, cashier's check, personal check, bank draft, or savings account. To be reported as cash on the balance sheet, the cash must be readily available for payment of current liabilities, and it must not include any contractual restrictions or limits on its use to pay current liabilities.

Cash Equivalents

Cash equivalents are marketable securities with maturities of less than three months at the time of acquisition. Short-term commercial paper is a common form of cash equivalent. Cash equivalents often are grouped with cash.

Restricted Cash

Restricted cash is cash that is set aside to fulfill the terms of an agreement or for some future use. Restricted cash may include compensating balances, dividend funds, or payroll funds. When the amounts are not material, they can be reported with cash, but if material, they are reported separately as a current or long-term asset. Restricted cash is a current asset if it will be used to pay liabilities within a year or the operating cycle, whichever is longer. Otherwise it is reported as a long-term asset, such as a plant expansion fund or fund for the retirement of a specific long-term debt.

Compensating Balances

Many lenders include a **compensating balance** requirement as part of a loan provision, especially in the case of open or revolving lines of credit. These compensating balances are minimum balance requirements designed to offset part of the risk of lending. Compensating balances may or may not be restricted. They can be used not only for loans but also for the assurance of available future credit and as indirect compensation for services such as check cashing or lockbox management.

The Securities and Exchange Commission (SEC) recommends that legally restricted compensating balances be reported as separate items under cash and cash equivalents if the balance is held against short-term borrowing arrangements and as noncurrent assets (investments or other assets) if the balance is held against long-term borrowing arrangements. Compensating balance arrangements that do not have legal restrictions on their use should be disclosed in the notes to the statements.

Marketable Securities

Investments in individual marketable securities that are expected to be converted to cash within one year are classified as current assets. Investments in marketable equity securities are valued at fair value on the balance sheet. The disposition of unrealized gains and losses that arise when these investments are marked to market value depends on whether the securities are classified as part of the trading or available-for-sale investment portfolios. Investments in marketable debt securities are accounted for similarly, except that certain debt investments are classified as held-to-maturity securities and valued at amortized cost rather than at fair value. Accounting for the gains and losses on equity and debt investments under Financial Accounting Standards Board (FASB) Accounting Standards Codification (ASC) Topic 320, *Investments: Debt and Equity Securities* (formerly addressed in FASB Statement No. 115) is discussed in more detail later in this topic. Money market funds, money market savings certificates, certificates of deposit (CDs), and short-term commercial paper are classified as temporary investments on the balance sheet because they contain restrictions on their availability or penalties for withdrawal.

Recording and Valuation

Marketable securities are initially recorded at their acquisition price plus all incidental costs, such as brokerage fees or taxes. If a marketable security is received as a noncash payment or trade, valuation can be based on the more reliable of the fair market value of either the stock or the item traded. Marketable securities are generally carried at market value because they are by definition generally tradable. However, in a limited number of situations, marketable securities could be reported at historical cost.

Market Value

Marketable securities are revalued at the current market price at the time of statement preparation. Rises and falls in the price are reported as gains and losses on the income statement if related to trading securities and as unrealized gains and losses in other comprehensive income (stockholders' equity) if related to available-for-sale securities. **Market value** is more relevant than historical cost for reporting liquidity and financial flexibility because it is the current price to acquire or sell the security. Market value is reliable because the price can be determined definitely. ASC Topic 320 prescribes (fair) market value accounting for all securities except held-to-maturity debt instruments.

Accounts Receivable

Receivables are claims against a customer for cash, goods, or services. Accounts receivable (A/R) is a subset of receivables and is detailed in this section. Receivables result from sellers extending credit to buyers in order to increase sales. Receivables are considered liquid but not as liquid as cash because some accounts probably will not be paid.

Types of Receivables

Receivables are classified as current or noncurrent, trade or nontrade. Trade receivables include accounts receivable and notes receivable. Each of these classifications is detailed below. Current receivables are due to be collected within the longer of a year or the current operating cycle. Noncurrent receivables are due after one year or the current operating cycle, whichever is longer.

Trade Receivables

Trade receivables are the most common form of receivable because they arise from the normal operations of an entity: credit sales of goods and services.

- **Accounts receivable (A/R).** Accounts receivable are promises to pay for a good or service delivered. Most receivables have 30- or 60-day net payment terms and therefore are usually current receivables, but wide variations exist in terms. Accounts receivable are also called "open accounts."
- **Notes receivable.** Notes receivable are more formal trade receivables because they require a written promise to pay on a specified date. They can be either current or noncurrent.

Nontrade Receivables

Nontrade receivables contain all types other than those involved in daily operations, including damage deposits and other guarantee deposits; advances to officers or to subsidiaries; dividends and interest receivable; and claims against insurance companies, common carriers, lawsuit defendants, the government, and customers for returned, lost, or damaged goods. Nontrade receivables usually are reported as separate items on the balance sheet.

Impact of Sales Practices on A/R Balances

Accounts receivable are subject to trade discounts and cash discounts.

Trade Discounts

Trade discounts (or volume or quantity discounts) allow a business to list a single price in a catalog and then sell the item to various types of customers, such as wholesale and retail customers, at different percentage discounts from the list price.

Cash Discounts

Cash discounts are incentives for early or prompt payment. Buyers can apply this type of discount automatically if they make payment by the specified deadline. Cash discounts are expressed in shorthand, such as 2/10, n/30 (2 in 10, net 30). This means a 2% discount is available if payment is made within 10 days or the net amount (undiscounted or gross amount) is due within 30 days. A discount of 2/10 net 30 not taken represents an opportunity cost of 37.25%:

$$\text{Effective Cost of Discount} = \frac{\text{Discount \%}}{(100 - \text{Discount \%})} \times \frac{365}{(\text{Net Period} - \text{Discount Period})}$$

$$= \frac{0.02}{(0.98)} \times \frac{365}{30 - 10} = 0.02041 \times 18.25 = 37.25\%$$

Because the firm presumably can borrow funds for less than this rate, it would be cheaper to borrow funds to pay within the discount period than to use the extended payment period.

Cash discounts can be recorded at either their gross amount or their net amount. Most companies record sales and receivables using the simpler gross method.

- **Gross method.** The gross method records each receivable and sale at the gross or undiscounted amount. Then sales discounts are recognized in accounting entries if the payment is received within the deadline for the discount. On the income statement, net sales are determined by deducting sales discounts from gross sales.
- **Net method.** The net method records each receivable and sale at the net amount, assuming all discounts are taken. It more fully embraces the matching

principle, because it provides an allowance for expected discounts to be taken and charges these against sales in the period of the sale, thus recording the sale at closer to its realizable value. To account for unused sales discounts, another revenue item account called sales discounts forfeited is created in which adjusting entries are recorded. Figure 1A-11 shows how a receivable of $100,000 with terms of 1/10, n/30 would be recorded under each method, assuming that half of the purchase is paid for within the discount period.

Figure 1A-11 Gross and Net Method Accounting for Cash Discounts on Accounts Receivable

Gross Method			Net Method		
On July 1, sale made:					
A/R	$100,000		A/R	$99,000	
Sales		$100,000	Sales		$99,000
On July 10, payment of $50,000 received:					
Cash	$49,500		Cash	$49,500	
Sales discounts	$500		A/R		$49,500
A/R		$50,000			
On July 30, payment of $50,000 received:					
Cash	$50,000		A/R	$500	
A/R		$50,000	Sales discounts forfeited		$500
			Cash	$50,000	
			A/R		$50,000

Sales Returns and Allowances

When a customer returns goods purchased on credit or receives an allowance (price discount) for imperfect goods, the seller credits accounts receivable and debits sales returns and allowances (a contra account to sales). However, certain companies experience such high rates of returns that they initially record sales net of an estimate for the expected returns and establish an allowance for sales returns as a contra account to accounts receivable. Sales returns and allowances are covered in more depth later in this topic.

Maturity Value versus Present Value in Trade Receivables

ASC Topic 835, *Interest* (formerly APB Opinion No. 21), indicates that long-term receivables should be recorded at their present values but specifically exempts trade receivables due to their short collection times. Trade receivables should instead be recorded at their maturity value, which in the case of a 30- or 60-day receivable is a small enough difference from the present value to make the difference immaterial. Generally accepted accounting principles (GAAP) allow for nonrecognition of present value for normal business receivables due in customary trade terms not exceeding one year.

However, trade receivables must be valued and reported at their net realizable value. The **net realizable value (NRV) for trade receivables** is the net amount of cash that the company expects to receive, excluding an estimate of uncollectible amounts (bad debt expense) and of expected returns (if there is a return policy). Note that NRV for trade receivables does not reflect the time value of money, and hence present value calculations are not included.

Valuation and Uncollectible Accounts

Sales made on account raise the possibility that a firm may not be able to collect the full amount of accounts receivable. The two most commonly used methods of recording bad debt expense are the direct write-off method and the allowance method.

Direct Write-off Method

The direct write-off method recognizes bad debt expense only after an account is deemed uncollectible. The direct write-off method has the advantage of simplicity and reliability, because no estimates are used. However, this method is generally not considered appropriate under GAAP because the costs are not matched against the revenues of the correct period and the receivables are overstated. The direct write-off method is required for federal income tax purposes.

Allowance Method

The allowance method makes an estimate of the expected uncollectible accounts from all credit sales or from all outstanding receivables. The allowance for doubtful accounts is netted against accounts receivable to determine net realizable value. This is the amount the company expects to collect. The bad debt expense is also reported as an operating expense. Under the allowance method, bad debt expense is estimated using either a balance sheet approach or an income statement approach.

- **Balance sheet approach (A/R relationship).** The balance sheet approach evaluates historical trends between actual bad debts recorded in the past and accounts receivable using one of two methods:
  1. **Percentage of outstanding A/R.** The goal of the percentage of outstanding accounts receivable method is to determine the net realizable value of receivables and report this information on the balance sheet. This method assesses the historical relationship between actual bad debts and accounts receivable over a period without identifying specific accounts. (Due dates of debts are not accounted for.) The resulting percentage of bad debts per average account receivable level is multiplied against the current accounts receivable at the end of a period to determine the required ending balance in the allowance for doubtful accounts. For example, if a company has $100,000 in accounts receivable at the end of a period and estimates that 4% of receivables result in bad debts, it multiplies that sum by 4%. The net realizable value in this example would be $96,000, and bad debt expense would be $4,000. However, if there is an existing credit balance in the allowance for doubtful accounts,

say of $1,000, then bad debt expense would be $3,000, because it is necessary to adjust the balance only to the desired level.

2. **Aging of A/R.** Accounts receivable become harder to collect as more time passes, a fact that the previous method of estimating bad debts ignores. Aging of accounts receivable using an aging schedule categorizes A/R by the length of time the debts have been outstanding. The older the debts are, the higher the estimated percentage of doubtful accounts.

Figure 1A-12 shows an example of an aging schedule.

Figure 1A-12 Accounts Receivable Aging Schedule

Bounce Sporting Goods Company
Aging Schedule

Name of Customer	Balance December 31	Under 60 Days	61–90 Days	91–120 Days	Over 120 Days
East Side Sport Supply	$54,880	$44,800	$10,080		
Rockford Gyms & Courts	179,200	179,200			
Freedom Tennis Supply	30,800				$30,800
Broadway Sporting Goods	41,440	33,600		$7,840	
	$306,320	$257,600	$10,080	$7,840	$30,800

Summary

Age	Amount	Percentage Estimated to Be Uncollectible	Required Balance in Allowance
Under 60 days old	$257,600	5%	$12,880
61–90 days old	10,080	15%	1,512
91–120 days old	7,840	20%	1,568
Over 120 days	30,800	25%	7,700
Year-end balance of allowance for doubtful accounts			$23,660

- **Income statement approach (sales relationship).** The income statement approach compares historical bad debts to sales using one of two methods:
  1. **Percentage of sales.** The percentage-of-sales method may be used when there is a stable relationship between cash and credit sales. This approach is based on the matching principle inherent in the income statement; expenses are matched against revenues in the same period. The historical percentage of bad debts to sales is used to calculate the estimated bad debts for the period. For example, if a company has $100,000 in sales and it estimates that 3% of sales result in bad debts, then bad debt expense is $3,000.
  2. **Percentage of net credit sales.** When the relationship between credit sales and total sales varies widely over time, the percentage of sales method cannot be used as it is. Instead, the method can be applied using net credit sales in place of total sales.

Both of these income statement methods focus on measuring the expense for the period, which is added to any existing balance in the allowance account.

Write-Offs and Collection of Write-Offs in Financial Statements

When using the allowance method, a specific uncollectible account receivable is written off by debiting the allowance for doubtful accounts and crediting accounts receivable. The write-off confirms the previously estimated loss, so the net carrying value of accounts receivable on the balance sheet is not affected. Bad debt expense is not recorded at the time of write-off. If a written-off receivable is subsequently collected, it is first reinstated by debiting accounts receivable and crediting the allowance for doubtful accounts. Then the receipt of cash and the reduction of accounts receivable is recorded.

If an account written off using the direct write-off method is subsequently collected, the amount is debited to cash and credited to a revenue account, such as uncollectible accounts recovered.

Sales Returns and Allowances

When a customer returns goods previously sold on credit, accounts receivable is credited and sales returns and allowances is debited, thus reducing net sales. However, in some industries, the return rate is so high that sales initially are recorded net of estimated sales returns, and an offsetting allowance for sales returns is established as a contra account to accounts receivable.

Notes Receivable

Accounts receivable are oral promises to pay; notes receivable involve written promises to pay. A **promissory note** documents a note receivable and is signed by a maker (the entity that will owe the money) as an unconditional promise to pay a specific sum of money at a particular date in the future.

Promissory notes are negotiable; they can be bought and sold by the current payee (the one who collects the payment and interest). Because notes are unconditional, they are considered fairly liquid. Notes generally are interest bearing within a stated rate of interest. Zero-interest-bearing notes include interest as part of their face value.

A note may be accepted from a customer that needs to extend the payment time on an existing receivable or to initiate a lending transaction.

Short-term notes receivable generally are recorded at face value. The interest that is implied in the maturity value for such notes is considered immaterial. Conversely, long-term notes must be reported at the present value of the expected amount to be received.

If a long-term interest-bearing note is issued and the interest stated on the note is equal to the effective (market) rate of interest, the note is issued at face value (future amount owed). When the stated rate differs from the current market rate, the note is issued at a discount or premium, and this amount is amortized over the life of a note to record the effective interest.

These two situations are further illustrated in the sections that follow.

Notes Issued at Face Value

When a note is issued at face value, the stated interest rate of the note would be the same as the going market rate for a new loan of similar risk, so no discount or premium is needed. For example, a lender will lend a borrower $100,000 in exchange for a $100,000 three-year note bearing 8% interest annually when the market rate for an investment of similar risk is also 8%.

The present value tables in Figures 1A-13 and 1A-14 are used to calculate the remaining examples in this section.

Figure 1A-13 Present Value of 1 (Present Value of a Single Sum)

$$\text{Present Value (PV)}_{n,i} = \frac{1}{(1+i)^n} = (1+i)^{-n}$$

(n) Periods	8%	9%	10%
1	.92593	.91743	.90909
2	.85734	.84168	.82645
3	.79383	.77218	.75132
4	.73503	.70843	.68301
5	.68058	.64993	.62092
6	.63017	.59627	.56447
7	.58349	.54703	.51316
8	.54027	.50187	.46651
9	.50025	.46043	.42410
10	.46319	.42241	.38554

Figure 1A-14 Present Value of an Ordinary Annuity of 1

$$\text{Present Value of an Ordinary Annuity (PV} - \text{OA)}_{n,i} = \frac{1 - \frac{1}{(1+i)^n}}{i}$$

(n) Periods	8%	9%	10%
1	.92593	.91743	.90909
2	1.78326	1.75911	1.73554
3	2.57710	2.53130	2.48685
4	3.31213	3.23972	3.16986
5	3.99271	3.88965	3.79079
6	4.62288	4.48592	4.35526
7	5.20637	5.03295	4.86842
8	5.74664	5.53482	5.33493
9	6.24689	5.99525	5.75902
10	6.71008	6.41766	6.14457

The exchange price (present value of the funds) of the note is calculated as shown in Figure 1A-15, where the interest charge for one period, or $8,000, is used to calculate the overall interest charge using the factor for an ordinary annuity (an annuity that uses compound interest charged at the end of each period).

Figure 1A-15 Note Issued at Face Value

Face value of the note		$100,000
Present value of the principal	$79,383	
($100,000 PV of $1_{3,8\%}$) = ($100,000 0.79383)		
Present value of the interest	$20,617	
($8,000 PV − OA of $1_{3,8\%}$) = ($8,000 2.57710)		
Present value of the note		$100,000
Difference		$0

The present value of the note and the face value are the same, so no discounting is needed.

Notes Issued at a Discount or Premium

A note is issued at a discount when the market rate is higher than the stated rate and at a premium when the market rate is lower than the stated rate.

Zero-Interest-Bearing Notes

Zero-interest-bearing notes have an implicit interest rate based on the difference between the face value (the future value) of the note and the actual amount received by the borrower. The difference between these present and future values is recorded as a discount. The discount must be amortized over the life of the note. For example, the borrower issues a three-year $100,000 zero-interest-bearing note with a present value (based on 8% current market rates) of $79,383. That is, the borrower will receive $79,383 and pay a total of $100,000 after three years. The difference of $20,617 is the total interest that must be paid at the end of the loan, an implicit interest rate of 8%.

Figure 1A-16 shows how the issuer of the zero-coupon bond records the transaction:

Figure 1A-16 Zero-Interest-Bearing Note

Note receivable	$100,000
Discount on notes receivable	
Cash	

The discount on notes receivable is recorded on the balance sheet as a contra asset (valuation) account to notes receivable. The discount is amortized over the term of the note. The effective interest method is used to recognize the annual interest revenue, using an amortization schedule as shown in Figure 1A-17.

Figure 1A-17 Amortizing a Discount on Notes Receivable

	Cash Received	Interest Revenue	Discount Amortized	Note Carrying Amount
Issue date				$79,383
Year 1 end	$0	$6,351	$6,351	85,734
Year 2 end	0	6,859	6,859	92,593
Year 3 end	0	7,407	7,407	100,000
	$0	$20,617	$20,617	

The interest revenue is calculated by multiplying the carrying amount at the beginning of the period by the 8% interest rate. The note's carrying amount at the end of the period is the sum of the discount amortized and the carrying value at the beginning of the period (e.g., $79,383 + $6,351 = $85,734). A small adjustment may be needed in the last period to compensate for rounding.

Interest revenue for the first year is recognized by debiting the discount amortized ($6,351 in the example) to discount on notes receivable and crediting interest revenue for the same amount.

Interest-Bearing Notes

If a company accepts a three-year $100,000 note bearing interest at 8% but the current market rate for a similar investment is 9%, the note will be exchanged at a discount, as calculated in Figure 1A-18.

Figure 1A-18 Discount on an Interest-Bearing Note

Face value of the note		$100,000
Present value of the principal		$77,218
($100,000 × PV of $1_{3,\ 9\%}$) = ($100,000 0.77218)		
Present value of the interest		$20,250
($8,000 × PV – OA of $1_{3,\ 9\%}$) = ($8,000 2.53130)		
Present value of the note		$97,468
Difference		$2,532

The receipt of the note will be recorded as shown in Figure 1A-19.

Figure 1A-19 Interest-Bearing Note Journal Entry

Notes receivable	$100,000	
Discount on notes receivable		$2,532
Cash		$97,468

The effective interest method is used to calculate interest revenue and determine the amount of discount amortized, as illustrated in Figure 1A-20.

Figure 1A-20 Amortized Discount Calculation

	Cash Received	Interest Revenue	Discount Amortized	Note Carrying Amount
Issue date				$97,468
Year 1 end	$8,000	$8,772	$772	98,240
Year 2 end	8,000	8,842	842	99,082
Year 3 end	8,000	8,918	918	100,000
	$24,000	$26,532	$2,532	

At the end of the first year, the buyer recognizes the receipt of $8,000 cash interest at the stated rate and effective interest revenue of $8,772. The difference between these amounts is the discount amortized, which is added to the note carrying amount to determine the year-end note carrying amount. So, in the first year, the buyer recognizes the cash receipt, the discount amortized, and the total interest revenue, as shown in Figure 1A-21.

Figure 1A-21 Interest-Bearing Note Journal Entry

Cash	$8,000	
Discount on notes receivable	$772	
Interest revenue		$8,772

Premiums are dealt with using the effective yield method as well, except that the premium on a note receivable is recognized as a debit and the amortization is an annual reduction in the amount of recognized interest revenue. (The discount amortized column in Figure 1A-21 would read premium amortized and be a negative number.)

Imputed Interest Rate

When the effective rate cannot be determined readily by means such as valuing the asset or services exchanged for the note, an imputed interest rate is used. An imputed interest rate is an approximation of the market interest rate. The imputed interest rate should be comparable to the prevailing rates based on the same lending risk level and a similar lending instrument. The imputed rate is determined at the time the note is received and is used for the term of the note.

Disposition of Accounts and Notes Receivable

Many companies continue to handle their own receivables until they are collected or written off, but companies often dispose of their trade receivables for immediate cash. Most companies need to extend credit, but not all companies can afford the full expense of a credit department. (However, most companies do not transfer their administrative functions when they sell receivables.) The purchasers of trade receivables specialize in account management and collection, so they can do so more efficiently than most companies. Companies may also dispose of receivables to generate cash to satisfy short-term liquidity needs without borrowing more or issuing more stock.

Purchasers of receivables do so mainly because they get a discount on the receivables and can specialize in efficient collection. Banks may purchase receivables to circumvent lending limits. Also, some purchasers desire the greater legal protections given to asset holders than the protections offered to a secured creditor.

Two types of trade receivable dispositions occur: secured borrowing and sales accomplished by factoring or securitization of receivables. Sales can be made with or without recourse.

Secured Borrowing

In a secured borrowing, receivables are collateral for a loan. This allows the company to keep its receivables and borrow against them. The individual debtors often are not notified of the transaction, and the borrower will continue to collect the receivables and record discounts, returns and allowances, and bad debts. The lender will charge interest on the note plus a finance charge on the accounts receivable.

Factoring and Securitization of Receivables

Factoring and securitization are two approaches companies can use to sell receivables. Factoring is generally on a nonrecourse basis, but some sales of receivables may be made with recourse. These topics are discussed separately after factoring and securitization.

Factoring

In factoring, factors buy receivables and often take on the billing and collection functions. Finance companies and banks are the most common factors. Factoring is common in the textile, furniture, and apparel industries. Credit cards are also a form of factoring. Companies that use factors get immediate cash (not as much as if secured borrowing were used) and can eliminate their credit departments, because factors usually take over these tasks. Factors conduct credit reviews for the company and extend or deny credit, take payments directly from customers, and remit cash minus a fee to the company for receivables purchased. The company continues all operational activities directly with the customers, such as order placement and fulfillment. Giving the power of credit decisions to the factor mitigates some of the risk for the factor, leading to a lower cost of service than would otherwise be the case, but the company will have to accept the credit decisions of the factor, and some sales will not be approved.

Most factors transfer only 80% to 90% of the value of the receivables to allow for sales returns and allowances and bad debts. In addition, factors charge a percentage commission dependent on the gross amount of receivables transferred and on the perceived risk of noncollection. The company records the factor's commission as an expense or a loss.

Securitization

Securitization is a bundling of similar receivables, such as mortgages, credit card receivables, or car loans, into an investment fund. The principal and interest payments collected on the receivables are available for payment to investors. Unlike factoring, the sellers of the receivables continue to service the receivables. Securitization usually involves a higher quality of receivables and lower fees.

Sale with Recourse

In a sale with recourse, the seller must pay the purchaser for any bad debts the purchaser incurs. Because the seller has a continuing involvement with the receivable, the transaction is recorded using the financial components approach. This approach allows the factor and the seller to recognize only the assets and liabilities they control after sale with recourse. All extinguished or sold assets and liabilities are not recognized. For example, using the financial components approach, $100,000 of receivables is sold with recourse to a factor, which assesses a finance charge of 2% of accounts receivable and withholds an additional 3% of accounts receivable as collateral against noncollection. The allowance for doubtful debts (also known as a recourse obligation) carries a fair value of $4,000. First, the net proceeds from sale are calculated, as in Figure 1A-22.

Figure 1A-22 Calculating Net Proceeds

Cash received ($100,000 less 2% + 3%)	$95,000	
Due from factor	3,000	$98,000
Less: Allowance for doubtful debts		(4,000)
Net proceeds		$94,000

The net proceeds are the assets received in the sale minus the incurred liabilities. A loss on the sale of receivable is recorded as in Figure 1A-23:

Figure 1A-23 Calculating the Loss on Sale

Carrying (book) value	$100,000
Net proceeds	94,000
Loss on sale of receivables	$6,000

Sale without Recourse

Factoring is most commonly a sale without recourse, meaning that the purchaser assumes the risk of bad debts. Because the sale transfers title, it is considered an outright sale in form, and because the sale transfers control of credit granting and collection, it is also an outright sale in substance. Accounting for a sale without recourse was covered above under "Factoring."

Secured Borrowing versus Sale

The FASB has set guidelines in ASC Topic 860, *Transfers and Servicing* (formerly covered in FASB Statement No. 140), to determine if a sale of receivables has occurred. Generally, a sale exists whenever surrender of control occurs. In addition, three criteria need to be met to recognize a sale of receivables:

1. The asset should be outside the reach of the seller and its creditors.
2. The buyer should be able to sell the assets or use them as collateral.
3. The seller should not have any agreement to repurchase the assets before their maturity.

According to the FASB, if these conditions are not met, the transfer should be recorded as a secured borrowing. Secured borrowings should be recorded as a liability, and the interest should be recorded as an expense. If the FASB criteria allow recognition of a sale and there is continuing involvement (sale with recourse), then the financial component approach detailed above is used. If the sale is final and there is no continuing involvement, the procedure is to record a reduction in receivables and either a loss or an expense.

Accounts Receivable Disclosure Requirements

Material receivables must be kept separate by type on the balance sheet and reported net of any valuation accounts. Receivables in the current assets section are expected to be converted to cash within the longer of a year or the operating cycle. Required disclosures include loss contingencies related to receivables, any pledges of receivables as collateral, any material concentrations of credit risk, and any related party receivables. A partial balance sheet with various types of receivables and disclosures is shown in Figure 1A-24.

Section A, Topic 2—Recognition, Measurement, Valuation, and Disclosure

Figure 1A-24 Receivables Disclosures

Bounce Sporting Goods Company
(Partial) Balance Sheet
For the Year Ended December 31, Year 1

Current assets		
Cash and cash equivalents		$1,383,985
Accounts receivable*	$6,643,478	
Less: Allowance for doubtful accounts	370,167	
	6,273,311	
Advances to subsidiaries due 9/30/XX	1,546,600	
Notes receivable—trade*	1,133,680	
Federal income taxes refundable	108,561	
Dividends and interest receivable	55,870	
Other receivables and claims (including debit balances in accounts payable)	129,219	9,247,241
Total current assets		10,631,226
Noncurrent receivables		
Notes receivable from officers and key employees		278,307
Claims receivable (settlement on litigation to be collected over five years)		432,900

*Note on accounts and notes receivable

In July Year 1, the company arranged with a finance company to refinance a part of its indebtedness. The loan is evidenced by a 8% note payable. The note is secured by substantially all the accounts receivable and is payable on demand.

Inventory

Inventory includes assets that are held for sale in the normal course of business, is work in the process of being produced for sale, or is the raw materials used to produce salable goods. Items that are not sold in the usual course of business are not inventory. Retail and manufacturing industries often report inventory as their largest asset.

Inventory is classified by its use. Retailers often have only one category—merchandise—which includes retail goods that were purchased ready for sale. Manufacturers often have three categories: raw materials, work in process, and finished goods. Costs of production, labor, fixed and variable overhead, and storage are divided among these categories as appropriate. Manufacturers often need inventory categories to account for internal use inventory types, such as manufacturing supplies, indirect materials, parts inventory, or factory supplies.

Perpetual and Periodic Inventory Systems

Today, companies are trying to reduce their inventories to the minimum levels required for sales to continue unhindered. Businesses need to have the inventory ready when it is ordered but want to avoid accumulating items because they require financing costs until sold and they could become obsolete or otherwise unsalable. Companies have installed enterprise databases, bar code scanning systems, and other technology to track inventory and keep records real time. Just-in-time (JIT) inventory systems reduce inventory holding times by setting up direct electronic links to suppliers so they know just when a particular raw material or finished good needs to be shipped.

Two approaches to inventory record keeping are in use: perpetual and periodic. The periodic system evolved before computers were used to track inventory and therefore is not widely used today.

Perpetual Inventory System

The perpetual inventory system keeps continuous track of the changes in the inventory accounts. All transactions are recorded as they occur. Sophisticated databases are used to update records of sales, purchases, conversions, and transfers in real time. Retail systems record inventory changes directly at the point of sale, updating both inventory and cost of goods sold. Purchases, returns and allowances, discounts taken, and freight-in are also updated.

When a company uses a perpetual inventory system, a journal entry is made with each sale to reduce inventory and increase cost of goods sold (an expense account). However, not all goods necessarily make it to the point of sale. Some goods are stolen, others are accidentally shipped without an invoice (overage in a shipment), and others are damaged and discarded without being recorded. Therefore, inventory recorded on the books generally will be higher than what is actually on hand. (However, overages also can and do occur.) So periodically companies using the perpetual system will count what inventory they do have on hand and write off the difference from what they have on the record, which increases cost of goods sold and decreases inventory. Because the size of the difference between actual and recorded inventory can be measured, management can determine the amount of such losses year to year. A primary drawback of the periodic system is that it cannot make this measurement.

The inventory account is a control account that contains a ledger of individual inventory records. Each individual record maintains the quantities and costs divided among the various categories of inventory. Other perpetual inventory accounting recognition guidelines include:

- Recognize cost of goods sold as a debit to cost of goods sold and a credit to inventory at the time of the sale.
- Recognize resale merchandise or production raw material purchases in inventory (not purchases).
- Recognize purchase discounts, freight-in, and purchase returns and allowances in inventory (not separate accounts).

The basic accounting for the perpetual system is:

Beginning Inventory + Purchases (Net) − Cost of Goods Sold = Ending Inventory

Periodic Inventory System

In contrast, the periodic system starts with the same two items but then subtracts ending inventory to arrive at goods sold (an amount already known under the perpetual system). The periodic inventory system is becoming obsolete as more companies in all industries adopt inventory tracking databases. Periodic inventory systems must count inventory on hand once a year to determine inventory levels. Acquisitions of inventory are debited to a purchases account. The balance of the purchases account at the end of the period is added to the beginning cost of inventory to determine cost of goods available for sale during the period. The cost of goods available for sale minus the ending inventory (determined at year-end count) equals cost of goods sold. Because cost of goods sold is determined only once a year, the information is not timely. To deal with this problem, a modified perpetual inventory system sometimes is used. The modified system keeps a detailed record of quantities (but not prices) in a memorandum account off the books.

Inventory Valuation

Inventory valuation is the process of determining what items to include in inventory, what costs should be included in inventory, and which cost flow assumptions should be used.

The overall cost of producing goods is allocated among the goods sold and the goods still on hand. The **cost of goods available for sale or use** is the cost of goods on hand at the start of the period plus the cost of goods acquired or produced throughout the period. The **cost of goods sold** is the cost of goods available for sale or use minus the cost of goods on hand at the end of the period. The cost of goods available for sale and the cost of goods sold are calculated as shown in Figure 1A-25.

Figure 1A-25 Cost of Goods Sold Calculation

Beginning inventory, January 1	$350,000
Cost of goods acquired or produced during the year	670,000
Total cost of goods available for sale	1,020,000
Ending inventory, December 31	400,000
Cost of goods sold during the year	$620,000

Which Goods to Include in Inventory

Purchases of inventory generally are recorded when the goods are received by the buyer, even though ownership legally transfers when the title passes to the buyer. Because the time of this transfer is hard to know, and because the result does not differ materially when the rule is applied consistently, the general practice is to record acquisitions to inventory when the goods are received. Exceptions to this generally accepted practice of recognizing ownership on delivery are detailed below.

- **Consigned goods.** Consigned goods are a way of mitigating the risk of unsalable inventory by allowing the wholesale seller (the consignor) to retain ownership of the property until a sale is recorded. Only then does the wholesaler receive payment for the goods from the retailer (the consignee). The consignee takes a selling commission for holding, marketing, and exercising due care of the goods. The consignor retains the item on its inventory until the sale to a third party. The consignee never records the item as inventory.
- **Goods in transit.** Goods in transit are those items that have been shipped but have not yet reached their destination at the end of a fiscal period. Who owns the goods in transit is determined by the shipping terms, which are either FOB (free on board) shipping point or FOB destination. Under FOB shipping point, title is transferred as soon as the seller delivers the item to a common carrier serving as an agent of the buyer. Under FOB destination, title is transferred when the goods arrive. The matter is of considerable importance because damages to the goods are the owner's responsibility. A designation such as FOB Minneapolis would indicate a specific city where title transferred. Before title transfers, the goods are the property of the seller; after transfer, they must be accounted for on the books of the buyer.
- **Sale agreements.** Some sale agreements involve a transfer of title at a different point from the transfer of the risks of ownership. Three particular situations are sales with high rates of return, sales with buyback agreements, and installment sales. Sales with high rates of return are not unusual in the publishing, sporting goods, music, and other seasonal industries, where customers are permitted to return unsold inventory for a full or partial refund. When the number of returns can be reasonably estimated, the goods should be considered sold and a sales return and allowances account established. However, when such an estimate is impossible, the seller should not record a sale until the amount of return is known.

    Sales with buyback agreements are a type of swap where a selling company sells its inventory to a buying company and agrees to repurchase the inventory at a specific price and at a specific time. Such a transaction is called a parking transaction because the seller "parks" inventory in the buyer's balance sheet for a short duration. Effectively the seller is financing its inventory and retaining the risks of ownership but transfers title to the goods. When a repurchase agreement has a set price that covers all of the buyer's costs plus the cost of the inventory, the inventory and the liability under the repurchase agreement still should be reported on the seller's balance sheet.

What Costs to Include in Inventory

Which costs should be allocated to inventory items when determining the price of the item? The types of costs allowed to be included in the determination of inventory value are discussed next.

- **Manufacturing overhead costs.** For entities that make their own goods for sale, the direct and indirect costs incurred in production are included in the cost of the inventory produced. ASC Topic 330, *Inventory* (formerly addressed in AICPA Accounting Research Bulletin No. 43), states that acquisition and production costs can be included, but general and administrative expenses should not be included except for any portion that is clearly related to production. It also states that selling expenses are not to be included. Both fixed and variable overhead items are included. Fixed overhead is allocated to goods manufactured using a traditional or activity-based approach. For example, a line manager's salary would be part of the fixed overhead pool attributable to a specific product line. However, an executive's salary would not be considered a product cost.

- **Product costs.** Product costs include all costs recorded as part of inventory, including shipping costs, labor costs, and direct costs of acquisition, production, and processing.
- **Cash discounts.** Cash discounts, as discussed earlier in this section under "Accounts Receivable," include discounts for early payment. The gross method records all purchases at the gross price, and discounts are recorded only if taken as deductions from net purchases. The net method records all purchases net of discounts. Purchase discounts lost are then charged to another expense account.
- **Period costs.** Items not included as part of inventory, such as selling, general, and administrative expenses, are considered period costs, because such costs are expensed in the period incurred. These costs sometimes are associated with production but in many cases are unrelated to it. Interest costs related to the preparation of inventory are also included in period costs, although some believe that interest should be capitalized as part of inventory. The FASB has decided that only interest costs of internally constructed assets or discrete projects, such as ships or real estate for sale or lease, can be capitalized. Financing costs associated with inventory that is routinely manufactured are not capitalized.

Cost Flow Assumptions

During an accounting period, inventory often is purchased at several different prices. Also, inventory from a prior period is included in the beginning inventory for a period, and then items are produced and added to the same inventory, each at different costs. Keeping the specific cost for each item separate may be impossible, given the permutations and various types of inventory involved. Several methods of accounting for inventory costs have evolved, called "cost flow assumptions." The cost flow assumptions are used for accounting and have nothing to do with the actual physical movement of goods. For example, first in, first out (FIFO) does not imply that the oldest inventory sold first. Cost flow assumptions simply determine which costs are allocated to inventory and which are allocated to cost of goods sold. Each method will have a different impact on income. However, the primary purpose in choosing a particular cost flow assumption should be to best approximate periodic income. The four cost flow assumptions currently in use are specific identification, average cost, FIFO, and last in, first out (LIFO).

- **Specific identification.** Specific identification tracks the cost of each individual item and records the item in cost of goods sold or inventory as appropriate. This method is feasible only if all items are uniquely tagged and works best with small numbers of expensive items, such as jewelry or automobiles in retail or with special orders and products in manufacturing using a job costing system. Specific identification works best with a perpetual inventory system that uses a real-time database for information storage. It matches costs directly with revenues and may become more popular as new technologies emerge to track individual items. Finally, specific identification can be abused to manipulate profits by selecting units at a particular price for sale to alter the gross profit for a period.
- **Average cost.** The average cost method aggregates costs for all similar inventory items and produces an average cost for the period. When using the perpetual inventory system, this method is called the moving average method, because a new average cost must be calculated after each purchase. This amount is used as the cost until another purchase is made. The average cost per unit is calculated as the cost of the units available for sale after each purchase divided by the number of units available for sale. Therefore, as of a particular day—for example, July 7—if the cost of goods available for sale equals $100,000 and the number of units available for sale is 2,000, then the average cost is $50. Whenever a purchase is made, the average cost of the good is recalculated. Figure 1A-26 shows the average costs for an entire month.

Figure 1A-26 Moving Average Inventory Cost Flow Assumption

Bounce Sporting Goods Company
Moving Average Invertory Cost Flow Assumption
(Perpetual Inventory System)

July 1, beginning inventory	1,000 units @ $40	$40,000
July 7, purchases	1,000 units @ $60	60,000
July 7, balance	2,000 units @ $50	$100,000
July 15, sales	(1,000) units @ $50	(50, 000)
July 15, balance	1,000 units @ $50	$50,000
July 20, purchases	500 units @ $56	28,000
July 20, balance	1,500 units @ $52	$78,000
July 28, sales	(300) units @ $52	(15, 600)
July 31, balance	1,200 units @ $52	$62,400
Cost of goods sold (1,300 units)	$50,000 + $15,600	$65,600
Ending inventory (1, 200 units @ $52)		$62,400

When used with the periodic system, average cost is called the "weighted average method." The total cost of the goods available for sale for a period is divided by the total number of units sold, to arrive at a weighted average cost per unit. Goods available for sale includes beginning inventory and purchases. Ending inventory is multiplied by the average cost to determine the value of ending inventory. Cost of goods sold can be determined by subtracting ending inventory from the cost of goods available for sale or by multiplying the units sold by the average cost.

The average cost method is objective and simple to use, and the results are not as subject to manipulation as other methods, so many businesses use it for practical reasons.

- **First-in, first-out.** The first-in, first-out (FIFO) method (which was discussed earlier in this book) makes the accounting assumption that goods purchased earlier are used or sold before goods purchased later. Therefore, the costs incurred farthest in the past should be included in the cost of goods sold, and the costs incurred most recently should be included in ending inventory.

When costs are increasing, FIFO yields a lower cost of goods sold because the oldest costs are used, but ending inventory has a relatively higher cost. If costs are going down, the converse is true; a higher cost of goods sold and lower ending inventory value will result.

Using the data from Figure 1A-26, the cost of goods sold and the ending inventory are calculated as shown in Figure 1A-27 under the perpetual method. When a quantity sold exceeds the number obtained at the earliest price, the price of the next most recent purchase is used. Cost of goods sold is always based on the earliest costs.

Figure 1A-27 Perpetual FIFO

Bounce Sporting Goods Company
First-In, First-Out Inventory Cost Flow Assumption
(Perpetual Inventory System)

Cost of goods sold (1,300 units):	
July 15 1,000 units @ $40	$40,000
July 28 300 units @ $60	18,000
Total	$58,000

Ending inventory (1,200 units):
Beginning Inventory + Purchases − Cost of Goods Sold = Ending Inventory
$40,000 + $88,000 − $58,000 = $70,000*

* 700 units @ $60	$42,000
500 units @ $56	28,000
	$70,000

If the periodic system is used, the cost of the ending inventory is calculated using the most recent costs. The total cost of goods available for sale minus the ending inventory is equal to the cost of goods sold. The same inventory and cost of goods sold will be computed under FIFO regardless of whether the perpetual or the periodic system is used, because the same costs will always be the first in. Figure 1A-28 shows periodic FIFO valuation.

Figure 1A-28 Periodic FIFO

Bounce Sporting Goods Company
First-In, First-Out Inventory Cost Flow Assumption
(Periodic Inventory System)

Ending inventory (1,200 units):	
700 units @ $60	$42,000
500 units @ $56	28,000
	$70,000

Cost of goods sold (1,300 units):
Beginning Inventory + Purchases − Ending Inventory = Cost of Goods Sold
$40,000 + $88,000 − $70,000 = $58,000

An objective of using FIFO is to approximate the actual flow of inventory. When the oldest goods are sold first, as is the case with all perishables, FIFO approximates the specific identification method. Also, FIFO ending inventory values provide a reasonable estimate of inventory replacement costs, especially when turnover is rapid or prices are stable. However, FIFO does not match current costs with current revenues on the income statement. Because the oldest costs are matched with revenue, FIFO can distort net income. When inventory prices are rising, FIFO produces phantom inventory profits.

- **Last-in, first-out.** Under the **last-in, first-out (LIFO)** method, the cost of the last goods bought are assigned to cost of goods sold, and the ending inventory will include the cost of the earliest purchases. When costs are increasing, LIFO produces the highest cost of goods sold and the lowest ending inventory. LIFO traditionally has been used in department stores and in other industries that carry a constant base stock, such as chemical and refining companies.

    When using the perpetual inventory system, which records events in the order they actually occur, the LIFO cost of the most recent purchase is determined as of the date of each sale. Using data from Figure 1A-28, Figure 1A-29 illustrates the perpetual LIFO method.

Figure 1A-29 Perpetual LIFO

Bounce Sporting Goods Company
Last-In, First-Out Inventory Cost Flow Assumption
(Perpetual Inventory System)

Cost of goods sold (1,300 units):		
July 15	1,000 units @ $60	$60,000
July 28	300 units @ $56	16,800
		$76,800

Ending inventory (1,200 units):
Beginning Inventory + Purchases − Cost of Goods Sold = Ending Inventory
$40,000 + $88,000 − $76,800 = $51,200*

*1,000 units @ $40 =	$40,000
200 units @ $56 =	11,200
	$51,200

Unlike FIFO, the LIFO perpetual inventory system and the LIFO periodic system will yield different costs of goods sold and ending inventory figures. This is because the periodic system measures LIFO cost as of the end of the accounting period while the perpetual method measures LIFO cost as of the date of each sale.

When using the periodic system, the cost of goods sold is calculated by subtracting the ending inventory from the cost of goods available for sale. Figure 1A-30 shows how inventory is valued using the periodic LIFO method.

Figure 1A-30 Periodic LIFO

Bounce Sporting Goods Company
Last-In, First-Out Inventory Cost Flow Assumption
(Periodic Inventory System)

Ending inventory (1,200 units):
1,000 units @ $40	$40,000
200 units @ $60	12,000
	$52,000

Cost of goods sold (140 units):
Beginning Inventory + Purchases − Ending Inventory = Cost of Goods Sold
$40,000 + $88,000 − $52,000 = $76,000

LIFO has the advantage of providing a better measure of current earnings because it matches recent costs against current revenues. LIFO also allows income tax deferrals when costs are rising, and inventory levels remain stable because cost of goods sold will be higher and net income lower compared with other methods. Lower taxes mean a higher cash flow for a company. LIFO can also be a hedge against price declines, because it rarely requires the markdowns to market value as a result of price decreases, which FIFO inventories may be subject to. However, the lower reported earnings that reduce taxes are a disadvantage to some companies wishing to report higher income. LIFO also distorts the balance sheet by understating inventory values and therefore working capital.

LIFO Liquidation

LIFO records inventory in layers separated by different purchase times and costs. The oldest costs are called the "base layer." For example, if Bounce Sporting Goods has a three-year history of purchasing raw rubber, the company might use its ending inventory and an average unit cost for its LIFO inventory. If usage of raw rubber exceeds purchases during a period, a situation called "LIFO liquidation" can occur. **LIFO liquidation** is the sale of multiple layers of inventory, resulting in revenues at current prices but costs at a mix of current and old prices. Assuming that prices are rising, LIFO liquidation results in higher income levels being reported and likely higher taxes as well.

Figure 1A-31 shows how this could occur when a shortage of raw rubber prevents a firm from purchasing as much of this direct material as is needed. Note that the beginning inventory is made from three layers of costs and that the first two layers are eliminated and the base-year layer is reduced permanently. Because these layers were purchased at a lower cost in each of the prior years, using these layers results in higher income levels and thus higher taxes than if the firm purchased the rubber at current market prices (assuming inflation), as illustrated by the footnote in the figure.

Figure 1A-31 LIFO Liquidation

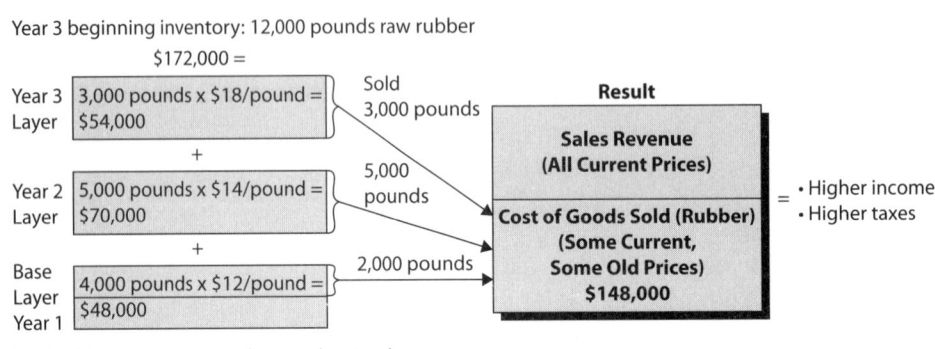

Year 3 beginning inventory: 12,000 pounds raw rubber

$172,000 =

- Year 3 Layer: 3,000 pounds x $18/pound = $54,000 — Sold 3,000 pounds
- Year 2 Layer: 5,000 pounds x $14/pound = $70,000 — 5,000 pounds
- Base Layer Year 1: 4,000 pounds x $12/pound = $48,000 — 2,000 pounds

Result:
Sales Revenue (All Current Prices)
Cost of Goods Sold (Rubber) (Some Current, Some Old Prices) $148,000
= • Higher income
• Higher taxes

During Year 3, 10,000 pounds raw ruber used; none available for purchase due to shortage.

* If 7,000 additional pounds of rubber were purchased in year 3 at $18 per pound, then COGS (rubber) would = $180,00, resulting in lower income and loer taxes.

LIFO liquidations can be quite common and can reduce the benefits of using LIFO. Therefore, a common solution is to use the **specific goods pooled LIFO approach**, which groups items into pools of substantially identical items to allow liquidation of one pool to be offset by increases in a different pool. Using pools can reduce fluctuations, but because most companies are continually changing product mixes and therefore inventory items, pools must also be redefined at some expense, and if item mixes change enough, new pools may need to be created, allowing the old pools to be subject to LIFO liquidation.

Dollar-Value LIFO

Another solution to LIFO liquidation and to the problems with using pools is to use **dollar-value LIFO**, which measures increases and decreases in a cost pool by their total dollar value instead of using physical quantities. This allows pools to be more vaguely defined to include interchangeable or similar items. The broader the pools, the lower the chances of LIFO liquidation. Dollar-value LIFO calculations are complex; they involve calculating inventory at end-of-year prices and then creating a price index set at 100% for the base year. Each layer above the base has a price index applied that reflects the increases (or decreases) in prices for the period (e.g., if prices increased by 16%, then the index would be 116% of the base layer). Using such an index allows each layer to be calculated at base-year prices. Figure 1A-32 shows how end-of-year inventory at base prices is determined.

Figure 1A-32 Dollar-Value LIFO—End-of-Year (EOY) Inventory at Base-Year Prices

December 31	Inventory at EOY Prices		Price Index	EOY Inventory at Base-Year Prices
Year 1 (base year)	$450,000	/	100%	$450,000
Year 2	$550,000	/	116%	$474,138

The EOY inventory at base-year prices less the beginning inventory at base-year prices (prior year's data) equals the increase (or decrease) in the quantity of goods. An increase would become a layer of cost. If the difference results in a decrease, then this amount must be subtracted from the most recently added layer. Subtractions are accounted for at the prices that were used to calculate costs for that layer. If a layer is reduced or eliminated, it cannot be rebuilt. Therefore, some years might not have a layer. As inventory is used, the most recent layer of costs is used first. Dollar-value LIFO calculations are outside the scope of this text. See an intermediate-level accounting textbook for more information on this subject.

LIFO Reserve

An AICPA task force has defined **LIFO reserve** as "the difference between (a) inventory or the lower of LIFO cost or market and (b) inventory at replacement cost or at the lower of cost determined by some acceptable inventory accounting method (such as FIFO or average cost) or market." This definition has been given authoritative status under GAAP. LIFO has advantages for tax preparation and external financial reporting; it is less useful for internal reporting because it does not approximate the physical flow of the product and is cumbersome when applied to interim periods because it relies on estimates of year-end quantities and prices.

Therefore, many companies use a combination of LIFO for taxes and external reporting and an average cost or FIFO method for internal reporting. The internal reporting method is generally followed, and any differences that arise between the two methods are recorded in an allowance to reduce inventory to LIFO account, also called a "LIFO reserve." Changes in the balance of the allowance account are called the "LIFO effect."

Effect of Converting from LIFO to FIFO

When a company decides to switch between inventory accounting methods, what will be the effect on the cost of sales? On income? Answering such questions will help determine if the change will be an advantage to the company.

For example, when comparing two possible companies to invest in, one reporting with FIFO and the other with LIFO, the analyst will need to convert one method to the other method for a true comparison. Because companies that report LIFO are required to disclose their LIFO reserve, it is easier to convert LIFO to FIFO than vice versa. Selected data from a LIFO-basis company is shown in Figure 1A-33.

Figure 1A-33 Selections from Financial Statements of Company with LIFO Inventory Accounting

	Year 2	Year 1
Excerpts from balance sheet:		
Inventories (approximate FIFO cost)	$338,757	$307,566
– LIFO reserve	–$32,231	–$11,820
LIFO cost	$306,526	$295,746
Excerpts from income statement:		
Cost of goods sold (COGS)	$2,590,650	
Net income	$108,690	

Because the LIFO reserve increased by $20,411 ($32,231 − $11,820 = $20,411), inventory costs are rising. (Otherwise the LIFO reserve would have fallen.) Also note that in both years, the FIFO cost of inventory was greater than the LIFO cost, another indication that costs are rising. (During rising costs, LIFO has the highest cost of goods sold and the lowest net income.) Therefore, the first distinction that can be made is that if the company had used FIFO, its COGS would have been lower and its net income higher, as calculated in Figure 1A-34. (The example assumes a 40% tax rate.)

Figure 1A-34 Converting from LIFO to FIFO

LIFO-basis COGS	$2,590,650
– Increase in LIFO reserve: $32,231 − $11,820 = $20,411	– $20,411
FIFO-basis COGS	$2,570,239
Net income under LIFO	$108,690
Pretax income differential (from COGS change)	+ $20,411
Taxes on differential	– $8,164
Net income under FIFO	$120,937

Using the net income under FIFO, a valid comparison to another FIFO-basis company could now be done. The LIFO reserve is an accumulation of total cost differences between LIFO and FIFO (or another method) since the LIFO method was adopted. Therefore, multiplying the current LIFO reserve by the tax rate will show the amount of income taxes that was saved by using LIFO (disregarding present values). To find this amount, multiply the tax rate by the LIFO reserve (see Figure

1A-33): 0.4 × $32,231 = $12,892. The company therefore has had this much more capital to invest in its operations over the long term.

Effect on Income and Assets of Using Different Cost Flow Assumptions

FIFO and LIFO represent extreme ends of a spectrum for their results on income while average costing falls in the middle. When costs are rising, LIFO will minimize income, which results in lower income tax payments. Because LIFO also matches recent costs with revenues first, some argue that it is the best measure of the COGS because it approximates replacement costs.

LIFO also excludes inventory holding gains from net income. Holding gains are the difference between the historical cost and the replacement cost of a unit when it is sold. Because LIFO costs approximate replacement costs, the holding gains are minimized and net income is closer to earnings on a current cost basis. In contrast, FIFO includes holding gains in income.

For example, if the most recent unit purchase cost is $90, the oldest cost is $80, and the sale price remains at $200 for a period, then FIFO would record gross profit of $120, which includes a holding gain of $10 (difference between current replacement cost and historical cost). LIFO would record gross profit of $110 and no holding gains. LIFO presents a more realistic picture of the income available for dividends after subtracting the amount needed to replace inventory at the new higher price.

The effects of FIFO, average cost, and LIFO methods are compared in Figure 1A-35 using the data from the preceding examples.

Figure 1A-35 Comparing Perpetual Inventory Cost Flow Assumptions

Bounce Sporting Goods Company
Effects of Inventory Cost Flow Assumptions

Cost Flow Assumption	Cost of Goods Available for Sale	Cost of Goods Sold	Ending Inventory
FIFO, perpetual	$128,000	$58,000	$70,000
Moving average, perpetual	128,000	65,600	62,400
LIFO, perpetual	128,000	76,800	51,200

Cost flow assumption advantages and disadvantages. All four cost flow assumptions are permitted under GAAP, but there is a wide amount of variance between them. A main disadvantage of allowing so many inventory valuation methods, each resulting in a different net income level, is that it is more difficult to compare various financial statements from different organizations. Because comparison is a primary purpose of financial reporting, this inconsistency complicates matters. However, LIFO companies disclose supplemental information that allows investors to determine what earnings would have been under FIFO.

The International Accounting Standards Board (IASB) considers the LIFO method to be a less acceptable method of inventory accounting. Consequently, as the IASB and the FASB progress in their convergence project, it is likely that inventory valuation methods could be affected.

Effects of Inventory Errors

Two main types of inventory errors are misstatements in ending inventory and misstatements in purchases and inventory. These misstatements can be in number of units or in valuation methods.

- **Misstated ending inventory.** When items are not included in ending inventory even though they should have been, the balance sheet will understate inventory, which in turn will understate retained earnings, working capital, and the current ratio. Also, income will be understated because cost of goods sold is overstated. If the error is not corrected in the following period, the opposite effect will result, but the two periods' statements viewed together will result in the same total income as if no error had occurred. However, the net income for each year will have been misstated when viewed individually. When ending inventory is overstated, the converse of this situation occurs; net income, inventory, retained earnings, working capital, and the current ratio are overstated while the cost of goods sold is understated.
- **Misstated purchases and inventory.** When a purchase is not recorded as a purchase and is not recorded in ending inventory, the balance sheet understates inventory and accounts payable and overstates the current ratio. On the income statement, both purchases and ending inventory are understated, which results in the correct cost of goods sold. Therefore, net income will not be affected. The current ratio calculation will be overstated because reducing the size of both current assets and current liabilities will yield a higher ratio. For example, if current assets were $200,000 and current liabilities were $100,000, the ratio would be 2 to 1. However, if both sums were reduced by an error of $50,000, the ratio would be 3 to 1, an overstatement. When both purchases and inventory are overstated, the converse of this situation is true.

    Consider a situation in which ending inventory is overstated by $10,000 in Year 0 (the current year). The effects of the error and its correction in Year 1 are shown in Figure 1A-36, with the resulting increases and decreases represented by up or down arrows.

Figure 1A-36 Correcting an Inventory Misstatement

Cause	Timing	Change
Effects (corrected in Year 1)		
Ending inventory misstated	Year 0	↑ $10,000
Cost of sales	Year 0	↓ $10,000
Operating income	Year 0	↑ $10,000
Tax expense (40% tax rate)	Year 0	↑ $4,000
Net income	Year 0	↑ $6,000
Retained earnings	Year 0	↑ $6,000

Beginning inventory	Year 1	↑ $10,000
Cost of sales	Year 1	↑ $10,000
Operating income	Year 1	↓ $10,000
Tax expense (40% tax rate)	Year 1	↓ $4,000
Net income	Year 1	↓ $6,000
Ending inventory	Year 1	Correct
Retained earnings	Year 1	Correct

This example shows how misstated purchases and inventory can have a material effect on financial statements and how restatements for accounting irregularities can have a large impact on reported numbers.

Lower of Cost or Market Rule

While inventory is initially recorded at historical cost, if inventory declines in value due to obsolescence, damage to the goods, or price level changes, then the inventory should be written down to its current value.

The **lower of cost or market (LCM) rule** comes into play when inventory becomes obsolete or declines in value (e.g., foreign competition brings prices down). In such situations, inventory is valued at its cost or market value, whichever is lower. Market value generally is considered the cost to replace the item by purchasing or reproducing it. (Thus it is the value in the purchase market, in not the sales market.) Inventory is written down in the period in which the value declines rather than in the period in which the item is sold. This method is based on the assumption that a decline in the replacement cost of an item normally means the selling price of an item will have to drop to stay competitive.

Net Realizable Value

Net realizable value (NRV) is the estimate of an item's sale price in an ordinary business situation (not a liquidation) minus all costs to complete the sale and dispose of the asset.

LCM Ceiling and Floor

When determining what market value should be, two constraints have been placed on the use of replacement cost as a measure of market value:

1. Ceiling—Market value should not be greater than the inventory's net realizable value.
2. Floor—Market value should not be less than the inventory's net realizable value less an allowance for a normal markup or profit margin.

The ceiling (or upper limit) is designed to make sure that the inventory is not overstated and the loss understated (thus avoiding the need to recognize further losses in future periods). The floor (or lower limit) is designed to make sure that the loss is not overstated and the inventory is not understated (preventing the recognition of excessive future profits).

Applying LCM

According to Accounting Research Bulletin No. 43, the lower of cost or market rule may be applied to individual items, to categories of items, or to the total inventory. When applying LCM to categories or the total inventory, increases in market price in one area tend to offset decreases in a different area, generally leading to a smaller restatement than if LCM is applied to individual items. Item-level LCM is the most common, partly because Internal Revenue Service (IRS) rules generally require its use. Item-level LCM also produces the most conservative inventory value. Figure 1A-37 shows how LCM can be applied in various ways.

Figure 1A-37 Applying LCM

Alternative Methods of Applying Lower of Cost or Market Rule

Inventory	Cost	Market	Individual Items	Category	Total
Rubber products department:					
Tennis balls (box)	$120	$84	$84		
Racquet balls (box)	144	156	144		
	$264	$240		$240	
Racquet department:					
Tennis racquet 1	$192	$230	192		
Tennis racquet 2	240	211	211		
	$432	$441		432	
Total	$696	$681			$681
Inventory valuation			$631	$672	$681
Loss recognition			$65	$24	$15

Recording LCM

When inventory is written down to market, either the direct method or the indirect (allowance) method can be used. The direct method simply substitutes the market value in place of the cost in the inventory, so the loss is not visible on the income statement but is included in cost of goods sold. The allowance method retains the cost in the inventory account and records the write-down in a contra asset account and a loss account.

Relative Sales Value Method

When a group of items is purchased for a lump-sum price and the items differ significantly in type or quality, the purchase price is allocated between the items based on their relative sales value. Figure 1A-38 illustrates the allocation of costs, and Figure 1A-39 illustrates the determination of gross profit using the relative sales value method.

Figure 1A-38 Allocation of Costs Using Relative Sales Value

Lots	Number of Lots	Sales Price Per Lot	Total Sales Price	Relative Sales Price	Total Cost	Cost Allocated to Lots	Cost Per Lot
A1	50	$6,000	$300,000	3/48	$2,000,000	$125,000	$2,500
A2	200	12,000	2,400,000	24/48	2,000,000	1,000,000	5,000
A3	300	7,000	2,100,000	21/48	2,000,000	875,000	2,917
			$4,800,000			$2,000,000	

Figure 1A-39 Calculation of Gross Profit Using Relative Sales Value

Lots	Number of Lots Sold	Sales	Cost of Lots Sold	Gross Profit
A1	25	$150,000	$62,500	$87,500
A2	120	1,440,000	600,000	840,000
A3	230	1,610,000	670,910	939,090
		3,200,000	$1,333,410	$1,866,590

Accounting Issues Related to Purchase Commitments

When customers ask for a product and it is out of stock, it is likely a lost sale. To make sure that their suppliers will have the items they need, some companies engage in purchase commitments, which are agreements to purchase inventory in the future. A purchase commitment does not transfer title to the buyer, and no entries are required for commitments that are optional or cancelable.

Noncancellable commitments are not recognized as assets or liabilities, because neither party has exchanged anything yet, but material commitments should be disclosed in the notes to the balance sheet. When the negotiated price is the same or less than the market price, no additional disclosure is required. However, if the contract price is greater than the market price, the amount of the estimated loss should be recorded and reported under other expenses and losses. Assuming the contract price was $300,000 and the market value declined to $200,000, an estimated liability for purchase commitments of $100,000 and an unrealized loss in the corresponding account is recorded. If some or all of the value is recovered, the estimated liability on purchase commitments account and the unrealized holding loss are adjusted.

Estimating Inventory

Although a physical inventory count is important from an internal control viewpoint, it is usually impractical to take a physical inventory more than once a year. When inventory is not known but needs to be estimated when preparing quarterly statements, either the gross profit method or the retail inventory method can be used.

Estimating Inventory Using the Gross Profit Method

The gross profit method (or gross margin method) of estimating inventory was developed for situations when it is impossible or impractical to get a precise inventory count. This method is used when preparing quarterly statements because it is not practical to perform physical inventory counts each quarter. The gross profit method also is used by auditors when an estimate of inventory is needed, such as when inventory records have been destroyed in a fire.

The gross profit method uses three assumptions:

1. Beginning inventory plus purchases equals total goods to be accounted for.
2. Goods not sold are in inventory (not stolen, etc.).
3. The ending inventory is equal to beginning inventory plus purchases minus sales at cost.

To determine sales at cost, the gross profit percentage is used. This percentage is determined based on records from prior periods. Figure 1A-40 shows how to approximate ending inventory using the gross profit method.

Figure 1A-40 Gross Profit Inventory Calculation

Beginning inventory (at cost)		$130,000
Purchases (at cost)		410,000
Goods available (at cost)		540,000
Sales (at selling price)	$570,000	
Less: Gross profit (24% of $570,000)	136,800	
Sales (at cost)		433,200
Approximate inventory (at cost)		$106,800

Estimating Inventory Using the Retail Inventory Method

- Retail stores often sell thousands of different items at high volumes, making the inventory tracking method of specific identification impractical. Therefore, the retail inventory method estimates inventory value using retail prices, converting this data to cost using a formula that reflects the firm's average markup. To use the retail inventory method, retail companies must track period sales.
- Total cost and retail value of purchased goods.
- Total cost and retail value of goods available for sale.

Figure 1A-41 shows how this data is applied at Bounce Sporting Goods to estimate the ending inventory value by using the cost to retail ratio for goods available for sale.

Figure 1A-41 Retail Inventory Method

Bounce Sporting Goods
Year 1

	Cost	Retail	Cost to Retail Ratio
Beginning inventory	$320,000	$510,000	
Purchases	1,250,000	2,075,000	
Goods available for sale	$1,570,000	$2,585,000 =	60.7%
Less sales		− $2,100,000	
Ending inventory (retail prices)		$485,000	
× Cost to retail ratio		× 0.607	
Ending inventory (cost)		$294,395	

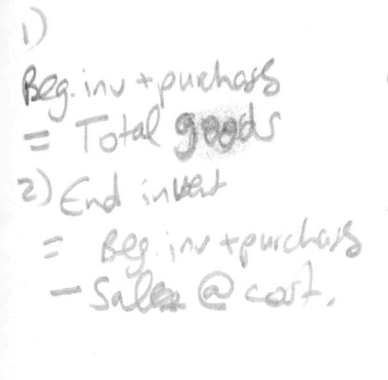

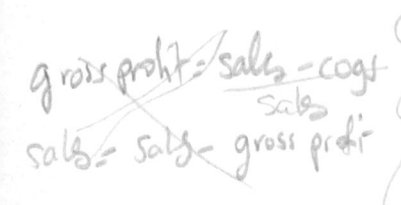

Investments

Accounting for investments in debt securities or equity securities of other companies is covered in this section.

Debt Securities

A debt security is a form of loan to another entity, including federal and municipal government securities, commercial paper, corporate bonds, securitized debt instruments, and convertible debt. Debt securities are categorized as follows according to ASC Topic 320:

- Held to maturity (those that the company has the intent and ability to hold until maturity)—Valued at amortized cost (acquisition cost plus/minus unamortized premium or discount), so no unrealized holding gains or losses are recognized.
- Trading (near-term sale is expected)—Valued at fair value and unrealized holding gains and losses are recognized in net income.
- Available for sale (all others)—Valued at fair value and unrealized holding gains and losses are recognized as other comprehensive income (and as a separate component of stockholders' equity).

On the balance sheet, companies report individual held-to-maturity, available-for-sale, and trading securities as either current or noncurrent, as appropriate, depending on whether they are expected to be converted to cash within a year or the operating cycle, if longer. For securities classified as available for sale and held to maturity, disclosure is required of the aggregate fair value, gross unrealized holding gains and losses, and amortized cost basis.

In adjusting a portfolio of trading and available-for-sale securities to market value, a valuation allowance (a contra or adjunct account) to the investment account is used. At each balance sheet date, the valuation allowance is adjusted so that the sum of the investment account (at cost) and the valuation allowance are equal to the fair value of the securities. An unrealized gain or unrealized loss is credited or debited as the other side of the adjusting entry. When the securities are sold, the cost is removed from the investment account and a realized gain or loss is recorded.

Held to Maturity

Because equity securities have no maturity date, only debt securities can be held to maturity. In order to classify securities as held to maturity, the reporting entity must have both the positive intent and the ability (financial flexibility, risk tolerance) to hold the securities to maturity.

ASC Topic 320 lists several exceptions to this rule, which allow an entity to sell a particular security without calling its intent to hold other securities to maturity into question. Some exceptions include deterioration of issuer's creditworthiness, changes in regulatory requirements altering permissible or maximum investments, or tax law changes that eliminate or reduce tax-exempt status of interest on the debt security.

Debt securities may not be classified as held to maturity when the intent is merely to hold them indefinitely (without the ability to do so) or if it is intended that the securities would be sold in response to changes in market interest rates or the security's prepayment risk, need for liquidity, yield or availability of alternative investments, financing, or foreign currency risk.

Other than such exceptions, sales of held-to-maturity securities should be rare. When they are sold, according to ASC Topic 320, the amortized cost amount of the sold or transferred security, the related gain or loss, and the circumstances leading to the decision to sell or transfer the security shall be disclosed in the notes to the financial statements for each period for which the results of operations are presented.

As covered earlier in the discussion of notes receivable, the unamortized discount or premium, if any, is deducted from or added to the acquisition cost to determine the carrying value. Unrealized gains and losses are not accounted for because the assets are not recorded at fair value. As with notes receivable, the effective interest method is used to compute interest income. See the section titled "Notes Receivable" for an example of this method (Figure 1A-20).

Trading

Trading securities are intended to be sold in the short term to generate income from short-term differences in price. Because it is the intention to trade such securities, trading securities are recorded at fair value, and any unrealized holding gains or losses resulting from marking the securities to market (e.g., fair value) at the balance sheet date must be included in net income. At the date of acquisition, the security is recorded at its cost including commissions, fees, and taxes. As of the next and all succeeding statement dates, the security is reported at its fair market value. Dividend or interest revenue recognized but not received is accounted for separately as a receivable.

Figure 1A-42 shows a sample debt security portfolio including the cost, the fair value, and the unrealized gain or loss (which is the difference between cost and fair value).

Figure 1A-42 Computation of Securities Fair Value Adjustment

Trading Debt Security Portfolio
For Year Ended December 31, Year 1

Investments	Cost	Fair Value	Unrealized Gain (Loss)
X Corporation 12% bonds	$54,386	$64,860	$10,474
Y Corporation 10% bonds	228,445	216,248	(12,197)
Z Corporation 8% bonds	107,086	114,600	7,514
Total of portfolio	$389,917	$395,708	5,791
Previous securities fair value adjustment balance			(3,201)
Securities fair value adjustment—debit			$2,590

Available for sale

Available-for-sale securities include all securities that do not fit in the trading and the held-to-maturity categories, such as securities that have an indeterminate use or indefinite holding time but are not being actively traded to take advantage of temporary differences in market prices. These securities are reported at fair value, and any unrealized gains and losses resulting from marking the securities to market at the balance sheet date are reported in other comprehensive income and as a separate component of stockholders' equity until realized by a sale.

Figure 1A-43 shows how a security would be adjusted to fair value. The example assumes that there was an unrealized loss of $14,257 the prior year. Because the unrealized loss at the end of the current year of $12,000 is $2,257 less than the prior year, an unrealized gain would be recorded.

Figure 1A-43 Calculation of Securities Fair Value Adjustment—Available for Sale

Available-for-Sale Debt Security Portfolio
For Year Ended December 31, Year 1

Investments	Amortized Cost	Fair Value	Unrealized Gain (Loss)
X Corporation 10% bonds (total portfolio)	$300,000	$288,000	$(12,000)
Previous securities fair value adjustment balance—credit			(14,257)
Securities fair value adjustment—debit			$2,257

The balance sheet and the income statement for the available-for-sale security in Figure 1A-43 is illustrated in Figure 1A-44. (The income statement includes a $6,212 loss on the sale of a security that was sold during the year.)

Figure 1A-44 Available-for-Sale Securities on the Balance Sheet and Income Statement

Balance Sheet

Current assets	
Interest receivable	$xxx
Investments	
Available-for-sale securities, at fair value	$288,000
Stockholders' equity	
Accumulated other comprehensive loss	$12,000

Income Statement

Other revenues and gains	
Interest revenue	$xxx
Other expenses and losses	
Loss on sale of securities	$6,212

Equity Securities

Debt securities are used primarily to preserve capital and generate income; equity securities are those securities that convey an ownership interest in another entity. They include common and preferred stock, other capital stock, and rights to buy or sell ownership interests at set prices (warrants, options, and rights).

Equity securities do not include convertible debt securities or redeemable preferred stocks. Initially they are valued at acquisition cost plus brokerage and other fees.

When the investor in a stock acquires an interest in the investee, the percentage of voting stock acquired determines the method of accounting for the security.

- **Holdings of less than 20% (passive interest)**—Investor uses the fair value method.
- **Holdings between 20% and 50% (significant influence)**—Investor uses the equity method.
- **Holdings of greater than 50% (controlling interest)**—Investor issues consolidated financial statements.

Holdings of Less than 20%

Equity securities held at a level of less than 20% ownership interest are accounted for as either available-for-sale or trading securities. (Having no maturity date, they cannot be classified as held-to-maturity securities.) The presumption is that investors with less than 20% interest have little or no influence over the investee. If the investor has significant influence over the investee even with less than 20% ownership interest, the equity method is used. (See the section titled "Holdings between 20% and 50%" below.)

Investments of less than 20% initially are recorded at their acquisition cost including fees and then are revalued to fair value at each balance sheet date. Securities acquired in a noncash exchange (such as for services or land) are recorded at the fair value of the noncash consideration paid or the fair value of the security received, whichever is more readily available. If neither value is easy to ascertain, an estimate must be made.

Available-for-Sale Security Portfolio

Cash dividends declared by the investee are reported as income by the investor. Securities initially are recorded at cost. At each balance sheet date, the portfolio is valued at fair value, with any net unrealized gain or loss calculated as shown in Figure 1A-45.

Figure 1A-45 Calculation of Securities Fair Value Adjustment

Available-for-Sale Equity Security Portfolio
For Year Ended December 31, Year 1

Investments	Cost	Fair Value	Unrealized Gain (Loss)
X Corporation	$228,536	$242,000	$13,464
Y Corporation	279,400	267,520	(11,880)
Z Corporation	124,388	91,520	(32,868)
Total of portfolio	$632,324	$601,040	(31,284)
Previous securities fair value adjustment balance			1,000
Securities fair value adjustment—credit			$(30,284)

The net unrealized gain or loss on the portfolio is reported as part of other comprehensive income and as a component of stockholders' equity (accumulated other comprehensive income). The entry to adjust the portfolio via the valuation allowance (securities fair value adjustment) and record an unrealized loss is illustrated in Figure 1A-46.

Figure 1A-46 Journal Entries for Securities Fair Value Adjustment

Unrealized holding gain or loss – equity	$30,28	
Securities fair value adjustment (available for sale)		

When a stock in the portfolio is sold, a realized gain or loss is calculated by deducting the acquisition cost from the net proceeds from sale. A realized gain would be accounted for as of the date of the sale, as shown in Figure 1A-47.

Figure 1A-47 Accounting Entries for a Realized Gain on Sale of a Security

Cash	$10,000	
Available-for-sale securities		$4,000
Gain on sale of stock		$6,000

Realized gains and losses are recorded when securities are sold. Sales and purchases of securities during the year will change the cost basis of the investment account. Companies often wait until year-end to calculate the net unrealized gain or loss on the portfolio as a whole. When an available-for-sale security is sold during the year, a reclassification adjustment also is required to avoid double-counting the gain or loss. These adjustments are discussed later in this topic.

Trading Securities

Accounting for trading securities is the same as the accounting for available-for-sale securities, with the exception that unrealized holding gains or losses are reported in net income instead of other comprehensive income. The account is therefore unrealized holding gain or loss income, and sale of the security requires any remainder of the gain or loss to be recognized in income.

Holdings between 20% and 50%

The equity method of accounting, described in ASC Topic 323, *Investments—Equity Method and Joint Ventures*, is required for any investor who is able to exercise significant influence over an investee's operating and financial policies. The term "significant influence" is not limited to a minimum percentage of ownership of 20% but also can be determined by the amount of representation on the board of directors, material intercompany transactions, and other factors.

However, unless evidence demonstrates otherwise, a 20% or greater investment is presumed to cause significant influence. Those holding greater than 20% interest in an investee can prove that they do not exert significant influence if situations such as the next ones are true:

- Investor signed a contract surrendering significant rights to the investee.
- Investee opposition, such as litigation or other challenges.
- Investee ownership is concentrated among a small group that does not heed the investor's opinions.
- Investor tried and failed to get representation on the board of directors.
- Investor is not allowed access to the required information for using the equity method.

In such a case, the investor would be required to report its equity investment similar to the way investments are accounted for when the investor holds a less than 20% ownership (i.e., available-for-sale security).

Equity Method Accounting

Under the equity method, an investment initially us recorded at acquisition cost plus fees. Subsequently, the investment's carrying amount is increased or decreased by the investor's percentage of the earnings or losses of the investee and is decreased by any dividends received from (or declared by) the investee. The investor records its share of the investee's income as an increase or decrease in the carrying value of the investment account obtained by multiplying the percentage of ownership in the investee by its reported income. The equity method presumes a material relationship between the two entities, so in addition to recognizing that the earnings and losses of the investee raise or lower the investor's net assets, several items must be removed from the investor's books to avoid double-counting of assets or liabilities:

- Any intercompany transactions that factor into the investor's net income must be eliminated to the extent of the investor's interest therein.
- The proportionate share of the difference between fair market values and book values of the investee's fixed assets should be depreciated. If investee assets cannot be determined at fair market value, the entire difference between acquisition price and book value is amortized as goodwill.

- The proportionate share of the investee's extraordinary items (discussed later in this topic), results of discontinued operations, and cumulative effects of accounting principles should be treated as the investor's extraordinary items.

To illustrate the accounting for an equity purchased by an investor company, assume that an investor company purchases a 30% share in an investee company for $20 million. On the date of the investment, the investee's book value is $50 million. The excess of purchase price over the proportionate share of the book value acquired is $5 million ($20 million minus 30% of $50 million). In this example, the difference is allocated among goodwill ($2.5 million), finite-lived intangibles ($1.5 million), and undervalued depreciable assets of the investee's company ($1 million). The intangibles are amortized over five years, and the assets are depreciated over ten years.

At the end of the first year when the investee company releases its end-of-period results, the investor company must account for both ordinary and extraordinary components of income. (Assume that the company reported $4.6 million in net income, which includes a $600,000 extraordinary loss.) A year-end dividend of $1.4 million also was declared. Finally, the amortization and depreciation resulting from the allocation of the excess purchase price must be accounted for. The entries for the end of the year are shown in Figure 1A-48.

Figure 1A-48 Year-End Accounting Entries for Securities Accounted for under the Equity Method

Investment in X Company stock		$1,380,000
Loss form investment (extraordinary)		$180,000
Income from investment (ordinary)		$
[To record share of X Company net income ($4,600,000 X 0.3) and extraordinary loss ($600,000 X 0.3)]		
Cash		$420,000
Investment in X Company stock		
[To record dividend received ($1,400,000 × 0.3) from X Company]		
Income from investment (ordinary)		$400,000
Investment in X Company stock		
To record amortization of investment cost in excess of book value represented by:		
Undervalued depreciable assets	$\dfrac{\$1\text{ million}}{10\text{ years}}$	= $100,000
Unrecorded intangibles	$\dfrac{\$1.5\text{ million}}{5\text{ years}}$	= $300,000
Total = $400,000		

The carrying amount of the investment is calculated as in Figure 1A-49 (assuming that a June dividend of $700,000 was also declared, 30% of which would have been recognized in June, or $210,000).

Figure 1A-49 Calculation of Investment Carrying Amount

Investment in Investee Company		
Acquisition cost, 1/1/Year 1	$20,000,000	
Plus: Share of Year 1 income before dividends and amortization	1,380,000	21,380,000
Less:		
Dividends received 6/30 and 12/31	(630,000)	
Amortization of undervalued depreciable assets	(100,000)	
Amortization of unrecorded intangibles	(300,000)	(1,030,000)
Carrying amount, 12/31/Year 1		$20,350,000

Holdings of Greater than 50%

When a company achieves a controlling interest in an investee's operations, usually indicated by owning greater than 50% of the investee's stock, each company continues to maintain separate accounting records. Interperiod statements are prepared using the equity accounting method, and the investment is treated as a long-term investment. At the end of the accounting period, the parent company consolidates its results with those of the subsidiary. In the consolidated balance sheet, the investment account is eliminated to avoid double-counting and is replaced with the individual assets and liabilities of the subsidiary. Consolidated statements treat the entities as a single accounting entity. Specifics of consolidated statements are not treated here.

Purchase Accounting

When one company acquires more than 50% of another through a merger, acquisition, or statutory consolidation, GAAP requires the use of **purchase accounting** to record the event. Purchase accounting records the value of the acquired firm at the fair market value of the consideration given (stock, cash, debt, or some combination). Also included in the cost of the acquisition are any fees paid to complete the transaction (e.g., a preacquisition audit or finder's fees paid to an investment banker). Purchase accounting requires that the net assets of the acquired companies be recorded in the consolidated financial statements at their fair market value. Any difference between the amount paid and the fair market value of the acquired company's net assets is recorded as goodwill. Goodwill is an intangible asset that must be tested for impairment annually and written down if impairment occurs. (Goodwill amortization is no longer acceptable under GAAP.)

If the transaction is structured so the acquired firm remains a separate legal entity, that firm is considered a subsidiary of the acquiring (parent) firm and keeps its own set of books. The parent firm carries the subsidiary on its books in an investment in a subsidiary (asset) account. After the date of acquisition, period adjustments are made to the investment in subsidiary account. If the holding company has between 20% and 50% control, the parent company usually tracks its investment in the subsidiary using the equity method. If the parent company has a controlling interest (usually greater than 50% ownership), use of consolidated financial statements and the equity method is required. Under the equity method, the investment account is increased by the subsidiary's net income, decreased for dividends paid, and adjusted for any additional expenses related to the step-up in basis to fair market value. Under the cost method, an adjustment to the investment in subsidiary account is made for a permanent decline in value and additional investments.

Consider an example in which Acme Diversified purchases 60% of Abco Inc.'s stock for $3.84 million. Figure 1A-50 compares the differences between the cost and equity methods by showing the accounting entries for the first year of the relationship. The example assumes that the $3.84 million investment exceeded Abco's book value by $480,000. Of this, $240,000 was considered goodwill and $240,000 was considered an excess of market value over book values for depreciable assets. (This amount is amortized over five years while goodwill is not amortized.) Furthermore, in Year 1, Abco reported income of $432,000 and a dividend of $144,000.

Income of $432,000 less the dividend leaves cumulative income after dividends of $288,000.

Figure 1A-50 Cost Method versus Equity Method—Parent Company Perspective

Cost Method	Equity Method
Year 1	**Year 1**

Investment in Abco $3,840,000
   Cash $3,840,000
To record the initial investment
Cash $86,400
   Dividend income $86,400
To record dividends received (0.6 × $144,000)
	Investment in Abco $3,840,000
	   Cash $3,840,000
	To record the initial investment
	Investment in Abco $259,200
	   Equity in subsidiary income $259,200
	To record equity in subsidiary income (0.6 × $432,000)
	Equity in subsidiary income $48,000
	   Investment in Abco $48,000
	To adjust equity in subsidiary income for excess depreciation ($240,000/5 years = $48,000)
	Cash $86,400
	   Investment in Abco $86,400
	To record dividends received (0.6 × $144,000)
	   Investment in Abco $86,400
	To record dividends received (0.6 × $144,000)

Figure 1A-51 shows how the investment account balances are determined in Year 1.

Figure 1A-51 Investment Accounts: Cost versus Equity Methods

Investment Account at Year 1 End

Cost Method		Equity Method		
Year 1 cost	$3,840,000	Year 1 cost	$3,840,000	
		Year 1 equity in subsidiary income	$259,200	Year 1 amortization of depreciable assets
				Year 1 share of dividend declared
Year 1 balance	$3,840,000	Year 1 balance	$3,964,800	

What does the comparison between the two methods tell us?

- Dividends paid or declared are considered income under the cost method but are recorded as a decrease in investment under the equity method.
- Income reported by the subsidiary increases the investment account (asset account) under the equity method but does not get recorded under the cost method.
- Additional depreciation expense of assets marked up during acquisition is included in the equity method but is not in the cost method.

Financial Statement Presentation Issues

Two specific issues in statement presentation have a significant impact on financial statements. These include impairment of value and reclassification adjustments.

Impairment of Value

Investments sometimes suffer **impairments** in value, which are losses that are other than temporary. All investments should be evaluated to determine if this is the case. The most common impairments are bankruptcies or other loss of liquidity on the part of an investee. When an impairment is judged to be other than temporary, it is written down to its new cost basis. Impairment losses are considered realized and are included in net income.

Impairment testing is performed in the following manner.

- **Debt securities**—Determine if it is probable that an investor will be unable to collect all of the amounts due as per the terms of contract.
- **Equity securities**—If the security's net realizable value is lower than the carrying amount of the investment, consider the duration of time and the extent to which the fair value has been less than cost, the intent and ability of the investor to hold the investment for the period anticipated for the fair value of the investee's stock to regain its value, and the investee's future prospects.

Assume a loss on available-for-sale securities was reported earlier as an unrealized loss in comprehensive income, say, of $100,000 on a $1 million bond. If the loss needs to be recorded as a realized loss because the impairment in value is considered other than temporary, the accounting entry (assuming an available-for-sale debt security) is as shown in Figure 1A-52.

Figure 1A-52 Realized Loss Due to Impairment

Loss on impairment	$100,000	
Securities fair value adjustment (available for sale)	$100,000	
Unrealized holding gain or loss – equity		$100,000
Available-for-sale securities		$100,000

Thus, the investment in the debt security has a new cost basis of $900,000.

Reclassification Adjustments

Unrealized gains and losses on available-for-sale securities are included in other comprehensive income. When the securities are sold, realized gains and losses are reported as part of net income, so double-counting occurs unless a reclassification adjustment is performed. For example, assume an investor holds the portfolio of stocks in Figure 1A-53 for Year 1.

Figure 1A-53 Available-for-Sale Security Portfolio

Investments	Cost	Fair Value	Unrealized Holding Gain (Loss)
X Corporation common stocks	$98,400	$129,150	$30,750
Y Corporation common stocks	147,600	166,050	18,450
Total of portfolio	$246,000	$295,200	49,200
Previous securities fair value adjustment balance			0
Securities fair value adjustment—debit			$49,200

The investor's statement of comprehensive income for the period would include the net holding gains for Year 1 as in Figure 1A-54.

Figure 1A-54 Statement of Comprehensive Income

Bounce Sporting Goods Company Statement of Comprehensive Income For Year Ended December 31, Year 1	
Net income	$430,500
Other comprehensive income	
Holding gains arising during period	
Comprehensive income	49,200
	$479,700

The X Corporation stock was sold with a realized gain of $30,750 in Year 2. The available-for-sale security portfolio at the end of Year 2 is illustrated in Figure 1A-55.

Figure 1A-55 Available-for-Sale Security Portfolio

Investments	Cost	Fair Value	Unrealized Holding Gain (Loss)
Y Corporation common stocks	$147,600	$190,000	$42,400
Previous securities fair value adjustment balance—debit			(49,200)
Securities fair value adjustment—credit			$(6,800)

The holding gain or loss is computed as in Figure 1A-56.

Figure 1A-56 Computation of Total Holding Gain (Loss)

Unrealized holding gain (loss)	$(6,800)
Realized holding gain	30,750
Total holding gain recognized	$23,950

The unrealized gain on the X Corporation stock was included in the Year 1 comprehensive income statement while in Year 2 the realized gain was reported in net income. Because comprehensive income is a component of net income, a reclassification adjustment is required in the Year 2 statement of comprehensive income to eliminate the realized gain from comprehensive income, as shown in Figure 1A-57.

Figure 1A-57 Statement of Comprehensive Income

Bounce Sporting Goods Company
Statement of Comprehensive Income
For Year Ended December 31, Year 2

Net income (includes $30,750 realized gain on X Corporation shares)		$885,600
Other comprehensive income		
Holding gains arising during period ($190,000 – $166,050)	$23,950	
Less: Reclassification adjustment for gains included in net income	(30,750)	(6,800)
Comprehensive income		$878,800

Property, Plant, and Equipment

Property, plant, and equipment (PP&E) covers all assets of durable nature, such as land, office and retail space, factories, warehouses, equipment, machinery, and company vehicles.

Major Characteristics of PP&E

To be considered PP&E, an asset must have these three characteristics:

1. **The asset is held for use in operations and not for resale.** PP&E includes assets held for use in operations. Assets acquired for investment or resale are

not considered PP&E. For example, a vacant building would be classified as an investment.
2. **The asset is long term in nature and if other than land is depreciable.** PP&E is expected to provide future benefits over a number of years. Based on the matching principle, the asset's cost is spread over its estimated life and charged to earnings as depreciation expense. Land, which typically does not decline in value, is not depreciated (but in some cases, its value may become impaired).
3. **The asset must be tangible.** Assets classified as PP&E have a physical substance, in contrast to intangible assets, such as copyrights or patents, which do not.

Cost Basis of Valuing PP&E at Acquisition

The historical cost, or acquisition cost, is the basis used to value PP&E. Issues related to costing land, buildings, equipment, and self-constructed assets also are considered in this section.

Historical Cost

Historical cost is measured by the cash or cash equivalent price paid to obtain or construct an asset, including transportation, installation costs, taxes, and related costs. The general rule for determining the cost of an asset, whether PP&E or inventory, is that all the costs necessary to get the asset in place and ready for its intended use are capitalized as part of the cost of the asset.

At the acquisition date, an asset's historical cost and fair value are equivalent. Subsequent to acquisition, changes in fair value are not recognized in the accounts (except when impairment occurs). Some accountants would argue that fair values constitute more relevant measures than historical costs. However, others are concerned that fair values may lack reliability. Consequently, under GAAP, PP&E is valued at amortized historical cost because of its reliability. The costs of additions or improvements are added to the cost of plant assets when an increase in future service potential will result. In contrast, the cost of routine repairs and maintenance would be expensed as incurred.

Cost of Land

The cost of land includes:

- The purchase price.
- Closing costs, including title, commissions, legal fees, past-due taxes, and insurance.
- Land preparation costs, such as grading, filling, demolition, draining, razing old buildings (net of salvage proceeds), and clear-cutting.
- Cost of surveys.
- Assumption of liens, mortgages, or other possible encumbrances.

Special assessments for municipal improvements, such as sewers and street lights, are charged to the land account because typically they are permanently maintained by the government. The cost of private improvements of a temporary nature, such as driveways and fences, would be recorded in a separate land improvements account and depreciated over the useful life of the improvement. Land held for speculative reasons is considered an investment; land held by a property developer for resale would be considered inventory.

Cost of Buildings

The cost of buildings includes all costs to buy or construct a building, including architect's fees, building permits, materials, labor, and overhead. If an old building is razed to make way for a new building, that cost is considered part of the cost of the land, which is being readied for its intended use as a building site, not part of the cost of the new building.

Cost of Equipment

All expenditures in purchasing, shipping, preparing a site, and installation of equipment are included in the cost of the equipment. For example, preparing a foundation for equipment is included in the cost. Equipment encompasses office equipment, machinery, delivery equipment, furniture, fixtures, and all other similar fixed assets.

Cost of Self-Constructed Assets

While most companies contract out construction projects to professional firms, some companies, such as those in the telecommunications, rail, and utilities industries, construct their own assets. Lacking an external purchase price, the cost of self-constructed assets is more difficult to determine. An entity must allocate costs and expenses carefully between operating and construction activities to determine the asset's cost.

Allocating direct construction costs, such as materials and direct labor, is straightforward. In theory, indirect costs, such as insurance, property taxes, utilities, depreciation of fixed assets, and supervisory factory labor, might be dealt with in different ways. In practice, a proportional amount of these overhead costs would be allocated to the self-constructed asset. However, some accountants would argue against allocating these overhead costs to construction, because they would be incurred whether the construction project was under way or not. Any costs incurred in excess of the asset's market value should not be capitalized but would be recorded as a loss.

Accounting for Interest Costs during Construction or Acquisition of PP&E

In theory, capitalization of interest costs arising during construction of PP&E can be handled in three ways:

1. **Capitalize only actual interest costs arising during construction.** With a few exceptions, GAAP requires this method because it uses the historical cost

principle of recording only actual transactions that are a part of the actual cost of construction. Under GAAP, the amount of interest capitalized is based on the lower of the amount of interest actually incurred during the construction period or the amount of interest that would have been avoidable if expenditures for the asset had not been made.

2. **Do not capitalize any interest charges during construction.** Those who favor this approach argue that if a firm had used equity rather than debt financing, no interest costs would have been incurred. Therefore, interest should be considered a financing cost rather than a construction cost. However, unless the related interest costs are immaterial, such an approach is unacceptable under GAAP.

3. **Capitalize all types of finance costs used to construct the asset, whether specifically identifiable or not.** Some argue that there is always an opportunity cost to funding construction, whether debt or equity financing is used, and that this should be considered part of the asset's cost. However, because this opportunity cost is a subjective measure that does not fit with the historical cost method, it is not used under GAAP.

Nonmonetary Exchanges

Exchanges of nonmonetary assets (such as inventory or PP&E) are recorded based on fair values, as long as the transaction has commercial substance. A transaction has commercial substance if the exchange will change the timing and amount of the firm's future cash flows. Future cash flows are likely to change when the assets exchanged are dissimilar (inventory for equipment) or when the assets are similar (truck for truck) but have different expected useful lives. In other words, if the two entities will have different economic positions after the exchange, the transaction has commercial substance and is reported at fair value with gains or losses on the exchange immediately recognized. If future cash flows are not expected to change significantly, the transaction lacks commercial substance and would be accounted for at book value. Losses on the exchange would be recognized, but no gains would be reported unless "boot" (e.g., cash) was received in the transaction; then a portion of the gain would be recognized.

Accounting for Exchanges with Commercial Substance—Gain Recorded

An asset acquired in a nonmonetary exchange is valued based on the fair values of the assets given up. Only in the case when it is more clearly evident would the fair value of the asset received be used instead. Figure 1A-58 illustrates the computation of a gain when a warehouse is acquired in exchange for a fleet of cars.

Figure 1A-58 Computation of Fair Value of Cars and Gain

Fair value of cars		$147,000
Cost of cars	$192,000	
Less: Accumulated depreciation	66,000	
Book value of car		126,000
Gain on disposal of cars		$21,000

The warehouse would be recorded for $147,000, the fair value of the cars given up. The cars and their related accumulated depreciation account would be written off, and a gain of $21,000 would be recorded as a result of the exchange.

Accounting for Exchanges with Commercial Substance—Loss Recorded

This situation is illustrated in Figures 1A-59 and 1A-60. The example assumes that a company acquires a new machine (B) with a list price of $25,000 by paying cash and trading in its old machine (A). An analysis of the future cash flow associated with the old and new machines indicates that the exchange has commercial substance. The old machine had an original cost of $18,000, and accumulated depreciation of $8,000 has been recorded on it. The fair value of the old machine is determined to be $7,000, but a trade-in allowance of $12,000 is negotiated for it as part of the purchase agreement.

Figure 1A-59 Computation of Cost of New Machine

List price of new machine	$25,000
Less: Trade-in allowance for used machine	12,000
Cash payment due	13,000
Fair value of used machine	7,000
Cost of new machine	$20,000

The accounting entry to record the exchange is shown in Figure 1A-60.

Figure 1A-60 Accounting Entry for Exchange

Machine B	$20,000	
Accumulated depreciation — machines	$8,000	
Loss on disposal of machine	$3,000	
[Fair value – book value: $7,000 – $10,000]		
Machine A		$18,000
Cash		$13,000

Accounting for Exchanges without Commercial Substance

When the company remains in the same economic position as before the exchange, the asset acquired should be recorded at the book value of the asset disposed of. Any losses on the exchange would be recognized, but generally no gains are recognized unless "boot" (e.g., cash) was received in the transaction. In this case a partial gain would be recognized. To illustrate a situation involving a nonmonetary exchange that lacks commercial substance (no boot received), assume that company A exchanges its iron stamping machine for company B's steel stamping machine. Company A's iron stamping machine has a:

- Fair value of $112,000.
- Book value of $94,500 (cost of $105,000 less accumulated depreciation of $10,500).

Company B's steel stamping machine has a:

- Fair value of $119,000.
- Book value of $95,200 (cost of $140,000 less accumulated depreciation of $44,800).

Company A also pays company B $7,000 in cash. From company A's perspective, the calculation of the unrealized gain on the swap is shown in Figure 1A-61.

Figure 1A-61 Calculation of Gain (Unrecognized)

Fair value of iron stamper exchanged	$112,000
Book value of iron stamper exchanged	94,500
Total gain (unrecognized)	$17,500

The new machine is expected to produce cash flows similar to those of the old machine, so the exchange is deemed to lack commercial substance. As a result, the total gain on disposal of the old machine is deferred. The cost recorded for the new machine can be calculated based either on the book value of the assets given up or on the fair value of the asset received less the amount of gain deferred, as illustrated in Figure 1A-62.

Figure 1A-62 Basis of Steel Stamper

Book Value Method			Fair Value Method	
Book value of iron stamper	$94,500		Fair value of steel stamper	$119,000
Cash paid	7,000	Or	Less: Gain deferred	(17,500)
Basis of steel stamper	$101,500		Basis of steel stamper	$101,500

The entry to record this exchange on company A's books is shown in Figure 1A-63.

Figure 1A-63 Company A's Entry for the Exchange

Steel stamper	$101,500	
Accumulated depreciation—old boiler	$10,500	
Iron stamper		$105,000
Cash		$7,200

If the steel stamping machine is later sold to an outside party, the deferred gain that reduced its basis will be recognized.

Nonmonetary exchanges should be disclosed in the financial statement notes. Disclosure should include the nature of the transaction, the accounting method used, and any gains or losses recognized.

Payment for PP&E in the Form of Stock

When PP&E assets are acquired through the issuance of stock or other securities, the par value of the stock will be inadequate to measure the true cost of the property.

Instead, if the stock is being actively traded, its current market value is used. If the stock value cannot be determined because the stock is not actively traded, an estimate of the market value of the property should be made and used as the basis for recording the value of both the asset and the issuance of the stock.

An example follows of an acquisition when the stock is being actively traded. Acme Company wants to build luxury condominiums and so purchases a warehouse from Robin Manufacturing by issuing Robin 10,000 shares of $1 par common stock currently trading at $20 per share. Acme's accounting entry would be as shown in Figure 1A-64.

Figure 1A-64 Acme Company Accounting Entry

Property (10,000 shares × $20/share)	$200,000
Common stock	$10,000
Additional paid-in capital	$190,000

Accounting for Costs Subsequent to Acquisition

Costs subsequent to the acquisition of PP&E are either capitalized or expensed as operating expenditures. To qualify as a cost to be capitalized (recorded to the asset account), the cost should provide future economic benefits above those that were expected from the existing asset. Future economic benefits can be increased either by extending the life of the asset or increasing the productivity of the asset by improving either the quantity or quality of the units produced.

Additions, improvements and replacements, reinstallations or rearrangements, and repairs each have special accounting implications.

Additions

Additions should be capitalized because they are effectively new assets. If the addition results in modifications to the existing structure, the cost of those modifications would be capitalized provided the addition had been planned when the existing structure was constructed; otherwise, the costs would be reported as an expense or loss.

Improvements and Replacements

An improvement substitutes a more effective asset for one in place; replacements replace aging assets with newer versions of the same thing. Both should be capitalized. Three approaches are used to account for such capitalizations: the substitution method, capitalizing the new cost, and charging the cost to accumulated depreciation.

1. **Substitution method.** Whenever the book value of the asset to be replaced is known, the substitution method should be used. The book value of the old asset is removed from the asset account and the new item is recorded. Assume that

an old boiler needs to be replaced with a new boiler. The old boiler has a scrap value of $300, a current book value of $4,500, and an original book value of $45,000 less accumulated depreciation of $40,500. The new boiler costs $37,500. The book entry for the substitution is shown in Figure 1A-65.

Figure 1A-65 Substitution Method Accounting Entries

New boiler	$37,500	
Accumulated depreciation—old boiler	$40,500	
Loss on disposal of old boiler ($4,500 − $300)	$4,200	
Old boiler		$45,000
Cash ($37,500 − $300)		$37,200

2. **Capitalizing the new cost.** Improvements usually are handled by capitalizing the cost of the new item without removing the carrying amount of the old item. This is justified by the assumption that sufficient depreciation was taken on the old item to make the carrying amount close to zero.
3. **Charge accumulated depreciation.** If the quality or quantity of an asset has not been improved but its useful life is extended, the costs are debited to accumulated depreciation because the previous reduction in carrying value has been restored. Such accounting will extend the depreciable life of the asset.

Reinstallations or Rearrangements

Movements of assets from one location to another are capitalized and expensed over the period of benefit. If certain of these costs cannot be separated from other operating benefits or if the costs are immaterial, they should be expensed immediately.

Repairs

Repairs that maintain a normal level of asset function are charged to the expense account in the period incurred. An allowance for repairs account sometimes is used when all repairs are performed during particular interim periods but benefit the entire year. For example, assume that a company estimates it will need to spend $1,000,000 on repairs during the year and allocates these costs over the four quarterly periods. Actual repair expenditures were incurred in the second quarter ($520,000), in the third quarter ($256,000), and in the fourth quarter ($235,000). The accounting for each quarter would be as shown in Figure 1A-66.

Figure 1A-66 Accounting Entries Using a Repair Expense Account

First-Quarter End

Repair expense	$250,000	
Allowance for repairs $\left(\dfrac{\$1,000,000}{4}\right)$		$250,000

(Continued)

Figure 1A-66 (*Continued*)

Second-Quarter End

Allowance for repairs	$520,000	
Cash, accrued payroll, inventory, etc.		$520,000
Repair expense	$250,000	
Allowance for repairs $\left(\dfrac{\$1,000,000}{4}\right)$		$250,000

Third-Quarter End

Allowance for repairs	$256,000	
Cash, accrued payroll, inventory, etc.		$256,000
Repair expense	$250,000	
Allowance for repairs $\left(\dfrac{\$1,000,000}{4}\right)$		$250,000

Fourth-Quarter End

Allowance for repairs	$235,000	
Cash, accrued payroll, inventory, etc.		$235,000
Repair expense	$261,000	
Allowance for repairs		$261,000
[$520,000 + $256,000 + $235,000 − ($250,000 × 3)]		

At the end of the year, the allowance for repairs account must have a zero balance, so any remaining balance should be closed to repairs expense. On interim statements, the allowance for repairs account is reported as a contra account to PP&E.

Depreciation

Depreciation is an accounting method of allocating costs over the useful life of a tangible asset to the periods the asset will benefit. Because depreciation is a method of cost allocation, not a method of asset valuation, the fair market value of an item generally has no relation to its depreciated book value. For natural resources and intangible assets, the terms "depletion" and "amortization" are used instead of depreciation.

In order to calculate depreciation, the following must be determined:

- Depreciable base
- Useful life
- Method of depreciation

An asset's depreciable base is its original cost minus its salvage (or residual) value, which is the estimated value of the asset at the end of its useful economic life. An asset's useful economic life may be shorter than its actual physical life, because, for example, it is expected to become obsolete before it actually wears out. A paper mill may shut down an old but still-functioning press because newer machines produce paper more efficiently and cheaply.

When assets are purchased or sold partway through a year, the annual depreciation expense is calculated and then prorated for the partial year (e.g., if a full year's depreciation is $120,000 and the asset was purchased on April 1, then 9/12 × $120,000 = $90,000).

We will consider depreciation methods based on expected units of use (the activity method) and expected years of use (the straight-line, sum-of-the-years'-digits, and declining balance methods). The sum-of-the-years'-digits and declining balance methods also are considered decreasing charge or accelerated depreciation methods because they result in high depreciation cost in earlier years and decreasing charges in later years.

For comparability, the same asset will be depreciated using each different method: a plastic extruder machine that cost $1,000,000 and has a $150,000 salvage value and an estimated life of 70,000 units produced or seven years of useful life.

Activity Method

The activity method (also known as the variable charge approach, units of production method, or units of output method) of depreciation does not depreciate assets by the passage of time but by units of use of the asset, either input units, such as the number of hours used, or output units, such as the number of items produced by the asset. Output measures associate costs with use more closely and should be used if easily determined.

The depreciation charge for a year is calculated in the following manner:

$$\text{Depreciation Charge} = \frac{\text{Depreciable Base} \times \text{Units Produced or Hours Used}}{\text{Total Units of Production or Total Hours Usable Over Life}}$$

If the plastic extruder machine actually produces 9,500 units in the first year and the asset has a depreciable base (cost less salvage) of $850,000, the depreciation charge for the first year is calculated as:

$$\frac{\$850,000 \times 9,500}{70,000} = \$115,357.14$$

The activity method is suitable for equipment and vehicles, but it is not useful for buildings because they depreciate primarily due to time rather than use. The activity method produces lower depreciation during periods of low use and higher depreciation during periods of high use and effectively matches costs with revenues for assets whose utility declines depending on the amount of usage. Therefore, the activity method is considered the best approach under GAAP for items that depreciate through wear or use.

Straight-Line Method

The straight-line method of depreciation is simple and therefore widely used. When obsolescence is a primary cause of depreciation, this time-based method that allocates equal depreciation to each period is often the most appropriate conceptually. It is also most appropriate for assets that generate revenue consistently over their lives.

Depreciation is calculated as follows:

$$\text{Annual Depreciation Charge} = \frac{\text{Depreciable Base}}{\text{Estimated Service Life}}$$

Referring to our example, this would result in:

$$\text{Annual Depreciation Charge} = \frac{\$850,000}{7} = \$121,428.57$$

One objection to this method is that it makes the unrealistic assumption that the asset's usefulness is the same every year and that repair costs are also the same each year. Also, as the depreciation reduces the asset's book value, if the revenue produced from use of the asset is steady each year, then the rate of return from the asset will continue to increase.

Accelerated Depreciation Methods

Accelerated depreciation or decreasing charge methods depreciate an asset more in the earlier years and less and less in the later years of the asset's life. The reasoning behind such methods is that assets lose the majority of their value in the first years of use and that repair costs will generally increase over the life of the asset. Repair costs increase as depreciation charges decrease, so that the total asset-related expenses are smoothed out. This method is also conceptually appropriate for assets that generate more revenue in their earlier years than in their later years.

Because depreciation is a noncash expense, it reduces a company's operating income and thereby reduces the company's tax liability. Hence, methods that record higher depreciation expenses early in the lifetime of the asset will reduce their tax liability sooner, which would result in a better cash flow in the earlier periods.

- **Sum-of-the-years'-digits method.** The sum-of-the-years'-digits method uses the depreciable base (cost less salvage value) and multiplies it by a fraction that decreases each year. The fraction is determined as follows:

$$\text{Depreciation Fraction} = \frac{\text{Years of Useful Life Remaining}}{\text{Sum of All Years of Useful Life}}$$

$$\text{First Year of 7-Year Life} = \frac{7}{7+6+5+4+3+2+1} = \frac{7}{28}$$

or

$$\text{Sum of All Years of Useful Life} = \frac{n(n+1)}{2} = \frac{7(7+1)}{2} = 28$$

(where n = all years of useful life)

Figure 1A-67 shows how this method is applied to the extruder machine. (Note: To avoid rounding issues, the depreciation expense was calculated by multiplying the depreciable base by the numerator of the depreciation fraction and then dividing the total by the denominator. The answers were rounded to the nearest dollar.)

Figure 1A-67 Sum-of-the-Years' Digits Method

Year	Depreciable Base	Years of Life Remaining	Depreciation Fraction	Depreciation Expense	End-of-Year Book Value
0					$1,000,000*
1	$850,000	7	7/28	$212,500	$787,500
2	$850,000	6	6/28	$182,143	$605,357
3	$850,000	5	5/28	$151,786	$453,571
4	$850,000	4	4/28	$121,429	$332,142
5	$850,000	3	3/28	$91,071	$241,071
6	$850,000	2	2/28	$60,714	$180,357
7	$850,000	1	1/28	$30,357	$150,000†
Totals		28	28/28	$850,000	

*Book value at date of purchase (i.e., cost).
†Salvage value. Final book value should always equal salvage value.

- **Declining balance method.** The declining balance method is applied using a percentage of a straight-line depreciation rate. In the straight-line method, an asset with a ten-year life is depreciated at 10% per year (1/10); the declining balance method is usually applied at 150% or 200% of the straight-line rate. (In the latter case, it is called the "double-declining balance method.")

  The declining balance method calculates depreciation based on the asset's book value without regard to salvage value (in contrast to the other methods that calculate depreciation based upon the depreciable base, or cost minus salvage value). As the asset's book value declines, applying the constant percentage rate of depreciation results in a lower amount of depreciation each year.

  For example, in the case of the plastic extruder machine with a life of seven years, its straight-line depreciation rate would be 1/7, or 14.29% per year. If 150% declining balance depreciation is used, the rate would be 1/7 × 1.5 = 1.5/7 = 21.43%. The double-declining balance would be 1/7 × 2 = 2/7 = 28.57%.

  Depreciation schedules using both 150% declining balance and double-declining balance rates are shown in Figure 1A-68. Note that as soon as the asset's residual value is reached, the depreciation ceases. As a result, in the figure, the normal declining balance computation requires an extra year under the 150% declining balance rate and the depreciation is settled a year early using the double-declining balance method.

Figure 1A-68 Declining Balance Depreciation Methods

Bounce Sporting Goods Company
Declining Balance Depreciation Methods

Year	Book Value of Asset at Beginning of Year	Rate	Depreciation Charge	Book Value at End of Year
		150% Declining Balance		
1	$1,000,000	21.43%	$214,300	$785,700
2	785,700	21.43%	168,376	617,324
3	617,324	21.43%	132,293	485,031
4	485,031	21.43%	103,942	381,089
5	381,089	21.43%	81,667	299,422
6	299,422	21.43%	64,166	235,256
7	235,256	21.43%	50,415	184,841
8	184,841	21.43%	34,841*1	50,000*
			$850,000	

*Depreciation charge of $39,611 in Year 8 reduced to arrive at salvage value of $150,000.

Year	Book Value of Asset at Beginning of Year	Rate	Depreciation Charge	Book Value at End of Year
		Double-Declining Balance		
1	$1,000,000	28.57%	$285,700	$714,300
2	714,300	28.57%	204,076	510,224
3	510,224	28.57%	145,771	364,453
4	364,453	28.57%	104,124	260,329
5	260,329	28.57%	74,376	185,953
6	185,953	28.57%	35,953*	150,000*
7	—		—	
			$850,000	

*Depreciation charge of $53,127 in Year 6 reduced to arrive at salvage value of $150,000.

To make sure that the asset is not depreciated below its salvage value or to complete the depreciation on the original schedule, some entities switch to a straight-line method near the end of the asset's useful life. For example, if in Year 5 of the 150% declining-balance example, the book value would be $299,422, and the depreciable base would be $249,422 ($299,422 − $150,000 = $149,422). The asset has two years left from its original estimate, so $149,422/2 = $74,711 is recorded in depreciation for Years 6 and 7.

Group and Composite Methods

The group and composite methods of depreciation are alternate methods that take a group of depreciable assets, average their service lives via a weighted average of the units, and then depreciate the group as if it were a single asset. Because the items are aggregated, gains and losses cannot be recognized when an asset is disposed of. Instead, gains and losses are netted into accumulated depreciation. The group method aggregates similar assets; the composite method aggregates dissimilar assets.

Both methods use the same formula:

$$\text{Depreciation Rate} = \frac{\text{Sum of Straight-Line Depreciation of Each Asset}}{\text{Total Asset Cost}}$$

$$\text{Depreciation Expense} = \text{Depreciation Rate} \times \text{Total Cost for Group or Composite}$$

Selecting a Depreciation Method

A company can select different depreciation methods for different classes of assets. For example, buildings that provide constant benefits over their useful life might be depreciated using the straight-line method while equipment that has a greater loss of utility in the initial years might be depreciated using the declining balance method.

Figure 1A-69 compares depreciation methods and notes their effect on depreciation expense, operating income (OI), tax expense and liability, and assets. The straight-line method is used as a baseline, and the other methods are compared to it.

Note that this comparison is for just one asset, but if the method was consistently applied, a similar result would be seen for the entire company. Note also that the activity method is omitted because if units of actual use match their expected values, this will result in the same depreciation as the straight-line method. (When it does not, each company will experience different results.)

Figure 1A-69 Comparison of Depreciation Methods to the Straight-Line Method

Method / Effect	Straight-Line Method	Sum-of-Years'-Digits Method	150% Declining Balance	Double-Declining Balance
Depreciation expense				
In Year 1	$121,429	$212,500	$214,300	$285,700
In Year 7	$121,429	$30,357	$50,415	$0
Effect on OI				
In Year 1	–	↓ $91,071	↓ $92,871	↓ $164,271
In Year 7	–	↑ $91,072	↑ $71,014	↑ $121,429
Effect on taxes (40%)				
In Year 1	–	↓ $36,428	↓ $37,148	↓ $65,708
In Year 7	–	↑ $36,429	↑ $28,406	↑ $48,571
Effect on assets				
In Year 1	–	↓ $91,071	↓ $92,871	↓ $164,271
In Year 7	–	↑ $91,072	↑ $71,014	↑ $121,429

For tax purposes, companies usually compute depreciation using the IRS's modified accelerated cost recovery system (MACRS), which sets different depreciation rates and methods depending on one of eight asset classes determined by asset life. The first four classes cover assets under 15 years of life and use the double-declining balance method; the next two classes cover assets between 15 and 27½ years and use the 150% declining balance method; and the last two classes cover assets with lives of 27½ years or longer and use the straight-line method.

Differences in depreciation methods for financial reporting and tax purposes often lead companies to record deferred tax liabilities. To illustrate the treatment of a tax liability here, assume that a firm used the straight-line method for financial reporting and the sum-of-the-years'-digits method for tax reporting (using the data in Figure 1A-67). If the operating income from before this depreciation charge is deducted (with all other depreciation items already deducted) was $1,000,000, then for book purposes, under the straight-line method, income before taxes would be $878,571, with tax owed of $351,428. For tax reporting under the sum-of-years'-digits method, resulting income before taxes would be $787,500, with tax owed of $315,000, for a deferred tax liability of $36,428 (i.e., you are paying less taxes now and therefore will owe more later).

Another way of saying this is that the additional $36,428 increases the company's annual depreciation tax shield (the total annual amount saved in taxes from taking depreciation deductions).

If the asset is retained for the seven years, the tax liability would be offset by corresponding increases in taxes owed (e.g., $35,429 in Year 7), removing this temporary difference. (If sold earlier for a taxable gain, the sale may result in having to pay this deferred tax liability.) However, due to the time value of money, companies prefer to pay lower taxes in earlier years. Companies will also have more money to reinvest in their business in these earlier years.

Deferred taxes are discussed in more detail later in this topic.

Impairment

Property, plant, and equipment (PP&E) is carried at historical cost and is not revalued at each balance sheet date to fair market value. However, when the book value of PP&E cannot be recovered through sale or use, the value of the asset has become impaired and the carrying value must be written down to fair value. Arriving at fair value for PP&E can be difficult and subjective.

ASC Topic 360, *Property, Plant, and Equipment* (previously addressed in FASB Statement No. 144) indicates that PP&E should be tested for impairment when one of the following circumstances exists:

- Significant decrease in the market value of an asset (asset group)
- Significant adverse change in the extent or manner in which an asset is used or its physical condition
- Significant adverse change in legal factors or in the business climate that could affect the value of a long-lived asset, including an adverse action or assessment by a regulatory body
- Accumulation of costs significantly in excess of the amount originally expected to acquire or construct a long-lived asset
- A current-period operating or cash flow loss combined with a history of such losses or a projection or forecast that demonstrates continuing losses associated with an asset
- The expectation that the asset is likely to be sold or retired significantly before the end of its previously estimated useful life

When one of these situations exists, a recoverability test is used to determine whether impairment has occurred. If the sum of the undiscounted future net cash flows expected from the use and disposition of the asset is less than the asset's carrying amount, the asset is impaired. If the undiscounted cash flows are greater than or equal to the carrying value, the asset is not impaired. If impairment exists, the asset is written down to its fair value and the write-down is recorded as an impairment loss. The fair value is the market value of the asset, if determinable; otherwise, the present value of the expected future net cash flows is used.

For example, if an asset has a book value of $1,000,000 and accumulated depreciation of $200,000 (thus a carrying amount of $800,000) and the undiscounted expected future net cash flows from use and disposition of the asset are $700,000, then an impairment has occurred. If the fair value of the asset is estimated to be $650,000, then an impairment loss of $150,000 ($800,000 − $650,000) must be recorded.

The impairment loss is recorded as part of income from continuing operations in a category such as other expenses and losses, not as an extraordinary item. Any recognized impairment loss should be disclosed, including information about the assets impaired, the reason for the impairment, the amount of the loss, and the method of determining fair value.

Disposition of PP&E

PP&E can be sold or exchanged, involuntarily converted, or abandoned. The company should depreciate the asset to the date of the disposal and then remove all related accounts from the books. At the time of disposition, any difference between the depreciated book value and the asset's disposal value must be recognized as a gain or loss. Gains or losses on dispositions of plant assets are reported as part of income from continuing operations unless the disposal is related to discontinued operations.

Sale

When PP&E is sold, depreciation must be recorded from the date of the last depreciation entry until the date of disposal. This brings the book value of the asset up to date in order to correctly measure the gain or loss from the sale of the asset. For example, say a firm has a plastic extrusion machine that originally cost $34,000 and has recorded $3,400 in depreciation for the past seven years. On April 1 of the eighth year (Year 8), the plastic extruder is sold for $10,000. What is the gain/loss on this sale? First, the firm must account for the depreciation for Year 8, which is $3,400 × 3/12 = $850. This amount normally would be added to the total depreciation amount at the end of the year, or it could be accounted for separately by debiting depreciation expense and crediting accumulated depreciation—machinery.

Figure 1A-70 shows how to calculate the gain/loss on the disposal of the extruder.

Figure 1A-70 Journal Entry on Sale of Machinery

Cash	$10,000	
Accumulated depreciation—machinery*	$24,650	
Machinery		$34,000
Gain (loss) on disposal of machinery[†]		$650

*($3,400 × 7) + $850 = $24,650

[†](Selling Price − Net Book Value) = Gain/Loss
Net Book Value = Cost − Accumulated Depreciation
$10,000 − ($34,000 − $24,650) = $650 gain

Because a company often makes multiple purchases and sales of equipment or other assets in a single period, a slightly more complex example follows. At the beginning of a year, Bounce Sporting Goods had equipment with a book value of $240,000 and $96,000 in accumulated depreciation. During the year, the company sold equipment costing $45,000 with a book value of $1,500 for $10,500. The year-end equipment balance was $330,000, and accumulated depreciation was $120,000. What were the equipment purchases for the year? To find out, first determine the cost from the given book value:

$$\text{Book Value} = \text{Cost} - \text{Depreciation}$$

Beginning Equipment
$$\$240{,}000 = x - \$96{,}000$$
$$x = \$336{,}000$$

Ending Equipment
$$\$330{,}000 = x - \$120{,}000$$
$$x = \$450{,}000$$

The next formula shows how to calculate the equipment purchases (or a different variable in the same equation):

Equipment Purchases
= Ending Equipment Balance Cost − Beginning Equipment Balance Cost + Equipment Sold
= $450,000 − $336,000 + $45,000 = $159,000

Involuntary Conversion

Flood, fire, earthquake, theft, and condemnation are types of involuntary conversions of assets. When the event that leads to such a conversion is considered to be both unusual in nature and infrequent in occurrence, the gain or loss on disposition would be reported as an extraordinary item on the income statement.

Even in situations where the asset converted is replaced immediately by another asset, a gain or loss on disposal must be recognized according to ASC Topic 605, *Revenue Recognition* (formerly outlined in FASB Interpretation [FIN] No. 30).

An example of an involuntary conversion is the loss of a plant by fire. In this example, the asset was bought for $1,600,000 and has accumulated depreciation of $600,000. Figure 1A-71 shows the accounting entry that would be used if an insurance settlement paid the firm $1,700,000.

Figure 1A-71 Journal Entry on Involuntary Conversion

Cash	$1,700,000	
Accumulated depreciation—Plant assets	$600,000	
Plant assets		$1,600,000
Gain (loss) on disposal of plant assets*		$700,000

*Insurance Payment – Net Book Value = Gain/Loss
Net Book Value = Cost – Accumulated Depreciation
$1,700,000 – ($1,600,000 – $600,000) = $700,000 Gain

Abandonment

Abandoned or scrapped items that do not result in any recovery of cash produce a loss equal to the book value of the asset. If any scrap value is received, a gain or loss is recognized for the difference between the scrap value and the asset's book value. Fully depreciated assets that are still in use should be disclosed in the notes to financial statements.

Depletion

Natural resources such as petroleum, minerals, and timber can be completely consumed and can be restored only by an act of nature, so they are called "wasting assets." Unlike other assets, wasting assets do not maintain their physical characteristics. The cost of natural resources is charged to income as depletion expense.

Depletion accounting requires establishing a depletion base, which includes acquisition costs, exploration costs, development costs, and restoration costs. Acquisition costs include the cost of purchasing property, rights to search for a resource, or rights to use a resource. Exploration costs include all costs of finding a resource. Intangible development costs such as drilling costs are included in the depletion base; tangible development costs for equipment that can be moved from one site to another are not included in the depletion base but are depreciated separately. Restoration costs are the costs of restoring the land to a usable state and are included in the depletion base. The salvage value of a property is deducted from the depletion base.

After establishing the depletion base, this amount is allocated to the appropriate accounting periods, normally using a units-of-production or activity-based approach, as discussed previously.

The depletion rate is determined using the following formula:

$$\text{Depletion Cost per Unit} = \frac{\text{Total Cost} - \text{Salvage Value}}{\text{Total Estimated Units Available}}$$

Thus, if depletion costs for an oil well are $5 per barrel and 5,000 barrels are extracted in the first year, depletion of $25,000 would be recorded.

Financial Statement Presentation and Disclosure Requirements for PP&E

For PP&E and natural resources, the basis of the valuation should be disclosed (e.g., historical cost) along with any commitments, pledges, and liens (such as use of the asset as collateral). Liabilities secured by PP&E are reported separately in the liability section of the balance sheet and not netted against the asset.

Also, PP&E used in operations should be segregated from PP&E not currently used in operations. Reporting accumulated depreciation separately informs statement users of the historical cost of the assets and the amount of depreciation recorded to date. Some entities use a similar accumulated depletion account, but others credit depletion directly to the natural resources account. The oil and gas industry has special disclosure requirements, including the accounting method used and the manner of disposing of such costs.

ASC Topic 360, *Property, Plant, and Equipment* (as previously addressed in APB Opinion No. 12), indicates that the following information about depreciable assets used should be disclosed:

- Depreciation expense for the period
- Balances of major classes of depreciable assets, classified by function and nature
- Accumulated depreciation, in total or by major classes of depreciable assets
- General descriptions of all methods used in calculating depreciation for each major class of depreciable asset

A sample of the disclosure requirements for PP&E is shown in Figure 1A-72.

Figure 1A-72 Disclosures for PP&E and Natural Resources for Year 2

Timber and Forest Corporation

	Year 2	Year 1
Property (Note 1)	(expressed in thousands)	
Property and equipment		
Land and land improvements	$46,847	$42,372
Buildings and improvements	425,877	403,087
Machinery and equipment	3,021,216	3,000,748
	3,493,940	3,446,207
Accumulated depreciation	(1,591,285)	(1,507,640)
	1,902,655	1,938,567
Timber, timberlands, and timber deposits	194,810	202,020
	$2,097,465	$2,140,587

Notes to Financial Statements

Note 1 (in part): Summary of Significant Accounting Policies

Property. Property and equipment are recorded at cost. Cost includes expenditures for major improvements and replacements and the net amount of interest cost associated with significant capital additions. Capitalized interest was $992,340 in Year 2, $7,825,500 in Year 1, and $13,155,720 in Year 0. Substantially all of our paper and wood products manufacturing facilities determine depreciation by the units-of-production method, and other operations use the straight-line method. Gains and losses from sales and retirements are included in income as they occur.

Depreciation is computed over the following estimated useful lives:

Buildings and improvements	5 to 40 years
Furniture and fixtures	5 to 10 years
Machinery, equipment, and delivery trucks	3 to 20 years
Leasehold improvements	5 to 10 years

Cost of company timber harvested and amortization of logging roads are determined on the basis of the annual amount of timber cut in relation to the total amount of recoverable timber. Timber and timberlands are stated at cost, less the accumulated cost of timber previously harvested.

Intangibles

The value of intangible assets continues to increase in today's economy. Many intangible assets, such as quality of management or customer loyalty, are difficult to value, so they are not reported on the financial statements. The balance sheet does include the value of purchased intangible assets, which are measured at amortized cost. This section covers the characteristics of intangibles and then explores valuation, amortization, impairment testing, and accounting for goodwill and research and development.

Characteristics of Intangibles

Intangible assets are defined by two main characteristics: They lack physical substance and are not financial instruments. Other factors distinguish intangible assets from tangible assets:

- Their values may fluctuate due to competitive conditions.
- They may be valuable only to the company possessing them.
- Their future benefits may not be readily determinable.
- They may have indeterminate lives.

Intangible assets typically are classified as noncurrent assets.

Types of Intangibles

ASC Topic 805, *Business Combinations* (formerly outlined in FASB Statement No. 141(R)), defines six categories of intangible assets. They are:

1. **Marketing intangibles.** Marketing intangibles include any assets used to market or promote a business, including trademarks, trade names, company names, Internet domain names, and agreements not to compete. They include words or symbols that identify products, services, or companies. The U.S. Patent and Trademark Office grants indefinite numbers of ten-year renewals for registered marks, but common law protects even unregistered marks. Purchased marketing intangibles are capitalized at their purchase price. Internally developed marketing intangibles are capitalized for the amount of legal fees, registration fees, design and consulting fees, and other costs, excluding research and development. Most marketing intangibles have indefinite lives; therefore, their cost cannot be amortized.

2. **Customer intangibles.** Customer lists, order or production backlogs, and other customer contracts and relationships are all customer intangibles because they relate to dealings with third parties. Most customer intangibles have a finite life and are amortized over that period.
3. **Artistic intangibles.** Copyrights on books, movies, plays, poems, music, photos, and audiovisual information are artistic intangibles. Copyrights granted to individuals are good for 70 years past the life of the creator and cannot be renewed. The costs to purchase and defend a copyright would be amortized over the period of expected benefit (which may be shorter than the legal life of the copyright).
4. **Contract intangibles.** Contract intangibles are the rights granted by contract arrangements, such as construction permits, broadcast rights, franchises and licensing agreements, and service contracts. The initial costs of securing a franchise (such as legal fees or an advance payment) are recorded in an intangible asset account and amortized over the life of the franchise, if it is limited. However, annual payments required under a franchise agreement are expensed as incurred.
5. **Technological intangibles.** Patented technology, trade secrets, and other innovations are technological intangibles. Patents, which include both product and process patents, have a legal life of 20 years. Purchased patents are capitalized at the purchase price; any legal fees required to secure or defend the patent are also capitalized. However, research and development (R&D) costs related to the patented product or process must be expensed as incurred. The capitalized cost of a patent is amortized over the shorter of its legal life or its useful life.
6. **Goodwill.** In short, goodwill is the difference between the price paid to acquire a business and the fair market value of its underlying identifiable assets. The amount paid for a company is allocated first to its identifiable tangible and intangible assets, and the remainder is recorded as goodwill, which is discussed more thoroughly later.

Valuation of Intangibles

Intangibles are recorded differently depending on whether they were purchased or created internally.

- **Purchased intangibles.** Purchased intangibles are recorded at cost, plus any additional costs, such as legal fees. If intangibles are acquired in exchange for stock or noncash assets, the exchange is recorded at the more reliable of the fair value of consideration given or the intangible asset received. If tangible assets are part of a basket purchase, the lump-sum price is allocated between the assets received based upon relative fair values.
- **Intangibles created internally.** R&D costs incurred to develop a patent internally are expensed as incurred. Only direct costs, such as legal fees, related to internally developed patents may be capitalized.

Amortization

Intangibles with an indefinite life are not amortized but are tested for impairment at least annually. The cost of intangible assets with a limited life is amortized over the period of expected benefit. An intangible's useful life is estimated using the following factors, which are described in more detail in ASC Topic 350, *Intangibles—Goodwill and Other* (formerly FASB Statement No. 142):

- Expected use of the intangible
- Limits placed on an intangible's life through legal, regulatory, or contractual provisions
- Extension rights or other provisions for renewal
- Provisions that allow for renewal or extension of the asset's life without substantial cost
- Effects of technological change, obsolescence, consumer demand, competition, and other economic factors
- Expected useful life of another asset related to the intangible asset
- Levels of maintenance expenditures required to gain the expected future benefits from the asset (if these are material compared to the carrying value of the asset, it suggests a limited life.)

When an intangible asset has a limited life, the capitalized cost minus any residual (salvage) value is amortized over that life. Residual value is usually zero unless the entity believes that the intangible will have some value to another entity at the end of the amortization period (such as a purchase commitment for a mailing list). Intangible assets are amortized using the straight-line method unless another method more clearly reflects the pattern of asset use. Amortization is debited to an expense account and credited either to the intangible asset account or to a separate accumulated amortization account.

Goodwill

According to ASC Topic 805, *Business Combinations* (formerly covered in FASB Statement No. 141(R)), goodwill is measured as the excess of (a) over (b):

a. The aggregate of the following:

1. The consideration (e.g. cash, stock, debt), measured at acquisition-date fair value, an acquirer company transfers in a business acquisition
2. The fair value of any noncontrolling interest in the acquiree company
3. The acquisition-date fair value of the acquirer company's previously held equity interest in the acquiree company (if being acquired in stages)

b. The net of the acquisition-date amounts of the identifiable assets acquired and the liabilities assumed from the acquiree company.

In essence, goodwill is the excess of the cost of an acquired entity over the net of the amounts assigned to assets acquired and liabilities assumed in a business acquisition transaction. This section deals with recording goodwill and testing it for impairment.

Recording Goodwill

Only purchased goodwill is capitalized. Internally created goodwill is never reported as an asset. Purchased goodwill is recorded as an asset only when an entire business is purchased; it cannot be separated from the business as a whole but is an integral part of the going concern.

When one company purchases another company, a price is determined based on the fair value of the new subsidiary's assets and liabilities, not on the amounts reported on its balance sheet, because these are listed at historical cost. An audit usually is conducted by the purchasing company or independent agents to arrive at the fair market value of the subsidiary's net assets. The long-term assets and liabilities usually have the greatest variance between book and fair value. The audit also seeks out any unrecorded assets or liabilities and accounts for the method of inventory valuation in its fair value estimate. Once the fair value is determined, the negotiators settle on a purchase price that usually accounts for intangibles that cannot be valued, such as management expertise, reputation, and the like. Therefore, the purchase price likely will be materially higher than the fair value. In very rare instances, negative goodwill occurs, which is a credit on the purchasing company's books in instances where the purchase price was less than the fair value. Also known as bargain purchase, this situation is rare because the seller is more likely to sell off the pieces of the business separately to get the market value.

As an example of goodwill, if a parent company purchases a company as a subsidiary and the net fair market value for the underlying assets and liabilities is $35 million but the purchase price is $40 million, the $5 million difference is accounted for as goodwill.

The calculation in Figure 1A-73 demonstrates the allocation of the purchase price.

Figure 1A-73 Calculation of Goodwill

Purchase price	$40,000,000
Less:	
Cash	$2,500,000
Receivables	$5,000,000
Inventories	$9,000,000
Property, plant, and equipment	$22,000,000
Patents	$1,500,000
Liabilities	($ 5,000,000)
Fair value of identifiable net assets	$35,000,000
Goodwill	$ 5,000,000

Impairment Testing of Goodwill

Goodwill is not amortized but is tested for impairment at least annually and is written down when impairment is determined to have occurred. The FASB does not believe that goodwill amortization helps investors analyze financial performance, and goodwill is considered to have an indefinite life.

A potential impairment of goodwill exists when the fair value of the reporting unit is less than its carrying value, including goodwill. When a potential impairment exists, the loss (if any) must be measured. An impairment loss is recognized for the excess of the carrying amount of the reporting unit goodwill over the implied fair value of that goodwill. The implied fair value of goodwill is determined in a similar manner as that in which it is determined in a business combination. The fair value of the reporting unit is allocated to identifiable net assets (including unrecognized intangibles), and any excess is considered implied goodwill.

For example, if a subsidiary had a fair value of $40 million including goodwill and valued its net identifiable assets (excluding goodwill) at $36 million, then the implied goodwill would be $4 million. If the goodwill recorded on the books was $5 million, it would be written down $1 million, with an impairment loss recorded for that amount. An impairment loss cannot exceed the carrying amount of goodwill, and after a loss is recognized, it cannot subsequently be reversed.

Accounting for Impairment of Intangible Assets

Intangible assets other than goodwill also are tested for impairment. Both limited-life and indefinite-life intangibles are tested.

Impairment Testing for Limited-Life Intangibles

Intangible assets that are subject to amortization are reviewed for impairment in the same way as property, plant, and equipment. (See the "Property, Plant, and Equipment" section for details on the recoverability test.) An impairment loss is recognized if the carrying amount of an intangible asset is not recoverable and its carrying amount exceeds its fair value. Once an intangible asset has been written down, any recovery in value cannot be recognized.

Impairment Testing for Indefinite-Life Intangibles

Intangibles that are not subject to amortization should be tested for impairment at least annually by comparing the fair value of the intangible asset with its carrying amount. If the carrying amount exceeds the fair value, an impairment loss is recognized for the excess. Once a loss is recognized, it cannot be reversed.

Research and Development

R&D costs are charged to expense when incurred. Although R&D expenditures may result in the creation of an intangible asset, such as a patent, the difficulty in identifying the costs associated with different projects and the uncertainties inherent in estimating the magnitude of expected benefits led the FASB to require firms to simply expense these costs.

ASC Topic 730, *Research and Development* (formerly addressed in FASB Statement No. 2), describes research as a planned search to discover new knowledge that may lead to the development of a new product or service. Development involves translating research findings into a plan for a new product or process, including design and testing phases. Routine alterations to existing products are not considered R&D.

Accounting for R&D

The costs of materials, equipment, facilities, and purchased intangibles are expensed as incurred, unless they have alternative future uses. In that case, they are capitalized and charged to expense as used. Personnel and contract services costs are expensed immediately. Other indirect costs are allocated to R&D on a reasonable basis, except that general and administrative costs usually are not included.

Costs Similar to R&D

Other costs that typically are expensed as incurred include start-up costs for a new operation or activity, initial operating losses incurred by development-stage entities, advertising costs, and costs of developing products or processes (such as computer software) that will be used in a firm's selling and administrative activities.

Financial Statement Presentation and Disclosure Requirements for Intangibles

On the balance sheet, goodwill should be reported separately, and all other intangible assets in the aggregate should, at a minimum, be reported separately. Unlike PP&E, accumulated amortization normally is not presented separately in the balance sheet for intangibles. All amortization charges and impairment losses should be reported as part of income from continuing operations, except for goodwill impairments related to discontinued operations. Disclosure in the footnotes of the following items is required for all intangibles subject to amortization:

- The gross carrying amount and accumulated amortization in total and by major intangible class
- Amortization expense for the periods presented
- Estimated amounts of amortization for each of the five succeeding years

For intangibles not subject to amortization, the total amount and the amounts by major class should be disclosed. Changes in goodwill during the period must also be disclosed, including the amount acquired and the amount of impairment losses recognized.

Current Liabilities

According to FASB Statement of Financial Accounting Concept (SFAC) No. 6, *Elements of Financial Statements*, liabilities are the "probable future sacrifices of economic benefits arising from present obligations of a particular entity to transfer assets or provide services to other entities in the future as a result of past transactions or events." According to ASC Topic 210, *Balance Sheet* (previously covered in the AICPA's Accounting Research Bulletin [ARB] No. 43), current liabilities are "obligations whose liquidation is reasonably expected to require use of existing resources properly classified as current assets, or the creation of other current liabilities."

Types of Current Lliabilities

Figure 1A-74 shows the types of current liabilities covered in this section.

Figure 1A-74 Current Liabilities

Accounts payable	Taxes payable from operations
Notes payable	• Sales taxes payable
• Interest-bearing	• Income taxes payable
• Zero-interest-bearing	Employee-related liabilities
Current maturities of long-term debt	• Payroll deductions
Short-term obligations to be refinanced*	• Compensated absences
Dividends payable	• Bonus obligations
Returnable deposits and advances	Estimated liabilities
Unearned or deferred revenues	• Property taxes payable

* Must show intent and ability to refinance obligation on long-term basis.

Accounts Payable

Accounts payable are amounts owed to suppliers for goods purchased on credit. A discount may be allowed for early payment, based on the invoice terms. Cash discounts, expressed in terms such as 2/10 net 30, were covered previously under "Accounts Receivable." Accounts payable should be recorded when title to the goods passes or the services have been received, so special attention must be paid to transactions near the end of the accounting period. Accounts payable are easily valued at the amount owed.

Notes Payable

Notes payable are more formal, written agreements to pay a certain sum on a certain date. Notes can be short or long term, interest bearing or zero interest bearing.

- **Interest-bearing notes payable.** Interest-bearing notes are recorded as the initial cash received from the lender. Interest expense and interest payable are recorded ratably over the period during which the note is outstanding. At maturity, the borrower pays back the face value of the note plus interest.
- **Zero-interest-bearing notes payable.** Zero-interest-bearing notes implicitly carry interest because the lender gives the borrower the present value of the note, which is less than the amount due at maturity. Figure 1A-75 shows how the transaction is recorded if a $1,050,000 note payable is signed and the present value of $1,000,000 is received from a lender.

Figure 1A-75 Accounting Entry for Zero-Interest-Bearing Notes Payable

Cash	$1,000,000	
Discount on notes payable	$50,000	
Notes payable		$1,050,000
(To record issuance of six-month zero-interest-bearing note to × Bank)		

The discount on notes payable account is used to record the difference between the cash received and the face value of the note. On the balance sheet, notes payable will be reported net of the discount (a contra liability account), as shown in Figure 1A-76.

Figure 1A-76 Balance Sheet Presentation of Discount

Current liabilities		
Notes payable	$1,050,000	
Less: Discount on notes payable	50,000	1,000,000

Over the term of the note, interest expense will be recorded with an accompanying credit to the discount account. As the contra account is reduced, the net liability is increased and will be equal to the face value by the maturity date.

Current Maturities of Long-Term Debt

Current maturities of long-term debts represent the portion of long-term liabilities, such as mortgages, that will become payable within the next year. The balance of these liabilities that is not maturing currently would be reported as a long-term liability. Also included with current liabilities would be debts that are callable on demand within one year. However, liabilities that are not expected to use current assets are not reported in the current liability section. Examples include debt to be retired using assets accumulated in a long-term asset account, debt to be refinanced on a long-term basis, and debt to be converted into capital stock.

Short-Term Obligations Expected to Be Refinanced

If a company intends to refinance a short-term obligation and demonstrates the ability to do this by having a refinancing agreement with clear terms, then the debt can be reported in the long-term liability section, according to SFAS No. 6. If the short-term debt is greater than the financing in place or arranged, only the portion of the debt that will be covered by the arrangement may be classified as long-term debt.

Dividends Payable

When a cash or property dividend is declared by the board of directors, it is recorded as a current liability and a reduction to retained earnings. When the dividend is paid, the liability is eliminated. Stock dividends do not lead to the creation of liabilities, because a firm's own equity securities, rather than its assets, will be transferred. Preferred stock dividends in arrears are not considered a liability until declared.

Returnable Deposits and Advances

Returnable cash deposits received from customers or employees are recorded as a liability, which may be classified as either current or noncurrent depending on when they are expected to be repaid. Such deposits might be made to cover performance or property loss or damage, for example.

Unearned or Deferred Revenues

Unearned or deferred revenues include prepayments for goods or services that the company is obligated to provide in the future. Cash received in advance for magazine subscriptions, airline tickets, or gift certificates would fall in this category. When the cash is received, the unearned revenue account is credited; when the service or product is actually delivered, the unearned revenue is debited and revenue is credited.

Taxes Payable from Operations

Taxes payable from operations include sales taxes and income taxes. Property taxes payable are discussed later.

- **Sales taxes payable.** Sales tax is collected from customers and, before the tax is remitted to the government, would be reported as a liability. If the amount owed the government differs from the amount recorded as sales taxes payable, a gain or loss is recognized. If sales taxes are not recorded separately at the time of sale, an adjusting entry must be made later to reduce the sales account for the amount of the tax and credit sales taxes payable.
- **Income taxes payable.** Corporate income taxes are computed based on the income reported on state and federal tax returns. The amount due is classified as a current liability until paid. If additional taxes from a prior year are assessed, income taxes payable is credited and current income is debited. Differences in measuring income for tax reporting and financial reporting lead to recording liabilities or assets for deferred income taxes.

Employee-Related Liabilities

Employee-related current liabilities include payroll deductions and accruals for compensated absences, retirement benefits, and bonus obligations.

- **Payroll deductions.** Payroll deductions include taxes, union dues, insurance premiums, employee savings plans, and other amounts that the employee agrees to have (or is legally obligated to have) withheld. If such amounts have not yet been remitted to the entities owed by the end of the accounting period, they are considered current liabilities. In addition to payroll taxes withheld from the employee's paycheck, the employer also has current liabilities for matching Social Security taxes and unemployment taxes.

- **Compensated absences.** Compensated absences include paid days off for vacations, holidays, or sick days. Such absences are recognized as expenses and related liabilities in the year that the benefits are earned, as long as the obligations are attributable to services already rendered, payment is probable, the obligations relate to rights that accumulate or vest, and the amount of the liabilities can be reasonably estimated. Accumulated rights are those that, if not used, can be carried forward to later periods. Vested rights are those that must be paid even if employment is terminated. Under ASC Topic 710, *Compensation—General* (formerly FASB Statement No. 43), firms are required to accrue vacation days earned and have the option of recording sick days earned. The FASB has made an exception for sick days because payment is not considered probable (because sickness may not occur).

  The accrual can be made either using the employee's current rate of pay or a projected future rate. If the pay rate used for the accrual differs from the rate in effect when the days are used, the difference is expensed in the period in which the days are used.

- **Bonus obligations.** Bonuses payable to employees are considered a form of additional wages. When earned, they are recorded as operating expenses and current liabilities.

Warranties, Premiums, and Coupons

Based on the matching principle, costs associated with certain product warranties and with coupon and premium offers are reported as expenses and liabilities in the period in which the related product is sold. Experience serves as a basis for developing estimates of the expected costs of repairing or replacing products covered under warranty. Similarly, the expected cost of fulfilling offers like cash rebates or delivering premiums in exchange for box tops or wrappers is estimated. When the product under warranty actually is repaired, the cash rebate paid, or the premium delivered, the estimated liability is reduced. Warranties are a type of loss contingency (discussed later in this topic).

Accounting for Warranty Costs

There are two basic ways to account for warranty costs, cash basis and accrual basis, and of the accrual basis, there are two methods, the expense warranty approach and the sales warranty approach.

- **Cash basis.** When it is improbable that a liability has been incurred or if the liability is not reasonably estimable, the cash basis method is required. This method is optional if warranty costs are immaterial or the warranty period is brief. In this method, no warranty liability is recognized in the period of sale, and warranty costs are charged during the period in which the warranty is exercised. The cash basis is the only method allowed for income taxes.

- **Accrual basis.** Accrual basis is required when it is probable that some amount of warranty claims will be exercised and the firm can make a reasonable estimate of the costs.
  - **Expense warranty approach.** The expense warranty approach makes an estimate of the warranty expense during the year of the sale. For example, a cash register company sells 1,200 Type A cash registers during a year (Year 1) for $1,000 each with a one-year warranty. It has determined from past warranty claims that approximately $40/unit will go toward warranty expense. During Year 1, the company incurs $20,000 in actual warranty costs, and, during Year 2, it anticipates incurring an additional $28,000 in actual warranty costs related to Year 1 sales of Type A cash registers. In Year 1, the sale would be recorded as shown in Figure 1A-77.

Figure 1A-77 Accounting Entry for Expense Warranty Approach

Cash or accounts receivable	$1,200,000	
Sales		$1,200,000

The warranty expense would also be recognized in Year 1, as shown in Figure 1A-78.

Figure 1A-78 Accounting Entry for Expense Warranty Approach

Warranty expense	$20,000	
Cash, inventory, accrued payroll		$20,000
To recognize warranty costs incurred		
Warranty expense	$28,000	
Estimated liability under warranties		$28,000
To accrue estimated warranty costs		

The Year 1 balance sheet would include this $28,000 as an estimated liability under warranty under current liabilities, whereas the Year 1 income statement would record warranty expense of $48,000. In Year 2, warranty costs on Type A units sold in Year 1 would be recognized, and after the warranty period expires, any difference between the estimate and the actual expense is netted out of the estimated liabilities under warranties account.

- **Sales warranty approach.** The sales warranty approach is used when the warranty (or extended warranty) is sold separately from the item. In this method, the item and the warranty are recorded separately. Sales revenue from selling the extended warranty is deferred and usually is recognized on a straight-line basis over the life of the warranty. Commissions and other costs that vary directly with the sale of the warranty also are deferred and amortized. Costs that would be incurred regardless of the sale, such as salaries, are expensed in the period incurred.

If the cash register company mentioned previously also offers an extended warranty on its Type A registers for an additional two years for $100 and it sells 100 of these in Year 1, the sale of the cash registers and the additional warranties are accounted for as shown in Figure 1A-79.

Figure 1A-79 Accounting Entry for Sales Warranty Approach

Cash or Accounts receivable	$1,210,000	
Sales		$1,200,000
Unearned warranty revenue		$10,000

At the end of Years 2 and 3 (the period in which the extended warranty begins), warranty revenue is recognized using straight-line amortization ($10,000/2 = $5,000 per year), as shown in Figure 1A-80.

Figure 1A-80 Accounting Entry for Sales Warranty Approach

Unearned warranty revenue	$5,000	
Warranty revenue		$5,000

The exception to the use of straight-line amortization is if the costs to be recognized fall in a predictable but irregular pattern, in which case the revenue is recognized in proportion to the costs expected to be incurred.

Valuing Current Liabilities

In theory, liabilities should be valued at the present value of future cash flows. However, current liabilities typically are recorded at their maturity or face amount, because the difference between this amount and the present value is rarely material.

Contingent Liabilities and Commitments

According to ASC Topic 450 *Contingencies for Gain and Loss* (formerly FASB Statement No. 5), a contingency is "an existing condition, situation, or set of circumstances involving uncertainty as to possible gain (gain contingency) or loss (loss contingency) to an enterprise that will ultimately be resolved when one or more future events occur or fail to occur."

Accounting for Gain Contingencies

Gain contingencies result if there is a possibility that an entity will receive assets (or reduce its debt) as a result of the receipts of gifts, donations, bonuses; disputed tax amounts; pending court cases (where the company is expected to receive a settlement); or tax-loss carryforwards. Gain contingencies are not recorded in the accounts but may be disclosed in the notes to the financial statements if it is likely that a material gain will occur.

Accounting for Loss Contingencies

Loss contingencies result when existing situations have the potential to lead to future losses. A **contingent liability** is recorded when it is probable a liability has been incurred as of the financial statement date and the amount of the loss can be reasonably estimated. Contingent losses are disclosed but not recorded in the financial statements when occurrence of the loss is considered only "reasonably possible" rather than "probable" or when the amount of a probable loss cannot be reasonably estimated. Losses with only a "remote" chance of occurring, or those whose amount is immaterial, need not be disclosed.

Types of loss contingencies include the risk of uncollectibility of receivables, warranty obligations, premiums, pending litigation, threatened expropriation of assets, pending claims or assessments, agreements to repurchase sold receivables, and guarantees of the indebtedness of others. Some contingencies, like the risk of uncollectible accounts and the threatened expropriation of assets, result in the reduction of an asset rather than the incurrence of a liability. General business risks and the risks of losses from fires, explosions, and other natural and workplace hazards are not considered contingencies, because an event triggering the possibility of loss has not yet occurred.

Financial Statement Presentation and Disclosure Requirements for Current Liabilities

Financial Statement Presentation of Current Liabilities

Current liabilities usually are reported in financial statements at their maturity value. They are presented on the balance sheet in order of liquidation preference or in order of maturity. An example of current liabilities on a balance sheet is presented in Figure 1A-81.

Figure 1A-81 Current Liabilities on the Balance Sheet

Bounce Sporting Goods Company		
	Current Year	**Prior Year**
Current liabilities		
Short-term borrowings	$4,214	$18,353
Accounts payable	1,929,825	1,268,743
Accrued payroll-related liabilities	1,331,374	808,778
Accrued liabilities	2,883,832	2,075,038
Deferred service revenues	1,080,614	678,315
Income taxes payable	1,031,201	482,920
Note payable	60,000	102,400
Total current liabilities	$8,321,060	$5,434,547

Supplemental information should be provided to grant full disclosure of current liabilities. Liabilities secured with collateral and the related collateral should be identified. Current liabilities should not be netted against assets intended to be used in their liquidation.

Financial Statement Presentation of Loss Contingencies

Disclosure of a loss contingency in the notes to the financial statements is illustrated in Figure 1A-82.

Figure 1A-82 Disclosure of Loss Contingency

XYZ Corporation

Note 1: Litigation. XYZ is a defendant or codefendant in a substantial number of lawsuits alleging wrongful injury and/or death from rupture of silicone breast implants. The following table summarizes the activity in these lawsuits:

Claims	
Pending at beginning of year	7,411
Received during year	3,775
Settled or otherwise disposed of	(1,213)
Pending at end of year	9,973
Average indemnification cost	$3,826
Average cost per case, including defense costs	$6,459
Trial activity	
Verdicts for the company	32
Total trials	46

The following table presents the cost of defending silicone breast implant litigation, together with related insurance and workers' compensation expenses.

Included in operating profit	$1,572,480
Nonoperating expense	7,624,680
Total	$9,197,160

The company is seeking to reasonably determine its liability. However, it is not possible to predict which theory of insurance will apply, the number of lawsuits still to be filed, the cost of settling and defending the existing and unfiled cases, or the ultimate impact of these lawsuits on the company's consolidated financial statements.

Long-Term Liabilities and Bonds Payable

Long-term liabilities are those that will not be paid with current assets or, in other words, those that are expected to be paid after one year or the operating cycle, whichever is longer. Bonds payable and notes payable are common types of long-term liabilities.

Valuation of and Accounting for Long-Term Notes Payable

Like short-term notes payable, long-term notes payable have a set maturity date and either a stated or implicit interest rate. Unlike short-term debt, which may be recorded at maturity amount, long-term liabilities are valued at the present value of their future cash flows, including payments for both interest and principal. Accounting for long-term notes payable mirrors accounting for long-term notes receivable, which was presented earlier. In this section we review the terminology related to notes. We examine accounting for bonds payable, which is similar to accounting for notes, in a subsequent section.

- **Notes issued at face value.** When a note is issued at face value, the stated interest rate and the effective interest rate are the same. The note is recorded at its face amount; no discount is recorded. Interest paid on the note (determined by multiplying the face value times the stated rate) is recorded as interest expense, which is recognized as time passes. For example, if a $24,000 8% note payable was issued on August 1, 20X5, with the first interest payment due on August 1, 20X6, the adjusting entry on December 31, 20X5, would record an $800 debit to interest expense and credit to interest payable:

$$\frac{\$24000 \times 8\%}{\left(\frac{12 \text{ Months}}{5 \text{ Months}}\right)} = \$800$$

- **Notes not issued at face value.** Notes not issued at face value have a stated rate that is different from the effective rate. One example would be a zero-interest-bearing note, which has a stated rate of zero. The amount of interest paid on these notes is based on the stated rate, whereas the amount of interest expense recorded is based on the effective, or imputed, rate. The effective rate is the rate that discounts the maturity amount and/or periodic payments to equal the amount borrowed.
- **Imputed interest.** Notes payable with rates substantially different from market rates have their rate imputed. See the section on accounts payable for a discussion of imputed interest.
- **Notes issued for property, goods, and services.** The value of a note issued for cash is readily determinable. However, this is not always the case when a note is issued in exchange for noncash assets or services. The stated rate on such notes is assumed to be fair unless the note has no stated interest rate, the stated rate is unreasonable, or the face amount of the note differs materially from the fair value of the assets or services for which it is exchanged. In that case, the note would be valued based on the fair value of the noncash consideration for which it is exchanged. If the fair value of that consideration is not readily determinable, the note would be valued by discounting its cash flows at an imputed interest rate. An imputed rate is determined by estimating what rate the borrower would be expected to pay for a similar type of debt instrument.

Mortgage Notes Payable

Mortgages are a common type of secured note payable that use property as collateral. Mortgages are either payable in full at maturity or payable in installments.

Points paid by the borrower at the inception of the loan reduce the amount of cash borrowed and thus increase the effective rate. Mortgages may be issued with either a fixed rate or a variable (floating) rate. The rate charged on variable rate mortgages fluctuates in tandem with a benchmark interest rate, such as the prime rate.

Mortgage notes payable at maturity are reported as long-term liabilities until the year prior to when they become due. If the mortgage is payable in installments, the principal amount of the payments due within the upcoming year would be reported as a current liability, and the remainder would be reported as a long-term liability.

Off-Balance Sheet Financing

Over the years, the financial community has developed various types of financing arrangements that enable companies to finance certain types of assets in a manner that permits both the assets and the related liabilities to be omitted from the balance sheet. Such transactions, which include certain operating leases and other transactions, are commonly referred to as off-balance sheet financing. Changes made to the SEC disclosure requirements after passage of the Sarbanes-Oxley Act require all off-balance sheet financing to be disclosed by public companies.

Project financing arrangements are a common form of off-balance sheet financing and typically are accomplished as follows:

- Two or more entities create a new entity for the sole purpose of constructing an operating plant to be used by both entities.
- The new entity borrows funds for the project and pays the debt back using completed project funds.
- The original entities secure the debt with guarantees.

This approach keeps the liability for the funds borrowed on the books of the separate entity rather than on the books of the investing entities. As a result, the companies initiating the project financing arrangement will have balance sheets that look more favorable. They are required to disclose only the loan guarantees.

Enron used a considerable amount of off-balance sheet financing, which led to one of the largest bankruptcies on record. In response to the Sarbanes-Oxley Act of 2002, the SEC required increased disclosures in the management's discussion and analysis section of the annual report, including tabular disclosure of all contractual obligations and disclosure of contingent liabilities and commitments. (SEC reporting requirements are covered in detail later in this topic.)

Types of Bonds

Bonds are long-term debt arrangements usually requiring the approval of the board of directors and involving covenants and restrictions for the protection of both the lender and the borrower. By issuing bonds, a borrower can obtain more cash than a single lender is able to supply. Once issued, bonds can be traded on an active bond market. The fair value of the bonds will fluctuate in this secondary market depending on the current market rate for instruments of similar risk. General economic conditions as well as perceptions about the borrower's level of risk will lead to value changes over time. For accounting purposes, however, the issuer of a bond payable does not recognize fair value changes until the period in which the bond is redeemed.

Some of the different types of bonds are listed next.

- **Secured and unsecured bonds.** Secured bonds are backed by collateral, such as real estate (mortgage bonds) or stocks and bonds of other corporations (collateral trust bonds). Unsecured bonds, or debenture bonds, are backed only by the word of the issuer.
- **Deep-discount bonds.** Deep-discount bonds are zero-interest debenture bonds that sell at a discount from face value.
- **Callable bonds.** Callable bonds have an option that allows the issuer to buy back the bonds at a call price set one or two percentage points above the par value (e.g., at 101 or 102). A firm issuing a callable bond has three options: wait until maturity to pay off or retire the bonds; buy them on the open market if the market price is less than the call price; or call them at the specified call price. A company may issue such bonds when interest rates are higher in hopes that it can retire the debt early and issue new bonds at a more favorable rate. The gain or loss on early retirement of the debt is recorded as other income (loss) on the income statement. For example, if a firm had issued $400 million in bonds callable at 101 that had an unamortized discount of $20 million at a time when the market price was 103, the gain or loss is calculated as shown in Figure 1A-83.

Figure 1A-83 Gain or Loss on Retiring a Callable Bond Early

Retire on Open Market	(in millions)	Retire by Calling	(in millions)
Par value of bonds being retired	$400	Par value of bonds being retired	$400
− Unamortized discount	− $20	− Unamortized discount	− $20
Carrying value of the bonds	$380	Carrying value of the bonds	$380
− Market price ($400 × 1.03)	− $412	− Call price ($400 × 1.01)	− $404
Loss on retirement of bonds payable	($32)		($24)

- **Other bond terminology.** Bonds that all mature on the same date are called "term bonds," and those that mature in installments are called "serial bonds." Some bonds are convertible into the issuer's stock at the option of the investor (as we discuss next).

Impact of Convertible Bonds

Convertible bonds are debt instruments that can be converted into a specific number of shares of common stock (equity). The issuer has the advantage of issuing the debt for lower interest rates than a straight debt issue would require, and potential dilution of stock is limited over a straight equity issuance. For example, to raise $5 million, a company with stock currently selling for $60 per share would need to issue more than 83,333 shares (more than this much because of issuance costs); if the company could sell 2,500 bonds at $2,000 par convertible into 30 shares of common stock apiece, it would risk diluting equity only by up to 75,000 shares. The next accounting for convertible bonds is from the perspective of the issuer.

Issuance of Convertible Bonds

The bond is recorded as a straight debt issuance with none of the amount being recorded as equity. Discounts and premiums are amortized to their maturity date as shown elsewhere in this section.

Conversion of Convertible Bonds

Accounting for conversion can be difficult because common stock or other equity securities fluctuate in value. The GAAP practice for recording the conversion is called the "book value method." This method recognizes no gain or loss upon conversion because at issuance the firm agreed either to pay the value of the bond at maturity or to issue a specific number of shares.

Note that the paid-in capital in excess of par is calculated as the bonds payable plus the premium on bonds payable (or less a discount) less the par value of the common stock. This is done because no gain or loss is recognized on the conversion. The market value of the bond and the market value of the stock are not considered under this method.

Valuation of and Accounting for Bonds

Prior to issuing bonds, the company establishes a maturity value (also known as par value, face value, or principal amount) and stated interest rate (also known as the coupon or nominal rate). The issuer will pay annual interest on the bond equal to the stated rate multiplied by the face value of the bonds. This interest may be paid semiannually, annually, or quarterly.

However, between the time the bonds are printed and finally come to market, the market interest rate for similar debt may have changed. Alternately, bonds can be planned to be issued at a discount or premium such as if management wanted to set a specific interest rate. In the case of either a timing difference or management choice to issue bonds not at par, investors will pay more (bonds are issued at a premium) or less (bonds are issued at a discount) than face value for the bonds in order to earn the current market rate (also called effective rate or yield). The issue price of a bond is determined by discounting its cash flows (the interest payments calculated at the stated rate and the maturity value) at the effective interest rate. When the effective rate is higher than the stated rate, the bond sells at a discount. When the effective rate is lower than the stated rate, the bond sells at a premium. If the effective rate is equal to the stated rate, the bond sells at par value.

Bonds Issued at Par on an Interest Payment Date

If a bond is issued at par on an interest payment date, there is no accrued interest and no premium or discount. The issuer debits cash and credits bonds payable for the face amount of the bonds. In subsequent years, the interest expense equals the amount of cash paid.

Bond Discounts or Premiums

Bonds Issued at a Premium or Discount on an Interest Payment Date

If a $1,000,000 bond was issued at 95 (95% of par value), then the issuer would debit cash for $950,000, credit bonds payable for $1,000,000, and debit discount on bonds payable for $50,000. The discount account is a contra liability, so the net carrying value of the bond at issuance would be $950,000.

If a $1,000,000 bond was issued at 105 (105% of par value), then the issuer would debit cash for $1,050,000, credit bonds payable for $1,000,000, and credit premium on bonds payable for $50,000. The premium account is a liability, so the net carrying value of the bond at issuance would be $1,050,000.

Interest on the bonds would be recorded using either the effective rate method or the straight-line method (if that produces results that are not materially different from the effective rate method). The effective rate method is discussed later in this section, and an amortization schedule is illustrated in Figure 1A-90. Under the effective rate method, interest expense recorded is higher than the interest paid, and the difference is amortized to the discount on bonds account (a contra liability account).

Bonds Issued between Interest Dates

For simplicity, bond issuers pay a full period's interest to all bond investors on each interest payment date. However, an investor who purchased bonds between interest payment dates would not be entitled to a full period's interest. To compensate for this, the investor prepays interest accrued since the last interest payment date at the time the bonds are purchased. The net result is that the investor is left with the amount he or she is entitled to for the period the bonds were held. If a ten-year, 8%, $1,000,000 bond, with interest payable semiannually on January 1 and July 1, was issued on April 1, Year 1, at par plus accrued interest, the issuer would record the entry shown in Figure 1A-84. (Interest payable also could be credited instead of interest expense.)

Figure 1A-84 Issuance of Bonds between Interest Dates

Cash	$1,020,000	
Bonds payable		$1,000,000
Bond interest expense ($1,000,000 $\times$ 0.08 $\times \frac{3}{12}$)		$20,000

When the issuer pays interest on July 1, the entry in Figure 1A-85 would be recorded.

Figure 1A-85 Entry at Interest Payment Date

Bond interest expense	$40,000	
Cash		$40,000

Interest expense would therefore be $20,000 ($40,000 minus $20,000) for the three months the bonds actually were outstanding. If the same bonds had been issued at 95 instead of at par, the entry would be as shown in Figure 1A-86.

Figure 1A-86 Issuance of Bonds at 95 between Interest Dates

Cash	$970,000	
$[(\$1,000,000 \times 0.95) + (\$1,000,000 \times 0.08 \times \frac{3}{12})]$		
Discount on bonds payable ($1,000,000 × 0.05)	$50,000	
Bonds payable		$1,000,000
Bond interest expense		$20,000

Effective Interest Rate Method

The effective rate method is the preferred method for computing bond interest expense and amortizing bond discounts and premiums. Under the effective rate method, interest expense is calculated by multiplying the effective rate by the carrying value of the debt at the beginning of the period. (Note that because interest rates are stated in annual terms, they must be adjusted if interest is paid more than once a year. Thus, an 8% annual rate translates to a 4% semiannual rate or a 2% quarterly rate.) The difference between bond interest paid (face value times the stated rate) and bond interest expense (beginning carrying value times effective rate) is the amount of discount or premium amortized. So the amount of discount or premium amortization can be expressed as shown:

Amortization Amount
= (Carrying Value of Bonds at Start of Period × Effective Interest Rate)
− (Face Amount of Bonds × Stated Interest Rate)

In the effective rate method, interest expense is a constant percentage of the bond's carrying value. If the bond was issued at a discount, the carrying value and interest expense will both increase over time. Conversely, if the bond was issued at a premium, the carrying value and interest expense will both decrease over the term of the bond. In contrast, the straight-line method would assign the same amount of interest expense to each period. Regardless of whether the effective rate or straight-line method is used to compute interest expense, over the life of the bond, the same total amount of expense will be reported.

The time value of money tables in Figures 1A-87 and 1A-88 are used in the examples that follow.

Figure 1A-87 Present Value of 1 (Present Value of a Single Sum)

$$PV_{n,i} = \frac{1}{(1+i)^n} = (1+i)^{-n}$$

(n) Periods	4%	5%	6%
1	.96154	.95238	.94340
2	.92456	.90703	.89000
3	.88900	.86384	.83962
4	.85480	.82270	.79209
5	.82193	.78353	.74726
6	.79031	.74622	.70496
7	.75992	.71068	.66506
8	.73069	.67684	.62741
9	.70259	.64461	.59190
10	.67556	.61391	.55839

Figure 1A-88 Present Value of an Ordinary Annuity of 1

$$PV-OA_{n,i} = \frac{1 - \frac{1}{(1+i)^n}}{i}$$

(n) Periods	4%	5%	6%
1	.96154	.95238	.94340
2	1.88609	1.85941	1.83339
3	2.77509	2.72325	2.67301
4	3.62990	3.54595	3.46511
5	4.95182	4.32948	4.21236
6	5.24214	5.07569	4.91732
7	6.00205	5.78637	5.58238
8	6.73274	6.46321	6.20979
9	7.43533	7.10782	6.80169
10	8.11090	7.72173	7.36009

Bonds Issued at a Discount

If a five-year, $100,000, 9% bond payable with semiannual interest dates is issued at a 12% effective rate, the issue price is calculated as shown in Figure 1A-89. Note that the five-year bond that pays semiannual interest includes ten interest payment dates, so the present value is determined using ten periods. The effective rate and stated rate also are adjusted to reflect semiannual interest rates.

Figure 1A-89 Computation of Discount on Bonds Payable

Maturity value of bonds payable		$100,000.00
Present value of $100,000 due in 5 years at 12%, interest payable semiannually; FV(PV$_{10, 6\%}$); ($100,000 × .55839)	$55,839.00	
Present value of $4,500 interest payable semiannually for 5 years at 12% annually; R(PV − OA$_{10, 6\%}$); ($4,500 × 7.36009)	33,120.41	
Proceeds from sale of bonds		88,959.41
Discount on bonds payable		$11,040.59

The amortization schedule for the bond is shown in Figure 1A-90. Based on the table amounts computed for each interest payment date, the issuer would record a credit to cash, a debit to interest expense, and a credit to discount on bonds payable. (Note: A company with a December 31 year-end would have to accrue interest prior to the scheduled January 1 payment date and in this adjusting entry would credit interest payable rather than cash for the amount payable.)

Figure 1A-90 Bond Discount Amortization Schedule

Schedule of Bond Discount Amortization, Effective Yield Method—
Semiannual Interest Payments (5-Year 9% Bonds Sold to Yield 12%)

Date	Cash Paid	Interest Expense	Discount Amortized	Carrying Amount of Bonds
1/1/Y1				$88,959.41
7/1/Y1	$4,500[a]	$5,337.56[b]	$837.56[c]	89,796.97[d]
1/1/Y2	4,500	5,387.82	887.82	90,684.79
7/1/Y2	4,500	5,441.09	941.09	91,625.88
1/1/Y3	4,500	5,497.55	997.55	92,623.43
7/1/Y3	4,500	5,557.41	1,057.41	93,680.84
1/1/Y4	4,500	5,620.85	1,120.85	94,801.69
7/1/Y4	4,500	5,688.10	1,188.10	95,989.79
1/1/Y5	4,500	5,759.39	1,259.39	97,249.18
7/1/Y5	4,500	5,834.95	1,334.95	98,584.13
1/1/Y6	4,500	5,915.05	1,415.87*	100,000.00
	$45,000	$56,039.77	$11,039.77	

[a] $4,500 = $100,000 × .09 × 6/12
[b] $5,337.56 = $88,959.41 × .12 × 6/12
[c] $837.56 = $5,337.56 − $4,500
[d] $89,796.97 = $88,959.41 + $837.56

* Note: The final discount amortized was adjusted for rounding errors in order to make the carrying amount of the bond equal to the bond's maturity value.

Bonds Issued at a Premium

If the five-year, 9%, $100,000 bond is instead issued at an effective rate of 8%, the premium is calculated as in Figure 1A-91.

Figure 1A-91 Calculation of Premium on Bonds Payable

Maturity value of bonds payable		$100,000.00
Present value of $100,000 due in 5 years at 8%, interest payable semiannually; FV(PV10, 4%); ($100,000 × .67556)	$67,556.00	
Present value of $4,500 interest payable semiannually for 5 years at 8% annually; R(PV – OA10, 4%); ($4,500 × 8.11090)	36,499.05	
Proceeds from sale of bonds		104,055.05
Premium on bonds payable		$4,055.05

The premium amortization schedule for the bond appears in Figure 1A-92. Based on the table amounts computed for each interest payment date, the issuer would record a credit to cash, a debit to interest expense, and a debit to premium on bonds payable. (Note: A company with a December 31 year-end would have to accrue interest prior to the scheduled January 1 payment date, and in this adjusting entry the company would credit interest payable rather than cash for the amount payable.)

Figure 1A-92 Bond Premium Amortization Schedule

Schedule of Bond Premium Amortization
Effective Yield Method—Semiannual Interest Payments
5-Year 9% Bonds Sold to Yield 8%

Date	Cash Paid	Interest Expense	Premium Amortized	Carrying Amount of Bonds
1/1/Y1				$104,055.05
7/1/Y1	$4,500[a]	$4,162.20[b]	$337.80[c]	103,717.25[d]
1/1/Y2	4,500	4,148.69	351.31	103,365.94
7/1/Y2	4,500	4,134.64	365.36	103,000.58
1/1/Y3	4,500	4,120.02	379.98	102,620.60
7/1/Y3	4,500	4,104.82	395.18	102,225.42
1/1/Y4	4,500	4,089.02	410.98	101,814.44
7/1/Y4	4,500	4,072.58	427.42	101,387.02
1/1/Y5	4,500	4,055.48	444.52	100,942.50
7/1/Y5	4,500	4,037.70	462.30	100,480.20
1/1/Y6	4,500	4,019.21	480.20*	100,000.00
	$45,000	$40,944.36	$4,055.64	

[a]$4,500 = $100,000 × .09 × 6/12
[b]$4,162.20 = $104,055.05 × .08 × 6/12
[c]$337.80 = $4,500 – $4,162.20
[d]$103,717.25 = $104,055.05 – $337.80

* Note: The final discount amortized was adjusted for rounding errors in order to make the carrying amount of the bond equal to the bond's maturity value.

Discount and Premium Classification

On the balance sheet, the bond is reported at its carrying value, which is the face amount less any discount or plus any premium. The discount and premium accounts are considered contra and adjunct liability accounts respectively.

Financial Statement Presentation and Disclosure Requirements for Notes and Bonds

Long-term debts maturing within a year are classified as current liabilities, whereas all other long-term debts are noncurrent or long-term liabilities. Entities with large numbers of debt securities often will report an aggregate amount on the balance sheet and attach a breakdown in a supporting schedule. Figure 1A-93 shows an example of several disclosures for long-term liabilities. (Current year is Year 2.)

Figure 1A-93 Disclosure of Long-Term Obligations for K-V Pharmaceutical Co. (Dates Genericized)

K-V Pharmaceutical Company—Long-Term Debt
Long-term debt as of March 31, Year 3, consists of:

	Year 3	Year 2
Building mortgages	$43,000	$10,740
Convertible notes	200,000	200,000
	$243,000	$210,740
Less current portion	(1,681)	(973)
	$241,319	$209,767

As of March 31, Year 3, the Company has credit agreements with two banks that provide revolving lines of credit for borrowing up to $140,000. The credit agreements provide for $80,000 in revolving lines of credit along with supplemental credit lines of $60,000 that are available for financing acquisitions. These credit facilities expire in October Year 3 and June Year 3, respectively. The revolving and supplemental credit lines are unsecured and interest is charged at the lower of the prime rate or the one-month LIBOR rate plus 175 basis points. At March 31, Year 3, the Company had $3,900 in an open letter of credit issued under the revolving credit line and no cash borrowings under either credit facility. The credit agreements contain financial covenants that impose minimum levels of earnings before interest, taxes, depreciation and amortization, a maximum funded debt ratio, a limit on capital expenditures and dividend payments, a minimum fixed charge coverage ratio, and a maximum senior leverage ratio.

In March Year 3, the Company entered into a $43,000 mortgage loan agreement with one of its primary lenders, in part, to refinance $9,859 of existing mortgages. The $32,764 of net proceeds the Company received from the new mortgage loan will be used for working capital and general corporate purposes. The new mortgage loan, which is secured by three of the Company's buildings, bears interest at a rate of 5.91% and matures on April 1, Year 16.

On May 16, Year 0, the Company issued $200,000 principal amount of Convertible Subordinated Notes (the "Notes") that are convertible, under certain circumstances, into shares of Class A common stock at an initial conversion price of $23.01 per share. The Notes, which are due May 16, year 31, bear interest that is payable on May 16 and November 16 of each year at a rate of 2.50% per annum. The Company also is obligated to pay contingent interest at a rate equal to 0.5% per annum during any six-month period from May 16 to November 15 and from November 16 to May 15, with the initial six-month period commencing Year 3, if the average trading price of the Notes per $1,000 principal amount for the five trading day period ending on the third trading day immediately preceding the first day of the applicable six-month period equals $1,200 or more. As this contingent interest feature is based on the underlying trading price of the Notes, the contingent interest meets the criteria of and qualifies as an embedded derivative. At the time of issuance and at March 31, Year 3, management determined that the fair value of this contingent interest embedded derivative was de minimis and, accordingly, no value has been assigned to this embedded derivative.

The Company may redeem some or all of the Notes at any time on or after May 21, Year 3, at a redemption price, payable in cash, of 100% of the principal amount of the Notes, plus accrued and unpaid interest, including contingent interest, if any. Holders may require the Company to repurchase all or a portion of their Notes on May 16, Year 5, Year 8, Year 13, Year 18 and Year 23 or upon a change in control, as defined in the indenture governing the Notes, at a purchase price, payable in cash, of 100% of the principal amount of the Notes, plus accrued and unpaid interest, including contingent interest, if any.

The Notes are subordinate to all of our existing and future senior obligations. The net proceeds to the Company were approximately $194,200, after deducting underwriting discounts, commissions and offering expenses. The Notes are convertible, at the holders' option, into shares of the Company's Class A common stock prior to the maturity date under the following circumstances:

- During any quarter commencing after June 30, Year 0, if the closing sale price of the Company's Class A common stock over a specified number of trading days during the previous quarter is more than 120% of the conversion price of the Notes on the last trading day of the previous quarter. The Notes are initially convertible at a conversion price of $23.01 per share, which is equal to a conversion rate of approximately 43.4594 shares per $1,000 principal amount of Notes;
- If the Company has called the Notes for redemption;
- During the five-trading day period immediately following any nine-consecutive-day trading period in which the trading price of the Notes per $1,000 principal amount for each day of such period was less than 95% of the product of the closing sale price of our Class A common stock on that day and the number of shares of our Class A common stock issuable upon conversion of $1,000 principal amount of the Notes; or
- Upon the occurrence of specified corporate transactions.

The Company has reserved 8,691,880 shares of Class A common stock for issuance in the event the Notes are converted into the Company's common shares.

The Notes, which are unsecured, do not contain any restrictions on the payment of dividends, the incurrence of additional indebtedness or the repurchase of the Company's securities, and do not contain any financial covenants.

The aggregate maturities of long-term debt as of March 31, Year 3, are as follows:

Due in one year	$1,681
Due in two years	1,941
Due in three years	2,058
Due in four years	2,182
Due in five years	2,315
Thereafter	$232,824

Weighted average limited partners' units outstanding—dilutive

The Company paid interest, net of capitalized interest, of $4,692 and $4,156 during the years ended March 31, Year 3 and Year 2, respectively. For the year ended March 31, Year 1, the Company paid interest of $3,215.

The notes to financial statements should include all relevant details of the debt securities, including their nature, maturity dates, interest rates, collateral used, and any other restrictions or rights provided such as call provisions. Companies must also disclose five years' worth of future payment information about principal repayment requirements and maturity closures (see end of Figure 1A-93). All off-balance sheet financing arrangements, such as project financing arrangements, must be disclosed in the notes as well. Companies with callable bonds must disclose on an unclassified balance sheet any bonds that have become callable due to a violation of a debt agreement, including a description of the violated covenants and disclosure of the long-term debt liabilities and their circumstances. Firms must also note if any such bonds are classified as noncurrent because the debt violation is likely to be cured.

Other items of note in Figure 1A-93 include the following:

- Disclosure of contractual agreements for the firm's various lines of credit and various covenants
- Disclosure of new long-term debt
- Disclosure of potentially dilutive notes convertible into common stock, including discussion of related contingencies and their likely impact
- Disclosure that notes are redeemable and states the rights of holders; the dates listed can be critical because they show when the company could have cash flow issues due to redemption of notes

Early Extinguishment of Debt

When debt is retired at scheduled maturity, any premium or discount will be fully amortized and the carrying amount will equal the face value. As a result, no gain or loss would be recorded. However, when debt is retired prior to scheduled maturity, a gain or loss may result. The gain or loss would be the difference between the carrying value of the debt (including any unamortized premium or discount and issue costs) and the reacquisition price. If the reacquisition price exceeds the carrying value, a loss results; if the carrying value exceeds the reacquisition price, a gain results.

ASC Topic 470, *Debt* (formerly FASB Statement No. 145), no longer allows classification of gains or losses on the extinguishment of debt to be treated as extraordinary items, although prior accounting standards required this type of classification.

An in-substance defeasance is the creation of an irrevocable trust account that contains funds (principal plus interest earned in the trust) sufficient to service the remainder of a debt. In-substance defeasances do not extinguish the liability on the debtor's balance sheet. (No gain or loss is recorded.)

Equity Transactions and Earnings per Share

Although equity is dealt with differently for proprietorships and partnerships, this section deals with equity for the most common form of business, the corporate form. This section also deals with earnings per share (EPS).

Corporate Capital

Equity in a corporation is called "corporate capital," "stockholders' equity," or "shareholders' equity." Corporate capital is made up of capital stock, additional paid-in capital, and retained earnings. Contributed capital, or paid-in capital, is capital stock plus additional paid-in capital, and it represents the total amount paid by investors for equity securities. Retained earnings represent earned capital, which is the result of profitable operations. Retained earnings are available (some restrictions apply) for shareholder dividends, which provide investors with a return on their investment.

Legal capital is defined as the par value of the capital stock. Par values are nominal amounts printed on the shares, which are unrelated to fair market values. However, an investor that buys stock for less than par value (an infrequent event) will have a contingent liability to the corporation's creditors in the event of bankruptcy. Par values are typically low to avoid this problem. Shares also can be issued without a par value. In that case, a stated value may be assigned to them, which is accounted for similarly to par value but does not trigger the same contingent liability.

Accounting for the Issuance of Shares of Stock

A corporation can issue stock after it has been granted a charter or certificate by the state of incorporation. The corporation can market its shares directly or through an underwriter. When the shares are sold, the corporation records the receipt of cash and the issuance of the shares. Details of specific types of stock issues follow.

Par Value Stock

When par value stock is sold, the par value is credited to a separate account. Par value accounts are maintained for different classes of stock, such as common and preferred. Any amount paid for the shares in excess of par is credited to additional paid-in capital (also called premium on stock). A discount account would be used for shares that sell for less than par.

For example, the accounting entry for an issuance of 1,000 shares of stock with a par value of $6 per share at a total price of $10,000 would be as shown in Figure 1A-94.

Figure 1A-94 Stock Issuance at Premium

Cash	$10,000	
Common stock		$6,000
Paid-in capital in excess of par (premium on common stock)		$4,000

No-Par Stock

No-par stock that has no stated value is recorded in a single account at the selling price, with no additional paid-in capital recorded, as illustrated in Figure 1A-95.

Figure 1A-95 No-Par Stock Issuance

Cash	$10,000	
Common stock		$10,000

No-par stock to which a stated value has been assigned is accounted for similarly to par value stock. The stated value is recorded in the capital stock account, and any excess above stated value is recorded in the additional paid-in capital account.

Stock Sold on a Subscription Basis

In cases where investors buy shares on a subscription basis, the purchase price is paid in installments. The shares are not issued until the price is paid in full. On the balance sheet, the amount of subscriptions receivable is reported as a contra equity account, not as an asset account.

Lump-Sum Sales

When several classes of stock are sold in a package for a lump-sum price, the total received is allocated between the different securities. If the fair values of each class of stock are known, then the allocation is based on relative fair values (the proportional method). The fair market value of each security divided by the aggregate fair market values of all securities determines the proportion of the purchase price assigned to that security, as shown in Figure 1A-96, where 10,000 shares of common stock and 5,000 shares of preferred stock are issued for a lump-sum price of $180,000. On that date the common stock was selling for $14 per share and the preferred stock for $10 per share.

Figure 1A-96 Proportional Method for Allocation of a Lump-Sum Price

Fair market value of common (10,000 × $14)	=	$140,000
Fair market value of preferred (5,000 × $10)	=	50,000
Aggregate fair market value		$190,000
Allocated to common: $\dfrac{\$140,000}{\$190,000} \times \$180,000$	=	$132,632
Allocated to preferred: $\dfrac{\$50,000}{\$190,000} \times \$180,000$	=	47,368
Total allocation		$180,000

When the fair value of only one security can be determined, that security is recorded at its fair value and the balance of the lump-sum price is allocated to the remaining security (the incremental method). If none of the fair values can be determined, the allocation may be based on an appraisal or estimate.

Stocks Issued in Noncash Transactions

As with all noncash transactions, the value of the exchange is determined by either the market value of the shares issued or the market value of the noncash items received. If neither of the values can be readily determined, an appraisal or estimate is required.

Stock Issuance Costs

Direct costs of issuing stock reduce the proceeds received from issuance and so are debited to additional paid-in capital (rather than being treated as expenses). These costs include the following:

- Printing costs
- Underwriting fees and marketing costs
- Legal and accounting fees involved in preparing a registration statement
- Filing fees and exchange listing fees
- Clerical, administrative, and mailing costs

Recurring costs, such as maintaining records on investors or registrar or agent fees, should be expensed in the period incurred.

Companies sometimes want to make just one registration of new securities even though they do not plan to issue all of the approved shares to the public immediately. This type of situation is called a "shelf registration." Companies can request permission from the SEC to obtain a shelf registration. A shelf registration helps reduce the filing costs when more than one issue of stock is planned. The unissued stock is treated as treasury stock unless it is issued at a subsequent date.

Capital Stock

Capital stock is divided into common stock and preferred stock unless the entity has only one type of stock, which is always called "common stock." Common stock has already been covered (par stock, no-par stock, etc.). Preferred stock characteristics are explained next.

Preferred Stock

Preferred stock gains certain preferences compared to common stock, but preferred shareholders do not have the right to vote. Some preferred stock is convertible into common stock, and other preferred stock is callable at a specified price and date. Preferred stock may be issued instead of debt when an entity's debt to equity ratio is too high. Various features of preferred stock are discussed next.

- **Preference to dividends.** Preferred shareholders are entitled to receive dividends before common shareholders. Before declaring a dividend, the board of directors should confirm that the company has an adequate balance in retained earnings and sufficient cash available to fund the dividend.

  The dividend rate on preferred stock is stated as a percentage of the par value. For example, 10% preferred stock with a par value of $50 will pay an annual dividend of $5 per share if declared by the board of directors. With cumulative preferred stock, if dividends are not declared during a year, these dividends in arrears accumulate and must be paid before dividends can be declared on common stock. Dividends in arrears are not considered a liability but would be disclosed in the notes to financial statements.

  Another type of preferred stock, participating preferred stock, calls for preferred and common shareholders to share in a total dividend declared based upon a stated allocation.

- **Voting rights.** Preferred stock usually does not allow any voting rights.
- **Preference in liquidation.** If the corporation is liquidated, assets will be distributed first to creditors, then to preferred stockholders, and last to common shareholders. As a result, in a bankruptcy situation, there may be insufficient assets for shareholder distributions.
- **Debt versus preferred stock.** Unlike debt, preferred stock has no maturity date and entails no legal obligation for payment. Therefore, it is classified as part of stockholders' equity. However, mandatorily redeemable preferred stock must be redeemed on a specific date and so is, in substance, debt rather than equity. Accordingly, ASC Topic 480, *Distinguishing Liabilities from Equity* (formerly FASB Statement No. 150), requires that such securities be classified as liabilities.

Treasury Stock (Reacquisition of Shares)

Shares that have been issued by a company and are later reacquired are called "treasury stock." Shares may be reacquired for the following reasons:

- To reduce the number of stockholders or prevent takeover attempts
- To have shares available for the exercise of employee stock options
- To increase earnings per share and return on equity
- To make a market in the company's stock and so stabilize or increase the stock price
- To distribute cash to shareholders at favorable capital gains rates

Treasury stock is reported as a reduction of stockholders' equity and is not an asset because an entity cannot own itself. Shares held as treasury stock have no voting or dividend rights. Reacquired shares are accounted for by either the cost method or the par value method. The cost method is more commonly used in practice.

- **Cost method.** In the cost method, the treasury stock account is debited for the cost of the shares reacquired. When treasury shares are reissued subsequently, treasury stock is credited for the cost of the shares, cash is debited for the selling price, and additional paid-in capital from treasury stock is credited for the excess of the cash received over the cost of the shares. If treasury shares are reissued for less than cost, the difference is debited either to additional paid-in capital from treasury stock or to retained earnings. Under the cost method, the reacquisition of 10,000 shares at $9 per share would be recorded as shown in Figure 1A-97.

Figure 1A-97 Reacquisition of Shares under Cost Method

Treasury stock	$90,000	
Cash		$90,000

The reissuance of 4,000 of these shares for $11 per share is recorded shown in Figure 1A-98.

Figure 1A-98 Reissuance of Shares under Cost Method

Cash	$44,000	
Treasury stock (4,000 shares at $9 per share)		$36,000
Additional paid-in capital from treasury stock		$8,000

- **Par (or stated value) method.** In the par value method, treasury stock is recorded at par value. When shares are reissued, cash is debited for the selling price, treasury stock is credited for the par value of the stock, and additional paid-in capital is credited for the excess.

Retiring Treasury Stock

Treasury stock actually is included in three accounts: in the treasury stock account at cost (in the cost method), in the common stock account (for the par value), and in additional paid-in capital on common stock (for the amount at which the stock originally sold in excess of par). When the shares are retired, an appropriate amount must be removed from all three accounts. This entry is illustrated in Figure 1A-99, which assumes that 10,000 shares of $5 par common stock are retired from the treasury. The shares had originally sold for $8 per share and had been repurchased as treasury stock at $9 per share.

Figure 1A-99 Cost Method of Retiring Treasury Stock

Common stock, $5 par	$50,000	
Additional paid-in capital on common stock*	$30,000	
Retained earnings	$10,000	
Treasury stock (10,000 shares at $9 per share)		$90,000

* ($8 − $5) × 10,000 = $30,000

If the par value method is used, the par value of the retired shares in the treasury stock account offsets the capital stock account. The accounting entry appears as shown in Figure 1A-100.

Figure 1A-100 Par Value Method of Retiring Treasury Stock

Common stock, $5 par	$50,000	
Treasury stock (10,000 shares at $5 par)		$50,000

Required Disclosures for Treasury Stock

Disclosures are required for each treasury stock transaction. When treasury stock is purchased or sold, companies should disclose the number of shares issued, the number in the treasury, and the number left outstanding. Additionally, if the treasury stock is accounted for under the cost method, the total cost of the treasury stock should be presented as a deduction of total stockholders' equity. If accounted under the par method, the par value of the treasury stock should be presented as a deduction from par value of issued shares of the same class. Additional paid-in capital from the treasury stock is netted with corresponding additional paid-in capital without needing separate disclosure.

Treasury stock being retired can be either an actual retirement, which means the shares were canceled through formal application, or a constructive retirement, which is a board-authorized retirement without formal cancellation. Constructive retirement method accounting requires disclosure of the number of shares held in treasury.

Paid-in Capital

Paid-in capital, or contributed capital, is recorded when capital stock is issued and can be affected by various other transactions, including:

- Sale of treasury stock at above or below cost.
- Revision of the capital structure to absorb a deficit (as in a quasi-reorganization).
- Conversion of convertible bonds or preferred stock to common stock.

Balance Sheet Presentation of Paid-in Capital

Capital stock and additional paid-in capital are reported in the stockholders' equity section of the balance sheet. Disclosure should be provided of the rights and privileges of each type of outstanding stock. After being paid in, the funds become part of a common pool for all shareholders, and no individual shareholder has any special claim on the amounts paid in. Changes in these account balances during the year are reported in the statement of stockholders' equity. An example of the stockholders' equity section of the balance sheet is shown in Figure 1A-101.

Figure 1A-101 Contributed Capital

Bounce Sporting Goods Company
Contributed Capital
For Year Ended December 31, Year 1

Stockholders' Equity

Contributed capital:	
Preferred stock, $70 par (9%, cumulative, convertible, 10,000 shares authorized, 5,500 shares issued and outstanding)	$385,000
Common stock, $4 par (70,000 shares authorized, 46,500 shares issued)	186,000
Treasury stock, at cost (1,000 shares common)	(18,400)
Additional paid-in capital	652,093
Total contributed capital	$1,204,693

Retained Earnings

Profitable operations are the primary source of retained earnings. In addition to net income and net losses, the other transactions that can affect retained earnings include prior-period adjustments (error corrections and certain changes in accounting principle), dividends of all types, some treasury stock transactions, and quasi-reorganizations.

Stock Options, Warrants, and Rights

Stock options, warrants, and rights are call options that give the holder the right to buy shares of stock at a set exercise price. Because these are equity instruments, accounting for them affects paid-in capital.

Shares Issued to Employees

Shares may be issued to employees who exercise stock options granted to them as a form of additional compensation. Employees can also purchase shares under an employee share purchase plan.

- **Employee stock ownership plans (noncompensatory plans).** Employee stock ownership plans (ESOPs), or employee share purchase plans, are intended to raise capital and provide employees with a sense of ownership rather than an additional source of compensation. To be considered noncompensatory, such plans should cover substantially all full-time employees and offer only a small discount from market price (comparable to what might be offered to current shareholders). The plan cannot offer any substantive option feature. Without all of these features, a plan cannot be considered noncompensatory. No compensation expense is recorded; the sale of the shares is recorded as for any other sale of stock.

Disclosures required for ESOPs include a description of the plan, the basis for making contributions, covered groups, and any notes to help comparability between periods. Significant accounting policies, compensation cost recognized, any repurchase obligations (at aggregate fair value), and the fair value of any unearned compensation must also be disclosed.

- **Equity share options.** According to ASC Topic 718, *Compensation—Stock Compensation* (previously addressed in FASB Statement No. 123 (R)), at the date that stock options are granted to employees, the fair value of the options is measured based on market prices of options with similar terms, if available, or estimated using an option pricing model. The fair value of the options is recorded as additional paid-in capital and as compensation expense over the service period. The service period is the period during which the employee renders services in exchange for the compensation and frequently is the period between the date of grant and the date that the options first become exercisable.

For example, assume that an executive is granted options for the purchase of 1,000 shares of $8 par common stock at $20 per share. There is a four-year service period before the options become exercisable. At the date of grant, the options are determined to have a fair value of $4 each. During each year of the service period, the employee will make the entry as illustrated in Figure 1A-102.

Figure 1A-102 Annual Entry Recognizing Compensation Expense

Compensation expense	$1,000	
Paid-in capital stock options		$1,000

When the option is exercised, the entry is as shown in Figure 1A-103.

Figure 1A-103 Entry for Option Exercise

Cash ($20 × 1,000 shares)	$20,000	
Paid-in capital stock options	$4,000	
Common stock, $8 par		$8,000
Additional paid-in capital on common stock		$16,000

Firms with stock compensation plans should disclose the nature and terms of the plans, the method of estimating fair value, the effect of the plans on the income statement, and the cash flows associated with the plans.

Warrants and Rights

Warrants allow the holder to acquire shares of stock at a certain price within a stated duration of time. Stock options issued to employees are a form of warrant, as are stock rights granted to shareholders. Warrants sometimes are issued in a package with other securities, such as bonds or preferred stock. When the stock price rises above the exercise price stated on the option, the potential for profit exists, either by exercising the option and selling the shares or by selling the option itself, which now has an intrinsic value.

Stock rights give current stockholders the right to purchase newly issued shares in proportion to those currently held, thus preventing their ownership stake and voting rights from being diluted without their permission. This right is also called the "preemptive right." No entry is recorded when the warrants are issued. When the warrants are exercised, the receipt of cash and the issuance of the shares is recorded, as for any other sale of shares.

Stock Warrants Issued with Other securities

A stock warrant sometimes is issued in a package with bonds or stock as an additional incentive to entice investors. As long as the warrants are detachable and thus can be sold separately from the other security, the issuer must allocate the proceeds of the package between the stock warrant and the other security. The allocation is based on either the proportional or the incremental method.

- **Proportional method.** The proportional method is used when the fair market values of both securities can be determined, often by relying on prices when the securities begin to trade separately after issuance. The total amount investors paid for the package is allocated between the two securities based on their relative market values. For example, assume that 1,000 shares of preferred stock are issued together with 1,000 warrants, for a total of $20,750. After the sale, the preferred stock is selling for $18.25 per share and the warrants are selling for $3 each. The allocation under the proportional method is shown in Figure 1A-104.

Figure 1A-104 Proportional Method of Valuing Stock Warrants Grouped with Securities

Fair market value of preferred (1,000 × $18.25)	=	$18,250
Fair market value of warrants (1,000 × $3)	=	3,000
Aggregate fair market value		$21,250
Allocated to preferred: $\frac{\$18,250}{\$21,250} \times \$20,750$	=	$17,821
Allocated to warrants: $\frac{\$3,000}{\$21,250} \times \$20,750$	=	2,929
Total allocation		$20,750

- **Incremental method.** When the fair value of one of the securities cannot be determined (e.g., the warrants are not being separately traded), the incremental method is used. In this approach, the fair value that is determinable is assigned to that security, and the remainder of the price is assigned to the other security. Figure 1A-105 illustrates this method, assuming that only the preferred stock in the last example was trading separately.

Figure 1A-105 Incremental Method of Valuing Stock Warrants Grouped with Securities

Lump-sum receipt	=	$20,750
Allocated to preferred (1,000 × $18.25)	=	18,250
Balance allocated to warrants		$2,500

Appropriation of Retained Earnings

An appropriation of retained earnings is a reclassification of these earnings for specific purposes. The board of directors must approve any appropriations of retained earnings. Appropriations reduce unappropriated retained earnings and must be displayed within the stockholders' equity section of the balance sheet. However, according to ASC Topic 450, costs or losses cannot be charged directly to appropriated retained earnings but must be reported on the income statement. Once such costs have been accounted for, the retained earnings appropriation would be reversed. An appropriation of retained earnings is just a means to signal that these earnings are unavailable for dividends. Alternately, a restriction on retained earnings can be disclosed. Reasons that a firm might appropriate or restrict retained earnings include:

- Loss contingencies (such as pending lawsuits).
- Legal restrictions related to treasury stock.
- Contractual restrictions related to bond indentures.
- Plant expansion or debt retirement.

Accounting for Appropriation of Retained Earnings

An account such as appropriated retained earnings is set up as a subclassification of retained earnings. When the appropriation is made, the accounting entry is as shown in Figure 1A-106.

Figure 1A-106 Accounting for Appropriations of Retained Earnings

Retained earnings	$10,000,000	
Retained earnings appropriated for Product x lawsuit loss contingency		$10,000,000

Dividends

Dividend distributions typically are made from retained earnings, but few companies distribute all of their retained earnings as dividends. Retained earnings may be restricted, or firms may wish to retain assets that might be used to pay dividends to fund future growth. Many companies try to maintain a steady record of dividend payments over time, consistent with investors' expectations. In contrast, some younger companies have never paid a dividend. To the extent that retained earnings are not distributed as dividends, they should contribute to increasing share prices. The types of dividends covered here include cash dividends, property dividends, liquidating dividends, cumulative dividends, scrip dividends, and stock dividends. Stock splits and reverse stock splits are also covered.

Cash Dividends

The cash dividend rate on preferred stock is fixed and stated either as a percentage of par or as a per-share amount. Dividends on common stock vary at the discretion of the board of directors. Cash dividends become a current liability on the date they are declared by the board of directors (the date of declaration). Dividends are payable to those stockholders who own shares as of the date of record and are distributed on the date of payment. Assuming that the board of directors declared a dividend of $1 per share on the 200,000 shares outstanding, the entry for the date of declaration is as shown in Figure 1A-107.

Figure 1A-107 Accounting for Cash Dividends at Date of Declaration

Retained earnings	$200,000	
Dividends payable		$200,000

No accounting entry is made of the date of record. On the date of payment, cash is credited and dividends payable debited.

Property Dividends

Any nonreciprocal transfer of nonmonetary assets from the entity to its owners is considered a property dividend. Dividends payable in property, merchandise, or investments are called "property dividends." Property dividends are accounted for at the fair value of the assets transferred. At the date of declaration, a gain or loss is recognized for the difference between the asset's cost and its carrying value.

Assume that a company declares a property dividend that calls for distribution of securities held as an investment. These securities have a cost and carrying value of $1,000,000 and a fair market value of $1,300,000 to stockholders. The entry at the date of declaration is as shown in Figure 1A-108.

Figure 1A-108 Accounting for Property Dividends at Date of Declaration

Investments in securities	$300,000	
Gain on appreciation of securities		$300,000
Retained earnings (property dividends declared)	$1,300,000	
Property dividends payable		$1,300,000

The entry at the date of distribution would be shown in Figure 1A-109.

Figure 1A-109 Accounting for Property Dividends at Date of Distribution

Property dividends payable	$1,300,000	
Investments in securities		$1,300,000

Liquidating Dividends

A dividend that is paid out of paid-in capital rather than retained earnings is a liquidating dividend. A liquidating dividend constitutes a return of the stockholders' investment rather than a return on their investment, as a normal dividend would be.

Liquidating dividends typically occur when a company is ceasing operations. The entry shown in Figure 1A-110 illustrates the accounting for a dividend that was partly paid from retained earnings (normal dividend) and partly from additional paid-in capital (liquidating dividend).

Figure 1A-110 Accounting for Liquidating Dividends at Date of Declaration

Retained earnings	$750,000	
Additional paid-in capital	$250,000	
Dividends payable		$1,000,000

The entry for the date of payment is shown in Figure 1A-111.

Figure 1A-111 Accounting for Liquidating Dividends at Date of Payment

Dividends payable	$1,000,000	
Cash		$1,000,000

Cumulative Dividends

A preferred stock can be cumulative, meaning that if a corporation fails to pay a dividend on this stock in a year and owes this dividend in arrears, then the corporation is legally obligated to pay the dividends in arrears plus the current year's dividend before the corporation can pay any dividends to common shareholders. Unless preferred stock is labeled as noncumulative, it is legally considered to be cumulative. Noncumulative stock carries no obligations to pay dividends (like common stock).

Scrip Dividends

Scrip is a type of note payable. Therefore, a scrip dividend is a promise to pay a specific dividend at a future date. A scrip dividend can be declared when a corporation has sufficient retained earnings for a dividend but is experiencing cash flow problems. A scrip dividend can be used instead of failing to make an expected dividend payment (a negative sign to the market). A shareholder with a scrip dividend can hold it until maturity or sell it on the open market.

Stock Dividends

Stock dividends are a nonreciprocal transfer of an entity's own stock to its shareholders on a pro rata basis. Unlike cash or property dividends, stock dividends do not affect total assets or total shareholders' equity. Retained earnings merely are reclassified as paid-in capital. This capitalization of earnings has the effect of retaining them in the corporation on a permanent basis. Small stock dividends involve the distribution of less than 20% to 25% of the number of shares outstanding on the date of declaration and are accounted for by debiting retained earnings for the market value of the shares on the declaration date. In contrast, large stock dividends involve the transfer of more than 20% to 25% of the number of shares outstanding and are accounted for by debiting retained earnings for the par value of the shares.

Stock dividends often are issued when the company wants to give something to the owners while still conserving cash. The company can reinvest its cash by reclassifying it from earned to contributed capital, retaining the funds in the business. Shareholders can sell these extra shares on the open market.

Although shareholders maintain their same proportional ownership in the company after the stock dividend, the fact that there are more shares outstanding will cause the book value per share and market price per share to adjust downward. The impact of this will be more noticeable in the case of large stock dividends, which, like stock splits, often are used to decrease the stock price to a more marketable level. Therefore, the market usually treats large stock dividends as if they were stock splits.

Stock Splits

A stock split is a tool to reduce the market price per share of a company's stock without changing ownership proportions by issuing a specific number of shares for each share outstanding and reducing the par value per share by the same proportion. For example, a 4-for-1 stock split on 100,000 shares of stock trading at $400 per share would result in 400,000 shares of stock trading at approximately $100. Thus there is no net change to stockholders' equity, unlike with a stock dividend, which increases the number of shares without lowering the par value (increasing the total par value of outstanding shares). The reason for using stock splits is to make the stock more affordable for certain investors, thus increasing the diversification of ownership and theoretically increasing overall trading. No entry is recorded for a stock split; instead, a memorandum notes the changed par value of the shares.

Although rare, a **reverse split** is the opposite of a stock split in that it reduces the number of outstanding shares and proportionally increases the per-share price. For example, a 1-for-20 reverse stock split would transform 200,000 shares at $1 per share into 10,000 shares at approximately $20 per share.

EPS Simple Capital Structure

A company with no potentially dilutive securities outstanding has a simple capital structure, whereas a company with such securities has a complex capital structure.

Potentially dilutive securities are those that have the potential to lead to the issuance of additional shares of common stock. These securities include convertible preferred stock, convertible bonds, contingent shares, and stock options, warrants, and rights.

Basic earnings per share (EPS) is reported for a company with a simple capital structure. It is computed as net income available to common stock (net income minus dividends on preferred stock) divided by the weighted average shares of common stock outstanding during the year:

$$\text{Basic Earnings Per Share} = \frac{\text{Net Income} - \text{Preferred Dividends}}{\text{Weighted Average Common Shares Outstanding}}$$

Preferred dividends and weighted average shares are discussed next.

Preferred Stock Dividends

Preferred stock dividends declared reduce the amount of earnings available for common stock. They therefore are subtracted from net income (or, if a company reports a net loss, serve to increase the loss). If the preferred stock is cumulative, the annual dividend affects the EPS numerator whether it has been declared or not.

Weighted Average Common Shares Outstanding

Anytime the number of shares outstanding changes during the year, a weighted average number of shares is determined for use in the EPS denominator. The shares outstanding at a given point are weighted by the portion of the year during which they are outstanding:

$$\text{Weighted Average Common Shares Outstanding} = \text{Shares Outstanding} \times \frac{\text{Months Outstanding}}{12 \, \text{Months}}$$

The sum of the weighted average common shares outstanding is totaled to find the weighted average shares for the year. For example, assume that a company had changes to its outstanding shares due to the issuance of additional shares and the purchase of shares for the treasury as shown in Figure 1A-112.

Figure 1A-112 Shares Outstanding and Ending Balance

Date	Share Changes	Shares Outstanding
January 1	Beginning balance	110,000
March 1	Issued 40,000 shares for cash	40,000
		150,000
June 1	Purchased 46,000 shares	46,000
		104,000
October 1	Issued 35,000 shares for cash	35,000
December 31	Ending balance	139,000

The computations in Figure 1A-113 are performed to determine the total weighted average.

Figure 1A-113 Weighted Average Common Shares Outstanding

Dates Outstanding	Shares Outstanding		Fraction of Year		Weighted Shares
January 1–March 1	110,000	×	2/12	=	18,333
March 1–June 1	150,000	×	3/12	=	37,500
June 1–October 1	104,000	×	4/12	=	34,667
October 1–December 31	139,000	×	3/12	=	34,750
Weighted average common shares outstanding					125,250

Assume that the company has income before extraordinary items of $300,000 and preferred dividends of $100,000. Therefore, income before extraordinary items available to common shareholders would be $200,000 and earnings per share would be calculated as in Figure 1A-114.

Figure 1A-114 Computation of Income Available to Common Stockholders

	Income Information		Weighted Shares		Earnings per Share
Income before extraordinary items available to common stockholders	$200,000	/	125,250	=	$1.60
Extraordinary gain (net of tax)	50,000	/	125,250	=	.40
Income available to common stockholders	$250,000	/	125,250	=	$2.00

Earnings per share related to extraordinary items must be disclosed separately, either on the face of the income statement or in the notes. Income statement disclosure is shown in Figure 1A-115.

Figure 1A-115 Earnings per Share with Extraordinary Item

Income before extraordinary item	$300,000
Extraordinary gain, net of tax	50,000
Net income	$350,000
Earnings per share:	
Income before extraordinary items	$1.60
Extraordinary item, net of tax	.40
Net income	$2.00

EPS Complex Capital Structure

Companies with potentially dilutive securities outstanding report both basic and diluted EPS. Diluted EPS reflects the hypothetical impact that conversion or exercise of outstanding potentially dilutive securities would have on earnings available to common shareholders.

Diluted EPS = Basic EPS + Impact of Convertibles + Impact of Warrants

The intent of diluted EPS is to show bad news, or a potential decrease in EPS. Sometimes conversion or exercise of a potentially dilutive security will cause EPS to increase. When that is the case, that security is considered antidilutive and is omitted from the calculation of diluted EPS. As a result, diluted EPS always will be smaller (or a loss per share larger) than basic EPS.

The impact of convertible bonds and convertible preferred stock on diluted EPS is calculated using the if-converted method, whereas the impact of warrants, options, and rights is determined using the treasury stock method.

If-Converted Method

The if-converted method assumes that convertible securities are converted to common stock at the beginning of the period (or at the date of issuance if issued during a period). The impact of the assumed conversion on the EPS numerator and denominator is then determined. In the case of a convertible bond, conversion to common stock would mean that no bond interest expense would have been incurred, so earnings available for common stock would increase by the after-tax amount of bond interest expense (because interest is deducted before computing tax expense). Conversion also would increase the number of common shares outstanding. Starting with basic EPS, the additional income would be added to the EPS numerator and the additional shares added to the EPS denominator in order to arrive at diluted EPS. Convertible preferred stock is treated similarly, except that dividends on preferred stock do not affect tax expense and so are not subject to the tax adjustment. (Net income is used in the numerator.)

For example, assume a 40% tax rate for a year in which two convertible debenture bonds are issued: a 6%, $1,000,000 bond that is convertible into 30,000 common shares is issued at par on January 1 and a 7%, $1,000,000 bond that is convertible into 35,000 common shares is issued at par on July 1. The net of tax adjustment for interest for the first bond is calculated as

$$\text{Annual Interest} \times (1 - \text{Tax Rate})$$
$$(\$1,000,000 \times 0.06) \times (1 - 0.40) = \$36,000$$

Because the 7% bond was issued in July, interest expense for only half of a year would have been recorded:

$$\text{Annual Interest} \times (1 - \text{Tax Rate}) \times \frac{\text{Months Outstanding}}{12 \text{ Months}}$$
$$(\$1,000,000 \times 0.07) \times (1 - 0.40) \times \frac{1}{2} = \$21,000$$

If income available for common shareholders from basic EPS was $300,000, the after-tax bond interest expense would be added to that to compute the numerator for diluted EPS: $300,000 + $36,000 + $21,000 = $357,000. The weighted average number of shares in the EPS denominator would be increased by the additional shares issued on conversion, weighted by the portion of the year outstanding (July through December):

$$\text{Convertible Number of Shares} \times \frac{\text{Months Outstanding}}{12 \text{ Months}}$$

$$30{,}000 \times 1 = 30{,}000$$

$$35{,}000 \times \frac{1}{2} = 17{,}500$$

If 100,000 weighted average shares were used in the calculation of basic EPS, the number of shares used for diluted EPS would be 100,000 + 30,000 + 17,500 = 147,500. As a result, diluted EPS is $357,000 divided by 147,500, or $2.42 per share.

Treasury Stock Method

The treasury stock method assumes that (1) warrants and options are exercised at the beginning of the year (or on the date of issuance if issued during the year) and (2) the proceeds from exercise are used to repurchase shares (at the average stock price for the year) for the treasury. The second assumption has the effect of mitigating the increase in the number of outstanding shares that otherwise would occur. The excess of the shares assumed to be issued in step 1 less the shares repurchased in step 2 is the number of incremental shares added to the EPS denominator. An incremental amount will exist when the exercise price is less than the stock's market price because the funds will not be enough to buy back all of the shares. Because warrants do not pay interest or dividends, they have no effect on the EPS numerator.

Any time the exercise price of the warrant or option is higher than the market price of the stock, the options will be antidilutive and are ignored for purposes of calculating diluted EPS. Therefore, when the exercise price of the warrant or option is greater than the market price of the stock, exercise is not assumed and no dilution need be accounted for.

For example, assume that a company has 2,000 warrants outstanding, each of which can be exercised for the purchase of one share of common stock at $15 per share, and the average market price of the common stock during the year is $45. The treasury stock method first assumes that all the warrants are exercised, which leads to the issuance of 2,000 shares of common stock, accompanied by a cash inflow of $30,000 (2,000 × $15). Next, the company is assumed to use the cash received to repurchase shares for the treasury. At the average market price, 667 shares can be repurchased ($30,000/$45). The net result is that 1,333 (2,000 − 667) incremental shares would be outstanding and are added to the EPS denominator in computing diluted EPS.

Alternately, the same result can be arrived at using the next formula.

$$\text{Number of Incremental Shares} = \text{Number of Options} \times \frac{\text{Market Price} - \text{Option Price}}{\text{Market Price}}$$

$$= 2{,}000 \times \frac{\$45 - \$15}{\$45} = 1{,}333$$

Assume that basic EPS was $3.00 per share, based on $300,000 in earnings and 100,000 shares outstanding. The incremental shares are added to the denominator, and diluted EPS would be calculated as follows:

$$\text{Diluted EPS} = \frac{\$300{,}000}{100{,}000 + 1{,}333} = \$2.96 \text{ per Share}$$

Diluted EPS with Convertible Debts and Stock Warrants

Assuming the examples used for the if-converted method and the treasury stock method were for the same company and period of time, the combined diluted EPS would be calculated as shown next.

$$\text{Diluted EPS} = \text{Basic EPS} + \text{Impact of Convertibles} + \text{Impact of Warrants}$$

$$= \frac{\$300{,}000 + \$36{,}000 + \$21{,}000}{100{,}000 + 47{,}500 + 1{,}333} = \frac{\$357{,}000}{148{,}833 \text{ Shares}} = \$2.40/\text{Share}$$

Income statement presentation of the basic and diluted EPS amounts is shown in Figure 1A-116.

Figure 1A-116 Earnings per Share Disclosure

Net income for the year	$300,000
Earnings per share (Note 1):	
Basic earnings per share ($300,000 / 100,000)	$3.00
Diluted earnings per share ($357,000 / 148,833)	$2.40

Financial Statement Presentation and Disclosure Requirements for Equity and EPS

Disclosures for simple and complex earnings per share on the income statement were illustrated previously. When irregular items appear on the income statement, per-share amounts should be shown for income from continuing operations, income before extraordinary items, income before accounting changes, and net income. EPS should be shown for each period presented on the statements.

EPS is covered in ASC Topic 260, *Earnings per Share* (previously covered in FASB Statement No. 128), and provides guidelines for computation and presentation of EPS for public companies and any nonpublic companies wishing to report EPS. The statement helps integrate EPS practices with international standards and simplifies reporting. Specific requirements of this Standard have been covered throughout this section, such as that both basic and dilutive EPS must be listed for any company with potentially dilutive securities. Furthermore, any presentation showing a complex capital structure requires the following disclosures:

- Rights and privileges of outstanding securities
- Reconciliation of the numerator and denominator used for basic and diluted EPS, showing the impact of each individual security
- Effect of conversions that occurred after year-end but before statement issuance
- Weight given to preferred dividends when calculating income available to common stockholders for basic EPS
- Antidilutive securities that were not included in basic or dilutive EPS that could affect EPS in the future

Revenue Recognition

Revenue recognition has been a continual topic of concern for the SEC, because it is often a source of restatements for companies that have recognized revenues prematurely or improperly. This section covers different accounting approaches used in various industries for recognizing revenues. CMA candidates should note that the FASB and International Accounting Standards Board (IASB) have been working on a joint project for several years now in their attempt to converge revenue recognition standards. The project proposes significant changes to the process for recognizing revenues and a single model to be applied consistently to various transactions. At its core is the requirement for an entity to recognize revenue to depict the transfer of goods or services to customers in an amount that reflects the consideration that the entity receives. To apply the model for revenue recognition, an entity follows a five-step process or approach as follows:

1. Identify the contract with the customer.
2. Identify separate performance obligations in the contract.
3. Determine the transaction price.
4. Allocate the transaction price to separate performance obligations.
5. Recognize revenue only when the entity satisfies each performance obligation.

The new Standard is scheduled to be finalized in the second quarter of 2014, so CMA candidates should continue to monitor the FASB website at www.fasb.org in order to keep abreast of the proposed changes. Regardless, it should be noted that the CMA examiners do not typically test new authoritative standards until (the earliest) one year from the effective date of the standard. Thus, the content of this topic in this section presents and focuses on revenue recognition standards and practices as they currently exist under U.S. GAAP.

The revenue recognition principle in FASB Concepts Statement No. 5 states that revenue is recognized when it is realized or realizable and earned. However, this approach is somewhat inconsistent with FASB Concepts Statement No. 6, which defines revenues in terms of inflows of assets or settlement of liabilities as a result of a firm's ongoing or central operations. As a result, the FASB has contemplated a redefinition of the revenue recognition concept in terms of changes in assets and liabilities.

The following are some common sources of revenue and the point at which recognition typically occurs:

- **Sales of products**—Recognized as of date of sale or delivery to customers
- **Services and fees**—Recognized after the service is performed and is billable
- **Interest, rents, and royalties from permitting others to use an asset**—Recognized as time passes or the assets are used
- **Gains or losses on disposition of noninventory assets**—Recognized as of the date of sale

The point of sale is the most common point for revenue recognition, but revenue for certain types of transactions can be recognized before delivery (before, during, or on completion of production) or after delivery (as cash is collected or after costs are recovered). These different approaches are discussed below.

Point-of-Sale Recognition Issues

Questions arise about revenue recognition at the point of sale in certain situations, such as when a buyback agreement or right of return exists.

- **Sales with buyback agreements.** A sale that includes an agreement to buy back the goods later has transferred the title legally, but the seller retains the risks of ownership, so therefore no sale should be recorded. (Note that this was covered earlier in the discussion of inventory.)
- **Sales when a right of return exists.** Book, magazine, and music publishers, perishable food dealers, and many other industries provide guarantees for return of unsold merchandise in order to increase overall sales. As long as the following conditions are met, firms should report sales less an allowance for estimated returns:

- The sales price is fixed or determinable.
- The buyer's obligation to pay the seller is not contingent on resale of the product.
- Theft, damage, or destruction of the product will not alter the liability of the buyer to the seller.
- The buyer has economic substance separate from the seller.
- The seller has no significant obligations for future performance to directly bring about the buyer's resale of the product.
- The amount of returns can be reasonably estimated.

- **Trade loading (channel stuffing).** Trade loading is the practice of convincing retailers to buy more wholesale product than they can sell in a reasonable amount of time to inflate revenues (and profits) in the near term. The effect is that tomorrow's or next year's revenues are booked today, which eventually will lead to lowered future revenues unless the practice is continued indefinitely. Such window-dressing policies are discouraged.

Recognition after Delivery

Three methods are used when revenue recognition is deferred because collectibility of the sales price is not reasonably assured: the installment sales method, the cost recovery method, and the deposit method.

1. **Installment sales method.** The installment sales method recognizes profit as cash is collected rather than at the point of sale. It is used when no reasonable estimate of the amount that can be collected is available. Thus this method often is used when payments for purchases of goods are required in installments (e.g., furniture, large, expensive machinery, land development sales). To protect the seller, such agreements may include provisions such as delaying transfer of title until full payment has been made.

   This method recognizes the revenues and costs of goods sold related to installment sales in the period of sale but defers gross profit until the cash is collected. A gross profit rate is computed based on each year's installment sales. As cash is collected, the profit realized is determined by multiplying the cash collections by the gross profit rate applicable to that year's installment sales. Any remaining gross profit not realized is deferred to future years.

   On the balance sheet, deferred gross profit generally is reported as a liability representing unearned revenue, although some accountants argue that it is preferable to treat it as a contra account to installment accounts receivable.

2. **Cost recovery method.** Under the cost recovery method, revenue is recognized only when the cash received by the seller exceeds the cost of goods sold. After this threshold, all cash collections lead to profit recognition. This method is applicable when collectibility cannot be reasonably estimated. In the year of sale, the income statement reports revenue, cost of goods sold, deferred gross profit, and recognized gross profit. For example, if a company had sales on credit of $100,000 and cost of goods sold of $70,000, the closing entry to defer gross profit for Year 1 sales would be as shown as in Figure 1A-117.

Figure 1A-117 Year 1 Closing Entry under Cost Recovery Method

Sales	$100,000	
Cost of sales		$70,000
Deferred gross profit		$30,000
(To close sales and cost of sales and to record deferred gross profit on sales accounted for under the cost recovery method)		

If, by the end of Year 2, cash collections on the Year 1 sales totaled $80,000, then $10,000 profit would be recognized as shown in Figure 1A-118.

Figure 1A-118 Year 2 Entry under Cost Recovery Method

Deferred gross profit	$10,000	
Realized gross profit		$10,000
(To recognize gross profit to the extent that cash collections in Year 2 exceed costs)		

The final entries would be made in Year 3 when the remaining profits are recorded. (See Figure 1A-119.)

Figure 1A-119 Year 3 Entry under Cost Recovery Method

Deferred gross profit	$20,000	
Realized gross profit		$20,000
(To recognize gross profit to the extent that cash collections in Year 3 exceed costs)		

3. **Deposit method.** The deposit method is not really a revenue recognition method but rather a procedure applied when advance payment is made for goods or property that have not yet been transferred by the seller. No revenue is recognized until the sale is complete. The cash collected is reported as a liability (customer deposits), and the inventory remains on the books of the seller. When the sale is complete, an appropriate revenue recognition method is applied.

Issues and Concerns Regarding Revenue Recognition

In addition to the issues addressed earlier, like channel stuffing, the SEC has become concerned about other issues. For example, some companies acting as intermediaries and earning a fee on the sales they facilitate have recorded the full amount of the sale in their revenues. The SEC has indicated that such companies should report only their own fee as revenues. Another issue concerns revenue on contracts that provide services over the course of several years. Revenue under such contracts should be recorded only as earned and not front-end-loaded at the inception of the contract. Another revenue recognition issue is recognizing all of the revenue as earned on a contract that provides services over the course of several years. Such contracts should record revenue only as it is earned.

Premature or excess revenue recognition has been one of the most common problems that the SEC has discovered in its review of the statements companies file with it. This became an even greater concern during the Internet boom, when the shares of development-stage Internet companies began to trade on revenues multiples instead of the more traditional earnings multiples. In response, the SEC, in Staff Accounting Bulletin (SAB) 101 (as updated by SAB No. 104 and further incorporated into ASC Topic 605, *Revenue Recognition*), summarized the four basic criteria under GAAP that must be met for revenue to be recognized:

1. Persuasive evidence of an arrangement exists.
2. Delivery has occurred or the services have been rendered.
3. There is a fixed or determinable price.
4. Collectibility is assured.

GAAP for revenue recognition has evolved, and issues including accounting for multideliverable arrangements (MDAs) covering contracts combining the delivery of goods and services, such as a sale of equipment with ongoing maintenance services, are being addressed in the context of the newly proposed revenue recognition

Standard mentioned previously. In such circumstances, currently it is necessary to break the transactions into their components and apply the revenue recognition principles to the component parts of the transaction. In the case of the sale of an automobile with lifetime maintenance, it would be necessary to distinguish the portion of the sales price that applies to the sale of the car from the amount that represents a prepayment of the regular maintenance service that is also included in the transaction. The revenue associated with the maintenance services would be deferred and recognized over the period during which the maintenance would be performed.

Accounting for Long-Term Construction Projects

Currently, two accounting methods can be applied in recognizing revenue on long-term construction contracts: the percentage-of-completion method and the completed contract method.

Percentage-of-Completion Method

The percentage-of-completion method is used for recognition of revenues from long-term construction contracts under GAAP, as long as estimates can be made of the extent of job completion and a contract with legally enforceable rights exists. Estimates of completion can be based on input measures, such as costs incurred or labor hours used, or output measures, such as stories completed or miles of road completed. A commonly used input measure (recommended by the Committee on Accounting Procedure in Accounting Research Bulletin No. 45) is based on the ratio of costs incurred to date to total estimated costs:

$$\text{Cost-to-Cost Percentage Complete} = \frac{\text{To-Date Costs}}{\text{Most Recent Estimate of Total Costs}}$$

This percentage is multiplied by the estimated total gross profit or revenue to determine the amount of revenue and profit to recognize to date. The amount of profit recognized to date less the amount of profit recognized at the end of the prior year determines the profit recognized for the current year.

An inventory account titled "contracts in progress" is used to collect construction costs plus gross profit earned to date. When the customer is billed, accounts receivable is increased together with billings on contract, which is netted against the construction in progress account on the balance sheet, with the total reported as either an asset or a liability.

For example, assume that a company has a construction contract for $11,250,000. During the first year, $2,500,000 of actual costs were incurred, which was 25% of the total estimated contract costs of $10,000,000. The total estimated gross profit on the contract is $1,250,000 ($11,250,000 − $10,000,000), and 25% of this amount, or $312,500, is recognized as gross profit the first year in relationship to the costs incurred to date.

The journal entries shown in Figure 1A-120 would be made during the year as costs are incurred, billings are made, and collections received.

Figure 1A-120 Percentage-of-Completion Entries

Contracts in progress	$2,500,000	
Materials, cash, payables, etc.		$2,500,000
(To record cost of construction)		
Accounts receivable	$2,250,000	
Billing on contracts in progress		$2,250,000
(To record progress billings)		
Cash	$1,875,000	
Accounts receivable		$1,875,000
(To record collections)		

At the end of the year, profit is recognized on the contract, along with expenses, and the total equals the amount of revenue to be recognized the first year. (See Figure 1A-121.)

Figure 1A-121 Year-End Percentage-of-Completion Entry

Contracts in progress (gross profit)	$312,500	
Construction expenses	$2,500,000	
Construction revenue		$2,812,500

At completion of the contract, construction in progress is credited and billings on contract are debited to close out the accounts.

Completed-Contract Method

The completed-contract method is used only when the entity has mostly short-term contracts, when the percentage-of-completion method is inappropriate because estimation of costs is not practical or when the contract has hazards that go beyond ordinary business risks.

Under the completed-contract method, revenue and gross profit are recognized only after the contract is complete. A contracts in progress (inventory) account is used to accumulate construction costs. A contra inventory account called "progress billings on construction in process" is used to accumulate progress billings.

Unlike the percentage-of-completion method, the completed-contract method makes no interim charges or credits for revenues, costs, or gross profit. However, when it is likely that a loss will be incurred on the contract, it should be recorded as discussed below.

In the final year of the contract, the accounting entries shown in Figure 1A-122 would be made.

Section A, Topic 2—Recognition, Measurement, Valuation, and Disclosure

Figure 1A-122 Contractor's Final Year Accounting Entry Using Completed-Contract Method

Billings on construction in process	$11,250,000	
Revenue from long-term contracts		$11,250,000
Costs of construction	$10,125,000	
Construction in process		$10,125,000

Losses on Long-Term Contracts

Long-term contracts can result in a current period loss on a project that is still going to be profitable or a loss on an unprofitable project.

Loss in a Current Period

Under the percentage-of-completion method, a change in estimate results if estimated expenses increase but the overall estimate for a project still results in a profit. A loss is recorded in the current period to offset the excess gross profit recognized previously. The current-period loss is calculated as shown in Figure 1A-123.

Figure 1A-123 Computation of Recognizable Loss in Current Period

Cost to date (12/31/Year 2)	$4,315,680
Estimated costs to complete (revised)	3,231,716
Estimated total costs	$7,547,396
Percentage complete ($4,315,680 / $7,547,396)	57.2%
Revenue recognized in Year 2: ($6,660,000* × 57.2%) − $1,665,000†	$2,144,520
Costs incurred in Year 2	2,797,360
Loss recognized in Year 2	$(652,840)

* Revenue recognized in Year 2 on project.

† Cumulative revenue recognized up to Year 1 on project.

The loss is recorded as shown in Figure 1A-124.

Figure 1A-124 Loss in Current Period on Long-Term Contract

Construction expense	$2,797,360	
Construction in process (loss)		$652,840
Revenue from long-term contract		$2,144,520

This loss is the difference between the reported revenue and the actual costs.

Loss on an Unprofitable Contract

No matter whether the completed-contract method or the percentage-of-completion method is used, if an overall loss on a project is expected, the entire amount of the loss that is estimated must be recognized in the current period.

- **Percentage-of-completion accounting.** Under the percentage-of-completion method, when a gross profit was recognized in a prior year, that amount has to be recognized as a loss, along with the currently projected loss on the contract. For example, if $100,000 in gross profit was recognized in the prior year and the total loss on the contract is now projected to be $50,000, then the loss recognized in the current year is $150,000. The entry to record the loss is shown in Figure 1A-125.

Figure 1A-125 Loss in Current Period Using Percentage-of-Completion Accounting

Construction expense	$1,000,000	
Construction in process (loss)		$150,000
Revenue from long-term contract		$850,000

- **Completed-contract accounting.** The completed-contract method simply recognizes the total loss in the year it becomes evident, as shown in Figure 1A-126.

Figure 1A-126 Accounting Entry for Loss under Completed-Contract Accounting

Loss from long-term contracts	$50,000	
Construction in process (loss)		$50,000

Neither the balance in construction in process nor the balance in the billings account can exceed the contract price. If the construction in process account exceeds the billings, the loss is deducted from the construction in process account and reported in a current liability account titled "estimated liability from long-term contracts."

Expense Recognition

The matching principle states that expenses are either to be matched to the revenues they create as in matching cost of sales to sales, construction costs of revenue to constructions revenue, or gross profits in the installment sales method or to matched to the period to which they pertain. Matching to the period would include such expenses as advertising, promotion, research and development, interest, and utilities.

Gains and Losses

A gain is the excess of revenue over cost from a transaction that is outside the normal course of business. Examples would be the gain from the sale of fixed assets or investments or the gain from early retirement of debt. A loss is the expiration of an asset without creating revenue. It occurs when there is an excess of cost over revenue from a transaction outside the normal course of business. Examples would be a fire loss, loss on sale of fixed assets or investments, or the loss on early debt retirement. Gains and losses preferably are shown in other revenues, expenses, gains, and losses shown below operating income on the income statement.

Comprehensive Income

Comprehensive Income Information

Comprehensive income is defined in FASB Concepts Statement No. 6 as "the change in equity [net assets] of a business enterprise during a period from transactions and other events and circumstances from non-owner sources. It includes all changes in equity during a period except those resulting from investments by owners and distributions to owners." These changes result from the effects of exchange transactions, the entity's productive efforts, price changes, and peripheral transactions.

So, comprehensive income includes all revenues, expenses, gains, and losses that affect a business during the period, including both realized gains and losses that are included in net income and unrealized gains and losses that are reported outside of net income as elements of other comprehensive income. The main items of other comprehensive income are:

- Unrealized gains and losses on investments in available-for-sale securities.
- Unrealized gains and losses on certain derivative financial instruments.
- Pension losses that result from the pension liability adjustment.
- Certain foreign currency translation adjustments.

Other Comprehensive Income

Comprehensive income is the sum of net income and the items of other comprehensive income. Per-share amounts are not reported for comprehensive income.

Net income is closed to retained earnings and other comprehensive income is closed to accumulated other comprehensive income, so each is separately accumulated as a component of shareholders' equity. To avoid double-counting when a gain or loss previously reported in other comprehensive income is later realized and reported in net income, a reclassification adjustment is required. This adjustment removes the effect of the gain or loss, once it has been realized, from accumulated other comprehensive income.

Comprehensive income can be presented either on a combined income statement or on a separate income statement. These two presentations are illustrated next.

- **Combined statement of income and comprehensive income.** A company can choose to present traditional net income as a subtotal, followed by the items of other comprehensive income, with comprehensive income as the total. Although straightforward, this approach gives less prominence to net income, which some companies view as a disadvantage. Figure 1A-127 illustrates a combined statement of income and comprehensive income.

Figure 1A-127 Combined Income Statement—Comprehensive Income

Bounce Sporting Goods Company
Statement of Income and Comprehensive Income
For Year Ended December 31, Year 1

Sales revenue	$1,120,000
Cost of goods sold	840,000
Gross profit	280,000
Operating expenses	126,000
Net income	154,000
Unrealized holding gain, net of tax	42,000
Comprehensive income	$196,000

- **Separate comprehensive income statement.** The starting point for this separate statement is net income, to which the items of other comprehensive income are added to arrive at the total comprehensive income. This presentation clarifies the relationship between net income and other comprehensive income. Figure 1A-128 illustrates separate statements of income and comprehensive income.

Figure 1A-128 Separate Income Statement and Comprehensive Income Statement

Bounce Sporting Goods Company
Income Statement
For Year Ended December 31, Year 1

Sales revenue	$1,120,000
Cost of goods sold	840,000
Gross profit	280,000
Operating expenses	126,000
Net income	$154,000

Bounce Sporting Goods Company
Comprehensive Income Statement
For Year Ended December 31, Year 1

Net income	$154,000
Other comprehensive income	
Unrealized holding gain, net of tax	42,000
Comprehensive income	$196,000

Leases

A **lease** is a contract between a lessor and a lessee in which the lessor gives the lessee the right to use the lessor's property for a certain period of time in exchange for rent payments that are usually periodic in nature. The lessor retains the title to the property, so the form of a lease agreement is different from a sale. Nevertheless, sometimes the substance of the lease agreement is comparable to a sale, which is the case when the lease transfers substantially all of the risks and benefits of asset ownership to the lessee.

From the perspective of the lessee, there are two types of leases: capital and operating.

Capital Leases

ASC Topic 840, *Leases* (formerly FASB Statement No. 13), lists four criteria used to determine whether a lease transfers substantially all of the risks and benefits of property ownership to the lessee.

A lease is capitalized by the lessee if it meets at least one of the following criteria:

1. **Transfer of title.** The lease transfers title in the asset to the lessee at the end of the lease term.
2. **Bargain purchase option.** The lease contains a bargain purchase option, which allows the lessee to purchase the property at a price that is significantly lower than its fair market value.
3. **75% of useful life.** The lease term is 75% or more of the remaining life of the property.
4. **90% of net FV.** The present value (PV) of the minimum lease payments is equal to 90% or more of the fair value (FV) of the property at the inception of the lease.

If the lease qualifies as a **capital lease**, the lessee records both a leased asset and a lease liability on its balance sheet. The asset is measured based on the present value of the minimum lease payments (excluding any executory costs, such as insurance or maintenance) or the lower fair market value of the leased asset. The leased asset, which is reported with property, plant, and equipment, is depreciated (or amortized) by the lessee. Lease payments reduce the lease liability, or **capital lease obligation**. A capital lease obligation is the PV of future lease payments. The future cash payment can be divided into an interest expense portion and a reduction in lease obligation portion (analogous to a principal payment for a regular loan). Interest expense is recorded on the liability using the effective rate method. (Therefore, the accounting is similar to that which would be applied if a company had purchased an asset by issuing a note payable.)

For example, say that on January 1, Year 1, Acme Company (the lessee) leases a plastic extrusion machine worth $150,000 (fair value at inception) from Plastcon (the lessor). The noncancellable lease is for four years and includes annual lease payments of $41,933.41 every January 1 starting at inception. The lease cannot be renewed, the equipment reverts back to the lessor at the end of the lease, and the equipment has no residual value due to an estimated economic life of four years. In addition, the equipment is depreciated on a straight-line basis. Acme's incremental borrowing rate is 9% per year, and Plastcon has informed Acme that it has built in an 8% per year rate of return on this asset. If the lessee knows the lessor's actual rate, it should be used in calculations, but only if it is lower than the lessee's incremental borrowing rate. Otherwise, the lessee's incremental borrowing rate should be used.

First, the four lease capitalization criteria must be tested to determine the proper accounting method:

1. **Transfer of title?** No. The lease does not transfer ownership of the asset.
2. **Bargain purchase option?** No. The lease does not contain a bargain purchase option.
3. **75% of useful life?** Yes. The four years of the lease divided by four years of useful life equals 100%.

4. **90% of net FV?** Yes. $41,33.41 × PV of an annuity due of $1 for four periods at 8% = $41,933.41 × 3.57710 (see Figure 1A-129) = $150,000.00. The FV at inception is also $150,000. $150,000 PV payments/$150,000 FV = 100% of net FV.

Note that an annuity due presumes that payments are made at the beginning of a period instead of the end (i.e., an ordinary annuity) and so uses different PV tables.

Figure 1A-129 Present Value of an Annuity Due of 1

$$\text{Present Value of an Annuity Due of 1 } (PV - AD)_{n,i} = \frac{1 - \frac{1}{(1+i)^{n-1}}}{i}$$

(n) Periods	8%	9%	10%
1	1.00000	1.00000	1.00000
2	1.92593	1.91743	1.90909
3	2.78326	2.75911	2.73554
4	3.57710	3.53130	3.48685
5	4.31213	4.23972	4.16986
6	4.99271	4.88965	4.79079
7	5.62288	5.48592	5.35526
8	6.20637	6.03295	5.86842
9	6.74664	6.53482	6.33493
10	7.24689	6.99525	6.75902

Because at least one of the criteria was answered by a yes, this lease qualifies as a capital lease. Therefore, the entry on January 1, Year 1, is as shown in Figure 1A-130.

Figure 1A-130 Entry to Record a Capital Lease (January 1, Year 1)

Leased equipment under capital leases	$150,000.00	
Obligations under capital leases		$108,066.59
Cash		$41,933.41

To record a capital lease at inception at the present value of future rental payments (for four periods at 8%: 41,933.41 × [3.57710 − 1]* = $108,066.59) and to record a capital lease payment.

* Amount reduced by 1 because the first payment is not being included in the PV calculations.

The $41,933.41 payment has an interest portion and a reduction in lease obligation portion.

Figure 1A-131 shows how the annuity due basis and the effective interest methods are used to determine the annual interest on the unpaid obligation and the resulting lease obligation.

Section A, Topic 2—Recognition, Measurement, Valuation, and Disclosure

Figure 1A-131 Lessee Perspective Lease Amortization Schedule on the Annuity Due Basis

Acme Company Lease Amortization Schedule

Date	Annual Lease Payment	Interest on Unpaid Obligation*	Reduction of Lease Obligation†	Lease Obligation
Inception				$150,000.00
1/1/Y1	$41,933.41	$0.00	$41,933.41	$108,066.59
1/1/Y2	$41,933.41	$8,645.33	$33,288.08	$74,778.51
1/1/Y3	$41,933.41	$5,982.28	$35,951.13	$38,827.38
1/1/Y4	$41,933.41	$3,106.03‡	$38,827.38	$0.00
Total	$167,733.64	$17,733.64¶	$150,000.00	

*8% interest applied to remaining lease obligation at the end of the year, e.g., (0.08 × $108,066.59 = $8,645.33). Note that the first payment is on the date of inception so no interest has accrued.

†Reduction in lease obligation calculated as annual lease payment less interest on unpaid obligation.

‡Interest reduced by $0.16 to account for rounding errors.

¶Note that $167,733.64 − $17,733.64 = $150,000.00.

At the end of Year 1, Acme records its accrued interest as shown in Figure 1A-132.

Figure 1A-132 Entry to Record Accrued Interest (December 31, Year 1)

Interest expense	$8,645.33	
Interest payable		$8,645.33
To record accrued interest on a leased plastic extrusion machine		

Also at the end of Year 1, Acme records its straight-line depreciation as shown in Figure 1A-133.

Figure 1A-133 Entry to Record Depreciation Expense (December 31, Year 1)

Depreciation expense—Capital leases	$37,500	
Accumulated depreciation—Capital leases		$37,500
To record depreciation expense ($150,000 / 4 years = $37,500)		

Portions of leases due within one year are classified as current liabilities (e.g., $33,288.08 in Year 1, which is the amount due within the next year), and longer-term portions are classified as noncurrent or long-term liabilities ($74,778.51 in Year 1, for a total obligation of $108,066.59). On the December 31, Year 1, balance sheet, assets with capital leases are separately identified, and the current liabilities section would list interest payable at $8,645.33 and obligations under capital leases at $33,288.08. Noncurrent liabilities would list obligations under capital leases at $74,778.51. Figure 1A-134 shows a lease payment in a year with interest payable (Year 2).

Figure 1A-134 Entry to Record Lease Payment (January 1, Year 2)

Interest payable	$8,645.33	
Obligations under capital leases	$33,288.08	
Cash		$41,933.41
To record a lease payment for a plastic extruder machine		

When the lease expires, the asset is returned to the lessor and the accumulated depreciation accounts and leased equipment accounts are removed from the books, as shown in Figure 1A-135.

Figure 1A-135 Entry to Remove Leased Asset from Books (January 1, Year 5)

Equipment	$150,000	
Accumulated depreciation—Capital leases	$150,000	
Leased equipment under capital leases		$150,000
Accumulated depreciation—Equipment		$150,000
To remove a leased asset from the books at the end of the lease		

Capital lease disclosures include gross amount by major class of assets under capital leases, future minimum payments for each of the next five years, including all of the separate categories of data shown in Figure 1A-135, information on noncancellable leases and contingent rentals, and depreciation on capital leases.

Operating Leases

Leases that do not meet the criteria for capitalization are recorded as operating leases. Operating leases are similar to ordinary rent. The expense accrues as time passes. Using the operating method, the liability for the rent expense accrues daily, and the rent is assigned to each period during which the firm benefited from using the asset. However, recognition of the expense or revenue generally is made on a straight-line basis over the lease term. Commitments to make future payments are not accounted for. If the asset from the prior example met none of the criteria for capitalization, then the payment would be recorded without any reference to the components making up the charge, as shown in Figure 1A-136. If there is multiyear agreement of a material amount with an operating lease, then the payment schedule has to be disclosed.

Figure 1A-136 Lessee's Entry to Record Rent Payment (January 1, Year 1)

Rent expense	$44,933.41	
Cash		$44,933.41
To record rent payment on a plastic extrusion machine		

Operating leases do not appear on the balance sheet. On the income statement, the lessee will report rental expense and the lessor will report rental revenue. If an operating lease has terms making it noncancellable for a year or more, this must be disclosed.

Lease Classifications from the Lessor's Perspective

There are four possible lease classifications from the perspective of the lessor:

1. Operating (discussed previously for both the lessor and the lessee)
2. Sales type
3. Direct financing
4. Leveraged

Referring to the four criteria for determining whether a lease is a capital lease, from the lessor's perspective, if a lease meets any of these four criteria and both of the next criteria, then it is a sales-type, a direct financing, or a leveraged lease. These leases must have both of the next properties:

- Collectibility of the minimum lease payments is reasonably predictable.
- No important uncertainties exist related to unreimbursable costs the lessor may yet incur.

The three nonoperating classifications depend on whether a profit or loss can be recognized due to issuance of the lease. In each of these three capital-type leases, the lessor removes the asset from the balance sheet and replaces it with a lease receivable (or net investment in the lease). The lessor will record interest revenue over the lease term.

Sales-Type Leases

Sales-type leases are transactions that are used as alternatives to a sale but are otherwise like a sale, such as leasing a new car from a dealership or re-leasing equipment when its prior lease is expiring. When the lessor is a manufacturer or dealer in the leased asset, the lease usually is a sales-type lease. In addition to interest revenue, the lessor also will recognize sales and cost of goods sold at the inception of the lease. Technically, a lease is considered a sales-type lease when the fair value (sales price) of the asset differs from the cost of the asset. The difference between the two is the gross profit (or loss). Sales-type lease transactions involving real estate must transfer the title by the end of the lease term.

Direct Financing Leases

Direct financing leases are transactions that are used as a form of loan, where the cost of the asset is equal to the fair value of the asset (sales price). Therefore, other than interest revenue, the lessor does not realize a profit or loss on the transaction. Lessors are commonly banks that purchase the asset and lease it out. Borrowing funds using the property being purchased as collateral would accomplish the same result, with the exception that with a direct financing lease, the lessor keeps title to the assets. Direct financing leases can be used when a borrower cannot otherwise finance 100% of the asset, when there are tax benefits to doing so, or when the residual value on the asset plus the interest earned is more favorable than outright sale for the lessor.

Leveraged Leases

Leveraged leases are a type of direct financing lease, but they have separate accounting treatment because they involve three or more parties. In addition to the lessor and the lessee, a long-term creditor serves as an intermediary. Here the lessor is called the "equity participant." The long-term creditor must provide financing without recourse to the lessor's general credit but can have recourse to the leased asset. A lease is not a leveraged lease unless the lessor has substantial financial leverage in the transaction. The behavior of a leveraged lease is that the net investment of the lessor will decline in early years and increase in later years.

Pensions and Other Postretirement Benefits

A **pension plan** provides benefits to employees after retirement based on services provided during the employees' working years. The matching principle dictates that the costs of these benefits be reported during the periods when employees work to earn the benefits rather than when they are paid. The employer typically makes payments to a separate entity, the pension fund, to accumulate the assets to pay future benefits. Some plans are contributory, with both employees and employers contributing to the pension fund. Other plans are noncontributory, or funded solely by the employer. Accounting for the sponsoring employer, rather than for the pension fund itself, is the topic discussed in this section.

Two major types of pension plans are defined contribution plans and defined benefit plans. In a defined contribution plan, the amount the employer agrees to contribute to the pension fund each period is defined by a formula. The formula may be based on factors such as age, length of service, employer profits, and compensation. No promise is made regarding the amount of future benefits to be paid, so the risk of pension variability rests with the employees. An independent third-party trustee usually collects funds from the employer, safeguards the accumulated income in the trust, and deals with forfeitures of funds from early termination in a manner dictated by the employer. The trustee's beneficiaries are the employees in the plan.

In a defined benefit plan, the employer promises that a specific benefit amount will be paid during the retirement years. This payment is based on a formula that may take into account the number of years worked and the compensation level near retirement. Trustees for defined benefit plans safeguard and invest the employer's contributed assets to build enough funds to pay the employer's obligations. The employer retains ownership of the trust assets. Therefore, the trustee's beneficiary for a defined benefit plan is the employer, not the employees. Employers are at risk with these types of plans because they have to make up any shortfall if the amount accumulated in the pension fund is insufficient to make the defined benefit payments. The present value of the promised payments is a pension liability; the fact that this liability can be measured using several different approaches (projected benefit obligation, accumulated benefit obligation, vested benefit obligation) further complicates the accounting.

Accounting for Defined Contribution Plans

Accounting by the employer sponsoring a defined contribution plan is simple: Pension expense is recorded for the amount of the annual contribution to the plan, cash is credited for the amount paid into the pension fund, and, if necessary, an asset or liability is recorded for any difference. The employer's cost is simply its minimum annual contribution. If the employer fails to make the full minimum contribution, a liability is created on the employer's balance sheet for the difference. If funds above the minimum are deposited, an asset is created on the balance sheet. Disclosures include a description of the plan with listings of covered employee groups, contribution formulas used, and any other significant matters that could affect comparability between periods.

Accounting for Defined Benefit Plans

Accounting for defined benefit plans is complex because the ultimate cost of the promised benefits can only be estimated during the working years. The employer measures pension expense in accordance with the provisions of ASC Topic 715, *Compensation–Retirement Benefits* (formerly FASB Statement No. 158).

Pension expense is the sum of several components, including service cost (the increase in the pension liability resulting from employees providing one more year of service) and interest cost (the increase in the pension liability due to the passage of time). Other components included in pension expense are the return on plan assets (FASB prescribes the "expected return"), amortization of prior service cost, and amortization of certain gains and losses (actuarial gains and losses). The employer debits pension expense for this total, credits cash for the amount contributed to the pension fund, and then records the difference as a liability (or asset) account, accrued (or prepaid) pension cost.

Additional adjustments may be required to recognize the funded status of the pension plan on the balance sheet. The funded status is equal to the difference between the projected benefit obligation (this is the highest level of pension obligation associated with the pension plan) and the fair value of the pension plan asset. Typically three measures of liability are computed and disclosed in connection with an employer's defined benefit pension plan.

1. **Vested benefit obligation.** The vested benefit obligation measures the benefit obligation only for vested employees and only at current salary levels. Employees become fully vested after a specific number of years on the job.
2. **Accumulated benefit obligation.** The accumulated benefit obligation uses current salary levels to determine the payment that would be required if the employee were to quit today but disregards whether employees are vested or nonvested. The accumulated benefit obligation measures the firm's payment obligation as of the current time without considering additional years of service or anticipated salary increases.
3. **Projected benefit obligation.** The projected benefit obligation measures the benefit obligation for vested and nonvested employees and makes a projection for future salary levels (i.e., basing the formula on projected final pay). This

method results in the highest estimates. The FASB recommends this method because it provides a more realistic measure of the employer's obligation. As mentioned previously, it is the projected benefit obligation that is used in the funded status computation.

In recognizing the funded status on the balance sheet, the employer will record an adjustment to other comprehensive income and the pension liability in order to account for any excess liability or asset not already recognized through pension expense. The discount rate used in the present value calculations has a significant influence on the projected pension obligation and so is required to be adjusted each measurement date to reflect current interest rates. Furthermore, actuaries include adjustments for deaths, withdrawals, early retirements, and disabilities in their present value calculations, technically making them actuarial present values.

Pension Expense

The annual payments made to a defined benefit plan are broken down into several components because of the need to match costs to the appropriate periods of benefit. The components are discussed next.

- **Service cost.** According to ASC Topic 715, service cost equals the actuarial present value of the benefits attributed by the pension benefit formula to employee service during the period (e.g., attributed to the current increase in the projected benefit obligation).
- **Interest expense.** Interest expense, or the interest on the pension liability, accrues on the projected benefit obligation outstanding for the period based on the settlement rate, which is an interest rate determined by actuaries that would effectively settle all projected benefit obligations if the plan were to be terminated (includes time value of money calculations).
- **Expected return on plan assets.** The return on plan assets will decrease pension expenses. The return is computed by using a market-related value of the plan assets multiplied by the expected return rate (as determined by actuaries). The expected return should be distinguished from the actual return, which is computed as follows:

$$\text{Actual Return} = (\text{Plan Assets [PA] Ending Balance} - \text{PA Beginning Balance}) - (\text{Contributions} - \text{Benefits Paid})$$

- **Amortization of unrecognized prior service cost.** Prior service costs arise from plan amendments that provide retroactive benefits for completed employee work. These costs are allocated to pension expense to the future remaining service years of the affected employees. The unrecognized or unamortized prior services costs reside in other comprehensive income until amortized through the pension expense computation.
- **Amortization of actuarial gains or losses.** Actuarial gains and losses arise from differences in the actual versus the expected return on plan assets. These gains or losses also can be caused by changes in the pension benefit obligation estimate or changes in the market value of the pension plan assets. Unamortized actuarial gains or losses also reside in other comprehensive

income until amortized through the pension expense computation. However, it should be noted that these gains or losses are not amortized unless they become "significant." Significance is determined by an approach called the "corridor" approach. Actuarial gains and losses are amortized only when they exceed the corridor (which is 10% of the greater of the projected benefit obligation or the fair market value of the pension plan assets).

Disclosure of Pensions on the Balance sheet

On the balance sheet, the funded status of the pension plan is presented. An underfunded pension plan (or one in which the projected benefit obligation exceeds the fair value of the pension plan assets) would be reflected as a liability (either current, noncurrent, or both).

Any overfunded amount (one in which the fair value of the pension plan assets exceeds the projected benefit obligation) would appear as an asset on the balance sheet. Overfunded plans are presented as noncurrent assets.

Pension Worksheet

Because not all of the aspects of pension expense are tracked through normal journal entries, a pension worksheet tracks the annual pension expense, cash, and prepaid or accrued pension cost accounts from the general ledger against the unrecognized pension items: projected benefit obligation and plan assets. Figure 1A-137 shows an example of a pension worksheet using sample numbers and a 10% settlement rate. Note that the prepaid accrued pensions cost balance should equal the memo record's net balance. Note also that the debits and credits for both records are used as if they were one journal. (Each transaction has debits equal credits across the two records.) The contributions item refers to the employer's current period contributions made to the pension plan, whereas the benefits refer to actual benefits disbursed to current retirees. The purpose of Figure 1A-137 is to show the format of the pension worksheet; it does not illustrate the underlying computations.

Figure 1A-137 Pension Worksheet (in Thousands)

	General Journal Entries			Memo Record	
Items	Annual Pension Expense	Cash	Prepaid/ Accrued Cost	Projected Benefit Obligation	Plan Assets
Balance, Jan 1, Year 1			$0	$200,000 Cr	$200,000 Dr
Service cost	$16,000 Dr			16,000 Cr	
Interest expense	20,000 Dr			20,000 Cr	
Return on plan assets	20,000 Cr*				20,000 Dr
Contributions		$14,000 Cr			14,000 Dr
Benefits				12,000 Dr	12,000 Cr
Journal entry for Year 1	$16,000 Dr	$14,000 Cr	2,000 Cr†		
Balance, Dec 31, Year 1			$2,000 Cr‡	$224,000 Cr	$222,000 Dr

Note: Dr = debit, Cr = credit.
*Return on plan assets = ($222,000 − $200,000) − ($14,000 − $12,000) = $20,000.
†Cash less annual pension expense equals the prepaid/accrued cost: $14,000 − $16,000 = ($2,000).
‡Plan assets less projected benefit obligation equals the end-of-year balance in the prepaid/accrued cost: $222,000 − $224,000 = ($2,000).

Financial Statement Disclosures

Disclosures related to pension plans should be made within the body of the financial statements or in the notes. Figure 1A-138 shows an example of a pension disclosure in the notes from a company's 10-Q.

Figure 1A-138 Pension Disclosures for New CF&I (Dates Genericized) fictional company

NEW CF&I, INC.
Notes to Consolidated Financial Statements [Pension Disclosures Excerpt]
(Unaudited)

Employee Benefit Plans

New CF&I has noncontributory defined benefit pension plans and postretirement health care and life insurance benefit plans that cover nearly all of its eligible employees. Certain management employees are no longer eligible to participate in the defined benefit plans if they were hired after September 1, Year 1 (Y1). Those employees are instead enrolled in an employer-funded defined contribution plan equal to 3% of annual wages. The new defined contribution plan is funded annually, and participants' benefits vest after five years of service. New CF&I also offers a qualified Thrift 401(k) plan to all of its employees.

Components of net periodic benefit cost related to the defined benefit pension plans are as follows:

	Defined Benefit Pension Plans			
	Three Months Ended June 30		Six Months Ended June 30	
	Year 2 (Y2)	Year 2 (Y2)	Y2	Y1
	(In thousands)		(In thousands)	
Service cost	$648	$579	$1,296	$1,158
Interest cost	1,057	1,001	2,114	2,002
Expected return on plan assets	(880)	(586)	(1,760)	(1,200)
Amortization of unrecognized net loss	115	38	230	76
Amortization of unrecognized prior service cost	609	609	1,218	1,218
Total net periodic benefit cost	$1,549	$1,641	$3,098	$3,254

Components of net periodic benefit cost related to the postretirement health care and life insurance benefit plans are as follows:

	Other Benefit Plans			
	Three Months Ended June 30		Six Months Ended June 30	
	Y2	Y1	Y2	Y1
	(In thousands)		(In thousands)	
Service cost	$60	$55	$117	$111
Interest cost	309	304	612	607
Amortization of unrecognized net loss	69	54	131	107
Amortization of unrecognized prior service cost	183	180	363	359
Total net periodic benefit cost	$621	$593	$1,223	$1,184

New CF&I made contributions of $7.5 million and $11.3 million, respectively, to its pension plans for the three and six months ended June 30, Y2, and contributions of $2.2 million and $5.6 million, respectively, during the three and six months ended June 30, Y1. New CF&I expects to make additional contributions of $8.1 million in Y2.

The first paragraph in Figure 1A-138 discloses the types of pension plans the company has and who is eligible. The employer is required to make these disclosures (see the top half of the figure): projected benefit obligation, pension plan assets, unrecognized (unamortized) prior service costs, and unrecognized (unamortized) actuarial net gain or loss. These items are not otherwise recorded on the financial statements. In addition, this information (although not all inclusive) should be disclosed:

- A schedule showing the components of pension expense
- The funded status of the plan (the difference between the projected benefit obligation measure of the pension liability and the fair value of the plan assets)
- A schedule showing the changes in the projected benefit obligation and the fair value of the plan assets during the year
- The estimates used for the discount rate, plan asset return rate, and rate of compensation increases

The final paragraph of the disclosures in Figure 1A-138 indicates the firm's actual and planned contributions.

Deferred Income Taxes

Because the IRS tax code has differences from GAAP (and there are many variations within GAAP), the usual result is that pretax financial income will differ from taxable income. **Pretax financial income** (or income before taxes/income for book purposes) is the income derived for financial reporting under GAAP for use by the investment community. **Taxable income** is a term in the Internal Revenue Code (the tax code) denoting the base amount of net income (after all allowed deductions) that is used to calculate income tax payable.

Temporary Differences

Many of the differences between the two methods are actually temporary differences. A **temporary difference** is a differential between an asset or liability's reported value (carrying or book) and its tax basis that will reverse itself in a later period, resulting in the same net tax being paid. For example, although GAAP uses full accrual accounting, the tax code allows the use of a modified cash basis for revenue recognition. This means that under GAAP, revenue generally is recognized in earlier periods than under the tax code. Figure 1A-139 shows how such a temporary difference in revenues can exist for a time due to differences in the timing of revenue recognition. The figure assumes a 40% tax rate and consistent revenues and expenses for GAAP reporting (for easier comparison).

Figure 1A-139 Financial versus Tax Reporting

	Acme Company			
	Year 1	Year 2	Year 3	Total
GAAP reporting				
Revenues	$100,000	$100,000	$100,000	
Expenses	$60,000	$60,000	$60,000	
Pretax financial income	$40,000	$40,000	$40,000	$120,000
Income tax expense	$16,000	$16,000	$16,000	$48,000
Tax reporting				
Revenues	$70,000	$110,000	$120,000	
Expenses	$60,000	$60,000	$60,000	
Taxable income	$10,000	$50,000	$60,000	$120,000
Income tax payable	$4,000	$20,000	$24,000	$48,000
Difference*	$12,000	($4,000)	($8,000)	

*Difference = Tax Expense − Tax Payable.

The temporary difference in Figure 1A-139 is a deferred tax liability offset by the two future increases in tax payable. A **deferred tax liability** is a difference that results in paying less taxes now (the $12,000) compensated by paying higher taxes in future periods (the $4,000 and $8,000 differences). A **deferred tax** asset is a difference that results in paying higher taxes now and lower taxes later.

Differences of these sorts result in needing to allocate tax between periods, called "interperiod tax allocation." Interperiod tax allocation refers to the allocation of total income tax expense or benefit between continuing operations, discontinued operations, extraordinary items, and items charged or credited directly to shareholders' equity between periods. It is needed when items are recorded in different periods for tax accounting and financial reporting (or book) purposes. For example, a company might accrue warranty expense in the period that a product is sold under warranty for financial reporting purposes but deduct the repair costs for tax purposes when warranty service actually is provided. Or the revenue from an installment sale might be reported in the period of sale for financial reporting purposes but reported as taxable income when cash is received. Under GAAP, the tax effects of these differences lead to the recording of deferred tax assets and liabilities. Stated a different way, deferred tax assets result when book-tax differences result in deductible amounts (like the warranty expense), and deferred tax liabilities result when book-tax differences result in taxable amounts (like the installment sales revenue). A **deductible amount** is an item that decreases taxable income in future periods. A **taxable amount** is an item that increases taxable income in future periods.

According to ASC Topic 740, *Income Taxes* (previously addressed in FASB Statement No. 109), under SFAS No. 109, deferred taxes are measured using the asset and liability method. This method measures the tax effects that arise when the carrying amounts of assets and liabilities differ for financial reporting and tax purposes.

Consider the case of a fixed asset that costs $1,500 and that is being depreciated using the straight-line method for financial accounting purposes and an accelerated method for tax purposes. As illustrated in Figure 1A-140, assume that at the end of the year (Year 1), the asset has a carrying value of $1,200 for financial reporting purposes and a tax basis of $1,000. This $200 difference would give rise to a deferred tax liability. Assuming that the tax rate was 40%, a deferred tax liability of $80 ($200 × 40%) would be recorded related to the depreciable asset. The nature of this liability can be understood by assuming that the asset had been sold for $1,200. No gain or loss would be reported on the income statement, but a taxable gain of $200 would result. So, a future sale of the asset may increase taxable income and taxes payable. Of course, any gain on the future asset sale may be more than offset by tax-deductible expenses or losses, so no tax payment may in fact result. Therefore, deferred taxes, although classified as assets and liabilities, are not receivables or payables in the usual sense.

Figure 1A-140 Carrying Value Difference

	Book	Tax
Asset cost	$1,500	$1,500
Depreciation to date	(300)	(500)
Basis at balance sheet date	$1,200	$1,000

Assume that the company had a tax rate of 40%, taxable income of $8,000, and no deferred tax assets or liability balances at the beginning of the year. Tax expense would be computed as the difference between the amount of tax payable with the tax return (taxable income times the tax rate) and the adjustment to the deferred tax liability account, as illustrated in Figure 1A-141.

Figure 1A-141 Entry to Record Tax Expense

Tax expense	$3,280	
Deferred tax liability		$80
Tax payable		$3,200

Tax expense reported on the income statement is the sum of the amount of tax payable with tax returns for the period and the net amount of adjustments made to deferred tax asset and liability balances from the beginning to the end of the year. Because companies that have been operating for more than a year may have interperiod differences over several years, the current year's income tax expense can be calculated as follows:

$$\text{Income Tax Expense} = \begin{pmatrix} \text{(End-of-Year Deferred Tax Liability (Asset))} \\ - \text{ Beginning-of-Year Tax Liability (Asset)} \\ + \text{ Current Period Income Tax Payable} \end{pmatrix}$$

In Year 2, the book depreciation to date is $600 and the tax depreciation is $750, so this $150 difference results in an additional $60 deferred tax liability. The ending deferred tax liability is therefore $140. If taxable income is $7,000, income tax expense = [$140 − $80] + $2,800 = $2,860. A similar accounting entry to Figure 1A-141 would be made crediting deferred tax liability by an additional $60. In Year 3, the book depreciation to date is $900 and the tax depreciation is $800, so this $100 difference × 40% = $40 taxable amount. and the end-of-year deferred tax liability will be $140 − $40 = $100. If taxable income is $8,000, income tax expense = ($100 − $140) + $3,200 = $3,160. Figure 1A-142 shows how the journal entry will partly reverse the amount in the deferred tax liability account.

Figure 1A-142 Entry to Record Tax Expense

Tax expense	$3,160	
Deferred tax liability	$ 40	
Tax payable		$3,200

Because the asset was being depreciated over a five-year life, in the fifth year, the difference would be completely reversed. Because the ability to realize the benefit of deferred tax assets is not a certainty, a valuation allowance is provided to reduce deferred tax assets to the extent that it is more likely than not—greater than 50% likelihood—that they will not be realized.

Examples of temporary differences include where different methods are used for:

- Installment sales method for taxes (cannot be used with GAAP).
- Long-term construction contracts.
- Depreciation.
- Goodwill (amortization over 15 years under tax code; not amortized under GAAP).
- Estimated costs such as warranty expense are not recorded until they actually occur under the tax code.
- Prepaid income is part of taxable income when received for taxes but is a liability until earned under GAAP.
- Accounting for investments uses the equity method for financial reporting and the cost method for taxes.
- Net capital loss is recognized currently under GAAP; it is carried forward to offset future capital gains for taxes.
- Deferred compensation accrues over employee's employment period for GAAP but cannot be deducted until actually paid for taxes.
- Accrued contingent liabilities cannot be deducted for taxes until they are fixed and determinable.
- Excess charitable contributions can be carried over to future years for taxes.
- Cash versus accrual basis: Taxes use modified cash; GAAP uses accrual accounting.

Permanent Differences

A number of differences between GAAP and tax accounting will never be reversed because some items always affect one method but never another or vice versa.

Examples of Permanent Differences

The following are some examples of permanent differences.

- **Changes in effective tax rate.** If the tax rates change, a portion of a temporary difference could become a permanent difference (e.g., if a 40% tax rate changes to a 35% tax rate, the 5% change would become a permanent difference because it would not need to be paid when the temporary difference reverses itself).
- **Deduction for dividends received.** Dependent on ownership interest, some percentage of dividends received by a corporation are nontaxable but must be fully taxed under financial reporting.
- **Municipal interest income.** 100% exclusion from taxes is allowed for qualified municipal securities (capital gains from the investment are taxable) but is not excluded from financial reporting.
- **Percentage depletion.** Excess of percentage depletion over cost depletion is allowable as a deduction for taxes but not for financial reporting.
- **Government tax exemptions.** Governments have passed laws that exempt certain revenues from taxation, permit special deductions above what is allowed by GAAP, or add special taxes on types of businesses to discourage their growth. To spur development in certain geographical areas, some local governments have created tax-free zones. In such situations, a company's effective tax rate will differ from the statutory tax rate (used for financial reporting). The differential will become permanent.

Permanent Difference Illustration

The best way to illustrate a permanent difference is to show it alongside temporary differences. This will help show how permanent differences are not included in a deferred tax liability or asset account. For example, say that Acme Company reported pretax financial income of $100,000 for Year 1, $110,000 for Year 2, and $120,000 for Year 3; has a 40% tax rate; and received municipal interest income of $20,000 in each of the three years, which is entirely tax deductible for taxes and not deductible for financial reporting. In addition, the company sells a $15,000 asset on an installment account, recognizing the entire sale in Year 1 for financial reporting, but it can recognize only a third of the amount per year for tax purposes. Figure 1A-143 shows how to calculate income taxes payable for each of the years.

Figure 1A-143 Calculating Income Taxes Payable with Temporary and Permanent Differences

	Year 1	Year 2	Year 3
Pretax financial income	$100,000	$110,000	$120,000
Permanent difference			
Deductible expense	($20,000)	($20,000)	($20,000)
Temporary difference			
Installment sale*	($10,000)	$5,000	$5,000
Taxable income	$70,000	$95,000	$105,000
Income tax payable (40%)	$28,000	$38,000	$42,000

*Installment sale in Year 1: ($15,000) recognized for book + $5,000 recognized for tax = ($10,000).

To determine taxes payable from pretax financial income, deduct those differences that make pretax financial income greater than taxable income and add those differences that make pretax financial income less than taxable income. Therefore, the $15,000 asset sold on the books increases Year 1 income by this amount but for taxes only $5,000 can be claimed, so the $10,000 difference is deducted because this is the amount by which pretax financial income exceeds taxable income for the temporary difference. Figure 1A-144 shows the journal entries for each of the three years and reflects how temporary differences require a deferred tax liability account but permanent differences simply are rolled into income tax payable and income tax expense.

Figure 1A-144 Acme Company Journal Entries for Income Taxes in Years 1, 2, and 3

December 31, Year 1

Income tax expense [$28,000 + ($10,000 × 40%)]	$32,000	
Deferred tax liability ($10,000 × 40%)		$ 4,000
Income tax payable		$28,000
To record income payment of income taxes		

December 31, Year 2

Income tax expense [$38,000 − ($5,000 × 40%)]	$36,000	
Deferred tax liability ($5,000 × 40%)		$ 2,000
Income tax payable		$38,000
To record income payment of income taxes		

December 31, Year 3

Income tax expense [$42,000 − ($5,000 × 40%)]	$40,000	
Deferred tax liability ($5,000 × 40%)		$ 2,000
Income tax payable		$42,000
To record income payment of income taxes		

Although the statutory tax rate for each of these years remains 40%, the effective tax rate differs. The effective tax rate formula and examples follow.

$$\text{Effective Tax Rate} = \frac{\text{Total Income Tax for Period}}{\text{Pretax Financial Income}}$$

For Year 1 = $\frac{\$32,000}{\$100,000} = 32\%$ For Year 2 = $\frac{\$36,000}{\$110,000} = 32.73\%$ For Year 3 = $\frac{\$40,000}{\$120,000} = 33.33\%$

Financial Statement Impact

Deferred tax amounts are separated on the balance sheet for financial reporting purposes into current and noncurrent amounts. Deferred tax balances that relate to a current asset or liability are classified as current, and deferred tax balances that relate to a noncurrent asset or liability are classified as noncurrent. For example, the deferred tax balance related to the depreciable asset in the last example would be classified as noncurrent because it relates to a plant asset. The net amount of any current deferred tax assets and liabilities is reported on the balance sheet, as is the net amount of any noncurrent deferred tax assets and liabilities.

The notes to the financial statements should include a reconciliation of the statutory tax rate and the effective tax rate and disclosure of the components of the net deferred tax liability or asset recognized in the balance sheet. Figure 1A-145 shows an example of income tax disclosures.

Figure 1A-145 Disclosure of Income Taxes

Bounce Sporting Goods Company, International (in Millions)

Note 13: Income Taxes

U.S. and foreign income from continuing operations before income taxes:

		Year 3	Year 2	Year 1
U.S.		$1,401	$1,489	$1,402
Foreign		545	497	(55)
		$1,946	$1,986	$1,347

Provision for income taxes on income from continuing operations:

Current:	Federal	$(166)	$514	$218
	Foreign	230	95	119
	State	40	51	62
		104	660	399
Deferred:	Federal	117	20	175
	Foreign	3	13	(35)
	State	9	11	(2)
		129	44	138
		$233	$704	$537

(Continued)

Figure 1A-145 (*Continued*)

Reconciliation of the U.S. federal statutory tax rate to our effective tax rate on continuing operations:

U.S. federal statutory tax rate	35.0%	35.0%	35.0%
State income tax, net of federal tax benefit	1.7	2.1	3.0
Effect of lower taxes on foreign results	(3.0)	(5.6)	(4.4)
Settlement of prior years' audit issues	(5.6)	(1.9)	(2.8)
Guatemala settlement	(21.4)	—	—
Effect of unusual impairment and other items	3.3	2.3	9.6
Other, net	2.5	3.5	(0.6)
Effective tax rate on continuing operations	12.5%	35.4%	39.8%

Deferred taxes are recorded to give recognition to temporary differences between the tax bases of assets or liabilities and their reported amounts in the financial statements. We record the tax effect of the temporary differences as deferred tax assets or deferred tax liabilities. Deferred tax assets generally represent items that can be used as a tax deduction or credit in future years. Deferred tax liabilities generally represent items that we have taken a tax deduction for but have not yet recorded in the income statement.

Deferred tax liabilities (assets):

Intangible assets other than nondeductible goodwill	$1,242	$1,172
Property, plant, and equipment	572	430
Safe harbor leases	94	99
Zero-coupon notes	68	72
Other	407	288
Gross deferred tax liabilities	2,383	2,061
Net operating loss carryforwards	(483)	(447)
Postretirement benefits	(212)	(212)
Various current liabilities	(604)	(439)
Gross deferred tax assets	(1,299)	(1,098)
Deferred tax assets valuation allowance	492	394
Net deferred tax assets	(807)	(704)
Net deferred tax liabilities	$1,576	$1,357

Included in:

Prepaid expenses, deferred income taxes, and other current assets	$(148)	$(102)
Deferred income taxes	1,724	1,459
	$1,576	$1,357

Deferred tax liabilities are not recognized for temporary differences related to investments in foreign subsidiaries and in unconsolidated foreign affiliates that are essentially permanent in duration. It would not be practical to determine the amount of any such deferred tax liabilities.

Net operating losses of $2.3 billion at year-end Year 3 were carried forward and are available to reduce future taxable income of certain subsidiaries in a number of foreign and state jurisdictions. These net operating losses will expire as follows: $83 million in Year 4, $2.1 billion between Year 5 and Year 17; $173 million may be carried forward indefinitely.

Stock Options

As discussed earlier, a stock option gives selected employees or directors the right to buy common stock at a set exercise price over a specified period of time. The objective of employee stock options is to encourage employees to take an ownership stake in improving the company. Stock options also help retain key employees; provide deferred, long-term compensation that maximizes the employee's after-tax benefits; and help tie employee and company performance to compensation.

Key terms for stock options include:

- **Grant date**—The date on which the employee receives the options; on the grant date, the exercise price and the market price of the stock should be the same (but may not be).
- **Vesting date**—A date after which the options are allowed to be exercised without any contingent clause of continued employment.
- **Service period**—The period of time between the grant date and the vesting date during which the employee must continue working for the company (unless otherwise specified).
- **Exercise price**—A price for the stock that is set on the grant date; it is the price the executive will pay for the stock if he or she exercises the options and buys the stock. If the stock price eventually rises above the exercise price, the employee can profit by purchasing shares at the exercise price and selling them at the higher market price.

Stock options can have an effect on the dilution of ownership of a company. Although a stock option is similar to issuing new shares of stock, issuing stock options does not require a company to give current shareholders first right of purchase as is done for normal issuances of new stock. Therefore, current shareholders may experience a drop in their percentage of ownership if large amounts of stock options are issued.

Accounting Issues

ASC Topic 718, *Compensation—Stock Compensation*, requires firms to recognize compensation expense based on the fair market value of the stock options expected to vest on the grant date. Determining expense using the fair value method is ideally performed by using actual market prices (market-observed) for the stock options. However, usually this is not available because employee stock options lack exchangeability. Therefore, fair value often is based on use of an option pricing model (e.g., the Black-Scholes model or binomial lattice model) that determines the fair value of the company (and thus its stock). Black-Scholes is a closed-form fair value model originally intended to value stocks on the public market (rather than stock options), which incorporate little variables. Therefore, companies now use models such as the binomial lattice model, which provides the flexibility to include or exclude variables as fits the situation. This model is complex but has become easier to apply as sophisticated computer software has evolved. ASC Topic 718 recommends use of lattice models, as they are more sensitive to the differences found in stock options.

The fair value method recognizes that there are three aspects to the value of a stock option: the intrinsic value (the difference between the stock price at the grant date and the current market price), the time value of money (investors can invest funds elsewhere while waiting to exercise the options), and the time value of the underlying stock's volatility (the employee may profit from appreciation of underlying stock but risks only the option premium, not the full value of the stock). This means that even if the intrinsic value is zero, the total of the other two items likely will show that the option provides some amount of compensation and must be so accounted for. Base data to calculate these three items includes the exercise price of the option, expected dividends, expected volatility of the price of the underlying share, risk-free interest rates for the term of the option, the current price of the underlying share, and the expected term of the option (including contractual term, vesting, and postvesting employee termination behaviors).

Once the fair value of the company has been determined and applied to the value of the stock options on the grant date, increases or decreases in the stock price do not cause adjustments in the value of the option. The expense is recognized in income over the service period, during which the employee provides services in exchange for the options.

Financial Statement Impact

Note disclosures related to stock options include the following:

- The method of estimating the fair value of goods or services received or the fair value of the equity instruments granted during the period.
- The cash flow effects from share-based payments.
- Vesting requirements, maximum term of options granted, and number of shares authorized for grants of options or other equity instruments.
- The number and weighted-average exercise prices of each group of options.
- The weighted-average grant-date fair value of options granted during the year, classified according to whether the exercise prices equals, exceeds, or is less than the fair value of the stock at the date of grant.
- A description of methods used and assumptions made in determining the fair values of the options.
- Total compensation cost recognized for the year.

Backdating is the practice of setting the exercise price on a date when the stock was relatively low. Required disclosures for stock options also include any backdating, which, while currently legal, must receive the permission of directors and be consistent with company policy and must provide full disclosure to investors and reduce earnings by the amount of the added costs. Backdating has been abused by many firms, such as by timing the announcement of news that will likely raise their stock price to just after stock options have been issued or by not properly reducing earnings when the backdating occurs. The SEC has forced numerous companies to restate their earnings and is well aware of this issue.

Expiration and Adjustment

If stock options expire without being exercised, no adjustment is made to compensation expense. However, if the employee fails to meet the necessary obligations under the agreement, compensation expense must be adjusted as a change in estimate to decrease compensation expense.

Discontinued Operations

A discontinued operation is a common type of irregular item reported on the income statement. When a segment is being disposed of, these operations become discontinued. The results of operations of a component of an entity that has been sold during the year or is being held for sale would be reported under **discontinued operations** net of taxes or benefit, as would losses or gains related to sale or impairment of the asset. Operations that are to be discontinued are transferred from the held-and-used category to the held-for-sale category on the balance sheet, which may result in gains or losses reported under discontinued operations.

Accounting Issues

ASC Topic 205, *Presentation of Financial Statements* (as previously addressed in FASB Statement No. 144), defines the accounting and disclosure provisions for discontinued operations. A discontinued operation is defined as a "component of an entity" that can be distinguished by its own cash flows and operations. To qualify as a discontinued operation, it is expected that, after disposition, the operations and cash flows of the component will no longer affect ongoing operations, and there will be no significant continuing involvement with the component disposed of. The component may be a segment of a business, a reporting unit, or an asset group, but it should have clearly distinguishable operations and cash flows.

If the component is considered impaired, a loss is recognized and the carrying value is written down to fair value less cost to sell. Subsequently, gains may be recognized based on increases in fair value less cost to sell—but not in excess of the total loss previously recognized. At the date of sale, any gain or loss not previously recognized would be recorded.

When a company decides to discontinue an operation, the date of this decision becomes the decision date. On or after the decision date, the operation is officially classified as held for sale. When the operation is officially disposed of, this becomes the disposal date.

Calculating the Ggain or Loss on Disposal

Two basic amounts must be known to calculate the gain or loss on operations: the loss or gain from operations of the discontinued operation (net of tax) and the loss or gain on disposal of the discontinued operation. The total of these amounts equals the loss or gain on the discontinued operation. The loss from operations is calculated by summing these items:

- The difference between the carrying value of the operations at the beginning of the year and the carrying value after GAAP adjustments are made to bring the operation up to the date it was classified as held for sale. Excluding long-lived assets, the carrying value of assets and liabilities must be adjusted according to GAAP. These adjustments are excluded from the gain or loss on disposal because they are included in the gain or loss from operations of the discontinued operation. GAAP adjustments include depreciation, amortization, and adjustment of valuation accounts. For example, the valuation allowance for bad debts on accounts receivable may need to be adjusted to reflect the probabilities of collection when the asset is classified as held for sale.
- Losses from operations from the beginning of the year until the date it was reclassified as held for sale (includes GAAP adjustments).
- Losses from operations from when it was classified as held for sale until sold or until the end of the year if not sold (i.e., subsequent to GAAP adjustments).

The gain or loss on disposal is determined by comparing the carrying value of the operation to the fair value less selling costs. The formula for the loss (gain) on disposal is shown next.

$$\text{Loss (Gain) on Disposal} = (\text{Carrying Value} - \text{GAAP Adjustments}) - (\text{Fair Value} - \text{Selling Costs})$$

"GAAP adjustments" refer to the adjustments mentioned in the first bullet on the previous page.

The first step in calculating a gain or loss on disposal of an operation is to determine the costs to sell the asset. These costs are deducted from the fair value of the asset. Incremental direct costs of transacting the sale (those costs that arise directly from the decision to sell) include:

- Brokers' commissions and other selling fees.
- Fees for fair value assessment of operation.
- Legal fees.
- Title transfer fees.
- Closing costs.

The next step in calculating the gain or loss on the disposal of an operation is to calculate the carrying value of the operation. This should include capitalization of interest and other costs. With certain exceptions, all material costs that were needed to get the asset ready for its initial use, including any interest costs from financing the asset, should be capitalized to show a more accurate initial investment cost.

Once the carrying value of the operation is determined, the fair value of the operation is assessed by an actuary. If the total carrying amount is greater than the fair value less these costs, then a loss on disposal is recognized in the period in which the asset is classified as held for sale. If the opposite is true and there is a gain on disposal, it is not recognized until the period of actual sale.

Financial Statement Impact

The results of discontinued operations, less applicable income taxes (benefit), are reported as a separate component of income before extraordinary items (if applicable). The gain or loss on disposal instead may be disclosed in the notes to the financial statements. Figure 1A-146 illustrates the presentation of discontinued operations on the income statement.

Figure 1A-146 Income Statement—Discontinued Operations

Income from continuing operations		$8,000,000
Discontinued operations		
Loss from operation of discontinued × division (net of tax)	$120,000	
Loss from disposal of × division (net of tax)	$200,000	$320,000
Net income		$7,680,000

Future-Period Adjustments

Future losses from the end of the fiscal year until the anticipated date of sale would be dealt with in the periods in which these losses occur in the same way they are accounted for in the prior discussion. In addition, amounts reported in discontinued operations may need to be adjusted in later periods by classifying them separately in discontinued operations for the current period. (The nature and amount of adjustments should be disclosed.)

Extraordinary Items

An extraordinary item is another type of irregular item reported on the income statement. To qualify as an **extraordinary item**, an event or transaction must have an unusual nature, occur infrequently, and be outside management control, taking into account the environment in which the entity operates. Such events typically are unrelated to the normal activities of the entity and are not expected to reoccur in the foreseeable future. So, for example, damage from a hurricane would be considered extraordinary only if it occurred in a part of the country where such damage was a rare occurrence.

Accounting Issues

Because restrictive criteria are applied in determining whether an item is considered extraordinary, a number of unusual or infrequent items are not reported as extraordinary items but are included in income from continuing operations.

Financial Statement Impact

Extraordinary items are listed net of taxes on a separate line of the income statement below income from continuing operations.

Accounting Changes and Error Corrections

Financial statements must reflect the results of:

- Changes in accounting principle.
- Changes in estimates.
- Changes in reporting entities.
- Error corrections.

Changes in accounting principle occur as a result of new rules issued by the FASB or because management has elected to change from one GAAP method to another GAAP method, where a choice is allowed. An example would be a company changing from the weighted average cost method for valuing inventory to the FIFO method. Note that changing from a cash-based method to a GAAP method is not considered a change in accounting principle as the cash-based method is not GAAP. This type of change would be considered an error correction (further discussed below) and would be treated as such. Further note that a change in depreciation method (e.g., changing from the straight-line method to the double-declining balance method) is not considered a change in accounting principle. Instead, it is considered a "change in accounting estimate effected by a change in principle." It is, therefore, treated as a change in estimate and accounted for in a similar manner as a change in estimate (further discussed below).

Changes in estimate involve the change in an estimated financial statement amount based on new information or experience. This might include, for instance, changing the bad debt percentage of sales estimate from 2% to 3% or changing the useful life of an asset from five to seven years.

Changes in reporting entities include changes that result in the financial statements representing a different entity. Some examples include presenting consolidated statements in place of individual statements, a change in subsidiaries, or a change in the use of the equity method for an investment.

A correction of an error occurs when a material error is made in a prior period's financial statements and requires an adjustment to restate the financial statements so that, cumulatively, they reflect an accurate retained earnings balance.

Accounting Issues and Impact

Under ASC Topic 250, *Accounting Changes and Error Corrections* (formerly covered in FASB Statement No. 154), changes in accounting principle require retrospective application. This approach requires the reporting of the cumulative effect of the impact on the carrying amounts of assets and liabilities (as if the new method had been used all along) with an offsetting adjustment to the opening balance of retained earnings as of the beginning of the first period presented.

Changes in estimates require prospective application, meaning that the financial statements are not restated but rather the change is reported in the current period and in future periods only.

Changes in reporting entities also require retrospective application similar to changes in accounting principle. Prior-period financial statements are reflected to show the financial information for the new reporting entity as if they entity had existed in that form all along. Cumulative earnings differences are reported through beginning retained earnings as of the beginning of the first period presented.

Errors made that affect the income or loss reporting in prior periods are corrected by adjusting the beginning balance of retained earnings. When financial statements of prior years are being reported on a comparative basis, they are restated to correct amounts. The effect of the error on earlier periods is presented as an adjustment of beginning retained earnings for the earliest period presented.

Business Combinations

ASC Topic 805, *Business Combinations*, states that a business combination is a transaction or other event in which an acquirer obtains control of one or more businesses. This is often accomplished when an entity (the acquirer) acquires the net assets that constitute a business or acquires the equity interests of one or more other entities and obtains controls over that entity or entities (the acquiree(s)).

Accounting Issues

The purchase method of accounting for business combinations is required under GAAP; the former pooling-of-interests method is no longer acceptable for new business acquisitions. However, if an entity is using the pooling-of-interests method for a former acquiree company, the entity may continue to do so. In the purchase method, the acquiring company allocates the acquisition purchase price to all tangible and identifiable intangible assets acquired and to liabilities assumed, based on their fair values. Any excess of the purchase price over the fair value of the underlying assets and liabilities is accounted for as goodwill. If the fair value of the net assets acquired exceeds the purchase price, then that negative difference is reported immediately through the income statement as a gain on the business acquisition.

In most cases, the entity to be considered the acquirer in a business combination is evident. The larger entity or the one that issues its equity is normally the acquirer. Business combinations of entities under common control were not affected by ASC Topic 805 guidance, so a method similar to the pooling-of-interests method is used. Common control exists when an individual, a direct family member, or a group of shareholders owns over 50% of the voting interests in each entity in the combination.

Financial Statement Impact

The notes to the financial statements would include disclosure of the name and a brief discussion of the entity acquired; the percentage interest acquired; the cost of the acquisition, including the number of shares, if any, issued to complete the transaction; the primary reason for the acquisition; and the period for which the results of operations of the acquired entity are included in the consolidated financial statements. Disclosure also is required of a summarized balance sheet of the acquired company, identifying the values allocated to each of the assets and liabilities. Specific disclosure is required of acquired intangible assets, both those that are subject to amortization and those that are not, as well as goodwill arising from the transaction, which should be broken down by the business segments to which it relates.

Consolidated Financial Statements

Consolidated financial statements are statements presenting the financial position and results of operations of a parent company and its subsidiaries as if the aggregate were a single entity with divisions. Consolidated financial statements are considered to be the most useful statements of the entity for shareholders and creditors of the entity. A **combined financial statement** is the same as a consolidated financial statement except that it consolidates the statements of legally separate entities related by common ownership. Consolidated and combined financial statements differ in the presentation of the equity section, where the legal status of the entities dictates the information displayed.

Accounting Issues

As required by ASC Topic 810, *Consolidation* (previously covered under FASB Statement No. 94), all companies with subsidiaries are required to issue consolidated statements, which should include each subsidiary they control. (Usually control is implied by a 50% or more ownership; however, control also can be exerted in other ways.) The limited exceptions that remain allowing the nonconsolidation of majority-owned subsidiaries principally relate to the absence of control over the subsidiary due to legal or other restrictions.

Financial Statement Impact

To create a consolidated financial statement, first the assets, liabilities, assets, revenue, and expenses of each formerly separate company are combined. Second, any intercompany transactions and balances are eliminated. Finally, the consolidated statements are issued. Intercompany transactions and balances are transactions and balances that appear on the books of both companies, such as the investment account, which contains the investment made to acquire the company (and any previous partial acquisitions) as well as the related stockholders' equity for the subsidiary. An eliminating entry is a workpaper entry (not an accounting entry) used to cancel the effects of intercompany transactions and therefore avoid double-counting of the net assets. The elimination substitutes the subsidiary's net assets for the investment account. In addition to eliminating entries, adjusting entries also occur. An adjusting entry is an entry to correct errors or to account for entries that were made by one party but not the other.

All of the primary financial statements—balance sheet, income statement, statement of cash flows, and statement of stockholders' equity—must be prepared on a consolidated basis, as such information is essential to an understanding of financial position and operating results of the entity by its stakeholders.

To begin the process of consolidating the financial statements, first determine the percentage of stock that has been acquired in the subsidiary if less than 100%. Second, if there is any purchase differential, or a difference between the purchase price and the book value of the acquisition, then this amount is allocated to adjust the underlying assets/liabilities of the acquisition. The percentage acquired times the net assets or of the equity of the acquisition equals the book value. When cost is greater than book value, the net assets will be adjusted upward (or vice versa).

For example, assume that Acme Company acquired 75% of Beta Company's stock for a cash payment of $330,000 (7,500 of 10,000 shares). The initial journal entry by Acme would record a debit of $330,000 to investment in Beta Company with a corresponding credit to cash. The book value of the firm is $400,000. Any difference between the cost and the book value would need to be allocated to specific accounts. When the cost is greater than the book value, some asset accounts would need to be increased in value (or vice versa). The accounts that can be increased are those that have a historical cost that is greater than the market value. Such accounts can be increased but not to the point where they exceed market value. (Any excess is marked as goodwill.) Therefore, in this example, we assume that the property and equipment account and the land account will each be allocated 50% of the excess of cost over book value. Figure 1A-147 shows how to determine if there is a difference between the cost and book value.

Figure 1A-147 Calculating Difference between Cost and Book Value and Allocating the Difference

Cost of investment (purchase price)	$330,000
Book value of equity acquired (75% × $400,000)	$300,000
Difference: cost greater than (less than) book value	$ 30,000
Adjust property and equipment upward* (50% × $30,000)	($15,000)
Adjust land upward* (50% × $30,000)	($15,000)
Balance	$ 0
*To mark toward market	

Figure 1A-148 shows how a workpaper is used to determine the necessary eliminations.

Figure 1A-148 Consolidated Balance Sheet Workpaper

Consolidated Balance Sheet Workpaper
Acme Company and Wholly Owned Subsidiary
January 1, Year 1 (Date of acquisition)

	Acme Co.	Beta Co.	Eliminations Debit	Eliminations Credit	Noncontrolling Interest	Consolidated Balances
Cash	$170,000	$100,000				$270,000
Other current assets	700,000	250,000				950,000
Plant and equipment	600,000	200,000	$15,000†			815,000
Land	200,000	100,000	15,000†			315,000
Investments in Beta Co.	330,000			$330,000*		
Difference between cost and book value			30,000*	$30,000†		
Total assets	$2,000,000	$650,000				$2,350,000
Liabilities	300,000	250,000				550,000
Common stock						
Acme Co.	1,000,000					1,000,000
Beta Co.		250,000	187,500*		$62,500*	
Other contributed capital						
Acme Co.	200,000					200,000
Beta Co.		50,000	37,500*		12,500*	
Retained earnings						
Acme Co.	500,000					500,000
Beta Co.		100,000	75,000*		25,000*	
Noncontrolling interest					$100,000	100,000
Total liabilities and equity	$2,000,000	$650,000	$360,000	$360,000		$2,350,000

*To eliminate investments in Beta Co: common stock = $250,000 × 0.75 = $187,500 owned, $62,500 not owned; other contributed capital = $50,000 × 0.75 = $37,500 owned, $12,500 not owned; retained earnings = $100,000 × 0.75 = $75,000 owned, $25,000 not owned; difference between cost and book value = $30,000.
†To distribute the difference between cost and book value ($30,000 × 50% to plant and equipment, × 50% to land).

Note also in Figure 1A-148 that assets and liabilities are summed to find the consolidated amounts (after factoring in eliminating entries). The fair value markups made to account for the difference between cost and book value would be amortized over the useful lives of the assets selected.

In the subsequent periods, the fair value markups would be amortized over the remaining life of the underlying assets. Similarly, intercompany transactions in the subsequent years will have to be reversed. Discussion of these topics is beyond the scope of the current text.

Derivatives

A **derivative** is a type of financial instrument or contract that generally requires no or minimal initial investment and permits net settlement. A derivative derives its value from changes in a benchmark known as an underlying, such as mortgage rates, commodity prices, exchange rates, interest rates, or indexes. Changes in the benchmark are measured based on a notional amount, or unit measure of currency, bushels, shares, and so on.

Derivative contracts include forwards, futures, swaps, and options. The stock options and warrants discussed earlier are a common type of derivative instrument. The market value of a stock option is derived from the value of the underlying stock that can be purchased at an established price. Derivative contracts should have terms that permit net settlement.

Derivatives might be purchased for speculative purposes. But they often are used to hedge, or offset, risks involved in other transactions. For example, the option to purchase a quantity of oil at a set price in the future can offset the risk of oil price variability. Therefore, derivatives are similar to insurance, because the mitigation of risk comes with a price. That price includes not only the cost of the derivative but the reduction of the potential for gain on favorable price changes for the item being hedged.

Accounting Issues

ASC Topic 815, *Derivatives and Hedging* (formerly addressed in FASB Statements No. 133 and 138), governs accounting for derivatives and hedging transactions. This authoritative literature requires that all derivative instruments be recognized at fair value in the balance sheet as assets or liabilities, depending on their nature.

How changes in the fair value (i.e., gains or losses) of a derivative are accounted for depends on whether the derivative instrument has been designated as, and qualifies as part of, a hedging relationship and the nature of the hedge.

- **No hedging designation.** When a derivative is held for speculative purposes, the gain or loss is recognized currently in earnings.
- **Fair-value hedge.** A fair-value hedge is used to offset the exposure to changes in the value of an asset, liability, or firm commitment (like a purchase commitment). The gain or loss on the hedging instrument as well as the offsetting loss or gain on the hedged item are recognized currently in earnings in the same accounting period.
- **Cash flow hedge.** A cash flow hedge is used to offset the exposure to variability in future cash flows from an anticipated transaction (such as an anticipated purchase of inventory). Gains and losses on cash flow hedges are reported in other comprehensive income and then reclassified into earnings when the forecasted transaction affects earnings.

- **Foreign currency hedge.** Gains or losses on a derivative instrument or non-derivative financial instrument designated and qualifying as a foreign currency hedging instrument are accounted for as follows:
  - The gain or loss on a hedge of a foreign-currency-denominated firm commitment and the offsetting loss or gain on the firm commitment hedged is recognized currently in earnings.
  - The gain or loss on a hedge of an available-for-sale security and the offsetting loss or gain on the hedged security is recognized currently in earnings.
  - The effective portion of the gain or loss on a hedge of a forecasted foreign-currency-denominated transaction is reported as a component of other comprehensive income and reclassified into earnings in the same period or periods during which the hedged forecasted transaction affects earnings. The remaining gain or loss on the hedging instrument is recognized currently in earnings.
  - The gain or loss on a hedge of a net investment in a foreign operation is reported in other comprehensive income as part of the cumulative translation adjustment to the extent that it is effective as a hedge, and any remaining gain or loss is recorded in earnings currently.

Financial Statement Impact

Disclosure for derivatives includes the objectives for holding or issuing the instruments (speculative or hedging), the context needed to understand the objectives, and the firm's strategy for achieving those objectives. Fair-value hedges, cash flow hedges, and other types of derivatives should be distinguished. The company's risk management policy should be described, as should the items or transactions for which risks are hedged. Disclosure of the gain or loss recognized in earnings is also required.

The requirements of ASC 815, *Derivatives and Hedging* (formerly SFAS No. 133) are complicated, and a clear understanding of hedging strategies is necessary to ensure that the appropriate accounting is made for an entity's transactions in this area.

Segment Reporting

Diversified entities and entities that grow by purchasing other entities are becoming ever more common, and readers of financial statements need more information on the components of such diversified entities in order to get a realistic picture of how each component contributes to the risk, profitability, and growth of the entity.

Some corporations object to releasing segment information, fearing that the information will be misinterpreted or used by competitors and unions. However, the FASB and the SEC feel that not reporting segment information leaves investors with an incomplete picture of a company's operating performance. ASC Topic 280, *Segment Reporting* (formerly FASB Statement No. 131), requires that the management approach be used to report financial information. The management approach requires that entities report information on a single basis of segmentation—the basis that is used by management in making capital allocation decisions, such as product line or geographic region.

Operating Segment

The operating segment is the basic division that requires disaggregated reporting.

Any component of an entity that meets the following criteria is considered an operating segment:

- The component has separate revenues and expenses earned from business activities.
- A chief decision maker for the entity reviews the component's activities and decides how to allocate funds to the component.
- An internal reporting system tracks individual financial data for the segment.
- The component is materially significant enough to warrant disclosure, as defined by at least one of the following:
  - Revenue is at least 10% of the revenue for the entire entity.
  - The absolute value of its profit or loss is at least 10% of the absolute value of the greater of either the total operating profit of all segments reporting a profit or the total loss of all segments reporting a loss.
  - Segment assets are at least 10% of the total assets of the entity.

Results of two or more segments may be aggregated provided that they share similar characteristics, in that they:

- Make the same products or services.
- Use the same production process.
- Share the same type of customers.
- Use similar methods of distribution.
- Share the same regulatory environment.

Required Segment Reporting

A maximum of ten segments would be identified, and the identified segments should account for at least 75% of the total sales to external customers. Allocation of common or corporate costs for financial reporting is not required.

ASC Topic 280 requires disclosure of general information about operating segments, segment assets, and segment income statement information, including sales (both internal and external), interest revenue and expense, tax expense, depreciation and amortization, and unusual and extraordinary items. Other required disclosures relate to operating results for different geographic areas (when segments are not defined on this basis) and information about major customers. Reconciliation of segment revenue, income, and assets to financial statement totals for those amounts is also required.

Differences in Financial Results: IFRS versus GAAP

The International Accounting Standards Board (IASB) was established in 2001 as part of the International Accounting Standards Committee Foundation. The IASB is responsible for the approval of IFRS and related documents. One of the primary objectives of the IASB is to bring about convergence between the national accounting standards and IFRS. Toward that end, the IASB has been working closely with the FASB to harmonize the international standards with U.S. GAAP.

The IASB's objective is to require like transactions and events to be accounted for and reported in a like way and unlike transactions and events to be accounted for and reported differently, both within an entity and among entities across industries and geographical boundaries. To that effect, the IASB considers those events where there is disparity or choice in accounting treatments with the objective of reducing the number of these choices or all alternative treatments for similar transactions or events. The next discussion covers some common financial statement elements that have been covered in this section, for which the IFRS Standards are different from U.S. GAAP. Candidates for the CMA exam are urged to review the current pronouncements from the IASB and FASB by visiting their respective Web sites (www.iasb.org and www.fasb.org) in preparation for the exam.

A listing of International Accounting Standards (IASs) and a comparison of IFRS and U.S. GAAP is provided next, with additional discussions after.

Topic	IFRS	U.S. GAAP	IAS
Revenue recognition, with respect to the sale of goods	Revenue recognized when risks and rewards of ownership have been transferred, buyer has control of the goods, revenues can be measured reliably, and it is probable that economic benefits will flow to the company.	Revenue recognized when delivery has occurred, risks and rewards of ownership have been transferred, there is persuasive evidence of a sale, the fee is determinable, and collectability is reasonably assured.	IAS No. 18, *Revenue*
Revenue recognition, with respect to deferred receipts	Considered a financing agreement; discount all future receipts at an imputed interest rate.	Discounting to present value required in limited situations.	IAS No. 18, *Revenue*
Revenue recognition, with respect to construction contracts	Percentage-of-completion method is allowed if specific criteria are met; otherwise, revenue is recognized using recoverable costs incurred. The completed contract method is prohibited.	Percentage-of-completion method is allowed if specific criteria are met; otherwise, use completed contract method.	IAS No. 18, *Revenue*
Expense recognition, with respect to share-based payments and employee benefits	Compensation cost is recognized on an accelerated basis.	Compensation cost can be recognized on a straight-line basis or over an accelerated basis.	IAS No. 19, *Employee Benefits* IFRS No. 2, *Share-Based Payment*

Topic	IFRS	U.S. GAAP	IAS
Intangible assets, with respect to development costs and revaluation	Development costs may be capitalized; revaluation permitted if the asset trades in an active market.	Generally, development costs are expensed as incurred; revaluation is prohibited.	IAS No. 38, *Intangible Assets*
Inventories, with respect to costing methods	LIFO is prohibited.	LIFO is permitted.	IAS No. 2, *Inventories*
Inventories, with respect to valuation	Inventory is carried at the lower of cost or net realizable value.	Inventory is carried at the lower of cost or market.	IAS No. 2, *Inventories*
Inventories, with respect to write-downs	Previous write-downs of inventory can be reversed if the impairment no longer exists.	Any write-downs of inventory become the new cost basis and cannot be reversed.	IAS No. 2, *Inventories*
Leases, with respect to leases of land and buildings	Land and building are considered separate units.	Land and building generally are accounted for as a single unit unless the land is more than 25% of the total fair value of the leased property.	IAS No. 17, *Leases*
Long-lived assets, with respect to revaluation, depreciation, and capitalization of borrowing costs	Long-lived assets are recorded at historical cost or a revalued amount (fair value).	Long-lived assets are recorded at historical cost. Revaluation is prohibited.	IAS No. 16, *Property, Plant, and Equipment*
Impairment of assets, with respect to determination, calculation, and reversal of loss	Impairment is recorded when an asset's carrying amount exceeds the discounted present value of the asset's expected future cash flows and fair value less costs to sell.	Impairment is recorded when an asset's carrying amount exceeds the expected future cash flows on an undiscounted basis.	IAS No. 36, *Impairment of Assets*
Financial statement presentation, with respect to extraordinary items and changes in equity	Extraordinary items are prohibited. Changes in equity presented in a separate statement, disclosed in notes, or a part of a single combined statement.	Extraordinary items are restricted to items that are unusual and infrequent. Changes in equity are presented in a footnote or separate statement.	IAS No. 36, *Impairment of Assets*

Revenue and Expense Recognition

As mentioned previously, the IASB is currently finalizing a joint project with FASB to develop a joint Standard for revenue recognition that will replace the existing Standards both internationally as well as in the United States. The Standard is expected to be issued in 2014, and candidates are urged to obtain up-to-date information from either IASB Web site (www.iasb.org) or FASB Web site (www.fasb.org) prior to taking the exam.

U.S. GAAP currently has numerous industry-specific standards relating to revenue recognition. Thus, it is possible that these different standards can produce conflicting results for similar economic transactions. The new Standard should remove inconsistencies and weaknesses in existing revenue recognition standards and practices and provide a more robust framework to address revenue recognition issues, thereby improving comparability of revenue across companies, industries, and geographical boundaries.

IFRS states that revenue recognition should be based on a contract with a customer—that is, revenue from that contractual arrangement should be recognized when it satisfies the performance obligations mentioned in the contract. Satisfying a performance obligation increases a company's net contract position. Usually a company satisfies a performance obligation only when it has transferred the good or service to the customer. This typically occurs when the customer takes physical possession of the good. However, in some situations, the transfer may be for multiple goods or services or is undertaken over a period of time. In such situations, revenue should be recognized as each promised good or service is delivered to the customer.

One of the primary areas that will be significantly affected by the new Standard is long-term (or multiyear) contracts. Currently, and as addressed earlier in this topic, U.S. GAAP allows for two methods for revenue recognition: percentage of completion and completed contract. Under the proposed Standard, the completed contract method could be used only for very stringent contracts between the firm and its customer on long-term contracts. Effectively, this would substantially reduce the use of the completed-contract method and increase the use of the percentage-of-completion method for long-term contracts.

Intangibles

IAS No. 38, *Intangible Assets*, prescribes accounting treatment for intangible assets and specifies how to measure the carrying amount and the required disclosures.

The Standard identifies intangible assets as items that are capable of being separated or divided from the entity and sold, transferred, licensed, rented, or exchanged either individually or together with a related contract. An intangible asset also must arise from contractual or other legal rights. In order for a firm to recognize an item as an intangible asset, it has to have control over the asset and be able to obtain the future economic benefit arising from that asset.

The IAS recognizes the capitalization of subsequent expenditure on in-process research and development projects provided these conditions are met:

- The technical feasibility of completing the project has been established.
- The firm has demonstrated the ability to use or sell the intangible.
- The firm intends to complete the project.
- Adequate technical, financial, and other resources are available to complete the development of the product.
- The expenditure attributable to the asset during its development can be reliably measured.

This set of criteria is more restrictive than that of U.S. GAAP, which primarily requires establishment of technical feasibility prior to capitalization of R&D costs.

Inventory

IAS No. 2, *Inventories*, prescribes accounting treatment for inventories. The primary issue in accounting for inventories is the amount of cost to be recognized as an asset and carried forward until the related revenues are recognized. Guidance is provided on determination of cost and its subsequent recognition as an expense.

The Standard requires that "cost of inventories that are not ordinarily interchangeable and goods or services produced and segregated for specific projects shall be assigned by using specific identification of their individual costs." The standards of specific identification are to be used when items are segregated for specific projects. When specific identification cannot be used, the cost of inventories "shall be assigned using either the first-in, first-out (FIFO) or weighted average cost formulas." The Standard does not permit the use of last-in, first-out (LIFO) method and in that respect differs from U.S. GAAP.

Leases

The current approach in both IFRS and U.S. GAAP is based on the assumption that finance leases (capital leases), unlike operating leases, are similar to the purchase of the underlying asset that is financed by a loan and therefore should be recognized as such. However, the structuring of lease arrangements as operating leases leads to comparability problems and is one of the techniques commonly used to attain off-balance sheet financing. Many believe that operating leases also give rise to assets and liabilities and should be recognized as such on the financial statement.

IAS No. 17, *Leases*, prescribes the appropriate accounting treatment for both the lessee and the lessor. A new Standard on lease accounting (proposed by the IASB) could affect any entity that leases items as a lessee. Accounting would change significantly for leases that are now classified as operating leases. Entities that lease assets under capital leases also would have to change the manner in which assets and liabilities are measured.

While still under discussion and not finalized, the IASB's position on lease accounting is that lease contracts create assets and liabilities that should be recognized as such on the financial statements of lessees. The IASB believes that through a rental/lease agreement, the lessee obtains the right of using the property and, therefore, should recognize it as an asset. Similarly, it also undertakes an obligation to pay the rental payments on a periodic basis, which should be recognized as a liability. If adopted, this Standard would be significantly different from what is permitted under U.S. GAAP for operating leases. Candidates for the CMA exam are urged to visit the IASB Web site at www.iasb.org for the most up-to-date information.

Property, Plant, and Equipment

IAS No. 16, *Property, Plant, and Equipment*, prescribes the accounting treatment for PPE and the related accounting for depreciation charges and impairment losses. It defines PPE as tangible items that are held for use in production or supply of goods or services and are expected to be used for more than one accounting period. Its recognition criteria are similar to U.S. GAAP in that it has to meet two conditions: future economic benefit and the cost can be measured reliably.

The Standard is specific on costs that can be capitalized as assets and those that have to be excluded. For example, an estimate of the costs of dismantling and removing the item can be capitalized at inception. Similarly, costs attributable to transporting the asset to the location have to be capitalized. Costs that cannot be capitalized as part of PPE include costs of opening a new facility and costs of conducting business at a new location.

The Standard allows the choice of either the cost model or the revaluation method for valuing PPE subsequent to initial acquisition.

- The cost method recognizes the value of PPE at its cost less accumulated depreciation.
- The revaluation method requires periodic estimation of the fair value, and the asset is carried at the fair value less any accumulated depreciation from the date of remeasurement.

Note the difference: In the cost method, the accumulated depreciation is from the date of purchase; in the revaluation method, it is from the date of remeasurement.

The Standard allows for a variety of depreciation methods to be used to allocate the cost of the asset over its useful life. These methods include the straight-line method, the diminishing balance method, and the units of production method.

Impairment

IAS No. 36, *Impairment of Assets*, provides guidance on determining the timing and amount of recognition of impairment of long-term assets. It explains the process of review for impairment, determination of the recoverable amount of asset, and when a firm should recognize (or reverse the recognition of) an impairment loss.

Procedures are prescribed to ensure that an entity carries its assets at no more than their recoverable amount. An asset is carried at more than its recoverable amount if its carrying value exceeds the amount to be recovered through use or sale of the asset. In these situations, the asset is described as impaired, and the IFRS requires the entity to recognize an impairment loss. The Standard also specifies when an entity should reverse an impairment loss. This is a departure from U.S. GAAP, in that GAAP is silent on reversals of impairment.

Knowledge Check: Recognition, Measurement, Valuation, and Disclosure

The next questions are intended to help you check your understanding of the material presented in this topic. They do not represent the type of questions that appear on the CMA exam.

Directions: Answer each question in the space provided. Correct answers and section references appear after the knowledge check questions.

Match the following types of receivables with their definitions.

1. __c__ Current receivables
2. __e__ Noncurrent receivables
3. __d__ Accounts receivable
4. __a__ Notes receivable
5. __b__ Nontrade receivables

a. Receivable evidenced by a written promise to pay on a particular date
b. Interest or dividends receivable
c. Receivables expected to be collected within a year or the operating cycle, whichever is longer
d. Informal customer promises to pay for goods sold on credit in the ordinary course of business
e. Receivables expected to be collected after one year or the operating cycle, whichever is longer

6. If inventory prices have been rising, which cost flow assumption would a firm choose in order to maximize its inventory value and its net income if it sells a high volume of inexpensive items?
   - ☐ a. LIFO
   - ☑ b. FIFO
   - ☐ c. Average cost
   - ☐ d. Specific identification

7. Trading securities should be valued at
   - ☐ a. historical cost.
   - ☑ b. market value.
   - ☐ c. present value.
   - ☐ d. net realizable value.

8. Which of the following costs should **not** be included in inventory valuation?
   - ☐ a. Manufacturing overhead costs
   - ☐ b. Cash discounts
   - ☐ c. Shipping costs (freight-in)
   - ☐ d. Interest costs related to inventory preparation

9. Which of the following methods of measuring depreciation would be based on units produced?

　☐ a.　Decreasing charge method

　☐ b.　Declining balance method

　☐ c.　Activity method

　☐ d.　Straight-line method

10. A loss contingency should be recorded if it is

　☐ a.　probable that a liability has been incurred and the loss can be reasonably estimated.

　☐ b.　reasonably possible that a liability has been incurred and the loss can be reasonably estimated.

　☐ c.　probable that a liability has been incurred and the amount of the loss is reliably documented.

　☐ d.　reasonably possible that a liability has been incurred and the amount of the loss is reliably documented.

Knowledge Check Answers: Recognition, Measurement, Valuation, and Disclosure

1. __c__ Current receivables [*See Types of Receivables.*]
2. __e__ Noncurrent receivables [*See Types of Receivables.*]
3. __d__ Accounts receivable [*See Types of Receivables.*]
4. __a__ Notes receivable [*See Types of Receivables.*]
5. __b__ Nontrade receivables [*See Types of Receivables.*]

6. If inventory prices have been rising, which cost flow assumption would a firm choose in order to maximize its inventory value and its net income if it sells a high volume of inexpensive items? [*See Cost Flow Assumptions.*]
   - ☐ a. LIFO
   - ☒ b. FIFO
   - ☐ c. Average cost
   - ☐ d. Specific identification

7. Trading securities should be valued at [*See Types of Receivables.*]
   - ☐ a. historical cost.
   - ☒ b. market value.
   - ☐ c. present value.
   - ☐ d. net realizable value.

8. Which of the following costs should **not** be included in inventory valuation? [*See What Costs to Include in Inventory.*]
   - ☐ a. Manufacturing overhead costs
   - ☐ b. Cash discounts
   - ☐ c. Shipping costs (freight-in)
   - ☒ d. Interest costs related to inventory preparation

9. Which of the following methods of measuring depreciation would be based on units produced? [*See Activity Method.*]
   - ☐ a. Decreasing charge method
   - ☐ b. Declining balance method
   - ☒ c. Activity method
   - ☐ d. Straight-line method

10. A loss contingency should be recorded if it is [See **Contingent Liabilities and Commitments**.]

    ☑ a. probable that a liability has been incurred and the loss can be reasonably estimated.

    ☐ b. reasonably possible that a liability has been incurred and the loss can be reasonably estimated.

    ☐ c. probable that a liability has been incurred and the amount of the loss is reliably documented.

    ☐ d. reasonably possible that a liability has been incurred and the amount of the loss is reliably documented.

Practice Questions: External Financial Reporting Decisions

Directions: This sampling of questions is designed to emulate actual exam questions. Read each question and write your response on another sheet of paper. Use the answer and explanation (given later in the book) to assess your response. Validate or improve the answer you wrote. For a more robust selection of practice questions, access the **Online Test Bank** at www.wileycma.com. See the "Answers to Section Practice Questions" section at the end of this book.

Question 1A1-W001
Topic: Financial Statements

The multistep income statement, with additional income statement items, for Harrington Technologies Inc. is shown next.

Net sales		$2,000,000
Less:	Cost of goods sold	890,000
Gross profit		1,110,000
Less:	Transportation and travel	45,000
	Depreciation	68,000
	Pension contributions	21,000
Operating income		976,000
Less:	Discontinued operations	76,000
Income before taxes		900,000
Less:	Tax expense @ 30%	270,000
Net Income		$630,000

Glen Hamilton, a financial analyst, analyzed the company's financial statements and concluded that the real net income should be $683,200 instead of $630,000. Which of the following arguments is **most** likely to support his conclusion?

- ☐ **a.** $53,200 due from a client was written off as irrecoverable after the finalization of accounts for the current period.
- ☐ **b.** The company valued its inventory using the specific identification method, whereas the financial analyst used the LIFO method for the current period.
- ☐ **c.** The company might have liquidated its LIFO reserve.
- ☐ **d.** The company has included expenses in relation to discontinued operations as part of income from continued operations.

Question 1A1-W002

Topic: Financial Statements

The current ratio for Garrett Inc. for the previous five years is as follows.

	Year 1	Year 2	Year 3	Year 4	Year 5
Current Ratio	5	4.5	4.9	1.2	4.2

Which of the following factor is the **most** likely reason for the low current ratio in Year 4?

- ☐ a. Materials were purchased on credit in Year 4 for which payment is due.
- ☐ b. Long-term debts were due for repayment in Year 4.
- ☐ c. The company reduced its credit period in Year 4.
- ☐ d. Working capital in Year 4 decreased due to an increase in accounts payable.

Question 1A1-W003

Topic: Financial Statements

The cash flows and net income from four business segments for Taylor Laboratories Inc. have been provided.

	Segment 1	Segment 2	Segment 3	Segment 4
Cash flow from operations	$3,000	$(250)	$(3,000)	$2,000
Cash flow from investing activities	(4,000)	6,000	8,000	(3,000)
Cash flow from financing activities	1,080	(1,000)	(1,000)	1,080
Net income	1,500	1,750	2,375	1,500

Based on the information, which segment should be discontinued by the company?

- ☐ a. Segment 3, because cash used in operations is high and cash inflow is predominantly from investing activities.
- ☐ b. Segment 1, because net income is lowest and requires high investments.
- ☐ c. Segment 4, because net income and cash inflow from operations are low.
- ☐ d. Segment 2, because cash used in operations is low and cash flow from investing activities is not properly utilized.

Question 1A1-W004
Topic: Financial Statements

The cash flow from operations for Charlene Energy Inc. is $25,000 for the current year. If the amortization expense increases by $5,000 and other factors remain same, under which of the following assumptions will the cash flow from operations remain unaffected?

- ☐ a. A change in amortization method will not have a retrospective effect.
- ☐ b. The company has an infinite life.
- ☐ c. The company is operating in a tax-free environment.
- ☐ d. The company can change the depreciation method in between a financial year.

Question 1A1-W005
Topic: Financial Statements

The following information is extracted from the latest financial information of Hines Materials Inc.

Tax rate	30%
Net Income	$15,000
Cash flow from operations	$45,000

Additional information:
1. The tax rate for the coming year is expected to increase by 2%.
2. The company is planning to purchase equipment worth $500,000 in the first quarter of next year.
3. 15% increase in capacity is expected with the use of new equipment.

Considering the given factors, which of the following would be an ideal strategy to decrease the tax liability for the next year?

- ☐ a. Defer the purchase of equipment to next year to take advantage of tax-loss carryforward.
- ☐ b. Depreciate the asset using the double-declining balance method to show higher cash flows from operations in initial years.
- ☐ c. Prepare the cash flow statement using the direct method to show lower cash from operations and lower net income.
- ☐ d. Defer the purchase of equipment to next year if a deferred tax liability can be reasonably estimated.

Question 1A1-W006
Topic: Financial Statements

The financial accountant of Eva Wolfe Corp. has ascertained the cash flows from operations as follows:

Net income	$15,000
Depreciation on equipment	2,500
Dividend income	2,500
Interest income	5,000
Increases in current assets	8,000
Increases in current liabilities	6,500
Cash flow from operations	$16,000

The company's management accountant argues that the cash flow from operations should be $8,500. Which of the following statements, if true, will support the management accountant's calculation?

- ☐ **a.** The company operates in a tax-free environment.
- ☐ **b.** The company uses IFRS to ascertain cash flow from operations.
- ☐ **c.** Cash flow from operations is ascertained using the direct method.
- ☐ **d.** Depreciation on equipment should not be added back to net income for calculating cash flows from operations.

Question 1A1-W007
Topic: Financial Statements

The management of Arthur Energy recognized a contingent liability of $50,000 in the current year. However, before the annual report was issued, the company resolved the issue, making a lump-sum payment of $42,000. The board of directors has decided to incorporate the transaction in the subsequent year's financial statements. Which of the following provisions of US GAAP, if applicable, is likely to prove the management decision wrong?

- ☐ **a.** Loss contingencies must be recognized when it is both probable that a loss has been incurred and the amount of the loss is reasonably estimable.
- ☐ **b.** Whenever GAAP or industry-specific regulations allow a choice between two or more accounting methods, the method selected should be disclosed.
- ☐ **c.** If an event alters the estimates used in preparing the financial statements, then the financial statements should be adjusted.
- ☐ **d.** If an event provides additional evidence about conditions that existed as of the balance sheet date and alters the estimates used, then the financial statements should be adjusted.

Question 1A1-W008
Topic: Financial Statements

Shelton Devin Corp. has two subsidiaries, of which 30% of ownership in each subsidiary lies with Shelton Devin. The CEO of the company is not in favor of presenting consolidated financial statements. Based on the information, which of the following is **most** likely true?

- a. The decision of the CEO is correct, as companies are required to issue consolidated statements only when the ownership exceeds 50%.
- b. The decision of the CEO is wrong, as companies are required to issue consolidated statements when the ownership exceeds 20%.
- c. The decision of the CEO is wrong, as companies are required to issue consolidated statements only if a company holds more than ten subsidiaries.
- d. The decision of the CEO is correct, as companies are required to issue consolidated statements when a company has three or more subsidiaries.

Question 1A2-W001
Topic: Recognition, Measurement, Valuation, and Disclosure

An extract of the footnotes of McGee Systems Inc., with ten subsidiaries across five countries, reads as follows:

> The company uses the temporal method for translation of subsidiary accounts. All nonmonetary balances and the expenses associated with them have been translated using historical exchange rates. Monetary assets and liabilities and other assets and liabilities measured at current values have been translated at the current exchange rate on the balance sheet date. Income statement accounts, other than nonmonetary accounts, have been translated using the historical exchange rate.

The company's CFO did not approve the financial statements, stating that the accounting policies followed are not in line with US GAAP. Which of the following statements support the CEO's decision?

- a. Income statement accounts should be translated based on the current exchange rate on the balance sheet date.
- b. Income statement accounts, other than nonmonetary accounts, should be translated based on the average rate for the current year.
- c. All assets and liabilities should be translated using the average rate for the current year.
- d. All assets and liabilities should be translated based on the spot rate for the current year.

Question 1A2-W002

Topic: Recognition, Measurement, Valuation, and Disclosure

Claire Enterprises has $150,000 in accounts receivable at the end of Year 1, and it estimates its bad debts to be 5% of the receivables. Hence, the accountant reports $7,500 as bad debts and the net realizable value as $142,500. Under which of the following circumstances will the amount of bad debts reported **most** likely reduce?

- ☐ a. If the company shortens the credit period allowed.
- ☐ b. If the company lengthens the credit period allowed.
- ☐ c. If the allowance for doubtful accounts has a credit balance of $1,500.
- ☐ d. If the allowance for doubtful accounts has a debit balance of $1,500.

Question 1A2-W003

Topic: Recognition, Measurement, Valuation, and Disclosure

The latest financial statements of Darlene Properties show 140,000 outstanding shares, par value $10. The current market value per share is $25. At the beginning of current year, the company reacquired 10,000 shares at $4 per share. The company follows the cost method for the accounting of treasury stock. The current year's books of accounts show the value of outstanding shares as follows:

Common stock, $10 par	$1,400,000
Less: Treasury stock	100,000
Net common stock, $10 par	$1,300,000

The company's CFO did not approve the financial statements. The **most** likely reason for CFO's disapproval is that:

- ☐ a. The treasury stock is incorrectly valued based on par value, instead of valuing at the acquisition price.
- ☐ b. The treasury stock is incorrectly valued based on par value, instead of valuing at the current market rate.
- ☐ c. The par value of the treasury stock should be presented as a deduction from par value of issued shares of the same class
- ☐ d. The treasury stock should be reported as an asset.

Practice Question: External Financial Reporting Decisions

Question 1A2-W004

Topic: Recognition, Measurement, Valuation, and Disclosure

Rogers Electronics is planning to make a market in the company's stock. The company's CFO suggests the reacquisition of shares. Which of the following is **most** likely to happen if the CFO's suggestion is implemented?

- ☐ a. The risk of takeovers by competitors will increase.
- ☐ b. This will hinder exercise of employee stock options.
- ☐ c. The stock price will increase.
- ☐ d. This could serve as an indication of the company's negative outlook about its future performance.

Question 1A2-W005

Topic: Recognition, Measurement, Valuation, and Disclosure

AWS Inc. is engaged in the construction of rail tracks. The CEO suggests allocating insurance, property taxes, and supervisory factory labor to construction. But the management accountant opines that a proportional amount of such indirect costs should be allocated to the rail tracks. Which of the following, if true, will support the management accountant's argument?

- ☐ a. The indirect costs were allocated to the extent of the difference between net realizable value and carrying value.
- ☐ b. The indirect costs were allocated to the extent of proportionate completion.
- ☐ c. The costs incurred on the rail tracks were in excess of their market value.
- ☐ d. The indirect costs were not capitalized to the rail tracks.

Question 1A2-W006

Topic: Recognition, Measurement, Valuation, and Disclosure

Calvin Software has invested in the equity stock of BioTech Corp. Its holdings consist of 35% of the voting stock. The CFO suggests acquiring more stock of BioTech. Based on the information, which of the following will be **true**?

- ☐ a. Additional acquisitions beyond 15% will require Calvin Software to issue consolidated financial statements.
- ☐ b. Calvin's total value will decrease as incidental costs of acquisition must be subtracted when holdings exceed 35%.
- ☐ c. The circumstances leading to the decision to acquire additional shares shall be disclosed in the notes to the financial statements.
- ☐ d. Any additional acquisition of assets up to 20% should be classified as held to maturity.

Question 1A2-W007

Topic: Recognition, Measurement, Valuation, and Disclosure

Warner Machines missed recording purchases worth $10,000 in the current year's income statement. While finalizing the financial statements, the company's accountant detected the error and partially corrected it. Under which of the following situations will the company report lower than actual net income?

- ☐ a. If the accountant has reduced cash by $10,000
- ☐ b. If the accountant has added the missing purchases worth only $10,000 to the cost of goods sold
- ☐ c. If the accountant has increased accounts payable only by $10,000
- ☐ d. If the accountant has reduced inventory by $10,000

Question 1A2-W008

Topic: Recognition, Measurement, Valuation, and Disclosure

Sandra Bellucci, a financial analyst, is analyzing inventory of companies from four different industries: consumer goods, sports goods manufacturers, electronics, and aircraft manufacturers. Assuming the inventory valuation methods reflect the actual flow of inventory and the inventory includes only finished goods, which of the following industries will **most** likely have zero LIFO reserve?

- ☐ a. Consumer goods
- ☐ b. Sports goods manufacturers
- ☐ c. Electronics
- ☐ d. Aircraft manufacturers

To further assess your understanding of the concepts and calculations covered in Part 1, Section A: External Financial Reporting Decisions, practice with the **Online Test Bank** for this section. REMINDER: See the "Answers to Section Practice Questions" section at the end of this book.

SECTION B

Planning, Budgeting, and Forecasting

How do some companies become great successes while others flounder? Successful companies have a strategy that is based on accurate information from both external and internal sources. They match their internal strengths to the best external opportunities available. But a good strategy is not enough. Companies need to convert an overall strategy into action. This is the purpose of a budget. A budget is a detailed plan for executing both long-term and short-term goals. A successful budget not only provides cost controls but also makes sure that day-to-day operations take the company where it wants to be in the future.

This section covers strategic planning as well as basic budgeting concepts and forecasting techniques that provide the assumptions on which budgets are based. It discusses various budget methodologies and their applications and explores the master budget in detail. It demonstrates, with case study examples, how a company can use components of a master budget to analyze its performance and operations.

Learning Outcome Statements Overview: Planning, Budgeting, and Forecasting

Section B.1. Strategic Planning

A. Discuss how strategic planning determines the path an organization chooses for attaining its long-term goals and mission.
   a. An organization's strategic plan is a long-term plan that flows directly from the organization's vision and mission. The strategic plan is used to develop long-term goals for the organization. The organization sets long-term objectives as milestones to be achieved on the way to attaining the objectives.
B. Identify the time frame appropriate for a strategic plan.
   a. The time frame for strategic planning is normally five to ten years. It may, however, be longer.
C. Identify the external factors that should be analyzed during the strategic planning process, and understand how this analysis leads to recognition of organizational opportunities, limitations, and threats.
   a. The external factors to consider are the external or environmental opportunities and threats that face the organization. Opportunities are those things that would enhance the organization's competitive position and profitability. Threats are risks that, if they occur, would be detrimental to the organization's competitive position and profitability.
D. Identify the internal factors that should be analyzed during the strategic planning process, and explain how this analysis leads to recognition of organizational strengths, weaknesses, and competitive advantages.
   a. The internal factors to consider are the organization's strengths and weaknesses. Strengths are those things that would enhance the organization's competitive position and profitability; weaknesses are those that detract from its competitive position and profitability.
E. Demonstrate an understanding of how mission leads to the formulation of long-term business objectives, such as business diversification, the addition or deletion of product lines, or the penetration of new markets.

      a. Long-term goals and objectives include such things as:
- Business diversification
- Product differentiation
- Cost leadership
- New markets

F. Explain why short-time objectives, tactics for achieving these objectives, and operational planning (master budget) must be congruent with the strategic plan and contribute to the achievement of long-term strategic goals.
      a. Short-term objectives and the tactics to achieve them should flow directly from the organization's strategic plan and should be designed to achieve the goals and objectives set forth in the strategic plan. The short-term objectives would be milestones along the road to the achievement of the long-term goals.

G. Identify the characteristics of a successful strategic plan.
      a. A successful strategic plan is one that assists the organization in achieving its long-term goals and objectives. It has well-defined goals consistent with the strategic plan and the mission from which the plan we derived. It also has SMART objectives, objectives that are:
- Specific
- Measurable
- Achievable
- Realistic
- Timely

H. Describe Porter's generic strategies, including cost leadership, differentiation, and focus.
      a. Cost leadership implies that the company has the lowest product costs in either the entire industry or within an industry segment.
      b. Differentiation implies that the company produces better products or services in the industry or within an industry segment.
      c. Focus implies attention to an industry segment.

I. Demonstrate an understanding of the following planning tools and techniques: SWOT analysis, Porter's five forces, situational analysis, PEST analysis, scenario planning, competitive analysis, contingency planning, and the BCG Growth Share Matrix.
      a. SWOT analysis involves identifying and understanding the organization's strengths and weaknesses (internal factors) and the opportunities and threats external to the organization. A SWOT analysis helps the organization utilize and maximize its strengths, minimize and correct its weaknesses, exploit opportunities, and avoid or minimize risks. Strengths and weaknesses were noted earlier in item D, while opportunities and threats were discussed in item C earlier.
      b. Michael Porter's five forces industry analysis involves analyzing the organization's environment to identify and minimize threats posed by the organization's competitors, supplies, and customers. The model is Porter's

reaction to the ad hoc nature and lack of rigor in the SWOT analysis. These are the five forces:
- The threat of new entrants to the marketplace
- The threat of the introduction of substitute products or services by competitors
- Rivalry among competitors.
- The bargaining power of customers
- The bargaining power of suppliers

c. Situational analysis is a collection of tools that an organization may use to analyze and understand both its internal and its external environments. It consists of SWOT analysis and Porter's five forces as well as 5C analysis. The 5Cs are: the company, its competitors, its customers, its collaborators, and the climate the company operates in. Company analysis covers the organization's goals and objectives, market position, performance related to its stated mission, and its product line. Competitor analysis looks at the positions of the organization's competition and the threats they may impose. Customer analysis encompasses an understanding of past, present, and future customers and their demographics. Collaborator analysis includes an understanding of agents, supplies, distributors, and business partners. The understanding of organization's climate includes understanding the political, regulatory, economic, social, cultural, and technological environments.

d. PEST analysis involves an understanding of the organization's political, economic, social, and technological environments. Its focus is on the opportunities and threats in the organization's environment.

e. Scenario planning, also called scenario thinking or scenario analysis, is a strategic planning methodology designed to assist the organization in developing flexible strategic plans. It involves simulating or gaming the expected behavior of what are called STEEEPA trends. STEEEPA is an acronym for plausible alternative social, technical, economic, environmental, educational, political, and aesthetic trends. These are the key driving forces in the organization's environment. Again, the focus is on opportunities and threats and developing coping mechanisms.

f. Competitive analysis, commonly called competitor analysis, focuses on understanding one's competition. It includes knowing who the competition really is rather than who the organization thinks it is. It involves profiling competitors regarding history, products and services, financial condition, corporate and marketing strategies, facilities, and personnel. It also encourages the organization to scan the environment for potential new customers.

g. Contingency planning, also called continuity or sustainability planning or plan B, is a process that helps prepare an organization to respond effectively to unplanned events. Contingency plans are part of risk management. They are used to respond to exceptional relatively unlikely risks that if they occur could have catastrophic effects on the organization.

h. The BCG (Boston Consulting Group) Growth Share Matrix looks at the company's products or services as one of the following: stars, cash cows, dogs, or question marks. Stars are products or services with high growth rates and high cash generation capabilities. Cash cows have high cash generation capabilities but low growth rates. Dogs have low cash generation capabilities and low growth rates. Question marks have high growth rates but low cash generation capabilities.

Section B.2. Budgeting Concepts

A. Describe the role that budgeting plays in the overall planning and performance evaluation process of an organization.
   a. Strategy is the organization's plan to match its strengths with the opportunities in the marketplace to accomplish its desired goals over the short and long term. A budget provides the foundation for planning, because a successful budget is created by a process of aligning the company's resources with its strategy. Budgets play a role in measuring performance against established goals.

B. Explain the interrelationships between economic conditions, industry situation, and a firm's plans and budgets.
   a. There are a significant number of interrelationships among economic conditions, industry situations, organizational plans, and the budgeting process. Budgeting is most effective when the budgeting process is linked to the overall strategy of the organization. Managers should build their strategy and organizational objectives to focus on all economic factors, including the financial impact of the decision-making process and understanding factors of competition.

C. Identify the role that budgeting plays in formulating short-term objectives and planning and controlling operations to meet those objectives.
   a. Short-term plans are established in order to meet the organization's long-term strategic objectives. Budgeting is a tool that an entity uses in order to identify the resources and commitments needed in order to satisfy the short-term goals. If done correctly, budgets are planned, maintained, and adjusted in order to control operations to meet those objectives.

D. Demonstrate an understanding of the role that budgets play in measuring performance against established goals.
   a. Budgets represent a quantitative map of how the organization is to accomplish its short- and long-term goals. At the end of an accounting period, an organization can use the actual results to measure the performance against the goal that it established in order to meet its goals. The variances can be analyzed so that adjustments can be made to operations to stay on track.

E. Identify the characteristics that define successful budgeting processes.
   a. Characteristics of a successful budget process include:
      i. Budget period—Management must consider what the most suitable length of time would be to suit the needs of the organization.
      ii. Participants in the budget process—Three groups make or break a budget: the board of directors, top management, and the budget committee. Middle and lower management also play a significant role, because they create detailed budgets based on upper management's plan.
      iii. Basic steps in budgeting—The steps that responsibility centers take in preparing their budgets include the initial budget proposal, budget negotiation, review and approval, and revision.
      iv. Use of cost standards—Organizations set different types of standards that they strive to achieve in order to meet their goals.
F. Explain how the budgeting process facilitates communication among organizational units and enhances coordination of organizational activities.
   a. Budgeting promotes communication and coordination of efforts within the organization. The different parts of the organization (production, marketing, materials management, etc.) must communicate their plans and needs to each other during the budget process so that all can evaluate the effect that the plans and needs of others have on their own.
G. Describe the concept of a controllable cost as it relates to both budgeting and performance evaluation.
   a. Costs are considered "controllable" or "discretionary" when the purchaser or manager has discretion in whether to incur the charge or alter the level of the charge in a short amount of time. Variable costs and other costs directly under the control of the manager are controllable costs. It is useful to identify these costs to evaluate the performance of a manager. A manager should not be evaluated on costs that are out of his or her control.
H. Explain how the efficient allocation of organizational resources are planned during the budgeting process.
   a. All entities have a finite amount of resources and want to make the most of their capital. The allocation of scarce resources among competing opportunities is accomplished through implementation of a strategy. When a budget exists without consideration of strategy, it usually begins with the prior year's budget and misses opportunities to change the direction of the company, causing stagnation.
I. Identify the appropriate time frame for various types of budgets.
   a. Long-term budgeting is usually a five- to ten-year plan of actions required to achieve the company's goals. Capital budgeting is the process of allocating resources to an entity's proposed long-term projects.
   b. Short-term budgeting is usually quarterly or annual results and represents variations in the long-term plan that result from capital budgeting, operating results of past periods, and expected future results caused by the current economic, social, industrial, and technological environment.

J. Identify who should participate in the budgeting process for optimum success.
   a. Three groups make or break a budget: the board of directors, top management, and the budget committee. Middle and lower management also play a significant role, because they create detailed budgets based on upper management's plan.

K. Describe the role of top management in successful budgeting.
   a. Top management is ultimately responsible for the budgets. The primary means top managers have of exercising this responsibility is to ensure that all levels of management understand and support the budget and the overall budget control process. If top management is not perceived to endorse a budget, line managers will be less likely to follow the budget precisely.
   b. Top management provides final budget approval.

L. Identify best practice guidelines for the budget process.
   a. There are two main methods of preparing budgets: the authoritative budget (top-down budget) and the participative budget (bottom-up budget). The ideal process combines the features of each and falls somewhere between these methods. The five steps in a combined approach include:
      i. Budget participants are identified, including representatives of all levels of management as well as key employees with expertise in particular areas.
      ii. Top management communicates the strategic direction to budget participants.
      iii. Budget participants create the first draft of their budget.
      iv. Lower levels submit budgets to the next higher level for review in an iterative process stressing communication in both directions.
      v. Rigorous but fair review and budget approval by top management sets the final budget.

M. Demonstrate an understanding of the use of cost standards in budgeting.
   a. Standards are any carefully determined price, quantity, service level, or cost. They are used in the budgeting process to align costs that an entity expects to incur with the final budget. Different types of standards (ideal or practical) can be used to set levels that management should attempt to reach in order to stay on budget.

N. Differentiate between ideal (theoretical) standards and currently attainable (practical) standards.
   a. Ideal standards—Forward-looking goals; they are currently attainable only if all circumstances result in the *best* possible outcome. Ideal standards work into a continuous improvement strategy and total quality management philosophies. They allow for no work delays, interruptions, waste, or machine breakdowns. Ideal standards require a level of effort that can be attained only by the most skilled and efficient employees working at their best efficiency all of the time.
   b. Currently attainable standards—Closer to historical standards; they set goals at a level that is attainable by properly trained individuals operating at a normal pace. The standards are expected to be reached most of the time. They allow for normal work delays, spoilage, waste, employee rest

periods, and machine downtime. Practical standards can be attained by efficient efforts from an average worker. Currently attainable standards are also called reasonably attainable standards.

O. Differentiate between authoritative standards and participative standards.
   a. Authoritative standards—Standards determined solely by management. They are set more speedily and can closely match overall company goals but may be a cause for resentment or may not be followed at all (top-down approach).
   b. Participative standards—Standards set by holding a dialogue between management and all involved parties. They are more likely to be adopted than authoritative standards, but they take more time and require negotiation to ensure that operating goals still are met.

P. Identify the steps to be taken in developing standards for both direct material and direct labor.
   a. Direct materials standards are determined by quality, quantity, and price objectives. Quality is determined first to align with the company's strategy (price leader, innovator, etc.). Once the quality is determined and standards have allowed for losses, spoilage, scrap, and waste, the quantity can be determined to align with management's estimates of demand. After quantity is determined, a price is set by selecting vendors in the supply chain that align with the company strategy.
   b. Direct labor standards are determined in a similar way as the materials for the product. The quality of the workforce should be determined based on the strategic goals of the company. Based on the quality of the workforce, the organization can align the amount and price that the labor will cost. Direct labor standards are adjusted for expected breaks, downtime, and spoilage.

Q. Demonstrate an understanding of the techniques that are used to develop standards, such as activity analysis and the use of historical data.
   a. Activity analysis—Identifies, codifies, and analyzes the activities needed to finish a job or operation. Activity analyses in activity-based costing are the most thorough costing method—and are the most expensive to implement.
   b. Historical data—Relying on historical data for determining costs is relatively inexpensive but is less reliable than activity analysis. When reliable, historical data can be used to find the average or median historical cost for an operation. To implement continuous improvement, the best performance recorded could be used as a standard or, at least, as an ideal standard.

R. Discuss the importance of a policy that allows budget revisions that accommodate the impact of significant changes in budget assumptions.
   a. Rigidly following a budget in the face of changing circumstances has the potential for disaster. Management should not be required to rely on the budget as the sole operational guideline. Regular revisions may provide better operating guidelines; however, this may lead managers to anticipate regular changes and not prepare budgets as carefully as they should.

S. Explain the role of budgets in monitoring and controlling expenditures to meet strategic objectives.

a. If the budget process is followed in accordance with best practices, the budget should be aligned with the overall long-term strategic objectives of upper management. If an organization takes the time to create, monitor, and improve budgets, they will serve as a tool to monitor and control expenditures that will eventually meet strategic objectives.
T. Define budgetary slack, and discuss its impact on goal congruence.
   a. Budgetary slack—Occurs when budgeted performance differs from actual performance because managers tend to build in some extra money for their budget to deal with unexpected events. Budgetary slack is built-in freedom to fail, and cumulative budgetary slack at each sublevel can result in a very inaccurate master budget.
   b. Budgetary slack usually involves over-budgeting expenses and under-budgeting revenues to allow "breathing" room.

Section B.3. Forecasting Techniques

A. Demonstrate an understanding of a simple regression equation.
   a. The simple regression equation attempts to measure the relationship between two variables (independent and dependent variables). For example, a simple linear regression can show how sales (dependent variable) are driven by each dollar spent on marketing (independent variable). Three common measures are used to evaluate the reliability of the regression equation: R-squared, T-value, and standard error of estimate.
      i. R-squared—A value between 0 and 1 indicating the degree to which changes in a dependent variable can be predicted by changes in independent variables (goodness of fit). It measures the percentage of the variability—the dependent variable explained by the variability in the independent variable(s).
      ii. T-value—Measures whether an independent variable (X) has a valid, long-term relationship to a dependent variable. Generally, the T-value should be more than 2. A variable with a low T-value indicates little or no statistically significant relationship between the independent and dependent variables.
      iii. Standard error of estimate—Measures the dispersion around the regression line and allows the user to assess the accuracy of predictions. That is, a user can build a confidence interval around the estimate.
B. Define a multiple regression equation and recognize when multiple regression is an appropriate tool to use for forecasting.
   a. A multiple regression model looks very similar to a simple regression model, except that it has two or more independent variables (X_1, X_2, etc). In the example above, more independent variables (i.e., economy, pricing, competitors, etc.) would be used to help determine, or explain, a change in the dependent variable (sales). Organizations should use multiple regression analysis when the dependent variable can't be well explained by just one independent variable.

C. Calculate the result of a simple regression equation.
   a. The simple regression equation is:

   $Y = a + bX$

   where

   Y = annual sales; it is the dependent variable to be forecast.

   a = amount of Y when X = 0. This value is also called the Y intercept, because when X = 0, Y = a, and on a graph, the line will intercept the Y axis at the value of a.

   b = slope of the line, also known as the regression coefficient. It represents the impact X has on Y. For every one unit change in X, Y is expected to change by b units.

   X = value for the independent variable (in this case, marketing costs) or the driver for the dependent variable to be forecast (in this case, annual sales).

   See Topic 3: Forecasting Techniques for applications of the formula.

D. Demonstrate an understanding of learning curve analysis.
   a. Learning curve analysis—A systematic method for estimating costs based on increased learning by the business, group, or individual, which allows them to become more efficient at completing tasks. As a result, costs will decrease as learning increases. The learning curve can be measured by the incremental unit-time learning model or the cumulative average-time learning model.

E. Calculate the results under a cumulative average-time learning model.
   a. Cumulative average-time model—Measures increased efficiency due to learning. It calculates cumulative total time by multiplying the incremental unit by the cumulative average time per unit. As the cumulative output doubles, the cumulative average output time per unit becomes the learning curve percentage times the previous cumulative average time. The fourth unit will take 6.4 hours (8 × .8).
   b. Incremental unit-time learning model—Measures increased efficiency by adding the incremental time for each unit to the previous total time. Average time per unit is then calculated by dividing total time by number of units. As the cumulative output doubles, the time for that unit becomes the learning curve percentage multiplied by the previous time.

      For example: Assume that one new worker can assemble the first widget in 10 hours. If one worker assembles both widgets, the first unit will take 10 hours, but because of the worker's learning experience, the second unit will take only 8 hours, assuming learning takes place at a rate of 80% (.8 × 10 hours = 8 hours). The total time to build the two widgets is 18 hours, so the average production time per widget is 9 hours.

Section B—Planning, Budgeting, and Forecasting

c. The two models are shown in the following two tables.

Under the cumulative average-time model, the 80% learning curve gets applied as follows:

X	Cumulative Average Time per Widget* (c)	Cumulative Total Time (c × X)	Individual Time for xth Widget
1	10 (value of c)	10 (10 × 1)	10
2	8 (10 × 0.8)	16 (8 × 2)	6 (16 − 10)
4	6.4 (8 × 0.8)	25.6 (6.4 × 4)	4.54†
8	5.12 (6.4 × 0.8)	40.96 (5.12 × 8)	3.55†

* Each c = rate (0.8 here) × the preceding value of variable c.

† Calculated by a formula not shown here.

F. List the benefits and shortcomings of regression analysis and learning curve analysis.
   a. Regression analysis
      i. Benefits
         - Gives management an objective measure to use in evaluating the precision and reliability of estimations.
      ii. Shortcomings
         - Can be influenced strongly by outliers.
         - Assumes a linear relationship between two or more variables.
         - Assumes past relationships will hold true in the future.
   b. Learning curve analysis
      i. Benefits
         - Helps organizations set prices based on increased learning.
         - Knowledge can help company gain market share by pricing lower.
      ii. Shortcomings
         - Not useful for machine-intensive jobs, as learning curve analysis only applies to labor hours.
         - Learning rate is assumed constant—likely not the case.
         - Conclusions might be unreliable.

G. Calculate the expected value of random variables.
   a. Expected value is a similar computation to a weighted average computation. The formula is the sum of the probability of occurrence multiplied by the amount of the outcome.

   Expected Value (EV) − $\Sigma S \times (P_x)$

   where:

   EV = expected value

   Σ = sum of the variables that follow in the equation

   S = amount associated with a specific outcome

   P_x = probability associated with a specific outcome

H. Identify the benefits and shortcomings of expected value techniques.
   a. Benefits
      - Helps an organization determine the average outcome of an event when faced with uncertainties.
   b. Shortcomings
      - The expected value calculation is only as good as the estimated potential outcomes for each scenario and the probability assigned to each scenario.
      - Doesn't take into account risk of the decision maker. It assumes the decision maker is risk neutral.
I. Use probability values to estimate future cash flows.
   a. The expected value computation can be used to estimate future cash flows as follows:

Economic Condition	Sales Forecast (a)	Probability (b)	Value (a × b)
Boom	$3,000,000	0.1	300,000
Average	$2,000,000	0.8	1,600,000
Recession	$600,000	0.1	60,000
	Expected Value		1,960,000

Section B.4. Budget Methodologies

For each of the budget systems identified (annual/master budget, project budget, activity-based budget, zero-based budget, continuous (rolling) budgets, and flexible budgeting), the candidate should be able to:

A. Define its purpose, appropriate use, and time frame.
   a. Annual/master budget—Comprehensive budget for a year or less to show every aspect of the company's revenue and cost flows to produce pro forma financial information.
   b. Project budgeting—Used when a project is completely separate from other elements of a company or is the only element of the company (i.e., construction of a building). The time frame is the duration of the project.
   c. Activity-based budgeting—Focuses on activities instead of departments or products. Each activity is matched with the most appropriate cost driver, which is any volume-based or activity-based unit of measurement of the cost of a job or activity needed to sustain operations. The time frame is usually short term but continuous.
   d. Zero-based budget—Focuses on constant cost justification of each and every item in a budget. Managers must conduct in-depth reviews of each area under their control to provide such justification instead of merely taking historical figures and making minor adjustments.
   e. Continuous (rolling) budget—Adds a new period onto the budget at the end of each period so there are always several periods planned for the future

and the budgets remain up to date with the operating environment. The time frame for this budget always remains the same since one period drops off as another is added.

    f. Flexible budgeting—Establishes a base cost budget for a particular level of output (a cost-volume relationship), plus an incremental cost-volume amount that shows the behavior of costs at various volumes. Only the variable costs are adjusted; fixed costs remain unchanged. The most common use of a flexible budget is to show the budget that would have been made if the organization had matched its sales forecast exactly.

B. Identify the budget components and explain the interrelationships among the components.

    a. The budget systems identified above all contain similar components and are interrelated to each other. Each of the systems attempts to derive an effective planning and management tool that supports and reinforces the overall company strategy. The budget system used is dependent on the complexity of the business, the maturity of the company, and the tone at the top. The availability of a range of budget methods enables an organization, and its constituent departments and divisions, to create budgets that are meaningful and appropriate to requirements. For more detailed information on what components can be found in a budget, see Topic 5: Annual Profit Plan and Supporting Schedules.

C. Demonstrate an understanding of how the budget is developed.

    a. Annual/master budget—The master budget is a compilation of each of the individual budgets (i.e., sales, production, general and administrative expenses, etc.). Those budgets are prepared based on forecasts and wrap up into the master budget to create the pro forma financial statements of a company.

    b. Project budget—A project budget is developed like a master budget except that the costs are focused on the individual project instead of the company as a whole. For example, a project budget to build a new building would include only the costs associated with that building, not any company overhead or sales items for that company that were not related to the new building.

    c. Activity-based budget—Costs are divided into cost pools, such as unit, batch, product, and facility. Cost pools include homogeneous costs that all vary in the same proportion to the rise and fall of production. Fixed costs are in one pool, and different levels of variable costs are in their own pools. Once the pools (activities) are defined, an activity rate is determined based on the estimated total usage to the overall cost. That activity rate can then be applied to activities based on their individual usage.

Activity	Usage	Activity Rate	Activity Cost
Machine setup	80 setup	$4000/setup	$320,000
Fabrication	1,700 DLH*	$5/DLH	8,500
Assembly	6,000 DLH	$12/DLH	72,000
Inspection	100 inspections	$2,500/inspection	250,000
Engineering changes	15 changes	$10,000/changes	150,000
Total overhead cost			$800,500

*DLH stands for direct labor hours.

d. Zero-based budgeting—The first step in developing a zero-based budget is to have each department manager rank all department activities from most to least important and assign a cost to each activity. Upper management asks questions, such as "Should the activity be performed? If it is not, what will happen?" or "Are there substitute methods of providing this function, such as outsourcing or customer self-service?" Benchmarks and standards can be used to develop the budget figures instead of just relying on historical numbers.

e. Continuous (rolling) budget—A continuous budget initially is developed just like any other budgets. The difference is that instead of preparing, for example, an annual budget at the beginning of each year, the budget is reviewed monthly as time passes. The most recent period is dropped off and a new period at the end is added.

f. Flexible budget—A flexible budget is used more as a variance analysis tool than a planning tool. A budget is created, using any of the methods described, with estimates of per-unit revenues and variable costs. At the end of the period, the budget is adjusted to reflect what it would have looked like had management been spot on with the units produced and sold. For example, if management estimated that 1,000 units were going to be produced and sold at a cost of $15 per unit, the original budget would have shown $15,000 in budgeted costs. If the demand came in lower, say, 800 units, at a total cost of $13,600, it would appear that the company came in under budget. However, after adjusting the budget to 800 units at $15 per unit (the flexible budget), the variance would be apparent. The company should have spent only $12,000 on those $800 instead of $13,600.

D. Compare and contrast the benefits and limitations of the budget system.
   a. Annual/master budget—As discussed, the master budget is extremely beneficial to the organization in order to align company strategy with operations. However, the exercise may be a waste of time if the process is not well implemented or the results are ignored.
   b. Project budget—Project budget advantages include the ability to contain all of a project's costs so that its individual impact can be easily measured. A potential limitation of a project budget occurs when projects use resources and staff that are committed to the entire organization rather than dedicated to the project.
   c. Activity-based budget—Proponents believe that traditional costing obscures the relationships between costs and outputs by oversimplifying the measurements into such categories as labor hours, machine hours, or output units for an entire process or department. Instead of using only volume drivers as a measurement tool, an activity-based budget uses activity-based cost drivers, such as number of setups, to make a clear connection between resource consumption and output. Although this may provide greater precision in determining costs, a potential drawback can occur if the cost of designing and maintaining the system exceeds the cost savings from better planning.

      d. Zero-based budget—Theoretically, a zero-based budget has the advantage of focusing on every line item instead of just the exceptions. Such a budget should motivate managers to identify and remove items that are more costly than the benefits provided. One issue with zero-based budgets is the time-consuming and expensive annual review process. As a result, the review often is less thorough than it should be.

      e. Continuous (rolling) budget—A continuous budget is more relevant than a budget prepared once a year. It can reflect current events and changes in its estimates, and it has the advantage of breaking down a large process into manageable steps. Potential disadvantages of a continuous budget include the need to have a budget coordinator and/or the opportunity cost of having managers use part of each month working on the next month's budget.

      f. Flexible budget—The benefits of using a flexible budget include the ability to make better use of historical budget information to improve future planning. There are few disadvantages to using a flexible budget, but there is the potential for the firm to focus principally on the flexible budget level of output and disregard the fact that the sales target was missed.

E. Evaluate a business situation and recommend the appropriate budget solution.
    a. From the information contained in this outline, you should be able to assess the appropriate budget for a given situation. For more detailed analysis, see Topic 4: Budgeting Methodologies.

F. Prepare budgets on the basis of information presented.
    a. From the information contained in this outline, you should be able to prepare budgets on the basis of information presented. For more detailed analysis, see Topic 4: Budgeting Methodologies.

G. Calculate the impact of incremental changes to budgets.
    a. An incremental budget is a general type of budget that starts with the prior year's budget and uses projected changes in sales and the operating environment to adjust individual items in the budget up or down. It is the opposite of a zero-based budget. For example, if sales last year were $1,500,000 and management estimates that there will be a 10% increase in sales, the budget would estimate sales of $1,650,000. The remaining components of the budgets are derived using similar logic.

Section B.5. Annual Profit Plan and Supporting Schedules

A. Explain the role of the sales budget in the development of an annual profit plan.
    a. A sales budget (or forecast) is a subjective estimate of the entity's future sales for the upcoming period. Without an accurate sales forecast, all other budget elements will be inaccurate since they are driven by estimated demand.

B. Identify the factors that should be considered when preparing a sales budget.
    a. Forecasters consider not only historical trends for sales but also economic and industry conditions and indicators, competitors' actions, rising costs, policies on pricing and extending credit, the amount of advertising and

marketing expenditures, the number of unfilled back orders, and sales in the sales pipeline (unsigned prospects). Sales forecasts should use statistical analysis techniques, such as regression analysis and time series analysis, and rely on sales managers' knowledge about their market and customer needs.

C. Identify the components of a sales budget and prepare a sales budget.
   a. The two key components of the sales budget are the projected number of units of sales and the projected selling prices. A sales budget may look like the next chart:

Robin Manufacturing Company Sales Budget for the Quarter Ended September 30, Year 1

	July	August	September	Quarter
Sales in units	70,000	72,000	77,000	219,000
Selling price per unit	$110.80	$110.80	$112.00	(varies)
Total sales	$7,756,000	$7,977,600	$8,624,000	$24,357,600

D. Explain the relationship between the sales budget and the production budget.
   a. Once the desired level of sales is determined (from the sales budget), the production budget is created to satisfy the expected demand, plus or minus desired changes in inventory levels.

E. Identify the role that inventory levels play in the preparation of a production budget, and define other factors that should be considered when preparing a production budget.
   a. The production budget is a plan for acquiring resources and combining them to meet sales goals and maintain a certain level of inventory. The budgeted production is calculated as:

   Budgeted Production = Budgeted Sales + Desired Ending Inventory − Beginning Inventory

F. Prepare a production budget.
   a. The production budget for Robin Manufacturing Company (above) would be derived from the estimated number of units sold from the sales budget. Adjustments are then made for desired changes in inventory levels.

Robin Manufacturing Company Production Budget for the Quarter Ended September 30, Year 1

	July	August	September	Quarter
Budgeted sales in units	70,000	72,000	77,000	219,000
Add: Desired ending inventory of finished goods	10,000	11,000	12,000	12,000
Total units needed	80,000	83,000	89,000	231,000
Less: Beginning inventory of finished goods	8,000	10,000	11,000	8,000
Budgeted production in units	72,000	73,000	78,000	223,000

G. Demonstrate an understanding of the relationship between the direct materials budget, the direct labor budget, and the production budget.
   a. After the production budget is completed, management can budget how much to spend on materials and how much labor is necessary to complete the desired units.
H. Explain how inventory levels and procurement policies affect the direct materials budget.
   a. The production budget specifies only the number of units to be produced. The usage budget specifies the amount and cost of materials needed for the production and the amount and cost of materials that must be purchased to meet the production requirement. The direct materials budget takes the production budget one step further based on the number of materials needed to make one finished good and the estimated cost of those materials.
I. Prepare direct materials and direct labor budgets based on relevant information, and evaluate the feasibility of achieving production goals on the basis of these budgets.
   a. The formula for determining the units of direct materials needed is the same as the production budget. The next chart illustrates Robin Manufacturing Company's direct material budget, assuming five units of materials for each finished unit.

Robin Manufacturing Company Direct Materials Purchase Budget for the Quarter Ended September 30, Year 1

	July	August	September	Quarter
Total direct materials needed in production	360,000	365,000	390,000	1,115,000
Add: Desired ending inventory	35,000	35,000	40,000	40,000
Total direct materials required	395,000	400,000	430,000	1,155,000
Less: Direct materials beginning inventory	35,000	35,000	35,000	35,000
Direct materials purchases	360,000	365,000	395,000	1,120,000
Purchase price per pound	$13.00	$13.25	$13.35	
Total cost for direct materials purchases	$4,680,000	$4,836,250	$5,253,500	$14,769,750

   b. The direct labor budget specifies the direct labor requirement needed to meet the production need based on the production budget. Total estimated direct labor hours required to produce one unit is multiplied total units to determine total direct labor hours. That number is then multiplied by the estimated cost of labor. The next chart illustrates Robin Manufacturing Company's direct labor budget.

Robin Manufacturing Company Direct Labor Budget for the Quarter Ended September 30, Year 1

	July	August	September	Quarter
Budgeted production	72,000	73,000	78,000	223,000
DLH* required per unit	× 0.5	× 0.5	× 0.5	
DLH needed	36,000	36,500	39,000	111,500
Hourly rate	× $15	× $15	× $15	
Total wages for direct labor	$540,000	$547,500	$585,000	$1,672,500

*DLH stands for direct labor hours.

J. Demonstrate an understanding of the relationship between the overhead budget and the production budget.
   a. All other production costs that are not in the direct materials and direct labor budgets are in the overhead budget. These account for costs that tend to be fixed instead of variable. They are not included in the other budgets as they typically don't vary based on production volumes.
K. Separate costs into their fixed and variable components.
   a. Variable costs vary with changes in production volume. Variable costs include: direct materials, direct labor, utilities, shipping, and the like.
   b. Fixed costs do not vary with changes in production volume. Fixed costs include: rent, insurance, manager's salaries, and the like.
L. Prepare an overhead budget.
   a. The variable portion of overhead complicates the overhead budget to some degree. Managers estimate the cost of the variable components based on the labor hours required from the direct labor budgets. (Machine hours also can be used.) The next chart illustrates Robin Manufacturing Company's overhead budget:

Robin Manufacturing Company Factory Overhead Budget for the Quarter Ended September 30, Year 1

	Rate per DLH*	July	August	September	Quarter
Total DLHs (See Figure 1B-34)		36,000	36,500	39,000	111,500
Variable factory overhead					
Supplies	$0.20	$7,200	$7,300	$7,800	$22,300
Fringe benefits	4.10	147,600	149,650	159,900	457,150
Utilities	1.00	36,000	36,500	39,000	111,500
Maintenance	0.50	18,000	18,250	19,500	55,750
Total variable factory overhead	$5.80	$208,800	$211,700	$226,200	$646,700
Fixed factory overhead					

	Rate per DLH*	July	August	September	Quarter
Depreciation		$20,000	$20,000	$20,000	$60,000
Plant insurance		800	800	800	2,400
Property taxes		1,200	1,200	1,200	3,600
Salary supervision		10,000	10,000	10,000	30,000
Indirect labor		72,000	72,000	72,000	216,000
Utilities		4,000	4,000	4,000	12,000
Maintenance		900	900	900	2,700
Total fixed factory overhead		$108,900	$108,900	$108,900	$326,700
Total factory overhead		$317,700	$320,600	$335,100	$973,400

*DLH stands for direct labor hours.

M. Identify the components of the cost of goods sold budget and prepare a cost of goods sold budget.

a. The cost of goods sold budget is produced after the production, direct materials, direct labor, and overhead budgets, as it is basically a summary of those budgets. The next chart illustrates Robin Manufacturing Company's cost of goods sold budget:

Robin Manufacturing Company Cost of Goods Sold Budget for the Quarter Ended September 30, Year 1

	July	August	September	Quarter
Beginning finished goods inventory, 7/1/Year 1				$626,400
Direct materials used (see the table in I.a., previously)	$4,680,000	$4,827,500	$5,185,250	14,692,750
Direct labor used (see the chart in I.b., previously)	540,000	547,500	585,000	1,672,500
Manufacturing overhead (see the chart in L.a., previously)	317,700	320,600	335,100	973,400
Cost of goods manufactured	$5,537,700	%5,695,600	$6,105,350	$17,338,650
Cost of goods available for sale				$17,965,050
Less: Ending finished goods inventory				939,600
Cost of goods sold				$17,025,450

N. Demonstrate an understanding of contribution margin per unit and total contribution margin, identify the appropriate use of these concepts, and calculate both unit and total contribution margin.

a. Contribution margin represents the portion of the revenue, less the total variable costs, that is used to recoup the fixed costs. This can be broken out on a per-unit basis or as a total. The contribution margin is used in break-even analysis to estimate the number of units that need to be sold in order to cover all the fixed costs in the organization's cost structure. It also can be used to estimate desired net income level based on unit sales. The formulas are shown next:

Unit Contribuion Margin = Price per Unit − Varibale Cost per Unit
Total Contribution Margin = Total Revenue − Total Variable Cost

O. Identify the components of the selling and administrative expense budget.
   a. Nonmanufacturing expenses are often grouped into a single budget called an selling and administrative (S&A) expense budget or nonmanufacturing costs budget. The selling expense components of this budget include salaries and commissions for the sales department, travel and entertainment, advertising expenditures, shipping supplies, postage and stationery, and the like.
P. Explain how specific components of the selling and administrative expense budget may affect the contribution margin.
   a. Just as with overhead expenses, S&A expenses can be categorized into fixed costs and variable costs. In general, selling expenses are made up of both fixed and variable cost components, whereas the administrative expenses tend to include mostly fixed costs. As such, the variable costs in the S&A budget need to be considered when computing contribution margin. Variable selling costs are mostly commissions and shipping costs.
Q. Prepare an operational (operating) budget.
   a. All of the budgets previously mentioned are components of the overall operating budget used to create pro forma income statements. An example of the pro forma income statement for Robin Manufacturing would look like this:

Sales	$24,357,600	From sales budget
Less: Cost of goods sold	17,026,650	From cost of goods sold budget
Gross margin	$7,330,950	
Less: S&A expenses	2,367,000	From S&A budget
Operating income	$4,963,950	
Less: Interest expenses	140,361	
Earnings before taxes	$4,823,589	
Less: Taxes	1,702,165	
Net income	$3,121,424	

R. Prepare a capital expenditure budget.
   a. The capital budget represents the amount of money the company plans to invest in selected capital projects, including purchased of property, plant, or equipment as well as new businesses. The budget shows details of how much will be spent in each category to determine the overall cash needs for capital expenditures.
S. Demonstrate an understanding of the relationship between the capital expenditure budget, the cash budget, and the pro forma financial statements.
   a. The pro forma income statement and the capital expenditure budget are used to derive the cash budget since those two budgets show sources and uses of cash.

T. Define the purposes of the cash budget, and describe the relationship between the cash budget and all other budgets.
  a. Maintaining adequate liquidity is a requirement for staying in business, and a cash budget is a plan to ensure liquidity. If a cash budget is prepared accurately, financing can be arranged in an orderly fashion, and investment durations can be planned so that they can be liquidated at the time the funds are needed. Because cash is needed in all areas of operations, the cash budget gets data from all parts of the master budget. A cash budget is divided into four sections: the cash receipt section, the cash disbursement section, the cash excess or deficiency section, and the financing section.

U. Demonstrate an understanding of the relationship between the credit policies and purchasing (payables) policies and the cash budget.
  a. The credit policies and purchasing policies play a large role in the development of the cash budget. Since the pro forma income statement is derived from the accrual basis of accounting, it doesn't always translate directly into cash. An organization must estimate the actual cash inflows from customers and outflows to suppliers, employees, and others in order to accurately manage its cash position.

V. Prepare a cash budget.
  a. A cash budget includes estimated cash receipts, followed by cash disbursements to compute the cash requirements of the company. For details on preparing the cash receipts and disbursement schedules, see Topic 5: Annual Profit Plan and Supporting Schedules.

Section B.6. Top-Level Planning and Analysis

A. Define the purpose of a pro forma income statement, a pro forma balance sheet, and a pro forma statement of cash flows, and demonstrate an understanding of the relationship among these statements and all other budgets.
  a. The pro forma income statement shows a company's projected sales revenue, costs, and profit derived from the individual operating budgets discussed in Topic 5. After the income statement is complete, the company can prepare the pro forma balance sheet based on estimated dividends and information from the other operating budgets. This will provide the company with projected solvency and liquidity figures for analysis purposes. After the balance sheet and income statement are complete, the company can complete the pro forma cash flow statement.

B. Prepare pro forma income statements based on several revenue and cost assumptions.
  a. Topic 5 addressed the preparation of the pro forma income statement based on the individual operating budgets. However, income statements also can be prepared using the percentage-of-sales method for a quicker way of forecasting year-end results.

b. The percentage-of-sales method is a simple approach that ties many of the items in the pro forma income statement and balance sheet to future sales revenue. It assumes that the relationship between these income statement and balance sheet items and sales revenue remains constant, which means that they grow proportionally with sales growth. See Topic 6: Top-Level Planning and Analysis for more detail on preparing pro forma statements using the percentage-of-sales method.

C. Evaluate whether a company has achieved strategic objectives based on pro forma income statements.
   a. After the pro forma statements have been compiled, they need to be analyzed to determine if the company is meeting its predetermined financial targets based on the estimates. The strategic objectives are defined prior to the formulation of the pro forma statements and are compared against the estimated results to determine if the company will meet goals if the estimates are achieved.

D. Use financial projections to prepare a pro forma balance sheet and a pro forma statement of cash flows.
   a. The percentage-of-sales method can be used to prepare pro forma balance sheets and the statement of cash flows. See Topic 6: Top-Level Planning and Analysis for more detail on preparing pro forma statements using the percentage-of-sales method.

E. Identify the factors required to prepare medium- and long-term cash forecasts.
   a. The capital expenditures budget and the operating budgets combine to assess the cash needs of the organization. It is also necessary to gather information on the company's collection pattern and purchases (payables) pattern in order to determine when inflows and outflows can be expected based on the capital and operating budgets. See Topic 5: Annual Profit Plan and Supporting Schedules for additional information.

F. Use financial projections to determine required outside financing and dividend policy.
   a. The pro forma income statements and balance sheets play a key role in determining the requirements for financing and dividend policy. If key line items on a balance sheet need to be maintained at a certain percentage of sales (i.e., cash 5% of sales, accounts receivable 15%, inventory 25%, and accounts payable 10%) in order to maintain company operations, management can derive the amount of funds available for dividends or the need for external financing. To derive those numbers, the balance sheet items are set at the percentage of sales as defined, and retained earnings is computed from the beginning-of-year amount plus pro forma net income less estimated dividends. The long-term debt isn't expected to change with changes in sales. After the computations are made, there will be a shortfall either in assets or in liabilities and equity. If assets are less than liabilities and equity, debt can be paid down or additional dividends can be paid. If assets are higher than liabilities and equity, external financing is needed in order to support the asset base.

TOPIC 1

Strategic Planning

STRATEGY DEFINES HOW A FIRM competes and sets forth the general direction an organization plans to follow to achieve its goals. It represents the collective soul of an organization. Strategies are developed by matching core competencies of the enterprise with industry opportunities and/or threats.

Strategic planning (sometimes referred to as **long-range planning**) involves a comprehensive look at an organization in relation to its industry, competitors, and environment. An organization charts its destination, assesses barriers that must be overcome to reach that destination, and identifies approaches for moving forward and dealing with the barriers. Although traditionally the responsibility of top management, all organizational members should be involved in the process. Well-thought-out strategic planning can help an organization adeptly navigate through turbulent times—both good and bad.

> **READ** the Learning Outcome Statements (LOS) for this topic as found in Appendix A and then study the concepts and calculations presented here to be sure you understand the content you could be tested on in the CMA exam.

Strategy and Strategic Planning

Every well-managed organization formulates both strategies and strategic plans at some level. Executives and managers typically spend considerable time thinking about strategies to achieve organizational goals; these strategies are then formally incorporated in a strategic plan.

Strategy

Strategy is a broad term. Organizations generally develop strategies at different levels. Figure 1B-1 shows three levels for which firms commonly develop organizational strategies:

1. Corporate (or multibusiness)
2. Competitive (or business unit)
3. Functional (within a business)

Figure 1B-1 Levels of Strategy

Corporate	Looks at the whole gamut of business opportunities, including international expansion and mergers and acquisitions
	Defines the organization's values, expressed in financial and nonfinancial terms
	Centers on identifying and building or acquiring key resources and capabilities
	Involves decisions about which industries the organization will compete in and how the businesses will be linked
	Determines how organizational resources will be allocated among the firm's businesses
	Determines constraints on what the firm will and will not do
Competitive	Defines how an organization competes in a given industry—how the firm creates value in an industry
	Involves a vision of what customers the organization serves and how it delivers value to them
	Combines specific activities and processes to enable the firm to create unique value
	Aligns organizational activities so all efforts consistently reinforce the potential advantage of the firm's competitive positioning
Functional	Reinforces the organization's competitive strategy
	Includes plans and objectives for marketing, finance, research, technology, operations, and so on
	Focuses on coordination among functions
	Defines activities and processes to help the organization maximize its competitive position
	Clarifies whether and how the organization's functions fit with the competitive strategy

Corporate strategy considers the big picture, determines the appropriate mix of businesses, and identifies where (in what markets) the firm competes. Competitive and functional strategies are more tactically focused on how the organization will compete in a given industry. Although the outcomes differ for the various levels of strategy, they all must be consistent and aligned.

Naturally, strategies differ between organizations. For example, how Dell, IBM, and Toshiba compete for market share in the same business computer arena is driven by different strategies. In turn, different strategies require different tasks, skills, priorities, and control systems.

In today's competitive environment, organizational strategies must be dynamic. The strength of an organization's strategy is not determined by the firm's initial move but rather by how well it:

- Anticipates competitors' actions.
- Anticipates and/or influences changing customer demands.
- Capitalizes on advantages in a changing competitive environment (e.g., regulations, technology, the economy, global opportunities and events).
- Reacts to, chooses, and executes alternative competitive strategies.

Anticipation and preparation are key to an effective strategy. Every eventuality with competitors and customers and other important factors must be met and addressed with rapid countermoves.

Strategic Planning

A conceptual representation of strategic planning is shown in Figure 1B-2.

Figure 1B-2 Key Elements of Strategic Planning

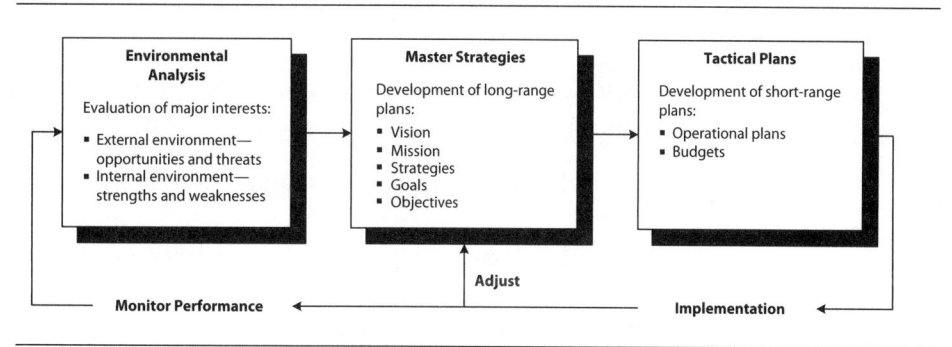

```
┌─────────────────────┐     ┌─────────────────────┐     ┌─────────────────────┐
│   Environmental     │     │  Master Strategies  │     │   Tactical Plans    │
│     Analysis        │     │                     │     │                     │
│ Evaluation of major │ ──▶ │ Development of      │ ──▶ │ Development of      │
│ interests:          │     │ long-range plans:   │     │ short-range plans:  │
│ ▪ External          │     │ ▪ Vision            │     │ ▪ Operational plans │
│   environment—      │     │ ▪ Mission           │     │ ▪ Budgets           │
│   opportunities     │     │ ▪ Strategies        │     │                     │
│   and threats       │     │ ▪ Goals             │     │                     │
│ ▪ Internal          │     │ ▪ Objectives        │     │                     │
│   environment—      │     │                     │     │                     │
│   strengths and     │     │                     │     │                     │
│   weaknesses        │     │                     │     │                     │
└─────────────────────┘     └─────────────────────┘     └─────────────────────┘
                                      ▲
                                    Adjust
     Monitor Performance ◀──────────────────────────── Implementation ◀──
```

Keep in mind that the representation shown here is conceptual; it is intended to provide a general view of the strategic planning process. In practice, strategic planning terminology and approaches differ across organizations. Organizations devise their own operational models that elaborate on the specifics of their strategic planning process. The nature of the enterprise, its marketplace and stakeholders; the size, resources, and capabilities of the organization; and other factors, such as the participants in the process and their power and interests ultimately dictate additional specifics that will shape the operational model.

What is the appropriate time frame for strategic planning? There is no rule regarding strategic plans being prepared at one-, three-, five-, or ten-year intervals. Organizations prepare strategic plans at different intervals depending on the industry, the level of competition (e.g., new entrants), and how fast products or services change. For example, technology-focused businesses prepare strategic plans at short time intervals to address the rapid changes and competitive pressure of their markets.

Typically, the strategic planning process is highly iterative. The core elements are interrelated; completion of one element requires a review of previous elements and entails some measure of fine-tuning. In the end, the resulting strategic plan yields insights into how an organization can position itself for sustainable competitive advantage.

The Relationship Between Strategy and Strategic Planning

In practice, strategy formulation and strategic planning have much overlap. But the two processes have important conceptual differences.

On a fundamental level, strategy formulation results in new strategies and strategic planning addresses how to implement the strategies. Additional distinctions can be made:

- Strategy formulation leads to organizational goals; management creates strategies to achieve those goals.
- Strategic planning develops plans to implement strategies and achieve the goals.
- Strategic planning is typically a systematic process with a timetable and some measure of prescribed procedures.
- Ideally, strategies are continually reevaluated based on perceived opportunities and threats.

Regardless of the overlap or variances in terms and processes, strategy formulation and strategic planning both address these core elements at some level:

- **External factors.** Recognition of organizational opportunities, limitations, and threats
- **Internal factors.** Recognition of organizational strengths, weaknesses, and competitive advantages
- **SWOT (*s*trengths, *w*eaknesses, *o*pportunities, and *t*hreats) analysis.** Identification of elements that will help or hinder the organization
- **Long-term vision, mission, and goals.** Development of the overall organizational vision and mission and the formulation of long-term business goals
- **Tactics to achieve long-term goals.** Development of short-term plans and tactics

Subsequent content looks at each of these elements in more detail.

Analysis of External Factors Affecting Strategy

Creating strategies without first assessing the organization's business environment—what is happening and what may happen inside and outside the organization—would be a futile exercise.

The specific external factors affecting an organization's strategy are determined by its industry and broader environment. Typically a variety of external factors typically make up an organization's business environment. Examples of key external factors shaping organizational strategy include:

- Legal and regulatory factors.
- Market forces, industry trends, and competition.
- Technological changes.
- Stakeholder groups and their social concerns.
- Globalization trends, emerging markets, and nongovernment organizations (e.g., United Nations, World Bank, etc.).

All of these external factors need to be examined during strategic planning.

Legal and Regulatory Factors

Depending on the industry, legal and regulatory factors may be interrelated. But the two factors also have some key distinctions.

Legal Factors

Legal factors are rules of conduct promulgated by legal entities (e.g., federal, state, county/provincial, or city laws); they are enforced by the threat of punishment. A host of legal factors can impact product/service success. Examples include:

- Patents
- Copyrights
- Trademarks
- Antitrust laws
- Trade protectionism
- Product/service liability issues
- Environmental liability concerns
- Employment law and litigation
- Compliance with the Sarbanes-Oxley Act (SOX)

Regulatory Factors

Regulatory factors (or regulations) are principles or rules designed to control or govern behavior. Theoretically, regulations are voluntary. But in many situations, regulations can have the force of law. For example, an organization may not be able to compete in a given market if it does not comply with regulatory factors.

Agencies under legal entities as well as nongovernmental entities (e.g., industry self-regulating bodies and professional societies) typically set regulations and sanctions. Unlike legal factors, which are always enforced by the threat of punishment, regulatory factors are enforced most often by some form of self-regulation, with the threat of fines and/or disenfranchisement.

General examples of regulatory factors that can affect an organization's strategy include:

Social Regulations

Examples include but are not limited to:

- Environmental Protection Agency (EPA) standards restrict pollution of air, water, and land.
- Occupational Safety and Health Administration (OSHA) standards protect the safety and health of American workers.
- Federal Trade Commission (FTC) regulations protect consumers, require truthful advertising by businesses, and prohibit collusion (e.g., price fixing and allocating markets).

Industry Regulations

Examples include but are not limited to:

- Federal Aviation Administration (FAA) requirements for airports, air traffic control, safety issues, and routes.
- Federal Communications Commission (FCC) regulations for radio and television frequencies.
- Food and Drug Administration (FDA) requirements for safety in the food and drug industry and in medical device manufacturing.

Linkage of Legal and Regulatory Factors to Strategic Planning

The influence of legal and regulatory factors on an organization's strategy can be quite pervasive. The following are just a few examples of how legal and regulatory factors can affect an organization:

- Influence how a firm chooses to compete (e.g., through antitrust laws and licensing requirements).
- Limit global operations (e.g., through trade protectionism).
- Thwart or promote technology innovations (e.g., through tax and patent policies).
- Impact human resource practices (e.g., through equal employment opportunity/antidiscrimination laws, wage and price controls, Family and Medical Leave Act legislation, and employee safety and health regulations).
- Restrict marketing campaigns (e.g., through FTC controls).
- Force environmental accountability (e.g., through EPA controls).
- Increase capital requirements (e.g., through required technical sophistication to meet governmental control requirements).

As seen above, many legal and regulatory factors are industry-specific; others may cut across a variety of industries. Some legal and regulatory factors may even be directed at an individual company.

To no small degree, the legal and regulatory factors already noted can directly affect management accounting due to significant cost incurrence implications. For example, changes in EPA or OSHA regulations can require significant capital investments.

Consider a few additional factors have specific implications for management accounting:

- Securities and Exchange Commission (SEC) laws and rules to protect investors and maintain the integrity of the securities markets
- The Sarbanes-Oxley Act changes regarding internal controls
- The Internal Revenue Service (IRS) code
- Congressional changes to minimum wage requirements and/or overtime compensation
- State-regulated insurance and banking commission regulations on how business is conducted and how various financial transactions are to be accounted for

Market Forces, Industry Trends, and Competition

History has shown how factors such as government deregulation, globalization, technological innovations, demanding customers, and changing demographics and social expectations can dramatically alter even stable business arenas. Thus, a critical part of strategic planning is an industry analysis—a thorough assessment of the competitive arena that includes the competitors the organization must face and the structure and boundaries of the competitive arena.

As in other aspects of strategic planning, there is no one single definitive method for identifying arena boundaries or anticipating rival actions. But most industry analyses consider the following factors:

- Entry of new competitors
- Threat of substitutes
- Bargaining power of buyers
- Bargaining power of suppliers
- Rivalry among existing competitors

Michael Porter developed a model examining these five forces and their collective role in determining the strength of competition and profitability. Figure 1B-3 depicts Porter's model.

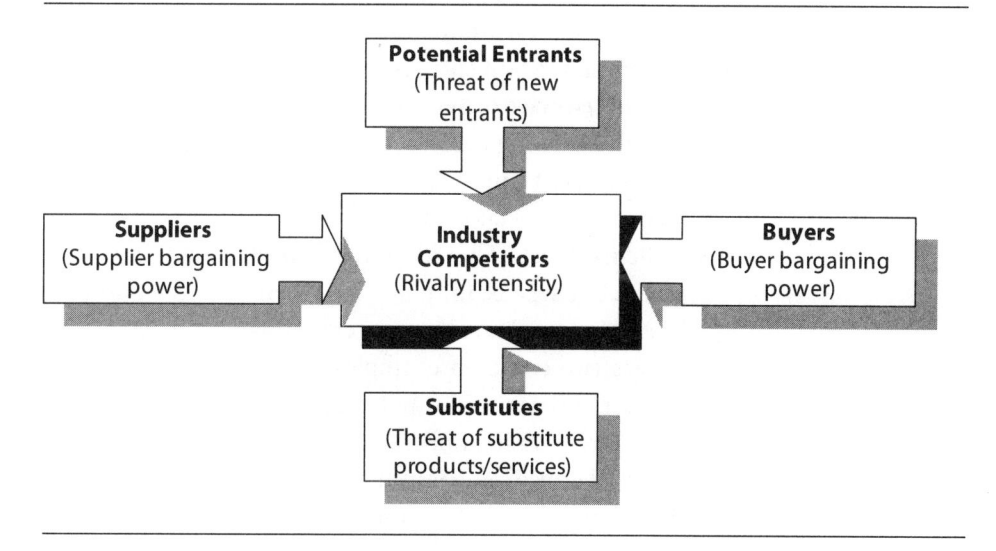

Figure 1B-3 Five Forces Driving Industry Profitability

```
                    Potential Entrants
                    (Threat of new
                        entrants)
                            |
                            v
  Suppliers         Industry Competitors        Buyers
  (Supplier    -->  (Rivalry intensity)   <--  (Buyer bargaining
  bargaining                                     power)
  power)
                            ^
                            |
                      Substitutes
                   (Threat of substitute
                     products/services)
```

Source: Adapted from Michael Porter, *Competitive Advantage—Creating and Sustaining Superior Performance*.

The discussion of Porter's five forces that follows is synthesized from two of Porter's books, *Competitive Strategy: Techniques for Analyzing Industries and Competitors* (1980) and *Competitive Advantage: Creating and Sustaining Superior Performance* (1985), and the collaborative text *Wharton on Dynamic Competitive Strategy* (Day and Reibstein, 1997).

Entry of New Competitors

A new player in a marketplace (an entrant) generally brings with them new capacity and resources. The profitability for an incumbent in the marketplace may be reduced if its sales prices are bid down or its product costs are increased in order to compete against this new entrant.

The threat of new competitors depends on the magnitude of entry barriers—factors that create a disadvantage for prospective entrants and lower their profit expectations.

Examples of entry barriers include these items:

- **Incumbent cost advantages.** These rewards are created when incumbents have advantages such as low labor or capital costs, preferred access to raw materials, government subsidies, favorable locations, proprietary technology and product designs, and accumulated learning experience. A start-up firm with no experience, for example, can expect higher costs than incumbents; heavy start-up losses and below- or near-cost pricing are often common in order to gain experience.
- **Economies of scale.** Generally defined as a decline in unit costs as volume per period increases, economies of scale can deter an entrant. A new entrant may need to come in at a larger scale and risk encountering strong reaction from the existing players. Or a new entrant may decide to come in at a smaller scale and incur a cost disadvantage. Facilities, research, marketing, sales force coverage, and distribution are all examples of areas of economies of scale that potentially require significant entry investments.
- **Product/service differentiation.** *Differentiation* refers to the brand identification and existing customer loyalties an entrant must overcome. Entrants will need to invest time and money to build a brand name. Such investments have no guarantee of success or "salvage value" should the entry fail.
- **Switching costs.** Should a buyer consider changing from an existing supplier's product or service to that of a new entrant, the one-time switching costs can be a deterrent. Having to purchase/install new equipment or retrain employees are two common examples of switching costs. A new entrant must offer a major cost savings or potential for performance improvement to warrant a switch from an incumbent.
- **Channel crowding.** Many distribution channels have limited capacity or exclusive relationships with manufacturers that restrict the number of product lines. Intense selling efforts generally are required to convince a distributor to take on a new product line. A new entrant may need to pay larger margins to offset the extra cost that distributors incur, or a new player may be forced to find a niche market.
- **Expected incumbent reactions.** Depending on how aggressively incumbents have defended their positions in the past, entry barriers may be raised or lowered. Incumbents with deep pockets and staying power who have demonstrated a willingness to take a short-term reduction in profits to defend market share discourage entrants. Incumbents who have ignored previous entrants or have been unwilling to defend their position can encourage entrants.

Threat of Substitutes

When an acceptable substitute product or service is available—one that provides the same functions and offers the same benefits—the average price that can be charged and the resulting profit margin is squeezed. The amount of product or service value is also limited. Less costly but acceptable substitutes also pose a threat.

How electronic surveillance and alarm systems have impacted security guard firms is but one example of industry threats posed by the availability of substitutes. Another example is how customers can now purchase products and services directly online in lieu of traditional distribution channels. The key in these situations is to account for similarities while looking for differentiation opportunities beyond product or service similarities. In the case of the security industry, firms offer guards and electronic surveillance systems as a value-added package, positioning the guards as skilled operators.

Bargaining Power of Buyers

Buyers (customers) and sellers (suppliers) of goods and services can have wide variance in their relationship. Relationships may involve tightly integrated, just-in-time manufacturing systems, or they may be at the other end of the spectrum, with mass marketing. Buyer power, in particular, is enhanced or deterred depending on bargaining leverage and price sensitivity.

Bargaining Leverage

Generally speaking, leverage is any strategic or tactical event that can be exploited to an advantage. A buyer's bargaining leverage is enhanced by the following factors:

- **Large-volume purchases made by a few key customers.** In this situation, the seller becomes somewhat dependent on the key buyers and would encounter problems if a relationship were severed.
- **Ability for customers to easily switch.** Customers may change suppliers if there is little product or service differentiation, low switching costs, or readily available low-cost substitutes.
- **Ability to backward-integrate.** Current prices and/or other terms can make an alternative more attractive than continuing to buy externally. (An example of this is the purchase of an upstream supplier or the ability to bring back in house something that was previously outsourced.)
- **Customer insider knowledge.** Bargaining leverage is gained if customers know the supplier's costs and profits or learn that the supplier needs their business to offset excess capacity or other mitigating circumstances.

Price Sensitivity

Price sensitivity is an indicator of how important lower prices are to customers. Price sensivilty is heightened by the following factors:

- **Product or service impact on end product quality.** A buyer pays more attention to price if the consequences of product or service failure are more severe

than in situations where the product/service has little impact on the quality of the end product.
- **Price of the product or service relative to a customer's total costs.** Big-ticket items tend to incur greater purchasing scrutiny; smaller incidental items often escape analysis of cost alternatives.
- **Buyer's profits.** When customers are suffering from poor profitability, they often seek price concessions from suppliers. The pressure for concessions can become intense if survival is at stake.

Price sensitivity is intensified further if buyers perceive little difference among competing suppliers.

Bargaining Power of Suppliers

A supplier's ability to withstand bargaining by customers tends to mirror those conditions making buyers powerful. A supplier's bargaining power depends on the following items:

- **Size of the supplier relative to the customer.** A larger supplier can have a distinct advantage and leverage in dealing with a small, dispersed customer base.
- **Customer's reliance on the supplier's product or service.** Reliance is influenced to the extent that a customer cannot buy an equivalent, the input is not storable (so the buyer cannot stockpile inventory), or switching costs are high.
- **Threat of forward integration.** If suppliers can sell directly to end users, customers will have less leverage to get better prices.

Rivalry Among Existing Competitors

In some environments, rivals coexist. In other environments, direct rivals constantly jockey for market share with tactics such as temporary price cuts, special promotions, advertising blitzes, aggressive new product launches, and increased customer service and extended warranties. Value often erodes as competitors match moves.

Telecommunication providers are notorious for price cutting in their efforts to secure new customers and cover fixed costs. Yet such actions often decrease profits and leave market share unchanged. The following factors typically influence the status of competitor relations.

- **Structure of competition.** Rivalry is generally most intense when there are a few balanced competitors or several small players serving the same market. Antagonism may run deep between top competitors; instability often results as firms may be prone to fight and retaliate. In the case of a proliferation of smaller players, these companies may try to make moves the others will not notice. But in situations where one competitor clearly dominates, rivalry often is subdued as followers learn to coexist under the leader's umbrella.

- **Structure of costs.** Capacity utilization is emphasized when fixed costs are high. Any excess capacity often leads to price cutting and a cycle of price matching.
- **Product or service differentiation.** In the absence of differentiation, customers often focus on price, terms, and the like, and rivalry intensifies. Conversely, rivalry is subdued when customers develop preferences and brand loyalty due to large perceived differentiation. Product differentiation can foster buyer preferences and loyalties to particular suppliers. Naturally, organizations seek differentiation that is sustainable (e.g., a feature that is difficult to imitate, remains useful, and customers are willing to pay for).
- **Customer switching costs.** Costs that tie a buyer to one supplier provide good protection against raids by rivals. Changing a computer operating system is an example of a situation in which a customer typically would incur a general disruption of operations and expensive costs.
- **Diversity of competitors' strategies and objectives.** It is much easier for competitors to anticipate another's intention or accurately anticipate reactions to market moves when all competitors have similar strategies, cost structures, management philosophies, and the like. When competitors come from diverse backgrounds (e.g., foreign-owned, government-owned, small owner-operated firms versus large enterprises), actions and activities are much less predictable.
- **High exit barriers.** Even when profits are depressed, exit barriers can keep players trapped. For example, firms may choose to endure the drain on profits caused by excess capacity rather than sell to other manufacturers that could threaten their other markets at a later point in time. Or management may resist an economically justified exit decision based on an emotional rationale, such as loyalty to a particular business or employees.

Linkage of the Five Forces to Strategic Planning

According to Porter, the five forces in total—entry of new competitors, threat of substitutes, bargaining power of buyers, bargaining power of suppliers, and rivalry among existing competitors—determine the intensity of industry competition and profitability. In other words, the collective strength of the five competitive forces determines the ability of firms to earn rates of return on investment in excess of the cost of capital.

In industries where the strength of the five forces is favorable (e.g., pharmaceuticals), profits are attractive. In industries where the strength of one or more of the forces is under fire (e.g., airlines), few firms have good returns in spite of management efforts. Porter notes that industry profitability is not a function of what a product looks like or whether a service incorporates high technology or low technology; but rather, it is determined by industry structure. That is why a product that looks mundane (e.g., an automotive aftermarket part) may be extremely profitable whereas a more glamorous high-tech product (e.g., a cellular handset) may not be highly profitable for all the market players.

To a large extent, the five forces are moving targets. In this respect, they:

- Can vary from industry to industry.
- Can change as an industry evolves.
- Are not equally important in any one industry.
- Are vulnerable to high growth and market demand (if a surplus of competitors is attracted, leading to overcrowding).

Naturally, different firms will have unique strengths and weaknesses that influence their ability to deal with or even alter industry structure. Understanding industry structure is a critical starting point during strategy formulation. Different forces take on prominence. The strongest force or forces assume increased importance during strategic planning and strategy formulation.

Technological Changes

No industry is immune to the strategic implications of technology. Consider the following points as proof:

- Technology can result in the creation of industry substitutes (e.g., wireless phones versus land lines).
- Technology can reduce the need for large-scale distribution and open a market up to new entrants (e.g., Web-based e-commerce technology versus traditional distribution channels).
- Technology can accelerate new product designs and facilitate short production runs in manufacturing-based industries, leading to either intense rivalry or monopoly.
- Technology can create a shift in the balance of power between an organization and a supplier or buyer, depending on where the technology is developed and exploited.
- Technology can change industry structure and thereby either improve or degrade average profitability.

Those firms savvy in recognizing and exploiting technological changes are generally more adept at gaining and sustaining competitive advantage. To a degree, technological change is both an external factor and an internal factor. Technology impacts what products and services an organization offers, how products and services are made, how customers are serviced, and with whom the firm must compete. As such, technology must reinforce a firm's strategic intent and competitive strategy.

Characteristics of a Technology Assessment

Technology cuts across all of the business units and activities of an enterprise. Given the span of technology and its importance to market success, an organization needs to assess its technology capabilities on an ongoing basis. *The Portable MBA* (Bruner et al., 1998) outlines a five-step process for a technology assessment:

1. Identify key technologies.
2. Analyze the potential changes in current and future technologies.
3. Analyze the competitive impact of technologies.
4. Analyze the organization's technical strengths and weaknesses.
5. Establish the organization's technology priorities.

Step 1. Identify Key Technologies

This initial phase in a technology assessment identifies all technologies that impact the organization. It involves current and future technologies as well as those used inside the firm or outside.

General categories that should be considered include:

- Product technology
- Manufacturing and/or service process technology
- Technology used by support functions (such as sales, customer service, finance and accounting)
- Information management technology
- Technologies used by competitors
- Technologies used by suppliers or buyers of the organization's products and services

Consideration should be given to technologies not currently used by the enterprise, especially if they might have future implications. For example, a small business not currently using e-commerce might well explore how the technology is used in other industries and how it could impact the firm's current products and processes.

Step 2. Analyze the Potential Changes in Current and Future Technologies

This next step involves evaluating short- and long-term changes in all the important technologies identified. Complex technologies may have many layers of subtechnologies. The evaluation must consider all of the subtechnologies.

In regard to analyzing potential changes, note that:

- People with expertise in the technologies should conduct the technology evaluation.
- Evaluations should be constructively examined and challenged by others to preclude the possibility of a forecast based on unquestioned conventional wisdom.
- The effort applied to technology development varies. A technology that is critical to a competitor will most likely evolve more quickly than technologies that are necessary but not an important source of competitive advantage.
- Mature technologies do not always change slowly, especially if the need for progress or replacement of the technology exists. Mature technologies will also change rapidly when a new technology offers opportunities for new entrants.

Step 3. Analyze the Competitive Impact of Technologies

The intent of this step is to answer the following key questions:

- What technologies or technological changes can give the organization the greatest source of competitive advantage?
- What technologies or technological changes would be the greatest threat in the hands of a competitor?
- What technologies or technological changes could significantly change the industry structure?

The competitive impact of different technologies generally is classified by base, key, or pacing characteristics.

- **Base technologies** are widely used throughout an industry. As such, they are well understood. They are considered necessary, but they do not provide competitive advantage.
- As implied by the name, **key technologies** are critical to competitive advantage. They help an organization differentiate its products or services. In some instances, they enable the firm to compete with lower costs. Patents, unpatented advances by the firm, or superior expertise in using the technology often make key technologies proprietary to an organization.
- **Pacing technologies** are those that have the potential to redefine an industry or change the whole basis of competition. Pacing technologies often replace key technologies. When firms that are not the market leader develop a pacing technology, the opportunity to change industry leadership exists. Market leaders have a dangerous tendency to overlook pacing technologies because they are often very different or they threaten to cannibalize existing products, services, and processes.

Step 4. Analyze the Organization's Technical Strengths and Weaknesses

Managers must assess the organization's strengths and weaknesses for each technology classification as well as the potential costs of developing each technology. The evaluation should compare findings with competitors' strengths and weaknesses (both current and future scenarios).

Just as in the overall organizational SWOT analysis, pride and unwillingness to acknowledge the organization's weaknesses or the strengths of a competitor can skew this assessment. To help ensure objectivity, it is best to have a team of technical specialists who understand the technologies and managers who are operations and market focused do the assessment together.

Step 5. Establish the Organization's Technology Priorities

Based on findings from the technology assessment process, a tentative set of priorities for the acquisition, development, and use of product, service, and process technologies can be created. A technology assessment should also consider the pros and cons of having highly integrated technology systems—whether or not the firm currently has highly integrated systems or is contemplating them.

- **Integration benefits.** Integration facilitates simultaneous updating of databases. Current data is available for decision making. The costs of data entry and processing are lower than for standalone applications.
- **Integration concerns.** System integration typically requires huge financial investments, comprehensive designs, and careful project management and execution as well as timely training on system features and the transition process. Integration is a big commitment. It often strains an organization's resources to the point of vulnerability to competitors by inhibiting growth and flexibility for a prolonged period of time (e.g., two or more years). Furthermore, failures can create customer dissatisfaction, lead to financial losses, and make the entire organization vulnerable.

Linkage of a Technology Assessment to Strategic Planning

Insights gained from the technology assessment evolve into an organizational technology strategy through a process of interaction between the firm's leaders and managers representing all the functional areas of the organization.

Characteristics of a sound technology strategy include:

- Enhancement of technology's strategic role in the organization.
- Support of the organization's corporate and competitive strategies.
- Plans for attaining short-term and long-term objectives and major projects, including goals and milestones.
- Resource allocation.
- Alignment to the organization's financial plan and budget.
- Metrics for measuring accomplishment.

A technology strategy also should be easily understood and well communicated. The commitment of key people must be secured.

The technology strategy establishes preliminary organizational priorities and commitments to innovation and technology development, always keeping the firm's strategic positioning in mind. It is in this manner that a technology assessment leads to a technology strategy and ultimately provides inputs for strategic plans.

Stakeholder Groups and Their Social Concerns

Stakeholders include people, departments, groups, organizations, or other bodies that have a "stake"—an investment or interest—in the success of or actions taken by an organization. Thus, stakeholders include:

- Executives
- Managers and employees (including their families)
- The organization's board of directors
- Shareholders (stockholders)
- The industry in which the organization operates
- Customers
- Competitors
- Suppliers
- Business partners

- Consulting and advisory services
- Creditors
- Special interest groups—industrial, political, consumer, and so on
- Unions
- Regulating government bodies
- The community in which the organization operates
- The nation
- The environment—plants, animals, ecosystems, natural resources
- Educational institutions
- The media
- Future generations

During strategic planning, it is important to identify the various stakeholders to understand their expectations and potential influences on the enterprise and to ensure that their needs and interests are addressed. If not on board, stakeholders can withhold resources and support and potentially undermine the legitimacy of the enterprise.

Maximizing Shareholder Value While Being Socially Responsible in Business

The idea of maximizing shareholder value is associated with for-profit corporations and generally refers to the market valuation of a firm. The idea of profit maximization requires consideration of marginal costs and a demand curve. Certainly, an organization must earn a profit that is at least equal to its cost of capital considering the risk. Although critical to organizational success, profit maximization and optimizing shareholder value are not the only goals for organizations.

The social responsibility approach in business implies that organizations should act as good corporate citizens and adopt socially responsible practices that will be a positive force for change and help improve the quality of people's lives. The premise behind this approach is that corporations have societal obligations that must complement—and not compete for—profit maximization. This philosophy suggests that corporate actions should balance the claims of all stakeholders; hence corporate leaders have a fiduciary responsibility to all stakeholders, not only the organization's executives and shareholders.

Organizations naturally encounter a host of challenges in attempts to be socially responsible. Consider a few common examples:

- Accounting practices—insider trading
- Advertising—accurate and truthful product/service representation
- Corporate restructuring—layoffs
- Diversity issues—race, ethnicity, gender, sexual orientation
- Employee privacy issues—drug testing, chemical dependency, AIDS
- Harassment issues—gender or age discrimination
- Environmental issues—pollution, animal rights

- International operations—conduct encountering bribery, nepotism, and other issues acceptable in other countries that challenge the organization's ethics
- Competition—predatory pricing, antitrust actions

Stakeholder Analysis

Most organizations use some type of model for stakeholder analysis to assess ethical challenges and how to best be socially responsible. Stakeholder analysis provides an organization with a framework for weighing all the various claims and stakeholder concerns to reach a socially responsible decision.

A common method of stakeholder analysis uses a matrix. The main steps of this type of stakeholder analysis are listed in Figure 1B-4.

Figure 1B-4 Steps in a Stakeholder Analysis Framework

Step 1.	Identify stakeholders; brainstorm a list of the main participants.
Step 2.	Determine stakeholder needs; collect input through interviews, focus groups, surveys, and so on.
Step 3.	Develop a matrix of the organization's objectives and the stakeholders' needs.
Step 4.	Code the effect of the organization's objectives versus the stakeholders' needs (e.g., using a plus or minus sign or question mark).
Step 5.	Make a decision based on the effects recorded.

A stakeholder analysis done in this manner sets the stage for decisions to change the organization's objectives, satisfy stakeholder demands, mitigate potential conflict, and pass if compatible or acceptable.

Figure 1B-5 shows an example of a stakeholder analysis. In this analysis, a produce distributor plans to build automated warehouses and install pricey high-tech gear. The matrix shown considers the stakeholders. The analysis points out that there is no one "right" way; differences in the weighting shown here can exist. The point of stakeholder analysis is to tackle such stakeholder issues and make informed and thoughtful decisions that are consistent and defensible.

Figure 1B-5 Stakeholder Analysis Example—Automating a Produce Warehouse

(+ or –)	Organization	Employees	Consuming Public	Suppliers	Government Inspectors
Harm and benefits	– Higher costs + Higher profits	+ More free time – Fewer hours/potential layoffs	+ Lower prices + Quick time to market; less spoilage	– New hardware	+ Power and influence
Rights and responsibilities	+ Value + Profits for owners and shareholders	+ Competitive market position	? Possible quality concerns ? Public good	? Ability to meet demand	+ Protect the public + Regulate industry

Other methods are available for conducting a stakeholder analysis. Some organizations do a stakeholder analysis by answering a series of guiding questions, such as:

- Who are the main stakeholders?
- What are the most important values of each stakeholder? (For example, what are the harm and benefits to each?)
- What rights and duties are at issue?
- What principles and rules are relevant?
- What are some relevant parallel cases?
- What should be done?

Linkage of a Stakeholder Analysis to Strategic Planning

There are many ways to manage an enterprise. The style of Xerox will differ from that of Fujitsu. Charles Schwab will approach things differently from E*Trade. But all firms will interact with their stakeholders.

Stakeholder analysis helps an organization frame its corporate social responsibility. It identifies the role good citizenship plays in a business. Through stakeholder analysis, a firm learns:

- How people feel about the organization and the industry it is in.
- What issues the organization should rethink/reevaluate its position on.
- What the organization should do differently to improve its position.

Shareholder value and stakeholder analysis are not mutually exclusive. Obvious decisions that balance expenses with revenues and are aligned to corporate goals are usually prudent courses for action. However, challenges can arise. For example, an organization may face a situation that violates the rights of one at the benefit for many. But most organizations also look for ways "to do the right thing" for all stakeholders while still achieving satisfactory profits for shareholders.

Globalization

Globalization describes an organization's migration to international operations. Globalization is a reflection of organizational strategy and an integrated progression of worldwide operations.

Although globalization is prevalent and a goal on which many organizations set their sights, an organization does not simply become a global entity overnight. The migration from domestic to global operations typically evolves through a series of relatively predictable stages.

- **Export.** This is the initial stage of globalization for most organizations. Firms begin to export their products or services abroad through direct sales to customers, import/export firms, and independent agents or distributors. International sales from exports generally represent a small portion of total revenue. They are seen as an adjunct to domestic sales.
- **International division and sales subsidiaries.** As international sales grow in importance, the organization is likely to establish a separate international

division and/or sales subsidiaries. At this stage of globalization, increased communication and coordination is required between domestic and international operations.

A sales subsidiary generally involves a branch operation in a country or countries where sales have become significantly large. Subsidiaries range from a relatively modest office to operations such as stores, service centers, or manufacturing plants, depending on the volume and the nature of the business.

- **Multinational corporation (MNC).** As sales volume and the number of countries significantly increase, an organization evolves to the stage of an MNC. The MNC generally operates in several countries and views and treats each one as a relatively separate entity. It often maintains global coordination of some functions, such as finance, staffing, and marketing. Or the firm may move to a regional structure with more regional headquarters and coordination.
- **Global organization.** To a global organization, the whole world is one market. National boundaries are seamless. The organization's headquarters may be located anywhere.

    The global organization is characterized by features such as but not limited to:

- Global strategic planning
- Products and services designed and marketed worldwide
- Pursuit of technology and innovation worldwide
- Sharing of global technology and innovation between all operations; application to individual markets
- Product and service development wherever cost, quality, and cycle time are favorable and demand is sufficient
- Pursuit of resources (such as money, materials, parts, insurance, and people) in locations where the best quality for cost can be found
- Employees moving freely between countries

- **Alliances, partnerships, joint ventures.** This stage of globalization does not necessarily replace the MNC or global organization, but it does offer an organization a channel to capitalize on resources (such as research and design, technology, personnel, manufacturing facilities) that would not otherwise be available. Two examples of this level of globalization are:
    - A large telecommunications firm subcontracting for technology resources in other countries, including from a major competitor
    - Two international electronics companies pooling resources to design and develop sophisticated computer chips and distribute them in more than 120 countries

Linkage of Globalization to Strategic Planning

The stages of globalization are sometimes named or categorized slightly differently than those just described. And, obviously, not every organization passes through each stage in exactly the same way. Some move at an accelerated pace—due to mergers, acquisitions, and so on. Others evolve slowly in a deliberate manner and may take years to move from export to MNC and global. Some organizations overlap the stages. For example, an organization with operations in multiple countries may be at the export stage in one country and at the MNC stage in another. But regardless of the nomenclature, the number of stages, and the time frame it takes for an organization to go global, it is helpful to recognize that globalization follows a progression.

An enterprise needs to acquire additional skills and competence as it moves through the stages of globalization. Various activities and functions evolve as an organization becomes a full-fledged multinational or global organization. For example, international financial skills and tax knowledge become increasingly important along the globalization spectrum.

To compete successfully in the global arena, organizations must make considerable investments in resources, and these investments should be carefully crafted during strategic planning.

Analysis of Internal Factors Affecting Strategy

To complement the assessment of external factors affecting strategy, an organization must conduct an internal capability analysis. Together these two assessments—external (looking from the outside in) and internal (looking from the inside out)—help an organization to establish its current capabilities and close the gap between current capabilities and those needed for industry success.

What to Assess in Internal Capability Analysis

In particular, an internal capability analysis helps to ensure that the organization has the resources, skills, and processes to reach its strategic and tactical goals.

- **Resources.** An internal assessment of resources looks at the finances, facilities, equipment, and other infrastructure issues that can support or impede organizational initiatives. Assessing resources requires review of financial statements and additional analytical work and quantitative information. Supporting growth strategies requires capital investment analysis. Supporting ongoing programs involves value chain analysis and review of activity-based costing (ABC) information. (Note: Additional information on value chain analysis is found in Section D, Topic 5: Business Process Performance.)
- **Skills.** Skills assessments examine the current education levels of employees, the core knowledge and skills required, and the specific technical or organizational skills required. As organizations face competitive pressures, employees must be prepared. As warranted, a commitment to training should be made.
- **Processes.** Cycle time and a variety of capacity issues are considered when assessing organizational processes necessary to gain competitive advantage. (Note: Process analysis is discussed further in Section D, Topic 5: Business Process Performance.)

How to Assess Internal Resources, Skills, and Processes

There is no one single method for analyzing internal capabilities, because every organization is unique. Examples of tools and techniques organizations may choose are listed next.

- Baldrige National Quality Program Criteria (for self-assessment)
- ISO 9001 quality system and ISO 14000 environmental management system requirements (for gap analysis)
- Benchmarking processes (to understand best-in-class)
- Competitive analysis (e.g., analysis of the five forces to understand competitors' businesses, market share, etc.)
- Employee competency assessments (to determine current knowledge, skills, experience, and aptitude)
- Training needs analysis (to identify training needs that can support organizational initiatives)
- Internal listening posts (to gather customer data, etc.)
- Employee surveys (to determine if employees understand the organization's focus and to assess conditions and/or issues in the current work environment, compensation approaches, management, etc.)
- Audits (to verify that processes are working within established limits)

No matter how an organization chooses to assess internal factors, internal issues should not be given a lower priority than the challenges the organization faces in the external environment. Without the internal capabilities in place, an organization is hard pressed to address external business issues. An internal gap can constrain an organization's ability to fulfill strategic external initiatives.

Linkage of Internal Capability Analysis to Strategic Planning

Conceptually, internal capability analysis has two phases. The first phase is establishing a snapshot of the present state and identifying gaps. The second phase involves making decisions about closing the critical gaps to desired states. Some gaps may be fairly simple and straightforward to address; others may require costly capital expenditures and time. The cost of developing new capabilities must be weighed against the potential payoffs.

Different capabilities support different sources of competitive advantage. An organization's future success often depends on the capabilities it develops. Capabilities that require financial investments can be risky because returns are uncertain; some investments may be irretrievable. But not investing can be just as risky as it may cause an organization to fall behind competitors, fail to sustain profits, or compromise existing capabilities, leading to lost opportunities.

Strategic planning stalls in many organizations because they fail to assess internal capabilities. Well-intended strategies become operational plans without an understanding of the internal requirements and capabilities to get the job done. In the end, due diligence in assessing internal capabilities and addressing them appropriately helps to position an organization for future opportunities.

SWOT Analysis

SWOT (or S.W.O.T.) is the acronym for strengths, weaknesses, opportunities, and threats. A **SWOT analysis** provides a framework to identify a variety of elements that will help or hinder an organization's progress in the environment in which it operates. SWOT analysis is sometimes called current state analysis.

An environmental analysis frames the proverbial big picture and identifies top issues an organization must deal with; a SWOT analysis takes the strategic planning process to the next level of focus. Organizations traditionally conduct a SWOT analysis to gather additional input for the strategic planning process.

Essentially, a SWOT analysis provides a means to organize the data gathered in the detailed internal and external analyses. Strengths and weakness are identified from an internal analysis of the organization; opportunities and threats are part of an external analysis of the environment in which the organization operates. (The external environment is essentially everything outside an organization that might affect it.)

Strengths

Identifying organizational strengths answers the question: What is the organization really good at? In other words, what are the skills, capabilities, and core competencies that help achieve the organization's goals and objectives and sustain its competitive position?

Organizational strengths might be any of the following:

- Strong leadership
- Financial soundness
- Organizational learning
- Research and development (R&D)
- Innovative product designs
- Breakthrough technology
- Product development
- Product assembly
- Strong distribution channel
- Strong market position

One or more strengths can provide a competitive advantage and help an organization differentiate itself in the marketplace. For example, if a company is exceptional at R&D, it might focus efforts on in-house product development to build or strengthen a competitive advantage. Conversely, spreading resources too thinly across too many areas can weaken an organization's competitive position.

Weaknesses

Identifying organizational weaknesses answers the question: What needs to improve? or What do we need that we do not currently have? More specifically, weaknesses are the skills, capabilities, and competencies that the organization lacks and that prevent the organization from achieving its goals and objectives. Weaknesses may be thought of as opportunities for improvement. Furthermore, any of the examples of strengths previously listed might be or become a weakness. In other words, an ability can become a disability.

Faced with a deficiency, an organization generally has three choices:

1. Modify the goal and objective into something achievable.
2. Invest the necessary capital to acquire the knowledge and/or skill required.
3. Find another organization that has the expertise needed, and outsource that requirement or develop an alliance.

For example, consider a small manufacturing company that does not have the funds or plant floor space for heat-treating furnaces. It would either have to outsource this "weakness" or invest capital funds if this capability was deemed critical for operations.

Opportunities and Threats

Opportunities generally are described as those events and trends that can help an organization meet goals and grow to new levels. Examples of opportunities are the chance to:

- Expand the customer base—based on growth in customer numbers due to demand, favorable demographic population shifts, and so on.
- Provide new avenues of customer access—such as distribution channels or bundling of services.
- Increase customer appeal of the product/service offering—new media for advertising or methods of packaging to entice customers to switch from competitors.
- Exploit a competitor's weakness—capitalize on windows of opportunity to strengthen customer acceptance of the firm's product/service.

Threats are barriers to an organization's growth. They are created mostly by events, trends, or competitor actions.

Examples of threats are situations that may:

- Reduce the size of a firm's customer base—due to economic downturns, unfavorable demographic population shifts, and in-sourcing by customers.
- Make customer access more difficult or costly—due to changes in customer buying practices or doing business with smaller numbers of suppliers.
- Reduce the customer appeal of a firm's product/service—price wars or other activities that can entice the customer to choose alternatives.
- Surpass the organization's product/service offering—price cutting or new offerings that provide significant improvements (e.g., technology leapfrogging).

Similar to strengths and weaknesses, opportunities and threats are dualistic—the same event or trend can be an opportunity or a threat. Organizations may address threats and opportunities in different ways. Overall, an organization should look to capitalize on opportunities and counter threats.

Example of a SWOT Weighted Average

A weighted average can be useful in implementing SWOT analysis data.

Example

This example shows one way to select strategies using a weighted average in conjunction with SWOT data.

ABC Company has identified the following factors that can impact market attractiveness and business strength for a product. Each item has a different proportionate weight, all summing to 1.0. The rating scale ranges from 1 (the highest) to 5 (the lowest).

Market Attractiveness	Weight	Rating (1–5)
Market size	0.3	4
Market profitability	0.4	5
Distribution structure	0.2	4
Government regulations	0.1	2
Business Strength	**Weight**	**Rating (1–5)**
Unit costs	0.4	3
Customer loyalty	0.5	2
Brand reputation	0.1	4

The calculated weighted average for market attractiveness is 4.2, and the calculated weighted average for business strength is 2.6, as shown below. Because the highly attractive market will presumably entice others to enter, planning strategies to build on the lower business strength (rather than attempting to exploit the higher market attractiveness) would be the most beneficial plan.

Market attractiveness = $(0.3 \times 4 + 0.4 \times 5 + 0.2 \times 4 + 0.1 \times 2 = 4.2)$

Business strength = $(0.4 \times 3 + 0.5 \times 2 + 0.1 \times 4 = 2.6)$

Use of a T.O.W.S. Matrix

A SWOT analysis provides a framework to identify elements that can help or hinder an organization; a **T.O.W.S. matrix** (*t*hreats, *o*pportunities, *w*eaknesses, and *s*trengths; or **TOWS matrix**), however, takes the process to the next level. Using SWOT analysis data, a T.O.W.S. matrix systematically identifies relationships and helps to develop strategies by matching strengths with opportunities, using opportunities to reduce weaknesses, using strengths to overcome threats, and reducing weaknesses and avoiding threats.

The variables in T.O.W.S. matrix are not new; they are direct outcomes of the SWOT analysis. The strategy formulation based on the systematic approach is what makes the T.O.W.S. matrix unique. T.O.W.S. is also referred to as situational analysis.

A basic T.O.W.S. is shown in Figure 1B-6.

Figure 1B-6 T.O.W.S. Matrix Example

Internal factors / External factors	Strengths (S) — A list of 5 to 10 internal strengths goes here	Weaknesses (W) — A list of 5 to 10 internal weaknesses goes here
Opportunities (O) — A list of 5 to 10 external opportunities goes here	**SO strategies** — Strategies here use strengths that take advantage of opportunities	**WO strategies** — Strategies here take advantage of opportunities by overcoming weaknesses
Threats (T) — A list of 5 to 10 external threats goes here	**ST strategies** — Strategies here use strengths to avoid threats	**WT strategies** — Strategies here minimize weaknesses and avoid threats

There are different ways of preparing a T.O.W.S. matrix and analyzing the situation. For example, an organization might begin by identifying important problems. Other approaches could be to start by identifying organizational objectives or by focusing on opportunities. Another consideration is whether to start by analyzing the external environment or to begin with the organization's internal resources. There is no single best way.

A T.O.W.S. matrix provides a good framework for identifying relationships, but it can become complex as multiple factors are being identified and the combinations examined increase. Once the combinations of relationships are identified, a weighting system may be used to help formulate the strategic choices. A plus sign ("+") can be used to indicate a match between the strengths of the company and external opportunities; a zero can be used to indicate a nonexistent relationship; or a minus sign can be used to indicate a weak relationship.

But management experts caution that you cannot simply add up the number of pluses, zeroes, and minuses in interpreting the matrix. Different relationships identified in a T.O.W.S. matrix often have different potential and merit further evaluation. Similar tables can be developed to analyze the strategy boxes (SO (strengths, opportunities), WO (weaknesses, opportunities), ST (strengths, threats), and WT (weaknesses, threats).

The point in time the matrix is prepared is another consideration. As noted previously, because internal and external environments are dynamic, multiple T.O.W.S. matrices may be warranted.

In spite of these potential complexities, a T.O.W.S. matrix offers a relatively straightforward way to identify promising strategies that use organizational strengths to take advantage of opportunities in the external environment.

Linkage of a SWOT Analysis to Strategic Planning

The outcomes of a SWOT analysis are usually lists that an organization needs to sort through. Organizations are faced with a number of questions, such as:

- What interrelationships exist among the strengths, weaknesses, opportunities, and threats?
- Does the organization have the necessary resources and capabilities to seize the opportunities and neutralize the threats?
- How many competitors already have the same resources and competencies?
- Are there barriers to market entry?
- Could the organization gain a source of competitive advantage?
- Will acquiring a particular resource or capability create a cost disadvantage for the firm?
- Are substitutes available?
- Does the organizational structure allow the firm to take full advantage of its resources and capabilities and support potential growth/change?

The challenge in evaluating all the strengths, weaknesses, opportunities, and threats is to prioritize them and then identify appropriate actions. The basic idea is to:

- Build on strengths.
- Eliminate or deal with weaknesses.
- Exploit opportunities.
- Minimize threats.

In addressing strengths and weaknesses, the outlook can change quickly. What is true or feasible now may differ in time. For example, something that is considered a strength today can be immediately neutralized by a technological innovation or a change in a government regulation.

A SWOT analysis is an important part of strategic planning because it incorporates both internal and external assessments about an organization into one summary that is practical and usable. It helps tie up any loose ends from the environmental analysis and answers many previously unresolved organizational issues. The opportunities and limitations identified provide information for reasonable goals and action plans in the strategic planning process.

Long-Term Vision, Mission, Goals, and Objectives

Organizational goals and strategies cannot be left to chance and intuition. They must be explicitly stated and clearly communicated to those in the organization responsible for their implementation. For that reason, an important step during strategic planning is to formally write out the organization's vision, mission, goals, and objectives.

Vision

An organization's **vision statement** is a guiding image of future success and achievement articulated in terms of the organization's contribution to society.

It is a succinct statement of what an organization will do for future generations and how it wants to be perceived.

Consider the vision statement example shown in Figure 1B-7.

Figure 1B-7 Vision Statement Example

Hilton Worldwide

To fill the earth with the light and warmth of hospitality.

PepsiCo

Our vision is put into action through programs and a focus on environmental stewardship, activities to benefit society, and a commitment to build shareholder value by making PepsiCo a truly sustainable company.

Unfortunately, too many vision statements tend to be soulless and easily transportable between companies by simply changing the organization's name (e.g., "XYZ strives to be a world-class organization committed to excellence and exceeding customer expectations"). A clear vision statement is compelling and unites everyone in the organization. It will reflect organizational values and inspire and challenge management and employees alike to action.

Mission

A **mission statement** provides the guiding compass for an organization. Similar to vision statements, mission statements are shaped by organizational values. A mission statement succinctly articulates an organization's business position. It expresses how the organization will continuously move toward its vision and provides a clear view of what the firm is trying to accomplish for its customers. A mission statement answers this question: Why are we in business? In answering this question, a mission statement must be accurate, easily understood, motivating, and transferable into action.

Figure 1B-8 shows an example of corporate mission statements.

Figure 1B-8 Corporate Mission Statement Example

Southwest Airlines

The mission of Southwest Airlines is dedication to the highest quality of customer service delivered with a sense of warmth, friendliness, individual pride, and company spirit.

Hilton Worldwide

To be the preeminent global hospitality company - the first choice of guests, team members, and owners alike.

PepsiCo

Our mission is to be the world's premier consumer products company focused on convenient foods and beverages. We seek to produce financial rewards to investors as we provide opportunities for growth and enrichment to our employees, our business partners and the communities in which we operate. And in everything we do, we strive for honesty, fairness and integrity.

Goals

Generally, goals may be thought of as aimed-at targets. They summarize what an organization hopes to achieve in order to fulfill its mission and achieve its vision. Goals serve as general guidelines; they tend not to be overly specific or quantifiable. A goal states the desired end result and/or the benefits of the result; it does not state the implementation plan. Organizations typically develop both strategic and tactical goals.

Strategic Goals

Strategic goals are established at the highest levels of an organization. As the name implies, strategic goals are part of the firm's strategic plan; they are long range in nature. Examples of strategic goals are business diversification, the addition or deletion of product lines, and the penetration of new markets. Strategic goals require additional goals to be achieved at the tactical level.

Tactical Goals

Tactical goals generally are established by business (also referred to as responsibility centers and strategic business units [SBUs]) or functional departments at middle and lower levels of an organization. Tactical goals are short range and usually span one year or less. An example of a tactical goal is "to increase product line profits by 10%."

Concepts Applying to Strategic and Tactical Goals

Just as organizational strategies must be dynamic, so too must strategic and tactical goals. New things are always on the competitive horizon: new entrants, technological changes, economic upheavals, to name but a few. Goals need to be modified or changed to reflect the internal and external changes taking place as well as threats and opportunities present. At a minimum, goals should be evaluated on an annual basis.

Objectives

Objectives provide the details or actions required to support goals. Well-conceived objectives specify the quantitative measures that will be used to track progress and performance—the desired action, the timing of the action, the level of performance desired, and the function or individual responsible for the action. Multiple objectives may support one goal. In this situation, all the objectives must be completed to realize the benefit of the goal; none of the objectives alone can ensure fulfillment of the goal. Expanding on the previous example, "to increase product line profits by 10%," a few supporting objectives might be:

- Marketing team member A determines customer quality perceptions of product X within 30 days. Team member A prioritizes these customer perceptions and assigns a relative weight to each.
- Production team member B develops a process flow diagram of product X within 30 days, including all equipment involved.
- Accounting team member C conducts a profitability analysis of product X within 30 days, determining the profit margin percentage and the investment turnover.

Additional objectives would need to be developed. In totality, all the objectives would support the goal of increasing product line profits by 10%.

As a reminder of the specificity objectives require, the acronym **SMART** often is applied. Objectives should be *s*pecific, *m*easurable, *a*ttainable, *r*ealistic, and *t*imely.

Alignment of Tactics with Long-Term Strategic Goals

As noted earlier, a strategic plan tends to have a long-range planning horizon—typically, somewhere between one and ten years, depending upon the nature of the business. By contrast, an **operational plan** focuses on the fiscal year ahead and involves more tactical issues. A strategic plan precedes an operational plan; the strategic plan provides the foundation upon which the more detailed operational plan is developed. In that sense, strategic plans are "macro" plans and operational plans are "micro" plans. An overview comparing strategic and operational plans is shown in Figure 1B-9.

Figure 1B-9 Comparison of Strategic and Operational Plans

	Strategic Plan	**Operational Plan**
Focus	Underlies both long- and short-run planning; provides the basis for the budget	Formulates specific goals for each business with detailed revenue and expense budgets
Issues Examined	Identifies and analyzes issues such as: • New global market entrants • Economic conditions • Plans for diversification	Identifies and analyzes issues such as: • Quarterly earnings • Inventory levels • Major capital expenditures • Marketing plans • Productions plans
Development	Flows from top down; reflects a comprehensive analysis of external and internal factors	Flows from bottom up; recommends specific options for the upcoming year
Control	Reviewed annually and updated as needed to reflect high-level changes	Reviewed and updated/modified periodically throughout the year to address changing needs (such as lagging major product sales, competitors' new pricing structures, newly opened distribution channel)

Linkage of Budgets to Strategic Plans

Strategic plans and operational plans lead to the formation of budgets. A **budget** represents a quantitative expression of proposed management actions for a set period of time. Budgets have numerous advantages. No matter what type or size an organization is, budgets can:

- Provide a blueprint for the organization to follow in an upcoming time period, identifying the resources and commitments required to meet organizational goals and objectives.

- Help to identify potential bottlenecks/problems and facilitate smoother operations across businesses.
- Serve as a communication device, indicating expected performance for all divisions and all employees for the specified time period.
- Provide a frame of reference with guidelines for operations and criteria for monitoring and control.
- Facilitate performance evaluation of divisions and employees through the comparison of expected operations with actual results.

Budgets quantify management expectations regarding income, cash flows, and financial position. An organization prepares a variety of operational budgets (production, research and design, marketing, distribution, administration, etc.). A master budget coordinates all these individual budgets into a comprehensive organization-wide budget on an annual basis.

Organizational strategies and the strategic plan provide the basis and starting point for preparing the annual master budget. Naturally, the master budget must be congruent with the strategies and strategic plan and contribute to the achievement of the organization's long-term strategic goals, mission, and vision.

How strategy flows from strategic planning through the budgeting process is shown in Figure 1B-10. Strategy starts with a broad perspective. At the budget level, the focus becomes quite specific.

Figure 1B-10 Flow of Organizational Strategy

Strategic Use of the Balanced Scorecard

The **balanced scorecard (BSC)**, developed by Robert Kaplan and David Norton during the early 1990s, was originally intended to help companies better manage intangible assets in conjunction with financial measures. Over time, companies have adapted their usage of the scorecard to help link long-term strategic planning objectives with short-term actions.

According to Kaplan and Norton, firms have introduced additional management processes to the BSC that, when used separately or collectively, facilitate a successful strategic management system. Figure 1B-11 summarizes this expanded use of the BSC.

Figure 1B-11 Use of the BSC as a Strategic Management System

Added BSC Process	Focus/Intent	Examples
Translating the organizational vision and strategy	Actions that senior executives take to translate long-term drivers of organizational success into integrated objectives and measures that can be acted on at operational levels throughout the organization	To build consensus and commitment to organizational strategy, a team of executives develops a BSC that converts the corporate vision statement into a meaningful strategy that can be readily understood terms such as *superior service* and *target customers* are further defined for people who will have to act on the strategy
Communicating the strategy and linking it to the organization	Actions that managers take to communicate organizational strategy throughout the organization and link it to departmental and individual objectives	Middle managers take the strategy to the next level by developing business unit scorecards and educating employees about them
		Internal business processes and learning and innovation objectives to support achievement of financial and customer goals are developed; goals are set, and rewards are linked to performance measures
Business planning	Actions that enable the organization to integrate all business initiatives and financial plans, setting priorities and allocating resources to support long-term strategic objectives	Steps are taken to link all change programs and resource allocation to long-term strategic priorities Short-term targets (milestones) are set for BSC measures Necessary investments to meet goals are identified and funded

(Continued)

Figure 1B-11 (*Continued*)

Added BSC Process	Focus/Intent	Examples
Feedback and learning	Actions that promote strategic learning through feedback and review processes of whether the company, its departments, and individual employees are meeting/have met budgeted goals	Appropriate reviews are conducted (monthly, quarterly, annually) to ensure that targets are being met
		Provisions are made for continuous review of BSC measures as well as market conditions, customer value propositions, competitors' behavior, and internal capabilities
		Ongoing viability of organizational strategy and strategic management system is assessed/reassessed

Kaplan and Norton note that companies have derived many benefits from this expanded BSC usage. Such an integrated and iterative strategic management system allows companies to:

- Clarify and update organizational strategy.
- More readily communicate strategy throughout the organization.
- Align business unit and individual goals to strategy.
- Link strategic objectives, long-term targets, and budgets.
- Identify and implement appropriate strategic initiatives.
- Monitor performance on an ongoing basis.
- Incorporate continuous learning into operating improvements.

Characteristics of Successful Strategic/Tactical Planning

Organizations and the industries they compete in are complex moving targets for strategists. Enterprises continually shift in response to anything that can upset the competitive balance.

The strategic planning process—no matter how large or small the organization or how formal or informal the methodology—offers several benefits in helping a firm frame its competitive strategy. It also has some limitations. Understanding both the advantages and disadvantages helps to recognize what constitutes successful strategic planning.

Benefits of Strategic Planning

Strategic planning provides the following benefits:

- A systematic approach to analyzing threats and opportunities and examining why some organizational strategies have better competitive and profit prospects than others
- A sound framework for developing an effective operating budget

- An organizational learning opportunity for managers to think about strategies and how to best implement them
- An exercise to align management decision making and actions with corporate strategies (e.g., to gain the buy-in of managers and show how their decisions and actions support corporate programs)
- A basis for both financial and nonfinancial performance measures
- A channel of communication among all levels of management about strategies, objectives, operational plans, and so on
- Guidance for approaching new situations

Limitations of Strategic Planning

Strategic planning is not the end-all panacea to all organizational woes. Some of the key shortcomings of strategic planning are listed next:

- The effort, time, and expense involved in the process
- The fact that planning based on predictions is not an exact science; due to a variety of factors, plans may prove to be incorrect and fail
- The potential for resistance to change resulting from entrenched ways of doing things
- The risk that planning can become a bureaucratic exercise devoid of fresh ideas and strategic thinking

Contingency Planning

Well-conceived strategic plans are based on events that have a high probability of occurring. But a strategic plan should not ignore the environmental uncertainties so prevalent in today's business environment.

Contingency Planning Defined

Increasingly, strategic plans include a section on contingency plans to help cope with the turbulence of conditions that could lead to serious difficulty for the enterprise.

Contingency plans are preparations for the what-if situations that might occur and are used for a specific unintended event. The purpose of contingency planning is to provide a quicker reaction time and supply much-needed guidance to managers faced with unexpected developments and possible times of crises.

Subjects of Contingency Plans

Many events and conditions can occur and wreak havoc in an organization. Typical subjects for contingency plans are:

- Lower sales or profit levels
- New entrants that can capture market share

- Government regulations
- Loss of a key executive or manager/succession planning for key employee replacement
- Damage to a critical facility
- Computer system hacking/information security issues
- Disaster recovery
- Sudden changes in interest rates
- Shrinking capital availability
- Union activity
- Mergers, acquisitions, and takeovers

Realistically, contingency plans cannot cover every scenario. Most organizations preparing contingency plans select no more than six critical events. The degree of criticality and the potential of probability usually influence which subjects should be addressed.

Steps in Contingency Planning

In most companies, contingency plans are prepared after the strategic plan is completed; the strategic planning process provides valuable data for developing the contingency plans. But contingency plans typically deal with short-range tactical strategies and not long-range strategies.

Figure 1B-12 outlines basic steps for contingency planning.

Figure 1B-12 Steps in Contingency Planning

Step 1.	Identify potential scenarios needing contingency plans (events, what-ifs).
Step 2.	Estimate the potential impact of the subjects identified (in financial terms, competitive position, etc.).
Step 3.	Develop strategies and tactical plans to deal with each possible occurrence.
Step 4.	Specify trigger points or warning signals.
Step 5.	Store plans off-site.
Step 6.	Routinely review plans and revise as warranted (at least as often as strategic planning).

No standard format for a contingency plan exists. Ideally, a contingency plan should be succinct but include enough detail to guide actions if needed. The more critical the threat, the more detail is warranted.

A few simple examples of accounting-related contingency plans are shown in Figure 1B-13.

Figure 1B-13 Examples of Accounting-Related Contingency Plans

Subject	Plan
Loss of a computer system during a general ledger (GL) close	Identification of off-site (outsourcing) location/service for computer usage
	Identification of company-trained associates who could work at the remote site
Loss of a chief financial officer or another key financial associate	Succession plan
	Identification of key associates to train
	Identification of backup personnel from another division
	Provisions/steps for an outside search
Declining major product/service sales	Identification of areas for analysis and/or change
	Plans for the alternate use of resources
	Layoff considerations

Other Planning Tools and Techniques

There are several other important tools and techniques an organization might use in its strategic planning efforts. These tool and techniques include situational analysis, scenario planning, competitive analysis, and the BCG Growth-Share matrix.

Situational Analysis

Situational analysis refers to a collection of methods that an organization uses to analyze its internal and external environment in order to enhance understanding of the organization's capabilities, customers, and business environment. The situational analysis looks at both the macroenvironmental factors that affect many organizations within the environment and the microenvironmental factors that specifically affect the organization. The purpose of the analysis is to identify the organization's position and to provide an assessment of the organization's ability to survive within the environment. Organizations must be able to summarize opportunities and problems within the environment so they can understand their capabilities within the market.

The methods used in conducting a situational analysis include: a SWOT analysis and Porter's five forces analysis (both previously discussed) as well as a 5C analysis. The 5C analysis is considered the most useful and common way to analyze the market environment, because of the extensive information it provides. It consists of five mini-analyses focused around the company, competitors, customers, collaborators, and the business climate—thus, the 5Cs.

The *company analysis* looks at evaluating the organization's objectives, strategy, and capabilities. The *competitor analysis* assesses competitor position within the industry and the potential threat it may pose to other businesses. The *customer analysis* is extensive, focusing on customer demographics (e.g., wants and needs, motivation to buy, quantity and frequency of purchase, target advertising, etc.). *Collaborator analysis* deals with identifying other key "middlemen" that might help increase the organization's likelihood of gaining more business opportunities. Collaborators include agencies, suppliers, distributors, and other business partners. Finally, a *climate analysis* focuses on researching factors within the business climate and environment that can have an effect on the organization. This analysis is also referred to as a **PEST analysis**, which includes conducting analyses of the following:

- **Political and regulatory environment**. How actively the government regulates the market with its policies and how this might affect the production, distribution, and sale of goods and services
- **Economic environment.** Analyzing trends regarding macroeconomics, such as exchange rates and inflation rate, which can prove to influence businesses
- **Social/cultural environment.** Focuses on interpreting societal trends, which include the study of demographics, education, and culture
- **Technological analysis.** Assessing current technological state and technological advances in order to be able to stay competitive and gain advantage over competitors

Scenario Planning

Scenario planning, also called scenario thinking or scenario analysis, is a strategic planning methodology designed to assist the organization in developing flexible strategic plans. It involves simulating or gaming the expected behavior of what are called STEEEPA trends. STEEEPA is an acronym for plausible alternative *s*ocial, *t*echnical, *e*conomic, *e*nvironmental, *e*ducational, *p*olitical, and *a*esthetic trends. These are the key driving forces in the organization's environment. Again, the focus is on assessing opportunities and threats and developing coping mechanisms.

Competitive Analysis

Competitive analysis, or competitor analysis, focuses on understanding an organization's competition. It includes recognizing who the competition really is rather than who the organization thinks it is. It involves profiling competitors regarding history, products and services, financial condition, corporate and marketing strategies, facilities, and personnel. It also encourages the organization to scan the environment for potential new customers. The steps in competitor analysis involve:

- Determining the organization's industry and its scope and nature
- Determining who the organization's real competitors are
- Determining the organization's customers and their needs

- Determining critical success factors (CSFs) or key performance indicators (KPIs) for the organization's industry
- Ranking the KPIs
- Ranking the organization's competition in relation to the KPIs

BCG Growth-Share Matrix

The **BCG Growth-Share matrix** is a chart/matrix created by Boston Consulting Group (BCG) in 1970 to help organizations analyze their business units, or product lines, so that they can allocate resources appropriately. The chart/matrix is an effective analytical tool in brand marketing and in product and strategic management. Through the matrix, an organization ranks its business units (or products) on the basis of their relative market shares and growth rates and places them into one of the following four quadrants:

1. **Cash cows.** Includes those business units or product lines that have high market share in a slow-growing industry. These units typically generate cash in excess of the amount of cash needed to maintain the business.
2. **Dogs.** Those business units or product lines that boast low market share in a mature, slow-growing industry. The units typically break even and generate barely enough cash to maintain the business's/product's market share.
3. **Stars.** Business units or products that have a high market share in a fast-growing industry.
4. **Question marks** (also known as problem children). Consist of businesses or product lines operating in a high-growth market but that have low market share. They are the starting point for most businesses and have the potential to gain market share, become stars and eventually cash cows when market growth slows.

Bruce Henderson of BCG has quoted the following with regard to the practical use of the matrix: "To be successful, a company should have a portfolio of products with different growth rates and different market shares. The portfolio composition is a function of the balance between cash flows. High-growth products require cash inputs to grow. Low-growth products should generate excess cash. Both kinds are needed simultaneously."

Knowledge Check: Strategic Planning

The next questions are intended to help you check your understanding and recall of the material presented in this topic. They do not represent the type of questions that appear on the CMA exam.

Directions: Answer each question in the space provided. Correct answers and section references appear after the knowledge check questions.

1. Corporate strategy is **best** described as
   - ☐ a. detailed plan describing what a firm will do to achieve superior return on investment.
   - ☐ b. definition of organizational values, expressed in financial and non-financial terms.
   - ☐ c. an analysis of industry attractiveness based on the five forces: buyer power, supplier power, competition, the threat of substitutes, and rivalry.
   - ☐ d. the big picture of how each activity in the firm's value chain affects costs and differentiation.

2. All of the following statements characterize the five forces driving industry profitability **except**:
   - ☐ a. They remain constant as an industry evolves.
   - ☐ b. They can vary from industry to industry.
   - ☐ c. They are vulnerable to high growth and market demand.
   - ☐ d. They are not equally important in any one industry.

Match the following determinants of industry profitability to the appropriate description.

3. _____ Differentiation — a. Leads to a decline in unit costs as the volume per period increases
4. _____ Economies of scale — b. Creates brand identification and existing customer loyalties an entrant must overcome
5. _____ Channel crowding — c. Results from limited capacity or exclusive relationships with manufacturers that restrict the number of product lines

6. "We believe the primary obligation of the company and its employees is to supply the public with the best modern utility service at reasonable rates." This statement exemplifies an organizational
   - ☐ a. vision.
   - ☐ b. mission.
   - ☐ c. strategic goal.
   - ☐ d. objective.

Knowledge Check Answers: Strategic Planning

1. Corporate strategy is best described as [See **Strategy**.]
   - ☐ a. detailed plan describing what a firm will do to achieve superior return on investment
   - ☑ b. definition of organizational values, expressed in financial and non-financial terms
   - ☐ c. an analysis of industry attractiveness based on the five forces: buyer power, supplier power, competition, the threat of substitutes, and rivalry
   - ☐ d. the big picture of how each activity in the firm's value chain affects costs and differentiation

2. All of the following statements characterize the five forces driving industry profitability **except** [See **Rivalry Among Existing Competitors**.]:
   - ☑ a. They remain constant as an industry evolves.
   - ☐ b. They can vary from industry to industry.
   - ☐ c. They are vulnerable to high growth and market demand.
   - ☐ d. They are not equally important in any one industry.

Match the following determinants of industry profitability to the appropriate description.

3. (b) Differentiation [See **Entry of New Competitors**.]	a.	Leads to a decline in unit costs as the volume per period increases
4. (a) Economies of scale [See **Entry of New Competitors**.]	b.	Creates brand identification and existing customer loyalties an entrant must overcome
5. (c) Channel crowding [See **Entry of New Competitors**.]	c.	Results from limited capacity or exclusive relationships with manufacturers that restrict the number of product lines

6. "We believe the primary obligation of the company and its employees is to supply the public with the best modern utility service at reasonable rates." This statement exemplifies an organizational [See **Vision**.]
   - ☑ a. vision.
   - ☐ b. mission.
   - ☐ c. strategic goal.
   - ☐ d. objective.

TOPIC 2

Budgeting Concepts

PLANNING IS THE PROCESS OF mapping out the organization's future direction to attain desired goals. Strategy is the organization's plan to match its strengths with the opportunities in the marketplace to accomplish its desired goals over the short and long term. A budget provides the foundation for planning, because a successful budget is created by a process of aligning the company's resources with its strategy.

This topic introduces the concepts underlying budgeting, the processes used, the people involved, and their roles. It also examines the standards that may be employed in developing budget expectations and evaluating performance against these expectations. This topic provides an overview of the elements of a budget that are explored in greater detail in subsequent topics.

> **READ** the Learning Outcome Statements (LOS) for this topic as found in Appendix A and then study the concepts and calculations presented here to be sure you understand the content you could be tested on in the CMA exam.

Fundamentals: Terminology, Budget Cycle, and Reasons for Budgeting

These budget terms are used in this section.

Budget. A budget is an operational plan and a control tool for an entity that identifies the resources and commitments needed to satisfy the entity's goals over a period. Budgets are primarily quantitative, not qualitative. They set specific goals for income, cash flows, and financial position.

Budgeting. Budgeting is undertaking the steps involved in preparing a budget. Along with clear communication of organizational goals, the ideal budget also contains budgetary controls.

Budgetary control. Without a formal system of control, a budget is little more than a forecast. Budgetary control is a management process to help ensure that a budget is achieved by instituting a systematic budget approval process, by coordinating the efforts of all involved parties and operations, and by analyzing variances from the plan and providing appropriate feedback to responsible parties. The goals identified in the budget must be perceived by employees as realistic if those employees are to be motivated to achieve the goals.

Pro forma statement. A pro forma statement is a budgeted financial statement based on historical documents that is adjusted for events as if they had occurred. Budgeted balance sheets, budgeted statements of cash flows, and budgeted income statements are forecasts of goals for a future period that assist in the allocation of resources.

Budget Cycle

A budget cycle usually involves four steps:

1. A budget is created that addresses the entity as a whole as well as its subunits, and all managers of the subunits agree to fulfill their part of the budget.
2. The budget is used to test current performance against expectations.
3. Variations from the plan are examined, and corrective actions are taken when possible.
4. Feedback is collected, and the plan is revisited and revised if needed. Figure 1B-14 shows how these steps revolve back to the beginning to form a cycle.

Figure 1B-14 Budget Cycle

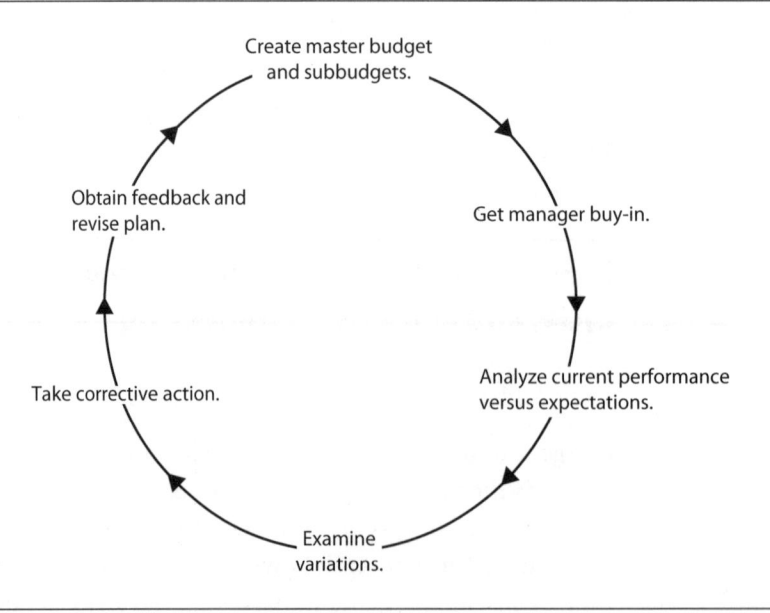

Reasons for Budgeting

There are four main reasons a company creates a budget: planning, communication and coordination, monitoring, and evaluation.

Planning

One of the major benefits of budgeting is that it forces the organization to examine the future. Expectations must be established for income, expenses, personnel needs, future growth (or contraction), and the like. Both strategic and tactical, or "operational," planning allow for the input of ideas from multiple sources within the organization and allow for input from different viewpoints. The planning process may generate new ideas for the organization's direction, or it may provide insight into better ways to achieve goals that have already been established. Budgets, an output of the planning process, provide a framework to achieve the goals of the organization. Without the budget framework, individual managers would improvise decisions and would operate in a reactive rather than a proactive manner. As a result, there would be a lack of direction and coordination of activities.

Communication and Coordination

Budgeting also promotes communication and coordination of efforts within the organization. The different parts of the organization (production, marketing, materials management, etc.) must communicate their plans and needs to each other during the budget process so that all can evaluate the effect that the plans and needs of others have on their own. Each part of the organization must coordinate its activities to attain the budgeted goals and objectives. For example, if new products are to be developed, funds must be provided for development, materials will have to be purchased to produce the products, marketing and sales must have sufficient resources to promote and sell the products, and shipping and distribution may need additional space to store the products or additional resources to distribute them. Budgeting also allows the organization to communicate its goals to everyone in the organization, including those not involved in the budget process. Budgeting sets the stage for everyone in the organization to work toward the goals of the organization.

Monitoring

The budget sets standards, or performance indicators, by which managers can monitor the organization's progress in meeting its goals. By comparing the actual results for a period to the budgeted results for that period, managers can see whether the organization is on track to achieving its goals. Breaking down the organization's master budget to divisional and departmental levels allows each level of the organization to be evaluated. The organization as a whole may be meeting its goals while individual divisions and departments are failing. The difference between the actual results and the expected results is called a variance. A negative, or unfavorable, variance may indicate a need to take corrective action. Positive, or favorable, variances can reflect opportunities to make adjustments to take advantage of the conditions creating the variance—that is, if sales are up, then perhaps production should be increased.

Evaluation

Budgets also serve as guides or instruments for employee evaluations. Once the budget is set and managers have been advised of their responsibilities in relation to budget performance, they can be held responsible for their portion of the budget. By comparing actual results to the budget for a given period, a manager's performance can be evaluated. Having negative or unfavorable results does not necessarily mean that a manager is not performing well, but it does provide an indication that a specific part of the business should be focused on, in order to determine the root cause of the unfavorable variance. Likewise, positive, or favorable, results do not necessarily mean that a manager is performing in an exceptional way. Performance evaluations allow an organization to motivate employees by rewarding them for good performance in a number of ways, such as through performance-based bonuses and/or by including performance evaluations in the decision process for future compensation or promotion decisions.

Economic Considerations in the Budgeting Process

There are a significant number of interrelationships among economic conditions, industry situations, organizational plans, and the budgeting process. Budgeting is most effective when the budgeting process is linked to the overall strategy of the organization. Managers should build their strategy and organizational objectives to focus on all economic factors, including the financial impact of the decision-making process and understanding factors of competition.

When developing an organizational strategy, managers should ask these questions:

- What are our organizational objectives?
- How can we relate our organizational objectives to the budgeting process?
- Who are our competitors, and how can we differentiate ourselves from them?
- How are we affected by the competition and trends in the marketplace?
- What organizational risks exist that may impact the budgeting process?
- What organizational opportunities exist that may impact the budgeting process?

Operations and Performance Goals

A prerequisite for budget development is a strategic analysis that matches an entity's capabilities with available marketplace opportunities. Strategy addresses the objectives of the organization; locates potential markets; considers the impact of events, competitors, and the economy; addresses the structure of the organization; and evaluates the risks of alternative strategies. Strategic analysis is the basis for both long-term and short-term planning. These plans lead, respectively, to long-term and short-term budgets (as summarized in Figure 1B-15), and these budgets in turn lead to the creation of a master budget and its components.

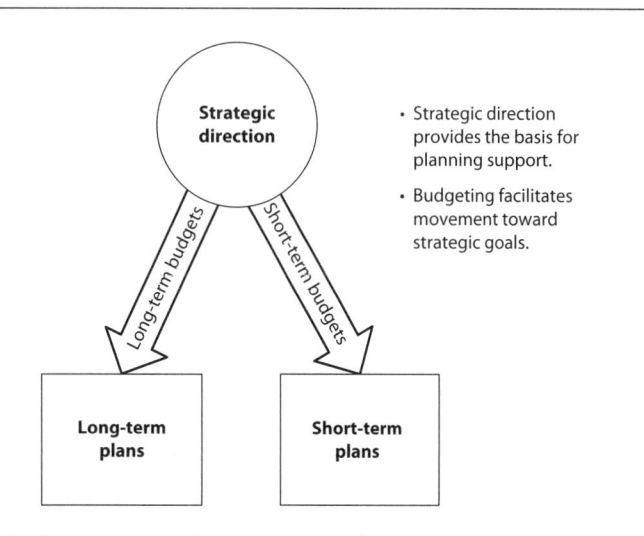

Figure 1B-15 Strategy, Planning, and Budgets

- Strategic direction provides the basis for planning support.
- Budgeting facilitates movement toward strategic goals.

Budgets play a role in measuring performance against established goals. When using past performance solely to evaluate present results, the mistakes and problems that occurred in the past are automatically factored in to the benchmark that is being used.

For example: A company reports poor sales because of a new and inexperienced sales force. If this year's data are used as the next year's sales benchmark, the mark would be set lower than necessary and the sales team would not be motivated to work as hard. However, if the benchmark is set too high, employees may not strive to achieve amounts they view as unrealistic. This can be the case when an anomaly produces better-than-average results one year.

Employing a forecasted budget as a plan allows for the use of the expected results as the benchmark. Another benefit of using a budget instead of historical results is that past performance is not always indicative of future results. A budget may be able to predict and account for such shifts, but relying only on historical data leads to a sense that the past year must always be improved on, no matter the circumstances.

Costs are considered "controllable" or "discretionary" when the purchaser or manager has discretion in whether to incur the charge or alter the level of the charge within a short amount of time. Variable costs and other costs directly under the control of the manager are controllable costs. The manager can cut workers' hours, use cheaper materials, or otherwise restrict such controllable costs. A division manager can control maintenance and advertising costs to a certain degree.

Fixed costs, such as administrative salaries or rent, usually are not controllable and are therefore called "committed" costs.

Controllable costs are useful for performance evaluation and budgeting.

- Rating a manager's use of funds based on divisional net revenue less controllable costs will be perceived, by those being rated, as a more reasonable approach than being held accountable for uncontrollable costs—which can be very unmotivating.

- Focusing on controllable costs places the emphasis where the most benefit can be achieved from the effort of budgeting.

Characteristics of Successful Budgeting

Many factors characterize a successful budget, but no single factor can lead to a successful budget. Here is a list of the common factors in a successful budget:

- The budget must be aligned with the corporate strategy.
- The budget process should be kept separate but should flow from the strategic planning and forecasting processes.
- **Strategic plans** are higher level, longer term, and structured in companywide terms, such as product lines, rather than responsibility centers. However, early budgeting steps can be used to refine the strategic direction of the company because they use more current information.
- **Forecasts** often have lower accountability than a budget, usually are not approved by management, and often are not formally analyzed against variances. For instance, a manager may create a forecast for direct materials needed in next week's production to ensure adequate inventory levels. However, budgets must use the forward-looking information from more comprehensive forecasts. Therefore, the forecasts directly used in the budgeting process, such as the sales forecast, must be kept accountable.
- The budget should be used to alleviate potential bottlenecks and to allocate resources to those areas that will use the funds most efficiently and effectively.
- The budget must contain technically correct and reasonably accurate numbers and facts.
- Management (including top management) must fully endorse the budget—it must accept responsibility for reaching the budget goals.
- Employees must consider the budget as a planning, communication, and coordinating tool, and not as a pressure or blame device.
- The budget must be characterized as a motivating tool to help employees work toward organizational goals.
- The budget must be seen as an internal control device, where internal-use budgets base employee evaluations on controllable or discretionary costs.
- Sales and administrative budgets need to be detailed in order that key assumptions can be better understood.
- A higher authority than the team that developed the budget must review and approve the budget.

The final budget should not be easily changed, but it must be flexible enough to be useful. Budgets should compel planning, promote communication and coordination, and provide performance criteria. The budget process must balance input from those who will need to follow the budget against a thorough and fair review of the budget by upper management.

Characteristics of a Successful Budget Process

Whether the organization and its budget are very simple or highly complex, the characteristics of a successful budget process include: the budget period, the participants in the budget process, the basic steps in budgeting, and the use of cost standards.

Budget Period

Budgets are most commonly prepared for the company's fiscal year, but often three-, five-, and ten-year budgets are planned, as well as budgets of shorter durations. Management must consider what the most suitable length of time would be to suit the needs of the organization. The most frequently used budget timeframe is one year, although often the year is divided into months and quarters. A different year basis other than fiscal year is possible but is not recommended because fiscal-year financial statements can be easily compared to the budget. Budgets are often further broken into continuous (rolling) budgets. A continuous budget has a month, quarter, or year basis, and as each period ends, the upcoming period's budget is revised and another period is added to the end of the budget. Software is available for implementing this type of budget.

Budget Process

Methods of budget preparation differ between companies, but all fall somewhere on a continuum between entirely authoritative and entirely participative. In an **authoritative budget** (top-down budget), top management sets everything from strategic goals down to the individual items of the budget for each department and expects lower managers and employees to adhere to the budget and meet the goals. In a **participative budget** (bottom-up or self-imposed budget), managers at all levels and certain key employees cooperate to set budgets for their areas, and top management usually retains final approval. The ideal process combines the features of each and falls somewhere between these methods.

Figure 1B-16 lists benefits and limitations of purely authoritative and participative budgeting and shows how a combined approach provides the greatest number of checks and balances over a budgetary process. Note that the combination approach sometimes is considered to be a form of the participative approach.

The five steps in a combined approach include:

1. Budget participants are identified, including representatives of all levels of management as well as key employees with expertise in particular areas.
2. Top management communicates the strategic direction to budget participants.
3. Budget participants create the first draft of their budget.
4. Lower levels submit budgets to the next higher level for review in an iterative process stressing communication in both directions.
5. Rigorous but fair review and budget approval sets the final budget.

Figure 1B-16 Comparison of Authoritative, Combined, and Participative Budgeting

Authoritative Approach	Combination Approach	Participative Approach
Top management incorporates strategic goals into its budgets.	Strategic goals are communicated topdown and implemented bottomup.	Strategic goals do not receive priority in the budgetary process.
Better control over decisions.	Control retained and expertise gained at cost of a slightly longer process.	Expertise leads to informed budget decisions.
Dictates instead of communicates.	Two-way communication: Top management understands participants' difficulties and needs. Participants understand management's dilemmas.	Communicates lower-level perspective (of product/service or market) to management.
Employees: Resentful Unmotivated	Personal control leads to acceptance, which leads to greater personal commitment.	Employees: Involved Empowered
Stringent budgets may not be strictly followed at lower levels.	Ownership of budget and thorough review leads to tight budgets that get followed.	Easy or abdicated approval can lead to loose budgets and budget slack.
Not a recommended approach but could work in small or slow-changing environments.	Best for most companies; provides balance between strategic and tactical inputs.	Best for responsibility centers with highly variable situations where area manager has best data.

Budget Participants

Three groups make or break a budget: the board of directors, top management, and the budget committee. Middle and lower management also play a significant role, because they create detailed budgets based on upper management's plan. Depending on the size of the company and the type of budget being created, a budget coordinator and process experts may be involved in budget development.

Board of Directors

The board of directors does not create the budget, but it cannot abdicate its responsibility to review the budget and either approve or send it back for revision. The board usually appoints the members of the budget committee.

Top Management

Top management is ultimately responsible for the budgets, and the primary means top managers have of exercising this responsibility is to ensure that all levels of management understand and support the budget and the overall budget control process. If top management is not perceived to endorse a budget, line managers will be less likely to follow the budget precisely. Also, top managers should pay close attention to how they are affecting each line manager's budget, because insensitive policies could result in creative budgeting on the part of staff.

Top managers should give their subordinates incentives for making truthful and complete budgets, such as rewarding accuracy. A common problem that needs to be avoided is budget slack. **Budget slack** occurs when budgeted performance differs from actual performance because managers tend to build in some extra money for their budget to deal with the unexpected. Budget slack is built-in freedom to fail, and cumulative budget slack at each sublevel can result in a very inaccurate master budget.

However, rigid enforcement of budgets will, in some situations, cost an organization more in the long run than if some flexibility is allowed. For example, a manufacturer could lose thousands of dollars if the maintenance manager refuses to approve overtime for its mechanics to make an urgent repair because "it would use up too much of the maintenance budget."

Budget Committee

Large corporations usually need to form a budget committee composed of senior management and often led by the chief executive officer (CEO) or a vice president. The size of the committee will vary depending on the organization. The committee directs budget preparation, approves budgets, rules on disagreements, monitors the budget, reviews results, and approves revisions.

Middle and Lower Management

Once the budget committee sets the tone for the budget process, many others in the organization have some role to play. Middle and lower management do much of the specific budgeting work. These managers follow budget guidelines, which are general guidelines for responsibility centers preparing individual budgets set by either top management or the budget committee. A responsibility center, cost center, or strategic business unit is a segment of a company in which the manager is vested with the authority to make cost, revenue, and/or investment decisions and therefore also set budgets. The budget guidelines are formed around the company's strategy and long-term plans. The guidelines govern preparation methods, layout, and new events that have occurred since the publication of the master budget, such as new downsizing needs, changes in the economy, and year-to-date operating results.

Budget Coordinator

The more people who are involved in a budget process, the greater the need for an individual or team who can identify and resolve discrepancies between the budgets of the various responsibility centers and between various portions of a master budget.

Process Experts

When participative budgeting is used, often certain key nonmanagerial employees are added to the team. Team participants tend to be those who have a detailed understanding of the costs for a particular area, especially those areas that are extremely complex or variable. Such participants will not only bring more focus to a budget but will also take ownership of the budget and increase its likelihood of being followed at the operational level.

Budgeting Steps

The steps that responsibility centers take in preparing their budgets include the initial budget proposal, budget negotiation, review and approval, and revision.

Budget Proposal

After the CEO decides on the company strategy, a memo or directive is sent to all line managers or responsibility centers so they can start aligning their budget process with the strategic plan (i.e., a top-down implementation). With this strategy in mind, each responsibility center prepares an initial budget, taking both internal and external factors into account. Internal factors include: changes in price, availability, and manufacturing processes; new products or services; changes in related or intertwined responsibility centers; and staff changes. External factors include changes in the economy and the labor market, the price and availability of goods and services, industry trends, and actions of competitors.

Budget Negotiation

When the initial budget proposal is submitted to a superior or to the budget committee, the budget is reviewed to see if it meets the organization's strategic goals, falls within an acceptable range, and is consistent with similar budgets. Reviewers also determine if the budget is feasible and if it fits within the goals of units the next level up. Negotiations take up the bulk of time in budget preparations because pushback from a superior will result in renegotiation of priorities for both the superior and the responsibility center.

Budget Review and Approval

Budgets are reviewed and approved up the chain of command to the level of the budget committee, where the combined budgets become the master budget, after review for consistency with the budget guidelines, short- and long-term goals, and strategic plans. Once the committee and the committee leader approve the plan, it is submitted to the board of directors for final approval.

Budget Revision

The rigidity of a budget varies from organization to organization. Some budgets must be followed absolutely; others can be revised only under specific circumstances; and others are subject to continuous revision. Rigidly following a budget in the face of changing circumstances has the potential for disaster. Management should not be required to rely on the budget as the sole operational guideline. Regular revisions may provide better operating guidelines; however, this may lead managers to anticipate regular changes and not prepare budgets as carefully as they should. Organizations that allow regular revisions should make sure that the threshold for revision is set high enough to keep employees working as efficiently as possible. When regular revisions occur, a copy of the original budget should be kept for comparison with actual results at the end of the period.

Cost Standards

Organizations set different types of standards that they strive to achieve. A **standard** is any carefully determined price, quantity, service level, or cost. Standards in manufacturing are usually set on a per-unit basis. A standard cost is how much an operation or service should cost, or the cost an entity expects to incur assuming that all goes as planned (e.g., expected time and capacity). Budget planners use standard costs to prepare budgets and then update standard costs as circumstances change. In practice, there is not a precise dividing line between a budgeted amount and a standard amount. With shorter time frames, there is little distinction between a budgeted amount and a standard amount.

Types of Standards

Standards can be either authoritative or participative.

Authoritative Standards

Authoritative standards are determined solely by management. They are more speedily set and can closely match overall company goals but may be a cause for resentment or may not be followed at all.

Participative Standards

Participative standards are set by holding a dialogue between management and all involved parties. They are more likely to be adopted than authoritative standards, but they take more time and require negotiation to ensure that operating goals are still met.

Specific types of standard costs include ideal standards and reasonably attainable standards.

Ideal Standards

An ideal standard is a forward-looking goal; it is currently attainable only if all circumstances result in the best possible outcome. Ideal standards work into a continuous improvement strategy and total quality management philosophies. They allow for no work delays, interruptions, waste, or machine breakdown. Ideal standards require a level of effort that can be attained only by the most skilled and efficient employees working at their best efficiency all of the time. Some firms use progress toward an ideal standard instead of deviations from the ideal to measure and reward success. However, ideal standards are very difficult to attain, and their frequent use can become frustrating. If difficult-to-attain ideal standards are constantly required, they can be a disincentive to productivity, because workers will not even attempt to meet such "impossible" goals and may become used to missing goals.

Reasonably Attainable Standards

A reasonably attainable standard is closer to a historical standard; it sets goals at a level that is attainable by properly trained individuals operating at a normal pace. The standard is expected to be reached most of the time. They allow for normal work delays, spoilage, waste, employee rest periods, and machine downtime. Practical standards can be attained by efficient efforts from an average worker. Variances from practical standards represent deviations caused by abnormal conditions and can be used in forecasting and inventory. In comparison, ideal standards cannot be used in forecasting and planning since they may result in unrealistic planning and forecasting figures that are not attainable even under the best of circumstances. Setting such a standard too low will encourage employees to work less diligently than needed. In addition, using reasonably attainable standards tends to discourage continuous improvement strategies.

Standard Costs for Direct Materials and Labor

Direct cost items, such as direct materials and direct labor, are measured by determining the number of units of each type of input required to get one unit of output. This amount is multiplied by the standard cost per input unit.

For example: If three input units are allowed for producing one output unit and an input unit costs $10, then the standard cost would be $30 per output unit. For direct labor, if 0.7 manufacturing labor hours of input are allowed for producing one output unit and labor hours cost $10, then the standard cost would be $7 per output unit.

Of course, real standard costs are developed by adding together multiple direct materials and labor costs. More specific guidelines for determining the prices for direct materials and labor are described next.

Standard Costs for Direct Materials

Standard costs are determined by quality, quantity, and price. Quality must be determined first, because it affects all the other variables. Quality level is determined by the product's targeted market niche. The standard is developed by engineers, production managers, and management accountants working together, on the basis of the production facilities, the quality of the product, the costs of manufacturing, and the equipment to be used. Direct material usage standards should allow for losses, spoilage, scrap, and waste normally expected in the production process. A price is set as a combination of all prior work done, including quality, quantity, and supply chain costs. Determining supply chain costs includes such considerations as whether to select the lowest-cost vendor each time (costs will vary) or to establish a relationship with one reliable vendor (costs will be more stable).

Standard Costs for Direct Labor

Product complexity, personnel skill levels, the type and condition of equipment, and the nature of the manufacturing process will all affect the direct labor costs. Management accountants, engineers, production managers, labor unions, human resources, and others affect the direct labor standards. Labor usage standards should consider normally expected equipment downtime and worker breaks that slow the production process. The cost of direct labor is based on gross base pay, not net base pay. Fringe benefits, overtime, and shift premiums are normally considered labor-related overhead costs.

Sources for Standards Setting

Several sources often are used simultaneously when setting standards: activity analysis, historical data, market expectations, strategic decisions, and benchmarking.

Activity Analysis

An activity analysis, as part of activity-based costing (ABC), identifies, codifies, and analyzes the activities needed to finish a job or operation. (ABC is discussed in more detail in Section D: Cost Management.) The most efficient combination of resources and other inputs is derived by interviewing personnel directly involved with various aspects of the operation. Engineers are involved in calculating the product ingredients and determining the specific steps required in the process. Management accountants help analyze the direct costs of the inputs and allocate an appropriate amount of the indirect costs (lighting, rent, repairs, etc.) to the operation. Such analyses also evaluate the skill levels required of those who perform the tasks. Activity analyses in activity-based costing are the most thorough costing method—and are the most expensive to implement.

Historical Data

Relying on historical data for determining costs is relatively inexpensive but is less reliable than activity analysis. When reliable, historical data can be used to find the average or median historical cost for an operation. To implement continuous improvement, the best performance recorded could be used as a standard or, at least, as an ideal standard. However, historical data can perpetuate past inefficiencies or fail to take into account the impact of new technologies.

Market Expectations and Strategic Decisions

Market expectations and strategic decisions can determine a maximum cost level that is allowed for a product, as is the case when using target costing. Target costing is a product design technique in which the product reaches a particular target cost at the end of the production process. However, when a company is a price taker in the market (in other words, it must take the going rate for materials or labor), target costing must take these actual costs into account when setting standards. Strategic objectives, such as a program of continuous improvement or zero defects, will be accomplished only if the standards are set high.

Benchmarking

Benchmarking is the continuous, systematic process of measuring products, services, and practices against the best levels of performance. Benchmarking is frequently thought of as capturing best-in-class information, but the practice has a much wider application. Quite often, "best levels" are comparisons to external benchmarks of industry leaders. However, they may also be based on internal benchmarking information or measures from other organizations (outside an industry) that have similar processes. Good benchmarks can lead a company toward continuous improvement. However, a poor benchmark can have significant negative results. For example, using an incompatible industry as a benchmark can produce either unreachable or unchallenging goals. Also, benchmarking typically does not produce breakthroughs that lead to sustainable competitive advantage.

Resource Allocation

All entities have a finite amount of resources and want to make the most of their capital. The allocation of scarce resources among competing opportunities is accomplished through implementation of a strategy.

Master Budget

A master budget is a plan based on a company's strategy for controlling its operations for a specific period of time. A key point is that master budgets are fixed at an expected level of business activity.

Strategy

A company analyzes external factors to identify opportunities and threats; it analyzes internal factors to identify competitive advantages and weaknesses. When a company sees how it can match its strengths to market opportunities, it has a strategy that can be applied to the budget.

When a budget exists without consideration of strategy, it usually begins with the prior year's budget and misses opportunities to change the direction of the company, causing stagnation. Many once-great companies have met their demise because they failed to change in response to market demands. Implementing the strategy requires formulation of long-term plans, and long-term plans are implemented using a budget process.

Long-Term Planning

While a strategy is the starting point for achieving organizational goals, a long-term plan is needed to ensure that the strategy is implemented. A long-term plan is usually a five- to ten-year plan of actions required to achieve the company's goals. Planning for the long term can involve discontinuing certain operations over time, arranging for equity or debt financing, and allocating resources gradually to new branches of business. Such major reorganizations can be accomplished only over a period of time and usually involve the use of capital budgeting (part of the master budget). Capital budgeting is the process of allocating resources to an entity's proposed long-term projects. Because buildings, equipment, and hiring and training staff are all extremely expensive, such allocations must be made in accordance with strategy.

Short-Term Objectives

Short-term objectives are the variations in the long-term plan that result from capital budgeting, the operating results of past periods, and expected future results caused by the current economic, social, industrial, and technological environment. These variations are fed into each year's master budget.

Components of a Master Budget

The **master budget** is the overall plan for operations for a company or business unit over a year, an operating period, or a shorter duration. The master budget sets quantitative goals for all operations, including detailed plans for raising the required capital. Figure 1B-17 shows how the factors behind a master budget relate to it.

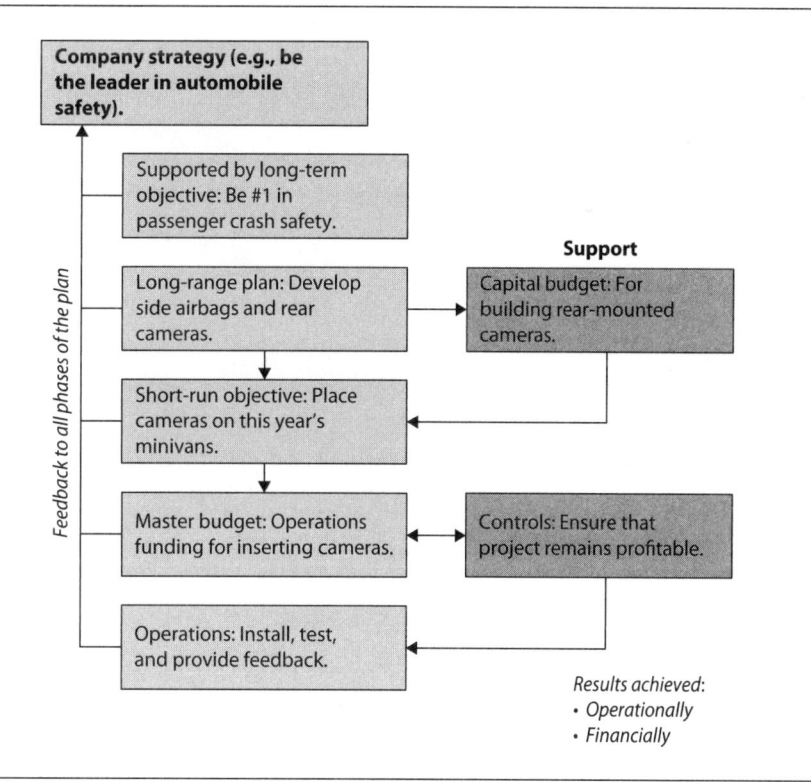

Figure 1B-17 Strategic Goals, Long-Term Objectives, Budgets, and Operations

The master budget is a map showing where the company is heading. If it is properly designed, it will show the company heading in the same direction as the strategy and the long-term plan. The budget is more precise and of shorter duration than long-term plans, and it is more focused on responsibility centers than longer-term planning tools.

A master budget is broken down into an operating and a financial budget.

- An **operating budget** identifies resources that are needed for operations and is concerned with the acquisition of these resources through purchase or manufacture. Production budgets, purchasing budgets, sales promotion budgets, and staffing budgets are all operating budgets.
- A **financial budget** matches sources of funds with uses of funds in order to achieve the goals of the firm, including budgets for cash inflows, outflows, financial position, operating income, and capital expenditures. A **capital budget** is used to plan how resources will be used to support significant investments in projects that have long-term implications. These projects could include the purchase of new equipment or investment in new facilities.

Knowledge Check: Budgeting Concepts

The next questions are intended to help you check your understanding and recall of the material presented in this topic. They do not represent the type of questions that appear on the CMA exam.

Directions: Answer each question in the space provided. Correct answers and section references appear after the knowledge check questions.

1. A management representative interviews the manager of the firm's tennis ball line and the tennis ball machine operators. The objective is to define a cost standard that each of these parties believes is the best result that could be achieved assuming that nothing went wrong. What sort of standard is being set?

    ☐ a. Authoritative ideal standard
    ☐ b. Participative ideal standard
    ☐ c. Authoritative currently attainable standard
    ☐ d. Participative currently attainable standard

2. Number the following steps in forming a master budget in the correct order:

    _____ Create master budget
    _____ Create long-term plans
    _____ Create short-term plans
    _____ Analyze the internal and external environment
    _____ Form strategic goals

3. Which of the following groups is most likely to introduce slack into a budget?

    ☐ a. Board of directors
    ☐ b. Top management
    ☐ c. Budget committee
    ☐ d. Middle and lower management

4. In setting standard costs for direct materials, what element must be determined first and why?

    _____

5. Identify at least three component budgets of a financial budget.

    _____, _____, and _____.

Knowledge Check Answers: Budgeting Concepts

1. A management representative interviews the manager of the firm's tennis ball line and the tennis ball machine operators. The objective is to define a cost standard that each of these parties believes is the best result that could be achieved assuming that nothing went wrong. What sort of standard is being set? [See *Types of Standards*.]
   - ☐ a. Authoritative ideal standard
   - ☒ b. Participative ideal standard
   - ☐ c. Authoritative currently attainable standard
   - ☐ d. Participative currently attainable standard

2. Number the following steps in forming a master budget in the correct order: [See *Master Budget*.]
   - 5 Create master budget.
   - 3 Create long-term plans.
   - 4 Create short-term plans.
   - 1 Analyze the internal and external environment.
   - 2 Form strategic goals.

3. Which of the following groups is most likely to introduce slack into a budget? [See *Middle and Lower Management*.]
   - ☐ a. Board of directors
   - ☐ b. Top management
   - ☐ c. Budget committee
   - ☒ d. Middle and lower management

4. In setting standard costs for direct materials, what element must be determined first and why? [See *Standard Costs for Direct Materials and Labor*.]

   Quality must be determined first, because it affects all the other variables.

5. Identify at least three component budgets of a financial budget. [See *Components of a Master Budget*.]

   Component budgets of a financial budget include budgets for: cash inflows, outflows, financial position, operating income, and capital expenditures.

TOPIC 3

Forecasting Techniques

A VITAL FUNCTION OF MANAGING any business is planning for the future. Experienced judgment, intuition, and awareness of economic conditions may give business leaders a rough idea of what may happen in the future. However, this experience must be supported by various quantitative methods that can be used to forecast such outcomes as next quarter's sales volume or the viability of introducing a new product line. In addition, a degree of uncertainty needs to be incorporated into the decision-making process.

This topic looks at a number of forecasting techniques that companies can use to plan for future financial performance. The quantitative methods discussed here are regression analysis, learning curve analysis, and expected value.

> **READ** the Learning Outcome Statements (LOS) for this topic as found in Appendix A and then study the concepts and calculations presented here to be sure you understand the content you could be tested on in the CMA exam.

Quantitative Methods

When planning for the future, a company faces some degree of uncertainty and will rely on a variety of quantitative methods to help it make better decisions. This content focuses on quantitative methods in three areas:

Data analysis involves analyzing a given set of data to establish the relationship and/or pattern in the data. These analyses can be used to predict the outcome based on a given set of conditions such as with regression analysis or they can be used to forecast the outcome based on an established pattern.

Model building involves creating a mathematical model that establishes the relationship between different factors. Learning curve analysis is one type of model that is used to determine how the amount of time required to produce a product changes as the number of units produced changes.

Decision theory deals with uncertainty by looking at various potential outcomes that can happen in the future, along with the likelihood of these outcomes occurring. Expected value is one method that deals with uncertainty.

Regression Analysis

Linear regression analysis is a statistical method used to determine the impact one variable (or a group of variables) has on another variable. It provides the best, linear, unbiased estimate of the relationship between the dependent variable (Y) and one or more independent variables (X or X's). Linear regression often is used by management accountants to analyze cost behavior (i.e., determine the fixed and variable portions of a total cost) or to forecast future events such as sales levels.

The assumptions underlying linear regression are:

- Linearity. The relationship between the dependent variable and the independent variable(s) is linear.
- Stationary. The process underlying the relationship is stationary. This assumption is often called the constant process assumption.
- The differences between the actual values of the dependent variable and its predicted values (the error or residual terms) are normally distributed with a mean of zero and a constant standard deviation. In other words, the dependent variable is not correlated with itself; that is, it is not autocorrelated or serialcorrelated.
- The independent variables (X's) in multiple regression analysis are independent of each other. There is no multi-colinearity.

Regression analysis creates a linear equation based on the relationship between a dependent variable and one or more independent variables. The dependent variable (Y) is the value being forecast, such as sales or total costs. The independent variables (X's) are the factors that are assumed to influence or drive the variations seen in the dependent variable. It is assumed that the relationship between the dependent variable and the independent variable remains constant (hence the linear relationship).

There are two main types of regression analysis: **simple regression analysis**, which uses only one independent variable, and **multiple regression analysis**, which uses two or more independent variables.

Regression analysis equations systematically reduce estimation errors and are therefore also called least square regression. Regression analysis fits a line (the regression line) through data points—a line that minimizes the difference between the line (prediction) and the data point (actual). The statistical formula that the regression is based on produces the least amount of error between these two items.

Simple Linear Regression

Simple linear regression analysis can be used to analyze the relationship between sales and marketing costs.

For example: A retail firm called Build and Fix is trying to forecast sales and believes that store sales depend on marketing costs. To forecast sales for year 4, Build and Fix management collects data about its past sales and marketing expenditures. Figure 1B-18 summarizes the data.

Figure 1B-18 Data on Marketing Costs and Sales for Build and Fix

	Marketing Costs ($000)	Sales ($000)	Marketing Costs ($000)	Sales ($000)	Marketing Costs ($000)	Sales ($000)
Quarter	Year 1		Year 2		Year 3	
Q1	$50	$48,000	$100	$89,000	$40	$62,000
Q2	30	40,000	90	105,000	90	130,000
Q3	40	62,000	80	73,000	70	80,000
Q4	60	75,000	110	105,000	50	50,000

Figure 1B-19 shows the data from Figure 1B-18 on a scatter diagram. Note in the scatter diagram that the data exhibit an upward trend, indicating that there is a positive relationship between sales and marketing costs. This means that when marketing costs increase, sales also increase. Regression analysis attempts to estimate the linear relationship between sales and marketing costs. The result is a linear regression line, shown in Figure 1B-19.

Figure 1B-19 Marketing Costs as a Predictor of Sales

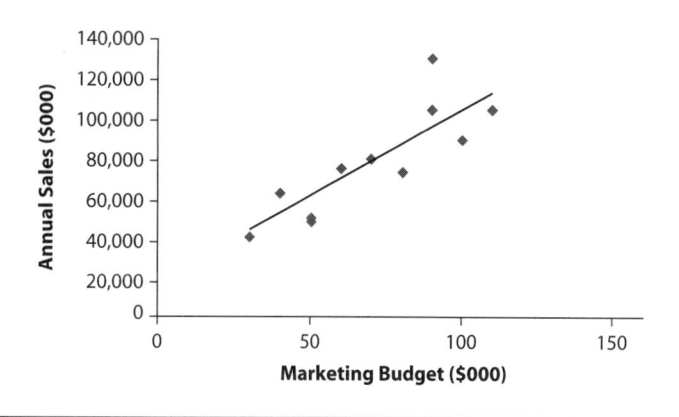

The dependent variable (Y), which is always plotted on the vertical axis, is sales. The independent variable (X) is plotted on the horizontal axis. In this example, it represents marketing costs. A mathematical expression of the original data points can be developed that can be used to forecast sales (Y) based on a given marketing budget. Since the regression line is a straight line that best fits the set of data points, it can be represented mathematically as the next equation:

$$Y = a + bX$$

where:
- Y = annual sales; it is the dependent variable to be forecast.
- a = amount of Y when X = 0. This value is also called the Y intercept, because when X = 0, Y = a, and on a graph, the line will intercept the Y axis at the value of a.
- b = slope of the line, also known as the regression coefficient. It represents the "impact" X has on Y. For every 1 unit change in X, Y is expected to change by b units.
- X = value for the independent variable (in this case, marketing costs) or the driver for the dependent variable to be forecast (in this case, annual sales).

Figure 1B-20 represents the results of the simple linear regression analysis performed on the given set of sales and marketing data in Figure 1B-18.

Figure 1B-20 Regression Values for Marketing Costs as Predictor of Sales

	Coefficients	T-Value	Standard Error
Intercept	$18,444,808.74	1.48	$12,460,200.96
Marketing costs	$861.31	4.98	$172.93

In the example shown in Figures 1B-19 and 1B-20, the regression equation is:

$$Y = \$18{,}444{,}809 + \$861(X)$$

where X represents the marketing budget. This formula can be used to go beyond the table and forecast sales with a marketing budget of $75,000.

$$Y = \$18{,}444{,}809 + \$861(75{,}000) = \$83{,}019{,}809 \text{ Forecast Sales}$$

Regression analysis also provides a number of objective benchmarks that allow users to evaluate the reliability of the regression equation. Three common measures are R-squared, T-value, and standard error of estimate (SE).

R-squared

R-squared (goodness of fit or coefficient of determination) is a value between 0 and 1 indicating the degree to which changes in a dependent variable can be predicted by changes in independent variables. R-squared shows how much of the variation in total cost is accounted for by the cost driver(s). It is the percentage of the variation in the dependent variable accounted for by the variability in the independent variable. A regression with an R-squared value closer to 1 has more explanatory power than a regression with an R-squared value closer to 0. Graphs of regressions with high R-squared values show data points lying near the regression line, while regressions with low R-squared values show more widely scattered data points.

The R-squared value for Build and Fix's sales and marketing costs is 0.7127. This means that approximately 71.27% of the variation in sales is accounted for by variation in marketing costs.

T-value

T-value measures whether an independent variable (X) has a valid, long-term relationship to a dependent variable. Generally, the T-value should be more than 2. A variable with a low T-value indicates little or no statistically significant relationship between the independent and dependent variables, and the variable should be removed from the regression because it can lead to inaccurate forecasts.

For Build and Fix, the T-value is greater than 2 for the marketing costs, which indicates that the impact marketing cost has on sales is statistically significant.

Standard Error of Estimate

The SE measures the dispersion around the regression line and allows the user to assess the accuracy of the predictions. That is, a user can build a confidence interval around the estimate. For normal (i.e., mound-shaped) distributions, approximately 68% of measurements will fall within plus or minus 1 standard error (depends on sample size). Approximately 95% will fall within plus or minus 2 standard errors.

Multiple Linear Regression

In the Build and Fix example, a simple linear regression analysis was used to estimate the impact that the amount of money spent on marketing would have on the company's sales. Using a simple regression analysis, it is assumed that marketing expenditures are the only factor that explain (or have an impact) on a company's sales level. Based on the results of the analysis, the R-squared is only 0.7127. That means only 71.27% of the variation in sales can be explained by changes in marketing expenditures, and the remaining 28.73% (100% − 71.27%) is explained by changes in other factors that are not included in the regression model.

In forecasting sales, an organization needs to take into consideration not only its marketing efforts but other factors, such as the economic conditions, its competitors' actions, its pricing strategy, and so on. All of these other factors can be incorporated into a multiple regression model, where they become the additional independent variables that can help to explain the other 28.73% in sales variation that cannot be explained by marketing expenditures.

In general, a multiple regression model looks very similar to a simple regression model, except that it has two or more independent variables (X_1, X_2, etc). The regression "line" from a multiple regression model can be represented mathematically as shown:

$$Y = a + b_1 X_1 + b_2 X_2 + b_3 X_3 + \ldots b_n X_n$$

For a multiple regression analysis, the interpretation of the Y-intercept (i.e., a), the regression coefficient of each of the independent variables (b_1, b_2, etc.), the R-square, and the T-value of each independent variable are similar to that of a simple regression analysis.

In addition to the R-squared, T-value, and standard error of the estimate, evaluating a multiple regression model requires the user to evaluate the correlation between the independent variables (X's) to assure the lack of multi-colinearity. A correlation matrix of the independent variables is used to accomplish this. As a general rule of thumb, as long as the correlation between any two independent variables is 0.7 or below, there is no problem. If the correlation between two of the independent variables is 0.7 or above, then one must be eliminated and the regression analysis must be run again.

Benefits and Shortcomings of Regression Analysis

Regression analysis gives management accountants an objective measure to use in evaluating the precision and reliability of estimations.

It is important to prepare a graph of the data prior to using regression analysis and to determine whether any unusual data points, called outliers, are present. Regression analysis can be influenced strongly by outliers, which may result in an estimation line that is not representative of most of the data. If present, each outlier should be reviewed to determine whether it is due to a data recording error, a normal operating condition, or a unique and nonrecurring event. Regression analysis requires a collection of data points—preferably 30 or more—to be accurate.

Regression analysis assumes a linear relationship between one dependent variable and one or more independent variables. In the case of analyzing cost behavior, this linear assumption can be problematic if it is expected that costs decline due to learning curves (see the Learning Curve Analysis later in this topic) or when there are different relevant ranges of activity that cause costs to shift.

Regression analysis also assumes that past relationships between dependent and independent variables will hold into the future. When using regression analysis as a forecasting tool, it is important to evaluate or make adjustments for changes in the relationship between the variables over time. For example, clear knowledge that one part of a variable cost element is increasing makes the b coefficient less reliable for future periods.

When using the results of a regression analysis to make any prediction, it is important to remember that the dependent variables used for the prediction must fall within the range of the data set used to establish the regression line. For the Build and Fix sales and marketing costs, the marketing costs used to estimate the regression line fall in the range of $30,000 and $110,000. The company can reliably predict its sales for any marketing cost that falls within this range, but it cannot rely on the result if the marketing cost used in the prediction falls outside this range (e.g., $10,000 or $200,000).

One caveat regarding regression analysis is that the user must evaluate the reasonableness of the relationship between the dependent and independent variables. Does it make sense that X causes Y to change? Any numbers can be input as X and Y variables and will result in an equation, but whether the equation makes sense must be based on the user's judgment.

Learning Curve Analysis

Learning curve analysis is a systematic method for estimating costs based on increased learning by the business, group, or individual, which allows them to become more efficient at completing tasks. As a result, costs will decrease as learning increases. However, this happens only to a certain point, and then costs level off. The learning curve is sometimes also called the experience curve.

Calculation of the learning curve is based on the learning rate, which is the percentage by which average time decreases from the previous level as output doubles. The learning curve can be measured in two ways:

1. Incremental unit-time learning model (also called the Crawford method)
2. Cumulative average-time learning model (also called the Wright method)

The cumulative average-time learning model (Wright method) is the generally accepted model.

Typical decreases in time based on learning range from 10% to 20% each time production doubles. A learning curve for a 20% reduction is called an 80% learning curve; a 10% reduction arises from a 90% curve.

Because of their different approaches, the incremental unit-time and cumulative average-time methods produce different results for the same data. The incremental method is considered more appropriate for large-scale, complex operations, while the cumulative method is considered to be simpler, and the one CMA Examination questions are likely to be focused on.

Incremental Unit-Time Learning Model

The incremental unit-time learning model measures increased efficiency by adding the incremental time for each unit to the previous total time. Average time per unit is then calculated by dividing total time by the number of units.

For example: Assume that one new worker can assemble his or her first widget in 10 hours. If two new workers each build one widget, then it would take 10 hours to assemble each widget, for a total of 20 hours of production time and an average production time of 10 hours per widget. However, if one worker assembles both widgets, the first unit will take 10 hours, but because of the worker's learning experience, the second unit will take only 8 hours—assuming learning takes place at a rate of 80% (.8 × 10 hours = 8 hours). The total time to build the two widgets is 18 hours, so the average production time per widget is 9 hours.

Figure 1B-21 shows the effect of the learning curve on average production time, as calculated by the incremental unit-time learning model. Assuming an 80% curve, production time (Y) decreases by 20% for each doubling of widget production (X). Total hours in column three results from adding the current production time (Y) to the previous total (a).

Figure 1B-22 is a graph of the average time, or cost, per widget with a learning curve. It is a visual representation of the impact of the 80% learning rate assumed in the example.

Figure 1B-21 Incremental Unit-Time Learning Model

Widget (X)	Hours for This Widget * (Y)	Total Hours ($c = a + Y$)	Average Time per Widget ($c \div X$)
1	10 (value of a)	10	10 (10 ÷ 1)
2	8 (10 × 0.8) = Y	18 (10 + 8)	9 (18 ÷ 2)
4	6.4 (8 × 0.8) = Y	31.42†	7.855 (31 ÷ 4)
8	5.12 (6.4 × 0.8) = Y	53.47†	6.68 (53.47 ÷ 8)

* Previous value of Y × learning curve rate (assumed to be 80% in this example).

† The total hours for four and eight widgets (31.42 and 53.47) are calculated by using a formula that is not shown here. The formula is complex, and calculations are usually done by software or numbers are read from standard tables. It may appear from this table that the total hours to produce eight widgets would simply be derived by multiplying 8 × 5.12. However, 5.12 is the amount of time that it took to produce the eighth unit. The seventh unit took more time to produce than the eighth unit; the sixth unit took more time to produce than the fifth unit, and so on. Learning curve calculators can be found through an Internet search.

Notice that the learning curve levels off. Learning increases efficiency up to a certain point, at which productivity reaches equilibrium and then levels off.

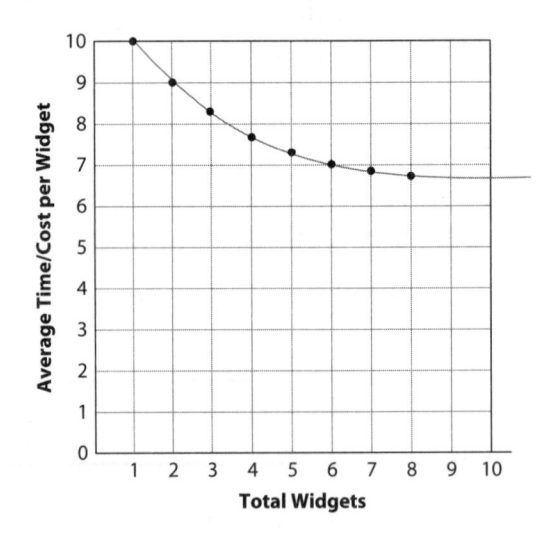

Figure 1B-22 Incremental Unit-Time Learning Curve

Cumulative Average-Time Learning Model

The cumulative average-time learning model also measures increased efficiency due to learning. It calculates cumulative total time by multiplying the incremental unit by the cumulative average time per unit.

For the widget learning curve example, the cumulative total time for assembling two widgets would be 16 hours (8 hours × 2 units). The individual unit time for the last unit then is 6 hours (16 hours total cumulative time minus the previous total of 10 hours).

Figure 1B-23 shows the previous learning curve example applied to the cumulative average-time learning model.

Figure 1B-23 Cumulative Average-Time Learning Model

X	Cumulative Average Time per Widget* (c)	Cumulative Total Time (c × X)	Individual Time for xth Widget
1	10 (value of c)	10 (10 × 1)	10
2	8 (10 × 0.8)	16 (8 × 2)	6 (16 − 10)
4	6.4 (8 × 0.8)	25.6 (6.4 × 4)	4.54[†]
8	5.12 (6.4 × 0.8)	40.96 (5.12 × 8)	3.55[†]

* Each c = rate (0.8 here) × the preceding value of the variable c.
[†] Calculated by a formula not shown here.

Note the difference in assumptions from before.

Here, for example, the first two units take an average time of 8 hours to produce (0.8 × 10 for the 80% curve). In the previous calculations, the second unit required 8 hours to produce, for an average of 9 hours when combined with the 10 hours required for the first unit.

Here the 0.8 multiplier is applied to the time required to produce all accumulated units, in other words, not only to the time required to produce the incremental unit.

Figure 1B-24 is a graph of the increase in efficiency from learning as measured by the cumulative average-time learning model.

Figure 1B-24 Cumulative Average-Time Learning Curve

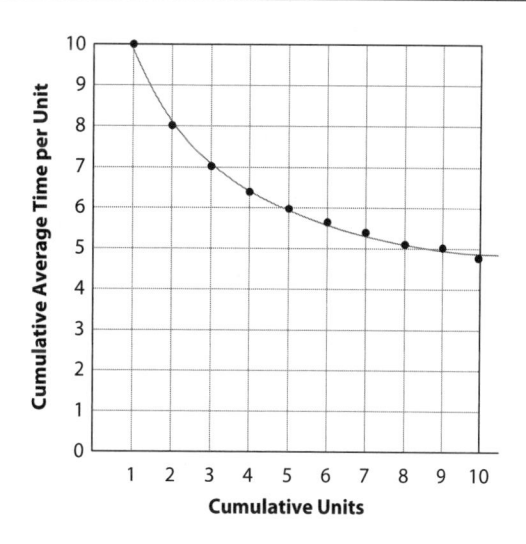

Benefits and Limitations of Learning Curve Analysis

Companies use learning curves to make a number of decisions, including setting prices. A company may set a price lower than the initial costs of production in order to gain market share, based on the assumption that as learning increases, production costs will decrease. Some companies use learning curve analysis when evaluating performance, because it expects an individual's productivity to increase with the individual's learning curve. Learning affects quality and improves productivity. Other factors contribute to the learning curve besides production output. These include job rotation, work teams, and total quality management.

The limitations of learning curve analysis are listed next.

- The learning curve approach is not as effective when machinery performs repetitive tasks, such as robotics. It is most appropriate for labor-intensive contexts that involve repetitive tasks, long production runs, and repeated trials.
- The learning rate is assumed to be constant in the calculations, but actual declines in labor time are not constant. The analyst needs to update projections based on the observed progression of learning.
- Conclusions might be unreliable because observed changes in productivity actually may be due to factors other than learning, such as a change in the labor mix, the product mix, or some combination of the two.

Expected Value

When a company is trying to forecast its sales for the upcoming year, the results can vary depending on the economic conditions. If the economy is booming, the company's sales may be higher, but if the economy is in a recession, the company's sales will likely be lower. Thus, future sales are considered to be a random variable because their outcome is uncertain.

After creating sales forecasts based on various economic conditions and assigning a probability for the likelihood of each economic scenario, the company can lay out the sales forecasts and probabilities for the various scenarios in a table. An example of such a table for Hardware Haven is presented in Figure 1B-25.

Figure 1B-25 Hardware Haven Sales Forecasts Based on Economic Conditions

Economic Condition	Sales Forecast	Probability
Boom	$3,000,000	0.1
Average	$2,000,000	0.8
Recession	$600,000	0.1

Using the information shown in the figure, the company can determine the expected value of its sales by using the next formula:

$$\text{Expected Value (EV)} = \Sigma\, S \times (P_x)$$

where:
    EV = expected value
    Σ = sum of the variables that follow in the equation
    S = amount associated with a specific outcome
    P_x = probability associated with a specific outcome

To calculate the expected value, simply multiply the outcome of each possible outcome by the probability associated with that possible outcome, and then add all of them together. The expected value of the sales in Figure 1B-25 is calculated as shown next:

$$\text{Expected sales} = \$3{,}000{,}000(0.1) + \$2{,}000{,}000(0.8) + \$600{,}000(0.1)$$
$$= \$1{,}960{,}000$$

In this example, given the uncertainties associated with the economic conditions, the company expects its sales, on average, to be $1,960,000 for the upcoming year. It is important to note that this is not the actual outcome the company will see in the upcoming year. The expected value simply represents the long-run average of the outcome (in this case, sales) based on the given uncertainties (represented by the probability assigned to the different outcomes).

Benefits and Limitations of Expected Value

The expected value technique helps an organization determine the average outcome of an event when faced with uncertainties. These averages often help the organization decide whether it should undertake certain actions.

For example: An organization may be presented with an investment option with a 60% chance of making a profit of $300,000 and a 40% chance of incurring a loss of $500,000. The calculation of the expected value of this investment reveals that the expected profit is:

$$\text{Expected Profit: } (\$300{,}000 \times 0.6) + (-\$500{,}000 \times 0.4) = -\$20{,}000$$

In other words, this investment is expected to lose, on average, $20,000. Given this information, it would not be a good idea for the organization to pursue this investment.

However, the expected value calculation is only as good as the estimated potential outcomes for each scenario and the probability assigned to each scenario. If any of these assumptions is unreliable, then the expected value that is calculated cannot be trusted in making sound decisions.

Expected value analysis assumes that the decision maker is risk neutral. If the decision maker is either a risk taker or risk averse, then the expected value model would not be appropriate.

Knowledge Check: Forecasting Techniques

The next questions are intended to help you check your understanding and recall of the material presented in this topic. They do not represent the type of questions that appear on the CMA exam.

Directions: Answer each question in the space provided. Correct answers and section references appear after the knowledge check questions.

1. An analyst generates a regression equation of Y = $1,125,000 + $2(X) as a predictor of a company's sales of cough syrup, where X = marketing costs. If the firm spends $50,000 on marketing, what will expected sales be?

   _____.

2. Using the cumulative average-time method and a 90% learning rate, what would be the total time required to produce 4 units of a product if the first unit was produced in 5 hours?

   - a. 20 total hours
   - b. 18 total hours
   - c. 17.6 total hours
   - ☑ d. 16.2 total hours

3. Which of the following is **not** an assumption of simple regression analysis?

   - a. There is a linear relationship between variables.
   - b. There is only one independent variable.
   - c. There may be several dependent variables.
   - d. Past relationships will continue in the future.

4. Match each measure to its description by drawing a line between them:

Measures	Definitions
R-squared	Measures the dispersion around the regression line and allows the user to assess the accuracy of the predictions.
SE	Measures whether an independent variable (X) is significant (i.e., does not equal zero).
T-value	Shows how much of the variation in the dependent variable is accounted for by variation in the independent variable(s).

5. Hardware Haven is considering expanding its product line to offer a full range of plants and garden supplies. The marketing director says that he is giving the project an 80% chance of delivering a profit of $600,000. The operations manager believes that the market for garden supplies will not support the investment, the facility is not well suited to maintaining plants

and that, overall, there is a 20% chance that they will lose $1.4 million. Strictly on the basis of these numbers, should the firm make the investment?

6. An organization has potential cash inflows of $10,000, $15,000, and $40,000. The probability of the entity receiving them is 50%, 35% and 15%, respectively. Using this information, compute the expected cash flow.

Knowledge Check Answers: Forecasting Techniques

1. An analyst generates a regression equation of Y = $1,125,000 + $2(X) as a predictor of a company's sales of cough syrup, where X = marketing costs. If the firm spends $50,000 on marketing, what will expected sales be? [See *Simple Linear Regression*.]

   $1,125,000 + $2($50,000) = $1,125,000 + $100,000 = $1,225,000

2. Using the cumulative average-time method and a 90% learning rate, what would be the total time required to produce 4 units of a product if the first unit was produced in 5 hours? [See *Cumulative Average-Time Learning Model*.]

   - ☐ a. 20 total hours
   - ☐ b. 18 total hours
   - ☐ c. 17.6 total hours
   - ☒ d. 16.2 total hours

   At a 90% learning rate, if the first unit takes 5 hours to produce, 2 units will take an average of 4.5 hours (0.9 × 5) and 4 will take an average of 4.05 hours each (0.9 × 4.5), for a total of 16.2 hours (4.05 × 4 units).

3. Which of the following is **not** an assumption of simple regression analysis? [See *Multiple Linear Regression*.]

   - ☐ a. There is a linear relationship between variables.
   - ☐ b. There is only one independent variable.
   - ☒ c. There may be several dependent variables.
   - ☐ d. Past relationships will continue in the future.

   Simple regression analysis assumes one dependent and one independent variable; multiple regression assumes more than one independent variable but only one dependent variable.

4. Match each measure to its description by drawing a line between them: (Correct matches are shown.) [See *Simple Linear Regression*.]

Measures	Definitions
R-squared	Shows how much of the variation in the dependent variable is accounted for by variation in the independent variable(s).
SE	Measures the dispersion around the regression line and allows the user to assess the accuracy of the predictions.
T-value	Measures whether an independent variable (X) is significant (i.e., does not equal zero).

5. Hardware Haven is considering expanding its product line to offer a full range of plants and garden supplies. The marketing director says that he is giving the project an 80% chance of delivering a profit of $600,000. The operations manager believes that the market for garden supplies will not support the investment, the facility is not well suited to maintaining plants and that overall there is a 20% chance that they will lose $1.4 million. Strictly on the basis of these numbers, should the firm make the investment? [See *Expected Value.*]

   Yes, based on calculation of expected value:

   Expected Value, Marketing Director Estimate = 0.8 × $600,000 = $480,000

   Expected Value, Operations Manager Estimate = 0.2 × $1,400,000 = $280,000

   Total Expected Value = $480,000 − $280,000 = $200,000

6. An organization has potential cash inflows of $10,000, $15,000, and $40,000. The probability of the entity receiving them is 50%, 35% and 15%, respectively. Using this information, compute the expected cash flow. [See *Expected Value.*]

   $10,000 × 50% = $5,000

   $15,000 × 35% = $5,250

   $40,000 × 15% = $6,000

   The expected cash flow is $16,250.

TOPIC 4

Budgeting Methodologies

To USE ITS BUDGET AS an effective planning and management tool, a company must choose a budget methodology that supports and reinforces its management approach. A firm looking to continuously improve and reinvent its operations may not be well served by an incremental budget system. For a stable operation with a few products, the investment in an activity-based budget effort may not be worth the effort. However, the availability of a range of budget methods enables an organization, and its constituent departments and divisions, to create budgets that are meaningful and appropriate to their requirements.

This topic covers the different types of budget systems, including annual/master budgets, project budgets, activity-based budgets, incremental budgets, zero-based budgets, continuous (rolling) budgets, and flexible budgets.

> **READ** the Learning Outcome Statements (LOS) for this topic as found in Appendix A and then study the concepts and calculations presented here to be sure you understand the content you could be tested on in the CMA exam.

Annual/Master Budget

An organization's **master budget**, also known as an annual business plan or profit plan, is a comprehensive budget for a year or less. Every aspect of the company's revenue and cost flows is projected, starting with the sales budget, based on its forecasted sales for the upcoming periods, and ending with a set of pro forma financial statements, which include the income statement and balance sheet. The benefits of having a master budget are numerous and the drawbacks are few. Virtually every company needs some form of master budget.

Depending on the types of business, organizational structure, complexity of operations, and management philosophy, a company can choose different approaches in formulating its master budget. The company can even adopt different approaches for different pieces of its master budget. Six different budgeting systems that a company can use to create its budgets are:

1. **Project budgeting.** Used for creating a budget for specific projects rather than for an entire company
2. **Activity-based budgeting.** Focuses on classifying costs based on activities rather than based on departments or products
3. **Incremental budgeting.** Starts with the prior year's budget and produces increments into the future based on the prior year's results and coming year's expectations
4. **Zero-based budgeting.** Starts each new budgeting cycle from scratch as though the budgets are prepared for the first time
5. **Continuous (or rolling) budgeting.** Allows the budget to be continually updated by removing information for the period just ended (e.g., March of this year) and adding estimated data for the same period next year (e.g., March of next year)
6. **Flexible budgeting.** Serves as a control mechanism that evaluates the performance of managers by comparing actual revenue and expenses to the budgeted amount for the actual activities (and not the budgeted activities)

These budgeting systems are not mutually exclusive; a company can choose to adopt several of them simultaneously.

Project Budgeting

Project budgets are used when a project is completely separate from other elements of a company or is the only element of the company. A motion picture has a crew and costs that are related solely to that movie. A ship, a road, an aircraft, or other major capital asset is also often budgeted using a project budget. The time frame for a project budget is simply the duration of the project, but a multiyear project could be broken down by year. Successful past project budgets for similar projects should be used as benchmarks when developing project budgets. Project budgets are developed using the same techniques and components as shown for master budgeting, except that the focus will be solely on costs related to the project instead of the company as a whole. The overhead budget is simplified because the company will allocate certain portions of the company's fixed and variable overhead to the project, and all remaining overhead for the company is excluded from the project budget.

Project budget advantages include the ability to contain all of a project's costs so that its individual impact can be easily measured. Project budgets work well on both large and small scales, and project management software can facilitate developing and tracking these budgets. A potential limitation of project budgets occurs when projects use resources and staff that are committed to the entire organization rather than dedicated to the project. In such situations, the budget will contain links to these resource centers, and affected individuals may be reporting to two or more supervisors. Care must be taken in dividing costs and lines of authority.

Activity-Based Budgeting

An **activity-based budget** (ABB) focuses on activities instead of departments or products. Each activity is matched with the most appropriate cost driver, which is any volume-based (e.g., labor hours or square feet) or activity-based (e.g., number of parts to assemble for a machine) unit of measurement of the cost of a job or activity needed to sustain operations. Costs are divided into cost pools, such as unit, batch, product, and facility. Cost pools include homogeneous costs that all vary in the same proportion to the rise and fall of production. Fixed costs are in one pool, and different levels of variable costs are in their own pools. The accuracy of these groupings should be evaluated each time a master budget is prepared. The concept of activity-based costing (ABC) is discussed in greater detail in Section D: Cost Management.

Whereas traditional budgeting focuses on input resources and expresses budgeting units in terms of functional areas, ABB focuses on value-added activities and expresses budgeting units in terms of activity costs. Traditional budgeting places emphasis on increasing management performance; ABB places emphasis on teamwork, synchronized activity, and customer satisfaction.

ABB proponents believe that traditional costing obscures the relationships between costs and outputs by oversimplifying the measurements into such categories as labor hours, machine hours, or output units for an entire process or department. Instead of using only volume drivers as a measurement tool, ABB uses activity-based cost drivers, such as number of setups, to make a clear connection between resource consumption and output. ABB will also use volume-based drivers if they are the most appropriate measurement unit for a particular activity. If the relationships are made clear, managers can see how resource demands are affected by changes in products offered, product designs, manufacturing techniques, customer base, and market share. Each planned activity will have its cost implications highlighted. Because of this, companies using ABB will be able to continuously improve their budgeting. Conversely, traditional budgets focus on past (historical) budgets and often continue funding items that would be cut if their cost-effectiveness were better known.

ABB can be used as the foundation of a master budgeting process. The resulting subbudgets would be based on different ways of measuring the costs, so the resulting proportions of costs would be weighted differently. For instance, some portion of the indirect materials or labor that would be part of overhead could be tracked more carefully and included in direct materials and direct labor amounts.

For example: Figure 1B-26 displays an overhead budget created for Bluejay Manufacturing Company using an activity-based approach. It shows overhead cost by activities, such as production setup, fabrication, assembly, quality control inspections, and engineering changes.

A key advantage of ABB is greater precision in determining costs, especially when multiple departments or products need to be tracked. This advantage comes at a cost, and a potential drawback to ABB can occur if the cost of designing and maintaining the ABB system exceeds the cost savings from better planning. Therefore,

Figure 1B-26 Activity-Based Overhead Budget for Bluejay Manufacturing Company

Activity	Usage	Activity Rate	Activity Cost
Machine setup	80 setup	$4000/setup	$320,000
Fabrication	1,700 DLH*	$5/DLH	8,500
Assembly	6,000 DLH	$12/DLH	72,000
Inspection	100 inspections	$2,500/inspection	250,000
Engineering changes	15 changes	$10,000/changes	150,000
Total overhead cost			**$800,500**

* DLH = direct labor hours.

ABB is most appropriate in businesses that have complexity in their number of products, number of departments, or other factors, such as setups. This is because the more complex a situation becomes, the less useful is the broad brush of traditional costing.

Incremental Budgeting

An **incremental budget** is a general type of budget that starts with the prior year's budget and uses projected changes in sales and the operating environment to adjust individual items in the budget upward or downward. It is the opposite of a zero-based budget. The main drawback to using this type of budget (and the reason that some companies use zero-based budgets) is that the budgets tend to only increase in size over the years. A sense of entitlement may also arise with the use of an incremental budget.

Zero-Based Budgeting

In order to avoid situations in which ineffective elements of a business continue to exist simply because they were on the prior budget, some companies use zero-based budgets, which, as the name implies, start with zero dollars allocated. While the traditional budget focuses on changes to the past budget, the **zero-based budget** focuses on constant cost justification of each and every item in a budget. Managers must conduct in-depth reviews of each area under their control to provide such justification.

The strength of the zero-based budget is that it forces review of all elements of a business. Zero-based budgets can create efficient, lean organizations and therefore are popular with government and nonprofit organizations. A zero-based budget is a way of taking a new look at an old problem.

The first step in developing a zero-based budget is to have each department manager rank all department activities from most to least important and assign a cost to each activity. Upper management reviews these lists, called "decision packages," and cuts items that lack justification or are less critical. Upper management asks questions, such as "Should the activity be performed and if it is not, what will happen?" or "Are there substitute methods of providing this function such as outsourcing or customer self-service?" Managers may also use benchmark figures and cost-benefit analysis to help decide what to cut. Only those items approved appear in the budget. The cost of the accepted items may be arrived at through discussion and negotiation with the department managers. Once the budget figures are determined, the zero-based budget becomes the basis for a master budget.

Theoretically, zero-based budgets have the advantage of focusing on every line item instead of just the exceptions. They should motivate managers to identify and remove items that are more costly than the benefits provided. These budgets are especially useful when new management is hired. Zero-based budgets have a major drawback in that they encourage managers to exhaust all of their resources during a budget period for fear that they will be allocated less during the next budget cycle. If a manager has incorporated budget slack into the budget, a zero-based budget can encourage a significant amount of waste and unnecessary purchasing.

One issue with zero-based budgeting is the time-consuming and expensive annual review process. As a result, the review often may be less thorough than it is intended to be. In addition, by not using prior budgets, the firm may be ignoring lessons learned from prior years. If used every year, a zero-based budget actually may become little more than an incremental budget with a little extra processing. Managers simply remember their old justifications and figures and use them the following year.

The time and expense of a zero-based budget often is mitigated by performing zero-based budgets only on a periodic basis, such as once every five years, and applying a different budget method in the other years. Or the firm might rotate the use of zero-based budgeting for a different division each year.

Continuous (Rolling) Budgets

A **continuous budget**, or rolling budget, adds a new period onto the budget at the end of each period so there are always several periods planned for the future and the budgets remain up-to-date with the operating environment. As with the other budget types, this budget becomes the master budget for an entity. However, while other budgets will expire at the end of the budgeted time period, the time frame for this budget always remains the same—for example, one year, no matter if it is viewed in January or July.

Therefore, if the period is a month, each month a new set of monthly financial statements is issued to each person responsible for preparing the budget. In a monthly budget meeting, managers report on the variances from the past month's budget and make projections for the next month. After review, a budget coordinator updates the master budget, performing the calculations not performed by line managers, such as depreciation or inventory valuation.

A continuous budget will be more relevant than a budget prepared once a year. It can reflect current events and changes in its estimates, and it has the advantage of breaking down a large process into manageable steps. Because managers always have a full period of budgeted data, they tend to view decisions in a longer-term perspective than with a one-year budget, which will cover a shorter and shorter period of time as the year progresses.

Potential disadvantages of continuous budgets include the need to have a budget coordinator and/or the opportunity cost of having managers use part of each month working on the next month's budget. Continuous budgets are appropriate for firms that cannot devote a large block of time to a once-a-year budget process. These types of budgets are also useful for companies that want their managers to have a longer-term view of the firm.

Flexible Budgeting

Flexible budgeting establishes a base cost budget for a particular level of output (a cost-volume relationship), plus an incremental cost-volume amount that shows the behavior of costs at various volumes. Only the variable costs are adjusted; fixed costs remain unchanged. The most common use of a flexible budget is to show the budget that would have been made if the organization had exactly matched its sales forecast. While flexible budgets from prior periods can be helpful in determining how to modify the next budget, a flexible budget that applies actual production output cannot be used as a type of master budget because the actual production output is not known until the period is complete. Therefore, flexible budgets are used more as an analysis tool for determining variances from plan than for creating the original budget.

The benefits of using a flexible budget include the ability to make better use of historical budget information to improve future planning. There are few disadvantages to using flexible budgeting, but there is the potential for the firm to focus principally on the flexible budget level of output and disregard the fact that the sales target was missed. However, most businesses use flexible budgets because they allow for extremely detailed variance analysis. The use of flexible budgeting in variance analysis is covered in Section D: Cost Management.

For example: Robin Manufacturing Company uses flexible budgeting to evaluate how closely its direct labor usage was to the budgeted amount (i.e., perform a variance analysis). For the month of July, the company has projected a production of 72,000 units each requiring 0.5 direct labor hours, with a budgeted hourly rate of $15. However, the actual production turns out to be only 68,000 units, and the actual hourly rate turns out to be $15.50. Figure 1B-27 presents the company's budgeted and actual cost of direct labor used.

Based on the information presented, it seems the company is $13,000 under its direct labor budget for the month of July. However, this is misleading because the company is not producing at its budgeted level of production. To truly evaluate its performance, the company needs to create a flexible budget where the standard cost

Figure 1B-27 Original Budget versus Actual Budget for Robin Manufacturing Company

	Original Budget	Actual Budget
Production (units)	72,000	68,000
DLH* per unit	× 0.5	× 0.5
DLH needed (or used)	36,000	34,000
Hourly rate	× $15	×$15.50
Total direct labor cost	$540,000	$527,000

*DLH = direct labor hours.

per unit (and not the actual cost per unit) is applied to the actual production and not the budgeted production. Figure 1B-28 shows the company's flexible budget.

Figure 1B-28 Flexible Budget versus Actual Budget

	Original Budget	Flexible Budget	Actual Budget
Production	72,000	68,000 ←	68,000
DLH* per unit	× 0.5	× 0.5	× 0.5
DLH needed (or used)	36,000	34,000	34,000
Hourly rate	× $15	× $15	$15.50
Total direct labor cost	$540,000	$510,000	$527,000

*DLH = direct labor hours.

From Figure 1B-28, it is clear that when evaluated at the actual production level of 68,000 units, Robin Manufacturing Company is actually $17,000 over its direct labor budget, not $13,000 under the budget.

Knowledge Check: Budgeting Methodologies

The next questions are intended to help you check your understanding and recall of the material presented in this topic. They do not represent the type of questions that appear on the CMA exam.

Directions: Answer each question in the space provided. Correct answers and section references appear after the knowledge check questions.

1. Which of the following budgeting methods might use a cost driver such as number of setups to measure the costs of a batch mixing production job?
   - ☐ a. Activity-based budgeting
   - ☐ b. Continuous (or rolling) budgeting
   - ☐ c. Flexible budgeting
   - ☐ d. Incremental budgeting
   - ☐ e. Project budgeting
   - ☐ f. Zero-based budgeting

2. Which of the following budgeting methods establishes a base cost budget for a particular level of output plus a marginal cost-volume amount that shows the behavior of costs at various volumes?
   - ☐ a. Activity-based budgeting
   - ☐ b. Continuous (or rolling) budgeting
   - ☐ c. Flexible budgeting
   - ☐ d. Incremental budgeting
   - ☐ e. Project budgeting
   - ☐ f. Zero-based budgeting

3. Department B must justify each of its programs annually to its parent agency, which then submits its budget request to the city council. Which budget system is most appropriate?
   - ☐ a. Activity-based budgeting
   - ☐ b. Continuous (or rolling) budgeting
   - ☐ c. Flexible budgeting
   - ☐ d. Incremental budgeting
   - ☐ e. Project budgeting
   - ☐ f. Zero-based budgeting

4. Company D completed its reorganization three years ago and has experienced steady sales in that time. It is now looking to add to its sales force, marketing, and production but maintain its current organization and direction. What budget method might be most appropriate?
    - ☐ a. Activity-based budgeting
    - ☐ b. Continuous (or rolling) budgeting
    - ☐ c. Flexible budgeting
    - ☐ d. Incremental budgeting
    - ☐ e. Project budgeting
    - ☐ f. Zero-based budgeting

5. Company C is a consulting firm that designs customized marketing plans and product launches for a variety of clients. Which budget system might work best for the firm, and what might be its disadvantages?

Knowledge Check Answers: Budgeting Methodologies

1. Which of the following budgeting methods might use a cost driver such as number of setups to measure the costs of a batch mixing production job? **[See *Activity-Based Budgeting*.]**
   - ☒ a. Activity-based budgeting
   - ☐ b. Continuous (or rolling) budgeting
   - ☐ c. Flexible budgeting
   - ☐ d. Incremental budgeting
   - ☐ e. Project budgeting
   - ☐ f. Zero-based budgeting

2. Which of the following budgeting methods establishes a base cost budget for a particular level of output plus a marginal cost-volume amount that shows the behavior of costs at various volumes? **[See *Flexible Budgeting*.]**
   - ☐ a. Activity-based budgeting
   - ☐ b. Continuous (or rolling) budgeting
   - ☒ c. Flexible budgeting
   - ☐ d. Incremental budgeting
   - ☐ e. Project budgeting
   - ☐ f. Zero-based budgeting

3. Department B must justify each of its programs annually to its parent agency, which then submits its budget request to the city council. Which budget system is most appropriate? **[See *Zero-Based Budgeting*.]**
   - ☐ a. Activity-based budgeting
   - ☐ b. Continuous (or rolling) budgeting
   - ☐ c. Flexible budgeting
   - ☐ d. Incremental budgeting
   - ☐ e. Project budgeting
   - ☒ f. Zero-based budgeting

4. Company D completed its reorganization three years ago and has experienced steady sales in that time. It is now looking to add to its sales force, marketing, and production but maintain its current organization and direction. What budget method might be most appropriate? **[See *Incremental Budgeting*.]**
   - ☐ a. Activity-based budgeting
   - ☐ b. Continuous (or rolling) budgeting

- ☐ **c.** Flexible budgeting
- ☑ **d.** Incremental budgeting
- ☐ **e.** Project budgeting
- ☐ **f.** Zero-based budgeting

5. Company C is a consulting firm that designs customized marketing plans and product launches for a variety of clients. Which budget system might work best for the firm, and what might be the disadvantages of that system? **[See *Project Budgeting*.]**

   Project budgeting would allow tracking and evaluating the costs of each client project, but shared resources would have to be allocated among the projects.

TOPIC 5

Annual Profit Plan and Supporting Schedules

THE MASTER BUDGET, OR ANNUAL profit plan, has many components and supporting schedules. Each of these pieces provides specific information that the organization can use to review its current operations and develop its plans for the short and long term. The forecasts and assumptions used in creating each component and the interplay of the components present not just an analytical challenge but an opportunity for effectively managing the organization toward its objectives.

This topic looks at the individual elements that come together to form the master budget. It describes the budgets for sales, production, direct materials, direct labor, overhead, cost of goods sold, and selling and administrative expenses that are used in developing the operating budget and the pro forma financial statement. It also discusses the cash budget, the capital expenditure budget, and the pro forma balance sheet and statement of cash flows and their place in the financial budget.

> **READ** the Learning Outcome Statements (LOS) for this topic as found in Appendix A and then study the concepts and calculations presented here to be sure you understand the content you could be tested on in the CMA exam.

Master Budget

The master budget provides a comprehensive summation of all of an entity's budgets and plans for the operating activities of its subunits. It is the place where everything must add up, where strategy and long-term plans meet up with short-term objectives and current realities.

The master budget is basically made up of financial projections of many different budgets for a company on an annual basis, although other short-duration time periods are also used. The master budget can be broken down into two major components: the operating budget and the financial budget.

The operating budget makes up the bulk of the master budget. It includes the sales budget, the production budget, the direct materials budget, the direct labor budget, the overhead budget, and the selling and administrative (S&A) expense budget. All of these budgets culminate in the formation of the pro forma (or budgeted) income statement. The financial budget includes the cash budget, the capital expenditure budget, and the pro forma (or budgeted) balance sheet and statement of cash flows.

Figure 1B-29 shows how the components of the master budget are related.

Figure 1B-29 Master Budget

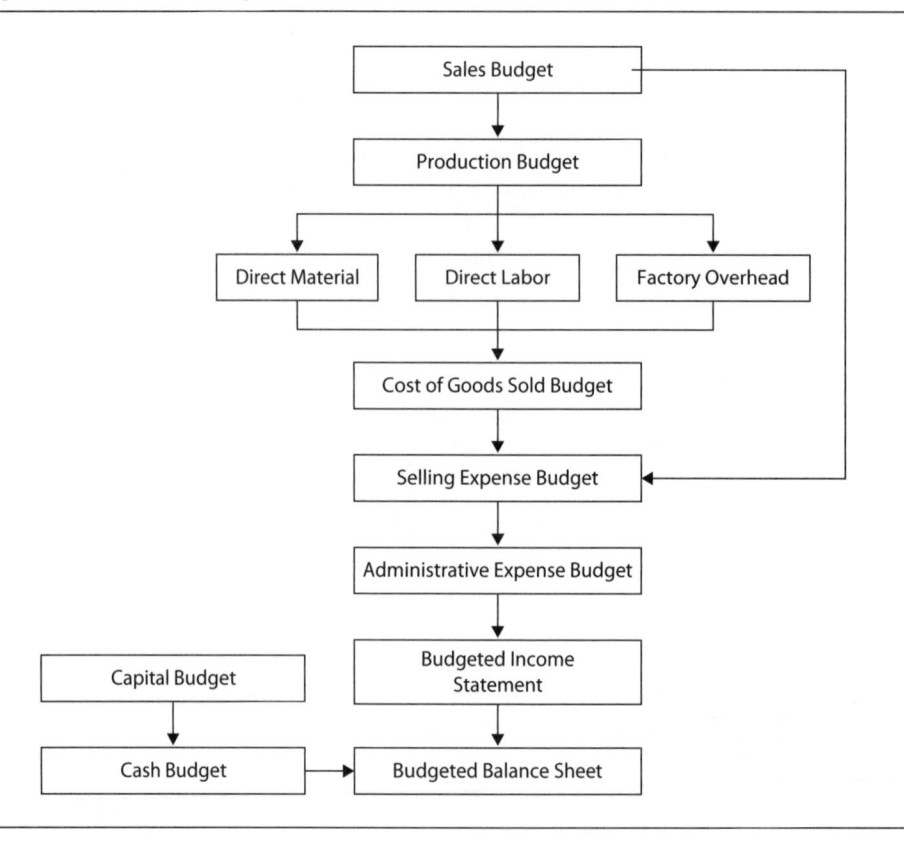

```
                    Sales Budget
                         |
                    Production Budget
                         |
        ┌────────────────┼────────────────┐
   Direct Material   Direct Labor    Factory Overhead
        └────────────────┼────────────────┘
                         |
                Cost of Goods Sold Budget
                         |
                 Selling Expense Budget  ←────
                         |
                Administrative Expense Budget
                         |
   Capital Budget   Budgeted Income Statement
        |                |
    Cash Budget  →  Budgeted Balance Sheet
```

Operating Budget

In creating an operating budget, the various pieces are assembled, including, for instance, the sales budget, the production budget, the direct materials budget, the direct labor budget, the overhead budget, and the S&A expense budget. All of these budgets are then used to create the pro forma (or budgeted) income statement.

Sales Budget

Before creating a sales budget, an accurate sales forecast is needed. A **sales forecast** is a subjective estimate of the entity's future sales for the upcoming period.

Without an accurate sales forecast, all other budget elements will be inaccurate. Forecasters consider not only historical trends for sales but also economic and industry conditions and indicators, competitors' actions, rising costs, policies on pricing and extending credit, the amount of advertising and marketing expenditures, the number of unfilled back orders, and sales in the sales pipeline (unsigned prospects).

Sales forecasts should use statistical analysis techniques such as regression analysis and rely on sales managers' knowledge about their market and customer needs. Once a company has determined its forecasted sales level, based on its long- and short-term objectives, it forms a sales budget to accomplish its goals. The two key components of the sales budget are the projected number of units of sales and the projected selling prices for the upcoming periods.

For example: Figure 1B-30 shows the sales budget of Robin Manufacturing Company for the third quarter.

Figure 1B-30 Sales Budget

Robin Manufacturing Company Sales Budget for the Quarter Ended September 30, Year 1				
	July	August	September	Quarter
Sales in units	70,000	72,000	77,000	219,000
Selling price per unit	$110.80	$110.80	$112.00	(varies)
Total sales	$7,756,000	$7,977,600	$8,624,000	$24,357,600

It is important to note that the sales budget basically drives the operating budget because it helps define the formation of the other budgets.

Production Budget

Once the desired level of sales is determined, the production budget is created to satisfy the expected demand. The **production budget** is a plan for acquiring resources and combining them to meet sales goals and maintain a certain level of inventory. The budgeted production is calculated as shown next.

> Budgeted Production = Budgeted Sales + Desired Ending Inventory − Beginning Inventory

Budgeted sales are an integral part of the production budget. Sales are the basis of what logistics managers use to plan resource needs for the coming year, develop manufacturing schedules, and create shipping policies. When actual sales either fall short or significantly exceed projected revenue, the entire inventory system is affected. Inventory on hand needs to be adjusted to reflect the change in production needs. Often inventory purchasing is planned in advance to take advantage of bulk pricing deals that may be negotiated with suppliers. If costs suddenly increase, the financial burden of buying and carrying inventory becomes greater. Changes in the operating and purchasing costs for a company can cause inventory purchase levels to change. For example, an organization may wish to increase or decrease purchasing volumes at various times during the year to try to take advantage of price fluctuations.

During the planning stages of a production budget, the production managers will complete a production schedule outlining how they will meet expected demand. The estimates should include the cost of production equipment, inventory, and personnel. Other factors that can affect the production budget include investment in new equipment, hiring necessary personnel, capacity constraints, and scheduling issues. *For example:* Figure 1B-31 shows a production budget for several months.

Figure 1B-31 Production Budget

Robin Manufacturing Company
Production Budget
for the Quarter Ended September 30, Year 1

	July	August	September	Quarter
Budgeted sales in units	70,000	72,000	77,000	219,000
Add: Desired ending inventory of finished goods	10,000	11,000	12,000	12,000
Total units needed	80,000	83,000	89,000	231,000
Less: Beginning inventory of finished goods	8,000	10,000	11,000	8,000
Budgeted production in units	72,000	73,000	78,000	223,000

Direct Materials Budget

The **direct materials budget** (or the direct materials usage budget) determines the required materials and the quality level of the materials used to meet production. While the production budget specifies only the number of units to be produced, the usage budget specifies the amount and cost of materials needed for the production and the amount and cost of materials that must be purchased to meet the production requirement. A direct materials purchase budget will need to be prepared to determine the amount and cost of materials that need to be purchased. This is determined as shown next.

> Direct Materials Purchased = Direct Materials Used in Production + Desired Ending Inventory of Direct Materials − Beginning Inventory of Direct Materials

For example: Figure 1B-32 illustrates Robin Manufacturing's direct materials usage budget. Figure 1B-33 illustrates the company's direct materials purchase budget.

Figure 1B-32 Direct Materials Usage Budget

Robin Manufacturing Company Direct Materials Usage Budget
for the Quarter Ended September 30, Year 1

	July	August	September	Quarter
Production requirement				
Budgeted production	72,000	73,000	78,000	223,000
Pounds of resin per unit of product	× 5	× 5	× 5	× 5
Total pounds of resin required	360,000	365,000	390,000	1,115,000
Pounds of resin in beginning inventory	35,000	35,000	35,000	35,000
Cost per pound	$13.00	$13.00	$13.25	$13.00
Total cost of beginning inventory	$455,000	$455,000	$463,750	$455,000
Total cost of resin purchases	4,680,000	4,836,250	5,253,500	14,769,750
Cost of resin available for production	$5,135,000	$5,291,250	$5,717,250	$15,224,750
Desired ending inventory in pounds	35,000	35,000	40,000	40,000
Cost of desired ending inventory per pound	× $13.00	× $13.25	× $13.30	× $13.30
Total cost of desired ending inventory	$455,000	$463,750	$532,000	$532,000
Cost of resin used in production (Cost Available for Production − Cost of Desired Ending Inventory)	$4,680,000	$4,827,500	$5,185,250	$14,692,750

Figure 1B-33 Direct Materials Purchase Budget

Robin Manufacturing Company Direct Materials Purchase Budget
for the Quarter Ended September 30, Year 1

	July	August	September	Quarter
Total direct materials needed in production	360,000	365,000	390,000	1,115,000
Add: Desired ending inventory	35,000	35,000	40,000	40,000
Total direct materials required	395,000	400,000	430,000	1,155,000
Less: Direct materials beginning inventory	35,000	35,000	35,000	35,000
Direct materials purchases	360,000	365,000	395,000	1,120,000
Purchase price per pound	$13.00	$13.25	$13.30	
Total cost for direct materials purchases	$4,680,000	$4,836,250	$5,253,500	$14,769,750

Direct Labor Budget

The production requirement laid out in the production budget, which determines the direct materials needed, also determines the direct labor needed for production. The **direct labor budget**, which is prepared by the production manager and human resources, specifies the direct labor requirement needed to meet the production need. The direct labor requirement is determined by multiplying the expected production by the number of direct labor hours (DLH) required to produce a unit. This number is then multiplied by the direct labor cost per hour to calculate the budgeted direct labor cost.

> Direct Labor Requirement = (Expected Production × Direct Labor Hours per Unit)
>
> Budgeted Direct Labor Cost = Direct Labor Requirement × Direct Labor Cost per Hour

The direct labor budget can help firms plan production processes to smooth out production over a year and keep a consistent workforce size throughout the year. Labor budgets are usually broken down into categories, such as semiskilled, unskilled, and skilled.

For example: Figure 1B-34 illustrates a direct labor budget for Robin Manufacturing.

Figure 1B-34 Direct Labor Budget

Robin Manufacturing Company Direct Labor Budget for the Quarter Ended September 30, Year 1

	July	August	September	Quarter
Budgeted production	72,000	73,000	78,000	223,000
DLH* required per unit	× 0.5	× 0.5	× 0.5	
DLH needed	36,000	36,500	39,000	111,500
Hourly rate	× $15	× $15	× $15	
Total wages for direct labor	$540,000	$547,500	$585,000	$1,672,500

* DLH = direct labor hours.

In addition to the cost of wages, an organization can estimate the cost of employee benefits. Employers match the Federal Insurance Contributions Act (FICA) contribution (7.65%) and may pay a share of health insurance, life insurance, or pension matching plans on behalf of their employees. Employee benefits can be included in direct labor costs or can be classified as overhead. The effect on cost of goods sold is the same regardless of whether it is classified as a direct labor cost or as overhead.

Overhead Budget (Factory Overhead Budget)

All other production costs that are not in the direct materials and direct labor budgets are in the **overhead budget**, sometimes called a fixed costs budget because most of the costs in this category do not vary with the rise and fall of production. Rent and insurance, for instance, remain stable even if production goes up or down. However, there are some overhead costs that do vary with production—variable costs such as batch setup costs or the costs of electricity and other utilities. Fixed costs are easy to budget, but variable costs require forecasting the number of units to be produced, the production methods used, and other external factors. *For example:* Figure 1B-35 illustrates Robin Manufacturing's overhead budget.

Figure 1B-35 Factory Overhead Budget

Robin Manufacturing Company Factory Overhead Budget for the Quarter Ended September 30, Year 1

	Rate per DLH*	July	August	September	Quarter
Total DLHs (See Figure 1B-34)		36,000	36,500	39,000	111,500
Variable factory overhead					
Supplies	$0.20	$7,200	$7,300	$7,800	$22,300
Fringe benefits	4.10	147,600	149,650	159,900	457,150
Utilities	1.00	36,000	36,500	39,000	111,500
Maintenance	0.50	18,000	18,250	19,500	55,750
Total variable factory overhead	$5.80	$208,800	$211,700	$226,200	$646,700
Fixed factory overhead					
Depreciation		$20,000	$20,000	$20,000	$60,000
Plant insurance		800	800	800	2,400
Property taxes		1,200	1,200	1,200	3,600
Salary supervision		10,000	10,000	10,000	30,000
Indirect labor		72,000	72,000	72,000	216,000
Utilities		4,000	4,000	4,000	12,000
Maintenance		900	900	900	2,700
Total fixed factory overhead		$108,900	$108,900	$108,900	$326,700
Total factory overhead		$317,700	$320,600	$335,100	$973,400

* Direct labor hour (DLH) is assumed to be the cost driver for factory overhead in this example.

For Robin Manufacturing, employee benefits such as health and dental insurance, short-term and long-term disability insurance, and retirement benefits, are considered to be part of the overhead budget, and they are rolled up as fringe benefits in Figure 1B-35. The company could also choose to allocate a portion of these employee benefits into the direct labor budget.

Cost of Goods Sold Budget

The **cost of goods sold budget** indicates the total cost of producing the product sold for a period. This budget is sometimes called the cost of goods manufactured and sold budget, because it often also includes items budgeted to be in inventory. This budget is created only after the production, direct materials, direct labor, and overhead budgets are formed, because it is basically a summary of these budgets.

For example: Figure 1B-36 illustrates a cost of goods sold budget for Robin Manufacturing.

In Figure 1B-36, the cost of goods manufactured is composed of the cost of direct materials used, costs of direct labor used, and the overhead cost. This means that the cost of goods manufactured can be recategorized into a variable cost component made up of the cost of direct materials used, the cost of direct labor materials used, and the variable overhead cost and a fixed cost component, or the fixed

Figure 1B-36 Cost of Goods Sold Budget

Robin Manufacturing Company Cost of Goods Sold Budget for the Quarter Ended September 30, Year 1

	July	August	September	Quarter
Beginning finished goods inventory, 7/1/Year 1				$626,400
Direct materials used (see Figure 1B-32)	$4,680,000	$4,827,500	$5,185,250	14,692,750
Direct labor used (see Figure 1B-34)	540,000	547,500	585,000	1,672,500
Manufacturing overhead (see Figure 1B-35)	317,700	320,600	335,100	973,400
Cost of goods manufactured	$5,537,700	$5,695,600	$6,105,350	$17,338,650
Cost of goods available for sale				$17,965,050
Less: Ending finished goods inventory				939,600
Cost of goods sold				$17,025,450

overhead cost. Dividing the costs of goods manufactured into the two components can assist the company in determining the unit and total contribution margins of its product, as shown next.

> Unit Contribution Margin = Price per Unit − Variable Cost per Unit
>
> Total Contribution Margin = Total Revenue − Total Variable Cost

The contribution margin represents the portion of the revenue, less the total variable costs, that is used to recoup the fixed costs. Once the fixed costs have been recouped, the remaining contribution margin will go toward the company's operating income. When calculating the contribution, both per unit and in total, other nonmanufacturing-related variable costs, such as variable selling or administrative expenses, need to be taken into consideration. For more information on calculating contribution margins, see Section D: Cost Management.

Selling and Administrative Expense Budget

Nonmanufacturing expenses are often grouped into a single budget called an S&A expense budget or nonmanufacturing costs budget. The selling expense components of this budget include salaries and commissions for the sales department, travel and entertainment, advertising expenditures, shipping supplies, postage and stationery (related to sales), and so on. Sales expenses are included in this category because they are not allowed to be allocated to production processes but must be expensed in the period in which they are incurred. The administrative expense components of this budget, however, include management salaries, legal and professional services, utilities, insurance expense, non–sales-related stationery, supplies, postage, and the like.

Just as with overhead expenses, S&A expenses can be categorized into fixed costs and variable costs. In general, selling expenses are made up of both fixed and variable cost components, whereas the administrative expenses tend to include more fixed costs.

The costs in this budget usually satisfy long-term goals, such as customer service, so it is not easy to make cuts in these expense items. When using a contribution margin format for S&A expenses, all variable selling and administrative costs as well as variable manufacturing costs are deducted from net sales to find the contribution margin. This allows the budget to be used for internal performance measurement and to help show where costs can be controlled.

For example: Robin Manufacturing Company's S&A expense budget (nonmanufacturing costs) is shown in Figure 1B-37.

Figure 1B-37 Selling and Administrative Expense Budget

Robin Manufacturing Company Selling and Administrative Expense Budget for the Quarter Ended September 30, Year 1

	July	August	September	Quarter
Research/design	$95,000	$95,000	$100,000	$290,000
Marketing	240,000	280,000	290,000	810,000
Shipping	135,000	140,000	150,000	425,000
Product support	90,000	90,000	95,000	275,000
Administration	185,000	190,000	192,000	567,000
Total	$745,000	$795,000	$827,000	$2,367,000

Pro Forma (or Budgeted) Income Statement

Various pieces of the operating budget developed earlier are used to put together the **pro forma (or budgeted) income statement**, which shows what the profits for the company will be at the end of the year if the company meets its budget and if its assumptions prove to be correct. When budgeted income falls short of the goal, management knows it must take corrective action. The budget is revised to account for these actions. A budgeted income statement is therefore a benchmark to use in evaluating progress.

For example: Figure 1B-38 shows the pro forma income statement for Robin Manufacturing Company compiled using information from the sales budget, the cost of goods sold budget, and the S&A expense budget. In addition, the company is expected to pay an interest expense of $140,361 and a tax installment of $1,702,165 for the quarter.

Financial Budgets

Once a company completes the various pieces of the operating budget and creates the pro forma (or budgeted) income statement, it next develops the necessary financial budgets to identify the assets and capital (both debt and equity) needed

Figure 1B-38 Pro Forma Income Statement

Robin Manufacturing Company
Pro Forma Income Statement
for the Quarter Ended September 30, Year 1

Sales (see Figure 1B-30)	$24,357,600
Less: Cost of goods sold (see Figure 1B-36)	17,026,650
Gross margin	$7,330,950
Less: S&A expenses (see Figure 1B-37)	2,367,000
Operating income	$4,963,950
Less: Interest expenses	140,361
Earnings before taxes	$4,823,589
Less: Taxes	1,702,165
Net income	$3,121,424

to support the operation. These financial budgets include the capital expenditure budget, the cash budget, the pro forma (or budgeted) balance sheet, and the pro forma (or budgeted) statement of cash flows. Figure 1B-39 shows the flow of the financial budgets.

Figure 1B-39 Financial Budget Flow

```
┌─────────────┐   ┌─────────────┐   ┌─────────────┐
│  Pro Forma  │   │   Capital   │   │    Cash     │
│   Income    │   │   Budget    │   │   Budget    │
│  Statement  │   │             │   │             │
└──────┬──────┘   └──────┬──────┘   └──────┬──────┘
       │                 │                 │
       └─────────────────┼─────────────────┘
                         │
              ┌──────────┴──────────┐
              ▼                     ▼
       ┌─────────────┐       ┌─────────────┐
       │  Pro Forma  │       │  Pro Forma  │
       │   Balance   │       │  Statement  │
       │    Sheet    │       │of Cash Flows│
       └─────────────┘       └─────────────┘
```

Capital Budget

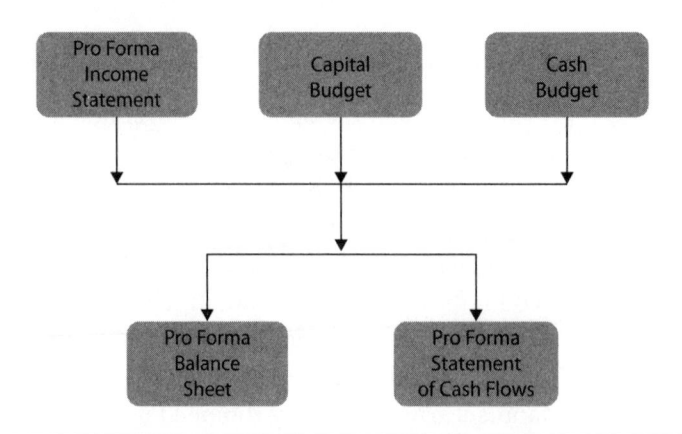

The **capital budget** represents the amount of money the company plans to invest in selected capital projects, which include purchases of property, plant, or equipment, as well as purchases of new businesses or operating capabilities. This budget often categorizes the capital projects by categories (e.g., machines, buildings, etc.), the amount of funding, the timing of the funding need, and the reasons for investing in the capital projects (e.g., process improvement, replacement of obsolete equipment, etc.).

The capital budget is used for evaluating and selecting projects that require large amounts of funding, which will provide benefits far into the future. Because all businesses face a scarcity of resources, capital must be rationed. Therefore, capital budgets must first be aligned with the company strategy, and that strategy must be continually refined to take advantage of internal strengths and external opportunities.

Cash Budget

Maintaining adequate liquidity is a requirement for staying in business, and a cash budget is a plan to ensure liquidity. Financing can be arranged in an orderly fashion, and investment durations can be planned so that they can be liquidated at the time the funds are needed. Cash budgets are commonly formulated for monthly periods, but many companies find it useful to have even finer divisions, such as by week or even by day.

Because cash is needed in all areas of operations, the cash budget gets data from all parts of the master budget. A cash budget is divided into four sections: the cash receipt section, the cash disbursement section, the cash excess or deficiency section, and the financing section.

Cash Receipts

Cash receipts are all collections in the current period from sales made in the current and prior periods (from collections of accounts receivable) and from other sources, such as interest income from investments.

Cash Disbursements

The cash disbursements section includes all outgoing cash payments. These include payments for purchases of materials, wages, operating expenses, taxes, and interest expenses.

Cash Excess or Deficiency

The cash excess or deficiency section is calculated as the beginning cash balance plus receipts and less disbursements and minimum cash balance requirements. The result is either an excess or a deficiency of cash for the period. Excess cash can be invested (per the company's policy) and deficiencies must be financed.

Financing

Financing includes finding sources of cash when liquidity levels fall below a point set by management or the board of directors as well as using excess cash for temporary and short-term investments to make use of cash above a certain level. Most firms value capital preservation over returns on investment when choosing investments, so they choose relatively safe investments, such as money market securities.

The more complex aspects of the financing section involve calculating interest and loan repayments. If financing is needed in one month, the amount of financing must include enough for the minimum cash balance to be satisfied. Conversely, when calculating the amount of principle and interest that can be repaid, the minimum cash balance must be deducted first. Furthermore, it is important to note when the principal and interest are to be repaid (at the beginning or the end of a period), in order to determine what principal the interest charge will be based on. Calculation of interest must take into account partial periods (e.g., 1/12th of 10% per annum for a month's interest).

The cash receipts and cash disbursements sections of the budget are influenced by a number of factors. Companies generally create a pro forma schedule to estimate their cash receipts and another to estimate cash disbursements. The pro forma cash receipts schedule estimates percentages of collections for each period using the same method as the accounts receivable balance pattern, which is discussed next. The pro forma cash disbursements schedule can also use payment percentage patterns, but these are based on payment history instead of collection history. Often these disbursements are broken down by materials purchases, direct wages (based on current sales), general and administrative expenses, and income taxes. Other schedules separate fixed and variable expenses.

An accounts receivable (A/R) balance pattern estimates cash inflows, but the same methods can be applied to cash outflows.

An A/R balance pattern is a forecasting tool to estimate timing of cash inflows and A/R levels resulting from making sales on credit. Companies use great care in analyzing historical collection trends and use such patterns as assumptions in forecasting cash collections. An A/R balance pattern is derived from a company's collection history and results in a percentage estimate of uncollected credit sales at the end of a specific period, such as a month.

For example: Figure 1B-40 shows an A/R sales collection history for Robin Manufacturing Company.

Figure 1B-40 A/R Sales Collection History

Robin Manufacturing Company A/R Sales Collection History

Interval Since Month Sales	Percentage Collected
Month 0 (current month)	40%
Month 1 (next month)	30%
Month 2 (month after next)	20%
Month 3 (three months after)	10%

Using this information, an A/R balance pattern can be applied to monthly sales to predict collections from an upcoming period.

Assume that Robin Manufacturing has actual March sales of $9,200,000, April sales of $9,500,000, May sales of $9,032,000, June sales of $8,520,000, and July through September estimated sales taken from the sales budget in Figure 1B-30. This is shown in Figure 1B-41.

Figure 1B-41 A/R Balance Pattern

Robin Manufacturing Company
A/R Balance Pattern for August with Forecast Inflows through September

Month Sales	Sales	Cash Inflows for Month	A/R Remaining from Month Sales at End of August	Remaining A/R as a % of Month Sales
June	$8,520,000	$8,937,600	$852,000	10%
July	$7,756,000	$8,414,800	$2,326,800	30%
August	$7,977,600	$8,125,040	$4,786,560	60%
September	$8,624,000	$8,246,080		

Cash inflows from sales for the month are calculated using the next formula.

> Cash Inflows for Month
> = (Month zero % Collected × Sales Current Month)
> + (Month one % Collected × Sales Last Month)
> + (Month two % Collected × Sales Two Months Ago)
> + (Month three % Collected × Sales Three Months Ago)

For example: The final forecast amount for September was determined using the next calculation.

For September = (0.4 × $8,624,000) + (0.3 × $7,977,600)
   + (0.2 × $7,756,000) + (0.1 × $8,520,000)
   = $3,449,600 + $2,393,280 + $1,551,200 + $852,000 = $8,246,080

Calculating accounts receivable from month sales at the end of the month and the remaining A/R percentage of month sales uses this formula:

> A/R Remaining from Month Sales at End of Current Month
> = (Month Sales − [(Month zero % Collected × Month Sales)
> + (Month one % Collected × Month Sales)
> + (Month two % Collected × Month Sales)
> + (Month three % Collected × Month Sales)]

A/R Remaining from June Sales at End of August

$$= \$8{,}520{,}000 - [(0.4 \times \$8{,}520{,}000)$$
$$+ (0.3 \times \$8{,}520{,}000) + (0.2 \times \$8{,}520{,}000) + 0^*]$$
$$= \$8{,}520{,}000 - (\$3{,}408{,}000 + \$2{,}556{,}000 + \$1{,}704{,}000)$$
$$= \$8{,}520{,}000 - \$7{,}668{,}000 = \$852{,}000$$

* Not yet collected.

For example: For Robin Manufacturing, A/R remaining from month sales at the end of August and the remaining A/R as a percentage of month sales are calculated as shown next.

A/R Remaining in Current Month as a % of Month Sales

$$= \frac{\text{A/R Remaining from Month Sales at End of Current Month}}{\text{Month Sales}}$$

A/R Remaining in August as a % of June Sales

$$= \frac{\$852{,}000}{\$8{,}520{,}000} = 0.1 = 10\%$$

Note that it is possible that the firm would have additional planned cash collections from nonsales sources, such as investment income. In this case, those cash receipts would be added to the cash receipts from sales to find total cash receipts. Using these methods, a pro forma schedule of cash receipts and disbursements can be made.

For example: Figure 1B-42 shows Robin Manufacturing's pro forma schedule of cash receipts and disbursements. In addition to the information stated previously in the direct materials, direct labor, and overhead budgets for Robin Manufacturing, assume that, in June, actual direct material purchases were $3,280,000, actual variable factory overhead was $188,500, actual fixed factory overhead (less depreciation) was $88,900, and actual S&A expenses were $705,000. Half of Robin Manufacturing's purchases are paid in the same month as the purchase, and the other half are paid one month later. Direct labor is paid in the same month. Overhead is paid the next month. In the meantime, the company's interest expense on its long-term debt for the quarter of $120,000 will be paid in July, and its tax installment for the quarter of $1,702,165 will be paid in August. The company has also budgeted the capital expenditures: July, $880,000; August, $5,360,000: September, $51,000. The amounts calculated on this schedule are used in the cash budget.

Once the company has determined its cash receipts and cash disbursements, and with the beginning cash balance for the quarter, it can then put together its cash budget for the quarter. The cash budget will help the company determine if it has surplus cash or insufficient cash.

Figure 1B-42 Pro Forma Schedule of Cash Receipts and Cash Disbursements

Robin Manufacturing Company Pro Forma Schedule of Cash Receipts and Cash Disbursements for the 3rd Quarter, Year 1

	July Expected	August Expected	September Expected
Sales (see Fig. 1B-30)	$7,756,000	$7,977,600	$8,624,000
DM* purchases (see Fig. 1B-32)	$4,680,000	$4,836,250	$5,253,500
Cash receipts			
Sales—40% same month	$3,102,400	$3,191,040	$3,449,600
30%—1-month lag	$2,556,000	$2,326,800	$2,393,280
20%—2-month lag	$1,806,400	$1,704,000	$1,551,200
10%—3-month lag	$950,000	$903,200	$852,000
Total cash receipts	$8,414,800	$8,125,040	$8,246,080
Cash disbursements			
DM purchases—50% same month	$2,340,000	$2,418,125	$2,626,750
50% following month	$1,640,000	$2,340,000	$2,418,125
Direct labor paid same month (see Fig. 1B-34)	$540,000	$547,500	$585,000
Variable factory overhead paid following month (see Fig. 1B-35)	$188,500	$208,800	$211,700
Fixed factory overhead paid following month[†] (see Fig. 1B-35)	$88,900	$88,900	$88,900
S&A expenses paid following month (see Fig. 1B-37)	$705,000	$745,000	$795,000
Interest expense on long-term debt	$120,000		
Tax installment		$1,702,165	
Capital expenditure	$880,000	$5,360,000	$51,000
Total cash disbursements	$6,502,400	$13,410,490	$6,776,475

*DM = direct materials.

[†]Since depreciation is a noncash expense, the $20,000 of depreciation was removed from each month's fixed factory overhead.

For example: It is assumed that Robin Manufacturing will not invest its surplus cash and will borrow with short-term loans to bring its cash balance to the minimum required level if it has insufficient cash. It is assumed that the company has an established policy to keep its minimum cash balance at $250,000. Figure 1B-43 illustrates the cash budget for Robin Manufacturing Company for the quarter ended September 30.

In Figures 1B-42 and 1B-43, the information from various pieces of the master budget is used to create the cash budget of Robin Manufacturing Company, which helps demonstrate the relationship between the cash budget and the rest of the master budget.

The cash receipt portion of the cash budget is influenced by the figures projected in the sales budget. The cash disbursement portion is influenced by the figures projected in the direct materials budget, the direct labor budget, the overhead budget, the S&A budget, and the capital expenditure budget.

Figure 1B-43 Cash Budget

Robin Manufacturing Company Cash Budget for the Quarter Ended September 30, Year 1

	July	August	September	Quarter
Cash balance, beginning	$1,587,000	$3,499,400	$250,000	$1,587,000
Add cash receipts	8,414,800	8,125,040	8,246,080	24,785,920
Total cash available for needs	$10,001,800	$11,624,440	$8,496,080	$26,372,920
Deduct cash disbursements	6,502,400	13,410,490	6,776,475	26,689,365
Minimum cash needed	250,000	250,000	250,000	250,000
Total cash needed	$6,752,400	$13,660,490	$7,026,475	$26,939,365
Cash excess (deficiency)	3,249,400	(2,036,050)	1,469,605	($566,445)
Financing				
Borrowing (beginning balance)	–	–	2,036,050	0
Borrowing	–	2,036,050	–	2,036,050
Repayment (end of period)	–	–	(1,449,244)*	(1,449,244)
Interest expense	–	–	(20,361)[†]	(20,361)
Borrowing (ending balance)		$2,036,050	$586,806[‡]	$586,806
Total financing needs (adjusted for interest payments)	–	2,036,050	(1,469,605)	586,806
Cash balance, ending	$3,499,400	$250,000	$250,000	$250,000

* Only $1,449,244 could be paid back at this time.

[†] Interest on short-term borrowings.

[‡] Note that interest for the following month will be $5,868.

General notes: Robin Manufacturing Company requires a cash balance of $250,000 at all times. In the month of August, the need to borrow over $2 million was financed with a short-term loan at 12% per annum interest. Note also that the example assumes that excess cash is not being invested (see July).

In the meantime, the cash budget is also influencing other pieces of the master budget. The financing portion of the cash budget will determine the borrowing needed (i.e., if the company has insufficient cash). This short-term borrowing will contribute to the current liabilities of the pro forma balance sheet, and the interest expense on the short-term borrowings will count toward the interest expense in the pro forma income statement. Similarly, any short-term investments made using surplus cash will contribute to the current assets of the pro forma balance sheet.

Pro Forma (or Budgeted) Balance Sheet

A pro forma balance sheet (also known as a budget balance sheet or statement of financial position) illustrates how operations should affect the company's assets, liabilities, and stockholders' equity. The budgeted balance sheet is usually the last item prepared in a master budget and is based in part on the budgeted balance sheet at the end of the current period. The effects of operations for the budget period are added to the data in the prior balance sheet.

Pro Forma (or Budgeted) Statement of Cash Flows

A company's pro forma statement of cash flows represents its projected sources and uses of funds. Using information from the income statement and balance sheet, it groups the company's cash flows into one of three activities: operating, investing, and financing activities.

The operating activity portion tracks the cash flows generated by the operation itself. Cash flows that are included in this category include net income (after adding back depreciation, because it is a noncash expense) plus net changes to its non-cash working capital accounts (i.e., accounts payable and receivable, inventory, accrued and prepaid expenses, and deferred taxes).

The investing activity portion tracks the cash flows associated with the buying and selling of capital assets.

The financing activity portion tracks the cash flows from the sale and repayment of the company's debt, both short term and long term, the sale and repurchase of its equity, both preferred and common stocks, and the payment of cash dividends. Note that the interest payments on debt appear in the operating activity portion and not in the financing activity portion.

Relationship Among Cash Budget, Capital Expenditure Budget, and Pro Forma Financial Statements

The cash budget combines the results of the operating, cash collections, and cash disbursements budgets to provide an overall picture of where an organization expects its cash to come from and be paid to for a given period. The capital expenditure budget is a line item that is included in the cash disbursements section of the cash budget. A pro forma income statement is completed to determine if an acceptable level of income is possible. This estimated income and changes to the cash budget are used to create a pro forma balance sheet. The pro forma cash flow statement classifies all of the cash receipts and disbursements based on activity: that is, operating activities, investing activities, and financial activities.

Comprehensive Problem: Budgeting Methodologies

Happy New Year! The date is January 2. You are the newly hired Assistant Controller for Pile Driver, Inc., and you have been asked to produce the following schedules and budgets for the current quarter:

a) Sales budget
b) Production budget
c) Finished goods inventory budget (in units)
d) Direct materials usage budget
e) Direct materials purchase budget
f) Direct labor budget
g) Factory overhead budget (variable and fixed)
h) Cost of goods sold budget and projected value of ending finished goods inventory
i) Selling and administrative budget
j) Pro forma schedule of cash receipts and cash disbursements
k) Cash budget
l) Pro forma income statement

After hours of research, you have collected the following information. Use this information to produce the required schedules in a format that will clearly document your calculations and communicate the important management accounting information.

Budgeted Sales Information

January	5,000 units
February	5,500 units
March	6,050 units
Selling price per unit	$60

Opening Balances as of January 1

Cash balance, January 1	$110,000
Accounts receivable balance, January 1	$39,150
Accounts payable balance, January 1	$11,750
Finished goods inventory quantity, January 1	900 units
Finished goods inventory value, January 1	$37,019
Direct materials inventory quantity, January 1	5,000 pounds
Direct materials inventory value, January 1	$3,750

Desired Monthly Closing Balances

Cash-desired minimum closing balance each month	$100,000
Finished goods inventory: 20% of next month's sales	
Direct materials inventory: 20% of next month's production	
The company uses a simple average cost method to calculate the value of the projected ending monthly finished goods inventory	

March 31—Special Assumptions

Desired finished goods inventory, March 31	1,230 units
Desired direct materials inventory, March 31	7,000 pounds

Production Cost Information

Direct materials needed per unit	6 pounds
Total direct labor hours needed per unit	2 hours
Direct materials cost per pound	$0.75
Direct labor cost per hour	$9.00

Overhead Costs

Variable

Supplies	$0.10 per DLH
Fringe benefits	$5.00 per DLH
Utilities	$0.80 per DLH
Maintenance	$0.75 per DLH

Fixed (monthly)

Depreciation	$15,000
Plant insurance	$800
Property taxes	$1,200
Salary supervision	$10,000
Indirect labor	$35,000
Utilities	$3,000
Maintenance	$1,100

Selling and Administrative Costs (monthly)

Research/design (January and February)	$5,000
Research/design (March)	$6,000
Marketing (monthly)	$1,000
Shipping	10% of sales
Product support (January and February)	$1,200
Product support (March)	$1,500
Administration (January)	$10,000
Administration (February)	$11,000
Administration (March)	$12,000

Additional Cash Flow Information

Collections: 70% of each month's sales are collected in the same month; 30% are collected the following month.

Payables: 50% of direct materials purchases are paid within the same month; 50% are paid the following month; assume all other cash expenses are paid in the month incurred.

Capital expenditures: no capital expenditures are planned for the quarter.

The company makes monthly payments of $5,000 on a term loan, with approximately $4,000 going against principal and $1,000 as interest.

The company also has access to a revolving line of credit with an interest rate of 10%.

As of January 1, the company had no borrowings against the line of credit.

Corporate income tax rate is 35% and the company pays quarterly installments.

Tax installment of $22,000 is due in January.

Use this information to create the required schedules. Good luck in your new position! Your success with this assignment will convince the management of Pile Driver, Inc. that they made a good decision when they hired you.

Solution to Comprehensive Problem: Budgeting Methodologies

a)

Sales Budget

	January	February	March	Quarter
Expected unit sales	5,000	5,500	6,050	16,550
Selling price per unit	$60	$60	$60	$60
Total Sales	$300,000	$330,000	$363,000	$993,000

b)

Production Budget

	January	February	March	Quarter
Budgeted unit sales	5,000	5,500	6,050	16,550
Add: desired ending finished goods inventory	1,100	1,210	1,230	
Total units needed	6,100	6,710	7,280	20,090
Less: beginning finished goods inventory	(900)	(1,100)	(1,210)	
Total budgeted production units	5,200	5,610	6,070	16,880

c)

Finished Goods Inventory Budget (units)

	January	February	March	Quarter
Beginning finished goods inventory	900	1,100	1,210	900
Units produced	5,200	5,610	6,070	16,880
Units available for sale	6,100	6,710	7,280	17,780
Budgeted unit sales	(5,000)	(5,500)	(6,050)	(16,550)
Ending finished goods inventory	1,100	1,210	1,230	1,230

d)

Direct Materials Usage Budget

	January	February	March	Quarter
Direct materials needed for production:				
Total budgeted production units	5,200	5,610	6,070	16,880
Direct materials needed per unit (pounds)	6	6	6	6
Direct materials needed for production (pounds)	31,200	33,660	36,420	101,280
Direct materials cost per pound	$0.75	$0.75	$0.75	$0.75
Total cost of direct materials used in production	$23,400	$25,245	$27,315	$75,960

e)

Direct Materials Purchase Budget

	January	February	March	Quarter
Direct materials needed for production	31,200	33,660	36,420	101,280
Add: Desired direct materials ending inventory	6,732	7,284	7,000	7,000
Less: beginning direct materials inventory	(5,000)	(6,732)	(7,284)	(5,000)
Direct materials to be purchased	32,932	34,212	36,136	103,280
Direct materials cost per pound	$0.75	$0.75	$0.75	$0.75
Total value of direct materials purchased	$24,699	$25,659	$27,102	$77,460

f)

Direct Labor Budget

	January	February	March	Quarter
Total budgeted production units	5,200	5,610	6,070	16,880
Direct labor hours needed per unit	2	2	2	2
Total hours needed for production	10,400	11,220	12,140	33,760
Labor rate per hour	$9.00	$9.00	$9.00	$9.00
Total direct labor cost	$93,600	$100,980	$109,260	$303,840

g)

Factory Overhead Budget

	Rate per direct labor hour	January	February	March	Quarter
Total direct labor hours		10,400	11,220	12,140	33,760
Variable Factory Overhead					
Supplies	$0.10	$1,040	$1,122	$1,214	$3,376
Fringe benefits	5.00	52,000	56,100	60,700	168,800
Utilities	0.80	8,320	8,976	9,712	27,008
Maintenance	0.75	7,800	8,415	9,105	25,320
Total variable factory overhead		$69,160	$74,613	$80,731	$224,504
Fixed Factory Overhead					
Depreciation		$15,000	$15,000	$15,000	$45,000
Plant insurance		$800	$800	$800	2,400
Property taxes		$1,200	$1,200	$1,200	3,600
Salary supervision		$10,000	$10,000	$10,000	30,000
Indirect labor		$35,000	$35,000	$35,000	105,000
Utilities		$3,000	$3,000	$3,000	9,000
Maintenance		$1,100	$1,100	$1,100	3,300
Total fixed factory overhead		$66,100	$66,100	$66,100	$198,300
Total overhead		$135,260	$140,713	$146,831	$422,804

h)

Cost of Goods Sold Budget

	January	February	March	Quarter
Direct materials used in production	$23,400	$25,245	$27,315	$75,960
Direct labor used in production	93,600	100,980	109,260	303,840
Manufacturing overhead (see schedule)	135,260	140,713	146,831	422,804
Cost of goods manufactured	252,260	266,938	283,406	$802,604
Beginning finished goods inventory	37,019	52,179	57,537	37,019
Cost of goods available for sale	$289,279	$319,117	$340,943	$839,623
Units available for sale	6,100	6,710	7,280	17,780
Average cost per unit available for sale	$47.42	$47.56	$46.83	n/a
Units sold	5,000	5,500	6,050	16,550
Cost of goods sold	$237,100	$261,580	$283,322	$782,002
Ending finished goods inventory	$52,179	$57,537	$57,621	$57,621

i)

Selling and Administrative Budget

	January	February	March	Quarter
Research/design	$5,000	$5,000	$6,000	$16,000
Marketing	1,000	1,000	1,000	$3,000
Shipping	30,000	33,000	36,300	$99,300
Product support	1,200	1,200	1,500	$3,900
Administration	10,000	11,000	12,000	$33,000
Total S&A	$47,200	$51,200	$56,800	$155,200

j)

Pro Forma Schedule of Cash Receipts and Cash Disbursements

	January	February	March	Quarter
Cash Receipts				
Collections from customers (70% same month)	$210,000	$231,000	$254,100	$695,100
Collections from customers (30% next month)	39,150	90,000	99,000	228,150
Total cash receipts	$249,150	$321,000	$353,100	$923,250
Cash Disbursements				
Direct materials purchases (50% same month)	$12,350	$12,830	$13,551	$38,731
Direct materials purchases (50% following month)	11,750	12,349	12,829	36,928
Direct labor (paid same month)	93,600	100,980	109,260	303,840
Variable factory overhead	69,160	74,613	80,731	224,504
Fixed factory overhead	66,100	66,100	66,100	198,300
Less depreciation (non-cash expense)	(15,000)	(15,000)	(15,000)	(45,000)
S&A expense	$47,200	$51,200	$56,800	$155,200

Pro Forma Schedule of Cash Receipts and Cash Disbursements (Continued)

	January	February	March	Quarter
Term loan payment	5,000	5,000	5,000	15,000
Tax installment	22,000	-	-	22,000
Capital expenditures	-	-	-	-
Total cash disbursements	$312,160	$308,072	$329,271	$949,503

k)
Cash Budget

	January	February	March	Quarter
Cash Balance, beginning	$110,000	$100,000	$100,000	$110,000
Add: Cash receipts	249,150	321,000	353,100	923,250
Total cash available for use	$359,150	$421,000	$453,100	$1,033,250
Cash disbursements	(312,160)	(308,072)	(329,271)	(949,503)
Cash balance before financing	$46,990	$112,928	$123,829	$83,747
Minimum cash required	(100,000)	(100,000)	(100,000)	(100,000)
Cash excess (deficiency)	$(53,010)	$12,928	$23,829	$(16,253)
Line of Credit (LOC)				
LOC interest expense	$-	$(442)	$(338)	$(780)
Borrowing (at end of month)	53,010	-	-	53,010
LOC repayment (at end of month)	-	(12,486)	(23,491)	(35,977)
Total effects of LOC financing	$53,010	$(12,928)	$(23,829)	$16,253
Cash balance, ending	$100,000	$100,000	$100,000	$100,000

l)
Pro Forma Income Statement

	January	February	March	Quarter
Sales	$300,000	$330,000	$363,000	$993,000
Cost of goods sold	(237,100)	(261,580)	(283,322)	(782,002)
Gross profit	$62,900	$68,420	$79,678	$210,998
Less: S&A expenses	(47,200)	(51,200)	(56,800)	(155,200)
Operating income (EBIT)	$15,700	$17,220	$22,878	$55,798
Less: Interest expense	$(1,000)	$(1,442)	$(1,338)	$(3,780)
Earnings before taxes	$14,700	$15,778	$21,540	$52,018
Less: Tax expense	(5,145)	(5,522)	(7,539)	(18,206)
Net income (loss)	$9,555	$10,256	$14,001	$33,812

Knowledge Check:
Annual Profit Plan and Supporting Schedules

The following questions are intended to help you check your understanding and recall of the material presented in this topic. They do not represent the type of questions that appear on the CMA exam.

Directions: Answer in the space provided. Correct answers and section references appear after the knowledge check questions.

1. Which of the following budgets is the first operating budget prepared because it defines needed capacity for operations?
   - ☐ a. Production/inventory budget
   - ☐ b. Direct labor budget
   - ☐ c. Sales budget
   - ☐ d. Overhead budget

2. Which of the following internal pro forma financial statements is usually the last budget prepared at the end of a period?
   - ☐ a. Pro forma income statement
   - ☐ b. Pro forma balance sheet
   - ☐ c. Pro forma statement of stockholders' equity
   - ☐ d. Cash budget

3. Which of the following budgets is designed to ensure that the company maintains adequate liquidity?
   - ☐ a. Overhead budget
   - ☐ b. Sales budget
   - ☐ c. Production/inventory budget
   - ☐ d. Cash budget

4. What factors are used to calculate the production budget? Complete the equation:

   Budgeted production = _____ + _____ − _____

5. Calculate the budgeted direct labor cost for Company D for January.

   Direct labor hours per unit = 7 direct labor hours

   Expected production = 5,700 units

   Direct labor cost per hour = $19 per hour

6. In a pro forma statement of cash flows, which activity tracks each of the following cash flows?

	Operating Activity	Investing Activity	Financing Activity
Net changes to non-cash working capital accounts			
Repayment of company debt			
Interest payment on debt			
Sales of capital assets			

Knowledge Check Answers: Annual Profit Plan and Supporting Schedules

1. Which of the following budgets is the first operating budget prepared because it defines needed capacity for operations? [**See *Sales Budget*.**]
    - ☐ a. Production/inventory budget
    - ☐ b. Direct labor budget
    - ☒ c. Sales budget
    - ☐ d. Overhead budget

2. Which of the following internal pro forma financial statements is usually the last budget prepared at the end of a period? [**See *Pro Forma (or Budgeted) Balance Sheet*.**]
    - ☐ a. Pro forma income statement
    - ☒ b. Pro forma balance sheet
    - ☐ c. Pro forma statement of stockholders' equity
    - ☐ d. Cash budget

3. Which of the following budgets is designed to ensure that the company maintains adequate liquidity? [**See *Cash Budget*.**]
    - ☐ a. Overhead budget
    - ☐ b. Sales budget
    - ☐ c. Production/inventory budget
    - ☒ d. Cash budget

4. What factors are used to calculate the production budget? Complete the equation: [**See *Production Budget*.**]

    Budgeted Production = Budgeted Sales + Desired Ending Inventory − Beginning Inventory

5. Calculate the budgeted direct labor cost for Company D for January. [**See *Direct Labor Budget*.**]

    Direct Labor Hours Requirement = 7 Direct Labor Hours × 5,700 units = 39,900 Direct Labor Hours

    Direct Labor Cost = 39,900 Direct Labor Hours × $19 per Hour = $758,100

6. In a pro forma statement of cash flows, which activity tracks each of the following cash flows? [See **Pro Forma (or Budgeted) Statement of Cash Flows.**]

	Operating Activity	Investing Activity	Financing Activity
Net changes to non-cash working capital accounts	X		
Repayment of company debt			X
Interest payment on debt	X		
Sales of capital assets		X	

TOPIC 6

Top-Level Planning and Analysis

THE MASTER BUDGET, OR ANNUAL profit plan, includes a set of pro forma financial statements. These financial statements are key elements in helping a company plan for the future. Based on these pro forma statements, a company can: determine if it is meeting its predetermined targets; estimate the amount of external funding needed to support its projected sales growth; and perform sensitivity analysis to identify the impacts of estimates, operating, and policy changes on selected financial ratios.

This topic traces the process of creating pro forma financial statements using the percentage-of-sales method, which builds a pro forma income statement and then a pro forma balance sheet, and it shows an example of creating a pro forma statement of cash flows. It describes the process of assessing anticipated performance using pro forma financial statements, including performing sensitivity analyses.

> **READ** the Learning Outcome Statements (LOS) for this topic as found in Appendix A and then study the concepts and calculations presented here to be sure you understand the content you could be tested on in the CMA exam.

Pro Forma Financial Statements and Budgets

The master budget is composed of the operating budgets and the financial budgets. The final product of the operating budget is the pro forma income statement, which basically shows a company's projected sales revenue, costs, and profit (i.e., net income). Once the company's dividend policy has been factored in to determine the amount of dividends to be paid, the amount of projected retained earnings will then be added to its current balance sheet to create the pro forma balance sheet. Information from the company's capital expenditure budget and cash budget will also be used to help formulate the pro forma balance sheet. Once the pro forma income statement and balance sheet are compiled, the information can then be used to create the pro forma statement of cash flows.

The relationships among the various pro forma financial statements and budgets are illustrated in Figure 1B-44.

Figure 1B-44 Relationships Among Pro Forma Financial Statements and Budgets

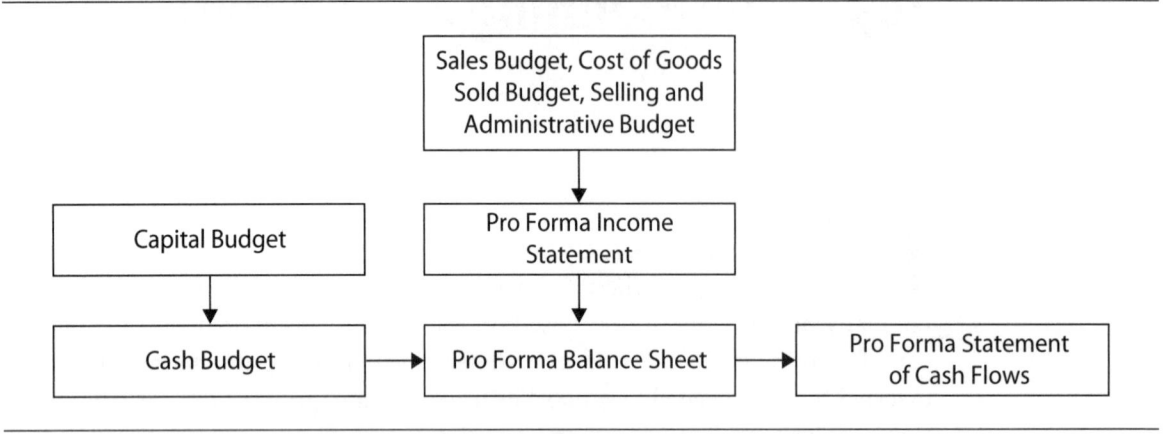

```
                    ┌─────────────────────────┐
                    │ Sales Budget, Cost of Goods │
                    │  Sold Budget, Selling and   │
                    │   Administrative Budget     │
                    └─────────────┬───────────────┘
                                  │
                                  ▼
┌──────────────┐        ┌──────────────────┐
│Capital Budget│        │ Pro Forma Income │
└──────┬───────┘        │    Statement     │
       │                └─────────┬────────┘
       ▼                          ▼
┌──────────────┐   ┌──────────────────────┐   ┌──────────────────┐
│ Cash Budget  │──▶│Pro Forma Balance Sheet│──▶│Pro Forma Statement│
└──────────────┘   └──────────────────────┘   │  of Cash Flows    │
                                              └──────────────────┘
```

Pro forma statements represent a company's projected financial statements. They are useful in the company's planning process because these statements support three major functions. They help a company to:

1. Assess whether its anticipated performance is in line with its established targets.
2. Anticipate the amount of funding needed to achieve its forecasted sales growth.
3. Estimate the effects of changes in assumptions of key numbers by performing sensitivity analysis (i.e., what-if analysis). Sensitivity analysis helps to identify potential conditions that could lead to major problems for the company. This enables the company to plan for appropriate actions in case such an event should occur. In addition, sensitivity analysis also provides the company with the opportunity to analyze the impact of changing its operating plans.

Creating a Pro Forma Income Statement with the Percentage-of-Sales Method

In Topic 5: Annual Profit Plan and Supporting Schedules, various pieces of the operating budget were projected and used to ultimately form the pro forma income statement. The process to complete these schedules is very complex and time consuming. Here a short-cut approach, known as the percentage-of-sales method, is used to create a pro forma income statement and a pro forma balance sheet.

The percentage-of-sales method is a simple approach that ties many of the items in the pro forma income statement and balance sheet to future sales revenue. It assumes that the relationship between these income statement and balance sheet items and sales revenue remains constant, which means that they grow proportionally with sales growth. Any activity that is needed to directly support the operations that will generate the specific sales level is assumed to grow proportionately with sales. On the income statement, these items include the cost of goods sold (COGS) and selling and administrative (S&A) expense; on the balance sheet, it includes current assets, net fixed assets, accounts payables, and accruals.

None of the financing activities—namely, notes payable (short-term borrowing), long-term debt, and owners' equity—is assumed to grow proportionately with sales.

For example: Heavenly Furniture Company uses the percentage-of-sales method to forecast its pro forma financial statements. Based on historical financial statements, these relationships can be established between several items and sales:

- COGS is 80% of sales.
- S&A expense is 5% of sales.
- Cash and equivalent are 3% of sales.
- Account receivables are 18% of sales.
- Inventories are 25% of sales.
- Net fixed assets are 35% of sales.
- Accounts payables are 12% of sales.
- Accruals are 8% of sales.

Heavenly Furniture is projecting a sales revenue growth of 18% in the upcoming year. The company currently has 12,000 shares of common stocks outstanding, and it plans on maintaining its dividend policy of paying out 40% of its net income as dividends. It is currently paying 8% interest on its notes payable and 10% on its long-term debt. The company has a 35% tax rate.

The process it uses is:

1. Create the pro forma income statement.
2. Create the pro forma balance sheet.
3. Create the pro forma statement of cash flows.

Creating a Pro Forma Income Statement

To create the pro forma income statement, it is necessary to first estimate the sales revenue for the upcoming year. Given the current-year sales revenue of $100,000 and a projected growth rate of 18%, the upcoming-year sale revenue will be $118,000. The projected sales revenue is then used to determine COGS and S&A. Since COGS is assumed to remain at 80% of sales, the forecasted COGS is projected to be $94,400. S&A is assumed to remain at 5% of sales, so the upcoming S&A is projected to be $5,900.

To simplify the calculations, it is assumed that Heavenly Furniture's interest expense is calculated based on its beginning-of-period debt balance. Since the company is carrying a $5,000 note payable and $20,000 of long-term debt at the beginning of the upcoming year, the total interest expense is $2,400—the interest expense on the note payable is $400 ($5,000 note payable multiplied by the 8% annual interest rate), and the interest expense on the long-term debt is $2,000 ($20,000 long-term debt multiplied by the 10% annual interest rate).

These numbers are then used to create the upcoming year's pro forma income statement, presented along with the current year's income statement in Figure 1B-45.

Figure 1B-45 Heavenly Furniture Company Pro Forma Income Statement

	Current Year	Upcoming Year
Sales	$100,000	$118,000
COGS	80,000	94,400
Gross Margin	20,000	23,600
S&A Expenses	5,000	5,900
EBIT (Operating Income)	15,000	17,700
Interest	1,800	2,400
EBT	13,200	15,300
Taxes (35%)	4,620	5,355
Net Income	$8,580	$9,945
EPS	$0.72	$0.83
Dividends (40%)	$3,432	$3,978
Addition to retained earnings	$5,148	$5,967

EBIT = earnings before interest and taxes; EBT = earnings before taxes; EPS = earnings per share.

With a projected 18% sales growth, Heavenly Furniture expects to generate a net income of $9,945 and EPS of $0.83 (= $9,945/12,000 shares). Given the current dividend policy of paying out 40% of earnings as dividends, the company will be paying out $3,978 (= $9,945 × 0.40) in dividends and retaining $5,967 (= $9,945 − $3,978) in earnings.

Creating a Pro Forma Balance Sheet and Determining Additional Funding Needed

After creating the pro forma income statement for the upcoming year, Heavenly Furniture Company's pro forma balance sheet can be created. Once again, based on a projected sales revenue of $118,000 and the assumed relationships:

Cash and cash equivalents are projected to be $3,540 (3% of sales).

Accounts receivables are projected to be $21,240 (18% of sales).

Inventories are projected to be $29,500 (25% of sales).

Net fixed assets are projected to be $41,300 (35% of sales).

Accounts payables are projected to be $14,160 (12% of sales).

Accruals are projected to be $9,440 (8% of sales).

In addition, based on the pro forma statement for the upcoming year, Heavenly Furniture Company is expected to retain $5,967 in earnings. The earnings will be added to the current year's retained earnings of $16,000 in the balance sheet to derive the upcoming year's retained earnings of $21,967.

Two iterations will be completed to derive Heavenly Furniture Company's pro forma balance sheet. In the first iteration, all financing activities (i.e., notes payables, long-term debt, and common stock) are assumed to remain at the current year's levels. This will help to determine if the company needs any additional external funding to support the projected sales growth. Once the level of external funding has been determined, it will be incorporated to create the final pro forma balance sheet in the second iteration.

Using the estimated balance sheet items calculated earlier, Heavenly Furniture's pro forma balance sheet (before any additional financing) is presented in Figure 1B-46.

Figure 1B-46 Heavenly Furniture Pro Forma Balance Sheet Before Additional Financing

	Current Year	Upcoming Year
Assets		
Cash and equivalents	$3,000	$3,540
Receivables	18,000	21,240
Inventories	25,000	29,500
Total Current Assets	46,000	54,280
Net Fixed Assets	35,000	41,300
Total Assets	$81,000	$95,580
Liabilities and Equity		
Accounts payable	$12,000	$14,160
Accruals	8,000	9,440
Notes payable	5,000	5,000
Total Current Liabilities	25,000	28,600
Long-term debt	20,000	20,000
Total Liabilities	45,000	48,600
Common stock	20,000	20,000
Retained earnings	16,000	21,967
Total Equity	36,000	41,967
Total liabilities and equity	$81,000	$90,567
Additional Funding Needed		$5,013

Since the company needed $95,580 in assets to support its estimated sales revenue of $118,000 but only has $90,567 in financing (i.e., total liabilities and equity), the company will need $5,013 ($95,580 − $90,567) in external funding.

Heavenly Furniture Company has several options for raising the $5,013 of external funding it needs. The company can raise the funds using notes payable, long-term debt, common stocks, or any combination of the three—such as $2,000 from notes payable and $3,013 from long-term debt. However, if the company is unwilling to seek that much external funding, it can lower its external funding need by increasing the amount of internal funding (i.e., retained earnings) available by altering its dividend policy. The company can lower its dividend payout ratio (e.g., from 40% to 30%) to reduce the amount of dividends paid out and to increase the amount of earnings retained. For every additional dollar of internal funding (in the form of retained earnings) raised, the company will need one less dollar of external funding.

In this scenario, it is assumed that Heavenly Furniture Company will acquire the $5,013 of external funding it needs using notes payable. This will be added to the company's current $5,000 of notes payable for a total of $10,013. Figure 1B-47 shows the company's pro forma balance sheet after taking on the additional funding.

Figure 1B-47   Heavenly Furniture Pro Forma Balance Sheet After Additional Financing

	Current Year	Upcoming Year
Assets		
Cash and equivalents	$3,000	$3,540
Receivables	18,000	21,240
Inventories	25,000	29,500
Total Current Assets	$46,000	$54,280
Net Fixed Assets	35,000	41,300
Total Assets	$81,000	$95,580
Liabilities and Equity		
Accounts payable	$12,000	$14,160
Accruals	8,000	9,440
Notes payable	5,000	10,013
Total Current Liabilities	$25,000	$33,613
Long-term debt	20,000	20,000
Total Liabilities	$45,000	$53,613
Common stock	20,000	20,000
Retained earnings	16,000	21,967
Total Equity	36,000	41,967
Total liabilities and equity	$81,000	$95,580

Creating a Pro Forma Statement of Cash Flows

Once Heavenly Furniture Company's pro forma income statement and balance sheet have been completed, that information can be used to create the company's pro forma statement of cash flows. There are two approaches to creating a statement of cash flows: the direct method and the indirect method. Heavenly Furniture Company's pro forma statement of cash flows will be created using the indirect method.

A key concept in dealing with cash flows is:

- Any increase in accounts receivables, inventories, net fixed assets, net income generated, and dividends paid represents a cash outflow, and vice versa.
- Any increase in accounts payables, accruals, and financing activities (i.e., notes payable, long-term debt, and common stock issued) represents a cash inflow, and vice versa.

For example: According to Figure 1B-47, Heavenly Furniture's accounts receivables increases by $3,240 (from $18,000 to $21,240). This represents a cash flow of −$3,240 (a cash outflow). Its accounts payable amount increases by $2,160 (from $12,000 to

$14,160). This represents a cash flow of +$2,160. The pro forma statement of cash flows groups cash flows as a result of various activities into three major categories:

1. Cash flows from operating activities
2. Cash flows from investing activities
3. Cash flows from financing activities

For example: Using information from the company's pro forma income statement and balance sheet (see Figures 1B-45 and 1B-46):

- Cash flow from operating activities = $5,805
- Cash flow from investing activities = −$6,300
- Cash flows from financing activities = $1,035

Heavenly Furniture's pro forma statement of cash flows is shown in Figure 1B-48.

Figure 1B-48 Heavenly Furniture Pro Forma Statement of Cash Flows

Net income	$9,945
Receivables	(3,240)
Inventories	(4,500)
Payables	2,160
Accruals	1,440
Cash flow from operating activities	$5,805
Capital expenditure (net fixed assets)	$(6,300)
Cash flow from investing activities	$(6,300)
Notes payables	$5,013
Dividends	(3,978)
Cash flow from financing activities	$1,035
Net change in cash flow	$540
Beginning cash	3,000
Ending cash	$3,540

The company's combined cash flow for the upcoming year totals $540 (= $5,805 − $6,300 + $1,035). Together with a beginning cash balance of $3,000, the additional cash flow of $3,000 will result in an ending cash balance of $3,540. This matches Heavenly Furniture Company's cash position in the pro forma balance sheet (see Figure 1B-47).

Assessing Anticipated Performance Using Pro Forma Financial Statements

Once a company creates its pro forma financial statements, the statements need to be analyzed to determine if the company is meeting its predetermined financial targets. This can be accomplished by calculating a variety of financial ratios and comparing them to predetermined targets and industry averages. These calculations can help answer questions such as:

- Is the company's leverage (as measured by its debt ratio) within an acceptable range?
- Is its return on equity (ROE) acceptable in relation to the industry average?

A more detailed discussion on financial statement analysis using ratios and the formulas for additional ratios is covered in Part 2 of the Wiley CMAexcel Learning System Exam Review.

For example: Figure 1B-49 presents a few selected financial ratios for Heavenly Furniture, calculated using the current and pro forma income statement and balance sheets (Figures 1B-45 and 1B-47).

Figure 1B-49 Heavenly Furniture Selected Financial Ratios

	Current Year	Upcoming Year
Current ratio	1.8400	1.6149
Quick ratio	0.8400	0.7372
Return on assets (ROA)	0.1059	0.1040
Return on equity (ROE)	0.2383	0.2370
Gross profit margin	0.2000	0.2000
Operating profit margin	0.1500	0.1500
Net profit margin	0.0858	0.0843
Debt ratio	0.5556	0.5609
Times interest earned (TIE)	8.3333	7.3750
EPS	$0.72	$0.83

The ratios shown are calculated using these formulas:

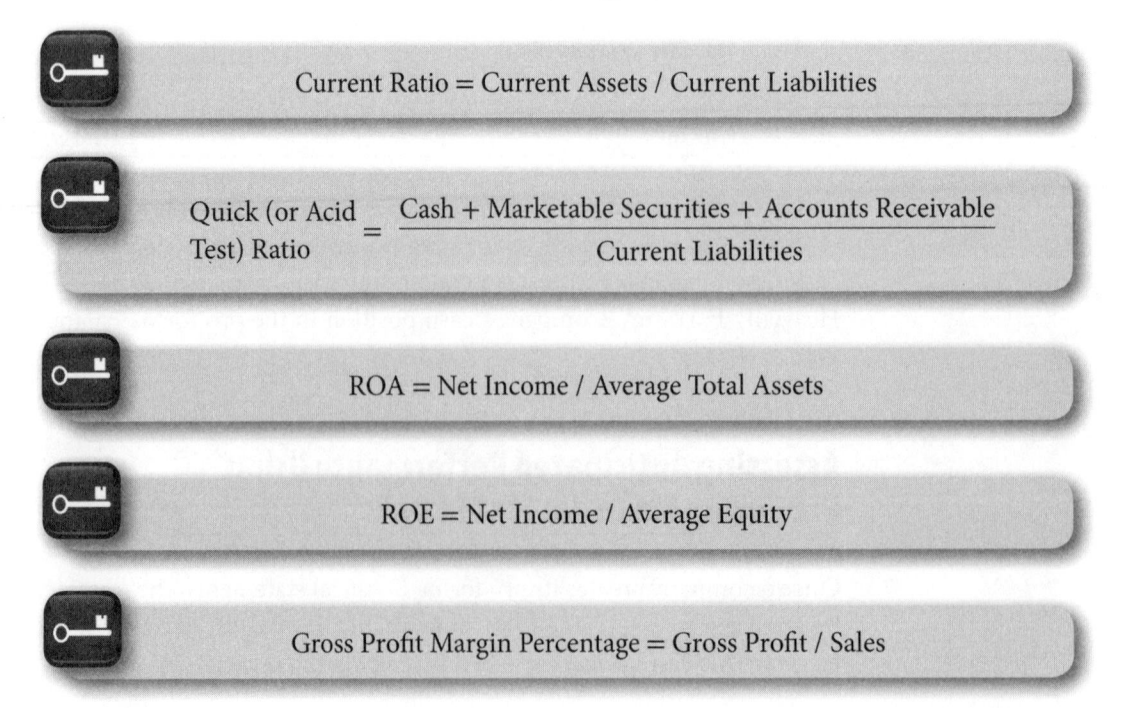

$$\text{Current Ratio} = \text{Current Assets} / \text{Current Liabilities}$$

$$\text{Quick (or Acid Test) Ratio} = \frac{\text{Cash} + \text{Marketable Securities} + \text{Accounts Receivable}}{\text{Current Liabilities}}$$

$$\text{ROA} = \text{Net Income} / \text{Average Total Assets}$$

$$\text{ROE} = \text{Net Income} / \text{Average Equity}$$

$$\text{Gross Profit Margin Percentage} = \text{Gross Profit} / \text{Sales}$$

Operating Profit Margin Percentage = Operating Income / Sales

Net Profit Margin Percentage = Net Income / Sales

Debt to Total Assets Ratio = Total Debt / Total Assets

Interest Coverage (or Times Interest Earned, TIE) = EBIT / Interest Expense

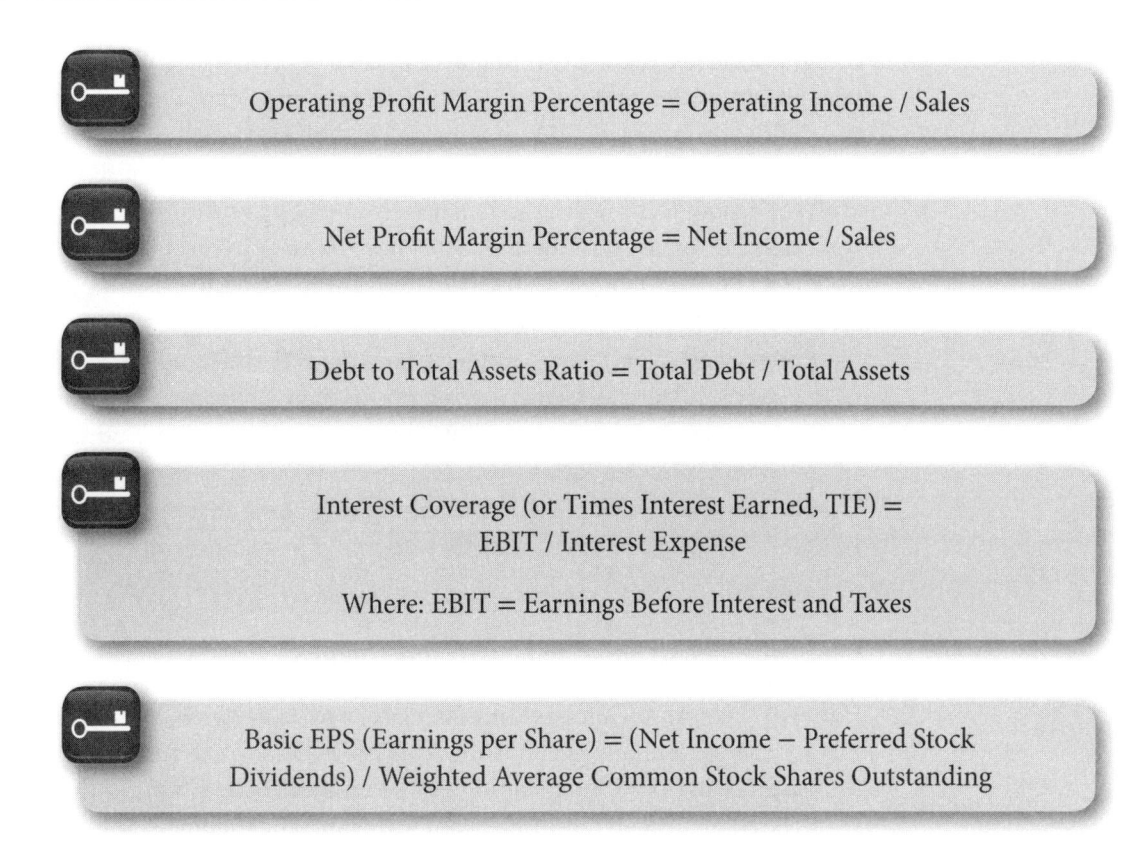

Where: EBIT = Earnings Before Interest and Taxes

Basic EPS (Earnings per Share) = (Net Income − Preferred Stock Dividends) / Weighted Average Common Stock Shares Outstanding

In order to support a projected 18% sales growth, Heavenly Furniture Company is raising $5,013 of external funding via notes payable. Because the company is tapping short-term borrowing for its external funding needs, its liquidity position will deteriorate as the current ratio and quick ratio are expected to decrease in the upcoming year. Its profit position, in terms of return on assets (ROA), return on equity (ROE), and net profit margin, is also expected to decrease in the upcoming year.

Because the company is relying on notes payable to raise its needed external funding, it is important that it pay close attention to its debt ratio and interest coverage (in terms of times interest earned [TIE]) to ensure that it has not violated its debt covenants. The company's debt ratio is expected to increase from 55.56% to 56.09%, and its TIE is expected to decrease from 8.333 to 7.3750. Both of these changes are relatively minor, so the company should be able to meet its debt covenant.

Earnings per share (EPS) is expected to increase from $0.72 to $0.83 (a 15.28% increase) as a result of the sales growth that is funded by additional debt.

Performing Sensitivity Analysis

The pro forma statements in Figures 1B-45, 1B-46, 1B-47, 1B-48, and the selected ratios in Figure 1B-49 are based on Heavenly Furniture Company's assumptions of a projected 18% sales growth and certain assumed relationships between sales revenue and selected items in the income statement and balance sheet. Since the company is dealing with the future when projecting its pro forma statements, there is always a chance that these initial assumptions will change. What if the projected sales growth is 20% rather than 18%? What if the cost of production has increased and the COGS is actually 85% of sales rather than 80% of sales?

The company can analyze these alternatives by performing a series of what-if analyses. Doing this involves systematically changing one of the assumptions and analyzing the impact that these changes have on the pro forma statements and on the selected financial ratios. What-if analysis that changes one assumption (or variable) at a time is also known as sensitivity analysis.

For example: Heavenly Furniture Company is performing a sensitivity analysis to determine the effects of changing one or more of its initial assumptions. The original pro forma income statement and balance sheet (from Figures 1B-45 and 1A-37) and the selected ratios (from Figure 1B-49) serve as the base scenario.

Their first analysis focuses on changing two of the income statement–related assumptions: sales revenue growth rate and the relationship between COGS and sales.

Sensitivity Analysis Based on Growth Rate Changes

Heavenly Furniture Company initially projected a sales revenue growth rate of 18% for the upcoming year. However, this projected growth rate might be as high as 20% or as low as 16%, depending on the economic conditions in the upcoming year. The company can reproject its pro forma income statement and balance sheet first based on a 16% growth rate and then based on a 20% growth rate. All other assumptions are assumed to remain the same.

The 16% growth rate will lead to projected sales of $116,000. The 20% growth rate will lead to projected sales of $120,000. Using the methods discussed earlier in creating the initial pro forma financial statements, the pro forma income statement and balance sheet for the various growth rate assumptions are presented in Figure 1B-50.

Figure 1B-50 Sensitivity Analysis with Different Growth Rates

Heavenly Furniture Company Pro Forma Income Statement

	Growth = 16%	Base =18%	Growth = 20%
Sales	$116,000	$118,000	$120,000
COGS	92,800	94,400	96,000
Gross Margin	23,200	23,600	24,000
S&A Expenses	5,800	5,900	6,000
EBIT (Operating Income)	17,400	17,700	18,000
Interest	2,400	2,400	2,400
EBT	15,000	15,300	15,600
Taxes	5,250	5,355	5,460
Net Income	$9,750	$9,945	$10,140
EPS	$0.81	$0.83	$0.85
Dividends	$3,900	$3,978	$4,056
Addition to retained earnings	$5,850	$5,967	$6,084

Heavenly Furniture Company Pro Forma Balance Sheet			
	Growth = 16%	Base=18%	Growth = 20%
Assets			
Cash and equivalents	$3,480	$3,540	$3,600
Receivables	20,880	21,240	21,600
Inventories	29,000	29,500	30,000
Total Current Assets	$53,360	$54,280	$55,200
Net Fixed Assets	40,600	41,300	42,000
Total Assets	$93,960	$95,580	$97,200
Liabilities and Equity			
Accounts payable	$13,920	$14,160	$14,400
Accruals	9,280	9,440	9,600
Notes payable	8,910	10,013	11,116
Total Current Liabilities	$32,110	$33,613	$35,116
Long-term debt	20,000	20,000	20,000
Total Liabilities	$52,110	$53,613	$55,116
Common stock	20,000	20,000	20,000
Retained earnings	21,850	21,967	22,084
Total Equity	$41,850	$41,967	$42,084
Total liabilities and equity	$93,960	$95,580	$97,200

The sensitivity analysis for Heavenly Furniture Company was done by varying its projected sales growth within the range of 16% to 20%. The pro forma income statement and balance sheet will provide the company an opportunity to determine how various items in the income statement and balance sheet change as the projected growth rate changes.

For example: In Figure 1B-50, the company's EPS drops to $0.81 when the growth rate is 16%, and the EPS rises to $0.85 when the growth rate is 20%. This means that a 2% change in growth rate leads to a $0.02 change in EPS.

The new pro forma income statement and balance sheet can also be used to create new sets of financial ratios, as shown in Figure 1B-51. Once again, the company will be able to analyze how each financial ratio changes when the growth rate changes.

In addition to the financial ratios, the additional amounts of external funding needed for the various growth rates are also presented in Figure 1B-51. Since the company relies solely on the use of notes payable to meet its external funding need, the amount of external funding needed can be determined by subtracting the amount of notes payable in the current year ($5,000) from the amount of notes payable in the upcoming year. For instance, the amount of notes payable is $8,910 when the growth rate is 16%, so the amount of external funding needed is $3,910 (= $8,910 − $5,000). It is important for Heavenly Furniture to pay close attention to how the amount of external funding needed changes when the growth rate assumption changes. The company might not be comfortable raising the amount

Figure 1B-51 Selected Financial Ratio Sensitivity Analysis with Different Growth Rates

	Growth = 16%	Base = 18%	Growth = 20%
Current ratio	1.6618	1.6149	1.5719
Quick ratio	0.7586	0.7372	0.7176
ROA	0.1038	0.1040	0.1043
ROE	0.2330	0.2370	0.2409
Gross profit margin	0.2000	0.2000	0.2000
Operating profit margin	0.1500	0.1500	0.1500
Net profit margin	0.0841	0.0843	0.0845
Debt ratio	0.5546	0.5609	0.5670
TIE	7.2500	7.3750	7.5000
Additional funding needed	$3,910	$5,013	$6,116

of external funding if the growth rate is higher than anticipated, or the company may need to arrange for a line of credit and be prepared to pursue other external funding options if needed.

Sensitivity Analysis Based on COGS Changes

In the previous scenario, a sensitivity analysis was performed by changing Heavenly Furniture Company's revenue (i.e., the sales growth rate). Now the analysis is repeated, but this time one of its expenses, namely COGS, will be changed.

In the base scenario, it was initially assumed that COGS is 80% of sales. However, the cost of its production (e.g., labor and materials) might increase in the upcoming year, and COGS could become 85% of sales. Due to a more streamlined production process or a drop in material costs, the COGS could decrease to 75% of sales in the upcoming year. Once again, assuming all the other assumptions remain the same (e.g., sales growth rate of 18%), the company's pro forma income statement and balance sheet can be prepared for each of the alternative COGS scenarios. The results are shown in Figure 1B-52.

Once again, the company can determine how various items in the income statement and balance sheet change when COGS changes. In Figure 1B-52, the company's EPS rises to $1.15 when COGS is 75% of sales, and the EPS drops to $0.51 when COGS is 85% of sales. This means that a 5% change in COGS (in relation to sales) leads to a $0.32 change in EPS.

Similarly, the new pro forma income statement and balance sheet, based on various COGS rates, are used to create new sets of financial ratios. The results (including the external funding needed) are presented in Figure 1B-53.

Heavenly Furniture Company can continue to perform additional sensitivity analysis by changing other income statement–related assumptions, such as the relationship between S&A and sales.

In addition, the company can analyze the impact of varying its operating plans by changing its balance sheet–related assumptions. For example, if the company

Figure 1B-52 Sensitivity Analysis with Different COGS Rates

Heavenly Furniture Company Pro Forma Income Statement

	COGS = 75%	Base = 80%	COGS = 85%
Sales	$118,000	$118,000	$118,000
COGS	88,500	94,400	100,300
Gross Margin	29,500	23,600	17,700
S&A Expenses	5,900	5,900	5,900
EBIT (Operating Income)	23,600	17,700	11,800
Interest	2,400	2,400	2,400
EBT	21,200	15,300	9,400
Taxes	7,420	5,355	3,290
Net Income	$13,780	$9,945	$6,110
EPS	$1.15	$0.83	$0.51
Dividends	$5,512	$3,978	$2,444
Addition to retained earnings	$8,268	$5,967	$3,666
Assets			
Cash and equivalents	$3,540	$3,540	$3,540
Receivables	21,240	21,240	21,240
Inventories	29,500	29,500	29,500
Total Current Assets	54,280	54,280	54,280
Net Fixed Assets	41,300	41,300	41,300
Total Assets	$95,580	$95,580	$95,580
Liabilities and Equity			
Accounts payable	$14,160	$14,160	$14,160
Accruals	9,440	9,440	9,440
Notes payable	7,712	10,013	12,314
Total Current Liabilities	31,312	33,613	35,914
Long-term debt	20,000	20,000	20,000
Total Liabilities	51,312	53,613	55,914
Common stocks	20,000	20,000	20,000
Retained earnings	24,268	21,967	19,666
Total Equity	44,268	41,967	39,666
Total liabilities and equity	$95,580	$95,580	$95,580

plans on installing a new inventory control system, how would that affect its pro forma financial statements, including additional funding needed and selected financial ratios? The company can accomplish this by varying the relationship between inventories and sales. Since the new inventory control system will allow the company to hold less inventory, the inventory assumption can be changed from 25% of sales to a lower number.

Figure 1B-53 Selected Financial Ratios Sensitivity Analysis with Different COGS Rates

	COGS = 75%	Base = 80%	COGS = 85%
Current ratio	1.7335	1.6149	1.5114
Quick ratio	0.7914	0.7372	0.6900
ROA	0.1442	0.1040	0.0639
ROE	0.3113	0.2370	0.1540
Gross profit margin	0.2500	0.2000	0.1500
Operating profit margin	0.2000	0.1500	0.1000
Net profit margin	0.1168	0.0843	0.0518
Debt ratio	0.5368	0.5609	0.5850
TIE	9.8333	7.3750	4.9167
Additional funding needed	$2,712	$5,013	$7,314

Overall, sensitivity analysis encourages a company to manage by exception. Performing sensitivity analysis by changing different variables allows a company to determine which sets of variables have the greatest impact on items of interest (e.g., EPS and additional funding needed) and which sets of variables have negligible impacts on the items of interest. This allows the company to focus its attention (and effort) on the most critical assumptions. In the Heavenly Furniture Company example, changes in COGS have a bigger impact on financial ratios (such as EPS) and additional funding needed than changes in the sales growth rate. As demonstrated, a 2% change in sales growth rate will lead to a $0.02 change in EPS, whereas a 5% change in COGS leads to a $0.32 change in EPS.

Knowledge Check: Top-Level Planning and Analysis

The next questions are intended to help you check your understanding and recall of the material presented in this topic. They do not represent the type of questions that appear on the CMA exam.

Directions: Answer in the space provided. Correct answers and section references appear after the knowledge check questions.

1. What planning functions do pro forma statements support?

    a. _____

    b. _____

    c. _____

2. Robin Manufacturing Company has projected a sales growth rate of 15% for the upcoming year. The pro forma balance sheet created based on this growth rate shows that total assets are $4,300,000 and the total liabilities and owner's equity are $3,950,000. This indicates that the amount of external funding the company needs is:

    ☐ a. $4,300,000

    ☐ b. $3,950,000

    ☐ c. $350,000

    ☐ d. $8,250,000

3. If the amount of external funding is too high for the company, which of the following actions can it take?

    ☐ a. Reduce its dividend payout.

    ☐ b. Increase its dividend payout.

    ☐ c. Increase its sales growth rate.

    ☐ d. Reduce its accounts payables (in relation to sales).

4. Which of the following actions is **not** permitted in a sensitivity analysis?

    ☐ a. Changing the projected growth rate

    ☐ b. Changing the dividend payout ratio

    ☐ c. Changing the cost of goods sold (COGS)

    ☐ d. Changing the projected growth rate and COGS

5. Indicate whether each situation listed represents a cash inflow or cash outflow.

Situation	Cash Inflow	Cash Outflow
Increase in inventories		
Increase in long-term debt		
Increase in accounts payable		
Decrease accruals		
Decrease in net fixed assets		
Decrease in accounts payable		

Knowledge Check Answers: Top-Level Planning and Analysis

1. What planning functions do pro forma statements support? [See *Creating a Pro Forma Income Statement with the Percentage-of-Sales Method.*]
   a. Assess whether anticipated performance is in line with its established targets
   b. Anticipate the amount of funding needed to achieve its forecasted sales growth
   c. Estimate effects of changes in assumptions of key numbers

2. Robin Manufacturing Company has projected a sales growth rate of 15% for the upcoming year. The pro forma balance sheet created based on this growth rate shows that total assets are $4,300,000 and the total liabilities and owner's equity are $3,950,000. This indicates that the amount of external funding the company needs is: [See *Creating a Pro Forma Balance Sheet and Determining Additional Funding Needed.*]
   - ☐ a. $4,300,000
   - ☐ b. $3,950,000
   - ☑ c. $350,000
   - ☐ d. $8,250,000

3. If the amount of external funding is too high for the company, which of the following actions can it take? [See *Creating a Pro Forma Balance Sheet and Determining Additional Funding Needed.*]
   - ☑ a. Reduce its dividend payout.
   - ☐ b. Increase its dividend payout.
   - ☐ c. Increase its sales growth rate.
   - ☐ d. Reduce its accounts payables (in relation to sales).

4. Which of the following actions is **not** permitted in a sensitivity analysis? [See *Performing Sensitivity Analysis.*]
   - ☐ a. Changing the projected growth rate
   - ☐ b. Changing the dividend payout ratio
   - ☐ c. Changing the cost of goods sold (COGS)
   - ☑ d. Changing the projected growth rate and COGS.

5. Indicate whether each situation listed represents a cash inflow or cash outflow. [See *Creating a Pro Forma Statement of Cash Flows*.]

Situation	Cash Inflow	Cash Outflow
Increase in inventories		X
Increase in long-term debt	X	
Increase in accounts payable	X	
Decrease accruals		X
Decrease in net fixed assets	X	
Decrease in accounts payable		X

Practice Questions: Planning, Budgeting, and Forecasting

Directions: This sampling of questions is designed to emulate actual exam questions. Read each question and write your response on another sheet of paper. Use the answer and explanation (given later in the book) to assess your response. Validate or improve the answer you wrote. For a more robust selection of practice questions, access the **Online Test Bank** found on www.wileycma.com. See the "Answers to Section Practice Questions" section at the end of this book.

Question 1B5-CQ02
Topic: Annual Profit Plan and Supporting Schedules

Troughton Company manufactures radio-controlled toy dogs. Summary budget financial data for Troughton for the current year are shown next.

Sales (5,000 units at $150 each)	$750,000
Variable manufacturing cost	400,000
Fixed manufacturing cost	100,000
Variable selling and administrative cost	80,000
Fixed selling and administrative cost	150,000

Troughton uses an absorption costing system with overhead applied based on the number of units produced, with a denominator level of activity of 5,000 units. Underapplied or overapplied manufacturing overhead is written off to cost of goods sold in the year incurred.

The $20,000 budgeted operating income from producing and selling 5,000 toy dogs planned for this year is of concern to Trudy George, Troughton's president. She believes she could increase operating income to $50,000 (her bonus threshold) if Troughton produces more units than it sells, thus building up the finished goods inventory.

How much of an increase in the number of units in the finished goods inventory would be needed to generate the $50,000 budgeted operating income?

- ☐ **a.** 556 units
- ☐ **b.** 600 units
- ☐ **c.** 1,500 units
- ☐ **d.** 7,500 units

Question 1B5-CQ04
Topic: Annual Profit Plan and Supporting Schedules

Hannon Retailing Company prices its products by adding 30% to its cost. Hannon anticipates sales of $715,000 in July, $728,000 in August, and $624,000 in

365

September. Hannon's policy is to have on hand enough inventory at the end of the month to cover 25% of the next month's sales. What will be the cost of the inventory that Hannon should budget for purchase in August?

- a. $509,600
- b. $540,000
- c. $560,000
- d. $680,000

Question 1B5-CQ06

Topic: Annual Profit Plan and Supporting Schedules

Tyler Company produces one product and budgeted 220,000 units for the month of August with these budgeted manufacturing costs:

	Total Costs	Cost per Unit
Variable costs	$1,408,000	$6.40
Batch setup cost	880,000	4.00
Fixed costs	1,210,000	5.50
Total	$3,498,000	$15.90

The variable cost per unit and the total fixed costs are unchanged within a production range of 200,000 to 300,000 units per month. The total for the batch setup cost in any month depends on the number of production batches that Tyler runs. A normal batch consists of 50,000 units unless production requires less volume. In the prior year, Tyler experienced a mixture of monthly batch sizes of 42,000 units, 45,000 units, and 50,000 units. Tyler consistently plans production each month in order to minimize the number of batches. For the month of September, Tyler plans to manufacture 260,000 units. What will be Tyler's total budgeted production costs for September?

- a. $3,754,000
- b. $3,930,000
- c. $3,974,000
- d. $4,134,000

Question 1B5-CQ08

Topic: Annual Profit Plan and Supporting Schedules

Savior Corporation assembles backup tape drive systems for home microcomputers. For the first quarter, the budget for sales is 67,500 units. Savior will finish the fourth quarter of last year with an inventory of 3,500 units, of which 200 are obsolete. The target ending inventory is 10 days of sales (based on 90 days in a quarter). What is the budgeted production for the first quarter?

- a. 75,000
- b. 71,700
- c. 71,500
- d. 64,350

Question 1B5-CQ09
Topic: Annual Profit Plan and Supporting Schedules

Streeter Company produces plastic microwave turntables. Sales for the next year are expected to be 65,000 units in the first quarter, 72,000 units in the second quarter, 84,000 units in the third quarter, and 66,000 units in the fourth quarter.

Streeter usually maintains a finished goods inventory at the end of each quarter equal to one half of the units expected to be sold in the next quarter. However, due to a work stoppage, the finished goods inventory at the end of the first quarter is 8,000 units less than it should be.

How many units should Streeter produce in the second quarter?

- a. 75,000 units
- b. 78,000 units
- c. 80,000 units
- d. 86,000 units

Question 1B5-CQ10
Topic: Annual Profit Plan and Supporting Schedules

Data regarding Rombus Company's budget are shown next.

Planned sales	4,000 units
Material cost	$2.50 per pound
Direct labor	3 hours per unit
Direct labor rate	$7 per hour
Finished goods beginning inventory	900 units
Finished goods ending inventory	600 units
Direct materials beginning inventory	4,300 units
Direct materials ending inventory	4,500 units
Materials used per unit	6 pounds

Rombus Company's production budget will show total units to be produced of:

- a. 3,700
- b. 4,000
- c. 4,300
- d. 4,600

Question 1B5-CQ11

Topic: Annual Profit Plan and Supporting Schedules

Krouse Company is in the process of developing its operating budget for the coming year. Given next are selected data regarding the company's two products, laminated putter heads and forged putter heads, sold through specialty golf shops.

	Putter Heads	
	Forged	**Laminated**
Raw materials		
Steel	2 pounds @ $5/pound	1 pound @ $5/pound
Copper	None	1 pound @ $15/pound
Direct labor	1/4 hour @ $20/hour	1 hour @ $22/hour
Expected sales	8,200 units	2,000 units
Selling price per unit	$30	$80
Ending inventory target	100 units	60 units
Beginning inventory	300 units	60 units
Beginning inventory (cost)	$5,250	$3,120

Manufacturing overhead is applied to units produced on the basis of direct labor hours. Variable manufacturing overhead is projected to be $25,000, and fixed manufacturing overhead is expected to be $15,000.

The estimated cost to produce one unit of the laminated putter head (PH) is:

- ☐ **a.** $42
- ☐ **b.** $46
- ☐ **c.** $52
- ☐ **d.** $62

Question 1B5-CQ12

Topic: Annual Profit Plan and Supporting Schedules

Tidwell Corporation sells a single product for $20 per unit. All sales are on account, with 60% collected in the month of sale and 40% collected in the following month. A partial schedule of cash collections for January through March of the coming year reveals these receipts for the period:

	Cash Receipts		
	January	**February**	**March**
December receivables	$32,000		
From January sales	$54,000	$36,000	
From February sales		$66,000	$44,000

Other information includes:

- Inventories are maintained at 30% of the following month's sales.
- Assume that March sales total $150,000.

The number of units to be purchased in February is

- ☐ a. 3,850 units
- ☐ b. 4,900 units
- ☐ c. 6,100 units
- ☐ d. 7,750 units

Question 1B5-CQ13

Topic: Annual Profit Plan and Supporting Schedules

Stevens Company manufactures electronic components used in automobile manufacturing. Each component uses two raw materials, Geo and Clio. Standard usage of the two materials required to produce one finished electronic component, as well as the current inventory, are shown next.

Material	Standard Usage per Unit	Price	Current Inventory
Geo	2.0 pounds	$15/pound	5,000 pounds
Clio	1.5 pounds	$10/pound	7,500 pounds

Stevens forecasts sales of 20,000 components for each of the next two production periods. Company policy dictates that 25% of the raw materials needed to produce the next period's projected sales be maintained in ending direct materials inventory.

Based on this information, what would the budgeted direct material purchases for the coming period be?

	Geo	Clio
☐ a.	$450,000	$450,000
☐ b.	$675,000	$300,000
☐ c.	$675,000	$400,000
☐ d.	$825,000	$450,000

Question 1B5-CQ14

Topic: Annual Profit Plan and Supporting Schedules

Petersons Planters Inc. budgeted these amounts for the coming year:

Beginning inventory, finished goods	$10,000
Cost of goods sold	400,000
Direct material used in production	100,000
Ending inventory, finished goods	25,000
Beginning and ending work-in-process inventory	Zero

Overhead is estimated to be two times the amount of direct labor dollars. The amount that should be budgeted for direct labor for the coming year is:

- ☐ a. $315,000
- ☐ b. $210,000
- ☐ c. $157,500
- ☐ d. $105,000

Question 1B5-CQ15

Topic: Annual Profit Plan and Supporting Schedules

Over the past several years, McFadden Industries has experienced the costs shown regarding the company's shipping expenses:

Fixed costs	$16,000
Average shipment	15 pounds
Cost per pound	$0.50

Shown next are McFadden's budget data for the coming year.

Number of units shipped	8,000
Number of sales orders	800
Number of shipments	800
Total sales	$1,200,000
Total pounds shipped	9,600

McFadden's expected shipping costs for the coming year are:

- ☐ a. $4,800
- ☐ b. $16,000
- ☐ c. $20,000
- ☐ d. $20,800

Question 1B5-CQ18

Topic: Annual Profit Plan and Supporting Schedules

In preparing the direct material purchases budget for next quarter, the plant controller has this information available:

Budgeted unit sales	2,000
Pounds of materials per unit	4
Cost of materials per pound	$3
Pounds of materials on hand	400
Finished units on hand	250
Target ending units inventory	325
Target ending inventory of pounds of materials	800

How many pounds of materials must be purchased?

- a. 2,475
- b. 7,900
- c. 8,700
- d. 9,300

Question 1B5-CQ22

Topic: Annual Profit Plan and Supporting Schedules

Given the next data for Scurry Company, what is the cost of goods sold?

Beginning inventory of finished goods	$100,000
Cost of goods manufactured	700,000
Ending inventory of finished goods	200,000
Beginning work-in-process inventory	300,000
Ending work-in-process inventory	50,000

- a. $500,000
- b. $600,000
- c. $800,000
- d. $950,000

Question 1B5-CQ23

Topic: Annual Profit Plan and Supporting Schedules

Tut Company's selling and administrative costs for the month of August, when it sold 20,000 units, were:

	Cost per Unit	Total Cost
Variable costs	$18.60	$372,000
Step costs	4.25	85,000
Fixed costs	8.80	176,000
Total selling and administrative costs	$31.65	$633,000

The variable costs represent sales commissions paid at the rate of 6.2% of sales.

The step costs depend on the number of salespersons employed by the company. In August there were 17 persons on the sales force. However, 2 members have taken early retirement effective August 31. It is anticipated that these positions will remain vacant for several months.

Total fixed costs are unchanged within a relevant range of 15,000 to 30,000 units per month.

Tut is planning a sales price cut of 10%, which it expects will increase sales volume to 24,000 units per month. If Tut implements the sales price reduction, the total budgeted selling and administrative costs for the month of September would be:

- ☐ a. $652,760
- ☐ b. $679,760
- ☐ c. $714,960
- ☐ d. $759,600

Question 1B5-CQ36

Topic: Annual Profit Plan and Supporting Schedules

Data regarding Johnsen Inc.'s forecasted dollar sales for the last seven months of the year and Johnsen's projected collection patterns are shown next.

Forecasted Sales

Month	Sales
June	$700,000
July	600,000
August	650,000
September	800,000
October	850,000
November	900,000
December	840,000

Types of Sales

Cash sales	30%
Credit sales	70%

Collection pattern on credit sales (5% determined to be uncollectible)

During the month of sale	20%
During the first month following the sale	50%
During the second month following the sale	25%

Johnsen's budgeted cash receipts from sales and collections on account for September are:

- ☐ a. $635,000
- ☐ b. $684,500
- ☐ c. $807,000
- ☐ d. $827,000

Question 1B5-CQ37

Topic: Annual Profit Plan and Supporting Schedules

The Mountain Mule Glove Company is in its first year of business. Mountain Mule had a beginning cash balance of $85,000 for the quarter. The company has a $50,000 short-term line of credit. The budgeted information for the first quarter is shown next.

	January	February	March
Sales	$60,000	$40,000	$50,000
Purchases	$35,000	$40,000	$75,000
Operating costs	$25,000	$25,000	$25,000

All sales are made on credit and are collected in the second month following the sale. Purchases are paid in the month following the purchase while operating costs are paid in the month that they are incurred. How much will Mountain Mule need to borrow at the end of the quarter if the company needs to maintain a minimum cash balance of $5,000 as required by a loan covenant agreement?

- a. $0
- b. $5,000
- c. $10,000
- d. $45,000

Question 1B3-CQ05
Topic: Forecasting Techniques

Aerosub, Inc., has developed a new product for spacecraft that includes the manufacture of a complex part. The manufacturing of this part requires a high degree of technical skill. Management believes there is a good opportunity for its technical force to learn and improve as it becomes accustomed to the production process. The production of the first unit requires 10,000 direct labor hours. If an 80% learning curve is used, the cumulative direct labor hours required for producing a total of eight units would be:

- a. 29,520 hours
- b. 40,960 hours
- c. 64,000 hours
- d. 80,000 hours

Question 1B3-CQ18
Topic: Forecasting Techniques

Scarf Corporation's controller has decided to use a decision model to cope with uncertainty. With a particular proposal, currently under consideration, Scarf has two possible actions: invest or not invest in a joint venture with an international firm. The controller has determined this information:

Action 1: Invest in the Joint Venture

    Events and Probabilities:

        Probability of success = 60%

        Cost of investment = $9.5 million

        Cash flow if investment is successful = $15.0 million

Cash flow if investment is unsuccessful = $2.0 million
Additional costs to be paid = $0
Costs incurred up to this point = $650,000

Action 2: Do Not Invest in the Joint Venture

Events:
Costs incurred up to this point = $650,000
Additional costs to be paid = $100,000

Which one of the next alternatives correctly reflects the respective expected values of investing versus not investing?

- a. $300,000 and ($750,000)
- b. ($350,000) and ($100,000)
- c. $300,000 and ($100,000)
- d. ($350,000) and ($750,000)

To further assess your understanding of the concepts and calculations covered in Part 1, Section B: Planning, Budgeting, and Forecasting, practice with the **Online Test Bank** for this section.
REMINDER: See the "Answers to Section Practice Questions" section at the end of this book.

SECTION C

Performance Management

Once an organization has established a master budget, it is critical to compare actual financial performance against the master budget plan to measure variances and in turn, success in achieving goals. This financial measure comparison or feedback process allows an organization to confirm the overall vision of where it wants to be against actual results. Without this feedback, the budgeting process is not very useful.

This section reviews the process of how to:

- Break down variances from the master budget into subcategories so an organization can better assess the specific reasons for the variance.
- Utilize performance feedback from responsibility centers or strategic business units (SBUs) to help manage profitability.
- Understand the financial measures of profitability used in responsibility centers and in the organization as a whole.

After covering financial measures, this section also shows a balanced approach to performance measurement. The balanced scorecard measures both financial and nonfinancial aspects of an organization and is integrated with strategy so that reading the scorecard will tell anyone in the organization what the strategy is and how the organization plans to achieve it.

Learning Outcome Statements Overview: Performance Management

Section C.1. Cost and Variance Measures

A. Analyze performance against operational goals using measures based on revenue, manufacturing costs, nonmanufacturing costs, and profit depending on the type of center or unit being measured.
   a. An organization can analyze performance against operational goals by studying variances at the end of the accounting period. Variances are differences in the actual results from the planned revenues and costs. For example, if the operating budget estimated manufacturing costs to be $150,000 and the actual results came in at $165,000, management can analyze the variance to determine what created the increase. The variance can be broken down into multiple factors as discussed below.
B. Explain the reasons for variances within a performance monitoring system.
   a. Variances create a starting point for management to assess why actual results were different from what was planned. The variances could be due to efficiency or effectiveness issues within the organization. Without computing variances, the forecast would be meaningless since it wouldn't require follow-up on differences to the budget.
C. Prepare a performance analysis by comparing actual results to the master budget, calculate favorable and unfavorable variances from budget, and provide explanations for variances.
   a. The next chart compares the actual results of a company to the master budget. The third column represents the variance from the budget.

	Actual Results	Static Budget	Variance (Actual – Static)	Favorable (F) Unfavorable (U)
Units sold	24,000	30,000	6,000	U
Revenues variable costs	$3,000,000	$3,600,000	$600,000	U
Direct materials	1,491,840	1,800,000	308,160	F
Direct manufacturing labor	475,200	480,000	4,800	F
Variable manufacturing overhead	313,200	360,000	46,800	F
Total variable costs	2,280,240	2,640,000	359,760	F
Contribution margin	719,760	960,000	240,240	U
Fixed costs	684,000	690,000	6,000	F
Operating income	$35,760	$270,000	$234,240	U

A favorable variance exceeds the planned amount of earnings or is less than the planned costs. An unfavorable variance is the opposite.

The analysis must be analyzed further to determine if the variances were due simply to a decrease in actual units sold or if there are effectiveness or efficiency problems with the organization's operational structure. For more information on the reasons for variances, see the discussion of price/rate and efficiency/usage variances later in this topic.

D. Identify and describe the benefits and limitations of measuring performance by comparing actual results to the master budget.
   a. The chart above provided management with the opportunity to measure actual performance with expectations and to determine where the major differences were. However, comparing the actual results to a static budget (master budget) doesn't provide answers on exactly why the results were different. For example, was the operating income variance due solely to a decrease in the demand of their product, or was it because they had cost overruns? Without adjusting the budget to what it would have been if the correct unit sales had been estimated, it is difficult to pinpoint the reasons. A flexible budget is used to adjust the master budget to standards based on the actual units sold.

E. Prepare a flexible budget based on actual sales (output) volume.
   a. The following chart summarizes what a flexible budget would look like for the company identified above. The sales and variable expenses are adjusted based on the per-unit cost and the actual units sold.

	Actual Results	Static Budget	Flexible Budget	Variance (Actual – Flexible)
Units sold	24,000	30,000	24,000	
Revenues	$3,000,000	$3,600,000	2,880,000	120,000 F
Direct materials	1,491,840	1,800,000	1,440,000	51,840 U
Direct manufacturing labor	475,200	480,000	384,000	91,200 U
Variable manufacturing overhead	313,200	360,000	288,000	25,200 U
Total variable costs	2,280,240	2,640,000	2,112,000	168,240 U
Contribution margin	719,760	960,000	768,000	48,240 U
Fixed costs	684,000	690,000	690,000	6,000 F
Operating income	$35,760	$270,000	78,000	42,240 U

   b. Notice from the chart that the variable expenses are adjusted to values assuming the company would have estimated 24,000 units. The fixed expenses are not changed since they do not vary based on actual output. The results using the flexible budget are much more meaningful than the static budget variance.

F. Calculate the sales-volume variance and the sales-price variance by comparing the flexible budget to the master (static) budget.
   a. The sales-volume variance is calculated by taking the flexible budget amount adjusted for the actual output ($78,000 from the chart above) less the static budget amount ($270,000 from chart). This variance provides information on how operating income is affected by the difference in the volume of budgeted sales compared to the volume of actual sales.

Sales Volume Variance = $78,000 − $270,000 = $192,000 U

G. Calculate the flexible-budget variance by comparing actual results to the flexible budget.
   a. The flexible budget variance is calculated by taking the actual results ($35,760 from the chart above) less the flexible budget amount adjusted for actual output ($78,000 from the chart). This variance identifies the difference in operating income when the budget is flexed, or adjusted to the actual level of sales.

   Flexible Budget Variance = $35,760 − $78,000 = $42,240 U

   Note: The sum of these two numbers equals the difference between the master budget and the actual results, or $234,240 (192,000 + 42,240).

H. Investigate the flexible-budget variance to determine individual differences between actual and budgeted input prices and input quantities.
   a. After the flexible budget is prepared, management can use the report to determine individual differences between actual and budgeted prices and quantities. For example, the flexible budget shows that the budgeted sales price per unit was $120 (2,880,000 / 24,000), but the actual per-unit sales price was $125 (3,000,000 / 24000). Despite a difference in the master budget due to lack of demand, the company actually was able to have a favorable sales price variance.

I. Explain how budget variance reporting is utilized in a management by exception environment.
   a. The breakdown of variances into flexible budget variances and sales budget variances can allow a firm to make business decisions based on these variances. Management by exception is a method of focusing management attention on only significant variances from the budget. Significant variances are the exceptions that require more attention than other areas.

J. Define a standard cost system, and identify the reasons for adopting a standard cost system.
   a. A standard cost is any carefully determined price, quantity, service level, or cost, usually expressed in a per-unit amount, which is determined before actual costs are available. A standard cost system can be a valuable management tool, because it enables the firm to identify variances from what was planned. When a variance arises between actual and standard costs, management becomes aware that costs have differed from the standard (planned, expected) costs.

K. Demonstrate an understanding of price (rate) variances and calculate the price variances related to direct material and direct labor inputs.
   a. A price variance measures the portion of a variance due to differences in the price paid for an item (either materials or labor). A price variance is the actual input quantity of an item multiplied by the difference between the actual input price and the budgeted (or standard) input price. Price variances are used for direct materials, and rate variances are used for direct labor.

Price (Rate) Variance = Actual Input Quantity × (Actual Input Price − Budgeted Input Price)

L. Demonstrate an understanding of efficiency (usage) variances, and calculate the efficiency variances related to direct material and direct labor inputs.
  a. An efficiency variance measures the portion of a variance due to differences in quantities consumed or hours used. An efficiency variance is the budgeted input price multiplied by the difference between the actual input quantity and the budgeted (or standard) input quantity.

Efficiency Variance = Budgeted Input Price × (Actual Input Quantity − Budgeted Input Quantity)

M. Demonstrate an understanding of spending and efficiency variances as they relate to fixed and variable overhead.
  a. The variable overhead spending variance is calculated by taking the difference between actual overhead cost and the actual quantity of cost driver multiplied by the standard variable overhead rate. This variance tells management how favorable or unfavorable spending on variable overhead costs was compared to how much "should have been spent" on those costs during the period based on an appropriate cost driver.

Variable Overhead Spending (or Price) Variance = Actual Overhead Cost − (Actual Quantity of Cost Driver × Standard Variable Overhead Rate)

  b. The variable overhead efficiency variance is the product of the actual quantity of the cost driver multiplied by the standard variable overhead rate, less the product of the standard quantity of cost driver allowed (for actual output) multiplied by the standard variable overhead rate.

Variable Overhead Efficiency Variance = (Actual Quantity of Cost Driver × Standard Variable Overhead Rate) − (Standard Quantity of Cost Driver Allowed (for Actual Output) × Standard Variable Overhead Rate)

  c. The total fixed overhead variance represents the difference between actual fixed overhead and applied fixed overhead. This variance can be broken down further into the fixed overhead production volume variance and the fixed overhead spending variance.

Fixed Overhead Spending Variance = Actual Fixed Overhead − Budgeted Fixed Overhead
Fixed Overhead Production Volume Variance = Budgeted Fixed Overhead − Applied Fixed Overhead

Applied fixed overhead is computed by taking the standard allowed quantity times the standard fixed overhead rate.
N. Calculate a sales mix variance, and explain its impact on revenue and contribution margin.
   a. A sales mix variance for a particular type of product is calculated by multiplying the budgeted contribution margin per unit for that merchandise, the total number of all merchandise sold, and the difference between the actual sales mix ratio and the budgeted sales mix ratio. The total sales mix variance is the sum of the sales mix variance of each type of merchandise sold by the company.

   Sales Mix Variance = (Actual Sales Mix Ratio for a Product − Budgeted Sales Mix Ratio for a Product) × Actual Units Sold × Budgeted Contribution Margin per Unit of Product

O. Calculate and explain a mix variance.
   a. The efficiency variance can be broken down into a direct materials (or labor) mix variance and a direct materials (or labor) yield variance. The mix variance results from using direct materials/labor inputs in a ratio that differs from standard specifications. Three amounts must be known to break an efficiency variance down into its subcomponents:
      i. Budgeted Cost / Unit × Actual Total Quantity Used × Actual Mix Ratio for the Item
      ii. Budgeted Cost / Unit × Actual Total Quantity Used × Budgeted Mix Ratio for the Item
      iii. Budgeted Cost / Unit × Budgeted Total Quantity Used × Budgeted Mix Ratio for the Item
   The mix variance is computed by subtracting item i from item ii above.

P. Calculate and explain a yield variance.
   a. The yield variance results because the yield (output) obtained differs from the expected on the basis of input.
   The yield variance is computed by subtracting item ii from item iii above.

Q. Demonstrate how price, efficiency, spending, and mix variances can be applied in service companies as well as manufacturing companies.
   a. The variance computations discussed above can be applied to service industries as well as manufacturing companies. However, the direct materials price and usage variances typically aren't used to the same extent because the amount of materials that are used is not a large portion of the business. The labor rate and efficiency variances as well as overhead variances play a larger role in service companies.

R. Analyze factory overhead variances by calculating variable overhead spending variance, variable overhead efficiency variance, fixed overhead spending variance, and production volume variance.

a. See item M above for the formulas for variable and fixed overhead variances.
S. Analyze variances, identify causes, and recommend corrective actions.
a. Variance analysis is an important aspect of performance measurement and helps to explain why certain goals weren't met. See the formulas listed above as well as Topic 1: Cost and Variance Measures for additional information.

Section C.2. Responsibility Centers and Reporting Segments

A. Identify and explain the different types of responsibility centers.
   a. Responsibility accounting is a method of defining segments or subunits in an organization as types of responsibility centers based on their level of autonomy and the responsibilities of their managers, and then basing performance evaluations on these factors. Responsibility centers are classified by their primary effect on the company as a whole. There are four main types of responsibility centers:
      i. Revenue centers—Responsible for sales but not for the manufacturing costs of the sales. Revenue centers are evaluated on their ability to provide a contribution: sales less the direct revenue center costs.
      ii. Cost centers—Responsible for controlling costs in a department that generates little or no revenue. Finance, administration, human resources, accounting, customer service, and help desks are all examples of cost centers.
      iii. Profit centers—Responsible for both costs and revenues. Since profit is a function of both revenue and costs, a manager for a profit center is responsible for generating profits, managing revenue, and controlling costs.
      iv. Investment centers—Responsible for investments, costs, and revenues in their department. Managers in such centers would be evaluated not only by the center's profit but by relating the profit to its invested capital.
B. Recommend appropriate responsibility centers given a business scenario.
   a. The four responsibility centers mentioned above are used to assess performance based on the actual items that a manager/department can control. It would not be appropriate to evaluate the human resource manager (a cost center) on how much profit was generated in the department. Likewise, a separate division or operating unit of a company should be evaluated on overall profit and return on investment, not just on revenues or costs.

C. Calculate a contribution margin.
   a. Contribution margin is the amount that contributes toward fixed expenses and profits. The contribution margin shows managers how profits are affected by changes in volume, because fixed costs and operating capacity are kept constant. To compute contribution margin, you subtract variable costs from revenue. Management performance can be evaluated more easily using a contribution income statement because the items outside managers' control are separated from the items within their control. However, many fixed costs are controllable, so managers often have their fixed costs further divided into controllable fixed costs and uncontrollable fixed costs.
D. Analyze a contribution margin report and evaluate performance.
   a. The next chart is an example of an income statement using the contribution margin approach:

Sales	31,200
Variable expenses	
Variable manufacturing	5,200
Variable selling & administration	2,600
Total variable	7,800
Contribution margin	23,400
Fixed expenses	
Fixed manufacturing	10,400
Fixed selling and administration	10,000
Total fixed expenses	20,400
Net income	3,000

Breaking costs out by their behavior (i.e., variable versus fixed) shows managers how profits are affected by changes in volume. Since the contribution margin is 75% (23,400 / 31,200), each additional dollar in sales will increase net income by 75 cents. This is because the fixed expenses should not change with changes in unit sales.

E. Identify segments that organizations evaluate, including product lines, geographical areas, or other meaningful segments.
   a. Reporting segments are portions of a business divided for reporting purposes along product lines, geographical areas, or other meaningful segments to provide individual information about that area. Segmented financial statements show the segment's own costs and revenues to indicate how profitable each segment is by itself.
F. Explain why the allocation of common costs among segments can be an issue in performance evaluation.
   a. Common fixed costs (such as the chief executive's salary) cannot be traced to a specific department because they are shared costs and must be apportioned between two or more departments using some allocation basis that

may or may not provide an accurate allocation. Because common costs often are uncontrollable to some extent by the department manager who is held responsible for them, they make it more difficult to determine the profitability of an individual segment.

G. Identify methods for allocating common costs, such as stand-alone cost allocation and incremental cost allocation.
   a. Stand-alone cost allocation—A method that determines the relative proportion of cost driver for each party that shares a common cost and allocates the costs by those percentages.
   b. Incremental cost allocation—A method that allocates costs by ranking the parties by a primary user and incremental users, or those users who add an additional cost due to the fact that there is now more than one user of the cost.

H. Define transfer pricing and identify the objectives of transfer pricing.
   a. Determining profits for a responsibility center or segment involves assigning pricing for the goods and services that pass between segments. Transfer pricing sets prices for these internally exchanged goods and services.

I. Identify the methods for determining transfer prices and list and explain the advantages and disadvantages of each method.
   a. Four models can be used to set transfer prices: market price, negotiated price, variable cost, and full cost.
      i. Market price model—A true arm's-length model because it sets the price for a good or service at going market prices. The market price model keeps business units autonomous, forces the selling unit to be competitive with external suppliers, and is preferred by tax authorities.
      ii. Negotiated price model—Sets the transfer price through negotiation between the buyer and the seller. Negotiated prices can make both buying and selling units less autonomous.
      iii. Variable cost model—Sets transfer prices at the unit's variable cost, or the actual cost to produce the good or service less all fixed costs. This model is advantageous for selling units that have excess capacity or for situations when a buying unit could purchase from external sources but the company wants to encourage internal purchases. Among the disadvantages of this method is the fact that it is not viewed favorably by tax authorities because it lowers the profits, and thereby taxes, for the location where the product was manufactured.
      iv. Full cost model—Starts with the seller's variable cost for the item and then allocates fixed costs to the price. This method may create less incentive for the buyer to purchase internally if the market price is less and may create less incentive for the seller to reduce costs.

In general, the market price method is preferred in situations when the market price for a good or service is available. When a market price is not available, the negotiated price method is preferred. When neither is acceptable, companies may turn to one of the cost models. Cost-based methods are not recommended because they can lead to motivation problems between parties, such as the seller not actively controlling costs because they are simply passed on to the buyer.

J. Identify and calculate transfer prices using variable cost, full cost, market price, negotiated price, and dual-rate pricing.

   a. Using the information above, computation of the appropriate price is relatively straightforward. The variable cost method is used when there is excess capacity and the seller is trying to cover additional fixed expenses by selling for a lower price over or equal to the variable costs. The full cost method takes into account all costs by the operating segment, predetermined with estimated fixed and variable expenses. Under the market price model, the price is set by what any willing third party would pay for the product. The negotiated price is set by both departments to determine what a product will be sold for.

K. Explain how transfer pricing is affected by business issues such as the presence of outside suppliers and the opportunity costs associated with capacity usage.

   a. The market price model is usually the preferred method as it is the most realistic approach for analysis and motivational reasons. However, when there are additional outside suppliers that may sell the same product for less, the buying segment may be tempted to purchase from an outside supplier if the segment is evaluated on its overall profitability. This would not be beneficial to the company as a whole. As such, a lower price can be negotiated. If the seller has excess capacity, it is better off reducing the selling price to a point between its variable cost and full market price since the sale of additional goods would cover some of the fixed expenses that don't fluctuate based on additional units being sold.

L. Describe how special issues such as tariffs, exchange rates, taxes, currency restrictions, expropriation risk, and the availability of materials and skills affect performance evaluation in multinational companies.

   a. Multinational companies must account for various concerns, such as how tariffs, exchange rates, taxes, currency restrictions, expropriation risk, and the availability and relative cost of materials and skills can affect performance evaluations. The use of transfer pricing by multinationals to gain tax and income advantages can conflict with the use of transfer pricing to evaluate performance or to create performance incentives. Selling products for above-market prices in a low-tax jurisdiction to a segment in a high-tax jurisdiction would save the company money on taxes. However, taxing entities scrutinize this practice.

Section C.3. Performance Measures

A. Explain why performance evaluation measures should be directly related to strategic and operational goals and objectives; why timely feedback is critical; and why performance measures should be related to the factors that drive the element being measured (e.g., cost drivers and revenue drivers).
   a. Responsibility centers and the individuals involved need to be analyzed based on the performance of actual results versus standards. In order for them to be effective, the standards and the evaluation measures need to be directly related to the goals and objectives of the organization. For example, if an organization's strategic goal is to become the industry cost leader, it should focus on short-term goals that will result in cost reductions company wide. It should then evaluate performance in accordance with that goal instead of focusing on other items that may be important in the goals of other organizations but not its own. For example, it shouldn't evaluate performance based on innovation or the number of new products brought to market. Additionally, the feedback should be timely in order to allow management to make appropriate adjustments if needed.

B. Explain the issues involved in determining product profitability, business unit profitability, and customer profitability, including cost measurement, cost allocation, investment measurement, and valuation.
   a. Profitability analysis focuses on the individual costs and revenues associated with a particular product, business unit, or customer. Whenever an organization is analyzing the profitability of a segment of its business, it must take into account all relevant revenues and costs associated with the segment. Some major issues that need to be considered include:
      - What costs can be eliminated and which will continue?
      - How will this decision affect the company strategy?
      - Can our efforts be focused elsewhere to provide a greater return?
      - Is this segment in line with our risk appetite, and are the returns adequate?

C. Calculate product-line profitability, business unit profitability, and customer profitability.
   a. Calculating the profitability for a product, business unit, or customer uses essentially the same factors and tools. In order to calculate them, you need to determine all relevant revenues and costs. You can essentially perform a what-if analysis assuming you were to get rid of the product, unit, or customer. To do so, you must adjust the income statement for the product, unit, or customer to include only the costs that are traceable to that segment. For example, allocated common costs, such as the chief executive's salary and company-wide administrative costs that should not be factored in the measure since they are outside of segment management and would continue if the segment was discontinued.

D. Evaluate customers and products on the basis of profitability, and recommend ways to improve profitability and/or drop unprofitable customers and products.
   a. After analyzing customers, products, or business units, an organization can determine all the possible actions it can take, such as increasing marketing costs, discontinuing the product, canceling the customer relationship, finding cost-cutting measures or other actions to increase the profitability of the company as a whole. Nonquantitative considerations need to be made as well to ensure that the overall impact on the company is not negative.
E. Define and calculate return on investment (ROI).
   a. Return on investment—Measures profitability by dividing the net profit of the business unit by the investment in assets made to attain that income.

$$\text{Return on Investment (ROI)} = \frac{\text{Income of a Business Unit}}{\text{Assets of a Business Unit}}$$

   Note that "Income" means operating income unless otherwise noted.
F. Analyze and interpret ROI calculations.
   a. The ROI calculation shows how much money is returned to shareholders for each $1 invested in assets. For example, an ROI of 25% means that for each dollar of assets invested in the company, the shareholders' return is 25 cents. An organization can compare the ROI with its cost of capital (or shareholder required rate of return) to determine whether the business segment should be continued, sold off, or discontinued.
G. Define and calculate residual income (RI).
   a. Residual income—The amount of income a business unit is able to earn above a required rate of return on its assets.

$$\text{Residual Income (RI)} = \text{Income of a Business Unit} - (\text{Assets of Business Unit} \times \text{Required Rate of Return})$$

   Note that "Income" means operating income unless otherwise noted.
H. Analyze and interpret RI calculations.
   a. Residual income is used to compute the excess return over and above the required rate of return. A positive RI means that the business unit is more profitable than the company's required rate of return and should be continued. A negative RI doesn't necessarily mean that the business unit isn't profitable. It just means that the rate of return is less than the company's required rate of return. For example, the ROI could be 10%, but the required rate may be 12%.
I. Compare and contrast the benefits and limitations of ROI and RI as measures of performance.
   a. ROI and RI shouldn't be the only tools used for comparison. They should be used in context with the industry and risk associated with the company. Additionally, both calculations may be skewed by accounting conventions for measuring assets and determining net income.

Generally accepted accounting principles (GAAP) and measurements may not be the best numbers to use for analysis. When managers are evaluated on the basis of ROI, they may reject projects that reduce their overall ROI, even though the projects may be beneficial to the company as a whole.

J. Explain how revenue and expense recognition policies may affect the measurement of income and reduce comparability among business units.
   a. Revenue and expense recognition policies need to be considered when computing return on investment (ROI) and residual income (RI). For example, in an inflationary environment, if a company reports inventory on a last-in, first-out (LIFO) basis, it will be running more expenses through the income statement than if inventory were reported on a first-in, first-out (FIFO) basis. Other accounting methods required by GAAP may skew the reported net income, such as the treatment of depreciation, research and development costs, and other items that may increase value but reduce accounting profits.

K. Explain how inventory measurement policies, joint asset sharing, and overall asset measurement policies may affect the measurement of investment and reduce comparability among business units.
   a. Both return on investment (ROI) and residual income (RI) are computed on the basis of assets invested in the organization. Much as revenues and expense recognition policies may skew results, invested assets may not be accurate with the true economic outlay for assets. For example, assets that may be reported at historical cost could have large off-balance sheet gains that are driving down the investment base and make ROI and RI better than they are. Inventory measurement policies—last-in, first-out (LIFO) versus first-in, first-out (FIFO)—also may report assets at a lower value than their true cost of acquisition.

L. Define key performance indicators (KPIs), and discuss the importance of these indicators in evaluating a firm.
   a. Key performance indicators (KPIs) are measures of factors critical to the success of the organization. Each KPI requires a defined business process, clear objectives for the process, quantitative or qualitative measurements for the objectives, and a plan for identifying and correcting variances from plan.

M. Define the concept of a balanced scorecard and identify its components.
   a. Balanced scorecard—A process of compiling and organizing the key performance indicators (KPIs) of an organization into four segments: financial, customer, internal business process, and learning and growth. Each KPI can be measured in a specific way so that it can be managed appropriately.

N. Identify and describe the perspectives of a balanced scorecard, including financial measures, customer satisfaction measures, internal business process measures, and innovation and learning measures.

a. Financial measures—Cover the traditional financial ratios, such as return on equity, sales growth, return on assets, earnings per share, and the like.

b. Customer satisfaction measures—Focusing on the customer is critical to accomplishing goals as the customer drives all of a company's revenue. The primary customer outcome measures include market share, acquisition, satisfaction, retention, and profitability.

c. Internal business process measures—Go beyond simple financial variance measures to include output measures, such as quality, cycle time, yield, order fulfillment, production planning, throughput, and turnover.

d. Innovation and learning measures—Focus on becoming efficient and effective at producing new products. The measures include time to market, percentage of sales from new products, and new products versus competitor's new products. Learning and growth measures focus on education and training of personnel and can be measured by training sessions provided, developing leadership skills, and reducing the number of defects.

O. Identify and describe the characteristics of successful implementation and use of a balanced scorecard.

a. Implementing the balanced scorecard basically involves executing strategy. Without execution, even the best vision remains a dream. The balanced scorecard lends itself well to strategy execution, because the scorecard itself is a method of describing strategy in a way that can be acted on. In order to be effective, the balanced scorecard needs to be tied to the organization's strategy and goals, and the performance measures need to be able to be quantified.

P. Analyze and interpret a balanced scorecard, and evaluate performance on the basis of the analysis.

a. The following chart is an example of a balanced scorecard for a company. Note that the main objective of the organization is to grow sales by 20% over the next two years. The organization has identified its KPIs in order to accomplish that goal so that all of the measures are tied to the firm's goal.

Overall goal: Grow sales by 20% over the next two years.

			Current Year (Y0)	Year 1 (Y1)	Year 2 (Y2)	
Revenues:			$400,000	$432,000	$484,000	
Perspective	**Strategic Objectives**	**Measurements**		**Y1 Target**	**Y2 Target**	**Programs**
Financial	F1: Maximize return on equity	Return on equity		9%	13%	
	F2: Positive economic value added (EVA)	EVA		$20,000	$30,000	
	F3: 10% revenue growth	% change in revenues		8%	12%	
	F4: Asset utilization	Utilization rates		85%	88%	
Customer	C1: Price	Competitive comparison		−4%	−5%	
	C2: Customer retention	Retention %		75%	75%	Implement customer relationship management (CRM) program
	C3: Lowest-cost suppliers	Total cost relative to competition		−6%	−7%	Implement supplier relationship management (SRM) program
	C4: Product innovation	% of sales from new products		10%	15%	
Internal business process	P1: Improve production work flow	Cycle time		0.3 days	0.25 days	Upgrade enterprise resource planning (ERP) system
	P2: New product success	Number of orders		1,000	1,500	
	P3: Sales penetration	Actual versus plan (variance)		0%	0%	
	P4: Reduce inventory	Inventory as a % of sales		30%	28%	
Learning and growth	L1: Link strategy to reward system	Net income per dollar of variable pay (aggregate)		65%	68%	Implement CRM
	L2: Fill critical competency gaps	% of critical competencies satisfied on tracking matrix		75%	80%	Tuition reimbursement
	L3: Become customer-driven culture	Survey index		77%	79%	Implement CRM
	L4: Quality leadership	Average ranking (on 10-point scale) of executives		8.9	9.2	Tuition reimbursement

Q. Recommend performance measures and a periodic reporting methodology given operational goals and actual results.
   a. No matter what performance measure or methodology a company uses, it must align the measures to its goals and strategy. The balanced scorecard is just one method that will help an organization develop and implement strategy. A company can also measure performance with the quantitative methods mentioned above, such as return on investment and residual income. For additional details and analysis, see Topic 3: Performance Measures.

TOPIC 1

Cost and Variance Measures

FEEDBACK IS A NECESSARY ELEMENT OF CONTROL. Feedback in financial management is the comparison of planned (expected) results or the budget to actual outcomes, and is known as a variance. A **variance** is the difference between the actual and planned results.

This topic covers how flexible budgets and variances aid in financial management control and planning, thereby making the business as efficient as possible. It includes a look at the use of flexible budgets in analyzing performance, a discussion of the role of management by exception, and an analysis of variation from standard cost expectations using a case study.

> **READ** the Learning Outcome Statements (LOS) for this topic as found in Appendix A and then study the concepts and calculations presented here to be sure you understand the content you could be tested on in the CMA exam.

Comparison of Actual to Planned Results

A successful budget cycle generally follows a process of:

- Creating a master budget that sets out plans for the performance of the organization as a whole as well as for each subunit.
- Establishing standards or specific expectations against which actual results can be compared.
- Investigating variations from plans and taking corrective action, if necessary.
- Planning for continuous improvement, taking into consideration feedback and changed conditions.

When comparing actual to planned results, managers are concerned with the efficiency of the operation and its effectiveness in meeting organizational goals.

Efficiency is the budgeted amounts or standards set for a particular resource compared to the actual resources consumed. Typically, resources are categorized into direct material, direct labor, and manufacturing overhead. For example, if a cost is estimated to be $2 per unit, an efficient operation that sells 1,000 units should have a cost of $2,000 or less. An inefficient operation would incur costs in excess of that amount.

Effectiveness is measured by how well a firm attains its goals. If the master budget calls for net operating income to be $300 million, an effective operation would have earned that amount or more and an ineffective operation would have earned less than that amount. An operation can be effective but not efficient or efficient but not effective. An inefficient but effective operation is one that meets its primary goals even though it had cost overruns.

In order to attain both objectives of efficiency and effectiveness, it is important to know how an operation is performing and how it should be performing. Determining how an operation is doing involves standard costing, but such methods will not alleviate any issues unless combined with variance analysis to determine actual operational behavior. Determining how the operation should perform depends on selecting appropriate benchmarks with an appropriate level of stringency—for example, whether to use kaizen with continually increasing goals, target costing with specific types of standards, and so on, in the measure.

A primary means of assessing effectiveness is through the **operating income variance**, or the difference between budgeted operating income and actual operating income. Such a measure looks at the bottom line of operations. A secondary means of assessing effectiveness is to do a line-by-line comparison of actual to planned results.

Figure 1C-1 shows variances from a **static budget**, which is a budget that is set at the beginning of the year and not changed. Flexible budgets are covered later in the topic.

Favorable/Unfavorable Variances

Some variances are favorable and others are unfavorable. A **favorable variance** exceeds the planned amount of earnings or was less than the planned costs. An **unfavorable variance** is the opposite. A general rule of thumb is that if a variance helps the bottom line, it is favorable; if it hurts the bottom line, it is unfavorable.

For example: Bounce Sporting Goods' budget analysis in Figure 1C-1 shows both favorable (F) and unfavorable (U) variances.

Note that in Figure 1C-1 there is a favorable direct materials variance, $1,491,840 − $1,800,000 = ($308,160), which is a negative but favorable amount. Positive and negative signs are very important to track for variance calculations but do not indicate favorableness or unfavorableness by themselves. Taken together with the fact that this is a cost, a negative number means that the cost is reduced, increasing net income, and therefore the variance is favorable.

In contrast, the $600,000 unfavorable revenue variance in Figure 1C-1 is unfavorable because it is lower than the planned revenue, adversely affecting net income. Some of the illustrations in this text drop the negative and positive signs to focus more on favorable and unfavorable variances, but if a favorable variance is added to an unfavorable variance, they have to be netted against each other.

Is the $308,160 favorable direct material variance a good thing for the company? Even though the operation was ineffective, was it at least efficient? Not necessarily.

Figure 1C-1 Analysis of Variance Between Actual and Static Budget for Bounce Sporting Goods Company

High-Level Analysis — Overview		
Actual operating income		$35,760
Budgeted operating income		270,000
Static-budget variance of operating income		$234,240 U*

Midlevel Analysis			
	Actual Results	**Static Budget**	**Variance (Actual − Static)**
Units sold	24,000	30,000	6,000 U
Revenues variable costs	$3,000,000	$3,600,000	$600,000 U
Direct materials	1,491,840	1,800,000	308,160 F†
Direct manufacturing labor	475,200	480,000	4,800 F
Variable manufacturing overhead	313,200	360,000	46,800 F
Total variable costs	2,280,240	2,640,000	359,760 F
Contribution margin	719,760	960,000	240,240 U
Fixed costs	684,000	690,000	6,000 F
Operating income	$35,760	$270,000	$234,240 U

*U = Unfavorable effect on operating income.
†F = Favorable effect on operating income.

Because the operation had an unfavorable number of units sold, the primary reason for the operation being ineffective was that sales were lower than budgeted. Because fewer goods were produced, the direct material costs were lower. The budgeted direct material costs were $1,800,000 for 30,000 units, or $60 per unit. The actual number of units produced was 24,000 units at an actual cost of $1,491,840, so the actual cost was $62.16 per unit.

Therefore, favorable and unfavorable are not necessarily indications of a good or bad result per se but show whether the firm is or is not meeting its plan. Budget variances on line items can be misleading and may not indicate either effectiveness or efficiency. Furthermore, variances should be tested against a materiality threshold. If they are individually immaterial, they should be ignored. However, several small variances could point to a much larger problem.

Consistent budget variances usually point to a systematic fault in the operation, which should be rectified to improve efficiency. However, budget variances can also occur because of flawed assumptions when preparing the budget, inefficiencies in execution of the budget, or unforeseen internal or external changes in the environment. Additional analyses that assess the efficiency of operations are needed to determine why targets were missed. One approach is to use a flexible budget.

Use of Flexible Budgets to Analyze Performance

Using a flexible budget provides more meaningful analysis than using a static budget when determining why a budget has variances.

The primary difference between a static budget and a flexible budget is that while both are planned and originally created in the same manner, at the end of the period, a **static budget** is left unchanged and all comparisons are made to the expected output, while a **flexible budget** alters the budget amounts to reflect actual output levels. Output levels and types of output vary across industries and businesses. A manufacturing company would base changes on units of output, but a hospital could use number of patient days, and a service company could use billed hours of service.

Referring again to the sales situation illustrated in Figure 1C-1, if sales were supposed to be 30,000 units but were actually 24,000 units, the flexible budget would be altered to show 24,000 units, and all other corresponding budgeted amounts would change accordingly. This means that variable costs would be adjusted to the actual output level and that fixed costs would most likely remain the same. The result would be a budget that is "flexed," or adjusted, to the actual level of output.

Creating a flexible budget from a static budget allows managers to make direct comparisons. Using a flexible budget, the favorable variance in direct material costs changes to an unfavorable variance, because instead of a budgeted amount of $1,800,000 for direct materials, the new budgeted amount of $1,440,000 ($60 per unit × 24,000 units) would be used, and the actual amount of $1,491,840 would be $51,840 unfavorable.

When compared to static budgets, flexible budgets yield better managerial control results. The reason for better control lies in the concept of variable and fixed expenses. In general, management has more control over variable costs because their cost behavior is directly tied to units of production. If a business lowers the number of units produced from the number suggested in the static budget, the variable costs incurred should go down in equal proportion with the drop in units of production.

Characteristics of Flexible Budgets

A detailed analysis of variances in a static budget can be misleading, because the static budget is prepared at the beginning of the budgeting period and is valid only for the planned level of activity. It is not adjusted to the actual level of activity. By contrast, analyzing a flexible budget's variances in detail can be informative. A flexible budget alters the output units and corresponding total variable costs related to a specific level of output but does not alter unit prices, unit costs, or other items not tied to output. Fixed expenses are also not usually changed because they are by nature fixed over the operating period.

For example: Bounce Sporting Goods' flexible budget has been altered for an unfavorable and a favorable variance in output units, along with changes in other items, and is shown in Figure 1C-2.

Figure 1C-2 shows how flexible budgets can be prepared either after the actual results are known or before, as a pro forma flexible budget. Unit changes alter total sales and total variable expenses. Therefore, the total contribution margin and operating income change correspondingly. However, the percentage of the contribution

Figure 1C-2 Flexible Budgets for Bounce Sporting Goods Company

	Flexible Budget at 80%		Flexible Budget at 100% Static or Master Budget		Flexible Budget at 110%	
Units sold	24,000		30,000		33,000	
Sales	$2,880,000		$3,600,000		$3,960,000	
Variable expenses	2,112,000		2,640,000		2,904,000	
Contribution margin	$768,000	26.67%	$960,000	26.67%	$1,056,000	26.67%
Fixed expenses	690,000		690,000		690,000	
Operating income	$78,000	2.7%	$270,000	7.5%	$366,000	9.2%

margin stays the same while the percentage of operating income changes. This is because when the flexible budget has an unfavorable output variance, the fixed costs assume a larger percentage of the costs. In a favorable output variance, the opposite is true.

Flexible budgets can be prepared without any reference to the master budget. A master budget must be prepared before the accounting period, but flexible budgets can be prepared any time and with varying levels of detail to highlight particular items that need attention. Managers can also use flexible budgets to analyze operating results and determine reasons for changes in operating conditions.

Steps in Preparing a Flexible Budget

Four steps are used when developing a flexible budget.

1. **Prepare a static master budget.** Determine a budgeted selling price, budgeted variable costs per unit, and budgeted fixed costs, as these amounts will continue to be used in the flexible budget. Additionally, output has to be estimated.
2. **Find the actual quantity of output.** The quantity of output is the cost driver for the variable costs.
3. **Calculate the flexible budget amounts for total sales.** The next formula is used to calculate total sales in a flexible budget:

> Total Sales = # of Units Sold × Budgeted Selling Price per Unit

For example: Bounce Sporting Goods' flexible budget revenues are calculated as shown:

$$\text{Flexible Budget Revenues} = \$120/\text{unit} \times 24,000 \text{ units}$$
$$= \$2,880,00$$

4. **Calculate the flexible budget amounts for expenses.** The next formula is used to calculate total expenses in a flexible budget:

> Total Expenses = Total Variable Expenses + Total Fixed Expenses

Total variable expenses equal the number of units sold multiplied by the budgeted variable costs per unit. *For example:* Bounce's flexible budget calculated for actual results is shown in Figure 1C-3.

Figure 1C-3 Flexible Budget Amounts for Expenses

Flexible budget variable costs	
Direct materials, $60 × 24,000	$1,440,000
Direct manufacturing labor, $16 × 24,000	384,000
Variable manufacturing overhead, $12 × 24,000	288,000
Total variable costs	2,112,000
Flexible budget fixed costs	690,000
Flexible budget total costs	$2,802,000

Flexible Budget Variance and Sales Volume Variance

A flexible budget can be used to analyze the efficiency of an operation.

The difference between the actual results and the static budget is called the **static budget variance**. This variance can be broken down into two different types of variances when a flexible budget is created:

1. The **flexible budget variance** is calculated by taking the actual results less the flexible budget amount (adjusted for actual output). This variance identifies the difference in operating income when the budget is flexed, or adjusted to the actual level of sales.
2. The **sales volume variance** is calculated by taking the flexible budget amount adjusted for actual output less the static budget amount. This variance provides information on how operating income is affected by the difference in the volume of budgeted sales compared to the volume of actual sales.

For example: Bounce's actual results are compared against the flexible and static budgets in Figure 1C-4. These comparisons provide the foundation for calculating the flexible budget variance and sales volume variance. A summary of these variances is included in Figure 1C-5.

The flexible budget variance is calculated as shown:

> Flexible Budget Variance = Actual Results − Flexible Budget Amount (adjusted for actual output)

Flexible Budget Variance = $35,760 − $78,000 = $42,240 U

Figure 1C-4 Calculating Flexible Budget Variance and Sales Volume Variance for Bounce Sporting Goods

	Actual Results	Flexible Budget	Flexible Budget Variances (Actual – Flexible)	Static Budget	Sales Volume Variances (Flexible – Static)
Units sold	24,000	24,000	0	30,000	6,000 U
Revenues	$3,000,000	$2,880,000	$120,00 F	$3,600,000	$720,000 U
Variable costs					
Direct materials	1,491,840	1,440,000	51,840 U	1,800,000	360,000 F
Direct manufacturing labor	475,200	384,000	91,200 U	480,000	96,000 F
Variable mfg. overhead	313,200	288,000	25,200 U	360,000	72,000 F
Total variable costs	2,280,240	2,112,000	168,240 U	2,640,000	528,000 F
Contribution margin	719,760	768,000	48,240 U	960,000	192,000 F
Fixed costs	684,000	690,000	6,000 F	690,000	0
Operating income	$35,760	$78,000	$42,240 U	$270,000	$192,000 U

$42,240 U Total flexible budget variance

$192,000 U Total sales volume variance

Total static budget variance $234,240 U

The sales volume variance is calculated as shown:

> Sales Volume Variance = Flexible Budget Amount (adjusted for actual output) − Static Budget Amount

Sales Volume Variance = $78,000 − $270,000 = $192,000 U

Figure 1C-5 Flexible Budget Variances and Sales Volume Variances for Bounce Sporting Goods

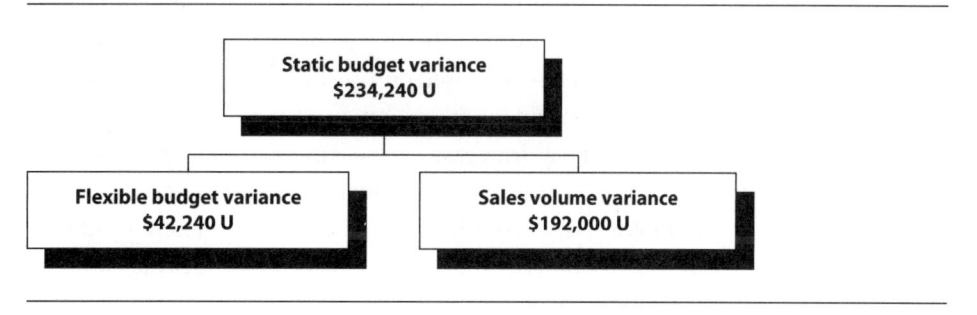

Static budget variance $234,240 U
- Flexible budget variance $42,240 U
- Sales volume variance $192,000 U

The sales volume variance shows the effect of the difference in actual output quantity from the budgeted amounts. The flexible budget variance, however, shows the effects of differences due to actual selling price, variable expenses, and fixed expenses. An unfavorable sales volume variance indicates that the firm does not have as much market share as was assumed or that the market is smaller than anticipated; favorable sales volume variance indicates higher-than-anticipated demand for the product. Insignificant sales volume variances mean that the budget predicted accurate sales. An unfavorable flexible budget variance indicates that the input costs were higher than budgeted. A favorable flexible budget variance indicates that the input costs were lower than budgeted. Analysis of both variances together will help assess whether an operation is effective and/or efficient.

Management by Exception

The breakdown of variances into flexible budget variances and sales budget variances can allow a firm to make business decisions based on these variances. **Management by exception** is a method of focusing management attention on only significant variances from the budget. Significant variances are the exceptions that require more attention than other areas. Some management software automatically creates exception reports. Management by exception flags unfavorable as well as favorable variances. Favorable variances should be tracked to determine if the performance is truly exceptional or perhaps the standard is set too low. Exceptional performance over time should be incorporated into standard practice.

Knowing which exceptions to investigate requires managerial experience, but the size and frequency of the variances are primary considerations. The relative size of the variance is more important than the absolute size, but managers often have set a general rule for both—for example, flag all variances over $30,000 or 5% of the budgeted cost.

Small but frequent variances are also worth investigating. Other considerations include following trends, such as a cost that continuously gets larger over time, and the level of control that can be directed to change the cost, such as not paying as much attention to a cost that is rising solely due to market demand.

Management by exception is a good management technique in that it focuses a manager's attention only on exceptions that are tracked, and each exception is tracked or not tracked based on a cost-benefit decision. However, because this method requires management discretion, poor management judgment can cause this benefit to become a drawback. For example, if management believes that a rising raw material cost cannot be controlled and therefore does not flag the cost, it might be overlooking an alternative, such as finding a different vendor or a replacement material. When properly implemented, exception tracking can reduce future costs when causes for unfavorable variances are removed or when causes for favorable variances can be extended.

Use of Standard Cost Systems

A **standard cost** is any carefully determined price, quantity, service level, or cost, usually expressed in a per-unit amount, which is determined before actual costs are available. Standard costs are used for planning purposes, because actual costs usually are not available until after a product is produced or a service is rendered. A standard cost is a predetermined amount based on experience and represents the amount that a unit of output is expected to cost. A standard costing system uses standard costs for all elements of a product or service, including standard expenses for manufacturing, administration, and sales. A standard costing system can be a valuable management tool, because it enables the firm to identify variances from what was planned. When a variance arises between actual and standard costs, management becomes aware that costs have differed from the standard (planned, expected) costs. Standard cost systems allow for the use of management by exception and provide the foundation for variance analysis, which allows management to gain an understanding of what is causing favorable or unfavorable performance.

Analysis of Variation from Standard Cost Expectations

A flexible budget provides a high-level overview of budget variances. Flexible budget and sales volume variances provide a more detailed view. A third level of detail is possible by analyzing the cause of these flexible budget variances.

Recall that all standards have two components:

1. A standard rate per unit of the cost driver. A cost driver is an activity, such as direct labor hours, machine hours, level of output, and so on, that affects the level of costs that are incurred.
2. A standard number of units of a cost driver for a given output level—the flexible budget level.

Focusing on changes in each of these two components allows flexible budget variances to be broken down into price (rate) variances and efficiency (usage) variances. The total of these two variances equals the flexible budget variance, as shown in Figure 1C-6 (where DM is direct materials and DL is direct labor).

Note that in Figure 1C-6, for direct materials, the price variance plus the efficiency variance will equal the flexible budget variance only when the amount of material purchased in the period exactly equals the amount used in production during the period, which means that the inventory balance does not change—and that is a rare event. This problem does not occur in direct labor or overhead because these items cannot be inventoried (i.e., the amount purchased always equals the amount used). Direct costs and fixed and variable overhead require different methods of calculating these variances.

A discussion of sales mix variances and their breakdown into mix variances and yield variances appears later in this topic.

Price and Efficiency Variances for Direct Labor and Direct Material Inputs

Price and efficiency variances result from variances from budgeted input prices or input quantities. A **standard input** is a predetermined quantity of direct inputs,

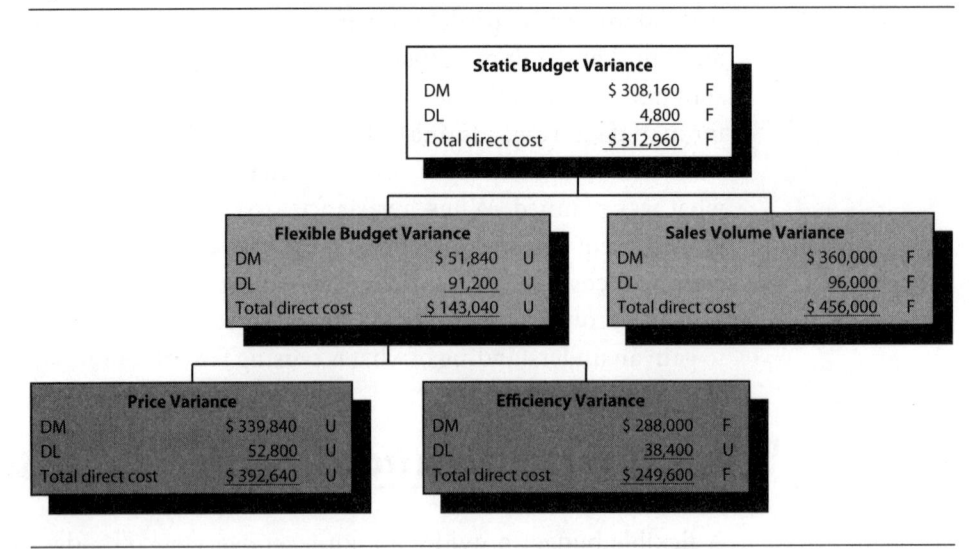

Figure 1C-6 Variance Breakdown for Direct Costs

Static Budget Variance
DM	$ 308,160	F
DL	4,800	F
Total direct cost	$ 312,960	F

Flexible Budget Variance
DM	$ 51,840	U
DL	91,200	U
Total direct cost	$ 143,040	U

Sales Volume Variance
DM	$ 360,000	F
DL	96,000	F
Total direct cost	$ 456,000	F

Price Variance
DM	$ 339,840	U
DL	52,800	U
Total direct cost	$ 392,640	U

Efficiency Variance
DM	$ 288,000	F
DL	38,400	U
Total direct cost	$ 249,600	F

such as labor hours or gallons of a fluid needed to make one unit of output. A price variance for direct labor is often referred to as a rate variance, and an efficiency variance for direct material is often referred to as a quantity or usage variance.

Price (Rate) Variances for Direct Costs

A **price variance** is the actual input quantity of an item multiplied by the difference between the actual input price and the budgeted (or standard) input price.

> Price (Rate) Variance = Actual Input Quantity × (Actual Input Price − Budgeted Input Price)

Suppose the standards for a unit were:

Direct Materials (DM): 10.0 Pounds DM/Unit @ $6.00/Pound = $60/Unit Standard
(24,000 Units × 10.0 Pounds/Unit = 240,000 Pounds Standard)

Direct Labor (DL): 2.0 Labor Hours/Unit @ $8.00/Hour = $16/Unit Standard
(24,000 Units × 2.0 Labor Hours/Unit = 48,000 Labor Hours Standard)

Assume that for a period, the actual price paid for direct materials was $7.77/pound and the process purchased and consumed 192,000 pounds of material to produce 24,000 units. The price variance for direct materials would be calculated as shown:

> DM Price Variance = Actual Input Quantity × (Actual Input Price − Budgeted Input Price)

DM Price Variance = 192,000 Pounds × ($7.77/Pound − $6/Pound)

= $339,840 U

If the quantity purchased is not equal to the quantity used, the quantity purchased should be used in the DM price variance calculation.

For the same period, if the actual price paid for labor hours was $9.00/hour and the number of hours logged was 52,800 to produce 24,000 units, the price (rate) variance for labor would be calculated as shown:

> DL Rate Variance = Actual Input Quantity × (Actual Input Price − Budgeted Input Price)

DL Rate Variance = 52,800 Hours × ($9/Hour − $8/Hour) = $52,800 U

Favorable direct materials price variances can be caused by quantity discounts, better negotiations, unforeseen price or shipping cost changes, or lack of demand for an item (high availability lowering the price). Unfavorable direct materials price variances can be caused by the opposite situations. Either type of variance could also be caused by poor budgeting or by receiving materials of better or worse quality than expected. Direct labor rate variances are caused by changes in market demand for the appropriate labor, labor shortages, overtime rates, or requiring different skill levels to be used, which requires different rates to be paid from those set in the standards.

The effect of a variance, whether it is favorable or unfavorable, should be studied. For example, a favorable materials price variance caused by purchasing in bulk could cause a firm to have greater inventory holding costs. Moreover, if the standards reflect the company's strategy, such as differentiation for quality, variations should be studied for their effect on the company's strategy and corrected when they differ from that strategy.

Efficiency (Quantity or Usage) Variances for Direct Costs

An **efficiency variance** is the budgeted input price multiplied by the difference between the actual input quantity and the budgeted (or standard) input quantity. This formula is:

> Efficiency Variance = Budgeted Input Price × (Actual Input Quantity − Budgeted Input Quantity)

Continuing with the prior example, for direct materials, the actual input quantity was 192,000 pounds, or 8 pounds/unit (192,000/24,000). Because the budgeted input quantity was 240,000 pounds and the budgeted price was $6/pound, the efficiency (quantity) variance would be calculated as shown:

> DM Efficiency (Quantity) Variance = Budgeted Input Price × (Actual Input Quantity − Budgeted Input Quantity)

DM Efficiency (Quantity) Variance = $6/Pound × (192,000 Pounds − 240,000 Pounds)
= $288,000 F

The direct materials efficiency variance is normally referred to as the direct materials quantity variance or the direct materials usage variance.

For direct labor, the actual input quantity was 52,800 labor hours, or 2.2 hours per unit (52,800/24,000). Because the budgeted input quantity was 48,000 labor hours and the budgeted price was $8/labor hour, the efficiency variance would be calculated as shown:

> DL Efficiency Variance = Budgeted Input Price × (Actual Input Quantity − Budgeted Input Quantity)

DL Efficiency Variance = $8/Hour × (52,800 Hours − 48,000 Hours)
= $38,400 U

Because the price variance plus the efficiency variance equals the flexible budget variance, the flexible budget variance can be verified by totaling the price and efficiency variances as shown:

DM Flexible Budget Variance = $339,840 U (price) + $288,000 F (efficiency)
= $51,840 U

DL Flexible Budget Variance = $52,800 U (price) + $38,400 F (efficiency)
= $91,200 U

Both direct material and direct labor efficiency variances can be caused by poor budgeting or by variances in worker skill level, scheduling, supervision, or setup efficiency. Improperly maintained machines or improper training can also lead to direct material and direct labor efficiency variances.

Spending and Efficiency Variances for Variable and Fixed Overhead

As with direct costs, variable overhead cost variances can be further broken down into price and efficiency variances. Because of the fixed nature of fixed overhead costs, the fixed overhead cost variances are further broken down into the fixed overhead spending variance and the fixed overhead production volume variance.

Variances for Variable Overhead

Breaking down the variable overhead flexible budget variance requires knowing three calculated amounts:

1. **Actual variable overhead:** Actual overhead incurred during the period
2. **Predicted variable overhead:** Actual quantity of cost driver times the standard variable overhead rate
3. **Applied variable overhead:** Standard quantity of cost driver allowed (for actual output) times the standard variable overhead rate

The variable overhead flexible budget variance can be broken down into a variable overhead spending variance (1 minus 2 in the list shown above) and a variable overhead efficiency variance (2 minus 3 in the list shown above).

Variable Overhead Spending Variance

The **variable overhead spending variance** is calculated by taking the difference between actual overhead cost and the actual quantity of cost driver multiplied by the standard variable overhead rate. This variance tells management how favorable or unfavorable spending on variable overhead costs was as compared to how much "should have been spent" on those costs during the period based on an appropriate cost driver.

> Variable Overhead Spending (or Price) Variance = Actual Overhead Cost − (Actual Quantity of Cost Driver × Standard Variable Overhead Rate)

Variable overhead standards are created using a cost driver and a number of units of the cost driver.

For example: If machine hours are used as the cost driver for variable overhead and 1.2 machine hours at $10/machine hour are set as the standard for one unit ($12/unit), then 24,000 units should require 28,800 machine hours, or $288,000 (see Figure 1C-4).

Actual variable overhead costs allocated to these 24,000 units are $313,200, which then makes the variable overhead flexible budget variance $25,200 unfavorable ($313,200 − $288,000 = $25,200 U).

Accordingly, if the actual number of machine hours is 28,000, the variable overhead spending variance would be calculated as:

Variable Overhead Spending Variance = $313,200 − (28,000 Machine Hours × $10/Machine Hour)
= $313,200 − $280,000
= $33,200 U

Variable Overhead Efficiency Variance

The **variable overhead efficiency variance** is the product of the actual quantity of the cost driver multiplied by the standard variable overhead rate, less the product of the standard quantity of cost driver allowed (for actual output) multiplied by the standard variable overhead rate.

> Variable Overhead Efficiency Variance =
> (Actual Quantity of Cost Driver × Standard Variable Overhead Rate) −
> (Standard Quantity of Cost Driver Allowed (for actual output) × Standard Variable Overhead Rate)

The variable overhead efficiency variance is shown next, along with an example.

$$\text{Variable Overhead Efficiency Variance}$$
$$= (28{,}000 \text{ Machine Hours} \times \$10/\text{Machine Hour})$$
$$- (28{,}800 \text{ Machine Hours} \times \$10/\text{Machine Hour})$$
$$= \$280{,}000 - \$288{,}000$$
$$= \$8{,}000 \text{ F}$$

> Variable Overhead Flexible Budget Variance = Variable Overhead Spending Variance + Variable Overhead Efficeincy Variance

The variable overhead spending plus efficiency variances aggregate to the variable overhead flexible budget variance.

$$\text{Variable Overhead Flexible Budget Variance} = \$33{,}200 \text{ U} + \$8{,}000 \text{ F}$$
$$= \$25{,}200 \text{ U}$$

A variable overhead variance is more likely caused by the imprecision inherent in choosing a single cost driver for overhead that is likely made up of very different costs. In contrast, variance measures for direct materials and direct labor have accurate cost drivers. For greater accuracy in calculating overhead, activity-based overhead variance measures could perform the variance measures using a variety of cost pools, each with its own cost driver, but the higher administrative cost may be prohibitive. Variable overhead may also have variances because many types of variable overhead costs are not based on output measures, such as units of output, but on input measures, such as number of setups or batches.

Variable Overhead Accounting

The unfavorable variable overhead flexible budget variance of $25,200 in the prior example represents the amount of underapplied overhead, because this is the amount by which actual costs exceed applied overhead. If favorable, the amount would represent the amount of overapplied overhead.

However, by breaking this variance down into spending and efficiency variances, the accounting for the differences can also become more specific. (See Figure 1C-7.)

Figure 1C-7 Journal Entries for Variable Overhead (Actual and Applied)

Variable Manufacturing Overhead Control	$313,200	
Accounts Payable Control and Other Accounts		$313,200
To record actual variable manufacturing overhead costs incurred.		
Work-in-Process Control	$288,000	
Variable Manufacturing Overhead Applied		$288,000
To record applied variable manufacturing overhead costs (1.2 machine hours/unit × $10/machine hour × 24,000 units).		

The costs in the work-in-process (WIP) control account would be transferred to the finished goods control account when production is finished. The costs of items sold are transferred from the finished goods control account to the cost of goods sold account when sales are made.

The entry shown in Figure 1C-8 would be made to record the variances. (Note that the two variance accounts now replace the single overhead applied account.)

Figure 1C-8 Journal Entry to Record Variable Overhead Variances

Variable Manufacturing Overhead Applied	$288,000	
Variable Manufacturing Overhead Spending Variance	$33,200	
Variable Manufacturing Overhead Control		$313,200
Variable Manufacturing Overhead Efficiency Variance		$8,000
To record variable overhead variances for the accounting period.		

Assuming that the amount of overhead that is underapplied (or overapplied) is immaterial, the accounting entries shown in Figure 1C-9 would be made to write off the difference to the cost of goods sold account at the end of the period.

Figure 1C-9 Disposition of Variable Overhead Variance Accounts

Cost of Goods Sold	$25,200	
Variable Manufacturing Overhead Efficiency Variance	$8,000	
Variable Manufacturing Overhead Spending Variance		$33,200
To record the disposition of variable overhead variance accounts.		

If the amount of overapplied or underapplied overhead is material and unavoidable, the amounts must be prorated among the ending WIP inventory, ending finished goods inventory, and the cost of goods sold based on the relative variable manufacturing overhead allocated to each account during the accounting period.

Variances for Fixed Overhead

The total **fixed overhead variance** represents the difference between actual fixed overhead and applied fixed overhead.

> Total Fixed Overhead Variance = Actual Fixed Overhead − Applied Fixed Overhead

The total fixed overhead variance is also called the underapplied or overapplied fixed overhead.

Just like the other cost variances, the fixed overhead variance can also be broken down further, so that management can gain a better understanding of performance for this cost category. To break down the total fixed overhead variance into two subcategories, three amounts must be known:

1. **Actual fixed overhead:** Actual overhead incurred in the period.
2. **Budgeted fixed overhead:** A fixed cost, usually assessed as a lump sum and not on a per-unit basis. The fixed overhead standard rate per unit is the total static budgeted quantity cost driver times the standard fixed overhead rate.
3. **Applied fixed overhead:** Actual quantity times the standard fixed overhead rate.

Actual fixed overhead is the actual amount of overhead incurred in a period. **Budgeted fixed overhead** uses the standard quantity set in the static budget. Note that the flexible budget cost for fixed overhead is equal to the static budget cost, as the fixed overhead cost is, by definition, fixed and is independent of output. Therefore, the sales volume variance for fixed overhead is always zero.

The fixed overhead flexible budget variance can be broken down into a fixed overhead spending variance (1 minus 2 in the prior list) and a fixed overhead production volume variance (2 minus 3 in the list). The fixed overhead spending variance is actual fixed overhead minus budgeted fixed overhead. The fixed overhead production volume variance is the budgeted fixed overhead minus applied fixed overhead.

Continuing the prior example (see Figure 1C-4), the actual fixed overhead is $684,000. The budgeted fixed overhead is calculated by taking 30,000 units and multiplying them by the standard fixed overhead rate of $23/unit ($690,000/30,000 = $23/unit), which equals $690,000. The applied fixed overhead is the actual quantity of 24,000 units multiplied by the standard rate of $23/unit, which equals $552,000.

The fixed overhead spending variance and the fixed overhead production volume variance are calculated as shown:

> Fixed Overhead Spending Variance = Actual Fixed Overhead − Budgeted Fixed Overhead

Fixed Overhead Spending Variance = $684,000 − $690,000 = $6,000 F

> Fixed Overhead Production Volume Variance = Budgeted Fixed Overhead − Applied Fixed Overhead

Fixed Overhead Volume Variance = $690,000 − $552,000 = $138,000 U

> Total Fixed Overhead Variance (Equal to the Amount of Overapplied or Underapplied Overhead) = Fixed Overhead Spending Variance + Fixed Overhead Production Volume Variance

Total Fixed Overhead Variance = $6,000 Favorable + $138,000 U

= $132,000 U

or

> Total Fixed Overhead Variance = Actual Fixed Overhead − Applied Fixed Overhead

Total Fixed Overhead Variance = $684,000 − $552,000 = $132,000 U

A fixed overhead spending variance shows that the budget procedure either missed or failed to predict changes in certain fixed costs. Unfavorable spending variances can also occur if inadequate control is exercised over departmental spending or because of accidents and unexpected repairs. The breakdown of fixed costs into these two categories can highlight when certain variable costs are misclassified as fixed costs, because changes in production volume will be accompanied by changes in some portion of the fixed costs that may be discretionary. Also, as with the variable overhead variances, the total fixed overhead variance of $132,000 unfavorable is the total amount of fixed overhead underapplied and would be accounted for using the combination of the fixed overhead spending variance and the fixed overhead production volume variance accounts. The entries would be similar to those shown previously for variable overhead, with the entry shown in Figure 1C-10 to record the variances.

Figure 1C-10 Journal Entry to Record Fixed Manufacturing Overhead Variances

Fixed Manufacturing Overhead Applied	$552,000	
Fixed Manufacturing Overhead Production Volume Variance	$138,000	
Fixed Manufacturing Overhead Control		$684,000
Fixed Manufacturing Overhead Spending Variance		$6,000
To record variances for the accounting period.		

The final entry to adjust the cost of goods sold (if immaterial) is shown in Figure 1C-11.

Figure 1C-11 Disposition of Fixed Overhead Variances

Cost of Goods Sold	$132,000	
Fixed Manufacturing Overhead Spending Variance	$6,000	
Fixed Manufacturing Overhead Production Volume Variance		$138,000
To record the disposition of fixed overhead variance account.		

Again, if material and unavoidable, such costs would be prorated among the inventory accounts and the cost of goods sold.

The fixed overhead production volume variance can occur when demand for a product changes from what was expected. Often some measurement of a production variable (e.g., labor hours or machine hours) is used as the allocation base for overhead. If the labor usage being measured (actual quantity of allocation base as measured in applied fixed overhead) differs from the budgeted amount used to compute the overhead rate (standard quantity of allocation base as measured in budgeted fixed overhead), this will result in fixed overhead variances being either overapplied or underapplied.

Other causes of the fixed overhead production volume variance include changes in strategy or unexpected breakdowns. If the company made as many units in the period as it budgeted, there should be no fixed overhead production volume variance. The production volume variance reflects the company's use of its capacity. When volume is low, the price per unit of fixed overhead is higher and capacity is underutilized. The production volume variance does not indicate efficiency but its effectiveness in attaining its cost goals.

Using Overhead Variance Data to Solve for Other Unknowns

Sometimes the variances for a situation are known but some other variables are not known. In such situations, the equation can be solved for the variable in question.

For example: Assume that Bounce Sporting Goods is benchmarking a competitor, SportCo. SportCo's actual variable overhead is $432,000, and its actual sales are 28,250 units. SportCo stated in a magazine article that it uses labor hours when allocating variable overhead, and it allows a budgeted input of 1.6 labor hours per unit. The article did not mention the variable overhead allocation rates or actual number of labor hours used for the period. SportCo's variable overhead variances are $58,000 unfavorable efficiency variance and $20,000 favorable spending variance. Standard flexible budget units of the cost driver can thus be derived: 28,250 actual units × 1.6 labor hours per unit = 45,200 labor hours.

Based on this information, what is the variable overhead allocation rate per unit? Per labor hour? What was the actual number of labor hours? To find the answers, input the known amounts into the formulas for variances and then solve for the unknown variable. Note that because the actual units of the labor hours cost driver is not known, the first calculation uses units as its cost driver and solves for the answer in units and then uses the answer to solve for the standard labor hours cost driver rate.

> Variable Overhead (OH) Spending Variance = Actual Cost − (Actual Units of Cost Driver × Standard Cost Driver Rate)

The variable overhead spending variance formula can be used to solve for the standard cost per unit as shown:

$$-\$20{,}000\text{ F} = \$432{,}000 - (28{,}250 \text{ Units} \times \$X/\text{Unit})$$

$$-\$20{,}000 - \$432{,}000 = -(28{,}250 \text{ Units} \times \$X/\text{Unit})$$

$$\$452{,}000 = 28{,}250 \text{ Units} \times \$X/\text{Unit}$$

$$\frac{\$452{,}000}{28{,}250 \text{ Units}} = \$X/\text{Unit} = \$16/\text{Unit}$$

> Budgeted Variable OH Cost Rate/Unit = Budgeted Input/Unit × Budgeted Variable OH Cost Rate/Input Unit

The last formula can be used to solve for the budgeted variable overhead rate as shown:

$$\$16/\text{Unit} = 1.6 \text{ Labor Hours/Unit} \times \$X/\text{Labor Hour}$$

$$\frac{\$16/\text{Unit}}{1.6 \text{ Labor Hours/Unit}} = \$X/\text{Labor Hour} = \$10/\text{Labor Hour}$$

Once the budgeted variable overhead cost rate per labor hour is known, the next steps show one way to determine the actual number of labor hours used based on the known variable overhead efficiency variance.

> Variable Overhead Efficiency Variance = (Actual Units of Cost Driver × Standard Cost Driver Rate) − (Standard Units of Cost Driver × Standard Cost Driver Rate)

The variable overhead efficiency variance is calculated as shown:

Variable Overhead Efficiency Variance

$= (\text{Labor Hours} \times \$10/\text{Labor Hour}) - (45{,}200 \text{ Labor Hours} \times \$10/\text{Labor Hour})$

$= \$58{,}000 \text{ Unfavorable}$

$= (\text{Labor Hours} \times \$10/\text{Labor Hour}) - \$452{,}000 = \$58{,}000 \text{ U}$

$= (\text{Labor Hours} \times \$10/\text{Labor Hour}) = \$58{,}000 \text{ U} + \$452{,}000$

$= (\text{Labor Hours} \times \$10/\text{Labor Hour}) = \$510{,}000$

$= \text{Labor Hours} = \dfrac{\$510{,}000}{\$10/\text{Labor Hour}} = 51{,}000 \text{ Labor Hours (Actual)}$

Sales Volume, Mix, and Quantity Variances

When there are multiple products, the sales volume variance can be broken down into a sales mix variance and a sales quantity variance.

> Sales Volume Variance = Sales Mix Variance × Sales Quantity Variance

The **sales volume variance** is the sum of the individual sales volume variances. Each individual sales volume variance is calculated as:

> Sales Volume Variance = (Units Sold − Units in Static Budget)
> × Budgeted Standard Contribution Margin per Unit

The contribution margin is calculated by taking total sales less all variable expenses. The portion of sales volume variance that is not attributable to sales quantity is caused by variations in the mix of various products a firm offers.

For example: If a tennis ball company also makes racquet balls, its sales mix variance would arise from variations in the actual sales mix of these two products compared to the budgeted sales mix. A sales mix is the ratio of any single product or service to the total of all products or services. Sales mix variance is a company-wide measure and is the sum of the sales mix variance of each type of merchandise sold by the company.

Sales Mix Variance

A sales mix variance for a particular type of product is calculated by multiplying the budgeted contribution margin per unit for that merchandise, the total number of all merchandise sold, and the difference between the actual sales mix ratio and the budgeted sales mix ratio. The sales mix variance formula is:

> Sales Mix Variance = (Actual Sales Mix Ratio for a Product − Budgeted Sales Mix Ratio for a Product) × Actual Units Sold × Budgeted Contribution Margin per Unit of Product

Consider a situation in which the master budget calls for 10,000 cans of tennis balls to be sold at a unit contribution margin of $8 each and for 6,000 cans of racquet balls to be sold at a contribution margin of $4 each. The budgeted sales mix ratio for tennis balls is 10,000/16,000, or 0.625, and for racquet balls is 6,000/16,000, or 0.375. Suppose the actual sales for the period were 9,000 cans of tennis balls and 9,000 cans of racquet balls. The sales mix ratios change to 0.5 for tennis balls and 0.5 for racquet balls.

> Product A Sales Volume Variance = Sales Mix Variance
> × Sales Quantity Variance

Tennis Ball Sales Volume Variance = (9,000 − 10,000) × 8

Tennis Ball Sales Volume Variance = −1,000 × 8

Tennis Ball Sales Volume Variance = $8,000 U

> Product B Sales Volume Variance = Sales Mix Variance
> × Sales Quantity Variance

Racquet Ball Sales Volume Variance = (9,000 − 6,000) × 4

Racquet Ball Sales Volume Variance = 3,000 × 4

Racquet Ball Sales Volume Variance = $12,000 F

> Total Sales Volume Variance = (Product A Sales Volume Variance
> × Product B Sales Volume Variance)

Total Sales Volume Variance = ($8,000 U) + ($12,000 F)

Total Sales Volume Variance = $4,000 F

> **Product A Sales Mix Variance** = (Actual Sales Mix Ratio for a Product − Budgeted Sales Mix Ratio for a Product) × Actual Units Sold × Budgeted Contribution Margin per Unit of Product

Tennis Ball Sales Mix Variance = (0.5 − 0.625) × 18,000 units × $8

Tennis Ball Sales Mix Variance = −0.125 × $144,000

Tennis Ball Sales Mix Variance = $18,000 U

Racquet Ball Sales Mix Variance = (0.5 − 0.375) × 18,000 units × $4

Racquet Ball Sales Mix Variance = 0.125 × $72,000

Racquet Ball Sales Mix Variance = $9,000 F

> **Total Sales Mix Variance** = (Product A Sales Mix Variance + Product B Sales Mix Variance)

Total Sales Mix Variance = ($18,000 U) + ($9,000 F)

Total Sales Mix Variance = 9,000 U

Total Quantity Variance

The next formula can be used to calculate the total quantity variance for each of the products:

> **Sales Quantity Variance** = Sales Volume Variance − Sales Mix Variance

Tennis Ball Sales Quantity Variance = $8,000 U − ($18,000 U)
= $10,000 F

Racquet Ball Sales Quantity Variance = $12,000 F − $9,000 F
= $3,000 F

The total quantity variances for each of the products can then be added together to arrive at a total quantity variance for both products.

> **Total Quantity Variance (Overall)** = Quantity Variance (Product A) + Quantity Variance (Product B)

Total Quantity Variance (Overall) = $10,000 Favorable + $3,000 Favorable

Total Quantity Variance (Overall) = $13,000 Favorable

Mix and Yield Variances for Direct Materials and Direct Labor

The efficiency (usage) variance for direct costs can be further broken down into two components when a product has two or more ingredients or labor costs that can be substituted for one another. The efficiency variance can be broken down into a direct materials (or labor) mix variance and a direct materials (or labor) yield variance. Three amounts must be known to break an efficiency variance down into its subcomponents:

1. Budgeted Cost/Unit × Actual Total Quantity Used × Actual Mix Ratio for the Item

2. Budgeted Cost/Unit × Actual Total Quantity Used × Budgeted Mix Ratio for the Item

3. Budgeted Cost/Unit × Budgeted Total Quantity Used × Budgeted Mix Ratio for the Item

The **mix variance** is calculated by taking the amount from item 1 above and subtracting the amount in item 2 above (1 − 2 = mix variance). The **yield variance** is calculated by taking the amount from item 2 above and subtracting the amount of item 3 above (2 − 3 = yield variance). The **mix ratio** is the amount of one substitutable item divided by the total of all substitutable items.

$$\text{Mix Ratio} = \frac{\text{Amount of Substitutable Items}}{\text{Total of All Substitutable Items}}$$

For example: Assume that synthetic rubber and natural rubber can be substituted to produce tennis balls and that the standard amounts and prices in the product mix call for 1,000 pounds of synthetic rubber at $2 per pound ($2,000 standard cost) and 600 pounds of natural rubber at $3 per pound ($1,800) to produce 1,000 cans of tennis balls ($3,800 total standard cost). The standard mix ratio for synthetic rubber would be 1,000/1,600 = 0.625, or 62.5%. Similarly the standard mix ratio for natural rubber would be 0.375, or 37.5%. Assume also that the production manager can substitute up to 5% of either product for the other product. In reality, only 988 pounds of synthetic rubber ($1,976 actual cost) and only 532 pounds of natural rubber ($1,596 actual cost) actually are used, for a total of 1,520 pounds (total cost = $3,572, a variance of $228 favorable). This makes the actual mix ratio 65% (988/1,520) for synthetic rubber and 35% for natural rubber.

Using these data, the mix variance is calculated as:

1. Budgeted Cost/Unit × Actual Total Quantity Used × Actual Mix Ratio for the item

   Synthetic Rubber = $2/Pound × 1,520 Pounds × 0.65 = $1,976
   Natural Rubber = $3/Pound × 1,520 Pounds × 0.35 = $1,596
   $3,572

2. Budgeted Cost/Unit × Actual Total Quantity Used × Budgeted Mix Ratio for the item

   Synthetic Rubber = $2/Pound × 1,520 Pounds × 0.625 = $1,900
   Natural Rubber = $3/Pound × 1,520 Pounds × 0.375 = $1,710
   $3,610

The yield variance is calculated as:

Step 1 − Step 2 = $3,572 − $3,610 = $38 Favorable Mix Variance

2. Budgeted Cost/Unit × Actual Total Quantity Used × Budgeted Mix Ratio for the item

   Synthetic Rubber = $2/Pound × 1,520 Pounds × 0.625 = $1,900
   Natural Rubber = $3/Pound × 1,520 Pounds × 0.375 = $1,710
   $3,610

3. Budgeted Cost/Unit × Actual Total Quantity Used × Budgeted Mix Ratio for the item

   Synthetic Rubber = $2/Pound × 1,600 Pounds × 0.625 = $2,000
   Natural Rubber = $3/Pound × 1,600 Pounds × 0.375 = $1,800
   $3,800

Step 2 − Step 3 = $3,610 − $3,800 = $190 Favorable Yield Variance

Total Efficiency Variance = ($38) + ($190) = $228 Favorable

The mix variance results from using direct material and/or labor inputs in a ratio that differs from standard specifications. The mix variance is favorable in the preceding example because a larger percentage of cheaper materials was used to create the product than was budgeted. The yield variance results because the yield (output) obtained differs from the one expected on the basis of input. The larger favorable amount for the yield variance in the example results from the fact that 10% less in materials was used than was expected in order to produce the 1,000 cans of tennis balls. Knowing the breakdown between mix and yield variances can help managers determine how an efficiency variance should be dealt with.

Extension of Variance Analyses

Each of the prior variances can be broken down into subclasses using the same formulas given. For example, the price (rate) variance can be used to differentiate labor classes to determine more specifically where a favorable or unfavorable variance originated.

Other similar breakdowns or variations include:

- Using mix variance to calculate labor substitution variance (e.g., professional versus unskilled labor substitution)
- Labor variance from using substandard materials
- Price (rate) variance formula to measure the sales price variance or the cost price variance without changing the formula

In some situations, some variances are known but other variables must be found. The next example shows a highly detailed variance analysis.

For example: The following description traces the variance analysis for Bounce Sporting Goods.

Bounce Sporting Goods had a very poor month in June, according to a flexible budget variance of $76,370 unfavorable. Key data for June follow.

Budgeted production was for 12,000 units, but a rush order for 8,000 units was added at the last minute, and the sales team promised end-of-month delivery.

Standard Costs:

Direct material (DM) (from supplier A): 1.5 pounds @ $8/pound = $12/unit

Direct labor (DL) (standard Class III, unskilled): 1.2 direct labor hours (DLH) @ $14/DLH = $16.80/unit

Total standard direct costs = $28.80/unit

Actual Costs:

After Bounce purchased (and used) 18,200 pounds of DM from supplier A for $144,690, the supplier could not provide more for the rush order, so the purchasing department had to use supplier B, which supplied 18,000 pounds for $142,200 (of which only 15,800 pounds were used, at a cost of $126,400).

Actual DM costs charged to production:

Supplier A DM—18,200 pounds × $8/pound = $145,600

Supplier B DM—15,800 pounds × $8/pound = $126,400

To meet the new production quota, Bounce had to transfer some Class II semi-skilled employees from a different department, paid on average $16/DLH. These employees, though more skilled, are not familiar with the task and will not be as efficient as employees who are trained in this task.

Actual DL costs charged to production:

Class III DL (15,200 hours) = $216,600

Class II DL (10,300 hours) = $163,770

Total production costs: $145,600 + $126,400 + $216,600 + $163,770 = $652,370

Total standard costs at flexible budget level: 20,000 units × $28.80/unit = $576,000

Flexible budget variance = $652,370 − $576,000 = $76,370 U

Because the DM from supplier B turned out to be very poor, the manager made a breakdown of the time spent by each class of labor in producing units with each set of DM, as shown in Figure 1C-12.

Figure 1C-12 Units Produced and Labor Used by DM Type

	Supplier A DM	Supplier B DM
DM used	18,200 pounds	15,800 pounds
Production output		
Class III	7,200 units	4,800 units
Class II	4,800 units	3,200 units
Total output	12,000 units	8,000 units
Actual DLH		
Class III DLH	8,600 hours	6,600 hours
Class II DLH	5,900 hours	4,400 hours
Total DLH	14,500 hours	11,000 hours

What is the DM efficiency (quantity or usage) variance for supplier A materials? For supplier B materials? Figure 1C-13 shows how these variances are calculated. Note that in the next calculations, the order of the variance calculations is reversed. Earlier the text presented this formula:

> Efficiency Variance = (Actual Input Quantity − Budgeted Input Quantity) × Budgeted Input Price

but the next calculations consistently reverse the order of budgeted versus actual inputs:

> Efficiency Variance = (Budgeted Input Quantity − Actual Input Quantity) × Budgeted Input Price

This formula will result in the same number, but it will be positive instead of negative (or vice versa). If this reversal is done for one of the variances, it must be done consistently for all of the variances in a set of data. Therefore, in Figure 1C-13, the $32,000 unfavorable material usage variance indicates that materials cost $32,000 more than was allocated in the flexible budget.

Bounce Sporting Goods also has enough data to break its direct labor variance down into four components: labor rate variance, labor substitution variance, labor variance from substandard materials (supplier B DM), and labor efficiency

Figure 1C-13 DM Efficiency (Quantity or Usage) Variance with Multiple Materials

	Supplier A DM	Supplier B DM	Total
Output—units produced	12,000	8,000	20,000
Material requirements per unit	× 1.5	× 1.5	
Total standard material requirements	18,000	12,000	30,000
Actual material consumed	− 18,200	− 15,800	− 34,000
Usage variance in units (unfavorable)	(200) U	(3,800) U	(4,000) U
Standard cost per unit	× $8	× $8	
Material usage variance	($1,600) U	($30,400) U	($32,000) U
Percent variance from standard	1.1% U	31.7% U	

variance on regular materials (supplier A DM). Figure 1C-14 shows the computation of these variances.

The Total Flexible Budget Variance of $76,370 Unfavorable is made up of:

- $32,000 Unfavorable Material Usage Variance (from Figure 1C-13)
- $2,770 Unfavorable Labor Rate Variance (from Figure 1C-14)
- $20,600 Unfavorable Labor Substitution Variance (from Figure 1C-14)
- $19,600 Unfavorable Substandard Material Labor Variance (from Figure 1C-14)
- $1,400 Unfavorable Labor Efficiency Variance on Regular Material (from Figure 1C-14)

Note that the final line of Figure 1C-14 is the sum of all variances for each column. What can be learned from this analysis? First, the rush order can be shown to have caused several of the problems. Supplier B's materials accounted for a material usage variance of $30,400 unfavorable (see Figure 1C-13), which is much greater than that for supplier A's materials, so the alternate supplies must have had much more scrap or waste. This could have been avoided if the rush order had not been submitted. Second, the labor substitution variance of $20,600 unfavorable is the result of needing to use labor that costs more than the regular workers. Third, the total direct labor variance from use of substandard materials is $19,600 unfavorable, which once again reinforces the conclusion that both types of workers had to waste time working with unsuitable materials.

A detailed analysis such as this can be used for performance evaluation. For example, in keeping with the tenets of responsibility accounting, perhaps the unfavorable variances related to the rush order could be charged to the sales department because it did not provide enough time to produce the rush order, or perhaps purchasing could be charged for the variances related to the substandard materials. Decisions such as these will force the other departments to work more carefully with the production department in the future.

Note that the measures used for the variances discussed here make direct use of the most likely cost drivers or revenue drivers that would be used in activity-based costing, such as measuring direct labor hours for a rate variance. Measuring performance against operational goals can take a variety of forms, and here,

Figure 1C-14 DL Variance with Multiple Materials and Multiple Types of Labor

	Class III DL	Class II DL	Total DL
Actual DL cost	$216,600	$163,770	$380,370
DL rate variance			
Actual direct labor hours	15,200	10,300	
Standard labor rate	$14.00	$16.00	
Actual labor rate (cost/hours)	− $14.25	− $15.90	
Rate variance per hour	($.25) U	$.10 F	
× Actual direct labor hours	× 15,200	× 10,300	
Labor rate variance	($3,800) U	$1,030 F	($2,770) U
Actual labor hours at standard rate	$212,800	$164,800	$377,600
DL substitution variance			
Class III standard labor rate		$14.00	
Class II standard labor rate		− $16.00	
Substitution rate variance per hour		($2.00) U	
× Actual direct labor hours		× 10,300	
Labor substitution variance		($20,600) U	($20,600) U
Actual labor hours at Class III standard rate	$212,800	$144,200	$357,000
DL variance from substandard materials (Supplier B)			
Units produced—alternative materials	4,800	3,200	
Labor standard per unit	× 1.2	× 1.2	
Standard hours allowed	5,760	3,840	
Actual hours	− 6,600	− 4,400	
Saved/(excess) hours	(840)	(560)	
× Class III standard rate	× $14.00	× $14.00	
Substandard materials labor variance	($11,760) U	($7,840) U	($19,600) U
Subtotal labor costs after substandard materials	$201,040	$136,360	$337,400
DL efficiency variance on regular materials (Supplier A)			
Units produced—regular materials	7,200	4,800	
Labor standard per unit	× 1.2	× 1.2	
Standard hours allowed	8,640	5,760	
Actual hours	− 8,600	− 5,900	
Saved/(excess) hours	40	(140)	
× Class III standard rate	× $14.00	× $14.00	
Labor efficiency variance on regular materials	$560 F	($1,960) U	($1,400) U
Flexible budget labor costs	$201,600	$134,400	$336,000
Total direct labor variances (Flexible − Actual)	($15,000) U	($29,370) U	($44,370) U

measuring performance was based mostly on manufacturing costs. However, other performance measures are based on revenue, nonmanufacturing costs, and profit, depending on the type of unit being measured.

Using Variance Analysis in Nonmanufacturing Organizations

Although the previous discussion focuses on calculating variances in a manufacturing organization, the concepts can also be applied to service industries, with minor modifications. Typically, in a service industry setting, the material price and usage variances are less significant, because direct materials constitute a very small percentage of total costs for firms in service industry. Consequently, the labor and overhead variances are more important. For example, in a hospital, the hours and costs of various categories of labor (e.g., nurses, interns, general practitioners, surgeons, etc.) and overhead (e.g., medical equipment, support staff, etc.) are of greater importance. Therefore, variance analysis in a service company will focus mostly on direct labor and overhead variances.

Many firms in service industries have implemented activity-based costing systems by going through the process of identifying various cost drivers within the organization. This causes some components of fixed costs (such as setup, quality assurance, secretarial services, etc.) to become variable with respect to the appropriate cost drivers. Analysis of the flexible budget could easily be extended to service companies to provide a more accurate benchmark against which to compare actual costs.

Furthermore, while the production volume variance is applicable to manufacturing companies, it has limited applicability to service companies, which have little or no production activity. However, certain service industries have developed their own well-accepted measures of production, such as the use of revenue passenger mile (RPM) or available seat mile (ASM) in the airline industry. Production volume variances can be modified to use these measures instead of units of output.

Knowledge Check: Cost and Variance Measures

The next questions are intended to help you check your understanding and recall of the material presented in this topic. They do not represent the type of questions that appear on the CMA exam.

Directions: Answer each question in the space provided. Correct answers and section references appear after the knowledge check questions.

1. The purpose of a flexible budget is to:
   - ☐ **a.** provide management with slack in their budget.
   - ☐ **b.** eliminate fluctuations in production reports.
   - ☐ **c.** compare actual and budgeted results at various levels of activity.
   - ☐ **d.** make the annual budget process more efficient.

2. Which variance would be added to the flexible budget variance to arrive at the total static budget variance?
   - ☐ **a.** Efficiency variance
   - ☐ **b.** Price variance
   - ☐ **c.** Sales mix variance
   - ☐ **d.** Sales volume variance

3. What is meant by the term *management by exception*?

4. What is the formula for calculating total fixed overhead variance?
   - ☐ **a.** Total Fixed Overhead Variance = Actual Fixed Overhead − Budgeted Fixed Overhead
   - ☐ **b.** Total Fixed Overhead Variance = Actual Fixed Overhead − Applied Fixed Overhead
   - ☐ **c.** Total Fixed Overhead Variance = Budgeted Fixed Overhead − Applied Fixed Overhead
   - ☐ **d.** Total Fixed Overhead Variance = Budgeted Fixed Overhead − Actual Fixed Overhead

5. Combo Company uses a standard cost system. Information for raw materials for Product #4 for the month of June is shown next:

Standard price per pound of raw materials	$1.60
Actual purchase price per pound of raw materials	$1.55
Actual quantity of raw materials purchased	2,000 pounds
Actual quantity of raw materials used	1,900 pounds
Standard quantity allowed for actual production	1,800 pounds

What is the materials purchase price variance?

- a. $90 favorable
- b. $90 unfavorable
- c. $100 favorable
- d. $100 unfavorable

6. Craig Corporation has provided the following data concerning its direct labor costs for January:

Standard wage rate	$13.30 per direct labor hour (DLH)
Standard hours	5.5 DLHs per unit
Actual wage rate	$13.20 per DLH
Actual hours	45,880 DLHs
Actual output	8,400 units

The labor rate variance for January would be:

- a. $4,588 unfavorable
- b. $4,588 favorable
- c. $4,620 unfavorable
- d. $4,620 favorable

7. The following labor standards have been established for product T3:

Standard labor hours per unit of output	5.0 hours
Standard labor rate	$18.25 per hour

The following data are for product T3 for the month of July:

Actual hours worked	9,800 hours
Actual total labor cost	$176,400
Actual output	1,900 units

What is the labor efficiency variance for the month?

- a. $3,025 unfavorable
- b. $5,400 unfavorable
- c. $3,025 favorable
- d. $5,475 unfavorable

Knowledge Check Answers: Cost and Variance Measures

1. The purpose of a flexible budget is to: [See **Characteristics of Flexible Budgets**.]
    - ☐ a. provide management with slack in their budget.
    - ☐ b. eliminate fluctuations in production reports.
    - ☑ c. compare actual and budgeted results at various levels of activity.
    - ☐ d. make the annual budget process more efficient.

2. Which variance would be added to the flexible budget variance to arrive at the total static budget variance? [See **Flexible Budget Variance and Sales Volume Variance**.]
    - ☐ a. Efficiency variance
    - ☐ b. Price variance
    - ☐ c. Sales mix variance
    - ☑ d. Sales volume variance

3. What is meant by the term *management by exception*? [See **Management by Exception**.]

    When using a management by exception approach, managers focus their attention on results that are different from what was expected. This approach assumes that results that meet expectations do not require investigation.

4. What is the formula for calculating total fixed overhead variance? [See **Variances for Fixed Overhead**.]
    - ☐ a. Total Fixed Overhead Variance = Actual Fixed Overhead − Budgeted Fixed Overhead
    - ☑ b. Total Fixed Overhead Variance = Actual Fixed Overhead − Applied Fixed Overhead
    - ☐ c. Total Fixed Overhead Variance = Budgeted Fixed Overhead − Applied Fixed Overhead
    - ☐ d. Total Fixed Overhead Variance = Budgeted Fixed Overhead − Actual Fixed Overhead

5. Combo Company uses a standard cost system. Information for raw materials for Product #4 for the month of June is shown next. [See **Price (Rate) Variances for Direct Costs**.]

Standard price per pound of raw materials	$1.60
Actual purchase price per pound of raw materials	$1.55
Actual quantity of raw materials purchased	2,000 pounds
Actual quantity of raw materials used	1,900 pounds
Standard quantity allowed for actual production	1,800 pounds

What is the materials purchase price variance?

- ☐ a. $90 favorable
- ☐ b. $90 unfavorable
- ☑ c. $100 favorable
- ☐ d. $100 unfavorable

Solution:

Materials Price Variance = Actual Quantity Purchased × (Actual Price − Standard Price)
Materials Price Variance = 2,000 × ($1.55 − $1.60)
Materials Price Variance = $100 Favorable

6. Craig Corporation has provided the following data concerning its direct labor costs for January: [See *Price and Efficiency Variances for Direct Labor and Direct Material Inputs*.]

Standard wage rate	$13.30 per direct labor hour (DLH)
Standard hours	5.5 DLHs per unit
Actual wage rate	$13.20 per DLH
Actual hours	45,880 DLHs
Actual output	8,400 units

The labor rate variance for January would be:

- ☐ a. $4,588 unfavorable
- ☑ b. $4,588 favorable
- ☐ c. $4,620 unfavorable
- ☐ d. $4,620 favorable

Solution:

Labor Rate Variance = Actual Hours × (Actual Rate − Standard Rate)
Labor Rate Variance = 45,880 × ($13.20 − $13.30)
Labor Rate Variance = $4,588 Favorable

7. The following labor standards have been established for product T3: [See *Efficiency (Quantity or Usage) Variances for Direct Costs*.]

Standard labor hours per unit of output	5.0 hours
Standard labor rate	$18.25 per hour

The following data are for product T3 for the month of July:

Actual hours worked	9,800 hours
Actual total labor cost	$176,400
Actual output	1,900 units

What is the labor efficiency variance for the month?

- [ ] a. $3,025 unfavorable
- [ ] b. $5,400 unfavorable
- [ ] c. $3,025 favorable
- [x] d. $5,475 unfavorable

Solution:

Standard Hours = Standard Hours per Unit × Actual Output

Standard Hours = 5 × 1,900 = 9,500

Labor Efficiency Variance = Standard Rate × (Actual Hours − Standard Hours)

= $18.25 × (9,800 − 9,500) = $5,475 Unfavorable

TOPIC 2

Responsibility Centers and Reporting Segments

A CENTRALIZED ORGANIZATION ALLOWS MANAGERS very little freedom to make decisions. In contrast, a decentralized organization spreads decision making to managers at different responsibility center levels. A responsibility center, also called a strategic business unit (SBU), is any portion of a business that grants the center's manager responsibility over costs, profits, revenues, or investments.

This topic covers different types of responsibility centers, including cost centers, profit centers, and investment centers. Reporting segments and contribution reporting are also discussed in this topic.

> **READ** the Learning Outcome Statements (LOS) for this topic as found in Appendix A and then study the concepts and calculations presented here to be sure you understand the content you could be tested on in the CMA exam.

Types of Responsibility Centers

Responsibility accounting is a method of defining segments or subunits in an organization as types of responsibility centers based on their level of autonomy and the responsibilities of their managers, and then basing performance evaluations on these factors. Responsibility centers are classified by their primary effect on the company as a whole. Revenue or profit centers sell their product or service to outside customers, generating revenues. Cost centers provide service to other parts of the organization and are not responsible for generating revenue through sales to outside customers. However, a cost center such as a service department may generate some revenues, but the department usually has a net cost. Investment centers not only generate revenues but also have authority on making investments.

Revenue Centers

Revenue centers are responsible for sales but not for the manufacturing costs of the sales. A revenue center obtains products from either a cost center or a profit center (discussed below). Revenue centers are evaluated on their ability to provide a contribution: sales less the direct revenue center costs. They are not responsible for the costs of the items obtained from cost or profit centers. A captive marketing division of a corporation would be an example of a revenue center.

Cost Centers

A manager for a **cost center** is responsible for controlling costs in a department that generates little or no revenue. Therefore, the manager is not responsible for revenue or investments but is rewarded whenever he or she can minimize costs while maintaining an expected level of quality. Finance, administration, human resources, accounting, customer service, and help desks are all examples of cost centers. If the cafeteria is not expected to make a profit, it is also a cost center. Even plants and manufacturing facilities sometimes are considered cost centers, assuming that the profit center would then be the sales department or a different production department.

Common costs are allocated among all cost centers involved in proportion to the amounts of a selected cost driver. Managers of cost centers usually are responsible for direct material and labor efficiency variances as well as the variable overhead variance. Removing unfavorable variances and analyzing favorable variances are often part of the manager's responsibility.

Profit Centers

Profit centers are responsible for both costs and revenues. Since profit is a function of both revenue and costs, a manager for a profit center is responsible for generating profits, managing revenue, and controlling costs. Managers of these departments usually do not have control over investments. Profit centers are often separate reporting segments. A grocery store that is part of a chain of stores could be a profit center and a separate reporting segment. Managers of profit centers would be evaluated based on actual profits versus expected profits.

Investment Centers

Managers for **investment centers** are responsible for investments, costs, and revenues in their department. Investment centers can be centered primarily on internal or external investments. Internal investment managers are responsible for reviewing and approving capital budgeting and other investments, such as in research and development. External investment managers are responsible for reviewing and approving temporary and long-term investments for capital maintenance, return on investment, and strategic investments. Managers in such centers would be evaluated not only by the center's profit but by relating the profit to its invested capital.

Strategic investments would be evaluated for their fit with company strategy, while other investments would be judged on their return on investment and preservation of capital.

For example: Consider an office supply store. If there is an employee cafeteria, it is probably a cost center, responsible only for controlling the costs of the cafeteria. Each product line, such as printers, is a revenue center, responsible to account for the revenues from the product line's sales. Each department is a profit center, such as paper supplies, which accounts for the revenues and the expenses (i.e., the profitability) of that department. Finally, each store is an investment center, responsible for the revenues and expenses and also for the capital project budgets and the assets and liabilities of the store.

Contribution and Segment Reporting

Managing the performance of the various responsibility centers depends on an analysis of their costs and revenue contributions to the organization. Two approaches that are used to aid in this type of analysis are contribution reporting and segment reporting.

Contribution Reporting

The contribution approach to reporting on an income statement is useful for internal decision making. It separates fixed from variable expenses, deducting variable expenses first to arrive at the contribution margin and then deducting fixed expenses to arrive at net operating income. The **contribution margin** is the amount that contributes toward fixed expenses and profits. The contribution margin shows managers how profits are affected by changes in volume, because fixed costs and operating capacity are kept constant.

The primary advantage of such an income statement format is that profit center managers can view the costs by their behavior (e.g., fixed or variable) instead of by departments, such as sales, administration, and production (cost of goods sold). Managers can use a contribution income statement when analyzing product lines and when deciding on prices for goods, whether to expand a segment or discontinue it, or whether to make or buy a good.

Evaluating a contribution margin report often involves the use of cost-volume-profit (CVP) ratios such as the contribution margin, the contribution margin ratio, and breakeven sales in dollars. Alternatively, a balanced scorecard is a more comprehensive tool used in evaluating performance.

Management performance can be evaluated more easily using a contribution income statement because the items outside managers' control are separated from the items within their control. However, many fixed costs are controllable, so managers often have their fixed costs further divided into controllable fixed costs and uncontrollable fixed costs. Controllable fixed costs are those that can be changed within a year; uncontrollable costs take over a year to influence. Uncontrollable fixed costs can also come from a nonnegotiable corporate allocation of headquarters expenses. The controllable margin is the contribution margin less the controllable fixed costs.

Figure 1C-15 shows two versions of the same income statement, in traditional and contribution formats. If a prior period's statement showed that the uncontrollable fixed production costs were rising and the variable production costs were falling, a traditional statement would not show this fact, but the contribution format could show that the manager has been successful at keeping costs relatively the same even in the face of rising fixed costs outside his or her control. Note also that the traditional income statement's cost of goods sold, selling, and administrative costs include both fixed and variable expenses, but there is no way to determine how the amounts are broken down.

Figure 1C-15 Income Statements in Traditional versus Contribution Format

Traditional Approach (Costs Organized by Function)			Contribution Approach (Costs Organized by Behavior)		
Sales		$31,200	Sales		$31,200
Less cost of goods sold		15,600	Less variable expenses:		
Gross margin		$15,600	Variable production	$5,200	
Less operating expenses:			Variable selling expenses	1,560	
Selling expenses	$8,060		Variable admin. expenses	1,040	$7,800
Administrative expenses	4,940	$13,000	Contribution margin		$23,400
Net operating income		$2,600	Less fixed expenses:		
			Fixed production	$10,400	
			Fixed selling	6,500	
			Fixed administrative	3,900	$ 20,800
			Net operating income		$2,600

Segment Reporting

Reporting segments are portions of a business divided for reporting purposes along product lines, geographical areas, or other meaningful segments to provide individual information about that area. *For example:* Consider a grocery chain. Each store is a segment. Also, if the accounting and decision-making systems evaluate product lines separately, each product line (such as produce, dairy, meats, etc.) is a segment as well.

Segmented financial statements are the same as nonsegmented statements except that each segment has its own costs traced back to it so that the report shows how profitable each segment is by itself. The **segment margin** is the segment's contribution margin less all traceable fixed costs for the segment. The segment margin is a useful indication of a segment's profitability. If it is not positive, the segment may need to be discontinued unless it adds value to other segments.

Traceable fixed costs that are included in a segment's margin are costs that would not exist were it not for the segment. Administrative salaries for segment managers are an example of a fixed cost that can be traced directly to a segment. Similarly, building maintenance costs or insurance premiums for a specific business segment can be traced to the segment.

Common Cost Allocation

Unlike traceable fixed costs, common fixed costs (such as the chief executive's salary) cannot be traced to a specific department because they are shared costs and must be apportioned between two or more departments using some allocation basis that may or may not provide an accurate allocation. Additionally, common costs are often uncontrollable to some extent by the department manager who is held responsible for the cost and thus make it more difficult to determine the profitability of an individual segment. A **common cost** is any cost that is shared by two or more segments or entities. When common costs are allocated to segments, the value of the segment margin on reporting profitability is diluted; therefore some businesses allocate common costs to segments only when all or most of the cost would disappear if the segment were to be discontinued. Two methods of allocating common costs are the stand-alone method and the incremental method.

Stand-alone cost allocation is a method that determines the relative proportion of cost driver for each party that shares a common cost and allocates the costs by those percentages.

For example: Company A has a new plant and an older plant, but both plants require some workers to be given on-site training. The traveling trainer's salary of $60,000 plus $10,000 travel and lodging expenses can be allocated based on the number of users who need to be trained at each location or some other cost driver, such as days spent at each location. If the old plant has 40 trainees and the new plant has 60 trainees, the old plant would receive $28,000 of the cost (40%) and the new plant would receive $42,000 of the cost. This method has the benefit of fairness and is easy to implement.

Incremental cost allocation is a method that allocates costs by ranking the parties by a primary user and incremental users, or those users who add an additional cost due to the fact that there is now more than one user of the cost.

For example: Company A, just described, hires a trainer because the new plant is being opened. The trainer is based in the new plant's city, so the new plant is the primary user of the trainer's time. If the trainer works at the new plant for three quarters of the time and at the old plant for one quarter of the time, the new plant is allocated $45,000 of the costs, while the old plant is allocated the remaining $15,000 plus all $10,000 of the travel expenses because these are an incremental cost of having the trainer relocate to serve the incremental user.

Conversely, if management wanted to reduce start-up costs for the new plant, it could choose to designate the old plant as the primary user and allocate only a small amount of the costs to the new plant. Because this method allows managers to manipulate how costs are allocated, it is not as balanced as the stand-alone method.

Also, when common costs are allocated in this manner, most of the segments want to be incremental users, so this method can cause interdepartmental contention.

Transfer Pricing Models

Allocating costs to a responsibility center or segment involves assigning pricing for the goods and services that pass between segments. **Transfer pricing** sets prices for internally exchanged goods and services. An **intermediate product** is a good or service that is transferred between two segments of a company. Company strategy is greatly affected by choice of transfer prices. If the company wants the business units to behave independently and keep managers motivated to achieve company goals, transfer prices should be set at arm's length, as if the party were any other external client. When no external suppliers or customers exist for a product or service, the arm's-length price (an impartial or fair market price) is more difficult to determine than simply checking market prices. The amounts set for transfer prices require cooperation among many departments, including finance, production, marketing, and tax planning.

Firms that have a high degree of vertical integration will need to set transfer prices carefully. For example, a corporation that owns farms, food warehouses, distributors, and grocery stores will need to set prices for each service that will be considered fair by all segments and also allow each portion of the business to be financially flexible.

Four models that can be used to set transfer prices are market price, negotiated price, variable cost, and full cost. Firms often combine various methods (dual pricing) to match their needs.

Market Price Model

The market price model is a true arm's-length model because it sets the price for a good or service at going market prices. This model can be used only when an item has a market; items such as work-in-process inventory may not have a market price. The market price model keeps business units autonomous, forces the selling unit to be competitive with external suppliers, and is preferred by tax authorities. Businesses that use this model should account for the reduced selling and marketing costs in the price.

Negotiated Price Model

The negotiated price model sets the transfer price through negotiation between the buyer and the seller. When different business units experience conflicts, negotiation or even arbitration may be needed to keep the company as a whole functioning efficiently. Negotiated prices can make both buying and selling units less autonomous.

Variable Cost Model

The variable cost model sets transfer prices at the unit's variable cost, or the actual cost to produce the good or service less all fixed costs. This method will lower the selling unit's profits and increase the buying unit's profits due to the low price. This model is advantageous for selling units that have excess capacity or for situations when a buying unit could purchase from external sources but the company wants to encourage internal purchases. Among the disadvantages of this method is the fact that it is not viewed favorably by tax authorities because it lowers the profits, and thereby taxes, for the location where the product was manufactured.

Full Cost (Absorption) Model

The full cost (absorption) model starts with the seller's variable cost for the item and then allocates fixed costs to the price. Some companies allocate standard fixed costs because this allows the buying unit to know the cost in advance and keeps the seller from becoming too inefficient due to a captive buyer that pays for the inefficiencies. Adding fixed costs is relatively straightforward and fair. However, it can alter a business unit's decision making.

Although fixed costs should not be included in the decision to purchase items internally or externally, often managers will purchase the "lower-cost" external item even though the internal fixed costs still will be incurred.

To illustrate: Hopkins Company has two operating divisions, North and South. One of the products of the North division is a raw material used in the South division. Income statements for the two divisions, excluding interdivisional operations, are shown in Figure 1C-16.

Figure 1C-16 North and South Division Income Statements

	North Division (30% Tax Rate)	North Division (40% Tax Rate)	Total Both Divisions
Sales			
10,000 units × $15 per unit	$ 150,000	–	$ 150,000
20,000 units × $18 per unit	–	$ 360,000	$ 360,000
Total sales	$ 150,000	$ 360,000	$ 510,000
Expenses			
Variable:			
10,000 units × $7 per unit	$ 70,000	–	$ 70,000
20,000 units × $10 per unit	–	$ 200,000	$ 200,000
Fixed:	50,000	65,000	$ 115,000
Total expenses	$ 120,000	$ 265,000	$ 385,000
Operating income	$ 30,000	$ 95,000	$ 125,000

Under the market price model, assuming that the North division is currently operating at full capacity and can sell all of the products it can produce, North will sell one unit to South for $15 (the price at which all products of North are sold).

Under the negotiated price model, assuming there is some excess capacity in the North division, if North sells to South at the market price ($15), South may prefer to purchase from an outside vendor, and company profit may not be maximized.

Therefore, North and South may negotiate a price between $15 (the market price) and $7 (the variable cost), which will provide some contribution toward North's fixed costs and contribute to overall company profits.

Under the variable cost model, North will sell to South at a price of $7 per unit (the variable costs).

Under the full cost (absorption) model, at this level of production and sales, North will sell to South at a price of $12 per unit ($7 variable plus $5 fixed costs per unit).

Choosing Transfer Price Models

In general, the market price method is preferred in situations when the market price for a good or service is available. When a market price is not available, the negotiated price method is preferred. When neither is acceptable, companies may turn to one of the cost models. Cost-based methods are not recommended because they can lead to motivation problems between parties such as the seller not actively controlling costs because they are simply passed on to the buyer.

The logic of choosing a transfer price model and setting transfer prices starts with a make-or-buy decision. If there are outside suppliers for a product or service, the market price model should be used. The company should compare the selling unit's variable costs to the market price for the external substitute. If the external market price is lower than the internal variable cost, the buyer should purchase externally to motivate the internal supplier to find ways to lower costs.

When the internal variable cost is less than the external market price, the buying unit should purchase internally, as long as the selling unit has excess capacity. The variable cost model is best for low capacity, and the market price model is best for high capacity. If the selling unit is at full capacity, the buying unit should purchase externally, as long as the selling unit can generate more profit from a sale to an external source than will be lost if the buying unit pays the external market price for the item. When the opposite is true, the buying unit should purchase internally and pay market price for the item.

Reporting of Organizational Segments

Performance measurement reports for various organizational segments are created for internal use and are focused on providing the information management needs to address problems and design improvements.

Performance Measurement Reports

Performance measurement reports should be tailored to the audience and level of management to which they are directed. Too much information can cloud an issue as easily as not enough information can, so the amount and timing of information delivery is critical to the success of each manager. Timing of performance measurement reports such as variance reports is critical; the information must be relevant for it to be useful. However, if a manager is flooded with information and cannot discern which information is important, reporting may be too frequent.

Effective performance measures lead to a desired strategic result by causing the manager and other employees to strive for organizational goals, simultaneously maximizing company goals and individual goals. The objectives of a performance evaluation system include:

- Goal congruence (e.g., aligning the individual's goals with those of the organization)
- Clear communication of expectations
- Opportunities to motivate the individual to perform in a way that will maximize organizational goals
- Providing communication between the individual and the organization
- Articulation of the organization's benchmarks

Improper motivation can occur when feedback is ineffective or when benchmarks are improperly matched with cost and/or revenue drivers of an operation, causing organizations to be counterproductive. Each performance measure selected needs to have these elements:

- A time period for performance measurement (e.g., view one year's results or several years' results simultaneously)
- Common definitions for items (e.g., assets are defined as total assets available regardless of function or usage)
- Definitions of specific measurement units used (e.g., historical cost, current cost)
- A target level of performance for each performance measure and each segment
- A feedback timing schedule (e.g., feedback supplied daily, weekly, quarterly)

Multinational Company Performance Measurement

The nonfinancial differences among countries—in economy, laws, customs, and politics—should play a part in evaluating a foreign division's results.

Multinational companies must account for additional concerns, such as how tariffs, exchange rates, taxes, currency restrictions, expropriation risk, and the availability and relative cost of materials and skills could affect performance evaluations. The use of transfer pricing by multinationals to gain tax and income advantages can conflict with the use of transfer pricing to evaluate performance or to create performance incentives.

For example: Some pharmaceutical companies produce their goods in Puerto Rico and sell the majority of the product in the mainland United States. Because Puerto Rico has a relatively lower tax status than the rest of the United States, the incentive is for the pharmaceutical company to charge the highest transfer price possible for drugs sold to their U.S. divisions (such as market price), thus retaining the profits in the territory that has a lower tax rate. Because the Puerto Rican subsidiary essentially has a captive market, it may not be as efficient as overall corporate management would like.

Conversely, if the producing country has relatively higher taxes than the primary country in which sales occur, the incentive will be to charge the lowest price possible (such as cost) for the goods so that the profits end up in the selling-country division. The resulting performance could be that the producing country fails to meet total demand. Also, if the price is actual cost, the producer will not have any incentive to control those costs because they are merely transferred to the other division. One solution to such a dilemma is to use standard costs instead of actual costs. (The standard could be made more stringent over time through continuous improvement efforts.) Another solution is to change the accountability structure of the segments, making them more centralized if decentralized transfer prices fail to create the desired incentives.

As with any performance evaluation, a multinational company should focus on separating controllable from noncontrollable costs, basing assessments only on costs that can be affected by the managers' choices. If a foreign currency becomes devalued, this will affect profits but is outside management's control. When foreign governments impose trade restrictions, such as tariffs, the performance measurement should take into account the reduced profits from such sources. When managers in foreign countries keep their books in a foreign country's currency, their supervisors should consider the effects of currency fluctuations, inflation, and differences in relative purchasing power in the foreign country. For example, a country with lower costs of labor and goods will also have to price goods for sale in that country much lower than in a country where labor and goods are more costly.

However, because performance evaluations should provide incentives for managers to improve overall operations, it is important to determine if any portion of a noncontrollable event actually could have been prevented or deflected. For example, if managers know they will not be held accountable for a devalued currency, they may not be as quick to move funds out of the country as if they were accountable for a portion of such losses. Managers evaluated in such a fashion might employ market analysts or economists specializing in currency exchange to help forecast such changes.

Another way of enhancing the value of performance measurement is by using benchmark values from other managers or companies in similar local environments. Each distinct area would have its own comparison group, which would provide an opportunity to evaluate performance across companies.

Finally, because profits can be so distorted by various international issues, performance evaluations could avoid focusing on profit and instead focus on more stable indicators, such as revenues, market share, or operating costs.

Knowledge Check: Responsibility Centers and Reporting Segments

The next questions are intended to help you check your understanding and recall of the material presented in this topic. They do not represent the type of questions that appear on the CMA exam.

Directions: Answer each question in the space provided. Correct answers and section references appear after the knowledge check questions.

1. Which of the following responsibility centers usually makes a manager responsible for all financial business decisions?
   - a. Revenue center
   - b. Cost center
   - c. Investment center
   - d. Profit center

2. Which of the following transfer pricing models sets prices at actual cost less all fixed costs?
   - a. Variable cost
   - b. Full cost (absorption)
   - c. Market price
   - d. Negotiated price

3. Match each of term to its corresponding description by drawing a line between them.

Term	Description
Common cost	Allows reporting based on product line or geographic location
Contribution margin	Shows how profits are affected by changes in volume
Incremental cost allocation	May allow managers to manipulate how costs are allocated
Segment reporting	Any cost that is shared by two or more segments or entities

Knowledge Check Answers: Responsibility Centers and Reporting Segments

1. Which of the following responsibility centers usually makes a manager responsible for all financial business decisions? **[See *Investment Centers*.]**
   - ☐ a. Revenue center
   - ☐ b. Cost center
   - ☒ c. Investment center
   - ☐ d. Profit center

2. Which of the following transfer pricing models sets prices at actual cost less all fixed costs? **[See *Variable Cost Model*.]**
   - ☒ a. Variable cost
   - ☐ b. Full cost (absorption)
   - ☐ c. Market price
   - ☐ d. Negotiated price

3. Match each of term to its corresponding description by drawing a line between them. (Correct matches of term and description are shown here.) **[See *Contribution and Segment Reporting*.]**

Term	Description
Common cost	Any cost that is shared by two or more segments or entities
Contribution margin	Shows how profits are affected by changes in volume
Incremental cost allocation	May allow managers to manipulate how costs are allocated
Segment reporting	Allows reporting based on product line or geographic location

TOPIC 3

Performance Measures

PROFITABILITY ANALYSES MEASURE THE RELATIVE success or failure of a company over a period. A variety of measures can be used to help an organization analyze the performance of specific products, business units, and customers. In addition to discussions of product, business unit, and customer profitability analysis, this topic covers performance analysis techniques, including return on investment, residual income, and balanced scorecard.

> **READ** the Learning Outcome Statements (LOS) for this topic as found in Appendix A and then study the concepts and calculations presented here to be sure you understand the content you could be tested on in the CMA exam.

Product Profitability Analysis

Product profitability analysis shows which products are the most profitable, which need to have their prices and costs reevaluated, and which should get the greatest amount of marketing and support attention. Product line managers often use a product profitability analysis as the basis for compensation or bonuses.

Product lines that are unprofitable in the long run will be discontinued. When determining whether to discontinue a product line, the first step is to remove from the analysis all per-unit fixed costs that would not be eliminated if the product line were discontinued. The product profitability analysis sums up the benefits of removing all fixed costs that are traceable to the affected unit, plus all variable costs for the unit. Then the analysis sums up the opportunity cost of all sales that would be lost if the product line were discontinued. The difference between these amounts is the increase or decrease in profit that would occur from discontinuing the product line.

For example: If Bounce Sporting Goods had a profitable tennis ball line and an unprofitable racquet ball line, the racquet ball line could be analyzed to determine what effect removing it would have on company profits. In Figure 1C-17, the contribution margin for both product lines shows a positive amount of profit. However, after traceable costs are allocated to each department, the racquet ball department shows a loss. Note that all common costs are deducted only from the total amount for the entire company, so these costs do not play a part in management's decision to discontinue the operation.

Figure 1C-17 Profitability Analysis for Bounce Sporting Goods

	Tennis Balls	Racquet Balls	Total
Last year's sales	$780,000	$195,000	$975,000
Relevant costs			
Variable cost	585,000	175,500	760,500
Contribution margin	$195,000	$19,500	$214,500
Other relevant costs (traceable)			
Advertising	19,500	26,000	45,500
Contribution after all relevant costs	$175,500	$(6,500)	$169,000
Nonrelevant costs (not traceable)			
Fixed cost			100,000
Net income with racquet balls			$69,000

In addition to financial measures, a product line profitability analysis needs to analyze how the line affects overall company strategy. These questions illustrate types of nonfinancial considerations:

- How will dropping the product line affect company morale?
- If the product line is dropped, how will sales of related product lines be affected?
- Is the product line used as a component of another, moreprofitable product?
- Would investing more resources into marketing and sales increase product profitability?
- Could the product become more profitable in the long run?
- Would increasing the price of the product increase profitability or just lower sales even more?

Business Unit Profitability Analysis

A business unit, often referred to as a **strategic business unit** or SBU, is an entity or operating unit within a larger organization. An SBU has its own business strategy and objectives, which may differ from that of its parent organization.

Business unit profitability analysis is measured using contribution margin, direct profit, controllable profit, income before taxes, or net income.

For example: Figure 1C-18 shows how an income statement could be formed to include these measures for a business unit.

Figure 1C-18 Business Unit Income Statement

Sales revenue	$780,000
Variable expenses	585,000
Contribution margin	195,000
Fixed expenses controllable by the profit center	19,500
Direct/controllable profit	175,500
Corporate charges allocated to the SBU	52,500
Income before taxes	123,000
Taxes	49,200
Net income	$73,800

Contribution Margin

Contribution margin measures the difference between revenue and variable expenses. It is useful for management performance analysis because it eliminates the fixed expenses that are perceived to be beyond the manager's control. However, not all fixed expenses are uncontrollable, so focusing on contribution margin can lead a manager to ignore possible cost reductions. Furthermore, even fixed costs that cannot be altered still must be managed for efficient use—for example, maintaining and improving performance standards for salaried employees.

Direct/Controllable Profit

Direct profit is the business unit's contribution margin less its fixed costs. Direct profit does not include fixed costs common to the organization as a whole. Managers evaluated using this measure may be content with a lower level of success than if common costs were also deducted from the measurement. This is the metric that should be used for the SBU's performance. Because corporate charges are beyond SBU management control, they should not be considered when measuring SBU performance.

Income Before Taxes

Income before taxes deducts all costs for a business unit other than taxes. However, using this measure makes the business unit manager seem accountable for costs that are not under the manager's control, such as the costs of the human resources department that are allocated to the business unit. Therefore, care must be exercised in conducting evaluations in this way. One advantage of using this measure is that the manager will have a realistic view of the level of profitability needed to make the business unit a successful part of the company, and thereby would affect its pricing and productivity decisions. The amount can be compared easily to the profitability of competitors. Managers rewarded for maintaining profitability in the face of all overhead may make better long-term decisions, such as decisions related to product mix and marketing.

Net Income

Net income is income after taxes. Using net income has the same benefits and drawbacks as using income before taxes in profitability analysis. It also has other drawbacks: First, tax rates are often the same for each area, so there may be little benefit to examining this amount. Second, when tax rates differ, it is usually a result of corporate manipulation for tax purposes, a factor beyond the manager's control. Third, taxes and tax-related decisions are made at the corporate level, not at the SBU level. Net income measurement is useful in evaluating foreign business units because the different tax rates in each country affect overall profitability for a business unit.

Organizational policies can alter the net income of a business unit and a company. For example, choosing the first-in, first-out (FIFO) method of cost flow assumption in valuing inventories causes the oldest inventory prices to be included in cost of goods sold on the income statement and the newest prices to be included in the balance sheet's inventory. In times of rising prices, FIFO will provide a higher inventory valuation and a higher net income than the last-in, first-out (LIFO) method or the average method. Similarly, the choice of depreciation methods (e.g., straight-line, declining balance, and units-of-production) will yield different amounts of expense that will, in turn, yield different balances in net income. In addition, when two companies have chosen different inventory or depreciation methods, comparability is more difficult because the same operations will yield different balance sheet and income statement results.

Customer Profitability Analysis

Customer profitability analysis evaluates the costs and benefits of providing goods or services to a particular customer or customer segment. This analysis is undertaken to enhance the overall profitability of the organization. This cost management tool is relatively new, although it is increasingly popular. This analysis has two primary objectives: measuring customer profitability and identifying effective and ineffective customer-related activities and services.

Measuring profitability at the level of the customer involves determining the benefits received from the customer and the costs incurred to service the customer. The benefits include nonfinancial and financial measures. Nonfinancial measures include customer acquisition, customer retention, customer satisfaction, and overall market share. Financial measures usually can be collected on a customer level only if the company uses financial software that breaks out costs by customer. This feature is typically found in activity-based costing (ABC) software. The financial measures serve as a balance to a company that puts customers first in its strategy, because retaining customers even when the costs outweigh the revenues is a losing strategy. Sometimes organizations seek to increase market share and customer satisfaction without fully evaluating the costs of doing so. This leads organizations to spend significant resources to satisfy customers, often without knowing whether such efforts will be profitable. The customer profitability analysis will show when a customer demand should be satisfied, when it should be declined, and when it should include an additional fee for the service. At the extreme, the organization may decide to drop unprofitable customers or find ways to serve them while making a profit. Some academic studies have shown that for a typical business, only 20% of customers contribute to profits; the remaining 80% either break even or generate losses.

For strategic reasons, some customer demands will be satisfied even when they are not financially profitable, but an advanced financial management software system such as ABC would at least bring the cost issue to the attention of managers so that a long-term solution can be formed. The emphasis should be on transforming the unprofitable customer into a profitable customer. Lifetime profitability is one reason to retain customers that are initially unprofitable. If customers can be retained for the long term, the overall profits can be very positive.

For example: A real estate agent who spends time with a client trying to purchase a lower-cost home may not realize much profit on the sale, but the customer's lifetime repeat business could be significant. Similarly, an unprofitable customer would be retained if having that customer attracts or influences other, more profitable customers.

The other objective of performing customer profitability analysis is to identify effective and ineffective customer-related activities, to determine which ones to enhance or eliminate, and to determine how such decisions will affect profitability. Banks, for example, may use this method to determine the classes of customers that are profitable or unprofitable and then use that information in deciding on the location of their branches, effectively adding or dropping customers.

Return on Investment

Return on investment (ROI) measures profitability by dividing the net profit of the business unit by the investment in assets made to attain that income. ROI is also called the accounting rate of return or the accrual accounting rate of return.

The formula used by the ICMA for ROI is:

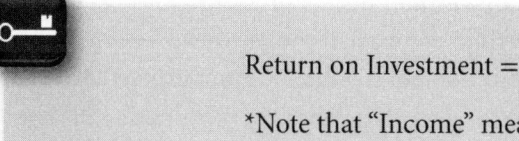

$$\text{Return on Investment} = \frac{\text{Income of a Business Unit}}{\text{Assets of a Business Unit}}$$

*Note that "Income" means operating income unless otherwise noted.

The formula used to calculate ROI may have many variations in regard to how to derive profit for the numerator and assets for the denominator. However, the formula shown here is the one that is tested on the CMA exam.

Although the timeline for the net profit and the investment in assets is not always equal—for example, investment in a bond in Year 1, with interest returns for the next five years—when comparing two or more investment opportunities, it is important that the time horizons be the same for each project so that a fair comparison can be made. When using ROI for a cost-benefit analysis, it is also important to account for any ongoing costs of the investment over the period that the benefits are tracked—that is, net benefit per year.

ROI can be measured for the short term (a single month or year) or the long term (e.g., investing in a computer system that will generate six years of benefits and six years of costs). However, when dealing with long-term analyses, using a discounted cash flow model will be more appropriate because such models take into account the time value of money.

Both the net profit and the assets of the business unit can be defined in different ways to measure different types of profitability, which are outlined in this topic.

ROI is a broad measure of what you get from what you put in. As mentioned earlier, the numerator and denominator of the ROI formula can be adapted in many different ways. How a particular company decides to calculate ROI may depend on industry conventions or internal company conventions. Knowing what figures were used to generate a ratio is the only way to be able to rely on those ratios. If the ratios for a firm are given without any context, it may be more reliable to generate ratios again, directly from the firm's financial statements. Doing this ensures that each ratio is computed using the same methodology and source data. Similarly, the disclosures to financial statements provide important information regarding what method the company used to, for example, account for inventory. Because of the various methods each firm may use, the results will not be comparable unless data is converted to a common methodology. For example, companies using LIFO for inventory valuation will report a FIFO equivalent in their disclosures, and this amount can be used when comparing results to another company also using FIFO.

ROI can be expressed as a percentage, and the greater the percentage, the greater the return on investment. ROI is a popular measure of profitability because it combines revenues, investments, and costs all in one figure. However, no financial ratio has meaning by itself; ROI should be used with other financial measures and should be compared to industry averages or to other possible investments.

For internal use, companies use various definitions of income (or profits) and investments. For external use, U. S. companies currently use generally accepted accounting principles (GAAP) definitions of each. However, both internal and external ratios may be hard to compare if the ratios were prepared using different methods of allocating common costs—that is, comparing ROI between business units.

When ROI uses average total assets in its investment denominator, it becomes **return on assets (ROA)**, which shows how successful a company is at making a profit using a given level of assets. Firms that are more efficient with their assets are more likely to be profitable.

When ROI uses ownership interest for the investment denominator, it is called **return on equity (ROE)**. ROE is calculated only for common equity because preferred stockholders have a set return that is the preferred dividend rate.

There is a relationship between ROE and ROA. In general, a company's ROE should be higher than its ROA, because this implies that the funds borrowed (e.g., at 9%) were reinvested to earn a higher rate of return (e.g., 15% ROE) than was used in borrowing the funds. A firm uses financial leverage to achieve this difference, which is called trading on the equity. Financial leverage is calculated as shown:

$$\text{Financial Leverage} = \frac{\text{Assets}}{\text{Equity}}$$

Having relatively more assets with relatively less equity increases the financial leverage ratio. From a shareholder's perspective, a higher financial leverage is preferred. For companies making profit above the financing costs, this would yield higher return on invested capital (equity). However, higher financial leverage also exposes the company to greater bankruptcy risk in situations when the company earns less than the interest costs. When revenues are increasing, profits for shareholders are multiplied. However, when revenues are decreasing, profits shrink at the same accelerated rate because interest costs must be paid regardless of profits.

For example: A sporting goods manufacturer analyzes ROI for two business units using operating income for income and net assets for investment:

Tennis ball business unit: income of $100,000; net assets of $400,000

$$\text{ROI} = \frac{\$100,000}{\$400,000} = 25\%$$

Racquet ball business unit: income of $60,000; net assets of $300,000

$$\text{ROI} = \frac{\$60,000}{\$300,000} = 20\%$$

Residual Income

Residual income (RI) is a dollar amount of income less a chosen required rate of return for an investment. The formula used by the ICMA for RI is:

Residual Income (RI) = Income of a Business Unit
− (Assets of Business Unit × Required Rate of Return)
*Note that "Income" means operating income unless otherwise noted.

The imputed cost of an investment (asset) is the required rate of return multiplied by the investment (asset), a measure of the opportunity cost of not being able to invest the funds elsewhere. Imputed costs attempt to add up the costs of an investment (asset) that are not always recognized under accrual accounting, such as the cost of raising capital, such as a 6% interest rate on long-term debt.

For example, assume that the same sporting goods manufacturer from the ROI example decided that the required rate of return for tennis balls was 10% but that the required rate of return for racquet balls was 12% due to greater risks involved in this business unit. The residual income of each business unit is calculated as shown:

$$\text{RI, tennis balls} = \$100,000 - (\$400,000 \times 0.1) = \$60,000$$

$$\text{RI, racquet balls} = \$60,000 - (\$300,000 \times 0.12) = \$24,000$$

RI implies that as long as the tennis ball unit earns more than $40,000 RI (0.1 × $400,000) and the racquet ball unit earns more than $36,000 RI (0.12 × $300,000), the sporting goods manufacturer should continue to invest in assets to grow these operations. Using RI instead of ROI makes managers aim for an actual dollar amount rather than a percentage.

Just as ROI can measure a specific business segment's returns, RI can be used for a business segment, in which case it uses segment income, segment investment, and a segment-specific required rate of return.

RI versus ROI

Financial ratios must be used in the context of the business and its industry. The nature of a company's business will affect how financial ratios such as ROI are perceived. For example, a particular industry may have lower average ROIs, and the market will view a slightly higher ROI favorably even though it is lower than ROIs for most industries. The maturity of the business also is considered; a firm in its first year of business is not expected to generate as high a return as an established business. Firms entering new markets must set their expectations appropriately. For example, a firm used to a particular ROI for its television division would have to use a different set of criteria for a new aerospace division. To get past these comparability issues, it is useful to compute the ratios for the company and for relevant benchmark firms (such as rivals) using the same methodology. Then the company can be compared to others at the same maturity level.

Focusing only on ROI is not a good general business policy. Instead, firms should take many factors into account, both financial and nonfinancial. Perhaps for business development reasons, a firm should take a low ROI project because it promises to add a new long-term client and therefore a long-term positive ROI.

When ROI is used as a primary performance evaluation tool, managers of business units with higher profits according to ROI may reject capital investments that do not promise as good or better an ROI than the rate being currently earned—even if the investment is strategically beneficial to the organization as a whole.

For example: If Bounce's tennis ball unit was considering purchasing a new machine for $100,000 that would produce additional revenue of $20,000, the ROI of 20% would lower the business unit's overall ROI of 25%:

$$\text{Tennis Ball Unit with Expansion} = \frac{\$100,000 + \$20,000}{\$400,000 + \$100,000} = 24\%$$

A manager compensated on ROI would be less likely to make this investment. Conversely, if the same situation used RI instead, the calculation is:

Tennis Ball Unit with Expansion = $120,000 − (0.1 × $500,000) = $70,000

Because RI increases with this investment, a manager compensated based on total RI would have the incentive to make this expansion. Assuming the expansion earns the revenue it promises to earn, the manager will be rewarded for increasing RI.

RI gives managers the incentive to select any project that generates returns above the required rate of return. However, RI is a flat dollar amount, so it is less useful for comparing business units of different sizes (using a percentage value). Also, large business units, even with poor efficiency, still will have a larger RI than a small business unit with good efficiency. Therefore, the measure tends to favor large business units over smaller ones. In contrast, ROI is a more robust measure in some ways because RI is very sensitive to the required rate of return and as the investments become larger, this sensitivity becomes more pronounced.

The objective of maximizing ROI may induce managers of highly profitable subunits to reject projects that, from the viewpoint of the organization as a whole, should be accepted. Such situations occur, as in the last example, when the subunit is operating at a higher ROI (22%) than the cost of capital for the organization (12%). In that case, a new project with an ROI of 18% would be beneficial to the organization but would be rejected by the subunit because it would reduce the overall ROI of the subunit. Conversely, a manager of an unprofitable subunit will accept projects that, from the viewpoint of the organization, should be rejected. Consider another subunit whose ROI is 8%, and the organization has a cost of capital of 12%. The manager of this subunit will accept a project with ROI of 10% even though it will yield a negative residual income for the organization. Generally, goal congruence between subunits and the organization is promoted by using RI rather than ROI as a measure of a manager's performance.

ROI and RI have similar problems. The maximization of either ROI or RI involves maximizing profits (maximizing sales while minimizing costs) and minimizing the investment base. Maximizing sales and minimizing costs promotes transfer price disputes among SBUs, because the transfer price is recorded as revenue to the seller and cost to the buyer. Cost minimization encourages SBUs to cut discretionary costs to maximize profits. The discretionary costs most likely to be cut in the short term are:

- Research and development
- Quality control
- Maintenance
- Human resource development
- Advertising and promotion

The cutting of such costs raises ROI or RI in the short run while creating long-term problems that could be quite detrimental to the SBU as well as to the overall organization.

Maximizing ROI or RI encourages SBU management to reduce the investment base by not replacing assets in need of replacement, not purchasing needed new assets or technology, or unwarranted disposal of assets. All of these actions tend to produce long-term problems.

Investment Base Issues

Using ROI and RI as performance measurement tools may present challenges when attempting to compare competing companies or various internal business units. This is due to the fact that organizations may use different approaches to measure their financial performance. Among the differences that may make these types of comparisons less useful are:

- Differing revenue and expense recognition policies
- Differing inventory measurement policies
- Possession of joint or shared assets between business units
- Differing choices on what to consider an asset and how to value those assets

Joint or shared assets are similar to other common costs that must be assigned to business units, as covered earlier in this section.

Balanced Scorecard

Traditionally, most companies focus the analysis of performance solely on financial measures. Although these measures are objective and quantitative, they are entirely historical in nature. Moreover, they are better at providing short-term forecasts than long-term ones. Although these lagging indicators are important in tracking what has been done, companies must now also focus on the leading indicators, or indicators of future success. The **balanced scorecard** (BSC) and similar holistic techniques provide this broader focus.

The BSC gives companies a simple tool that shows them specific financial and nonfinancial indicators. It is a strategic measurement and management system that translates a company's strategy into four balanced categories: Financial measures show the past performance of a firm; customer, internal business process, and learning and growth measures drive future financial performance.

BSC was created by Robert Kaplan and David Norton as a means of moving organizations away from concentrating solely on financial data. The objective is to focus simultaneously on financial information and on creating the abilities and intangible assets required for long-term growth. This is done by translating a company's strategy into specific measures within each category. Companies use the BSC as a management tool to:

- Clarify and communicate strategy
- Align individual and unit goals to strategy
- Link strategy to the budgeting process
- Get feedback for continuous strategy improvement

Key Performance Indicators for a Balanced Scorecard

To effectively develop its strategies, a firm needs to analyze its internal **strengths** and **weaknesses** and then analyze its external **opportunities** and **threats**. Combined, this effort is termed a **SWOT analysis**.

Strengths include the organization's core competencies, or skills the company performs especially well. Weaknesses are those characteristics that place the company at some disadvantage. Opportunities are chances to increase revenues or profits, and threats are elements in the company environment that may provide trouble for the company. Analysis of these factors helps a company determine its key performance indicators (KPIs).

KPIs are specific, measurable goals that must be met in order to achieve a firm's strategy. The BSC identifies KPIs and arranges them into the SWOT categories.

Figure 1C-19 presents an example of one company's KPIs.

Figure 1C-19 KPI Measurement

Factor	Key Performance Indicator	Measurement Examples
Financial	Sales	Sales forecast accuracy, return on sales, sales trends
	Liquidity	Asset, inventory, and receivables turnover; cash flow
	Profitability	ROI, residual income, economic value added
	Market value	Market value added, share price
Customer	Market share	Trade association analyses, market definitions
	Customer acquisition	Number of new customers, total sales to new customers
	Customer satisfaction	Customer returns, complaints, surveys
	Customer retention	Customer retention by category, percentage growth with existing customers
	Quality	Warranty expense
	Timeliness	Time from order to door, number of on-time deliveries
Internal business process	Productivity	Cycle time, effectiveness, efficiency, variances, scrap
	Quality	Defects, returns, scrap, rework, surveys, warranty
	Safety	Accidents, insurance claims, result of accidents
	Process time	Setup time, turnaround, lead time
	Brand management	Number of advertisements, surveys, new accounts
Learning and growth	Skill development	Training hours or trainees, skill improvement
	Motivation, empowerment	Suggestions per employee, suggestions implemented
	New products	New patents, number of design changes, research and development skills
	Competence	Employee turnover, experience, customer satisfaction
	Team performance	Surveys, number of gains shared with other teams, number of multi-team projects, percentage of shared incentives

After defining the KPIs, a measurement unit must be assigned to each one. According to Kaplan and Norton, "If you can't measure it, you can't manage it."

In developing KPIs, it is very possible that some measures may conflict with or be counterproductive to others. To avoid this, the BSC uses a process of integrating the KPIs into the firm's strategy.

Effective Use of a Balanced Scorecard

Once the KPIs and their measurements are defined, they must be linked back to the strategy of the firm. No set of measurement tools will be successful if each manager is motivated to achieve his or her goals at the expense of the other goals. A successful BSC will create a shared understanding within the organization. The BSC creates an overall view of how the individual contributes to strategic success. The elements of the BSC not only should be created from the strategy; study of the factors should show what the strategy is. Linking the four categories together with strategy requires understanding three principles: cause-and-effect relationships; outcome measures and performance drivers; and links to financial measures.

Cause-and-Effect Relationships

All of the KPIs just described should fit within an overall cause-and-effect relationship chain that ends with a relevant financial measure and the achievement of part of the company's strategy. Cause-and-effect situations can be hypothesized using if-then statements: If the firm introduces a new product line, then the firm will attract a new customer base. If the firm attracts a new customer base, then all existing product lines will have new customers . . . and so on. These chains of cause-and-effect relationships should progress through each of the four areas where possible, and the net result of all of the chains should explicitly describe the company's strategy, how to measure each element, and, therefore, how to provide feedback to the process. In the end, all KPIs should be incorporated into one of these cause-and-effect chains.

Outcome Measures and Performance Drivers

For the cause-and-effect chains of KPIs to be useful, they must be linked to a definite outcome and a performance driver that says how the outcome can be met. Outcome measures are lagging indicators, or historic indicators of success such as measures of profitability, market share, employee skills, or customer retention. Outcome measures tend to be general measures of what must be achieved at the end of several cause-and-effect chains. Performance drivers are leading indicators, or drivers that are specific to the strategy of a particular business unit, such as cycle times, setup times, or new patents. Performance drivers without outcome measures will show how to perform in the short term but will not indicate whether the strategy is successful in the long term. Outcome measures without performance drivers will indicate where the department or team needs to be but will not show the path to achieve the goal and will not give relevant information at the time the information is needed.

Links to Financial Measures

No matter how focused an organization is on an initiative such as total quality management or employee empowerment, without linkage to the bottom line, such programs can become goals in themselves. Furthermore, the lack of a link to a tangible benefit from the program can cause disillusionment because there is no way of measuring its success. Therefore, all cause-and-effect chains need to be linked to financial outcome measures.

Nonfinancial Balanced Scorecard Measures

To drive future financial performance, the BSC requires assessment of customer, internal business process, and learning and growth measures.

Customer Measures

Because customers create all of a company's revenue, customer identification and classification into market segments are of vital importance to all companies. The customer perspective must include specific outcome measures and specific performance drivers. Because a company cannot target everyone without losing its focus on its core customers, a company must shape performance drivers (also known as value propositions) that are specific to market segments and their strategy.

The primary customer outcome measures include:

- Market share
- Acquisition
- Satisfaction
- Retention
- Profitability

These elements work together in a cause-and-effect relationship chain, as shown in Figure 1C-20.

Figure 1C-20 Customer Outcome Measures

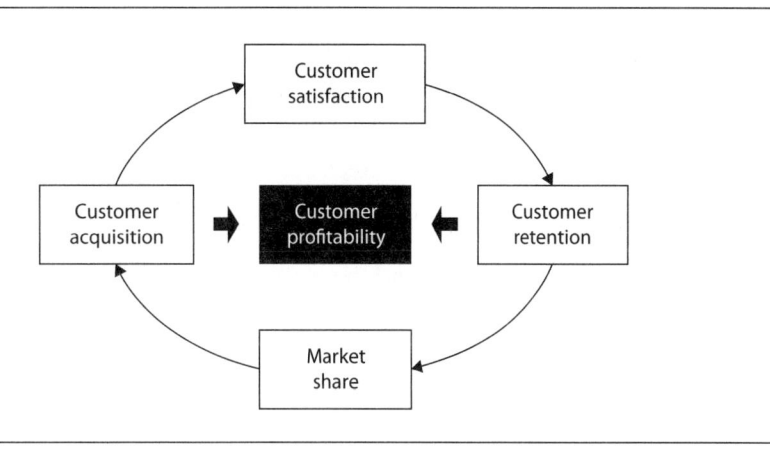

Market share is the proportion of customers that use a company's product or service out of the total of all users in that particular market segment. A subdivision of market share is account share. **Account share** is the proportion of a customer's business out of its total spending in the area the company represents. For example, a food distributor may measure the amount of purchases of its products over all of the targeted customers' food purchases as "share of the pantry."

Data on the size of the total market segment for a business can be gained from trade associations, industry groups, government studies, and customer surveys. The share of this market controlled by the company can be measured using metrics such as total number of customers, unit volume sold, or dollars spent. Account share is measured using surveys or approximation techniques that estimate the spending of an average user compared to the spending with the company itself. Companies with few customers can track individual customers, whereas companies with many customers must track customer segments.

Customer Acquisition

Companies with a growth strategy will focus strongly on the customer acquisition measure, but all companies need to add new customers because customer retention is never 100%. Customer acquisition is a measure of the success of the funds spent on acquiring the new customers, such as advertising costs and other marketing efforts. Customer acquisition can be measured in absolute terms (number of new customers) or relative terms (net gain in customers). It can also be measured as total sales to customers and acquisition divided by customer market segment. Other measures focus on customer conversion rate: the number of new customers divided by the total number of prospect contacts.

Customer Satisfaction

Measures of customer satisfaction show how successfully a company has met the needs of its consumers. When a firm's customers are corporations, a measurement of customer satisfaction often can be acquired through a formal process of having the customer rank its vendors on a variety of factors. Retail customer satisfaction similarly can be measured using surveys or, conversely, customer complaints. Customer surveys range from relatively inexpensive to very expensive, depending on the medium used and the number of desired responses. Web-based surveys and Web tracking have made the data-gathering process relatively inexpensive.

Customer Retention

Customer retention is an ongoing process that can be measured directly by companies that maintain lists of their customers, such as magazines, auto dealerships, distributors, and banks. Similar to account share, customer retention can be further broken down into the percentage change of business with each customer. For retailers, some customer retention data can be gained from credit card receipts. A major source of retention data for some retailers are "loyalty" programs that provide enrolled customers with discounts and enable the firm to precisely track customer purchases.

Customer Performance Drivers

Although outcome measures may be broadly defined for most industries, performance drivers are specific to each company's strategy and market. The performance drivers for customer acquisition, retention, and satisfaction are based on meeting the needs of customers. Examples of some common performance drivers include:

- Response time
- Delivery performance
- Defects
- Lead time

Internal Business Process Measures

After the financial and customer measures are created to meet company strategy, the internal business process measures can be designed to link to these metrics and achieve customer and shareholder value. Instead of creating measures that merely attempt to improve existing business processes, the BSC suggests that companies start with current and future customer needs, progressing through the cause-and-effect chain via operations, marketing, and other areas all the way to sales and service, keeping only the elements that add value to customers.

Internal business process measures go beyond simple financial variance measures to include output measures such as quality, cycle time, yield, order fulfillment, production planning, throughput, and turnover. However, improving such measures may not be enough to differentiate a company from its competitors, when these firms are working toward the same goals. Entirely new internal processes may be needed to make the company a leader in all of these measures simultaneously. A SWOT analysis can help identify weaknesses that require new solutions rather than just incremental improvements. For example, a business could radically improve cycle time by eliminating its warehouse and directly shipping goods to retail locations on a just-in-time basis.

The BSC identifies three business process areas that contribute to most companies' business strategies for internal business processes: innovation, operations, and postsale service.

Innovation

The innovation process starts with the SWOT analysis to identify customer needs that the company can satisfy. Research and development can be extremely expensive and must be written off as a period expense. Therefore, becoming efficient and effective at producing new products can be just as or more important than concentrating on the efficiency of ongoing production operations. Because the first company to introduce a new product has a distinct edge in market share, time to market is a key metric for evaluating the success of a new product introduction. Other measures employed include percentage of sales from new or proprietary products, new products versus competitors' new products, and variation from project budgets.

Product development processes can include performance measurements, such as yield, cycle time, and cost. For example, research into new computer chips could test numerous materials, and the yield of materials to warrant further study can be judged against the total number tested. The material in each stage can have its time in that phase measured (cycle time), and the overall cost of processing and research can be measured. Thus, the progress toward the outcome measurement of time to market and overall cost can be measured.

Operations

The operations process is the area that has garnered the majority of performance measurements in the past, and it continues to be important in reducing costs or increasing capabilities. Using only financial measures for operations, such as variances and standard costs, can lead to line managers making decisions that run counter to the organization's strategy—for example, creating too much inventory to keep a financial ratio in line with expectations rather than adjusting it to fit customer demand. Although the financial measurements continue to be important, the BSC recommends supplementing them with measures of quality, technological capabilities, and reducing cycle time to build the company's long-term strategy for differentiation over its competitors.

Postsale Service

Postsale service is a method of adding value to a product or service while simultaneously gaining feedback on customer satisfaction. Many companies that sell complex goods or services include postsale service in their strategic plans. Metrics such as response time for equipment failures and promptness of maintenance calls can be employed to measure the success of postsale service.

Learning and Growth Measures

A company develops learning and growth measures after identifying its financial, customer, and internal process strategic needs. If the company created its strategy with ambition and innovation, the company will need to achieve new capabilities through learning and growth. Although it is the last step designed in a BSC strategy, it will be the first step performed. Learning and growth measures are performance drivers for the desired strategic outcomes. Measuring learning and growth using financial measures alone usually tends to show only the short-term results, and short-term training results usually show that the training is unprofitable. However, because the long-term consequences of ignoring this element of an organization can be devastating, new measures must be introduced to guide management's decisions in this area.

The learning and growth perspective can be broken down into three categories: employee skill sets; information system capabilities; and empowerment, motivation, and organizational alignment.

Employee Skill Sets

The automation of repetitive tasks has transformed employee management from an industrial model to a knowledge-based model. Specific outcome measurements of employee results include employee satisfaction, employee retention, and employee productivity. Satisfied employees produce satisfied customers. Employee satisfaction can be measured through employee annual reviews or surveys. Employee retention is measured by employee turnover and by numbers of years of service. Employees with greater investment in a company tend to be more satisfied. The employee productivity outcome measure is a product of performance drivers, such as employee training, autonomy in decision making versus results, and output versus numbers of employees needed to produce the output. Another common and simple productivity measure is revenue per employee, but it should not be the sole measure because overly stressing revenue can lead employees to accept revenue even while the profit level is negative, such as salespersons offering huge price discounts to make sales.

Employees needing new skill sets can be measured using the amount of training needed per employee, the proportion of the workforce needing training, or the training and experience required to advance from an unqualified to a qualified employee. Such measures will indicate the amount of work required to raise the organization's capabilities to the desired strategic level. The strategic job coverage ratio is another metric that tracks the number of employees qualified for a strategic job divided by total organizational needs. This ratio exposes gaps in organizational skill sets.

Information System Capabilities

Measurements of the time needed to access or process business information can assess the capabilities of the current information systems and indicate need for continued investment in such infrastructure. A strategic information coverage ratio can be used to measure current information system capabilities divided by anticipated system needs.

Empowerment, Motivation, and Organizational Alignment

Empowerment and motivation can be measured using metrics such as the number and impact of employee-initiated improvements and innovations. Empowerment and motivation can be enhanced when employees are encouraged in and recognized for suggesting improvements in the organization's products and processes. Organizational alignment, organizational learning, and teamwork measurements include the goals set versus goals achieved for a department and team-based measures that include team-based rewards. The linking of personal goals and rewards to organizational outcomes is key to achieving the overall company strategy. Performance drivers for organizational alignment include periodic surveys of employees to determine their level of motivation to achieve the key performance indicators in the BSC.

A Balanced Scorecard Example

Acme Company's BSC, shown in Figure 1C-21, gives the company's overall strategic goal and the associated targets. It then covers the specific objectives from each of the four perspectives. Each objective has a specific measurable tool and a target for each of the next two years. The "Programs" column is the result of a survey Acme performed that matched planned programs to particular strategic objectives. The targets were set under the assumption that these programs would go forward.

Figure 1C-21 Acme Company's Balanced Scorecard (Planned Results)

Overall goal: Grow sales by 20% over the next two years.
Targets

		Current Year (Y0)	Year 1 (Y1)	Year 2 (Y2)	
Revenues:		$400,000	$432,000	$484,000	
Perspective	**Strategic Objectives**	**Measurements**	**Y1 Target**	**Y2 Target**	**Programs**
Financial	F1: Maximize return on equity	Return on equity	9%	13%	
	F2: Positive economic value added (EVA)	EVA	$20,000	$30,000	
	F3: 10% revenue growth	% change in revenues	8%	12%	
	F4: Asset utilization	Utilization rates	85%	88%	
Customer	C1: Price	Competitive comparison	−4%	−5%	
	C2: Customer retention	Retention %	75%	75%	Implement customer relationship management (CRM) program
	C3: Lowest-cost suppliers	Total cost relative to competition	−6%	−7%	Implement supplier relationship management (SRM) program
	C4: Product innovation	% of sales from new products	10%	15%	
Internal business process	P1: Improve production work flow	Cycle time	0.3 days	0.25 days	Upgrade enterprise resource planning (ERP) system
	P2: New product success	Number of orders	1,000	1,500	
	P3: Sales penetration	Actual versus plan (variance)	0%	0%	
	P4: Reduce inventory	Inventory as a % of sales	30%	28%	
Learning and growth	L1: Link strategy to reward system	Net income per dollar of variable pay (aggregate)	65%	68%	Implement CRM
	L2: Fill critical competency gaps	% of critical competencies satisfied on tracking matrix	75%	80%	Tuition reimbursement
	L3: Become customer-driven culture	Survey index	77%	79%	Implement CRM
	L4: Quality leadership	Average ranking (on 10-point scale) of executives	8.9	9.2	Tuition reimbursement

At the end of Year 1, the results were as shown in Figure 1C-22.

Figure 1C-22 Acme Company's Balanced Scorecard (Actual Results)

		Y1 Target	Y1 Actual	Variance*	
Revenues:		$432,000	$424,000	$8,000	U
Perspective	**Strategic Objectives**				
Financial	F1: Maximize return on equity	9%	8%	1%	U
	F2: Positive EVA	$20,000	$18,000	$2,000	U
	F3: 10% revenue growth	8%	6%	2%	U
	F4: Asset utilization	85%	87%	2%	F
Customer	C1: Price	−4%	−4%	0	
	C2: Customer retention	75%	70%	5%	U
	C3: Lowest-cost suppliers	−6%	−7%	−1%	F
	C4: Product innovation	10%	8%	2%	U
Internal business process	P1: Improve production work flow	0.3 days	0.25 days	0.05 days	F
	P2: New product success	1,000 orders	800 orders	200 orders	U
	P3: Sales penetration	0%	−7%	−7%	U
	P4: Reduce inventory	30%	29%	1%	F
Learning and growth	L1: Link strategy to reward system	65%	63%	2%	U
	L2: Fill critical competency gaps	75%	75%	0	
	L3: Become customer-driven culture	77%	74%	3%	U
	L4: Quality leadership	8.9	8.9	0	

Overall goal: Grow sales by 20% over the next two years. (Actual)

*U = Unfavorable variance; F = Favorable variance.

What can Acme learn from the results of Year 1? It may have had trouble implementing its CRM program (poorly planned, project canceled, delayed, etc.) because each of the measures that was linked to that program had an unfavorable variance. A reexamination of that program may find ways to refocus on the customers' needs.

Acme's production costs and production efficiencies all have favorable variances, meaning that the SRM and ERP initiatives seem to have been successful. Acme's workforce is progressing on pace, and its tuition reimbursement program is a likely aid to this success. However, although the workforce is strong in core competencies and in leadership, its members have not become customer-oriented enough, which is the primary reason for Acme's loss of customers and its inability to penetrate new markets and sell new products (which were likely designed with poor information on actual market needs). If Acme wants to turn things around and meet its goals, it must increase its investment in its CRM initiative, including training to change its employees' mind-sets toward a customer orientation.

Implementing the Balanced Scorecard

The next information on implementing the BSC was drawn from *The Strategy-Focused Organization* by Kaplan and Norton (Harvard Business Review Press,

2000). Implementing the BSC is basically executing strategy. Without execution, even the best vision remains a dream. In the past few decades, the average company has gone from about two-thirds of its value being based on tangible assets to about one-third, meaning that companies are moving from being able to describe and measure their success solely in financial terms to needing knowledge-based strategies that rely on more than just slow-reacting tools such as budgets. The BSC lends itself well to strategy execution, because the scorecard itself is a method of describing strategy in a way that can be acted on. A strategy-focused organization has these aspects:

- All of the measures used in the BSC (financial and nonfinancial) should be derived from the firm's vision and strategy.
- Processes become participative rather than directive.
- Change is not limited to cost cutting and downsizing but includes repositioning the firm (new or more specialized competitive markets, a customer focus, a performance mind-set, etc.).
- The organization must adopt new cultural values and priorities.

Aligning and Focusing Resources on Strategy

Rather than encouraging a general effort toward "improvement" or "efficiency," the executive team, business units, information technology, human resources, budgets, and capital investments must all be aligned and focused toward narrower and more intense (but not necessarily more capital-intensive) goals. To accomplish this, a firm must implement continuous improvement cycle consisting of five steps:

1. Translate the strategy into operational terms.
2. Align the organization to the firm's strategy.
3. Make strategy everybody's everyday job.
4. Make strategy a continual process.
5. Mobilize change through executive leadership.

1. **Translate the strategy into operational terms using strategy maps and the BSC.** A **strategy map** helps provide a high-level view of the organization's strategy and associated priorities so that it can design metrics that will enable it to evaluate its performance against strategies.

    For example: Figure 1C-23 shows a strategy map that Mobil North America Marketing and Refining (NAM&R) created to address a new focus on the customer and on those factors aimed at making customers want to use Mobil stations and products more.

2. **Align the organization to the firm's strategy using corporate scorecards as well as business unit and support unit synergies.** Synergies make the whole worth more than the sum of its parts. Break down functional area silos not by replacing departments or organizational charts but by replacing formal reporting structures with strategic priorities across business units (e.g., by having common themes across each unit's different scorecards). Examples of linked scorecards can be found in Kaplan and Norton's *The Strategy-Focused Organization*.

3. **Make strategy everyone's daily job using personal scorecards, strategic awareness, and balanced paychecks.** Replacing top-down direction with top-down communication means that every employee has a clear set of expectations that are already in line with strategy. The BSC becomes the educational tool showing how to measure success, but it may need to be backed up with more formal training (e.g., if employees must refine customer segments, they must first be taught about customer segmentation). Also, the lowest or personal-level scorecards can be left to the end users to create based on the higher-level priorities communicated. Often this leads to unsought-for synergies when an individual finds ways to help other areas of the company. Such a process helps create a strategic awareness at every level.

    Balanced paychecks link pay to the BSC measures, usually by business unit performance instead of individual performance. Balanced paychecks apply financial and nonfinancial BSC measures by weighting their importance. Some measures have an individual performance portion and a unit performance portion; and most also tie the compensation to some external factors, such as an industry benchmark to compensate for factors outside of employees' control. Using some form of balanced paycheck raises the interest level of all employees in using the BSC. Although employees may be studying the BSC to see what their compensation will be, they are also simultaneously working to improve corporate goals through their diligence. In the Mobil example in Figure 1C-23, when truck drivers delivered gasoline to stores, they started reporting poor station conditions because they knew their own compensation was partly based on customer perceptions at the stations.

4. **Make strategy a continual process by linking strategy to budgeting, using analytical automation, holding strategy meetings, and implementing strategic learning.** Strategy often is neglected in favor of tactical decisions, such as setting a budget, so the BSC uses a "double-loop" process. For example, two budgets are created, a strategic budget and an operational budget, thus protecting the long-term objectives from suboptimization in the short term. Regular strategy meetings organized around the BSC allow input from a broader group of managers while keeping the meeting focused. Instead of talking about variances or other specifics, managers will use their own BSC to measure their own performance and then use the meeting to talk about what has gone right and/or wrong and what should be continued or discontinued.

    Analytical tool automation found in today's enterprise resource and other sophisticated analytical systems can provide feedback to a broader audience than was traditionally possible, and a BSC can include such analysis. The firm must teach employees how to learn and adapt the strategy, such as by providing simple internal brochures explaining how to use a particular type of measure in its specific business context. Other firms may have employees use and then test the cause-and-effect linkages in a scorecard by analyzing actual results.

5. **Mobilize change through executive leadership using mobilization, governance processes, and a strategic management system.** Active executive

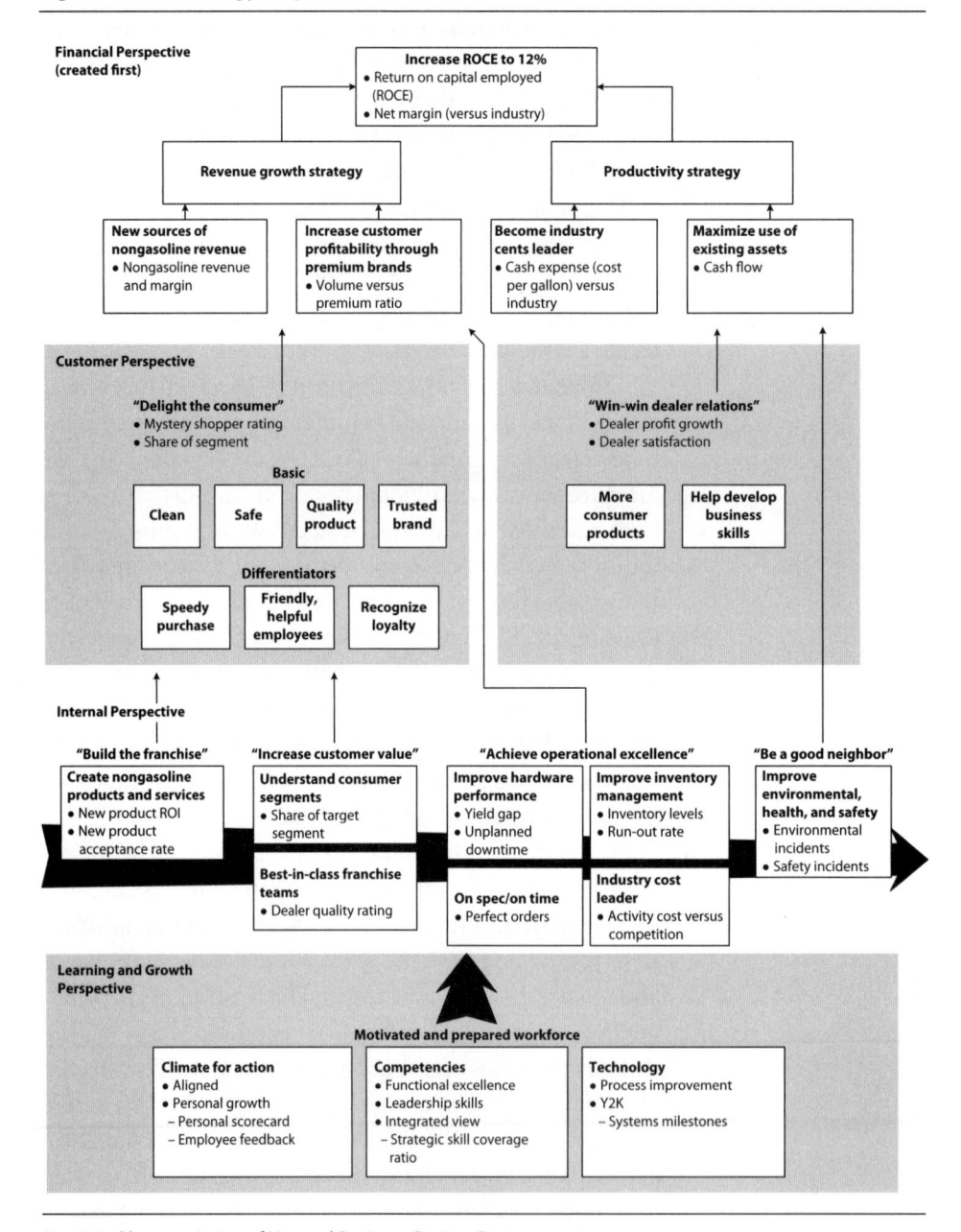

Figure 1C-23 Strategy Maps for Mobil NAM&R

Financial Perspective (created first)

- Increase ROCE to 12%
  - Return on capital employed (ROCE)
  - Net margin (versus industry)

- **Revenue growth strategy**
  - New sources of nongasoline revenue
    - Nongasoline revenue and margin
  - Increase customer profitability through premium brands
    - Volume versus premium ratio

- **Productivity strategy**
  - Become industry cents leader
    - Cash expense (cost per gallon) versus industry
  - Maximize use of existing assets
    - Cash flow

Customer Perspective

- "Delight the consumer"
  - Mystery shopper rating
  - Share of segment

  Basic: Clean | Safe | Quality product | Trusted brand

  Differentiators: Speedy purchase | Friendly, helpful employees | Recognize loyalty

- "Win-win dealer relations"
  - Dealer profit growth
  - Dealer satisfaction

  More consumer products | Help develop business skills

Internal Perspective

- "Build the franchise"
  - Create nongasoline products and services
    - New product ROI
    - New product acceptance rate

- "Increase customer value"
  - Understand consumer segments
    - Share of target segment
  - Best-in-class franchise teams
    - Dealer quality rating

- "Achieve operational excellence"
  - Improve hardware performance
    - Yield gap
    - Unplanned downtime
  - On spec/on time
    - Perfect orders
  - Improve inventory management
    - Inventory levels
    - Run-out rate
  - Industry cost leader
    - Activity cost versus competition

- "Be a good neighbor"
  - Improve environmental, health, and safety
    - Environmental incidents
    - Safety incidents

Learning and Growth Perspective

Motivated and prepared workforce

- **Climate for action**
  - Aligned
  - Personal growth
    – Personal scorecard
    – Employee feedback

- **Competencies**
  - Functional excellence
  - Leadership skills
  - Integrated view
    – Strategic skill coverage ratio

- **Technology**
  - Process improvement
  - Y2K
    – Systems milestones

Reprinted by permission of Harvard Business Review Press.

Source: *The Strategy-Focused Organization: How Balance Scorecard Companies Thrive in the New Business Environment* by Robert S. Kaplan and David P. Norton, Boston, MA: 2001

Copyright ©2001 by Harvard Business Publishing Corporation; all rights reserved.

involvement is a must, and it involves a focus more on mobilization or getting momentum started than on the metrics in the BSC itself. Governance processes involve how to manage the process once it has begun, using team-based approaches that break up old power structures and focus on executing strategy. In the final phase of implementing the BSC, governance becomes a strategic management system that transforms the new methods and values into the new business culture. Governance processes reinforce positive changes, such as by determining when and how to link the executive level and other levels of the firm to the BSC, for example, using executive compensation. This last phase is dangerous, as the desire for stability can make future changes more difficult. However, this tendency toward setting standards is universal in organizations and so should be planned for, embraced for a time, and then evaluated and changed to fit evolving strategy.

Performance Measures and Reporting Mechanisms

Management control systems, such as the BSC, aid in communication and coordination of an organization's goals to all employees. If carefully designed and properly implemented, these systems also can motivate employee behavior. Implementing a thorough BSC or any other strategic mechanism requires the development of a corresponding performance measurement system that supports the achievement of strategic goals and prevents dysfunctional behaviors that are not in alignment with strategic goals. A well-designed management control system will measure and report both financial as well as nonfinancial metrics of performance.

For performance measures to be effective in achieving the organization's goals, they must be related to the strategic goals of the organization. When performance measures are not aligned with the goals of the organization, they may induce behavior that is detrimental to the organization. It is often said that "You get what you reward." Hence, when performance measures are not linked to organizational goals, employees receive a mixed message as to which objectives management deems important. Measuring and rewarding behavior not aligned to organizational goals would induce behavior that is detrimental to the goals of the organization.

Performance measures need to be reasonably objective and easy to measure. Very complex performance measurement systems traditionally have not been successful in practice. Employees should be able to comprehend what is being measured, how the measurement system works, and how to relate the effects of their actions to those measures. This knowledge will help employees align their actions with the organization's goals.

It is important that performance measures be applied in a uniform, consistent, and regular manner. Inconsistent or irregular application of these measures has a negative impact on employee morale and motivation.

While traditional performance measurement systems focus more on financial measures, such as profits and cost variances, lately the emphasis has shifted toward the use of nonfinancial measures, such as those obtained from a BSC. It has been demonstrated that focusing on nonfinancial measures improves operational control. Moreover, such measures are more directly linked to the performance of lower-level employees.

Finally, the cost of measurement has to be considered. Since measuring performance requires the collection and analysis of data, the cost of such processes has to be considered prior to implementing a performance measurement system. A very costly performance measurement system may report very accurate results, but the additional costs may not be justified. Hence, the performance measurement system is the result of a trade-off between accuracy and cost.

Knowledge Check: Performance Measures

The next questions are intended to help you check your understanding and recall of the material presented in this topic. They do not represent the type of questions that appear on the CMA exam.

Directions: Answer each question in the space provided. Correct answers and section references appear after the knowledge check questions.

1. A business unit has $100,000 in net profit, assets of $500,000, and revenues of $200,000. Calculate its ROI.

   _____

2. Complete the following equation:

   Income of a Business Unit − (Assets of Business Unit × _____)
   = Residual Income

3. Which of the following perspectives of the balanced scorecard should every cause-and-effect chain be linked to?
   - a. Financial
   - b. Customer
   - c. Internal business process
   - d. Learning and growth

4. Which of the following is a customer performance driver?
   - a. Market share
   - b. Lead time
   - c. Retention
   - d. Profitability

5. Periodic surveys of employee motivation are an example of a
   - a. learning and growth outcome measure.
   - b. learning and growth performance driver.
   - c. customer outcome measure.
   - d. customer performance driver.

6. The process time key performance indicator would be measured best by which of the following?
   - a. Surveys
   - b. ROI
   - c. Customer returns
   - d. Turnaround

7. Define the five steps firms must use to implement a continuous improvement cycle.

   1. _____
   2. _____
   3. _____
   4. _____
   5. _____

Knowledge Check Answers: Performance Measures

1. A business unit has $100,000 in net profit, assets of $500,000, and revenues of $200,000. Calculate its ROI. **[See *Return on Investment*.]**

$$\text{Return on Investment (ROI)} = \frac{\text{Net profit of business unit}}{\text{Assets of busniess unit}}$$

   ROI = $100,000/$500,000

   ROI = 20%

2. Complete the following equation: **[See *Residual Income*.]**

   Income of a Business Unit − (Assets of Business Unit × Required Rate of Return) = Residual Income

3. Which of the following perspectives of the balanced scorecard should every cause-and-effect chain be linked to? **[See *Links to Financial Measures*.]**
   - ☑ a. Financial
   - ☐ b. Customer
   - ☐ c. Internal business process
   - ☐ d. Learning and growth

4. Which of the following is a customer performance driver? **[See *Customer Performance Drivers*.]**
   - ☐ a. Market share
   - ☑ b. Lead time
   - ☐ c. Retention
   - ☐ d. Profitability

5. Periodic surveys of employee motivation are an example of a **[See *Empowerment, Motivation, and Organizational Alignment*.]**
   - ☐ a. learning and growth outcome measure.
   - ☑ b. learning and growth performance driver.
   - ☐ c. customer outcome measure.
   - ☐ d. customer performance driver.

6. The process time key performance indicator would be measured best by which of the following? **[See *Key Performance Indicators for a Balanced Scorecard*.]**
   - ☐ a. Surveys
   - ☐ b. ROI
   - ☐ c. Customer returns
   - ☑ d. Turnaround

7. Define the five steps firms must use to implement a continuous improvement cycle. [See *Aligning and Focusing Resources on Strategy*.]
    1. Translate the strategy in operational terms.
    2. Align the organization to the firm's strategy.
    3. Make strategy everybody's everyday job.
    4. Make strategy a continual process.
    5. Mobilize change through executive leadership.

Practice Questions: Performance Management

Directions: This sampling of questions is designed to emulate actual exam questions. Read each question and write your response on another sheet of paper. Use the answer and explanation (given later in the book) to assess your response. Validate or improve the answer you wrote. For a more robust selection of practice questions, access the **Online Test Bank** found at www.wileycma.com. See the "Answers to Section Practice Questions" section at the end of the book.

Question 1C1-CQ22

Topic: Cost and Variance Measures

The following performance report was prepared for Dale Manufacturing for the month of April.

	Actual Results	Static Budget	Variance
Sales units	100,000	80,000	20,000F
Sales dollars	$190,000	$160,000	$30,000F
Variable costs	125,000	96,000	29,000U
Fixed costs	45,000	40,000	5,000U
Operating income	$20,000	$24,000	$4,000U

Using a flexible budget, Dale's total sales-volume variance is:

- a. $4,000 unfavorable.
- b. $6,000 favorable.
- c. $16,000 favorable.
- d. $20,000 unfavorable.

Question 1C1-CQ17

Topic: Cost and Variance Measures

MinnOil performs oil changes and other minor maintenance services (e.g., tire pressure checks) for cars. The company advertises that all services are completed within 15 minutes for each service.

On a recent Saturday, 160 cars were serviced resulting in the following labor variances: rate, $19 unfavorable; efficiency, $14 favorable. If MinnOil's standard labor rate is $7 per hour, determine the actual wage rate per hour and the actual hours worked.

	Wage Rate	Hours Worked
a.	$6.55	42.00
b.	$6.67	42.71
c.	$7.45	42.00
d.	$7.50	38.00

Question 1C1-CQ03

Topic: Cost and Variance Measures

Frisco Company recently purchased 108,000 units of raw material for $583,200. Three units of raw materials are budgeted for use in each finished good manufactured, with the raw material standard set at $16.50 for each completed product.

Frisco manufactured 32,700 finished units during the period just ended and used 99,200 units of raw material. If management is concerned about the timely reporting of variances in an effort to improve cost control and bottom-line performance, the materials purchase price variance should be reported as

- a. $6,050 unfavorable.
- b. $9,920 favorable.
- c. $10,800 unfavorable.
- d. $10,800 favorable.

Question 1C1-CQ18

Topic: Cost and Variance Measures

Christopher Akers is the chief executive officer of SBL Inc., a masonry contractor. The financial statements have just arrived showing a $3,000 loss on the new stadium job that was budgeted to show a $6,000 profit. Actual and budget information relating to the materials for the job are shown next.

	Actual	Budget
Bricks — number of bundles	3,000	2,850
Bricks — cost per bundle	$7.90	$8.00

Which one of the following is a **correct** statement regarding the stadium job for SBL?

- a. The price variance was favorable by $285.
- b. The price variance was favorable by $300.

☐ c. The efficiency variance was unfavorable by $1,185.
☐ d. The flexible budget variance was unfavorable by $900.

Question 1C1-CQ19
Topic: Cost and Variance Measures

A company isolates its raw material price variance in order to provide the earliest possible information to the manager responsible for the variance. The budgeted amount of material usage for the year was computed as shown:

150,000 Units of Finished Goods × 3 Pounds/Unit × $2.00/Pound = $900,000

Actual results for the year were the following:

Finished goods produced	160,000 units
Raw materials purchased	500,000 pounds
Raw materials used	490,000 pounds
Cost per pound	$2.02

The raw material price variance for the year was

☐ a. $9,600 unfavorable.
☐ b. $9,800 unfavorable.
☐ c. $10,000 unfavorable.
☐ d. $20,000 unfavorable.

Question 1C1-CQ20
Topic: Cost and Variance Measures

At the beginning of the year, Douglas Company prepared this monthly budget for direct materials.

Units produced and sold	10,000	15,000
Direct material cost	$15,000	$22,500

At the end of the month, the company's records showed that 12,000 units were produced and sold and $20,000 was spent for direct materials. The variance for direct materials is:

☐ a. $2,000 favorable.
☐ b. $2,000 unfavorable.
☐ c. $5,000 favorable.
☐ d. $5,000 unfavorable.

Question 1C1-CQ21
Topic: Cost and Variance Measures

Cordell Company uses a standard cost system. On January 1 of the current year, Cordell budgeted fixed manufacturing overhead cost of $600,000 and production at 200,000 units. During the year, the firm produced 190,000 units and incurred fixed manufacturing overhead of $595,000. The production volume variance for the year was:

- ☐ a. $5,000 unfavorable.
- ☐ b. $10,000 unfavorable.
- ☐ c. $25,000 unfavorable.
- ☐ d. $30,000 unfavorable.

Question 1C1-CQ22
Topic: Cost and Variance Measures

Harper Company's performance report indicated this information for the past month:

Actual total overhead	$1,600,000
Budgeted fixed overhead	$1,500,000
Applied fixed overhead at $3 per labor hour	$1,200,000
Applied variable overhead at $.50 per labor hour	$200,000
Actual labor hours	430,000

Harper's total overhead spending variance for the month was:

- ☐ a. $100,000 favorable.
- ☐ b. $115,000 favorable.
- ☐ c. $185,000 unfavorable.
- ☐ d. $200,000 unfavorable.

Question 1C1-CQ23
Topic: Cost and Variance Measures

The JoyT Company manufactures Maxi Dolls for sale in toy stores. In planning for this year, JoyT estimated variable factory overhead of $600,000 and fixed factory overhead of $400,000. JoyT uses a standard costing system, and factory overhead is allocated to units produced on the basis of standard direct labor hours. The denominator level of activity budgeted for this year was 10,000 direct labor hours, and JoyT used 10,300 actual direct labor hours.

Based on the output accomplished during this year, 9,900 standard direct labor hours should have been used. Actual variable factory overhead was

$596,000, and actual fixed factory overhead was $410,000 for the year. Based on this information, the variable overhead spending variance for JoyT for this year was:

- ☐ a. $24,000 unfavorable.
- ☐ b. $2,000 unfavorable.
- ☐ c. $4,000 favorable.
- ☐ d. $22,000 favorable.

Question 1C1-CQ24

Topic: Cost and Variance Measures

Johnson Inc. has established per-unit standards for material and labor for its production department based on 900 units normal production capacity as shown.

3 pounds of direct materials @ $4 per pound	$12
1 direct labor hour @ $15 per hour	15
Standard cost per unit	$27

During the year, 1,000 units were produced. The accounting department has charged the production department supervisor with the next unfavorable variances.

Material Quantity Variance		Material Price Variance	
Actual usage	3,300 pounds	Actual cost	$4,200
Standard usage	3,000 pounds	Standard cost	4,000
Unfavorable	300 pounds	Unfavorable	$200

Bob Sterling, the production supervisor, has received a memorandum from his boss stating that he did not meet the established standards for material prices and quantity and corrective action should be taken. Sterling is very unhappy about the situation and is preparing to reply to the memorandum explaining the reasons for his dissatisfaction.

All of the following are valid reasons for Sterling's dissatisfaction **except** that the:

- ☐ a. material price variance is the responsibility of the purchasing department.
- ☐ b. cause of the unfavorable material usage variance was the acquisition of substandard material.
- ☐ c. standards have not been adjusted to the engineering changes.
- ☐ d. variance calculations fail to properly reflect that actual production exceeded normal production capacity.

Question 1C3-AT35
Topic: Cost and Variance Measures

Teaneck Inc. sells two products, Product E and Product F, and had these data for last month:

	Product E		Product F	
	Budget	Actual	Budget	Actual
Unit sales	5,500	6,000	4,500	6,000
Unit contribution margin (CM)	$4.50	$4.80	$10.00	$10.50

The company's sales mix variance is:

- a. $3,300 favorable.
- b. $3,420 favorable.
- c. $17,250 favorable.
- d. $18,150 favorable.

Question 1C2-CQ17
Topic: Responsibility Centers and Reporting Segments

Manhattan Corporation has several divisions that operate as decentralized profit centers. At the present time, the Fabrication Division has excess capacity of 5,000 units with respect to the UT-371 circuit board, a popular item in many digital applications. Information about the circuit board is presented next.

Market price	$48
Variable selling/distribution costs on external sales	$5
Variable manufacturing cost	$21
Fixed manufacturing cost	$10

Manhattan's Electronic Assembly Division wants to purchase 4,500 circuit boards either internally or else use a similar board in the marketplace that sells for $46. The Electronic Assembly Division's management feels that if the first alternative is pursued, a price concession is justified, given that both divisions are part of the same firm. To optimize the overall goals of Manhattan, the minimum price to be charged for the board from the Fabrication Division to the Electronic Assembly Division should be:

- a. $21.
- b. $26.
- c. $31.
- d. $46.

Question 1C3-CQ12
Topic: Performance Measures

Performance results for four geographic divisions of a manufacturing company are shown next.

Division	Target Return on Investment	Actual Return on Investment	Return on Sales
A	18%	18.1%	8%
B	16%	20.0%	8%
C	14%	15.8%	6%
D	12%	11.0%	9%

The division with the **best** performance is:

- ☐ a. Division A.
- ☐ b. Division B.
- ☐ c. Division C.
- ☐ d. Division D.

Question 1C3-CQ13
Topic: Performance Measures

KHD Industries is a multidivisional firm that evaluates its managers based on the return on investment (ROI) earned by its divisions. The evaluation and compensation plans use a targeted ROI of 15% (equal to the cost of capital), and managers receive a bonus of 5% of basic compensation for every one percentage point that the division's ROI exceeds 15%.

Dale Evans, manager of the Consumer Products Division, has made a forecast of the division's operations and finances for next year that indicates the ROI would be 24%. In addition, new short-term programs were identified by the Consumer Products Division and evaluated by the finance staff as shown.

Program	Projected ROI
A	13%
B	19%
C	22%
D	31%

Assuming no restrictions on expenditures, what is the optimal mix of new programs that would add value to KHD Industries?

- ☐ a. A, B, C, and D
- ☐ b. B, C, and D only
- ☐ c. C and D only
- ☐ d. D only

Question 1C1-AT03

Topic: Cost and Variance Measures

Franklin Products has an estimated practical capacity of 90,000 machine hours, and each unit requires two machine hours. The next data apply to a recent accounting period.

Actual variable overhead	$240,000
Actual fixed overhead	$442,000
Actual machine **hours** worked	88,000
Actual finished **units** produced	42,000
Budgeted variable overhead at 90,000 machine hours	$200,000
Budgeted fixed overhead	$450,000

Of the following factors, the production volume variance is **most** likely to have been caused by:

- ☐ a. acceptance of an unexpected sales order.
- ☐ b. a wage hike granted to a production supervisor.
- ☐ c. a newly imposed initiative to reduce finished goods inventory levels.
- ☐ d. temporary employment of workers with lower skill levels than originally anticipated.

Question 1C3-AT19

Topic: Performance Measures

Which one of the following **best** identifies a profit center?

- ☐ a. A new car sales division for a large local auto agency
- ☐ b. The information technology department of a large consumer products company
- ☐ c. A large toy company
- ☐ d. The production operations department of a small job-order machine shop company

Question 1C3-AT21

Topic: Performance Measures

The balanced scorecard provides an action plan for achieving competitive success by focusing management attention on key performance indicators. Which one of the following is **not** one of the key performance indicators commonly focused on in the balanced scorecard?

- **a.** Financial performance measures
- **b.** Internal business processes
- **c.** Competitor business strategies
- **d.** Employee innovation and learning

> To further assess your understanding of the concepts and calculations covered in Part 1, Section C: Performance Management, practice with the **Online Test Bank** for this section. REMINDER: See the "Answers to Section Practice Questions" section at the end of this book.

SECTION D

Cost Management

Cost management requires the ability to measure, accumulate, assign, and classify all of the costs involved in running a modern business enterprise. A costing system is used to monitor a company's costs, thereby providing management with information on operations and performance. Various costing systems, such as job order costing, process costing, activity-based costing (ABC), throughput costing, and life-cycle costing, can be implemented to monitor costs.

Cost management involves the actions undertaken by managers to satisfy customers while also monitoring and controlling costs. In the modern manufacturing environment, every resource is monitored very closely to ensure the company is receiving the best return for its investment. The use of resources, such as direct materials, direct labor, and manufacturing overhead, are analyzed carefully with the appropriate measurement system. Operational efficiency and overall business performance can be sustained and improved through the knowledgeable application of the right systems.

Learning Outcome Statements Overview: Cost Management

Section D.1. Measurement Concepts

A. Demonstrate an understanding of the behavior of fixed and variable costs in the long and short terms and how a change in assumptions regarding cost type or relevant range affects these costs.
   a. The first step in classifying a cost is to understand its behavior over a specific period of time. This period of time is called the "relevant range," and the cost may be fixed or variable over the relevant range. A fixed cost remains the same over the relevant range. A variable cost varies in proportion to activity, volume, or some other cost driver. Total cost is the sum of all variable and fixed costs.

B. Identify cost objects and cost pools and assign costs to appropriate activities.
   a. Cost objects include anything within the organization for which the cost needs to be measured, such as a job, project, activity, or service. Cost pools are created to aggregate all of the costs required to perform a certain task for a cost object. By accounting for all of the costs incurred in a specific activity with a cost pool, it is easier to assign those costs to products in a systematic manner. Different methods for accumulating and allocating those costs include: job-order costing, process costing, standard costing, and the like.

C. Demonstrate an understanding of the nature and types of cost drivers and the causal relationship that exists between cost drivers and costs incurred.
   a. Four types of cost drivers affect the costing of particular cost objects:
      i. Activity-based cost drivers—Focus on *operations* that involve manufacturing or service activity, such as machine setup, machine use, or packaging.
      ii. Volume-based cost drivers—Focus on *output*, which involves aggregate measures, such as units produced or labor hours.
      iii. Structural cost drivers—Focus on company *strategy*, which involves long-term plans for scale, complexity, amount of experience in an area, or level of technical expertise.
      iv. Executional cost drivers—Focus on *short-term operations*, which involve reducing costs through concern with workforce commitment and involvement, production design, and supplier relationships.

D. Demonstrate an understanding of the various methods for measuring costs and accumulating work-in-process and finished goods inventories.
   a. In order to measure costs accurately, it is necessary to understand how the cost reacts to changes in levels of activity, also known as its cost behavior. A variable cost remains constant on a per-unit basis over a relevant range. A fixed cost decreases on a per-unit basis as activity levels increase. Variable and fixed costs can be period or product costs. Product costs are those costs that are accumulated as inventory and held on the balance sheet until the product is sold. Product costs are direct materials, direct labor, and manufacturing overhead. Period costs are expensed as incurred and include items such as advertising, management salaries, and other administrative items. The different methods for accounting for product costs are described in more detail below and in Topic 1: Measurement Concepts.
E. Identify and define cost measurement techniques such as actual costing, normal costing, and standard costing; calculate costs using each of these techniques; identify the appropriate use of each technique; and describe the benefits and limitations of each technique.
   a. Actual costing—Costing system records the actual costs incurred for *all* costs, including direct labor, direct material, and overhead. The actual costs are determined by waiting until the end of the accounting period and then calculating the actual costs based on the recorded amounts. The total actual costs are divided by the total number of units produced to get a per-unit cost. This method is more accurate than other methods but is more time consuming and may result in reporting delays as all the costs may not be known until sometime after the reporting period.
   b. Normal costing—Applies actual costs for direct materials and direct labor to a job, process, or other cost object and then uses a predetermined overhead rate to assign overhead to a cost object. The direct materials and labor are applied just like actual costing, and overhead is applied using a predetermined rate calculated as follows:
      i. Create an annual budget for overhead costs.
      ii. Choose a cost driver for charging overhead (i.e., machine hours, labor hours).
      iii. Estimate the total amount of the cost driver (estimated total machine hours).
      iv. Calculate the rate by dividing the total estimated cost by the total amount of the cost driver. Then multiply the rate by the actual volume of driver for a particular product.

      Using a normal costing system allows a company to identify actual cost for product costs that are easily traceable and apply a predetermined rate for the overhead costs. At the end of the period, usually there is a balance left unallocated or overallocated. This allows the company to see how estimates varied from actual results. This could be because either the volume or the costs were different from what was planned.

c. Standard costing—Applies all product costs (direct materials, direct labor, and overhead) using a predetermined (standard) rate. A standard cost is an expected or target cost for an operation. By using a standard rate, a company can see where variances occur so that the company can achieve better operating results. The rate is computed by estimating standard units allowed and standard rates (either ideal or practical standards) for each product produced. Knowing the standard rate and the number of units produced allows calculation of the standard cost of direct labor or direct materials. Standard costs (e.g., standard number of hours times the standard rate per hour) then can be compared to actual total costs (e.g., total direct labor costs). Two advantages of using standard costs are they are less likely to incorporate past inefficiencies and that they can be adapted as new data indicate expected changes during the budget period. The disadvantages in standard costing include the problems associated with unreasonable standards, when the process used to set the standards are authoritarian or secretive, or when the standards are poorly communicated. Inflexible standards or those that place undue emphasis on profits are likely to fail.

F. Demonstrate an understanding of variable (direct) costing and absorption (full) costing and the benefits and limitations of these measurement concepts.
   a. Variable (direct) costing—Inventory costing method that includes only the variable manufacturing costs in the inventory costs and excludes fixed manufacturing costs. This method is not compliant with external reporting based on generally accepted accounting principles (GAAP). If this method is used for internal reporting purposes, it must be adjusted to account for fixed manufacturing costs as inventoriable costs. However, this method allows a company to compute contribution margin for cost-volume profit and other analysis tools.
   b. Absorption (full) costing—Inventory costing system that includes both variable and fixed manufacturing costs. Under absorption costing, inventory absorbs all costs of manufacturing. This method is required for external reporting. Management can skew accounting profits by adjusting inventory levels since fixed manufacturing costs are included in inventory. If inventory levels increase, then some of the costs are on the balance sheet instead of the income statement.
   c. These two methods differ only the how they account for fixed manufacturing costs.

G. Calculate inventory costs, cost of goods sold, and operating profit using both variable costing and absorption costing.
   a. The only difference in variable and absorption costing is the difference in how fixed manufacturing costs are treated. Under the absorption method, the fixed manufacturing costs are inventoried and added to costs on a per-unit basis. If inventory levels rise, those costs are left on the balance sheet and not run through the income statement. The difference between variable and absorption net income can be computed by computing

the per-unit fixed manufacturing costs left in inventory (i.e., the rise in number of units from the previous period). For more detailed examples of computing inventory costs, cost of goods sold, and operating profit using these methods, see Topic 1: Measurement Concepts.

H. Demonstrate an understanding of how the use of variable costing or absorption costing affects the value of inventory, cost of goods sold, and operating income.
   a. If inventory levels rise, the value of inventory and operating income will be higher under absorption costing, and cost of goods sold will be lower. This is because fixed manufacturing costs are treated as inventoriable costs under absorption costing.

I. Prepare summary income statements using variable costing and absorption costing.
   a. For detailed examples of preparing an income statement using variable and absorption costing, see Topic 1: Measurement Concepts.

J. Determine the appropriate use of joint product and by-product costing.
   a. Joint product—Products that share a portion of the production process and have relatively the same sales value.
   b. By-products—Products that share the same production process with a product or joint product but have relatively minor value in comparison to the main product.

K. Demonstrate an understanding of concepts such as split-off point and separable costs.
   a. Split-off point—The point at which products diverge and become separately identifiable.
   b. Additional processing costs (separable costs)—Any costs that can be specifically identified with a product because the cost occurs after the split-off point where the costs are assigned to the separate products.

L. Determine the allocation of joint product and by-product costs using the physical measure method, the sales value at split-off method, constant gross profit (gross margin) method, and the net realizable value method; and describe the benefits and limitations of each method.
   a. Physical measure method—Uses a physical measurement to allocate joint costs to joint products. Physical measures include weight, number, and volume. The physical measure method can produce gross profit margins that could frustrate managers and distort profits. This is because the value of the joint product is not accounted for at all unless the relevant physical measure conveys the value of each of the items.
   b. Sales value at split-off method—Allocates joint costs to joint products using their proportional sales value at the split-off point. This is the most widely used method because it is simple to calculate and allocates costs according to value. The sales value method has the limitation of not being useful for products that need additional processing after the split-off point before a sales value is established.
   c. Constant gross profit (gross margin) method—Allocates joint costs so as to provide the same gross margin percentage of profit for each joint product.

One benefit of the gross profit method is that it can be used even when there are additional processing costs. The amount of the joint costs allocated to each product is not always a positive number; a joint product could get a negative allocation of joint costs in order to make the gross margin percentage equal to the overall average for the entity. This is an advantage for companies that wish to keep the same margin for each product, but it could lead to a distortion in the fairness of how costs are allocated.

d. Net realizable value method—Allocates joint costs according to the final sales value less additional processing costs. The net realizable value method is used when the market price for one or more of the joint products cannot be determined at the split-off point, usually because additional processing is needed. The benefit of this method is it takes into account additional processing costs.

Section D.2. Costing Systems

For each cost accumulation system identified (job order costing, process costing, activity-based costing [ABC], life-cycle costing), the candidate should be able to:

A. Define the nature of the system, understand the cost flows of the system, and identify its appropriate use.
   a. Job order costing—Assigns costs to a specific job (a distinct unit, batch, or lot of a product or service). As costs are incurred, they are accumulated and assigned to that particular job. Job order costing is used when the product or service has costs that can be, and often need to be, tracked and assigned to a specific job or service.
   b. Process costing—Accumulates product or service costs by process or department and then assigns them to a large number of nearly identical products by dividing the total costs by the total number of units produced. Process costing is used for multiple, nearly identical units that can be organized into a flow. These products tend to be homogeneous in nature, meaning they are all alike or very similar. Therefore, it is not necessary to track costs to a specific unit of product or service.
   c. Activity-based costing—A method of assigning costs to customers, services, and products based on an activity's consumption of resources. An activity is any type of action, work, or movement performed within an entity. The basis for ABC is that activities use resources but produce products or services. The resource cost is calculated using a cost driver; the amount of an activity consumed in a period is multiplied by the cost of the activity. The calculated costs are assigned to the product or service. ABC is especially appropriate for companies that have expanded to multiple products and/or products that use varying amounts of resources, which include not only raw materials and other direct costs but also indirect costs, such as customer service, quality control, and supervision.

d. Life-cycle costing—Considers the entire life cycle of a product or service, from concept through sales and warranty service. Life-cycle costing is sometimes used on a strategic basis for cost planning and product pricing. It is designed to allow a firm to focus on the overall costs for a product or service.
- **B.** Calculate inventory values and cost of goods sold.
    - a. Job order costing—Job order costing can use any of the previously mentioned cost measurement systems such as actual, normal, and standard costing to accumulate costs and allocate cost of goods sold. Cost of goods sold can be computed as

    Beginning Inventory + Current Period Costs − Ending Inventory

    - b. Process costing—In process costing, costs are accumulated by departments and applied to the total number of units produced. Usually there are partially completed units in the batch at the end of the period that need to be allocated some costs but shouldn't be counted as a whole unit. In order to do so, process costing uses a concept of equivalent units (EUs). An EU is a measure of the amount of work done on partially completed units expressed in terms of how many complete units could have been created with the same amount of work. The cost of goods sold computation is the same as job order costing except the beginning and the ending inventory are computed on the basis of EU instead of whole units. For more detailed analysis, see item F below and Topic 2: Costing Systems.
    - c. Activity-based costing—In ABC, costs are accumulated and allocated based on the predetermined rate for each activity. The predetermined rate is estimated based on the total costs in the pool divided by the total cost driver. Costs are then added to products based on the use of that particular activity. All the activities that a particular product will use in order for it to get to the point where it can be sold are added together to determine the total cost.
    - d. Life-cycle costing—Can determine inventory and cost of goods sold under any of the methods previously mentioned. The only difference between life-cycle costing and other methods is that a longer-term perspective is used instead of an annual accounting period. However, reporting based on generally accepted accounting principles (GAAP) still must be followed. Entire life costs are estimated including research and development, manufacturing, and distribution in order to come up with the estimated cost per unit.
- **C.** Demonstrate an understanding of the proper accounting for normal and abnormal spoilage.
    - a. Spoilage is any material or good that is considered unacceptable and is discarded or sold for its disposal value. Spoilage can be normal or abnormal. Normal spoilage is any unit of production that is deemed unacceptable during the normal production process, assuming *efficient* operating conditions. Abnormal spoilage is any unacceptable product that should not normally exist under efficient and normal operating conditions.

Normal spoilage is considered a cost of operations and charged to the cost of the units produced. Abnormal spoilage is directly expensed through the income statement in a separate loss account.

D. Discuss the strategic value of cost information regarding products and services, pricing, overhead allocations, and other issues.
   a. Job order costing—Can have a strategic value for a business because it gives a detailed breakdown of all of the different types of costs. The gross margin and gross profit margin can be used to compare the company's profitability across different jobs. For jobs that did poorly, the company can analyze whether the cost overruns were from direct labor costs, direct materials costs, or one of the indirect cost pools.
   b. Process costing—Can have a strategic value for a business because it accurately captures and assigns costs to mass produced products. The cost flow system also requires departments to create production reports and analyze costs accordingly. Cost overruns can be identified easily and compared to estimates.
   c. Activity-based costing—Helps managers understand their costs, thus highlighting the competitive advantages and weaknesses of their process or product. As more firms adopt ABC, it will become increasingly difficult for companies using a less accurate costing system to compete, because they will find themselves at a competitive disadvantage.
   d. Life-cycle costing—Sometimes used on a strategic basis for cost planning and product pricing. It is designed to allow a firm to focus on the overall costs for a product or service. Poor early design could lead to much higher marketing costs, lower sales, and higher service costs.

E. Identify and describe the benefits and limitations of each cost accumulation system.
   a. Job order costing—Can provide very detailed results of a specific job or operation so it is ideal for specific jobs. For large processes, job order costing is less valuable because it is impractical to assign individual costs to mass-produced items on a daily basis.
   b. Process costing—Useful for any highly repetitive flow process, such as mass production of homogeneous items. Conversely, it is not useful for custom orders or other individual jobs. Process costing allocates costs not only by cost per unit but also to specific departments, allowing individual managers to control their own costs.
   c. Activity-based costing—Reduces distortions found in traditional cost allocation methods that allocate overhead by department and helps determine more accurate costs of low-volume products that use similar volumes of costly activities. However, ABC requires substantial development and maintenance time and may add more data than necessary to create usable reports.
   d. Life-cycle costing—Allows an organization to price the product appropriately, considering all the upstream, manufacturing and downstream costs. In other costing methods, research and development costs usually are disregarded on the overall profitability of a product.

F. Demonstrate an understanding of the concept of equivalent units in process costing, and calculate the value of equivalent units.
   a. An equivalent unit (EU) is a measure of the amount of work done on partially completed units expressed in terms of how many complete units could have been created with the same amount of work. For example, 10 units that are 50% complete are equal to 5 completed units (EUs). EUs are calculated separately for direct materials, direct labor, and overhead (conversion costs). There are two different methods of computed EUs: the weighted average method and the first in, first out (FIFO) method. Both methods are similar in calculating EUs. The difference is in how to account for the beginning inventory. Under the weighted average method, prior-period costs are considered in the computation of cost per unit, and the EUs of beginning work in process (WIP) is set to 100% of total units. The FIFO method does not take into account prior-period costs or the work already completed in prior periods. The steps for calculating EUs under both methods are:
      i. Determine the flow of physical units.
      ii. Determine the EUs.
      iii. Calculate total manufacturing costs. (FIFO is current period costs only; weighted average is current and prior).
      iv. Calculate unit costs (step iii / step ii).
      v. Assign total manufacturing costs to units (need to be assigned to units transferred and ending WIP).
   b. The next chart demonstrates how EUs would be calculated (step ii) under both methods:

	Weighted Average			FIFO		
	Total	%	EUs	Total	%	EUs
Beginning WIP	100	100% (a)	100	100	0% (c)	0
Started and Completed	500	100% (a)	500	500	100% (a)	500
Ending WIP	200	80% (b)	160	200	80% (b)	160
	800		760	800		660

(a) Will always be equal to 100%
(b) Percent complete
(c) Percent not complete at beginning of period

G. Define the elements of activity-based costing such as cost pool, cost driver, resource driver, activity driver, and value-added activity.
   a. Cost pool—A set of costs incurred when a particular activity is performed. (i.e., compliance testing or packaging)
   b. Cost driver—Something that drives the cost of an activity in a cost pool (i.e., number of setups or machine activities, or number of hours worked)

c. Resource driver—Measures the amount of resources consumed by an activity (i.e., the amount of rubber required to make a batch of tennis balls).
d. Activity driver—Measurement of the amount of an activity used by a cost object. (i.e., number of labor hours required for the activity of performing a setup).
e. Value-added activity—An activity that increases the value (in the customer's eyes) of a product at any stage in the development of the product.

H. Calculate product cost using an activity-based system, and compare and analyze the results with costs calculated using a traditional system.
  a. Three steps are used to determine the product cost using an ABC system:
     i. Identify activities and resource costs.
     ii. Assign resource costs to activities.
     iii. Assign activity costs to cost objects.
  b. Once activity costs are calculated, compute the rate to be applied to each product:

  $$\text{Rate} = \frac{\text{Cost Pool}}{\text{Driver}}$$

  c. The next chart compares the cost drivers, overhead, and focus of an ABC system as opposed to a traditional costing system:

	ABC	**Traditional Costing**
Cost drivers	Multiple cost drivers: activity- and volume-based drivers (whichever fits the cost best)	Up to three cost drivers: only volume based, chosen for best general fit
Overhead	Overhead assigned to activities and then from activities to products or services	Overhead assigned to departments and then from departments to products or services
Focus	Focus on solving costing and processing issues that cross departmental lines	Focus on assigning responsibility to departmental managers for individual cost and process improvements within their department

I. Explain how activity-based costing can be utilized in service firms.
  a. ABC is not only used in manufacturing companies. The same methods can be applied to service firms where resources are consumed (usually labor) completed a specific activity.

J. Demonstrate an understanding of the concept of life-cycle costing and the strategic value of including upstream costs, manufacturing costs, and downstream costs.
  a. Life-cycle costing sometimes is used on a strategic basis for cost planning and product pricing. It is designed to allow a firm to focus on the overall costs for a product or service. Poor early design could lead to much higher

marketing costs, lower sales, and higher service costs. The total costs for a product's life cycle have three phases:
  i. Upstream costs—Costs that are prior to the manufacturing of the product or sale of the service, such as research and development or design (prototypes, tests, and engineering).
  ii. Manufacturing costs—Costs involved in producing a product or service, such as purchasing and direct and indirect manufacturing costs.
  iii. Downstream costs—Costs subsequent to (or coincident with) manufacturing costs, such as marketing, distribution (packaging, shipping and handling, promotions, and advertising), service costs, and warranty costs (defect recalls, returns, and liability).

Section D.3. Overhead Costs

A. Distinguish between fixed and variable overhead expenses.
  a. Fixed overhead expenses—Costs that do not change during an accounting period, provided the relevant range is consistent with the level of production. Fixed costs include depreciation on assets, rentals, leasing costs, and indirect labor incurred in manufacturing.
  b. Variable overhead expenses—Costs that change in proportion to the changes in a particular cost driver, and the cost drivers can be either volume or activity based. Variable costs include power, water, sewage, engineering support, machine maintenance, and indirect materials.
B. Determine the appropriate time frame for classifying both variable and fixed overhead expenses.
  a. Variable overhead costs are usually short term in nature as they fluctuate with levels of production and can be adjusted accordingly. Fixed overhead expenses have a longer time frame and can't be adjusted in the short run when production levels fluctuate.
C. Demonstrate an understanding of the different methods of determining overhead rates, e.g., plant-wide rates, departmental rates, and individual cost driver rates.
  a. Plant-wide overhead rate—A single rate used for all overhead costs incurred at a production facility.
  b. Departmental overhead rate—A single overhead rate calculated for a particular department. Each department could have its own rate calculated based on its own cost drivers.
  c. Individual cost driver overhead rate—Also known as activity-based costing (ABC). ABC assigns factory overhead costs to products or services using multiple cost pools and multiple cost drivers. The cost drivers are selected based on a cause-and-effect relationship and can be both activity based and volume based.

D. Describe the benefits and limitations of each of the methods used to determine overhead rates.
   a. Plant-wide overhead rate—This allocation method is much simpler to calculate and allocate to products but tends not to be as accurate. If one department in a plant is highly automated and another department is labor intensive, different cost drivers should be used for each department instead of a plant-wide overhead rate.
   b. Departmental overhead rate—Departmental overhead rates are more accurate than plant-wide rates, but they still are fairly general, so misallocations of costs can occur if the cost driver chosen does not truly relate to all activities for a department.
   c. Activity-based costing—Activity-based overhead allocation may help management identify inefficient products, departments, and activities when it attempts to eliminate activities that do not provide value to products and services. Activity-based overhead allocation may encourage focusing resources on profitable products, departments and activities, and controlling costs.
E. Identify the components of variable overhead expense.
   a. Variable overhead expenses include power, water, sewage, engineering support, machine maintenance, and indirect materials.
F. Determine the appropriate allocation base for variable overhead expenses.
   a. Variable overhead expenses should be allocated based on an appropriate cost driver. The cost driver should be selected based on the activity that tends to have a cause-and-effect relationship on the variable overhead expenses. For example, an appropriate allocation base could be machine hours or direct labor hours.
G. Calculate the per unit variable overhead expense.
   a. After a cost pool and cost driver is determined, it is simple to determine the per-unit application rate.

$$\text{Variable Overhead Application Rate} = \frac{\text{Total Cost in Variable Overhead Cost Pool}}{\text{Total Quantity of Allocation Base}}$$

H. Identify the components of fixed overhead expense.
   a. Fixed overhead includes depreciation, rentals, leasing costs, and indirect labor incurred in manufacturing.
I. Identify the appropriate allocation base for fixed overhead expense.
   a. Although fixed costs do not vary, they still must be allocated in proportion to the value they are providing to each cost pool.
J. Calculate the fixed overhead application rate.
   a. After a cost pool and cost driver is determined, it is simple to determine the per-unit application rate.

$$\text{Fixed Overhead Application Rate} = \frac{\text{Total Cost in Fixed Overhead Cost Pool}}{\text{Total Quantity of Allocation Base}}$$

K. Describe how fixed overhead can be over or under applied and how this difference should be accounted for in the cost of goods sold, work in process, and finished goods accounts.
   a. The application rate calculated above is usually an annual estimate of the total costs to be incurred divided the total estimated quantity of the cost driver. When fixed expenses or production is different from planned, it results in some overhead costs being over- or underapplied to products. If the amount is not material, the over- or underapplied overhead should be written off to cost of goods sold. However, if the amount is large, it should be allocated proportionately to cost of goods sold, work in process, and finished goods accounts.
L. Compare and contrast traditional overhead allocation with activity-based overhead allocation.
   a. The next chart compares the cost drivers, overhead, and focus of an ABC system as opposed to a traditional costing system:

	ABC	**Traditional Costing**
Cost drivers	Multiple cost drivers: activity and volume-based drivers (whichever fits the cost best)	Up to three cost drivers: only volume based, chosen for best general fit
Overhead	Overhead assigned to activities and then from activities to products or services	Overhead assigned to departments and then from departments to products or services
Focus	Focus on solving costing and processing issues that cross departmental lines	Focus on assigning responsibility to departmental managers for individual cost and process improvements within their department

M. Calculate overhead expense in an activity-based costing setting.
   a. Activity-based costing was described in detail in Section D.2: Costing Systems. See outline above as well as the chapter materials.
N. Identify and describe the benefits derived from activity-based overhead allocation.
   a. Activity-based overhead allocation may help management identify inefficient products, departments, and activities when it attempts to eliminate activities that do not provide value to products and services. Activity-based overhead allocation may encourage focusing resources on profitable products, departments, and activities, and controlling costs.
O. Explain why companies allocate the cost of service departments such as Human Resources or Information Technology to divisions, departments, or activities.
   a. Service department costs are allocated because most service departments do not generate any revenue (i.e., they are cost centers). Although a service

department may not directly add value to a product, it provides a service to other departments within a company that may directly add value to the products and services that the company offers. Managers may determine that service department costs should be allocated back to the operating departments because an operating department may not be able to provide its products without the support of the service department.

P. Calculate service or support department cost allocations using the direct method, the reciprocal method, the step-down method, and the dual allocation method.

a. Direct method—Allocates service department costs directly to production departments, ignoring the services it provides to other service departments. The formula for allocating service department costs under the direct method is:

$$\text{Department Allocation} = \frac{\text{Production Department Units}}{\text{Total Units for All Production Departments}} \times \text{Departments Costs}$$

b. Reciprocal method—The most complicated method of the allocation methods, as it fully recognizes all interdepartmental service costs using simultaneous equations. To calculate, a system of equations beginning with the total service department costs and the portions for each of the other departments needs to be set up. See Topic 3: Overhead Costs in the topic materials for more detailed computations.

c. Step-down method—Allocates a service department's costs to service departments and production departments. This method sequentially allocates service department costs, starting with the department that provides the most services to other service departments and finishing with the department that provides the least services to other service departments. Each successive department's allocation is a step down in costs that need to be allocated. See Topic 3: Overhead Costs in the chapter materials for more detailed computations.

Q. Estimate fixed costs using the high-low method and demonstrate an understanding of how regression can be used to estimate fixed costs.

a. The high-low method is a cost accounting technique that separates fixed costs from variable costs. It uses the highest and lowest observed cost driver (i.e., machine hours) values within the relevant range and their respective costs to estimate the slope coefficient and the constant of the cost function. Using the next chart, the fixed and variable costs can be calculated by taking the difference between the highest and lowest months of production, or 300 units (2,100 − 1,800). The difference in cost between those two months is $3,000 (31,000 − 28,000), which means the variable costs are $10 per unit (3,000 / 300). The fixed costs can then be calculated by subtracting the variable costs from the total costs for any given month.

Month	Production Activity	Wages
July	2,000 units	$30,000
August	1,800 units	$28,000
September	1,900 units	$29,000
October	2,100 units	$31,000

    b. The high-low method also can be determined using regression analysis. A constant (or fixed costs) can be determined by rearranging the regression equation of

$y = a + bX$ to $a = y - bX$

where
y = total costs
a = fixed costs
b = variable costs per unit
X = units of production

Section D.4. Supply Chain Management

A. Explain supply chain management.
    a. "Supply chain management (SCM) is the management of the flow of goods, which includes the movement and storage of raw materials, work-in-process inventory, and finished goods from the point of origin to the point of consumption. It involves the planning and management of all activities involved in sourcing and procuring raw materials, converting those materials to a finished product, and delivering that finished product to consumers. In a broad sense, SCM strives to integrate procurement, operations management, logistics, and information technology, while creating value through this 'chain of key processes and activities.'"

B. Define lean manufacturing and describe its central purpose.
    a. Lean manufacturing, also called lean enterprise or lean production, focuses on the creation of value for the end customer. Any expenditure for any goal other than creating customer value is considered waste and should be eliminated.

C. Identify and describe the operational benefits of implementing lean manufacturing.
    a. The primary benefits of lean manufacturing are reduced waste and improved production flow (throughput). Both waste reduction and increased throughput reduce costs.

D. Define materials requirements planning (MRP).
    a. Instead of a pull-through system like a just-in-time environment, MRP is a push-through system where demand forecasts are created for the

estimated total of finished goods needed. The production schedule is then built according to the demand forecast, and products are made according to schedule regardless of demand.

E. Identify and describe the operational benefits of implementing a just-in-time (JIT) system.
   a. Some of the general benefits of JIT are listed next:
      - Obvious production priorities
      - Reduced setup and manufacturing lead time
      - No overproduction occurrences
      - Improved quality control (faster feedback) and less materials waste
      - Easier inventory control (low or even zero inventory)
      - Less paperwork
      - Strong supplier relationships

F. Identify and describe the operational benefits of enterprise resource planning (ERP).
   a. The benefits of ERP are improved business effectiveness and efficiency, better and timelier decisions, a more flexible agile organization, improved data integrity and security, and improved collaboration between organizational functions.

G. Explain the concept of outsourcing, and identify the benefits and limitations of choosing this option.
   a. Outsourcing is the obtaining of goods or services from an outside supplier rather than producing them internally. Outsourcing may be short term or long term. The advantages of outsourcing are:
      - It frees the organization to focus on its core competencies.
      - It helps the organization to mitigate risk by sharing it with the supplier.
      - It allows the organization to use another's knowledge and expertise.
      - It can decrease the time it takes the organization to enter a market or to meet competition
      - It may reduce the organization's costs.
      - It allows the organization to convert a committed fixed cost to a potentially avoidable variable cost.

      The disadvantages of outsourcing are:
      - Increased risk of exposing confidential data and information.
      - Reliance on suppliers.
      - Increased costs.
      - Possible loss of customer focus.
      - Lowering of employee morale and commitment.

H. Demonstrate a general understanding of the theory of constraints.
   a. The overriding goal of the TOC is to improve speed in the manufacturing process by optimizing throughput rather than simply measuring output. The premise behind the TOC is that every system is pursuing a goal and that every goal is constrained by a limit. If a system is a series of connecting processes that work together to accomplish some aim, a constraint is a limiting factor, bottleneck, or barrier that slows a

product's total cycle time. Cycle time is the time it takes to complete a process from beginning to end. Constraint management is the process of identifying process barriers, analyzing and understanding the barriers, and removing them so as to reduce cycle time and optimize the system's efficiency.

I. Identify the five steps involved in theory of constraints analysis.

Step 1—Identify the system constraint

Step 2—Decide how to exploit the constraint

Step 3—Subordinate everything else

Step 4—Elevate the constraint

Step 5—Go back to Step 1, but beware of inertia.

J. Define throughput costing (super-variable costing) and calculate inventory costs using throughput costing.

    a. Throughput costing, also called supervariable costing, is a costing method where the only costs included in inventory are the costs of direct materials. In throughput costing, *inventory* refers to the total investment in inventory and includes:

All Direct Materials + Research and Development Costs + Cost of Buildings and Equipment

K. Define and calculate throughput contribution.

    a. Throughput contribution—The markup on direct materials costs. It is calculated as:

Throughput Contribution = Sales Revenue − Direct Material Costs

L. Describe how capacity level affects product costing, capacity management, pricing decisions and financial statements.

    a. Managers can use ideal or practical capacity levels when allocating overhead to products. If ideal capacity levels are used, less would be allocated to products and more would be left at the end of the accounting period, which eventually needs to get flushed through the income statement (or in remaining inventory). The choice of capacity level used to allocate overhead can have a great effect on product cost information that managers use. If a company has capacity in excess of what it needs, it will incur large costs of unused capacity. Likewise, if a company has too little capacity to meet demand, it may have trouble filling customer orders.

M. Explain how using practical capacity as denominator for fixed costs rate enhances capacity management.

    a. Practical capacity is a better choice to use as the denominator activity level for allocating overhead because it is realistic and will generate product costs that accurately reflect the cost of the product. By using practical capacity to calculate product costs, the company is not over- or underallocating costs to each unit of product.

N. Calculate the financial impact of implementing the above-mentioned methods.
   a. To illustrate the difference in the above methods, consider the following: A company has the ability, without machine breakdowns, delays, or the like (ideal capacity), to produce 10,000 widgets. However, the highest level of capacity that can be achieved while allowing for unavoidable losses of productive time, such as machine breakdowns, employee vacations, maintenance, and so on (practical capacity), is only 8,000 widgets. If the total overhead to be allocated to units is $500,000, then $50 would be allocated to each unit under the ideal capacity and $62.50 under the practical capacity. That is a $12.50 difference allocated to each product, which will skew the profitability of the product.

Section D.5. Business Process Improvement

A. Define value chain analysis.
   a. Value chain analysis—A continuous process of gathering, evaluating, and communicating information. The basic intent of value chain analysis is to help managers envision an organization's future and implement business decisions to gain and sustain competitive advantage.
   b. The value chain begins with research and development, then proceeds through product design, procurement, production, marketing and distribution, customer service, and back to research and development.
B. Identify the steps in value chain analysis.
   Step 1—Internal cost analysis
   Step 2—Internal differentiation analysis
   Step 3—Vertical linkage analysis
C. Explain how value chain analysis is used to better understand a firm's competitive advantage.
   a. The purpose of a value chain analysis is to focus on the total value chain of each product or service and to determine which selected part or parts support the firm's competitive advantage and strategy. Theoretically, competitive advantage and competitive strategy cannot be examined meaningfully at the organizational level as a whole or even at the business unit level. Because a value chain separates the firm into distinct strategic activities, organizations can use value chain analysis to determine where in the operations—from design to distribution and customer service—customer value can be enhanced and costs lowered.
D. Define, identify, and provide examples of a value-added activity and explain how the value-added concept is related to improving performance.
   a. Value-added activities—Activities that convert resources into products and services consistent with external customer requirements. If a customer requirement is the timely delivery of goods and exceptional customer

support, a company would focus its efforts on improving those areas of the business while eliminating any non-value-added activities that have no value in the eyes of the end user. By removing non-value-added activities, work processes can be more efficient and ultimately yield a better-quality product or service.

E. Demonstrate an understanding of process analysis and business process reengineering.
   a. Process analysis—A collection of analytic methods that can be used to examine and measure the basic elements for a process to operate. It also can identify those processes with the greatest need for improvement.
   b. Business process reengineering—The fundamental analysis and radical redesign of business processes within and between enterprises to achieve dramatic improvements in performance.

F. Define best practice analysis, and discuss how it can be used by an organization to improve performance.
   a. Best practice analysis involves assessing how a firm's given performance level measures up to a best practice and then defining the logical next steps in transitioning to the desired performance level. Best practice analysis enables firms to identify and undertake performance improvements.

G. Demonstrate an understanding of benchmarking process performance.
   a. Benchmarking can be used in coordination with process analysis to develop measures to use in assessing an organization's effectiveness, efficiency, and adaptability. The term *benchmarking* describes a continuous, systematic process of measuring products, services, and practices against the best levels of performance.

H. Identify the benefits of benchmarking in creating a competitive advantage.
   a. Well-designed and properly applied benchmarking can be a powerful tool in helping an organization to be competitive. Through benchmarking, a firm identifies best-in-class levels and conducts a study to determine how those levels can be adopted and lead to improved performance.

I. Apply activity-based management principles to recommend process performance improvements.
   a. Activity-based management—Focuses on the management of activities as the way of improving the value received by the customer and the profit achieved by providing this value. ABM helps make performance evaluation measures relate to the factors that drive the element being measured. Based on ABM information, organizations generally can make better decisions, improve performance, and increase earnings on total resources deployed.

J. Explain the relationship among continuous improvement techniques, activity-based management, and quality performance.
   a. ABM sometimes is erroneously thought of as a replacement for quality efforts, just-in-time systems, process reengineering, business process reengineering, and benchmarking. To the contrary, ABM *supports* quality management and the other initiatives by providing an integrated

information system that establishes accountability, facilitates measuring of results, and enables setting of priorities. ABM also facilitates quality implementation by identifying activity costs, increasing the visibility of associated costs to quality, and provides quality cost measures that can be easily incorporated in cost-of-quality reports.

K. Explain the concept of continuous improvement and how it relates to implementing ideal standards and quality improvements.
   a. Continuous improvement (kaizen)—Focuses on examining, working on, and improving every process throughout the organization by making continuous incremental improvements. The kaizen process is often described as a staircase of improvement. Moving from step to step, an organization uses a continuous process of following an improvement, maintaining an improvement, following an improvement, maintaining an improvement, and so on. Although the steps may be small, each step moves the organization upward toward sustained improvements.

L. Describe and identify the components of the costs of quality, commonly referred to as prevention costs, appraisal costs, internal failure costs, and external failure costs.

M. Calculate the financial impact of implementing the above-mentioned processes.

N. Identify and discuss ways to make accounting operations more efficient, including process walk-throughs, process training, identification of waste and overcapacity, identifying the root cause of errors, reducing the accounting close cycle (fast close), and shared services.
   a. Process walk-throughs increase one's understanding of processes and help one to enhance process effectiveness and efficiency. Process training enhances employees' effectiveness and efficiency in performing processes. Increased understanding of processes and process training help identify wasteful steps, excess capacity, and the root causes of process errors. Increased effectiveness and efficiency of processes should decrease the time it takes the organization to complete its period closing cycle and reduce the need for shared services.

TOPIC 1

Measurement Concepts

MEASUREMENT CONCEPTS MAKE USE OF cost behavior relationships to analyze the effect that changes in costs will have on the firm's profitability. Defining and classifying costs is essential to understanding how they can be used to measure performance.

This topic discusses types and classification of costs, including fixed, variable, and step costs; cost drivers; actual, normal, and standard costing; absorption and variable costing; and joint and by-product costing.

> **READ** the Learning Outcome Statements (LOS) for this topic as found in Appendix A and then study the concepts and calculations presented here to be sure you understand the content you could be tested on in the CMA exam.

Cost Behavior and Cost Objects

The first step in classifying a cost is to understand its behavior over what is referred to as the *relevant range*. The relevant range is the range of activity where assumptions of cost behavior reasonably hold true, over which the company plans to operate. Within the relevant range, costs will either be fixed or variable. A fixed cost will remain constant (in total) over the relevant range, but will vary on a per unit basis in proportion to activity, volume, or some other cost driver. This can be contrasted to variable costs which will vary (in total) in proportion to activity, volume, or some other cost driver, but will remain constant on a per unit basis over the relevant range. Total cost is the sum of all variable and fixed costs.

For example: A manufacturing plant has fixed costs, such as rent and management salaries, and variable costs, such as production labor and material costs. The fixed costs will remain constant (in total) regardless of whether the plant has zero output or full production; however, on a per unit basis, the fixed costs will change inversely to production changes. Variable costs, on the other hand, will not be incurred until production starts and then will increase as production increases or decrease as production decreases. Again, it is important to note that it is the total variable costs that change with production increases and decreases; the variable costs on a per unit basis remain constant.

Variable Costs

A **variable cost** includes changes in total for a cost object in proportion to each change in the quantity of a cost driver over a relevant range. Variable cost measured on a per-unit basis will remain constant over a relevant range (e.g., $5/unit within a relevant range of 1 to 5,000 units). Direct materials and direct labor are both variable costs because more materials and labor are needed if more units of a product are produced. Some indirect costs are also variable costs, such as sealants and adhesives used in the process that are difficult to track per unit but must be accounted for in the cost of each item.

For example: For a tennis ball manufacturer, as the quantity of tennis balls increases, the quantity of direct materials, such as rubber, and the quantity of direct labor will increase across the relevant range defined as the minimum and maximum output of the tennis ball machine (without having to change the size of the workforce).

Fixed Costs

Fixed costs are the portion of total costs that do not change when the quantity of a cost driver changes over a relevant range and duration. The duration is important because fixed costs may be constant one year and at a constant but higher level the next year. Fixed cost measured on a per-unit basis will decline (become less significant) as quantities increase: At 100 units, a $1,000 fixed cost is $10/unit, but at 1,000 units, it is only $1/unit.

Fixed costs can also be further classified as discretionary or committed:

- **Discretionary costs**, which are also known as managed or budgeted fixed costs, can be included or excluded from the budget at the discretion of the managers. Examples of discretionary costs include advertising, training, or internships, as well as indirect manufacturing labor and selling and administrative labor.
- **Committed costs** are costs that cannot be omitted due to strategic or operational priorities in the short run. An example is depreciation on equipment previously purchased. Committed fixed costs tend to be facilities related and result from prior capacity-related decisions.

Fixed costs include many indirect costs, such as depreciation, taxes, employees paid on salary, insurance, and lease costs. These costs usually are fixed because no matter the level of output within the relevant range, these costs will remain the same.

Figure 1D-1 shows both fixed and variable costs over a relevant range.

Figure 1D-1 Fixed and Variable Costs

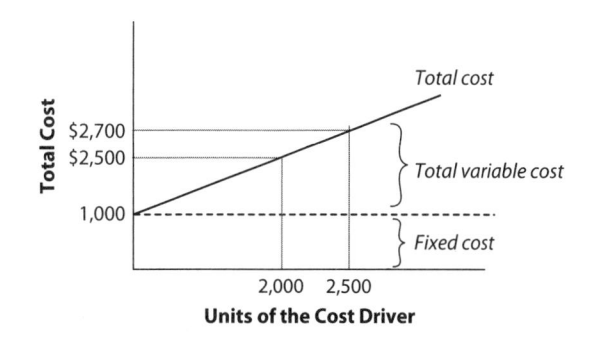

[Graph showing Total Cost on y-axis with values $2,700, $2,500, and 1,000 marked; Units of the Cost Driver on x-axis with 2,000 and 2,500 marked. Total cost line rises from 1,000 fixed cost baseline, with Total variable cost and Fixed cost brackets indicated.]

For a given output level, the next formula holds true:

> Total Cost/Unit at a Given Output Level = Fixed Cost/Unit + Variable Cost/Unit

Total cost per unit will decline as output increases because the fixed costs are being allocated over greater quantities.

Step Costs

Step costs are fixed costs with very narrow relevant ranges. Step costs tend to be considered fixed costs over the short run but become variable costs over the long run.

For example: A company operates one plant. In the short run, the plant overhead is a fixed cost. If the plant's capacity is 100 units a day, an additional plant must be purchased to produce 200 units per day. A doubling in production capacity will also double the plant overhead cost (assuming that each plant has the same capacity and costs). In the long run, plant overhead becomes a variable cost.

The narrow relevant ranges on step costs can be step-fixed or step-variable. Step-fixed ranges increase in equal-size chunks over an equal number of cost drivers, such as plant overhead increasing by $100,000 for each plant added. Step-variable ranges go up to a higher constant cost in either increasingly larger or increasingly smaller amounts of a cost driver. Step-variable costs can increase or decrease at a predictable rate when they are caused by factors such as increasing learning curve rates for workers, diminishing marginal returns, or economies of scale.

For example, if one worker can produce 0.5 units per day, two workers can produce 1.0 unit, three workers can produce 1.5 units, and four workers can produce 3.0 units, the resulting step-variable costs would look like those in the right side of Figure 1D-2. The left side of this figure shows step-fixed costs using the plant overhead example.

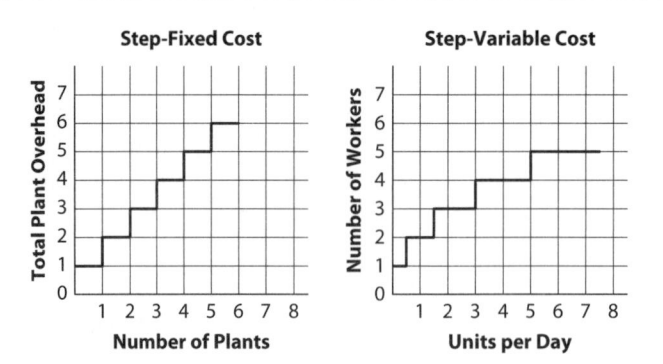

Figure 1D-2 Step-Fixed and Step-Variable Costs

Total Cost and Mixed Cost

Total costs are all fixed and variable costs for a cost object. Total costs are also called **mixed costs** when they include both fixed and variable components.

Cost Type Relationships

Direct costs can be fixed or variable, and indirect costs can also be fixed or variable.

Capacity

Capacity measures the constraints or bottlenecks keeping a system from expanding in output or some other measure. Manufacturing capacity can be increased by adding plants, employees, or equipment. Financial capacity can be increased by gaining access to new debt or equity. Capacity relates to the relevant range, because the capacity limits often are reached at the upper limit of the relevant range. Furthermore, as capacity limits are approached, operations lose efficiency and increase in cost. This leads to the need to define a company's **practical capacity**, which is the highest output level a resource such as a plant can achieve without increasing its costs due to bottlenecks. When output exceeds the practical capacity, marginal costs begin to exceed marginal benefits. Practical capacity also takes into account normal operating conditions, such as the average number of errors or breakdowns, holidays and vacation time, and other realistic factors.

When such real-world factors are omitted, capacity is defined as **theoretical capacity**, or the upper limit on output assuming that nothing goes wrong, everything operates at full speed, and no holidays or other scheduling conflicts are included. Theoretical capacity is an ideal.

Capacity decisions made in the past generally will determine a company's present fixed costs. Fixed costs related to capacity choices include everything from the amount of space and resources devoted to each business unit, the size and cost of plants, to the amount of depreciation. These fixed costs are generally noncontrollable by division managers, who nevertheless feel the effect of these costs. If too much capacity is created, there are opportunity costs and high fixed costs at risk. If too little capacity is created, companies face other costs, such as overtime, lost sales, and higher wear and tear on facilities. Tracking the cost of excess capacity separately from the overall cost of an item can help show the cost of underutilized assets.

For example: If a plant's budgeted fixed overhead is $500,000 and overhead is applied by the units produced, the plant has a practical capacity level of 5,000 units per period, and overhead would by applied at $100/unit. If the plant budgeted only 4,000 units at $100/unit, $400,000 would be allocated to operations, and the remaining $100,000 would be treated as a separate period expense, tracked as the cost of having excess capacity. It is important to match the manager's incentives to the plant's practical capacity so that any decisions made to increase output can be weighed against the costs of increasing that output, holding inventory, and the like.

Although the prior definitions of capacity hinged on output, when capacity is defined by the expected demand for output or budgeted demand, it is called capacity utilization. **Normal capacity utilization** is a level of capacity utilization that will meet the average customer demand over a period, including the seasonal and cyclical variations or trends. Normal capacity utilization is a long-term tool that often is used over a period of several years. **Master budget capacity utilization** is normal capacity utilization for the current budget period, such as a year. It is important to use normal capacity utilization for long-term planning and master budget capacity utilization for shorter-term planning, or else the end costs can be inaccurate. Each of these capacity levels can be used to allocate costs, and each generally shows a different amount.

For example: In a plant with $500,000 in budgeted fixed overhead, if theoretical capacity is 8,000 units/period, practical capacity is 5,000 units/period, normal capacity utilization is 4,500 units/period, and master budget capacity is 4,000 units/period, the budgeted fixed cost per case would be $62.50, $100, $111, and $125 respectively. Similar results can be found with variable costs. Correct choice of capacity is therefore the key to cost analysis, management incentives, and performance evaluation decisions.

Cost Drivers

Firms manage their costs by determining how cost drivers affect a particular cost object. There are four types of cost drivers:

1. **Activity-based cost drivers** focus on operations that involve manufacturing or service activity, such as machine setup, machine use, or packaging.
2. **Volume-based cost drivers** focus on output, which involves aggregate measures, such as units produced or labor hours.
3. **Structural cost drivers** focus on company strategy, which involves long-term plans for scale, complexity, amount of experience in an area, or level of technical expertise.

4. **Executional cost drivers** focus on short-term operations, which involve reducing costs through concern with workforce commitment and involvement, production design, and supplier relationships.

Activity-Based Cost Drivers

Firms use an activity analysis to determine a detailed description of each type of activity. These descriptions form the basis for the activity-based cost drivers. The descriptions then are broken down into steps, and each step in the description becomes a different cost driver. The intent is to determine how changing the steps will change the overall cost of the operation. The cost of each step or activity can also be determined, and therefore the overall cost of a cost object can be determined. This detailed breakdown can help firms determine which activities add value for customers and which do not. Furthermore, when an activity costs more than is expected, activity-based cost drivers will highlight this discrepancy.

For example: Figure 1D-3 illustrates a few of the activities and cost drivers for a retailer.

Figure 1D-3 Retailer Activities and Cost Drivers

Activity	Cost Driver
Accepting cash	Number of cash transactions
Processing of credit card	Number of credit transactions
Payment of credit card fee	Dollar size of transactions
Close-out and supervisor review of clerk	Number of close-outs
Consolidation and deposit of receipts	Number of deposits
Bank account reconciliation	Number of accounts
Updating of customer account balances via computer	Number of accounts updated
Investigation of unusual transactions	Number of transactions investigated
Processing of returns and chargebacks	Number of chargebacks
Maintenance of computer equipment	Number of computer terminals
Training	Number of stores
Mailing of customer statements	Number of accounts

Volume-Based Cost Drivers

Volume-based cost drivers are aggregations of activities based on volume of use. Some cost drivers, such as direct materials and direct labor, are inherently volume-based. Direct labor is, by definition, the level of output for a volume of work at an hourly rate. Volume-based drivers such as direct labor often have a sloped curve in relation to output levels, as shown in Figure 1D-4.

Figure 1D-4 Total Cost and the Effect of Capacity Limits

[Graph showing Total Cost on y-axis and Units of the Cost Driver on x-axis, with a curve rising slowly then sharply near the Capacity limit]

When a volume-based cost driver is very low, factors such as learning curves and efficient use of resources will cause costs to increase more slowly as production increases. This is called increasing marginal productivity, because the increasing output will use the inputs more efficiently. At a certain level, the total costs will level off, and a rise in volume will have a proportional rise in cost within the relevant range, until a certain point at which the capacity of the persons or equipment will reach the limit. As the volume increases toward the limit, the costs will rise dramatically because of increased need for repairs, more overtime, and other similar factors. This is called the law of diminishing marginal capacity.

Determining costs across the entire range of productivity would be hard to estimate without using complex calculations, which is why the relevant range is an important element of cost drivers.

Structural Cost Drivers

Structural cost drivers are long-term cost drivers based on the overall strategy of the company. There are four types of structural cost drivers: scale, experience level, technology, and complexity.

Scale

The scale of a project or the speed at which a company grows will affect all of the costs of the company overall. Deciding how many stores to open, how many employees to hire, or how much capital to devote to a project will affect costs directly.

Experience Level

The experience level of the company for a particular strategic desire will affect the overall cost of achieving that goal. The areas in which the company has the most expertise will be the cheapest areas to develop further, but if the market no longer needs such expertise, developing a new area of expertise could be more cost effective in the long run.

Technology

Changing the level of technology for a process can make that process more efficient and therefore less costly. The other benefit of investing in technology is that the products may be of higher quality; therefore, the firm may be able to increase market share with a cheaper and better product.

Complexity

The more complex a firm gets (more products, more levels of hierarchy), the more it costs to sustain that complexity. Reducing complexity will reduce both the costs of product development and the costs of distribution and service. Strategic decisions related to complexity usually are made to reduce overall complexity and cost. Conversely, a firm that has too few products or too small a staff may be missing out on market opportunities.

Executional Cost Drivers

Executional cost drivers are the short-term decisions that can be made to reduce operational costs. There are three types: workforce involvement, production process design, and supplier relationships.

Workforce Involvement

The greater the commitment of the workforce, the lower the labor costs will be in proportion to the amount of work that gets done. Many firms have been successful in improving quality and reducing labor costs by working to foster pride and commitment in the workplace through creative team building and an emphasis on consensus and employee input.

Production Process Design

Analyzing and redesigning production processes and incorporating software applications to streamline workflow have been key factors in reducing production costs for many firms.

Supplier Relationships

Close relationships with suppliers can reduce overall costs, especially inventory costs. With electronic data interchange (EDI) and similar applications, a firm can allow its supplier to view the company's inventory levels directly and automatically ship items as needed, resulting in a more efficient production flow.

Actual, Normal, and Standard Costing

Cost allocation is a method of applying costs to products, jobs, or services. Actual, normal, and standard costing are types of cost allocation. The terms *actual* and *normal* refer to the means of applying or allocating overhead costs to cost objects.

Actual costing uses the actual amounts for overhead costs. **Normal costing** uses the actual costs for labor and direct materials and uses a predetermined overhead rate for overhead. **Standard costing** uses a predetermined standard cost, also known as a "should" cost, for overhead, direct materials, and direct labor. All three of these methods are types of job order costing, in which costs are accumulated in inventory accounts (such as work-in-process [WIP] and finished goods inventory) and are recorded on the income statement as cost of goods sold (COGS) once the product is sold.

Actual Costing

An actual costing system records the actual costs incurred for *all* costs—including direct labor, direct material, and overhead. The actual costs are determined by waiting until the end of the accounting period and then calculating the actual costs based on the recorded amounts.

The primary benefit of actual costs is that they are more accurate than other costing systems. However, this reliability also means a delay in information, because the costs cannot be known until all of the invoices are received, which may not be until the end of the fiscal year or later. Because the number of units produced varies from period to period, and because the fixed costs do not vary with these production changes, actual costing makes costs per unit vary for products produced in different periods. To smooth out these fluctuations in the actual cost per unit, firms often turn to normal costing as an alternative method.

Normal Costing

Similar to actual costing, normal costing applies actual costs for direct materials and direct labor to a job, process, or other cost object and then uses a predetermined overhead rate to assign overhead to a cost object. This method allows current calculation of product costs and, by normalizing the fluctuations in overhead rates, enables comparisons between periods.

A predetermined factory overhead rate is applied to a job or other cost object, as determined in four steps:

1. Create an annual (or other period) budget for overhead costs.
2. Choose cost drivers (usually activity or volume) for charging overhead.
3. Estimate the total annual amount or volume of the selected cost driver for the total overhead costs or each cost pool.
4. Calculate the predetermined factory overhead rate by dividing the budgeted factory overhead costs by the estimated cost driver activity level:

$$\text{Predetermined Factory Overhead Rate} = \frac{\text{Budgeted Factory Overhead Costs}}{\text{Estimated Cost Driver Activity Level}}$$

Factory overhead using normal costing will be underapplied in some months and overapplied in others. The net amount overapplied is the amount of applied overhead that exceeds actual costs, and the net amount underapplied is the opposite. The net amount over- or underapplied is disposed of either by adjusting the COGS account or by prorating the net difference between the current period's applied overhead balances in the WIP inventory, finished goods inventory, and COGS accounts.

Adjusting Cost of Goods Sold

Suppose that $1,530,000 of actual overhead was incurred and $1,490,000 of overhead was allocated to products under normal costing. This means that overhead was underapplied by $40,000. Assuming that this underapplied amount is not material, the COGS should be increased by $40,000. The adjusting entry to the COGS account is shown in Figure 1D-5.

Figure 1D-5 Journal Entry to Record Disposition of Underapplied Overhead

	COGS Method	
Cost of Goods Sold	$40,000	
Factory Overhead Applied	$1,490,000	
Factory Overhead		$1,530,000

To record the disposition of underapplied overhead.

This entry closes the factory overhead applied and factory overhead accounts and debits (or increases) the cost of goods sold.

Under a different scenario, if $1,600,000 of overhead was allocated under normal costing and the actual overhead remained the same at $1,530,000 and if the $70,000 in overapplied overhead is not material, the adjusting entry to the COGS account would be as shown in Figure 1D-6. Note that the entry credits (decreases) cost of goods sold.

Figure 1D-6 Journal Entry to Record Disposition of Overapplied Overhead

	COGS Method	
Factory Overhead Applied	$1,600,000	
Factory Overhead		$1,530,000
Costs of Goods Sold		$70,000

To record the disposition of overapplied overhead.

Prorating Net Difference Between Inventories and Cost of Goods Sold

Factory overhead is accounted for in the WIP inventory, finished goods inventory, and COGS accounts, so when the net variance is material, it should be accounted for in each of these accounts in proportion to their relative size. If all production is complete, all goods are sold by the end of a period, and there is no balance in the WIP and finished goods inventory accounts, the simple COGS approach can be used. However, because production usually never ceases, the amount to be prorated to each account should be calculated. To determine the amount of overhead to apply to each account, the applied overhead in the ending inventories of each of these three accounts at the end of the period is divided by the sum of the applied overhead in the three accounts together.

For example: Assume that the applied overhead for each account is:

- Ending WIP inventory is $200,000.
- Ending finished goods inventory is $300,000.
- COGS is $1,000,000.

The ending WIP inventory proration is calculated as:

$$\frac{\$200,000}{\$1,500,000} = 0.133 = 13.3\%$$

If the finished goods are prorated at 20% and the COGS at 66.7% and if the variance were an underapplied overhead of $100,000, the WIP account would need to be increased by $13,300. Figure 1D-7 shows the adjusting entries.

Figure 1D-7 Journal Entry to Record Disposition of Underapplied Overhead

Inventory Account Allocation Method		
Factory Overhead Applied	$1,500,000	
Work-in-Process Inventory	$13,300	
Finished Goods Inventory	$20,000	
Cost of Goods Sold	$66,700	
Factory Overhead		$1,600,000
To record the disposition of underapplied overhead.		

Each inventory account is debited (or increased) by the amount shown. If $100,000 of overhead was overapplied (other factors staying the same), the adjusting entries would be as shown in Figure 1D-8.

Figure 1D-8 Journal Entry to Record Disposition of Overapplied Overhead

Inventory Account Allocation Method		
Factory Overhead Applied	$1,500,000	
Work-in-Process Inventory		$13,300
Finished Goods Inventory		$20,000
Cost of Goods Sold		$66,700
Factory Overhead		$1,400,000
To record the disposition of overapplied overhead.		

Each inventory account is credited (or decreased) by the amount shown. If the difference is immaterial, COGS is adjusted; if the difference is material, the prorated method is used.

Standard Costing

Standard costing applies all product costs (direct materials, direct labor, and overhead) using a predetermined (standard) rate. A standard cost is an expected or target cost for an operation. Standard costing is designed to point out where variances occur so that the company can achieve a better operating result. Each standard cost is usually broken down into these two parts:

1. A standard number of units of a cost driver adjusted for actual unit production (e.g., labor hours divided by the units produced, such as 40,000 labor hours divided by 80,000 units produced = 0.5 labor hours per unit).
2. A standard rate per unit of the cost driver (e.g., $20 per labor hour)

Knowing the standard rate and the number of units produced allows calculation of the standard cost of direct labor or direct materials. Standard costs (e.g., standard number of hours times the standard rate per hour) then can be compared to actual total costs (e.g., total direct labor costs).

For example: In a given month with the same 80,000 units produced, actual labor hours may have been 42,000 at an actual rate of $18 per labor hour. These differences between standard costs and actual costs lead to budget variances.

Standards can be ideal or currently attainable, as set by company policy, activity analysis, historical data, market expectations, strategy, and benchmarking.

Two of the advantages of using standard costs are they are less likely to incorporate past inefficiencies and that they can be adapted as new data indicate expected changes during the budget period.

The disadvantages in standard costing include the problems associated with unreasonable standards, when the process used to set the standards are authoritarian or secretive, or when the standards are poorly communicated. Inflexible standards or those that place undue emphasis on profits are likely to fail.

Absorption (Full) and Variable (Direct) Costing

Absorption costing (or full costing) is an inventory costing system that includes both variable and fixed manufacturing costs. Under absorption costing, inventory absorbs all costs of manufacturing. **Variable costing** (or direct costing) is an inventory costing method that includes only the variable manufacturing costs in the inventory costs and excludes fixed manufacturing costs. Variable costing expenses fixed manufacturing costs in the period in which the costs are incurred. Each method expenses all nonmanufacturing costs (both fixed and variable) in the period in which they occur. Therefore, these two methods differ only in how they account for fixed manufacturing costs.

Figure 1D-9 Variable versus Absorption Costing

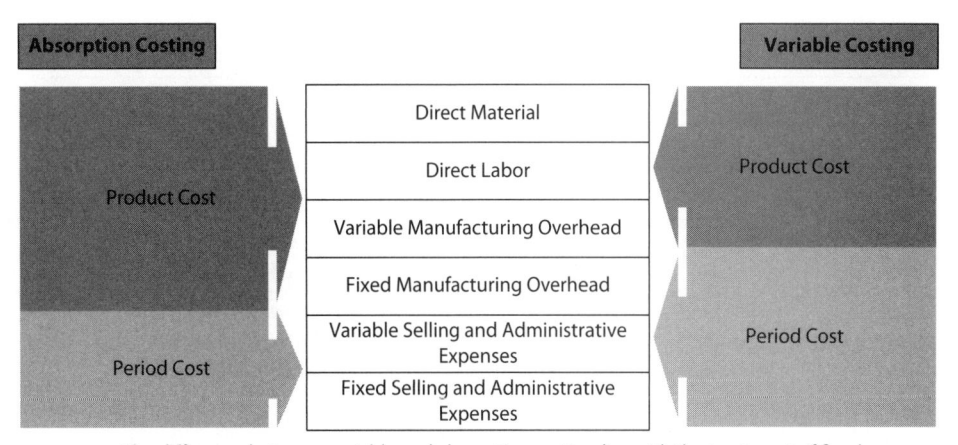

Absorption Costing		Variable Costing
Product Cost	Direct Material	Product Cost
	Direct Labor	
	Variable Manufacturing Overhead	
	Fixed Manufacturing Overhead	Period Cost
Period Cost	Variable Selling and Administrative Expenses	
	Fixed Selling and Administrative Expenses	

The difference between variable and absorption costing lies with the treatment of fixed manufacturing overhead. Absorption costing treats fixed manufacturing overhead as a product cost. Variable costing treats it as a period cost.

Income Statement Preparation Using Absorption and Variable Costing

Because variable costing and absorption costing have different objectives concerning the importance of the information presented on the income statement, each is usually presented in its own format. The variable costing method uses a contribution margin format, which highlights the distinction between fixed and variable costs. The absorption method uses the gross margin format, which highlights the differences between manufacturing and nonmanufacturing costs. The variable manufacturing costs are accounted for in the same manner in both income statements. The absorption method is the format required for external reporting.

The primary differences between the two statements are that under variable costing, the fixed manufacturing costs are deducted as an expense, whereas under absorption costing, each finished unit absorbs its share of the fixed manufacturing costs, which flows through to the finished goods inventory accounts. When production does not equal sales, net income will differ between absorption and variable costing. If more units are produced than sold, absorption costing will have higher net income because costs are all sitting in inventory, whereas variable costing will have lower net income because not as many costs end up in inventory compared to cost of goods sold.

Another difference is that when using absorption costing, fixed manufacturing costs in ending inventory are deferred to future periods whereas variable costing expenses the entire amount in the period in which the inventory is created.

Figure 1D-10 Variable Costing versus Absorption Costing Example

Variable Costing			Absorption Costing		
Revenues:			**Revenues:**		
$200 × 500 units		$100,000	$200 × 500 units		$100,000
Variable costs			**Costs of goods sold**		
Beginning inventory	$0		Beginning inventory	$0	
+ Variable manufacturing costs: $30 × 700	+21,000		+ Variable manufacturing costs: $30 × 700	+21,000	
= Cost of goods available for sale	21,000		+ Fixed manufacturing costs: $25 × 700	+17,500	
− Ending inventory: $30 × 200	− 6,000		= Cost of goods available for sale	38,500	
= Variable cost of goods Sold	15,000		− Ending inventory: ($30 variable + $25 fixed) × 200	−11,000	
+ Variable marketing costs: $20 × 500	+10,000		= Cost of goods sold		−27,500
= Total variable costs		−25,000			
= Contribution margin		75,000	= Gross margin		72,500
Fixed costs			**Operating costs**		
Fixed manufacturing costs: $25 × 700	17,500		Variable marketing costs: $20 × 500	10,000	
+ = Fixed marketing costs	+14,000		+ Fixed marketing costs	+14,000	
+/− Adjustment for fixed cost variances	0		+/− Adjustment for operating cost variances	0	
= Total fixed costs		−31,500	= Total operating costs		−24,000
= **Operating income**		**$43,500**	= **Operating income**		**$48,500**

For example: Figure 1D-10 shows each type of costing and each type of format. The data used for both sides of the table are the same.

- Units made: 700
- Units sold: 500
- Variable manufacturing costs per unit: $30
- Variable selling (marketing) costs per unit: $20
- Fixed manufacturing costs per unit: $25
- Fixed selling (marketing) costs: $14,000

In summary, when inventory increases, net income under absorption costing will be greater than under variable costing by the amount of the fixed cost of the change in inventory (200 units × $25 = $5,000 in Figure 1D-10). When inventory decreases, net income under absorption costing will be less than under variable costing by the amount of the change in inventory fixed cost. However, as methods such as just-in-time production and other inventory reduction methods increase in importance, the differences between variable and absorption costing will grow less material because inventory levels are less significant. In fact, if a company has zero inventory at the beginning and end of each accounting period, there is no difference between these two methods of costing.

Benefits and Limitations of Absorption and Variable Costing

Absorption costing is the standard method because both the U. S. Internal Revenue Service (IRS) and generally accepted accounting principles (GAAP) require its use. However, absorption costing allows managers to manipulate operating income simply by increasing production. If bonuses or other incentives are tied to operating income, managers may increase inventory even if no additional demand exists. Managers also may choose to produce items that absorb the highest fixed manufacturing costs instead of what is best for the company. To fix this and other improper management incentives, the company could switch to variable costing for internal reporting, allow managers less latitude in selecting what to produce, or provide a disincentive for accumulating inventory, such as a percentage carrying charge for all ending inventory.

Variable costing is used when the emphasis is on what items can be traced to and controlled by a responsibility center. Because fixed costs generally are outside the control of the center's manager, many companies focus only on the areas that can be controlled.

Variable costing is very effective in supporting internal decision making and is required for cost-volume-profit analysis.

Joint Product and By-Product Costing

Joint products are products that share a portion of the production process and have relatively the same sales value. **By-products** are products that share the same production process with a product or joint product but have relatively minor value in comparison to the main product. The oil industry uses a joint manufacturing process, where crude oil is refined into joint products, such as diesel, gasoline, motor oil, and plastic. A lumber mill may have finished boards and the scrap that could be used in plywood (a joint product), whereas the sawdust is used in other products (by-products). Both joint products and by-products share at least some of the same raw materials and initial processing costs. The split-off point is the point at which products diverge and become separately identifiable. The split-off point is not necessarily the point at which the products become finished goods.

Costing for joint products and by-products includes all manufacturing costs incurred before and after the split-off point. For financial reporting, joint costs incurred before the split-off point are allocated among the joint products. Additional processing costs (separable costs) are any costs that can be specifically identified with a product because the cost occurs after the split-off point where the costs are assigned to the separate products.

Two basic approaches can be taken for allocating joint costs to joint products: using data based on the market (such as revenues) or using data based on physical measures (such as weight or volume).

Market-Based Methods of Allocating Joint Costs to Joint Products

The market-based methods include:

- Sales value at split-off method
- Gross profit method
- NRV method

Sales Value at Split-off Method

The **sales value at split-off method** (also known as the sales value method) is widely used because of its simplicity. The sales value method can be used only when sales values are available at the split-off point. It allocates joint costs to joint products using their proportional sales value at the split-off point.

For example: A paper mill incurs $8,000 in joint costs when selling finished paper for $4 a pound and semifinished paper for $2 a pound. The process produces 1,000 pounds of finished paper and 3,000 pounds of semifinished paper. The steps for allocating this cost to each product are described next.

1. Calculate the total sales value for each joint product, which is the price per unit multiplied by the number of units. The sales value is not the record of actual sales but a calculation of value.

$$1{,}000 \text{ pounds} \times \$4 = \$4{,}000$$
$$3{,}000 \text{ pounds} \times \$2 = \$6{,}000$$

2. Calculate the proportion of the sales value for each joint product to the total sales value.

$$\frac{\$4{,}000}{\$10{,}000} = 0.4 = 40\% \qquad \frac{\$6{,}000}{\$10{,}000} = 0.6 = 60\%$$

3. Multiply the joint cost by the proportional amount of the sales value. This becomes the COGS and is the amount allocated to each product cost.

$$\$8{,}000 \times 0.4 = \$3{,}200 \qquad \$8{,}000 \times 0.6 = \$4{,}800$$

4. Calculate the cost per unit (pound) by dividing the COGS (proportional cost) from the previous step by the number of units (pounds). (Note that although the remaining methods do not show this step, the cost per unit can be calculated in the same manner.)

$$\frac{\$3{,}200}{1{,}000 \text{ pounds}} = \$3.20/\text{pound} \qquad \frac{\$4{,}800}{3{,}000 \text{ pounds}} = \$1.60/\text{pound}$$

5. Calculate the gross margin for each product by subtracting the sales value from the proportional cost:

$$\$4{,}000 - \$3{,}200 = \$800 \qquad \$6{,}000 - \$4{,}800 = \$1{,}200$$

Assuming that the sales prices are accurate estimates and if no extra processing is needed on the joint products, the sales value method has the advantage of providing the same gross margin percentage for both joint products. The gross margin percentage is calculated by dividing the gross margin by the sales value:

$$\frac{\$800}{\$4,000} = 0.2 = 20\% \qquad \frac{\$1,200}{\$6,000} = 0.2 = 20\%$$

The sales value method is widely used because it is both simple to calculate and allocates costs according to the value of the products. Other methods, such as the physical measure method, do not allocate costs according to value and therefore sometimes can allocate so much cost to a product that it has no gross profit margin whereas its counterpart joint product has a huge profit margin. The sales value method has the limitation of not being useful for products that need additional processing after the split-off point before a sales value is established. This method also may be less useful for products that have frequent market price fluctuations.

Gross Profit (Constant Gross Margin Percentage) Method

The **gross profit method,** also called the constant gross margin percentage method, allocates joint costs so as to provide the same gross margin percentage of profit for each joint product.

For example: Assume the same data from the paper mill example, except that in this case, the joint products share $5,000 in joint costs, finished paper has $2,000 in additional processing costs, and semifinished paper has $1,000 in additional processing costs after the split-off point. The steps for the gross profit method are:

1. Calculate the total gross margin percentage. To do this, first determine the final sales value by multiplying the price per unit by the number of units produced.

$$1,000 \text{ Pounds} \times \$4 = \$4,000$$
$$3,000 \text{ Pounds} \times \$2 = \$6,000$$

The total of these amounts ($10,000) less all joint and separable costs is the gross margin:

$$\$10,000 - \$5,000 - \$2,000 - \$1,000 = \$2,000 \text{ Gross Margin}$$

The gross margin percentage is the gross margin divided by the total sales value:

$$\frac{\$2,000}{\$10,000} = 0.2 = 20\%$$

2. To determine the total costs that each product will bear, multiply the gross margin percentage by each individual sales value amount, and then deduct this amount from the sales value to determine the cost:

$$\$4,000 \times 0.2 = \$800 \qquad \$6,000 \times 0.2 = \$1,200$$
$$\$4,000 - \$800 = \$3,200 \qquad \$6,000 - \$1,200 = \$4,800$$

3. Deduct the additional processing costs from the total costs to determine the joint cost that must be allocated to each product:

$3,200 − $2,000 = $1,200 Joint Cost Allocated to Finished Paper
$4,800 − $1,000 = $3,800 Joint Cost Allocated to Semifinished Paper
              $5,000 Total Joint Costs

The final step in this method distinguishes the gross profit method from the other methods because it takes into account the costs incurred before and after the split-off point. Thus, this method is not only a joint cost allocation method but also a profit allocation method. Both the joint costs and the total gross margin are allocated to a joint product to maintain a constant gross margin.

One benefit of the gross profit method is that it can be used even when there are additional processing costs. The amount of the joint costs allocated to each product is not always a positive number; a joint product could get a negative allocation of joint costs in order to make the gross margin percentage equal to the overall average for the entity. This is an advantage for companies that wish to keep the same margin for each product, but it could lead to a distortion in the fairness of how costs are allocated.

Net Realizable Value Method

The **net realizable value** (NRV) method, also known as the estimated NRV method, is used when the market price for one or more of the joint products cannot be determined at the split-off point, usually because additional processing is needed. The product's final sales value less additional processing costs is its NRV.

$$\text{NRV} = \text{Sales Value} - \text{Additional Processing Cost}$$

For example: Assume the same paper mill example, except that an additional 1,000 pounds of scrap can now be sold directly to a paper recycling business, with no additional cost, for $1 per pound.

The steps for calculating the NRV are shown next.

1. Calculate the NRV for each joint product. To do this, start by calculating the sales value for each unit, which is the price per unit multiplied by the number of units.

Finished Paper 1,000 Pounds × $4 = $4,000
Semifinished Paper 3,000 Pounds × $2 = $6,000
By-Products 1,000 Pounds × $1 = $1,000

The NRV is calculated using this final sales value. (For products with no additional processing cost, the sales value is the NRV.)

	Final Sales Value	–	Additional Processing Costs	=	NRV
Finished Paper	$4,000	–	$2,000	=	$2,000
Semifinished Paper	$6,000	–	$1,000	=	$5,000
By-Products					$1,000
			Total NRV		$8,000

2. Calculate the proportion of the NRV for each joint and by-product to the total NRV:

   Finished Paper   Semifinished Paper   By-Products

   $$\frac{\$2,000}{\$8,000} = 25\% \qquad \frac{\$5,000}{\$8,000} = 62.5\% \qquad \frac{\$1,000}{\$8,000} = 12.5\%$$

3. Multiply the joint cost by the proportional amount of the NRV. This is the amount allocated to each product cost.

   $$\$5,000 \times 0.25 = \$1,250$$
   $$\$5,000 \times 0.625 = \$3,125$$
   $$\$5,000 \times 0.25 = \$625$$

   Like the sales value method, this method allocates values in proportion to the value of the product and produces predictable profit margins.

Physical Measure Method of Allocating Joint Costs to Joint Products

The physical measure, or units-of-production, method uses a physical measurement to allocate joint costs to joint products. Physical measures include weight, number, and volume. Measures can be input measures, such as pounds of paper, or output measures, such as pounds, cans, packages, or crates. The physical measure method is called the average cost method when output is used to allocate joint costs.

For example: A paper mill sells finished paper for $4 a pound and semifinished paper for $2 a pound; the process produces 1,000 pounds of finished paper, 3,000 pounds of semifinished paper, and 1,000 pounds of scrap. It costs $8,000 for the entire process, with no additional processing costs.

The steps for allocating joint costs using the physical measure method with an input measure of pounds are shown next.

1. Calculate the average cost per unit of the total joint cost by dividing the total joint costs by the total number of pounds (ignoring scrap, waste, and by-products):

   $$\text{Average Cost/Unit} = \frac{\$8,000}{4,000 \text{ Pounds}} = \$2/\text{Pound}$$

2. Multiply the average cost per unit by the total number of units to determine the amount of the joint cost to allocate to each product:

$2/Pound × 1,000 Pounds = $2,000 Cost Allocated to Finished Paper
$2/Pound × 3,000 Pounds = $6,000 Cost Allocated to Semifinished Paper

Thus the gross margin for finished paper is $2,000 ($4,000 gross profit − $2,000 cost), making the profit margin for finished paper 50% ($2,000/ $4,000). The gross margin for semifinished paper is $0 ($6,000 gross profit − $6,000 cost). Semifinished paper has no profit margin.

Although the physical measure method is easy to use and employs objective criteria for measurement, it has more drawbacks than benefits. As shown in the example, the physical measure method can produce gross profit margins that could frustrate managers and distort profits. This is because the value of the joint product is not accounted for at all, unless the relevant physical measure conveys the value of each of the items. For example, gold melted into ounces or bars measured by weight would still be correctly valued (unless the processing added artistic or utilitarian value). Another limitation would be for processes that cannot all be measured using the same units, such as pounds and gallons. Last, the physical units method is not considered GAAP.

Accounting Treatment of Joint Products and By-Products

Joint product costs, once allocated using one of the methods just discussed, become part of inventory costs and are divided among the various finished goods. According to GAAP, all joint costs that can be considered manufacturing costs should be allocated to joint products for purposes of financial reporting and taxation.

By-products can be accounted for in two different ways: the asset recognition approach or the revenue method. If the firm can assign an inventoriable value to by-products at the split-off point, it uses an asset recognition approach. In this case, in the period in which the by-product is produced, it can record the NRV (NRV = Sales Value − Additional Processing Cost) of the by-products as inventory on the balance sheet and as a deduction from the total manufacturing cost on the income statement.

Alternatively, in the period in which the by-product is produced, the firm can record the NRV of the by-products as other income (or other sales revenue item) on the income statement. These methods follow the matching principle of accrual accounting because the firm matches the value of the by-product with its cost to manufacture. Therefore, recognition at the time of production is considered more appropriate if the amounts are material. When by-product is sold, the inventory cost is recorded as the cost of sales.

If the firm cannot assign an inventoriable value to by-products at the split-off point, it can recognize the by-product at the time of sale using a revenue method. The firm can record the net sales revenue from a by-product as other income (or other sales revenue item) on the income statement. Alternately, at the time of sale, it can record the net sales revenue as a reduction of the total manufacturing cost on the income statement.

The revenue methods are simpler to use and are based on the concepts of revenue realization but should be reserved for immaterial amounts.

Exercise: Absorption versus Full Costing

Consider the following information:

Units made	1,000
Units sold	750
Variable manufacturing costs per unit	$ 35
Variable selling costs per unit	$ 25
Fixed manufacturing costs per unit	$ 20
Fixed selling costs	$ 20,000
Beginning inventory (in units)	0
Ending inventory (in units)	250
Unit selling price	$150

In the space provided, prepare a variable costing and absorption costing income statement.

Exercise Solution

Variable Costing Operating Income Statement

Revenues		$ 112,500
Variable cost of goods sold:		
Beginning inventory	$ –	
Variable manufacturing costs	35,000	
Cost of goods available for sale	35,000	
Less ending inventory	(8,750)	
Variable cost of goods sold	26,250	
Variable selling costs	18,750	
Total variable costs		45,000
Contribution margin		$ 67,500
Fixed costs		
Fixed manufacturing costs	$ 20,000	
Fixed selling costs	20,000	
Total fixed costs		$ 40,000
Operating income		$ 27,500

Absorption Costing Operating Income Statement

Revenues		$112,500
Variable cost of goods sold:		
Beginning inventory	0	
Variable manufacturing costs	$ 35,000	
Fixed manufacturing costs	20,000	
Cost of goods available for sale	$ 55,000	
Less: ending inventory*	(13,750)	
Cost of goods sold		$ 41,250
Gross margin		$ 71,250
Operating costs:		
Variable selling costs	18,750	
Fixed selling costs	20,000	
Total operating costs		$ 38,750
Operating income		$ 32,500
Difference in absorption costing versus variable Costing		$ 5,000

*Includes both fixed and variable costs.

Knowledge Check: Measurement Concepts

The next questions are intended to help you check your understanding and recall of the material presented in this topic. They do not represent the type of questions that appear on the CMA exam.

Directions: Answer each question in the space provided. Correct answers and section references appear after the knowledge check questions.

1. Match the following types of cost drivers with an appropriate example of that cost driver.

    _____ Activity-based cost driver

    _____ Volume-based cost driver

    _____ Structural cost driver

    _____ Executional cost drivers

    a. Redesigning a production process to remove unnecessary steps

    b. High-technology machine replacing an older unit

    c. Labor hours spent driving a truck

    d. Number of invoices processed for billing

2. A plant meters electricity usage at the department level. The department contains several product operations, including the manufacturing of tennis balls. For a can of tennis balls, electricity is considered which of the following?

    ☐ a. A variable indirect cost

    ☐ b. A variable direct cost

    ☐ c. A fixed indirect cost

    ☐ d. A fixed direct cost

3. If a firm is more concerned with reliability of data than with the speed at which the data are available, which of the following costing methods would be the best fit?

    ☐ a. Variable (direct) costing

    ☐ b. Standard costing

    ☐ c. Normal costing

    ☐ d. Actual costing

4. Using variable costing, fixed manufacturing overhead costs are treated as _____ costs. Using absorption costing, fixed manufacturing overhead costs are treated as _____ costs.

5. Three market-based methods of allocating joint costs to joint products are:
   a. NRV method
   b. Sales value at split-off method
   c. _____

6. Complete the equation for NRV:

   NRV = Sales Value − _____

Knowledge Check Answers: Measurement Concepts

1. Match the following types of cost drivers with an appropriate example of that cost driver. [See **Cost Drivers**.]

   d Activity-based cost driver   a. Redesigning a production process to remove unnecessary steps

   c Volume-based cost driver   b. High technology machine replacing an older unit

   b Structural cost driver   c. Labor hours spent driving a truck

   a Executional cost drivers   d. Number of invoices processed for billing

2. A plant meters electricity usage at the department level. The department contains several product operations, including the manufacturing of tennis balls. For a can of tennis balls, electricity is considered which of the following? [See **Variable Costing**.]
   - ☑ **a.** A variable indirect cost
   - ☐ **b.** A variable direct cost
   - ☐ **c.** A fixed indirect cost
   - ☐ **d.** A fixed direct cost

3. If a firm is more concerned with reliability of data than with the speed at which the data are available, which of the following costing methods would be the best fit? [See **Actual Costing**.]
   - ☐ **a.** Variable (direct) costing
   - ☐ **b.** Standard costing
   - ☐ **c.** Normal costing
   - ☑ **d.** Actual costing

4. Using variable costing, fixed manufacturing overhead costs are treated as **period** costs. Using absorption costing, fixed manufacturing overhead costs are treated as **product** costs. [See **Absorption (Full) and Variable (Direct) Costing**.]

5. Three market-based methods of allocating joint costs to joint products are: [See **Market-Based Methods of Allocating Joint Costs to Joint Products**.]
   a. NRV method
   b. Sales value at split-off method
   c. **Gross profit method**

6. Complete the equation for net realizable value: [See **Net Realizable Value Method**.]
   NRV = Sales Value − Additional Processing Cost

TOPIC 2

Costing Systems

COSTING SYSTEMS ARE USED TO accumulate costs and assign them to a particular cost object, such as a product or service. Costing systems and the cost data they contain provide strategic value by helping businesses manage costs and price their products and services appropriately.

This topic covers job order costing, process costing, activity-based costing (ABC), life-cycle costing, and other methods of cost accumulation.

> **READ** the Learning Outcome Statements (LOS) for this topic as found in Appendix A and then study the concepts and calculations presented here to be sure you understand the content you could be tested on in the CMA exam.

Cost Flows in a Manufacturing Organization

It is important to understand how cost flows are processed in a manufacturing organization. Certain inputs are fed into the cost of the product to determine the product's total cost. A representation of this cost flow is presented in Figure 1D-11.

Figure 1D-11 Cost Flows in a Manufacturing Organization

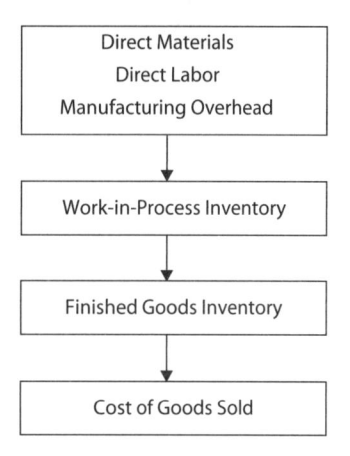

```
   Direct Materials
   Direct Labor
   Manufacturing Overhead
          │
          ▼
   Work-in-Process Inventory
          │
          ▼
   Finished Goods Inventory
          │
          ▼
   Cost of Goods Sold
```

Job Order versus Process Costing

Companies typically adopt one of two basic types of costing systems when they need to assign costs to products or services:

1. **Job order costing (job costing)** assigns costs to a specific job (a distinct unit, batch, or lot of a product or service).
2. **Process costing** accumulates product or service costs by process or department and then assigns them to a large number of nearly identical products by dividing the total costs by the total number of units produced.

Job order costing is used when the product or service has costs that can be, and often need to be, tracked and assigned to a specific job or service. For example, job costing is used for capital asset construction (buildings, ships) in the manufacturing sector; advertising campaigns, research and development, and repair jobs in the service sector; and custom mail-order items and special promotions in the merchandising sector. Costs for these products, projects, or services can be easily tracked to the product, project, or service.

Process costing is used for multiple, nearly identical units that can be organized into a flow. A process costing system would be suitable for products and services such as newspapers, books, and soft drinks in the manufacturing sector; check processing and postal delivery in the service sector; and magazine subscription receipts in the merchandising sector. These products tend to be homogeneous in nature, meaning they are all alike or very similar, and therefore it is not necessary to track costs to a specific unit of product or service.

Both costing systems share the overall purpose of assigning direct materials, direct labor, and manufacturing overhead to products. Both use the same accounts, including direct materials inventory, work-in-process (WIP) inventory, finished goods inventory, and cost of goods sold (COGS). Job costing differs from process costing in how costs are accumulated. In a job costing system, costs are accumulated by job. In a process costing system, costs are accumulated by department. Job costing uses a job sheet or equivalent software to track specific items, whereas process costing uses a production cost report to track all department costs. Job costing computes unit cost by job at the end of the job. Under process costing, unit costs are computed at the end of the accounting period, after total department costs are available. Most companies use a combination of the two methods, especially when they have some specific and some mass-produced products or services.

Job Order Costing

The procedures outlined previously for actual, normal, and standard costing can be used in job order costing. The basic steps in using job costing to assign costs to a job are:

1. Identify the job, typically with a unique code or hierarchical reference, including a date.
2. Trace the direct costs for the job (direct materials, direct labor).

3. Identify indirect cost pools associated with the job (overhead).
4. Select the cost allocation base (cost drivers) to be used in allocating indirect cost pools to the job.
5. Calculate the rate per unit of each cost allocation base. The actual indirect cost rate is calculated as shown:

$$\text{Actual Indirect Cost Rate} = \frac{\text{Actual Total Cost in Indirect Cost Pool}}{\text{Actual Total Quantity of Cost Driver}}$$

6. Assign cost to the cost object by adding all direct costs and indirect costs.

For example: Smith Company is a shipbuilding firm that manufactures yachts. It uses actual costing.

1. The yacht in question is identified as job number 123.
2. The direct costs for the job are $40,000 in direct materials and $60,000 in direct labor.
3. The total annual indirect cost for all projects is $60,000 for the first pool and $120,000 for the second pool.
4. The first pool is measured in machine hours: 20,000. The second pool is measured in direct labor hours: 30,000 for all projects for the entire year.
5. The actual indirect cost rate is calculated as:

$$\text{Actual Indirect Cost Rate} = \frac{\$60,000}{20,000 \text{ Machine Hours}} = \$3/\text{Machine Hour}$$

$$= \frac{\$120,000}{30,000 \text{ Labor Hours}} = \$4/\text{Labor Hour}$$

6. All direct costs are added to indirect costs. Indirect costs are based on a combination of machine and labor hours:

Direct costs:	
Direct materials	$40,000
Direct labor	60,000
Total direct costs	100,000
Indirect costs:	
2,000 machine hours @ $3/MH	$6,000
3,000 direct labor hours @ $4/DLH	12,000
Total indirect costs	18,000
Total manufacturing costs	$118,000
Yacht selling price	$140,000
Less total manufacturing costs	118,000
Gross profit margin	$22,000

Gross margin % = $22,000 / $140,000 = 15.7%

Spoilage, Rework, and Scrap in Job Costing

Companies want to reduce the amount of spoilage, rework, and scrap they produce in order to maximize the value of their raw materials.

Spoilage

Spoilage is any material or good that is considered unacceptable and is discarded or sold for its disposal value. Spoilage can be normal or abnormal. Normal spoilage is any unit of production that is deemed unacceptable during the normal production process, assuming efficient operating conditions. Normal spoilage is considered part of the cost of operations and therefore is part of the cost of good units produced. Normal spoilage can be a direct cost to a particular job or an indirect cost to production in general (allocated to factory overhead). If charged directly to a job, spoilage can be reduced by any estimated salvage value.

Abnormal spoilage is any unacceptable product that should not normally exist under efficient and normal operating conditions. Any spoilage over the amount considered normal is allocated to a loss from abnormal spoilage account.

Use the next formula to calculate total spoilage:

> Total Spoilage = Beginning Inventory + Units Started − Units Completed and Transferred Out − Ending Inventory

For example: At Peter's Plastics, the manufacturing cost per unit is $15. During the month, Peter's produces 10,000 good units. Despite efficient operations, limitations on the plastic molds produces 100 units of normal spoilage. In addition, 50 units spoiled because of unusual machine breakdowns.

The calculation of total good units completed (including normal spoilage) is:

Manufacturing costs of good units (units × manufacturing costs per unit)	$150,000
Normal spoilage costs (normal spoilage units × manufacturing costs per unit)	1,500
	$151,500

The calculation of total good units completed (including normal spoilage) is:

Manufacturing costs per good unit (total cost with spoilage/good units)	$15.15
Normal spoilage rate (spoiled units/good units)	1%

The cost of abnormal spoilage is calculated as:

Units lost from abnormal spoilage	50
Manufacturing cost per unit	$15
Cost of abnormal spoilage	$750

Rework

Rework is any finished product that must have additional work performed on it before it can be sold. It is divided into categories as rework needed on:

- Normal defective units for a specific job. Charged to a specific job's WIP inventory account (increasing the cost and reducing profits)
- Normal defective units common with all jobs. Charged to factory overhead
- Abnormal defective units. Charged to loss from abnormal rework account

Scrap

Scrap is a portion of a product or leftover material that has no economic value. It can be categorized by whether it relates to a specific job or is common to all jobs. Specific job scrap is charged to the job's WIP inventory account. Scrap that is common to all jobs is charged to factory overhead. Either method increases the cost from the affected account. Scrap costs are not accounted for separately, but if scrap is sold, the accountant will credit (reduce) either WIP inventory or overhead accounts by the price received for the scrap.

Job Order Costing Benefits and Limitations

Job order costing can provide very detailed results of a specific job or operation so it is ideal for specific jobs. For large processes, job order costing is less valuable because it is impractical to assign individual costs to mass-produced items on a daily basis. Job order costing can accommodate multiple costing methods, such as actual, normal, and standard costing, so it is flexible enough to be used by a wide variety of companies.

Job order costing can have a strategic value for a business because it gives a detailed breakdown of all of the different types of costs. The gross margin and gross profit margin can be used to compare the company's profitability across different jobs. For jobs that did poorly, the company can analyze whether the cost overruns were from direct labor costs, direct materials costs, or one of the indirect cost pools.

Process Costing

Process costing is recommended for companies that have mass production processes of identical or nearly identical products. Such companies track their quantities and costs on a departmental production cost report and calculate the unit cost at the end of a period by dividing the total cost of an operation or department by the total units produced.

Process costing is good for any highly automated or repetitive process. The strategic value of process costing for such companies is that they can be in continuous operations while still receiving timely, accurate, and relatively inexpensive cost information each period, due in part to the use of equivalent units. Process costing also uses production cost reports, which have built-in checks, such as balancing units to be accounted for against units accounted for.

Equivalent Units in Process Costing

Unlike job costing, in which partially completed units have a cost already attached to them, process costing cannot easily determine values for partially completed units because the accounting highlights costs for processes or departments, not jobs or items. Therefore, process costing must find the combined cost for all units, including all units partially complete at the beginning and end of the accounting period. *Partially complete* means that the item is still in WIP inventory so items that are considered complete by one department are not actually complete until they enter finished goods inventory. At the end of the period, either a production manager or an engineer gives an estimate of what percentage of units remains on the production line or in WIP inventory.

Because product cost is calculated by determining the cost per unit in each department, partially completed units must be factored into these calculations. At the end of an accounting period, a process costing system accounts for any WIP inventory as equivalent units. An **equivalent unit (EU)** is a measure of the amount of work done on partially completed units expressed in terms of how many complete units could have been created with the same amount of work. EUs are necessary because a continuous process is being divided into artificial time periods.

Engineers calculate EUs separately for direct labor, direct materials, and overhead because one category may be more complete than another for the same product. Each category is calculated in a similar fashion: Multiply the number of units that are partially complete by the estimated percentage that are complete overall.

For example: If direct labor on 1,000 cans of tennis balls is 30% complete, they would total 300 equivalent direct labor units. If the same tennis balls were complete but needed to be canned, the material costs could be 90% complete and therefore would total 900 equivalent direct materials units.

Beginning Inventory

Beginning inventory items that are a certain percentage complete were accounted for in the last accounting period at that percentage of completion, so the remaining percentage that needs to be completed is used instead. Therefore, if an item in beginning inventory is 30% complete, the remaining 70% incomplete is the basis for the EU calculation. (1,000 actual units would be 700 EUs.) However, not all methods account for beginning inventory in their calculations.

The formula for calculating the total EUs of production is:

> Equivalent Production Units = [Beginning Inventory Units × (100% − % Complete Beginning Inventory)] + Units Started and Completed During the Period + Equivalent Units in Ending WIP Inventory

Conversion Costs

Some firms measure only direct materials separately and combine direct labor and overhead, which are collectively called **conversion costs**. When the direct labor is not a significant portion of the costs due to a highly automated environment, such firms combine direct labor with overhead when performing calculations, such as determining EUs.

Conversion cost works well for companies using labor-based cost drivers, but those companies that use nonlabor-based drivers, such as number of setups or machine hours, find it better to calculate labor and overhead separately.

Process Costing Cost Flows

Unlike job costing, which moves costs through jobs directly, the cost flow in process costing is routed through processes and departments. In process costing, each department must have its own WIP inventory account. Because direct materials, direct labor, and overhead are incurred by each department involved, these charges can be made to each department, not just the first department. When departments complete their portion of work on a product, all of the costs are transferred to the next department's WIP inventory account by debiting a transferred-in costs account on the next department's books. When goods are completed, the cost of goods completed is transferred to finished goods inventory.

For example: The accounting entries for two different departments working on the same product are shown in Figure 1D-12.

Steps in Preparing a Production Cost Report

Individual departments prepare production cost reports that contain all physical units and EUs, ending WIP inventories, costs incurred during the period, costs assigned to units completed, and costs assigned to units transferred out.

Production cost reports are prepared using five steps:

1. Determine the flow of physical units. Both input and output units are accounted for when determining the units that are on hand at the beginning of the period, the units that are initiated or received, the units that are finished and transferred out, and the units that are in ending WIP inventory. Beginning WIP inventory and the units that enter the production department during the period are input units. For a particular department, units that are completed and transferred out and units remaining in WIP inventory at the end of the period are output units.
2. Determine the equivalent units.
   (Steps 1 and 2 analyze production quantities and measure the total work effort for production.)

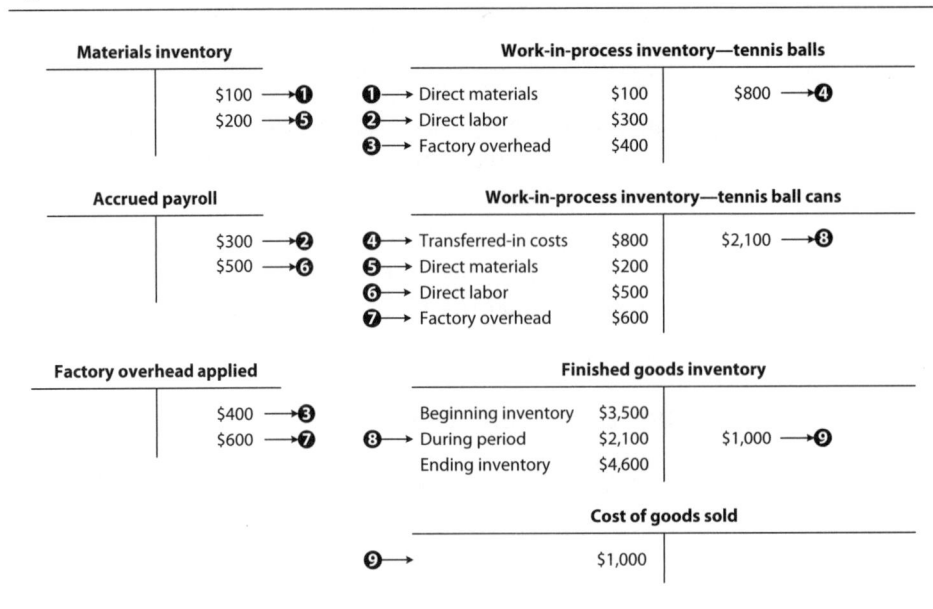

Figure 1D-12 T-Account Cost Flow Model Using Process Costing

Materials inventory		Work-in-process inventory—tennis balls			
$100 → ❶		❶→ Direct materials	$100	$800 → ❹	
$200 → ❺		❷→ Direct labor	$300		
		❸→ Factory overhead	$400		

Accrued payroll		Work-in-process inventory—tennis ball cans			
$300 → ❷		❹→ Transferred-in costs	$800	$2,100 → ❽	
$500 → ❻		❺→ Direct materials	$200		
		❻→ Direct labor	$500		
		❼→ Factory overhead	$600		

Factory overhead applied		Finished goods inventory			
$400 → ❸		Beginning inventory	$3,500		
$600 → ❼		❽→ During period	$2,100	$1,000 → ❾	
		Ending inventory	$4,600		

Cost of goods sold	
❾→ $1,000	

Note: Circled numbers indicate cost inputs and outputs of the process.

3. Calculate total manufacturing costs. The costs of any items in the WIP beginning inventory and any current costs are included in the total manufacturing costs that must be accounted for. Material requisition forms, time tickets, and factory overhead allocation sheets collect these costs.
4. Calculate unit costs. To determine product costing and income for a period, the costs per unit are calculated for overall costs as well as for direct materials, direct labor, and factory overhead.
   (Steps 3 and 4 are sometimes called unit cost determination.)
5. Assign total manufacturing costs to units (cost assignment). Units completed and transferred out and units remaining in WIP inventory receive the period's manufacturing costs.

Production Cost Report Preparation Methods

When using process costing, the production cost report can be prepared according to the first-in, first-out (FIFO) method or the weighted-average method.

First-In, First-Out Costing Method

The **FIFO** costing method is an inventory valuation method that calculates the unit cost using only costs incurred and work performed during the current period.

FIFO keeps the beginning WIP inventory separated from the inventory that begins and ends during the current period. FIFO also assumes that the beginning

WIP inventory is the first inventory to be completed in the period and therefore must be complete by the end of the period. The method requires two categories of completed units to correctly cost all inventory: beginning WIP units, and units started and completed during the current period.

The costs of work done before the current period on beginning WIP inventory are kept separate from work done in the current period. However, these prior-period costs are still included when calculating the costs of units completed from beginning inventory.

EU costing is a five-step process:

1. Determine the flow of physical units ("units to be accounted for").
2. Determine the EUs ("units accounted for").
3. Calculate total manufacturing costs (using work done in the current period only).
4. Calculate unit costs (beginning WIP plus current-period costs; "costs to be accounted for").
5. Assign total manufacturing costs to units (cost assignment; "costs accounted for").

Note that units to be accounted for should equal the units accounted for; similarly, the costs to be accounted for should equal the costs accounted for.

By definition, the beginning WIP will always be partially complete; otherwise, it would have been moved to the next department. Therefore, the objective is to obtain the correct cost of items completed during the month and items left in WIP at the end of the month.

For example: The EU costing for the firm described in Figure 1D-13 starts with an assumption that 100% of the material is added to the product at the beginning of the production process and is thus 100% complete for beginning inventory but that beginning WIP conversion costs are only 40% complete. The example also shows how to deal with a partially complete ending inventory (100% complete direct materials and 80% complete conversion costs).

Note that in the costs to be accounted for area, the beginning WIP costs are determined using the prior month's direct material (DM) and conversion costs.

1. **Determine the flow of physical units.**

    Input units:
    WIP beginning of month: 100 units
    Units started in production: 700 units
    Units to be accounted for: 800 units

    Output units:
    Units completed: 600 units
    Ending WIP inventory: 200 units
    Units accounted for: 800 units (should match the units to be accounted for)

2. **Determine the equivalent units.**

   Because direct materials are 100% complete and conversion costs are 40% complete, the beginning inventory of 100 physical units calculates to zero EUs of direct materials [100 × (100% − 100%)] and 60 EU of conversion costs [100 × (100% − 40%)].

   In addition, because direct materials are 100% complete and conversion costs are 80% complete, the ending inventory of 200 physical units calculates to 200 EUs of direct materials and 160 EUs of conversion costs.

   Taking into account the 500 units completed, direct materials EUs equal 700 and conversion cost EUs equal 660.

3. **Calculate costs accounted for.**

   To calculate the cost of the units transferred to next department (600 units):

   Determine the costs accounted for in the WIP beginning for (100 units), which is $5,800 plus the DM cost of $0.00 plus the conversion cost of $1,916.40 equals the WIP beginning total cost of $7,716.40.

   The cost of the units started and completed (500 units) is $37,400.00.

   The cost of the total units completed and transferred is $7,716.40 plus $37,400.00 equals $45,116.40.

   To calculate the cost of the WIP month-end (200 units): Take the DM cost of $8,572.00 plus the conversion cost of $5,110.40, which equals the total cost of the WIP month-end of $13,682.40.

   The total of costs accounted for is the cost of the total units completed and transferred of $45,116.40 plus the total cost of the WIP month-end of $13,682.40, which equals $58,798.80.

4. **Calculate unit costs (beginning WIP plus current-period costs; "costs to be accounted for").**

   Take the $29,998.80 cost of EUs DM added in the current month divided by the 700 units EUs of production to find the cost per EU of $42.86.

   Take the $23,000 cost of EU conversion added in the current month divided by the 720 EUs of production to find the cost per EU of $31.94.

5. **Assign total manufacturing costs to units (cost assignment; "costs accounted for").**

   Add the EU DM of $42.86 to the EU conversion of $31.94 to determine the whole cost per unit of $74.80.

Weighted-Average Method

The **weighted-average inventory valuation method** calculates the unit cost using all costs including both those for the current period and those for prior periods that are part of the current period's beginning WIP inventory. The weighted-average method finds the average of cost for prior periods and the current period. Whereas the FIFO method is concerned with both input and output measures (i.e., the beginning and ending status of products for the period), the weighted-average method is concerned only with the status of the products at the end of the period.

Figure 1D-13 FIFO Method Production Cost Report

		Physical Quantity	EU DM	EU Conversion	
Units to be accounted for	WIP beginning of month	100			
	Units started in production	700			
	Total units	800			
Units accounted for	Transfers to next department:				
	From beginning WIP, direct material (DM) 100 × (100% − 100%); conversion 100 × (100% − 40%):	100	0	60	
	Started and completed (800 units − 200 ending WIP − 100 beginning WIP completed first)	500	500	500	
	From WIP month-end, DM 200 × 100%, conversion 200 × 80%	200	200	160	
	Accounted for:	800			
	Work done in current period only:		700	720	

		Total Cost	Direct Materials Cost	Conversion Costs	Whole Unit
Calculate EU/Unit costs and costs to be accounted for	WIP, Beginning of month (cost of work done before current period: (100 DM × $40) + (40 conversion × $30)):	$5,200.00	Not included	Not included	
	Costs added in the current month:	52,998.80	$29,998.80	$23,000.00	
	EUs of production (see above):		700	720	
	Cost per EU:		$42.86	$31.94	$74.80
	Total costs to account for:	**$58,198.80**			
Costs accounted for	Transferred to next department (600 units):				
	WIP, beginning (100 units)	$5,200.00			
	DM	$0	0 × $42.86		
	Conversion	$1,916.40		60 × $31.94	
	WIP, beginning total	$7,116.40			
	Started and completed (500 units):	$37,400.00	500 × $42.86	500 × $31.94	
	Total units completed and transferred:	$44,516.40			
	WIP, month-end (200 units):				
	DM	$8,572.00	200 × $42.86		
	Conversion	$5,110.40		160 × $31.94	
	Total WIP, month-end	$13,682.40			
	Total cost	**$58,198.80**			

For example: For this firm, all costs on the current period's production cost sheet are included in cost calculations, whether the cost actually was incurred in the current period or not. The production cost report using the weighted-average method can be prepared using the same five steps that were used in the FIFO example:

1. Determine the flow of physical units ("units to be accounted for").
2. Determine the equivalent units ("units accounted for").
3. Calculate total manufacturing costs (using work done in the current period only).
4. Calculate unit costs (beginning WIP plus current-period costs; "costs to be accounted for").
5. Assign total manufacturing costs to units (cost assignment; "costs accounted for").

1. **Determine the flow of physical units.**
    Input units:

    Partially complete beginning WIP inventory: 5,000 units

    Work begun or received during the period: 30,000 units

These 35,000 units are called "units to be accounted for."

Output units:

Units completed: 20,000 units

Ending WIP inventory: 15,000 units

These 35,000 units are called "number of units accounted for" and should match the units to account for.

2. **Determine the equivalent units.** Beginning WIP inventory units are not included in EUs because they are already included in physical units under this method. Because direct materials are 100% complete and conversion costs are 47% complete, the ending inventory of 15,000 physical units calculates to 15,000 EUs of direct materials and 7,050 EUs of conversion costs (direct labor plus factory overhead). This, plus the 20,000 units completed, equals 35,000 direct materials EUs and 27,050 conversion cost EUs.

3. **Calculate total manufacturing costs.** The beginning WIP for direct materials, $10,000, is added to conversion costs, $10,043, for a total of $20,043. The current period's costs for direct materials, $60,000, are added to conversion costs, $40,000, for a total of $100,000. Total manufacturing costs are $120,043.

4. **Calculate equivalent unit costs as shown:**

    Direct Materials = $10,000 Beginning WIP Inventory
    $60,000 Current-Period Costs
    $70,000 Total Costs

    $$\frac{\$70,000}{35,000 \text{ Units}} = \$2/\text{Unit Direct Materials}$$

    $$\frac{\$50,043}{27,050 \text{ Units}} = \$1.85/\text{Unit Conversion Costs}$$

    $2.00 + $1.85 = $3.85/Unit Total Cost

5. **Assign total manufacturing costs to units in the ending inventory and to units transferred out.** The unit costs just calculated are multiplied by the number of units in each category, as shown at the bottom of Figure 1D-14 in a sample production cost report.

Figure 1D-14 Production Cost Report—Weighted-Average Method

1. Quantity Schedule and Equivalent Units (EUs)

Quantity Schedule

Units to be accounted for:	
Work in process, January 1	5,000
Started into production	30,000
Total units	35,000

		EUs Materials Units	%	EUs Conversion Units	%
Units accounted for as follows:					
Units completed and transferred out	20,000	20,000	100%	20,000	100%
Work in process, ending	15,000	15,000	100%	7,050	47%
Total units and EUs of production	35,000	35,000		27,050	

2. Costs per EU

	Total Cost	Materials	Conversion Costs	Whole Unit
Cost to be accounted for:				
Work in process, beginning	$20,043	$10,000	$10,043	
Cost added during the month	100,000	60,000	40,000	
Total cost (a)	$120,043	$70,000	$50,043	
EUs of production (b)		35,000	27,050	
Cost per EU (a/b)		$2.00 +	$1.85 =	$3.85

3. Cost Reconciliation

	Total Cost	EUs (above) Materials	Conversion
Cost accounted for as follows:			
Transferred out (20,000 × $3.85)	$77,000	20,000	20,000
Work in process, ending			
Materials (15,000 × $2.00)	30,000	15,000	
Conversion (7,050 × $1.85)	13,043		7,050
Total work in process, ending	43,043		
Total Cost	**$120,043**		

Note that the total costs calculated using unit costs should match the total costs calculated in the third step of $120,043.

Production Costing in a Multi-department Company

Because most processes usually involve more than one department, a more complex example will help show how to deal with costs transferred in from a prior department. This example also illustrates how to calculate inventory values and the COGS in process costing using both the FIFO and the weighted-average methods.

Transferred-in costs are any costs accumulated by prior departments. These are charged to the current department upon assumption of the partially completed units. Thus, each department is treated as a separate entity, and the prior department is like a vendor that supplies a semifinished good for a price (cost).

Unlike job order costing, with process costing, each production department will have its own WIP account. The completed production of a prior department is transferred to the next department's WIP account.

For example: Robusto Soup Company has three departments that operate in a continuous process, starting with the mixing department, then the cooking department, and finally the canning department. When each department finishes its work (measured in cans' worth of finished product) and transfers the materials to the next department, it also transfers the costs of the batch to that department as transferred-in costs (or prior department costs).

Figure 1D-15 shows how Robusto's materials and conversion costs are added by department.

Figure 1D-15 Percentage of Costs by Department

	Mixing Department	Cooking Department	Canning Department
Direct materials	90%	0%	10%
Conversion costs	60%	20%	20%
Transferred-in costs	N/A	100%	100%

Robusto Soup moves inventory between its accounts as shown in Figure 1D-16.

Figure 1D-16 Movement of Robusto's Inventory in Units for July

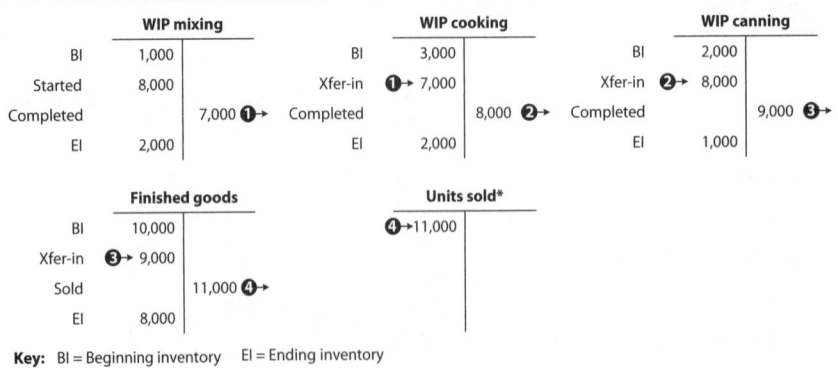

WIP mixing			WIP cooking			WIP canning		
BI	1,000		BI	3,000		BI	2,000	
Started	8,000		Xfer-in	❶→ 7,000		Xfer-in	❷→ 8,000	
Completed		7,000 ❶→	Completed		8,000 ❷→	Completed		9,000 ❸→
EI	2,000		EI	2,000		EI	1,000	

Finished goods			Units sold*	
BI	10,000		❹→11,000	
Xfer-in	❸→ 9,000			
Sold		11,000 ❹→		
EI	8,000			

Key: BI = Beginning inventory   EI = Ending inventory
      Xfer-in = Transferred in

*This account corresponds to cost of goods sold when viewed in dollars instead of in units.

Note: Circled numbers indicate flow of cost inputs and outputs.

Note that this figure shows movements in units and not in costs.

FIFO Method for the Canning Department at Robusto

If the company uses the FIFO method, its canning department has these costs:

Work-in-process (WIP) beginning (2,000 units):
- Cost of work done before current month: (1,800 DM × $1.25/unit) + (1,600 conversion × $2.50/unit) = $6,250

Costs added in current month:
- Transferred in from cooking department = $24,000
- DM = $990
- Conversion = $4,000

Figure 1D-17 shows a completed FIFO method production cost report using this data.

Figure 1D-17 Canning Department Equivalent Unit Calculation—FIFO Method

1. Quantity Schedule and Equivalent Units (EUs)

Quantity Schedule

Units to be accounted for:		
Work in process, beginning of month	2,000	
Started into production	8,000	
Total units	10,000	

		Transferred In		Materials		Conversion	
		units	%	units	%	units	%
Units accounted for as follows:							
From beginning WIP	2,000	-	100%	200	10%	400	20%
Units completed and transferred out	7,000	7,000	100%	7,000	100%	7,000	100%
Work in process, ending	1,000	1,000	100%	900	90%	800	80%
Total units and EUs of production	10,000	8,000		8,100		8,200	

2. Costs per EU

	Total Cost	Transferred In	Materials	Conversion Costs	Whole Unit
Cost to be accounted for:					
Work in process, beginning	$6,250	not included	not included	not included	
Cost added during the month	28,990	$24,000	$990	$4,000	
Total cost (a)	$35,240	$24,000	$990	$4,000	
EUs of production (b)		8,000	8,100	8,200	
Cost per EU (a/b)		$3.00 +	$0.12 +	$0.49 =	$3.61

3. Cost Reconciliation

	Total Cost	EUs Transferred In	Materials	Conversion	Whole Units
Cost accounted for as follows:					
Work in process, beginning (2,000 units)	$6,250				
Transferred in (0 × $3.00):	–	–			
Direct materials (200 × $0.12)	24		200		
Conversion (400 × $0.49)	196			400	
Total work in process, beginning:	$6,470				
Started and completed (7,000 × $3.61)	$25,270				7,000
Total of units completed and transferred out:	$31,740				
Work in process, ending					
Transferred in (1,000 × $3.00)	$3,000	1,000			
Direct materials (900 × $0.12)	108		900		
Conversion (800 × $0.49)	392			800	
Total work in process, ending	$3,500				
Total Cost	$35,240				

Weighted-Average Method for the Canning Department at Robusto

If the weighted-average method were used instead, the number of units transferred (Figure 1D-18) would remain the same, but the transferred-in costs would differ because each department would include the work done in prior periods (whereas the FIFO method includes only the work done in the current period). Therefore, although all other aspects of the example remain the same, assume that the transferred-in costs to the canning department are now $25,005. Figure 1D-18 shows a completed weighted-average method production cost report.

Figure 1D-18 Canning Department Production Cost Report—Weighted-Average Method

1. Quantity Schedule and Equivalent Units (EUs)

	Quantity Schedule						
Units to be accounted for:							
Work in process, beginning	2,000						
Transferred in	8,000						
Total units	10,000						

		EUs					
		Transferred In		Materials		Conversion	
		Units	%	units	%	units	%
Units accounted for as follows:							
Units completed and transferred out	9,000	9,000	100%	9,000	100%	9,000	100%
Work in process, ending	1,000	1,000	100%	900	90%	800	80%
Total units and EUs of production	10,000	10,000		9,900		9,800	

2. Costs per EU

	Total Cost	Transferred-In	Materials	Conversion Costs	Whole Unit
Cost to be accounted for:					
Work in process, beginning	$7,500	$6,250	$250	$1,000	
Cost added during the month	29,995	25,005	990	4,000	
Total cost (a)	$ 37,495	$ 31,255	$1,240	$5,000	
EUs of production (b)		10,000	9,900	9,800	
Cost per EU (a/b)		$3.13 +	$0.13 +	$0.51 =	$3.76

3. Cost Reconciliation

	Total Cost	EUs Transferred In	Materials	Conversion	Whole Units
Cost accounted for as follows:					
Goods completed and transferred out (9,000 × $3.76):	$33,840				9,000
Work in process, ending					
Transferred in (1,000 × $3.13)	3,130	1,000			
Direct materials (900 × $0.13)	117		900		
Conversion (800 × $0.51)	408			800	
Total work in process, ending	3,655				
Total Cost	$37,495				

Figure 1D-19 summarizes the data for Robusto Soup, showing the types of T-account transactions and journal entries that would coincide with the data from the weighted-average production cost report.

Separate production cost reports for the mixing department and the cooking department would also be needed. (Data for these two accounts are for illustrative purposes only.)

Note that each of the base accounts (raw materials, wages payable, and factory overhead) feeds not only into the first department but into the other departments, as indicated by the percentage of inputs shown in Figure 1D-19. The costs transferred out by that department do not directly equal the costs added during the current period; however, beginning inventory plus the costs added in the current month always equal the ending inventory plus the costs transferred out.

Note also that each inventory account's beginning and ending inventory levels are broken down by direct materials, conversion costs, and transferred-in costs.

Determining Inventory Levels in Process Costing

There may be considerable complexity in determining inventory levels in process costing.

For example: Bounce Sporting Goods buys rubber as a direct material for racquet balls. The molding department processes the racquet balls and then transfers the balls to the finishing department, where a coating and a label are applied. The

Figure 1D-19 T-Account and Journal Entries for Robusto (Weighted-Average Method)

Raw materials
BI	$15,000		
CM	$5,000	$9,000 →❶	
		$990 →❽	
EI	$10,010		

Wages payable
		$8,000	$4,800 →❷
			$1,600 →❺
			$1,600 →❾

Factory overhead
	$12,000	$7,200 →❸	
		$2,400 →❻	
		$2,400 →❿	

WIP mixing
BI	DM $1,250		
	Conv $2,500		
CM ❶→	DM $9,000		
❷❸→	Conv $12,000	$18,375 →❹	
EI	DM $2,375		
	Conv $4,000		
	Total $6,375		

WIP cooking
BI	DM $0		
	Conv $1,875		
	Xfer-in $9,375		
CM ❹→	Xfer-in $18,375		
	DM $0	$25,005 →❼	
❺❻→	Conv $4,000		
EI	Xfer-in $7,125		
	DM $0		
	Conv $1,500		
	Total $8,620		

WIP canning
BI	DM $250		
	Conv $1,000		
	Xfer-in $6,250		
CM ❼→	Xfer-in $25,005		
❽→	DM $990	$33,853 →⓫	
❾❿→	Conv $4,000		
EI	Xfer-in $3,125		
	DM $114		
	Conv $408		
	Total $3,647		

Finished goods
BI	$37,500		
⓫→ Xfer-in	$33,853	$41,371 →⓬	
CM			
EI	$29,982		

Cost of goods sold
⓬→	$41,371	

Selected journal entries:

❶→ WIP mixing $9,000
    Raw materials $9,000

❸→ WIP mixing $7,200
    Factory overhead $7,200

⓫→ Finished goods $33,853
    WIP canning $33,853

❷→ WIP mixing $4,800
    Salaries & wages payable $4,800

❼→ WIP canning $25,005
    WIP cooking $25,005

⓬→ Cost of goods sold $41,371
    Finished goods $41,371
    Accounts receivable $55,000
        Sales $55,000
To record 11,000 units sold at $5/unit

Key: Xfer-in = Transferred-in costs
CM = Current month
BI = Beginning inventory
WIP = Work-in-process inventory
EI = Ending inventory

Note: Circled numbers indicate flow of cost inputs and outputs.

---

forming department began manufacturing 15,000 balls (called "Bouncers") during the month of June. There was no beginning inventory.

Costs for the molding department for the month of June are:

Direct materials:	$60,000
Conversion costs:	46,200
Total	$106,200

A total of 12,000 balls were completed and transferred to the finishing department; the remaining 3,000 balls were still in the molding process at the end of the month. All of the molding department's direct materials were placed in process but, on average, only 40% of the conversion cost was applied to the ending WIP inventory.

What is the cost of the units transferred to the finishing department? To find the answer, first determine whether the operation uses the weighted-average or FIFO method. In this example, either method will arrive at the same answer because there is no beginning inventory: Beginning WIP EUs are 0 for DMs and 0 for conversion costs.

The answer, $90,000, is calculated as shown:

Determine units started and completed:

DM: 12,000 Units × 100% Complete = 12,000 EU

Conv: 12,000 Units × 100% Complete = 12,000 EU

Determine WIP month-end:

DM: 3,000 Units × 100% Complete = 3,000 EU

Conv: 3,000 Units × 40% Complete = 1,200 EU

Determine total EU:

DM: 0 + 12,000 + 3,000 = 15,000 EU

Conv: 0 + 12,000 + 1,200 = 13,200 EU

Calculate EU/unit costs:

DM: $\dfrac{\$60,000}{15,000 \text{ EU}} = \$4.00/\text{EU}$

Conv: $\dfrac{\$46,200}{13,200 \text{ EU}} = \$3.50/\text{EU}$

Cost of units started and completed (transferred to finishing department):

(12,000 × $4) + (12,000 × $3.50) = $90,000

To verify, calculate ending WIP:

(3,000 EU DM × $4) + (1,200 EU conv × $3.50) = $16,200

Note that $90,000 + $16,200 = $106,200, the total cost.

Spoilage in Process Costing

Process costing can have normal and abnormal spoilage (as defined in the discussion of job costing). Spoilage in process costing is handled in one of two ways. The first method counts the number of spoiled units, separately computes the total cost per unit, and then allocates this cost to the good units. The second method omits the spoiled units in the totals so that the cost per unit does not include any spoiled units, making the spoilage cost part of the total manufacturing costs. The first method provides more precise product costs because the individually calculated spoilage cost is spread over only the good units produced. The second method is less precise because the costs are spread to all units including good completed units, units in ending WIP inventory, and abnormal spoiled units.

Benefits and Limitations of Process Costing

Process costing is useful for any highly repetitive flow process, such as mass production of homogeneous items. Conversely, it is not useful for custom orders or other individual jobs. Process costing allocates costs not only by cost per unit but also to specific departments, allowing individual managers to control their own costs.

Another commonly used costing system is ABC, which allows companies to gain a more accurate understanding of its overhead costs, leading to better information about the profitability of its products and services.

Activity-Based Costing

ABC is a method of assigning costs to customers, services, and products based on an activity's consumption of resources. An activity is any type of action, work, or movement performed within an entity. An activity center is a logical grouping of activities, actions, movements, or sequences of work. A resource is an element with economic value that is consumed or applied when performing an activity.

Other terms important to ABC include resource cost drivers and activity cost drivers.

A resource cost driver measures the amount of resources consumed by an activity. Resource costs used in an activity are assigned to a cost pool using a resource cost driver. In manufacturing, a resource cost driver could be the amount of rubber required to make a batch of tennis balls. In an engineering services firm, a resource cost driver could be the number of hours used by an engineer to design, build, and maintain a project schedule.

An activity cost driver is a measurement of the amount of an activity used by a cost object. Activity cost drivers assign costs in cost pools to cost objects. For example, an activity cost driver is the number of labor hours required for the activity of performing a setup for a particular product.

The basis for ABC is that activities use resources but produce products or services. The resource cost is calculated using a cost driver; the amount of an activity consumed in a period is multiplied by the cost of the activity. The calculated costs are assigned to the product or service.

ABC is especially appropriate for companies that have expanded to multiple products and/or products that use varying amounts of resources, which include not only raw materials and other direct costs but also indirect costs such as customer service, quality control, and supervision. When each product or product line consumes each of these costs at different rates, a broad brush or uniform cost allocation for all items will make some products appear more profitable and others less profitable than they are. As a result, products can be overcosted or undercosted: Overcosted items consume few actual resources but are charged as if they had consumed more; undercosted items consume more actual resources than they are charged for.

Strategically, ABC should be used when the cost of making decisions based on inaccurate costing data exceeds the added expense of collecting more information and implementing the system. An effective ABC system can be particularly important to a firm in its decision to drop or add a product line. It can also aid in decisions related to product pricing and where to allocate funds to improve processes.

ABC uses a two-stage approach to allocate costs:

Stage 1: Resource cost assignment of overhead costs to activity cost pools or activity centers using pertinent resource cost drivers

Stage 2: Activity cost assignment of activity costs to cost objects using pertinent activity cost drivers (to measure a cost object's drain on an activity)

Key Steps in ABC

The steps for designing an ABC system are: identifying activities and resource costs, assigning resource costs to activities, and assigning activity costs to cost objects.

Step 1. Identify Activities and Resource Costs

An activity analysis identifies the resource costs of performing particular activities by determining the work performed for each activity. The project team makes detailed lists of activities and organizes them into activity centers as well as into these levels:

Unit-level activities include activities that are performed for each unit produced, such as direct materials or direct labor hours. In other words, these are the same as volume-based or unit-based activities.

Batch-level activities include activities that are performed for each batch of units, such as machine setup, purchase orders, batch inspections, batch mixing, or production scheduling.

Product-sustaining activities include activities that are performed to support the production process, such as product design, expediting, and implementing engineering changes.

Facility-sustaining activities include activities that support production for an entire facility, such as environmental health and safety, security, plant management, depreciation, property taxes, and insurance.

Customer-level activities include activities that are performed to support customer needs, such as customer service, phone banks, or custom orders.

Step 2. Assign Resource Costs to Activities

Resource costs are assigned to activities using resource cost drivers. A cause-and-effect relationship must be established between the driver and the activity. Resource cost drivers and the related activity that companies often use include:

- Number of employees: personnel activities
- Time worked: personnel activities
- Setup hours: setup or machine activities
- Number or distance of movements: materials-handling activities
- Meters: utilities (flow meters, electricity meters, etc.)
- Machine hours: machine-running activities
- Number of orders: production orders
- Square feet: cleaning activities
- Amount of value added: general and administrative

Step 3. Assign Activity Costs to Cost Objects

After determining activity costs, the activity costs per unit are measured using an appropriate cost driver. The activity cost driver should show a cause-and-effect relationship or, in other words, be directly related to the rise and fall of the cost.

The activity cost drivers determine the proportion of a cost to allocate to each product or service using the next formula:

$$\text{Rate} = \frac{\text{Cost Pool}}{\text{Driver}}$$

When to Use ABC

ABC helps managers understand their costs, thus highlighting the competitive advantages and weaknesses of their process or product. As more firms adopt ABC, it will become increasingly difficult for companies using a less accurate costing system to compete, because they will find themselves at a competitive disadvantage.

ABC is particularly important for:

- Firms that have high product diversity, complexity, or volume
- Firms that have a high likelihood of cost distortion, such as those with both mass-produced and custom orders, both mature and new products, and both custom delivery and standard delivery channels

ABC was first adopted by manufacturing companies. Now it is also used by service companies such as hospitals, banks, and insurance companies, not only to account for costs but also to make strategic decisions by analyzing processes, assessing management performance, and assessing profitability.

Differences between ABC and Traditional Costing

The three primary differences between ABC and traditional costing are shown in Figure 1D-20.

Figure 1D-20 ABC versus Traditional Costing

	ABC	Traditional Costing
Cost drivers	Multiple cost drivers: activity and volume-based drivers (whichever fits the cost best)	Up to three cost drivers: only volume-based, chosen for best general fit
Overhead	Overhead assigned to activities and then from activities to products or services	Overhead assigned to departments and then from departments to products or services
Focus	Focus on solving costing and processing issues that cross departmental lines	Focus on assigning responsibility to departmental managers for individual cost and process improvements within their department

Benefits and Limitations of ABC

Benefits of using ABC include these:

- ABC reduces distortions found in traditional cost allocation methods that allocate overhead by department. ABC gives managers access to relevant costs so they can compete better in the marketplace.
- ABC measures activity-driving costs, allowing management to alter product designs and activity designs and know how overall cost and value are affected.
- ABC normally results in substantially greater unit costs for low-volume products than is reported by traditional product costing (meaning better decisions can be made to add or drop a product line).

The limitations of ABC include these:

- Not all overhead costs can be related to a particular cost driver and some may need to be arbitrarily allocated, especially when the cost of tracing is greater than the benefit.
- ABC requires substantial development and maintenance time, even with available software. ABC changes the rules for managers, so resistance to change is common. Without top management support, managers could find workarounds.
- ABC, if viewed only as an accounting initiative, will likely fail.
- ABC generates vast amounts of information. Too much information can mislead managers into concentrating on the wrong data.
- ABC reports do not conform to generally accepted accounting principles (GAAP), so restating financial data adds an expense and causes confusion, leaving users unsure as to whether they should rely on the ABC or external data.

Life-Cycle Costing

When a longer-term perspective is needed than other costing methods provide (usually a year), life-cycle costing may be used. Life-cycle costing considers the entire life cycle of a product or service, from concept through sales and warranty service.

For example: The life cycle for a pharmaceutical product starts with research and development and moves through multiple stages of testing and approvals, product design, manufacturing, marketing and distribution, and customer service. In this case, the cycle may be defined as the life span of the patent on the product or the life span of its marketability.

Life-cycle costing is sometimes used on a strategic basis for cost planning and product pricing. It is designed to allow a firm to focus on the overall costs for a product or service. Poor early design could lead to much higher marketing costs, lower sales, and higher service costs. The total costs for a product's life cycle have three phases.

1. Upstream costs: costs that are prior to the manufacturing of the product or sale of the service, such as research and development or design (prototypes, tests, and engineering)
2. Manufacturing costs: costs involved in producing a product or service, such as purchasing and direct and indirect manufacturing costs
3. Downstream costs: costs subsequent to (or coincident with) manufacturing costs, such as marketing, distribution (packaging, shipping and handling, promotions, and advertising), service costs, and warranty costs (defect recalls, returns, and liability)

Life-cycle costing places its strategic focus on improving costs in all three phases. Improving product design is the key to the upstream phase. Improving the manufacturing process and relationships with suppliers is highlighted in the manufacturing phase. Improving the first two phases is the key to lowering downstream costs because actions taken in these phases limit the downstream choices. In other words, life-cycle costing attempts to make managers proactive in the earlier phases so they do not have to be reactive later.

Other Costing Methods

Two other costing methods are **operation costing**—which combines job costing with process costing—and **backflush costing**—which is used in just-in-time production systems.

Operation Costing

Operation costing is a costing system that combines job costing with process costing. Similar to job costing, operation costing assigns direct materials to each job or batch, but direct labor and overhead (conversion costs) are assigned similarly to process costing. This hybrid system is most suitable for manufacturers that have similar processes for high-volume activities but that need to use different materials for different jobs. Clothing manufacturers, for example, have standard operations—choosing patterns, cutting, and sewing—but the fabrics used vary by item, size, color and price, among other factors. Other industries that are suitable for operation costing include textiles, metalworking, furniture, shoes, and electronic equipment.

For example: A metalworking company produces handrails that are either unfinished (for painting) or chrome-plated. The company has one department create all of the metal rails and then transfers some to the chrome-plating department.

Assume that the company produced 1,000 unfinished rails and 500 chrome rails during a month and that it had no beginning or ending inventory for the month. Operation costing tracks direct materials by job and tracks conversion costs (direct labor and overhead) by department, as shown in Figure 1D-21.

Figure 1D-21 Total Cost Calculation

Direct Materials		$30,000
Job 1 — Unfinished Rails (1,000)		
Job 2 — Chrome Rails (500)		
Materials for Rails in Metal Department	15,000	
Chrome Plating Added to Rails in Chrome Department	10,000	25,000
Total Direct Materials		$55,000
Conversion Costs		
Metal Department		$45,000
Chrome Department		10,000
Total Conversion Costs		$55,000
Total Costs		$110,000

The product costs for unfinished rails and chrome rails are calculated in Figure 1D-22. Note that the conversion costs for the metal department groups all rails together because they are all processed the same in that department.

Note that the total cost of $110,000 is the same as in Figure 1D-21, proving that the calculations are correct.

Backflush Costing

Backflush costing is a costing system tailored to just-in-time production systems. A **just-in-time (JIT)** system produces materials just as they are needed for the next step in production. The trigger for manufacturing at a particular work area is the demand from the next station down the line. As a result, organizations using JIT production have very little inventory, making the choice of inventory valuation methods (FIFO or weighted-average) and inventory costing methods (absorption costing or variable costing) irrelevant because the costs flow directly to cost of goods sold during an accounting period.

Figure 1D-22 Product Cost Calculation

	Unfinished Rails	Chrome Rails
Direct Materials		
Job1 $\left(\dfrac{\$30,000}{1,000}\right)$	$30/Rail	
Job2 $\left(\dfrac{\$25,000}{500}\right)$		$50/Rail
Conversion – Metal Department $\left(\dfrac{\$45,000}{1,500}\right)$	$30/Rail	$30/Rail
Conversion – Chrome Department $\left(\dfrac{\$10,000}{500}\right)$		$20/Rail
Total Cost per Rail	$60/Rail	$100/Rail

Total Product Cost

Unfinished Rails $60 × 1,000 = $60,000
Chrome Rails $100 × 500 = 50,000
Total = $110,000

Backflush costing contrasts with traditional costing systems that use sequential tracking to record purchases and movements of costs between inventories and accounts in the order in which they occur. Sequential tracking tracks costs through a four-stage cycle:

Stage A: Purchase of direct materials (journal entry in materials inventory)

Stage B: Production (journal entry in WIP inventory)

Stage C: Completion of a good finished unit (journal entry in finished goods inventory)

Stage D: Sale of finished good (journal entry in cost of goods sold)

The journal entries made at each stage are called trigger points. Backflush costing omits some or all of the journal entries for the production cycle. When the journal entries are omitted from certain stages of the cycle, normal or standard costs are used to work backward and flush out the costs and then make the required journal entries for the missing steps.

Backflush costing skips the journal entry for WIP inventory, because JIT systems reduce the time that materials remain in this stage.

The use of backflush costing may not be in strict accordance with GAAP because backflush costing entries ignore WIP inventory, which still exists and should be recorded as an asset. However, many companies justify the use of backflush costing because under JIT production, such items are immaterial. When they are material, these unrecorded costs need to be approximated and adjusting entries made.

Backflush costing can save a company money on accounting, but some critics find the lack of a clear audit trail to be a risk because it limits the ability to pinpoint resources at each stage of the manufacturing process. Many inventories are so low under JIT production, however, that managers can track operations by simple observation and computer monitoring.

Companies that use JIT production systems are prime candidates for using backflush costing, but any industry that has fast manufacturing lead times and/or very stable inventory levels can use backflush costing.

Section D, Topic 2—Costing Systems   549

Knowledge Check: Costing Systems

The next questions are intended to help you check your understanding and recall of the material presented in this topic. They do not represent the type of questions that appear on the CMA exam.

Directions: Answer each question in the space provided. Correct answers and section references appear after the knowledge check questions.

1. Which of the following costing systems would work best for a firm that spends a considerable percentage of its overall costs on research and development?
   - a. Job order costing
   - b. Process costing
   - c. Activity-based costing
   - d. Life-cycle costing

2. A post office wants to implement a cost accumulation system for its bulk mail sorting warehouse. Which of the following methods would be best suited to this situation?
   - a. Life-cycle costing
   - b. Activity-based costing
   - c. Process costing
   - d. Job costing

3. Which of the following terms refers to an item with little economic value for the firm?
   - a. Abnormal spoilage
   - b. Normal spoilage
   - c. Rework
   - d. Scrap

4. A company is using process costing with FIFO. For a particular period, there is no beginning WIP inventory, the ending WIP inventory includes 10,000 physical units that are 60% complete, and there are 20,000 units completed during the period. How many equivalent units are there in total at the end of the period?
   - a. 20,000
   - b. 26,000
   - c. 32,000
   - d. 34,000

5. Five steps are used to develop a production cost report using the weighted-average method. Number the steps in the correct order:

   Assign total manufacturing costs to units.

   Calculate total manufacturing costs.

   Calculate unit costs.

   Determine the equivalent units.

   Determine the flow of physical units.

6. When a company moves from a traditional cost system in which manufacturing overhead is applied based on machine hours to an activity-based costing system in which there are batch-level and product-level costs, the unit product costs of high-volume products typically will _____ while the unit product costs of low-volume products typically will _____.

Knowledge Check Answers: Costing Systems

1. Which of the following costing systems would work best for a firm that spends a considerable percentage of its overall costs on research and development? [See *Life-Cycle Costing*.]
   - a. Job order costing
   - b. Process costing
   - c. Activity-based costing
   - ☑ d. Life-cycle costing

2. A post office wants to implement a cost accumulation system for its bulk mail sorting warehouse. Which of the following methods would be best suited to this situation? [See *Job Order versus Process Costing*.]
   - a. Life-cycle costing
   - b. Activity-based costing
   - ☑ c. Process costing
   - d. Job costing

3. Which of the following terms refers to an item with little economic value for the firm? [See *Scrap*.]
   - a. Abnormal spoilage
   - b. Normal spoilage
   - c. Rework
   - ☑ d. Scrap

4. A company is using process costing (with FIFO). For a particular period, there is no beginning WIP inventory, the ending WIP inventory includes 10,000 physical units that are 60% complete, and there are 20,000 units completed during the period. How many equivalent units are there in total at the end of the period? [See *Equivalent Units in Process Costing*.]
   - a. 20,000
   - ☑ b. 26,000
   - c. 32,000
   - d. 34,000

5. Five steps are used to develop a production cost report using the weighted average method. Number the steps in the correct order: [See **Steps in Preparing a Production Cost Report**.]

   (5) Assign total manufacturing costs to units.

   (3) Calculate total manufacturing costs.

   (4) Calculate unit costs.

   (2) Determine the equivalent units.

   (1) Determine the flow of physical units.

6. When a company moves from a traditional cost system in which manufacturing overhead is applied based on machine hours to an activity-based costing system in which there are batch-level and product-level costs, the unit product costs of high-volume products typically will **decrease** while the unit product costs of low volume products typically will **increase**. [See **Differences between ABC and Traditional Costing**.]

TOPIC 3

Overhead Costs

MANUFACTURING OVERHEAD COSTS CAN BE very significant for a business because they include all manufacturing costs except direct materials and direct labor. Overhead costs are product costs, which flow through inventory accounts such as raw materials inventory, work-in-process inventory, and finished goods inventory. Product costs flow to the income statement once the product has been sold.

This topic covers fixed and variable overhead, plant-wide versus departmental overhead, and activity-based costing overhead allocation. It also discusses determining an allocation base (i.e., choosing a cost driver) and the allocation of service department costs.

READ the Learning Outcome Statements (LOS) for this topic as found in Appendix A and then study the concepts and calculations presented here to be sure you understand the content you could be tested on in the CMA exam.

Fixed and Variable Overhead Expenses

All overhead expenses are either fixed or variable costs. **Fixed costs** include depreciation on assets, rentals, leasing costs, and indirect labor incurred in manufacturing. These costs do not change during an accounting period, provided the relevant range is consistent with the level of production. **Variable costs** include power, water, sewage, engineering support, machine maintenance, and indirect materials. Variable costs change in proportion to the changes in a particular cost driver and the cost drivers can be either volume or activity based.

Fixed Overhead Costs

Most fixed costs are set for a certain performance period, so, by definition, the day-to-day operations of a business have little effect on fixed costs. The time frame for planning fixed overhead costs has two phases: setting priorities and being efficient in the pursuit of those priorities. Setting priorities means that the firm should determine which fixed overhead costs should or must be undertaken, which fixed costs add no value and should be eliminated, and which fixed costs are most important to get right.

The second phase is pursuing efficiency in the fixed overhead costs that are on the list of priorities and determining which costs are most likely to be reduced through more careful planning.

For example: An auto rental company might set its highest fixed cost priority as the leasing or purchase of the proper number of rental vehicles for a period so that each facility has enough cars to satisfy demand without leaving too much unused capacity. The rental company can decide whether leasing or purchasing is the most cost-effective option, by choosing the most trouble-free brands of cars or negotiating the best deals with the auto manufacturers.

Variable Overhead Costs

The time frame for planning variable overhead costs has the same two phases: setting priorities and being efficient in the pursuit of those priorities. Setting priorities for variable costs involves determining which activities add value for customers and which can be eliminated. Unlike fixed costs, variable costs can be influenced on a day-to-day basis, so the efficient pursuit of priorities can be an ongoing process.

For example: The car rental company might eliminate several paperwork steps for customers or automate the entire process to both reduce its variable administrative costs and improve customer service. It could then implement efficiency measures, such as scheduling car maintenance activities during times of low rental demand, so that these activities do not hamper business.

Budgeted Fixed Overhead Cost Allocation Rates

Fixed overhead costs are a lump-sum amount that will not change over the course of a period even if wide variations occur in activity. The four steps in determining the budgeted fixed allocation rate are:

1. Determine the proper accounting period. A year basis is usually preferable to a monthly basis because most companies want to smooth over variations due to seasonality or different numbers of days per month. Using an annual period also keeps managers from having to create a new budget each month.
2. Determine the allocation base (cost driver) to use when allocating fixed overhead. A firm could use a volume- or activity-based cost driver. Although fixed costs do not vary, they still must be allocated in proportion to the value they are providing to each cost pool.
3. Determine the fixed overhead costs associated with each cost allocation base (cost driver). Fixed overhead costs could be grouped into any number of pools divided according to which allocation base best measures the value provided by the set of fixed costs.

4. Calculate the rate per unit of each allocation base used when allocating fixed overhead costs to cost objects:

$$\text{Fixed Overhead Application Rate} = \frac{\text{Total Cost in Fixed Overhead Cost Pool}}{\text{Total Quantity of Allocation Base}}$$

In this way, more of the fixed cost is assigned to operations that use more of the allocation base than other operations.

For example: A tennis ball manufacturer uses machine hours as its fixed cost driver (step 2, above). The company budgets 40,000 machine hours annually to produce 200,000 cans of tennis balls.

All fixed manufacturing overhead costs relate to the machine hours allocation base (step 3, above). The budgeted fixed overhead costs total $1,000,000 for the year. The rate per unit is calculated as:

$$\text{Fixed Overhead Application Rate} = \frac{\$1,000,000}{40,000 \text{ Machine Hours}} = \$25/\text{Machine Hour}$$

Planning for fixed overhead expenses is similar to planning for variable overhead expenses. Managers must attempt to eliminate activities that do not add value to a product or service to effectively plan fixed overhead costs and fixed overhead rates. Common fixed overhead costs include plant leasing costs, machine depreciation costs, and plant manager salaries. Management should select the appropriate allocation base for fixed overhead expenses based on operations. Common appropriate allocation bases may include machine hours, labor hours, or labor dollars.

Budgeted Variable Overhead Cost Allocation Rates

The steps and calculations listed for budgeting fixed overhead cost allocation rates are the same for variable rates. Simply substitute "variable" in place of "fixed" in the text to determine how to develop an applicable rate.

$$\text{Variable Overhead Application Rate} = \frac{\text{Total Costs in Variable Overhead Cost Pool}}{\text{Total Quantity of Allocation Base}}$$

Managers must attempt to eliminate activities that do not add value to a product or service to effectively plan variable overhead costs and variable overhead rates. Common variable overhead costs include indirect materials, indirect labor, utility costs, maintenance costs, and engineering support. Management should select the appropriate allocation base for variable overhead expenses based on operations. Common appropriate allocation bases may include machine hours, labor hours, or labor dollars.

Job Costing Using the High-Low Method

The high-low method is a cost accounting technique that separates the fixed and variable cost components of a mixed cost (e.g., a cost that contains both a fixed and variable component, such as rental car cost, which may include a fixed amount per day plus a variable amount based on miles driven). It uses, within a relevant range of activity, the highest and lowest amounts of the cost driver (e.g., machine hours) and the highest and lowest respective cost amounts in order to estimate a slope coefficient (e.g., the variable cost component) and the constant (or fixed amount/component) of the cost function. By performing a high-low analysis, interested parties gain an initial understanding of the relationship between a cost driver and costs (semivariable cost).

To illustrate the use of the high-low method, consider the next scenario.

Plate, Inc. has the following four months' worth of wage activity associated with production:

Month	Production Activity	Wages
July	2,000 units	$30,000
August	1,800 units	$28,000
September	1,900 units	$29,000
October	2,100 units	$31,000

The highest production for Plate, Inc. is 2,100 units. The lowest production for Plate, Inc. is 1,800 units. The difference in production is 300 units.

The highest wage cost for Plate, Inc. is $31,000. The lowest wage cost is $28,000. The difference in wage costs is $3,000.

Now we use the high-low method to determine the variable costs associated with production. We take the $3,000 difference in wage cost and divide by the difference in production of 300 units, arriving at variable costs per unit of $10.

The fixed costs assigned can then be calculated by subtracting variable costs from total costs. In September, for example, the total cost was $29,000. Variable costs were $19,000 ($10 × 1,900 units). Therefore, fixed costs for the month of September are $10,000.

High-Low Method and Regression Analysis

We can also use the high-low method using regression analysis. This quantitative analysis will show the best fit line associated with the data points. Using the same example, we can compute the cost function in this way:

$$y = a + bX$$

or

$$a = y - bX$$

where:
  y = the total cost associated with the observed activity;
  b = the slope coefficient (or variable cost per unit component)
  X = the observed activity
  a = the constant (or fixed cost component)

To compute the constant, we can use either the highest or the lowest observation of the cost driver.

At the highest observation of the cost driver, the constant, a, is calculated as:

$$\text{Constant} = \$31{,}000 - (\$10.00 \text{ per machine hours} \times 2{,}100 \text{ units}) = \$10{,}000$$

And at the lowest observation of the cost driver, the constant, a, is calculated as:

$$\text{Constant} = \$28{,}000 - (\$10 \times 1{,}800) = \$10{,}000$$

Thus, the high-low estimate of the cost function is:

$$y = a + bX$$
$$y = \$10{,}000 + (10 \times \text{Number of production units})$$

Advantage and Disadvantage of the High-Low Method

The advantage of the high-low method is that it is simple to use and, from a logical standpoint, easy to understand. The speed and initial understanding provided into how the cost driver affects indirect manufacturing labor costs is beneficial. The disadvantage is that this method relies on only two observations to estimate a cost function. The method ignores information that may change the results going forward.

Plant-Wide, Departmental, and Activity-Based Overhead Costing

Firms with two or more production departments can assign factory overhead costs to jobs or products in these ways:

- Plant-wide overhead rate
- Departmental overhead rate
- Activity-based overhead costing

Plant-Wide Overhead Rate

A **plant-wide overhead rate** is a single rate used for all overhead costs incurred at a production facility. The total plant factory overhead is determined using the next calculation:

$$\text{Plant-Wide Overhead} = \frac{\text{Total Plant Overhead}}{\text{Total Units of Cost Driver (Allocation Base) Common to All Jobs}}$$

Because plant-wide allocation is, by its nature, very general, it can be used only by facilities that have a strong single cost driver that relates to all types of production.

If one department in a plant is highly automated and another department is labor-intensive, different cost drivers should be used for each department instead of a plant-wide overhead rate.

Departmental Overhead Rate

A **departmental overhead** rate is a single overhead rate calculated for a particular department. Departmental overhead rates are more accurate than plant-wide rates.

Each department could have its own rate calculated based on its own cost drivers. The departmental overhead rate is calculated as shown:

$$\text{Departmental Overhead} = \frac{\text{Total Department Overhead}}{\text{Total Units of Cost Driver Common to All Jobs for the Department}}$$

Accounting for each overhead amount is tracked by keeping separate factory overhead and applied overhead accounts for each department. As with the plant-wide rate, the departmental overhead rate is still a fairly general rate, so misallocations of costs can occur if the cost driver chosen does not truly relate to all activities for a department.

Departmental overhead rates should be used only if the department is homogeneous and if a cause-and-effect relationship can be defined between each job and the selected cost driver. When this is not true, several sets of cost drivers and associated cost pools should be used. The dangers of improperly allocating costs have been elaborated on earlier—that is, certain products will appear less profitable than they really are and vice versa, thereby risking mismanagement of the product lines.

Activity-Based Overhead Costing

When plant-wide and departmental overhead allocation methods are not accurate enough, an **activity-based costing** (ABC) method can be used. ABC assigns factory overhead costs to products or services using multiple cost pools and multiple cost drivers. The cost drivers are selected based on a cause-and-effect relationship and can be both activity based and volume based.

For example: Figure 1D-23 shows the cost pools and cost drivers for a sample production facility.

Figure 1D-23 Cost Pools, Drivers, and Predetermined Driver Rate

Overhead Cost Pool	Budgeted Overhead Cost	Cost Driver	Units	Predetermined Driver Rate
Utilities	$100,000	Machine hrs.	10,000	$10/machine hr.
Materials handling	120,000	Materials weight (pounds)	40,000	$3/pound
Setups	90,000	Number of setups	300	$300/setup
	$310,000			

In the table, the predetermined driver rate is calculated by dividing the budgeted overhead cost by the total number of units of the cost driver. The precision in this system is apparent when two or more jobs or products share these costs.

Assume that the facility described has two jobs for the current period. Job 1 uses 4,000 machine hours and 30,000 pounds in direct materials weight and has 100 setups. Job 2 uses 6,000 machine hours and 10,000 pounds in direct materials weight and has 200 setups. The costs assigned to each job are calculated as shown in Figure 1D-24.

For comparison, if a plant-wide rate had been used with machine hours as the sole cost driver, the total overhead of $310,000 divided by 10,000 machine hours would be $31/machine hour, multiplied by 4,000 hours for job 1 ($124,000) and 6,000 hours for job 2 ($186,000).

Note that the ABC method produces very different costs for the two products compared to the plant-wide method.

Figure 1D-24 ABC versus Plant-Wide Overhead Allocation

	ABC	Plant-wide
Job 1 Utilities $10/machine hr. × 4,000 hrs. =	$40,000	
Job 1 Materials handling $3/lb. × 30,000 lbs. =	90,000	
Job 1 Setups $300/setup × 100 setups =	30,000	
Total =	$160,000	124,000
Job 2 Utilities $10/machine hr. × 6,000 hrs. =	$60,000	
Job 2 Materials handling $3/lb. × 10,000 lbs. =	30,000	
Job 2 Setups $300/setup × 200 setups =	60,000	
Total =	$150,000	186,000
	$310,000	$310,000

Benefits of ABC

Activity-based overhead allocation may help management identify inefficient products, departments, and activities when it attempts to eliminate activities that do not provide value to products and services. Activity-based overhead allocation may encourage focusing resources on profitable products, departments and activities, and controlling costs.

Allocation of Service Department Costs

There are two basic types of departments in a company: production departments and service departments. In contrast to production departments (which have been the focus of the discussion to this point), service departments do not directly perform operating activities. Instead, they assist production departments, customers, and employees. Examples of service departments include maintenance, internal auditing, cafeterias, information technology, human resources, purchasing, company stores, customer service, engineering, and cost accounting.

Allocation of service department costs has three phases:

Phase 1: Trace all direct costs and allocate overhead costs to all departments (production departments and other service departments).

Phase 2: Allocate service department costs to production departments or other service departments.

Phase 3: Allocate production department costs to products.

Service department costs are allocated because most service departments do not generate any revenue (i.e., they are cost centers). When a service department does generate revenue, such as the cafeteria or a repairs department, these revenues offset the costs, and any net cost is transferred to the production departments, which are revenue-producing departments. Managers must decide whether they should allocate service department costs to operating departments. If costs are allocated, the fixed and variable costs should be allocated in the same way.

Although a service department may not directly add value to a product, a service department provides a service to other departments within a company that may directly add value to the products and services that the company offers. Managers may determine that service department costs should be allocated back to the operating departments because an operating department may not be able to provide its products without the support of the service department.

Phase 1: Trace Direct Costs and Allocate Overhead Costs to Departments

The first activity in Phase 1 is to trace direct costs to production and service departments. This is the same process as tracing direct costs to production departments.

Similarly, overhead costs can be allocated to service departments in the same way as they are allocated to production departments. However, the cost drivers (allocation bases) may be slightly different in type. Common cost drivers for various service departments are listed next.

Cost accounting—labor hours, customers served

Data processing—number of personal computers, central processing unit minutes, disk storage used

Janitorial services—square feet of building space

Maintenance—machine hours

Materials handling—labor hours, volume handled

Medical facilities—cases handled

Shipping and receiving—units handled, number of requisitions, labor hours

Overall, the cost drivers selected should be easily understood by the managers who will have these costs allocated to them. Note that both the cost driver rate selected and the total units of the cost drivers can use actual or standard (budgeted) rates or units (or some combination, such as standard cost driver rate times actual units of the cost driver). Use of standard amounts for cost driver rates can motivate service department managers to control costs because the amounts can be calculated during a period. However, variances between standard and actual results will cause amounts to be underapplied or overapplied. Using actual cost drivers or actual amounts will allow for precise cost allocation but can be done only after the period is complete, so the method cannot be used for control purposes during the period.

There are two basic methods of allocating costs: the single-rate method and the contribution margin method.

Single-Rate Cost Allocation Method

The **single-rate cost allocation method** creates a single allocation base for a service department's combined fixed and variable costs, providing a single rate per unit for cost allocation. However, when fixed costs are grouped with variable costs, the entire cost seems to be a variable cost, and managers might be tempted to outsource to a provider with a lower rate. Because the fixed department costs would be incurred regardless of use (at least in the short term), outsourcing would cause the department to add new external costs while still continuing to incur the original fixed portion of the internal costs.

For example: If a project has $1 million in fixed costs plus variable costs of $50/machine hour and 5,000 machine hours, the total rate per machine hour would be [$1,000,000 + (5,000 × $50)]/5,000 = $250/machine hour. The single-rate cost can appear to overstate the rate.

Contribution Margin Cost Allocation Method

The **contribution margin cost allocation method**, also called the dual-rate method, creates separate fixed and variable cost pools for allocation of service department costs. Each pool can have its own allocation base, such as labor hours for variable costs and machine hours for fixed costs. By using different cost drivers and different rates, and using standard or actual amounts for each variable, the contribution margin method may produce a different estimate of total costs than if the single-rate method were used.

For example: By this method, with $1,000,000 in fixed costs allocated based on labor hours, and with 4,900 labor hours used, then the fixed allocation rate would be about $204/labor hour. The variable allocation rate would be $50/machine hour.

Each type of cost would be separately calculated using one of the allocation methods detailed in Phase 2 (discussed next), thus doubling the number of calculations required to find the total costs allocated. This method should lead to more precise allocation of costs and allow better managerial decision making, but it could also result in higher administrative costs due to more complex calculations and difficulty in determining proper classification of costs.

Phase 2: Allocate Service Department Costs to Production Departments or Other Service Departments

The second phase is to allocate the service department costs to the production departments or to other service departments. Allocating costs to other service departments, such as the cost for janitorial services to clean the cafeteria, are called interdepartmental or reciprocal services. Three methods can be used to allocate service costs to other departments: the direct method, the step-down method, and the reciprocal method. To keep the focus on the allocation methods, the single-rate method is used in all of the next examples. However, the contribution method can be applied to any of the methods.

Direct Method

The direct method, as its name implies, is the most direct and simple method of allocating service department costs. This method cannot be used to allocate costs to other service departments; it can be used only to allocate costs to production departments. Even when one service department does perform a significant amount of service for another department, this method bypasses such considerations and assigns all costs directly to the production departments. The direct method ignores the cost drivers that are related to the service departments and concentrates only on the cost drivers attributable to the production departments.

For example: Consider Figure 1D-25, showing four individual departments in a metalworking company.

Figure 1D-25 Department Costs and Cost Drivers

	Service		Production	
	HR	Janitorial	Metal Department	Chrome Department
Dept. Costs before Allocation	$200,000	$80,000	$400,000	$100,000
Labor Hours	10,000	5,000	20,000	5,000
Space (sq. ft.)	15,000	500	60,000	20,000

In this example, the human resources (HR) department's costs use the production department's labor hours, and the janitorial department uses the production department's space measurements, as calculated next:

$$\text{Department Allocation} = \frac{\text{Production Department Units}}{\text{Total Units for All Production Departments}} \times \text{Department Costs}$$

$$\text{HR Costs to Metal Dept.} = \frac{20{,}000}{20{,}000 + 5{,}000} \times \$200{,}000 = 0.8 \times \$200{,}000 = \$160{,}000$$

$$\text{HR Costs to Chrome Dept.} = 0.2 \times \$200{,}000 = \$40{,}000$$

$$\text{Janitorial Costs to Metal Dept.} = \frac{60{,}000}{60{,}000 + 20{,}000} \times \$80{,}000 = 0.75 \times \$80{,}000 = \$60{,}000$$

$$\text{Janitorial Costs to Chrome Dept.} = 0.25 \times \$80{,}000 = \$20{,}000$$

The total cost to the metal department is $620,000 ($400,000 + $160,000 + $60,000), and the total cost to the chrome department is $160,000 ($100,000 + $40,000 + $20,000). These allocations assume that there are only two production departments. Even so, the direct method does not take into account the services performed for other service departments. For example, the janitorial service also cleans the HR department, which means that the two production departments are receiving an inaccurate percentage of these costs.

Step-Down Method

The step-down method allocates a service department's costs to service departments and production departments. This method sequentially allocates service department costs, starting with the department that provides the most services to other service departments and finishing with the department that provides the least services to other service departments. Each successive department's allocation is a step down in costs that need to be allocated.

The step-down method also takes into account the proportion of work performed for each of the other service departments. As with the direct method, only the departments receiving the allocation are included in the calculation of cost driver proportions to be allocated.

For example: For the metalworking shop, the HR costs would be allocated first, followed by janitorial services. An actual company might have hundreds of service departments.

Figure 1D-26 illustrates allocation using the step-down method.

Figure 1D-26 Step-Down Method Allocation

	Service		Production	
	HR	Janitorial	Metal Department	Chrome Department
Dept. Costs before Allocation	$200,000	$80,000	$400,000	$100,000
First Step	(200,000)	33,333	133,334	33,333
Subtotal	0	113,333	533,334	133,333
Second Step		(113,333)	85,000	28,333
Total	$0	$0	$618,334	$161,666
Labor Hours	10,000	5,000	20,000	5,000
Space (sq. ft.)	15,000	500	60,000	20,000

Some figures are rounded.

The HR department costs are allocated to the three other departments in this way:

Step 1. A factor (or percentage) is created for each of the receiving departments by taking each of the receiving department's labor hours and dividing that number by the total number of labor hours for the three departments that will receive the allocation from the HR department.

- The janitorial department's allocation percentage is calculated by using 5,000 hours as the numerator and 30,000 (5,000 + 20,000 + 5,000 = 30,000) as the denominator, to create an allocation factor of 5,000/30,000, or 0.167.
- The factors for the metal and chrome departments are 0.667 and 0.167, respectively.
- These factors are then applied to the $200,000 in HR department costs that need to be allocated to the three departments. The HR department's service costs are then allocated to each of the three departments that benefit from its services.
- The janitorial department receives an allocation of $33,333 in costs from the HR department.
- The metal department receives an allocation of $133,334 in costs from the HR department.
- The chrome department receives an allocation of $33,333 in costs from the HR department.

Step 2. The new total of $113,333 for the janitorial costs is allocated to the two production departments based on square feet.

Comparing these costs to those provided by the direct method, the costs are slightly higher for the metal department and slightly lower for the chrome department. The step-down method provides a more accurate measure of how costs should be allocated. However, as can be seen, some costs still can be distorted. For example, janitorial costs still are not allocated to the HR department, even though it has many square feet of space that are cleaned.

In a realistic situation, these costs would be allocated to many service departments (ones with lower costs) other than just the production departments. However, all of the costs eventually end up in the revenue-producing production departments.

Reciprocal Method

The reciprocal method fully recognizes all interdepartmental service costs using simultaneous equations. In contrast, the step-down method provides only partial recognition because it does not allocate costs backward, only forward. Although the reciprocal method is a true recognition method and is most accurate, it is rarely used because of the complexity of its calculations and because the step-down method provides a more cost-effective and reasonable approximation of costs. Software applications make the reciprocal method easier to calculate, but most companies still do not use it.

For example: Apply the reciprocal method to the metalworking shop.

Step 1. Set up a system of equations beginning with the total service department costs and the portions for each of the other departments.

$$HR = \$200,000 + \left(\frac{15,000}{15,000 + 60,000 + 20,000} \times \text{Janitorial}\right)$$

$$\text{Janitorial (J)} = \$80,000 + \left(\frac{5,000}{5,000 + 20,000 + 5,000} \times HR\right)$$

$$HR = \$200,000 + 0.15789(J)$$

$$J = \$80,000 + 0.16667(HR)$$

$$HR = \$200,000 + 0.15789\left[\$80,000 + 0.16667(HR)\right]$$

$$HR = \$200,000 + \$12,631.20 + 0.02632(HR)$$

$$1(HR) - 0.02632(HR) = \$212,631.20$$

$$0.97368(HR) = \$212,631.20$$

$$HR = \frac{\$212,631.20}{0.97368} = \$218,378.93$$

$$HR \approx \$218,379$$

Step 2. Solve for HR's total cost and allocate this to the janitorial, metal, and chrome departments. This amount will be more than the $200,000 department costs.

Step 3. Allocate the new total in janitorial to HR, metal, and chrome departments. At this point, all costs will be allocated to production departments only.

	HR Department	Janitorial Department	Metal Department	Chrome Department
Costs	$200,000	$80,000	$400,000	$100,000
Step 1	(218,379)	36,397	145,586	36,397
Step 2	18,379*	(116,397)	73,514*	24,505*
	$0	$0	$619,100	$160,902

*Slightly off due to rounding.

Phase 3: Allocate Production Department Costs to Products

This phase has already been covered under the various costing methods described in this section.

Knowledge Check: Overhead Costs

The next questions are intended to help you check your understanding and recall of the material presented in this topic. They do not represent the type of questions that appear on the CMA exam.

Directions: Answer each question in the space provided. Correct answers and section references appear after the knowledge check questions.

1. To calculate a department's overhead rate that is based on machine hours, which of the following would be used in the numerator and denominator?

	Numerator	Denominator
☐ a.	Actual manufacturing overhead	Actual machine hours
☐ b.	Actual manufacturing overhead	Estimated machine hours
☐ c.	Estimated manufacturing overhead	Actual machine hours
☐ d.	Estimated manufacturing overhead	Estimated machine hours

2. Which of the terms below would make the next sentence correct? Multiple overhead rate costing systems are usually more _____ than plant-wide overhead rates.

    ☐ a. accurate and complex
    ☐ b. accurate
    ☐ c. complex

3. Which of the following allocates service department costs sequentially to both production and other service departments, starting with the department that provides the most services, and finishes in a single pass (does not allocate costs to items higher in the sequence)?

    ☐ a. Direct method
    ☐ b. Step-down method
    ☐ c. Reciprocal method
    ☐ d. Indirect method

4. Complete the following formula for calculating the fixed overhead application rate.

$$\text{Fixed Overhead Application Rate} = \left[\frac{}{\text{Total Quantity of Allocation Base}} \right]$$

5. Select the appropriate rate calculation method for each of these firms:

	Plant-wide overhead rate	Departmental overhead rate	ABC overhead costing
A firm manufactures and installs playground equipment			
A firm converts wastewater sludge into fertilizer			
A firm produces 17 types of power tools			

6. Determine if each of the following statements regarding allocation of service department costs is true or false.

	True	False
The reciprocal method provides a highly accurate view of costs.		
The direct method provides a simple means of allocating costs to production departments and to other service departments.		
The step-down method is used because it provides a more cost-effective and reasonable approximation of costs.		

Knowledge Check Answers: Overhead Costs

1. To calculate a department's overhead rate that is based on machine hours, which of the following would be used in the numerator and denominator? **[See *Departmental Overhead Rate*.]**

	Numerator	Denominator
☐ a.	Actual manufacturing overhead	Actual machine hours
☐ b.	Actual manufacturing overhead	Estimated machine hours
☐ c.	Estimated manufacturing overhead	Actual machine hours
☒ d.	Estimated manufacturing overhead	Estimated machine hours

2. Which of the terms below would make the next sentence correct? **[See *Phase 2: Allocate Service Department Costs to Production Department or Other Service Departments*.]**
   Multiple overhead rate costing systems are usually more _____ than plant-wide overhead rates.

   ☒ a. accurate and complex
   ☐ b. accurate
   ☐ c. complex

3. Which of the following allocates service department costs sequentially to both production and other service departments, starting with the department that provides the most services, and finishes in a single pass (does not allocate costs to items higher in the sequence)? **[See *Step-Down Method*.]**

   ☐ a. Direct method
   ☒ b. Step-down method
   ☐ c. Reciprocal method
   ☐ d. Indirect method

4. Complete the following formula for calculating the fixed overhead application rate. **[See *Budgeted Fixed Overhead Cost Allocation Rates*.]**

$$\text{Fixed Overhead Application Rate} = \frac{\text{Total Costs in Fixed Overhead Cost Pool}}{\text{Total Quantity of Allocation Base}}$$

5. Select the appropriate rate calculation method for each of these firms: [See *Plant-Wide, Departmental, and Activity-Based Overhead Costing*.]

	Plant-wide overhead rate	Departmental overhead rate	ABC overhead costing
A firm manufactures and installs playground equipment		X	
A firm converts wastewater sludge into fertilizer	X		
A firm produces 17 types of power tools			X

6. Determine if each of the following statements regarding allocation of service department costs is true or false. [See *Phase 2: Allocate Service Department Costs to Production Department or Other Service Departments*.]

	True	False
The reciprocal method provides a highly accurate view of costs.	X	
The direct method provides a simple means of allocating costs to production departments and to other service departments.		X
The step-down method is used because it provides a more cost-effective and reasonable approximation of costs.	X	

TOPIC 4

Supply Chain Management

A PARADIGM IS AN EXAMPLE OR a model, and a paradigm shift refers to a significant change in the model that people use to organize or understand what they are doing. At their inception, supply chain management, lean manufacturing, just-in-time production systems, theory of constraints, and outsourcing represented paradigm shifts in manufacturing. These manufacturing practices changed the type of information needed for decision making and the methods used to collect that data. Ultimately, these practices changed the role of the management accountant and improved the efficiency and effectiveness of information reporting.

This topic looks first at supply chain management and lean manufacturing. Then it discusses a traditional materials requirement planning systems as well as just-in-time and outsourcing systems and enterprise resource planning systems built on the theory of constraints. It also discusses capacity concepts and other production management theories.

READ the Learning Outcome Statements (LOS) for this topic as found in Appendix A and then study the concepts and calculations presented here to be sure you understand the content you could be tested on in the CMA exam.

Supply Chain Management

Supply chain management involves the management of the flow of goods, which includes the movement and storage of raw materials, work-in-process inventory, and finished goods from the point of origin to the point of consumption. It involves the planning and management of all activities involved in sourcing and procuring raw materials, converting those materials to a finished product, and delivering that finished product to consumers. Coordinating and collaborating with suppliers, intermediaries, third parties, and customers is critical in the execution of these activities.

In essence, the objective of supply chain management is to integrate procurement, operations management, logistics, and information technology while creating value through this chain of key processes and activities.

Lean Manufacturing

Lean manufacturing, also called lean enterprise or lean production, focuses on the creation of value for the end customer. Any expenditure for any goal other than creating customer value is considered waste and should be eliminated. The primary benefits of lean manufacturing are reduced waste and improved production flow (throughput). Both waste reduction and increased throughput reduce costs.

Materials Requirement Planning

The system of production traditionally used in manufacturing is **materials requirement planning** (MRP). Taking a product from raw material through delivery often is treated as a series of discrete events. The concept is to "push" the product through production to reach a market.

The premises underlying MRP push-through systems include:

- Demand forecasts
- A materials order specifying the materials, components, and subunit tasks required to produce a final product
- A production order specifying the quantities of materials, components, subunits, and product inventories needed to meet the demand forecast

In MRP systems, a master production schedule indicates the quantities and timing of each part to be produced. Once the scheduled production run begins, departments push output through a system, regardless of whether that output is needed.

For example: Using an MRP system, here is how a company might calculate subunits (parts) to produce Product P and offset lead times.

Product P is made from:	Part A is made from:	Part B is made from:
2 parts A	1 part C	2 parts C
3 parts B	2 parts D	2 parts E

If 100 units of Product P are required:

Part A	2 × number of Ps	= 2 × 100	= 200
Part B	3 × number of Ps	= 3 × 100	= 300
Part C	1 × number of As	= 1 × 200	
	+ 2 × number of Bs	+ 2 × 300	= 800
Part D	2 × number of As	= 2 × 200	= 400
Part E	2 × number of Bs	= 2 × 300	= 600

The lead times required are:

Product P	1 week
Part A	2 weeks
Part B	2 weeks
Part C	3 weeks
Part D	1 week
Part E	1 week

Once the date for Product P delivery is known, a schedule can be created, specifying when all the parts must be ordered and received to meet the demand for Product P.

		\multicolumn{7}{c	}{Weeks}	
		1	2	3	4	5	6	7	
P	Required date							100	P lead time = 1 week
	Order placement						100		
A	Required date						200		A lead time = 2 weeks
	Order placement				200				
B	Required date						300		B lead time = 2 weeks
	Order placement				300				
C	Required date				800				C lead time = 3 weeks
	Order placement	800							
D	Required date				400				D lead time = 1 week
	Order placement			400					
E	Required date				600				E lead time = 1 week
	Order placement			600					

In this example, the MRP is based on the demand for P, the parts or subunits that compose P, and the lead times needed to obtain each part either internally or from an outside supplier.

Benefits of MRP Systems

The benefits of MRP systems include:

- Less coordination required between functional areas; everyone follows the bill of materials.
- Scheduling improvements; levels load when demand is variable or relatively unpredictable.
- Predictable raw material needs; can take advantage of bulk purchasing and other price breaks.
- More efficient inventory control; schedules to use up raw materials or build finished goods.

- Additional inventory on hand to cover orders should product be damaged or lost in transit to a customer.
- Quick response to new customer demand; can supply new customers from existing inventory rather than building product after the order is received.
- Better manufacturing process control; minimizes retooling and machine setup time.

The primary disadvantage of an MRP environment is potential inventory accumulation. Workstations may receive parts that they are not ready to process.

Just-in-Time Manufacturing

A **just-in-time (JIT) system** refers to a comprehensive production and inventory control methodology in which materials arrive exactly as they are needed for each stage in a production process. The goal of JIT is to create lean manufacturing, reducing or eliminating waste of resources by producing production line components as they are required rather than holding large safety stocks of inventory. Nothing is produced until it is needed.

In a JIT system, need is created by demand for a product. Theoretically, the market "pulls" a replacement product from the last position in the system. Demand triggers every step and pulls a product through production—from customer demand for a finished product at one end working all the way back to the demand for raw materials at the other end. This "demand-pull" feature of a JIT system requires high levels of quality at each point in the system because only the minimum number of items demanded will be produced. Close coordination is required among all participants to ensure a smooth flow of goods and operations.

Characteristics of JIT Systems

The major characteristics of a JIT environment are:

- Production organized into manufacturing work cells. Organization of the related manufacturing processes necessary to create a final product into clusters and then logical grouping of clusters into small groups for close proximity, improved communication, and immediate feedback.
- Multiskilled workers. Cross-functional training of workers so they can perform a variety of operations and tasks on an as-needed basis to maintain smooth production flow.
- Reduced setup times. Reduction of the time required to get tools, equipment, and materials ready for a production run.
- Reduced manufacturing lead times. Reduction of the time from when an order is initiated to when a finished good is produced.
- Reliable suppliers. Careful screening of suppliers to ensure on-time deliveries of high-quality goods for JIT use possibly within a day or less.

Use of Kanban in JIT Implementation

Kanban is a Japanese term that describes a visual record or a card and is one of the most common methods used to implement JIT systems. In JIT environments, workers use a kanban to signal the need for a specified quantity of materials or parts to move from one work cell operation or department to another in sequence. Workers respond only after receiving a kanban. When production is complete, the kanban is attached to the finished order and sent downstream to the next work cell.

A kanban traditionally was a card with information identifying the part, the number needed, the delivery location, and similar information. E-kanban applications provide an automated approach that can be integrated with communications and enterprise resource planning (ERP) systems.

JIT Benefits and Limitations

Some of the general benefits of JIT are:

- Obvious production priorities
- Reduced setup and manufacturing lead time
- No overproduction occurrences
- Improved quality control (faster feedback) and less materials waste
- Easier inventory control (low or even zero inventory)
- Less paperwork
- Strong supplier relationships

JIT systems focus on controlling total manufacturing costs versus individual costs, such as raw materials or direct manufacturing labor. Typically, manufacturing costs decline, and cash flow and working capital levels improve. Specific financial benefits are possible; these include:

- Lower inventory investments.
- Reduced costs for carrying and handling inventories.
- Reduced risk of inventory obsolescence, damage, or "shrinkage."
- Lower investments in space (for production and inventories).
- Higher revenues resulting from a quicker response time to customers.
- Direct tracing of some costs that would otherwise be classified as overhead is also possible. Labor, shipping, and other costs arbitrarily allocated under another method are potentially traceable.

For all the benefits, JIT systems are not without their limitations, which may include:

- No buffer inventory; potential for increased idle time if production needs to wait for materials.
- Reliance on suppliers to maintain adequate stock to meet unpredictable demands; highly dependent on supply chain.
- Potential stockouts at suppliers; critical parts shortages can shut down an entire line.
- Potential overtime expenses from unanticipated orders.

It should be noted that in some markets and under certain conditions, occasional stockouts are preferable to the alternatives.

Enterprise Resource Planning

Enterprise resource planning (ERP), typically discussed in the context of an ERP system, gives organizations an information technology tool that combines and integrates various information systems it uses into one comprehensive system to manage operations. ERP, which evolved from the MRP systems developed for manufacturing in the 1980s, often includes modules such as accounting, human resources, supply chain and inventory, as well as manufacturing information systems. Its purpose is to facilitate the flow of information among departments within an organization, and manage data sharing with outside stakeholder systems, such as suppliers, clients, and regulatory agencies. ERP is intended to improve operational efficiency and reduce waste by allowing departments and functions across an organization to use resources and send work flow through a single computer system.

The fundamental advantage of ERP is that integrating myriad business processes saves time and expense. Examples of specific tasks that benefit from ERP integration include: sales forecasting, which allows inventory optimization, matching purchase orders, inventory receipts, and vendor invoicing; order tracking, from acceptance through fulfillment; and revenue tracking, from billing through cash receipt. Operational benefits achieved from this integration encompass:

- Improved business effectiveness and efficiency. By keeping an organization's internal business process running smoothly, ERP can lead to better outputs.
- Better and timelier decisions. ERP supports upper-level management, providing critical real-time decision-making information.
- A more flexible and agile organization that can better adapt to change. ERP allows a company to become less rigidly structured so organization components operate more cohesively.
- Improved data integrity and security. A common control system, such as that provided by ERP systems, allows organizations the ability to more easily ensure key company data is not compromised.
- Improved collaboration between organizational functions. ERP provides a platform that allows employees to spend more time collaborating on content rather than focusing on learning how to communicate in various formats across distributed systems.

While an organization's implementation of ERP allows it to realize many advantages and benefits for improved operational efficiency, there are disadvantages associated with ERP implementation. Some of those disadvantages include: problems with customization, higher costs than less integrated or less comprehensive solutions, extensive training, overcoming resistance to sharing sensitive information between departments, and diversion of focus on critical activities associated with the reengineering of business processes to fit the ERP system.

Outsourcing

Outsourcing describes a company's decision to purchase a product or service from an outside supplier rather than producing it in house. Through this option, an organization can concentrate resources on its core business competencies while capitalizing on the expertise of other firms that are more efficient, effective, or knowledgeable at specialized tasks that are peripheral to those core business competencies. Today, many firms outsource significant parts of their support services, such as information technology, customer service, and human resource functions.

The term *make versus buy* is often used in reference to outsourcing. Make-versus-buy analysis examines the relevant costs of keeping activities in-house versus outsourcing to external suppliers. Some firms have extended the idea of outsourcing to **contract manufacturing,** in which another company actually manufactures a portion of the first firm's products. Contract manufacturing can provide a win-win relationship if one firm has excess capacity or expertise and another company lacks capacity or knowledge.

Benefits and Limitations of Outsourcing

There are many strategic reasons an organization may choose to outsource work. For smaller business, outsourcing may provide access to resources and expertise for capabilities they may not have internally. For larger businesses, outsourcing can improve specific functions. Outsourcing may provide these benefits:

- Can allow management and employees to focus on core competencies and strategic revenue-generating activities
- Can improve efficiency and effectiveness by gaining outside expertise or scale
- Can provide access to current technologies at reasonable cost without the risk of obsolescence
- Can reduce expenses by gaining capabilities without incurring overhead costs (e.g., staffing, benefits, space)
- May improve the quality and/or timeliness of products or services

Despite many attractive advantages, outsourcing is not the answer for all activities or functions. Companies thinking of outsourcing should consider these key cautions:

- May cost more to go outside for specific expertise
- Can result in a loss of in-house expertise and capabilities
- Can reduce process control
- May reduce control over quality
- May lead to less flexibility (depending on the external supplier)
- May result in less personalized service
- Creates privacy and confidentiality issues
- Can result in giving knowledge away and lead to competitors obtaining expertise, scale, customers, and the like.
- Potential for employee morale and loyalty issues

Theory of Constraints

In the 1990s, Dr. Eliyahu Goldratt, a physicist turned business management consultant, countered the adage of "A penny saved is a penny earned" with "The goal is not to save money but to make money."

Goldratt developed the **theory of constraints (TOC)** as an overall management philosophy with a basis in the manufacturing environment. The overriding goal of the TOC is to improve speed in the manufacturing process by optimizing throughput rather than simply measuring output.

The premise behind the TOC is that every system is pursuing a goal and that every goal is constrained by a limit. If a system is a series of connecting processes that work together to accomplish some aim, a constraint is a limiting factor, bottleneck, or barrier that slows a product's total cycle time. Cycle time is the time it takes to complete a process from beginning to end. Constraint management is the process of identifying process barriers, analyzing and understanding the barriers, and removing them so as to reduce cycle time and optimize the system's efficiency.

Goldratt maintains that that there is only one constraint in a system at any given time but that this bottleneck limits the output of the entire system. The remaining components of the system are known as nonconstraints (non-bottlenecks). Overall, the TOC emphasizes fixing the system constraint and temporarily ignoring the nonconstraints. In this way, the theory has a profound impact on cycle time and process improvement rather than spreading limited time, energy, and resources across an entire system, which may or may not have tangible results.

However, when one constraint is strengthened, the system does not become infinitely stronger. The constraint simply migrates to a different component of the system (i.e., some other factor becomes a bottleneck or barrier). The system is stronger than it was but still not as strong as it could be.

Basic Principles in the Theory of Constraints

Inventory, operational expenses, throughput contribution, and the drum-buffer-rope system are the principal concepts underlying the TOC.

Inventory

Inventory refers to all the money the system invests in purchasing items it intends to resell. Typically, this referred to all physical inventory items, but the term now is more broadly defined to include all assets.

Operating Expenses

In the TOC, *operating* (or operational) *expenses* refer to the money the system spends to convert inventory into throughput. Operating expenses include expenditures such as direct and indirect labor, supplies, outside contractors, interest payments, and depreciation. Employees are responsible for turning inventory into throughput.

Throughput Contribution

Throughput contribution, also known as throughput margin or simply throughput, is a TOC measure of product profitability. It is the rate at which the entire system generates money through product and/or service sales.

Throughput contribution is represented by the next formula:

> Throughput Contribution = Sales Revenue − Direct ~~Material~~ *Variable* Costs

Throughput contribution assumes that the material costs include all purchased components and material handling costs. TOC analysis also assumes that labor is a fixed cost, not a direct and variable cost. The relationship between TOC and throughput contribution is explained in further detail later in this section.

Drum-Buffer-Rope System

The drum-buffer-rope (DBR) system is a TOC method for balancing the flow of production through the constraint. The drum connotes the constraint, the rope is the sequence of processes prior to and including the constraint, and the buffer is the minimum amount of work-in-process input needed to keep the drum busy. The objective of the drum-buffer-rope system is to keep the process flow running smoothly through the constraint by careful timing and scheduling of the processes in the rope leading up to the constraint.

Steps in the Theory of Constraints

The TOC includes five focusing steps designed to concentrate improvement efforts on the constraint most likely to have a positive impact on a system. Figure 1D-27 summarizes the five steps.

Figure 1D-27 Five Focusing Steps of the Theory of Constraints

Step 1	**Identify the system constraint.**
	In the first step, an organization identifies what part of the system constitutes the weakest link, or the constraint, and determines whether it is a physical constraint or a policy constraint.
	Example: A management accountant works with managers and engineers to flowchart a manufacturing process for a product line. They identify the sequence and the amount of time each step requires. A system constraint is identified where one step in the process is taking too long to complete or is idle too long.
Step 2	**Decide how to exploit the constraint.**
	The organization "exploits" the constraint by utilizing every bit of the constraining component without committing to potentially expensive changes and/or upgrades.
	Example: Scheduling of key machine time is changed, and employees are redeployed.

Step 3 **Subordinate everything else.**

With a plan in place for exploiting the constraint, an organization adjusts the rest of the system to enable the constraint to operate at maximum effectiveness and then evaluates the results to see if the constraint is still holding back system performance. If it is, the organization proceeds to Step 4. If it is not, the constraint has been eliminated, and the organization skips ahead to Step 5.

Example: Further analysis looks at actions to maximize flow through the constraint. With a focus on throughput, the review team suggests ways to speed up the process, such as reduced setup times and use of the DBR system. Non-value-added activities are eliminated. The idea is to keep the constraint busy without accumulating inventory or accumulating work in the process.

Step 4 **Elevate the constraint.**

If an organization reaches Step 4, it means that Steps 2 and 3 were not sufficient in eliminating the constraint. At this point, the organization elevates the constraint by taking whatever action is needed to eliminate it. This may involve major changes to the existing system, such as reorganization, divestiture, or capital improvements. Because these typically require a substantial up-front investment, the organization should be certain that the constraint cannot be broken in Steps 1 through 3 before proceeding.

Example: Management considers how to increase capacity of the system (should Steps 2 and 3 prove unsatisfactory in alleviating the constraint). Additional labor or more/new equipment may be necessary.

Step 5 **Go back to Step 1, but beware of inertia.**

After a constraint is broken, the organization repeats the steps all over again, looking for the next thing constraining system performance. At the same time, it monitors how changes related to subsequent constraints may impact the constraints that are already broken, thus preventing solution inertia.

Example: The organization considers a strategic response to the constraint. The goal is to improve throughput. The product or the process may be redesigned or hard-to-manufacture products may be eliminated, and so on.

In the theory of constraints, throughput (T), inventory (I), and operating expenses (OE) link operational and financial measures. As discussed in the Statement on Management Accounting "Theory of Constraints (TOC) Management System Fundamentals" (Copyright © 1999 Institute of Management Accountants):

- Net profit increases when throughput goes up or operating expenses go down.
- Throughput can go up by increasing sales revenues or reducing variable costs of production.
- Measures that increase net profit increase return on investment—as long as inventory remains the same.
- If inventory can be decreased then ROI will increase even without an increase in net profit.
- Cash flow increases when either throughput goes up or the time to generate throughput is reduced, assuming the time save is applied toward generating more throughput.

The TOC attempts to maximize throughput while decreasing inventory, operational expenses, and other investments. Unlike traditional performance measures, which focus on direct labor efficiency and unit costs and how efficiently the company must produce a product, TOC emphasizes how efficiently an organization must manufacture products for optimum market success. The flow of product is dictated by market demand, not by the forces influencing traditional mass production: cheap sources of materials, machine efficiencies, or low direct labor.

Stated another way, T, I, and OE measurements enable a company to understand how much money it is making and how to best leverage capabilities to improve profitability.

Theory of Constraints Reports

The TOC focuses on eliminating constraints and decreasing cycle time or delivery time. Performance measures used in implementing the TOC also will identify key performance indicators (KPIs). Organizations often prepare a TOC report to highlight select operating data and the throughput margin. TOC reports are valuable in identifying both profitability and KPIs.

Figure 1D-28 presents a sample TOC report.

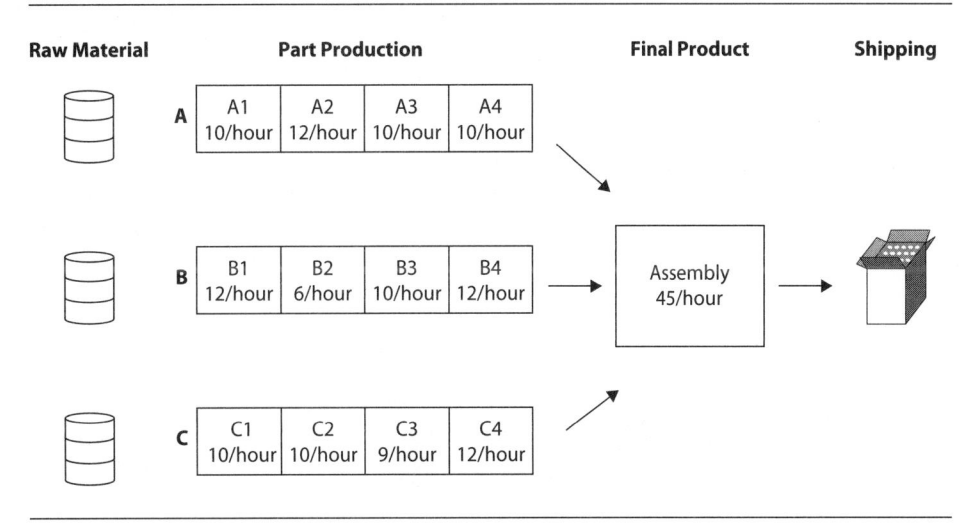

Figure 1D-28 Sample Theory of Constraints Report

Raw Material	Part Production				Final Product	Shipping
A	A1 10/hour	A2 12/hour	A3 10/hour	A4 10/hour		
B	B1 12/hour	B2 6/hour	B3 10/hour	B4 12/hour	Assembly 45/hour	
C	C1 10/hour	C2 10/hour	C3 9/hour	C4 12/hour		

Various formats are possible for TOC reports. In looking at this sample, the key points include:

- The final product is assembled from three component parts: A, B, and C.
- Each part is the result of a different series of linear operations. For example, part A starts with the raw material and goes through operations A1, A2, A3, and A4; raw material for part B goes through B1, B2, B3, B4, and so forth.
- The slowest operation is B2 (six per hour); therefore, the output of this operation is the weakest link and is constraining the output of the entire system.

Having successfully identified the system constraint, steps can be taken to lessen or eliminate it. The organization may "exploit" the constraint by changing how it uses the constraint without spending more money—such as by reducing setup times to improve efficiency and optimize the activity. The organization may "elevate" the constraint by investing money to increase the capacity of the constrained resources—such as buying another piece of equipment or outsourcing an activity.

Naturally, an organization should spend additional money to elevate a constraint only after exploiting the constraint to the fullest potential.

Theory of Constraints and Activity-Based Costing

Organizations that implement the TOC often use activity-based costing (ABC) as well. TOC and ABC are both used by organizations to assess product profitability, but there are a few differences in how these two cost management methods are used.

- TOC takes a short-term approach to profitability analysis with an emphasis on materials-related costs. ABC examines long-term costing, including all product costs.
- TOC considers how to improve short-term profitability by focusing on production constraints and plausible short-term product mix adjustments.
- ABC does not consider resource constraints and process capability; it analyzes cost drivers and accurate unit costs for long-term strategic pricing and profit planning decisions.
- ABC is generally used as a tool for planning and control.

The short-term aspects of TOC and the long-range focus of ABC make them complementary profitability analysis methods.

Although the TOC has its roots in the manufacturing environment, applications have been developed for service industries. Measures of speed and cycle time must be defined appropriately for the nature of the enterprise. Additionally, specific TOC implications for management accounting have been assessed to consider the benefits of throughput accounting in business rather than using traditional cost accounting methods.

Theory of Constraints and Throughput Costing

The TOC focuses on improving a company's profits by managing its operating constraints. Companies that employ a TOC approach use a form of variable costing called throughput costing. Throughput costing, also called super-variable costing, is a costing method where the only costs included in inventory are the costs of direct materials. All other costs are classified as period costs. In many companies, it is quite accurate to say that direct labor behaves like a committed fixed cost in the short run, not like a variable cost that adjusts to changes in output. The TOC has a short time focus; an assumption is made that all operating costs are fixed in the short term and are therefore categorized as fixed costs. Like variable costing, throughput costing is an internal reporting tool.

Three items that are measured in the TOC are **throughput contribution**, **inventory (or investments)**, and **operating expenses**.

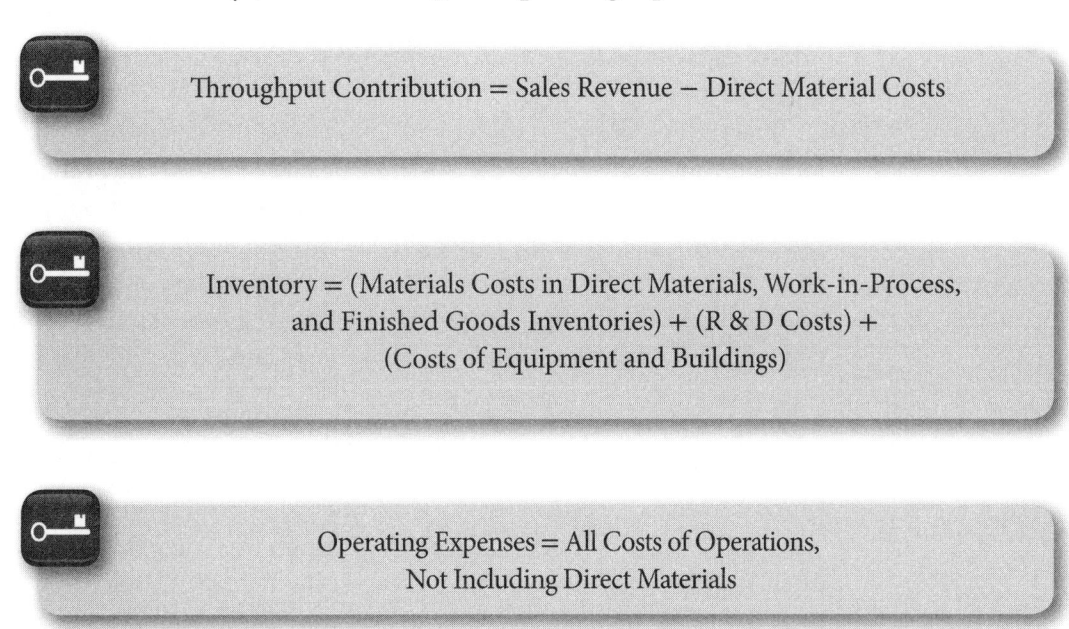

> Throughput Contribution = Sales Revenue − Direct Material Costs

> Inventory = (Materials Costs in Direct Materials, Work-in-Process, and Finished Goods Inventories) + (R & D Costs) + (Costs of Equipment and Buildings)

> Operating Expenses = All Costs of Operations, Not Including Direct Materials

Using this method, the objective is to maximize throughput contribution while reducing investments and operating costs.

Capacity Concepts

A key issue in costing is choosing the capacity level for computing the allocation of manufacturing overhead. Determining the correct level of capacity to use is a difficult strategic decision for managers. The choice of capacity level used to allocate overhead can have a great effect on product cost information used by managers. If a company has capacity in excess of what it needs, it will incur large costs of unused capacity. Likewise, if a company has too little capacity to meet demand, it may have trouble filling customer orders.

Theoretical capacity (also known as ideal capacity) is the level of capacity that can be achieved under ideal conditions, when there are no machine breakdowns or maintenance, delays, or the like. Theoretical capacity represents the largest volume of output possible but is unattainable and unrealistic.

Practical capacity represents the highest level of capacity that can be achieved while allowing for unavoidable losses of productive time, such as machine breakdowns, employee vacations, maintenance, and so on. Unlike theoretical capacity, it is the level of capacity that can realistically be achieved.

Using theoretical capacity when calculating overhead allocations would mean that a large-denominator activity level would be used, resulting in a lower overhead allocation to individual units of product. This would distort the allocated costs (making them too low) and provide management with product cost information that is not representative of actual costs. Practical capacity does not take into consideration the amount of unused capacity in allocating costs. The benefit of this approach is that it encourages managers to focus their attention on the amount of unused capacity, and user departments are not overcharged for a portion of costs related to unused capacity.

Practical capacity is a better choice to use as the denominator activity level for allocating overhead because it is realistic and will generate product costs that accurately reflect the cost of the product. By using practical capacity to calculate product costs, the company is not over- or underallocating costs to each unit of product. Instead, a "practical" or "realistic" amount of overhead is allocated to each unit produced. As a result, many companies prefer to use practical capacity as the denominator to calculate the allocated overhead rate.

Other Production Management Theories

Competitiveness... productivity... continuous improvement... profitability...

Organizations constantly strive to improve on what they already do well and to capitalize on growth opportunities. Beyond the manufacturing paradigms previously discussed, organizations have a wide array of other production management techniques to consider in their quest for better, faster, and more profitable operations.

Many organizations have adopted some or all of the approaches listed in Figure 1D-29 in an attempt to reduce costs, increase productivity, improve quality, and increase their overall responsiveness to customers.

Figure 1D-29 Contemporary Productivity Approaches

Technique	Description
Automation/robots	Uses reprogrammable, multifunctional robots (machines) designed to manipulate materials, parts, tools, or specialized devices through variable programmed motions
	Applies robots to the performance of a variety of repetitive tasks
Capacity management and analysis (capacity planning)	Represents an important decision-making area involving strategic, tactical, and operational aspects
	Includes an iterative procedure that:
	• Reviews long-term demand forecasts
	• Translates forecasts into capacity requirements
	• Matches the capacity requirements to present facilities
	• Identifies mismatches between capacity requirements and projected availability
	• Devises plans to overcome mismatches and selects the best alternative

Computer-aided design (CAD)	Uses computers in product development, analysis, and design modification to improve the quality and performance of the product
	Usually entails the drawing or physical layout steps of engineering design
Computer-aided manufacturing (CAM)	Applies the computer to the planning, control, and operation of a production facility
Computer-integrated manufacturing (CIM)	Involves a manufacturing system that completely integrates all factory and office functions within a company via a computer-based information network
	Uses computers to control the integration and flow of information between design, engineering, manufacturing, logistics, warehousing and distribution, customers and suppliers, sales and marketing activities, and accounting
	Facilitates hour-by-hour manufacturing management
Concurrent engineering (simultaneous engineering)	Integrates product or service design with input from all business units and functions throughout a product's or service's life cycle
	Emphasizes upstream prevention versus downstream correction
	Attempts to balance the needs of all parties in product or service design while maintaining customer requirements
Flexible manufacturing system (FMS)	Uses a computerized network of automated equipment that produces one or more groups of parts or variations of a product in a flexible manner

Knowledge Check: Supply Chain Management

The next questions are intended to help you check your understanding and recall of the material presented in this topic. They do not represent the type of questions that appear on the CMA exam.

Directions: Answer each question in the space provided. Correct answers and section references appear after the knowledge check questions.

1. What is the primary benefit of just-in-time (JIT) systems compared with traditional materials requirement planning systems?
    - ☐ a. Increased stock quantities at all levels in a system
    - ☐ b. Maximization of production runs to accommodate complete product lines
    - ☐ c. Replacement of a push-through manufacturing strategy with a demand-pull strategy
    - ☑ d. Reduced risk of overproduction and savings from holding less inventory

2. A large semiconductor manufacturer plans to apply the theory of constraints methodology to increase production capacity. How could a management accountant **best** support the initiative?
    - ☐ a. Determine outsourcing costs to offload long-term critical constraints.
    - ☐ b. Design buffer management worksheets to facilitate quantitative analysis.
    - ☐ c. Provide net profit, return on investment, and cash flow data.
    - ☑ d. Supply activity-based cost data.

For Questions 3 through 6, match the following terms to their appropriate description.

   a. An iterative decision-making process intended to overcome supply and demand mismatches

   b. A decision to purchase a product or service from an external supplier rather than producing it in-house

   c. JIT system feature requiring close coordination to ensure a smooth flow of goods and operations despite low inventory quantities

   d. A visual signal indicating the need for a specified quantity of materials or parts to move from one operation or department to another in sequence

3. _____c_____ Demand-pull

4. _____d_____ Kanban

5. ____b____ Outsourcing

6. ____a____ Capacity management

7. An organization will directly gain all of the following benefits from the TOC methodology **except**:
   - a. reduced bottlenecks.
   - b. increased profitability.
   - c. improved long-term planning and control.
   - d. improved quality of products and services.

8. In a TOC model, what does this calculate?

   Sales Revenue − Direct Material Costs = _____

9. In TOC, what factors link operational and financial measures?
   a. _____
   b. _____
   c. _____

10. What concern would there be in using theoretical capacity to allocate overhead? What should be used instead?
    _____

Knowledge Check Answers: Supply Chain Management

1. What is the primary benefit of just-in-time (JIT) systems compared with traditional materials requirement planning systems? [See **JIT Benefits and Limitations**.]
   - ☐ a. Increased stock quantities at all levels in a system
   - ☐ b. Maximization of production runs to accommodate complete product lines
   - ☐ c. Replacement of a push-through manufacturing strategy with a demand-pull strategy
   - ☒ d. Reduced risk of overproduction and savings from holding less inventory.

2. A large semiconductor manufacturer plans to apply the theory of constraints methodology to increase production capacity. How could a management accountant best support the initiative? [See **Theory of Constraints and Activity-Based Costing**.]
   - ☐ a. Determine outsourcing costs to offload long-term critical constraints.
   - ☐ b. Design buffer management worksheets to facilitate quantitative analysis.
   - ☐ c. Provide net profit, return on investment, and cash flow data.
   - ☒ d. Supply activity-based cost data.

For Questions 3 through 6, match the following terms to their appropriate description. [See **Just-in-Time Manufacturing, Outsourcing,** and **Capacity Concepts**.]

   a. An iterative decision-making process intended to overcome supply and demand mismatches
   b. A decision to purchase a product or service from an external supplier rather than producing it in-house
   c. JIT system feature requiring close coordination to ensure a smooth flow of goods and operations despite low inventory quantities
   d. A visual signal indicating the need for a specified quantity of materials or parts to move from one operation or department to another in sequence

3. __c__ Demand-pull
4. __d__ Kanban
5. __b__ Outsourcing
6. __a__ Capacity management

7. An organization will directly gain all of the following benefits from the TOC methodology **except**: [See *Theory of Constraints*.]
   - ☐ a. reduced bottlenecks.
   - ☐ b. increased profitability.
   - ☒ c. improved long-term planning and control.
   - ☐ d. improved quality of products and services.

8. In a TOC model, what does this calculate? [See *Theory of Constraints and Throughput Costing*.]

   Sales Revenue − Direct Material Costs = **Throughput Contribution**

9. In TOC, what factors link operational and financial measures? [See *Steps in the Theory of Constraints*.]
   a. **Throughput (T)**
   b. **Inventory (I)**
   c. **Operating expenses (OE)**

10. What concern would there be in using theoretical capacity to allocate overhead? What should be used instead? [See *Capacity Concepts*.]

    Using theoretical capacity results in a lower overhead allocation to individual units of product. Practical capacity reduces theoretical capacity by including unavoidable interruption, such as machine maintenance, plant shutdowns, and the like. Therefore, practical capacity is more realistic and will generate product costs that more accurately reflect the cost of the product than if theoretical capacity is used to allocate overhead.

TOPIC 5

Business Process Improvement

BUSINESS PERFORMANCE HAS ORGANIZATIONAL RAMIFICATIONS beyond matching or surpassing the competition in your industry. Customers are generally better informed and have virtually unlimited sources of quality goods and services at acceptable prices. Customers today demand more for less. Organizations are constantly challenged to address these rising customer expectations, and the analysis of business process improvement is one way to meet those challenges.

This topic addresses some of the techniques used to analyze business process improvement: value chain analysis, process analysis, process reengineering, benchmarking, activity-based management, continuous improvement, best practice analysis, and cost-of-quality analysis.

> **READ** the Learning Outcome Statements (LOS) for this topic as found in Appendix A and then study the concepts and calculations presented here to be sure you understand the content you could be tested on in the CMA exam.

Value Chain Analysis

How do organizations make intelligent choices about where to focus their energy and how to best create value in the eyes of their customers? Many organizations have found success through value chain analysis, which has become an integral part of the strategic planning process. Similar to strategic planning, value chain analysis is a continuous process of gathering, evaluating, and communicating information. The basic intent of value chain analysis is to help managers envision an organization's future and implement business decisions to gain and sustain competitive advantage.

The concept underlying this system is **value**, which is generally used to describe the worth, desirability, or utility of a particular asset. It may be applied to an individual product or a service rendered, to a group of assets, or to an entire business unit. Value may also be applied as a metric, such as in market value, shareholders' value, and so on.

Value activities describe the collective activities performed by organizations in a given industry, from the processing of raw material (in a manufacturing industry) to the production and servicing of a final product. Depending on the industry, some firms may be involved in several activities whereas others may have responsibility for only a single activity. Within an organization, business units may be a further subset. A clothing company, for example, may start with the raw textiles, design and manufacture clothing articles, and contract advertising and sales to retailers. Another clothing company may contract out manufacturing, concentrate on sales and marketing through organizational business units, and rely on retailers for distribution.

A **cost driver** is any factor that causes a change in the cost of an activity. Direct labor hours, machine hours, computer time, and beds occupied in a hospital are all examples of cost drivers. For more meaningful analysis, beyond the total costs of each value-creating activity, the causes for significant costs need to be identified. Firms examine structural cost drivers and executional cost drivers. Structural cost drivers are long-term organizational decisions that determine the economic structure driving the cost of the firm's product or service. Executional cost drivers reflect a firm's operational decisions on how to best use its resources, both human and physical, to achieve organizational goals and objectives.

A **supply chain** is the extended network of distributors, transporters, storage facilities, and suppliers that participate in the production, design, sale, delivery, and use of a company's product or service. During value chain analysis, an organization examines the entire supply chain.

A **value chain** is a system of interdependent activities, each of which is intended to add value to the final product or service. Naturally, the development of a value chain depends on the industry. Figure 1D-30 shows a typical value chain for a manufacturing environment. In a service environment, the acquisition of raw materials would be absent, and other activities and operations might vary and/or assume different degrees of importance.

Value chain analysis (VCA) is a strategic analysis tool organizations use to assess the importance of their customers' value perceptions. It consists of an integrated set of tools and processes that define current costs and performance measures and evaluate where customer value can be increased and where costs can be reduced throughout the supply chain.

The distinct benefit of VCA is that it looks at the entire value chain, not just the activities in which the organization participates. Suppliers, distributors, and others involved in a value chain each have costs and profit margins, which affect the final price to end users and the marketing strategy for the product or service.

Steps in Value Chain Analysis

The purpose of a VCA is to focus on the total value chain of each product or service and to determine which selected part or parts support the firm's competitive advantage and strategy. Theoretically, competitive advantage and competitive strategy cannot be examined meaningfully at the organizational level as a whole or even at the business unit level. Because a value chain separates the firm into distinct

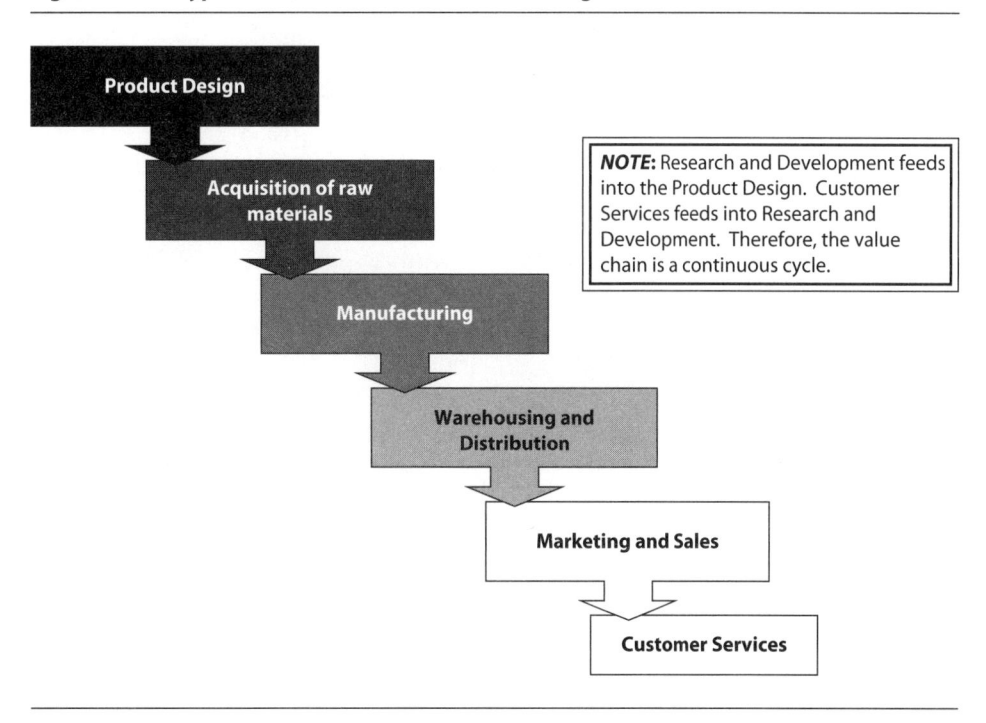

Figure 1D-30 Typical Value Chain for a Manufacturing Environment

```
Product Design
      ↓
Acquisition of raw materials
      ↓
Manufacturing
      ↓
Warehousing and Distribution
      ↓
Marketing and Sales
      ↓
Customer Services
```

NOTE: Research and Development feeds into the Product Design. Customer Services feeds into Research and Development. Therefore, the value chain is a continuous cycle.

strategic activities, organizations are able to use VCA to determine where in the operations—from design to distribution and customer service—customer value can be enhanced and costs lowered. In this way, VCA helps to identify sources of profitability and to understand the costs of the related activities and processes.

VCA requires a strategic framework as a starting point for organizing and analyzing internal and external information and for summarizing findings and recommendations.

There is no one standard process to conduct a VCA, and practices will vary among companies. The general steps in VCA discussed on the IMA Web site in Statement on Management Accounting, "Value Chain Analysis for Assessing Competitive Advantage" (Copyright © 1996 Institute of Management Accountants) are summarized in Figure 1D-31.

Figure 1D-31 Value Chain Approach for Assessing Competitive Advantage

Step 1	Internal cost analysis
	This step determines the sources of profitability and the relative cost of internal processes or activities. An internal cost analysis will: • Identify the firm's value-creating processes. • Determine the portion of the total cost of the product or service attributable to each value-creating process. • Identify the cost drivers for each process. • Identify the links between processes. • Evaluate opportunities for achieving relative cost advantages.

(Continued)

Figure 1D-31 (Continued)

Step 2	**Internal differentiation analysis**
	During this part of the analysis, sources for creating and sustaining superior differentiation are examined. The primary focus is the customer's value perceptions of the firm's products and services. Similar to Step 1, an internal differentiation analysis first requires identifying internal value-creating processes and cost drivers. With this information, a firm can perform a differentiation analysis to:
	Identify customers' value-creating processes.
	Evaluate differentiation strategies for enhancing customer value.
	Determine the best sustainable differentiation strategies.
Step 3	**Vertical linkage analysis**
	Vertical linkage analysis is a broader application of Steps 1 and 2; it includes all upstream and downstream value-creating processes in an industry. Vertical linkage can identify which activities are the most/least critical to competitive advantage or disadvantage. It considers all links, from the source of raw materials to the disposal and/or recycling of a product. A vertical linkage analysis will:
	Identify the industry's value chain and assign costs, revenues, and assets to value-creating processes.
	Diagnose the cost drivers for each value-creating process.
	Evaluate the opportunities for sustainable competitive advantage.

These three types of analysis—internal cost analysis, internal differentiation analysis, and vertical linkage analysis—are complementary. Organizations begin by examining their internal operations and then broaden their focus to evaluate their competitive position within their industry.

Typically, a large amount of data is generated during a VCA study, and these data require careful interpretation to discern the key messages of how to best create customer-perceived value.

Value-Added Concepts and Quality

Quality, like strategy and strategic planning, has many definitions and descriptions and a variety of approaches. The customer ultimately defines what constitutes product or service quality, but this is not a static perception; instead, it is constantly evolving based on factors such as product innovation and market changes.

Internal and External Customers

In quality terms, a customer is anyone who is affected by an organization's processes, products, and services. Therefore, a firm has both internal and external customers.

An **internal customer** is an employee, department, or business unit that receives an output in the form of information, a product, or a service from another employee, department, or business unit. Even the next person in a work process is an internal customer. Based on this concept, all work-related activities may be considered as a series of transactions between employees or between internal customers and internal suppliers.

An **external customer** is a person or entity outside of the organization who receives information, a product, or a service. Generally, external customers are thought of as being end users outside the organization.

Value Chain Analysis and Quality Performance

As organizations strive for quality performance, everyone, from the top executives to an employee on the front line, has a responsibility to create or contribute to the value of the firm's processes, products, and services for the external customer or end user.

Suppliers also have a crucial role. An organization starts with external customer requirements as determined by its industry analysis and/or strategies. The firm proceeds to identify internal customer–supplier relationships and requirements and continues with external suppliers. A chain of operations produces the final product or service. The external customer is best served when every internal customer and supplier receives what they need along the chain.

Figure 1D-32 illustrates the customer–supplier value chain as represented in IMA Statement on Management Accounting "Managing Quality Improvements" (Copyright © 1993 Institute of Management Accountants).

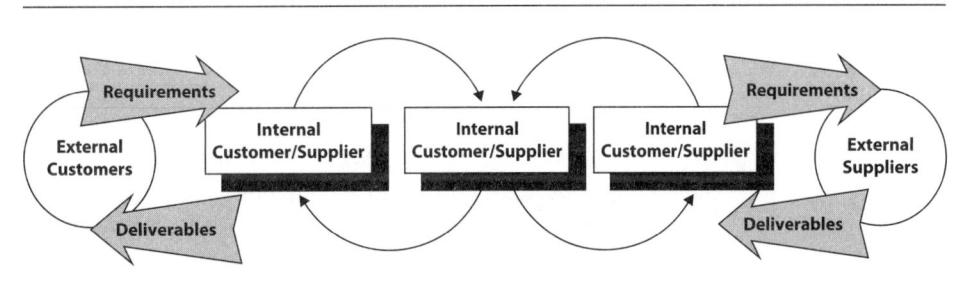

Figure 1D-32 Customer–Supplier Value Chain

The concept of **value added** refers to activities that convert resources into products and services consistent with external customer requirements. Non-value-added activities can be eliminated with no deterioration in product or service functionality, performance, or quality in the eyes of the end user. In industries in which product and service parity is prevalent or outputs are perceived as commodities, examples of value-added activities might be some extra fabrication or customization before the sale to a customer or providing more service with the sale. Activities related to materials movement or rework would most likely be non-value-added.

The goal of the customer–supplier value chain is to integrate value into every aspect of a work process. By removing non-value-added activities, work processes can be more efficient and ultimately yield a better-quality product or service.

Process Analysis

A **process** is an activity or a group of interrelated activities that takes an input of materials and/or resources, adds value to it, and provides an output to internal or external customers. A process often spans several departmental units, such as accounting, sales, production, and shipping.

A firm should recognize and understand the array of business processes that contribute to its business profitability. One way to do this is through process analysis. **Process analysis** refers to a collection of analytic methods that can be used to examine and measure the basic elements for a process to operate. It can also identify those processes with the greatest need for improvement.

Process Characteristics

Three characteristics that help to identify a good process fit are:

1. **Effectiveness.** A process is effective when it produces the desired result and meets or exceeds customers' requirements. Customers perceive an effective process as being of high quality.
2. **Efficiency.** A process is efficient when it achieves results with minimal waste, expense, and/or cycle time. It has a high ratio of output to input.
3. **Adaptability.** A process is adaptable when it is flexible and can react quickly to changing requirements or new competition.

A process needs to address all three areas: A cost-efficient process is of little use if it does not produce an effective product, or if it cannot adapt to changing needs.

An assumption from the early days of quality improvement programs was that process improvements could be gained only at the expense of productivity. Although experience has shown that quality improvements usually increase productivity by decreasing waste and the need for rework, the fact is that quality does have a cost, but it is a cost that management can influence and control.

A quality-oriented approach to product design, manufacturing, and service will consider upstream and downstream effects of all decisions. Cost drivers from all the company's departments, plus additional outside costs, must be accurately understood to ensure that sufficient resources are available for the transition to a quality enterprise.

Process Reengineering/Business Process Reengineering

Process improvements and productivity gains achieved through total quality management (TQM) generally are incremental gains achieved by tweaking a system and reducing inputs. In contrast, process reengineering and business process reengineering offer deeper, more sweeping gains.

Process reengineering diagrams a process in detail, evaluates and questions the process flow, and then completely redesigns the process to eliminate unnecessary steps, reduce opportunities for errors, and reduce costs. All activities that do not add value are eliminated.

Business process reengineering (BPR) is the fundamental analysis and radical redesign of business processes within and between enterprises to achieve dramatic improvements in performance (e.g., cost, quality, speed, and service). Michael Hammer and James Champy brought BPR to the forefront in the early 1990s with their book *Reengineering the Corporation* (HarperBusiness, 2003, rev. ed.). BPR promotes the idea that sometimes wiping the slate clean and radically redesigning and reorganizing an enterprise is necessary to lower costs and increase the quality of a product or service.

According to Hammer and Champy, BPR involves changes that are:

Fundamental. BPR forces people to look at tacit rules and assumptions underlying the way they currently do business. Firms must answer two questions: Why do we do what we do? Why do we do it the way we do it?

Radical. BPR is about reinvention, not improvement or modification. A radical redesign means disregarding existing processes and inventing new ways of doing work.

Dramatic. BPR is not for the faint of heart. It should be used when "heavy blasting" is needed to alleviate a dire situation. If you need only a slight bump in process improvement, there is no need to reengineer.

Process. BPR is about a process orientation with a heavy emphasis on the chain of activities that take input and create output of value to the customer.

The BPR model espouses that process workflow in most large corporations is based on assumptions about technology, people, and organizational goals that are no longer valid. It also maintains that information is a key enabler to achieve radical change.

Figure 1D-33 lists the common tools and tactics underpinning successful BPR efforts.

Figure 1D-33 Fundamentals of Business Process Reengineering

Process orientation	Organizations look at entire processes that cut across organizational boundaries, not narrowly defined tasks with predefined organizational boundaries.
Ambition	Companies aim for breakthroughs, not minor improvements.
Rule breaking	Old traditions and assumptions are deliberately abandoned.
Creative use of technology	Current/state-of-the-art technology serves as an enabler that allows organizations to do work in radically different ways.

Process reengineering and BPR are strong medicine. Many well-intended reengineering efforts have failed for any number of reasons. In a bit of a backlash to Hammer and Champy's initial foray, reengineering was even accused of being a cover for downsizing and layoffs. Yet the success stories show that although boldness may have perils and may create some pain, the end gains of reengineering can be dramatic.

Process analysis looks at the linkage of quality, productivity, and process improvements:

1. Productivity implies trying to improve on what already exists.
2. Improving productivity requires continuous quality improvement.
3. Continuous improvement necessitates ongoing organizational learning, process improvements, and reengineering.

These continuous productivity improvements, then, can help an organization be competitive in the long term.

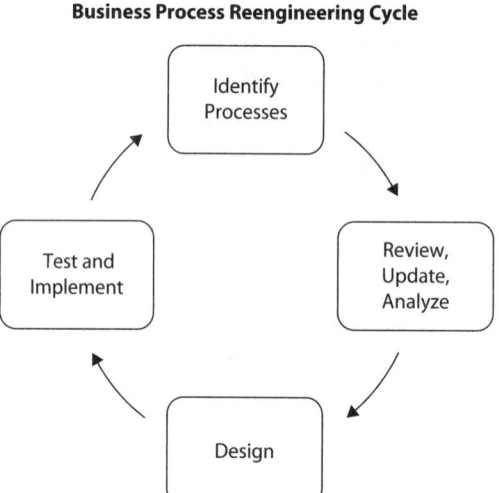

Business Process Reengineering Cycle

Identify Processes → Review, Update, Analyze → Design → Test and Implement → (back to Identify Processes)

Benchmarking

Benchmarking can be used in coordination with process analysis to develop measures to use in assessing an organization's effectiveness, efficiency, and adaptability. The term **benchmarking** describes a continuous, systematic process of measuring products, services, and practices against the best levels of performance. Many people think of benchmarking as simply capturing best-in-class information, but the practice has a much wider application. Quite often, best-in-class levels are comparisons to external benchmarks of industry leaders. However, they may also be based on internal benchmarking information or measures from other organizations (outside an industry) that have similar processes.

Benchmarking Process Performance

Best-in-class levels may be financial or nonfinancial measures. Statement on Management Accounting "Effective Benchmarking" (Copyright © 1995 Institute of Management Accountants) describes benchmarking as having seven phases with associated activities, as illustrated in Figure 1D-34.

Figure 1D-34 Benchmarking Phases and Activities

Phases	Activities
Selecting and prioritizing benchmarking projects	Identify and prioritize areas to be benchmarked. → Identify customers of benchmarking and their requirements.
Organizing benchmarking teams	Establish benchmarking teams.
Documenting own work processes	Determine relevant benchmarking measurements. → Study proposed internal benchmark process(es).
Researching and identifying best-in-class performance	Determine data-gathering method. → Identify organizations to be benchmarked. → Gather benchmark performance and enabler data.
Analyzing benchmarking data and identifying enablers	Determine current performance gap. → Identify causes for current and future gaps. → Estimate future attainable performance.
Implementing benchmarking study recommendations and recalibrating benchmarks	Gain management acceptance of conclusions and actions to close gap. → Establish performance goals and objectives. → Implement actions. → Assess progress toward goals. → Revise goals if necessary. → Validate/update benchmarks.

Benchmarking and Creating Competitive Advantage

The 1990s saw a proliferation in benchmarking studies, but, unfortunately, many organizations misused benchmarking. Benchmarking studies in various forms (best practice, functional, process, and competitive) were freely conducted, generally without a context. Invalid comparisons were often made (e.g., comparing the growth of a highly leveraged company to one internally financed from earnings, or comparing the growth of a company in a low-cost environment to one in Silicon Valley).

Given such misapplications, most of these benchmarking studies were not particularly cost-effective.

However, well-designed and properly applied benchmarking can be a powerful tool in helping an organization to be competitive. Through benchmarking, a firm identifies best-in-class levels and conducts a study to determine how those levels can be adopted and lead to improved performance. It provides a rational method for setting performance goals and gaining market leadership; important decisions are based on facts and data rather than on emotions. Because benchmarking is based on what the best are doing, it provides an accurate assessment of what needs to change.

Strategic Benchmarking

Although many benchmarking studies have an operational focus, a benchmarking project also may have a strategic focus. Strategic benchmarking applies process benchmarking to the level of business strategy by incorporating benchmarking results in the strategic planning process. As such, it helps an organization develop an increased understanding and ability to address strategic business issues, such as:

- Building core competencies to help sustain competitive advantage
- Developing a new business line
- Targeting a specific shift in strategy (e.g., entering new markets or developing a new service)
- Making an acquisition
- Creating an organization that can quickly respond to uncertainties

Activity-Based Management

Activity-based management is another type of strategic analysis aimed at yielding process improvements.

Activity-based costing and activity-based management are related concepts.

- **Activity-based costing (ABC)** is a measure of the costs and performance of activities, resources, and cost objects. It assigns resources to activities and assigns activities to cost objects. It focuses on a causal relationship between cost drivers and activities.
- **Activity-based management (ABM)** focuses on the management of activities as the way of improving the value received by the customer and the profit achieved by providing this value. ABC provides the data used by ABM for cost driver analysis, activity analysis, and performance measurement.
- While ABC designates and uses cost drivers for each activity, ABM analyzes these cost drivers for their effectiveness in defining the root causes of activity costs. To explain the effects of cost drivers, ABM uses internal interviews, observation, and quality control tools such as theory of constraints benchmarking, and other analytical tools. The result will be an assessment of how well cost drivers reflect actual costs and actual areas of profitability.

- Another aspect of ABM is performance measurement. ABM helps make performance evaluation measures relate to the factors that drive the element being measured (i.e., costs drivers and revenue drivers). Such measures include revenue, manufacturing cost, nonmanufacturing cost, and profit as well as nonfinancial measures.

The bottom line is that both ABC and ABM are valuable practices for any firm striving to maintain or improve its competitive position. ABC answers the question "What do things cost?" ABM takes a process view and asks "What causes costs to occur?"

ABM Principles and Process Improvements

ABM is forward-looking and change-oriented. It seeks ways to avoid unnecessary costs and put existing resources to maximum use.

Based on ABM information, organizations generally can:

- Make better decisions.
- Improve performance.
- Increase earnings on total resources deployed.

Overall, ABM supports both process reengineering and BPR by analyzing the organizational processes and by facilitating the measurement of the impact of reengineering efforts, thereby increasing the value created for the resources consumed.

Organizations implement ABM for a variety of reasons. Figure 1D-35 summarizes general situations where a firm can benefit from ABM, depending on its stage of evolution.

Figure 1D-35 General Applications for ABM

If a firm's operations are...	Then ABM can be useful to...
Growing	Redeploy non-value-added work.
	Improve processes and activities.
Flat	Identify non-value-added costs.
	Set priorities for improvement and effect improvement.
	Isolate/eliminate cost drivers.
	Determine product/service costs.
Declining	Cut costs.
	Downsize.
	Effect layoffs.
Constrained as to capacity	Determine product/service costs.
	Make product/service decisions.
	Determine activity capacity.
	Identify bottlenecks.

ABM and Quality Improvements

ABM is sometimes erroneously thought of as a replacement for quality efforts, just-in-time systems, process reengineering, BPR, and benchmarking. To the contrary, ABM supports quality management and the other initiatives by providing an integrated information system that:

- Establishes accountability
- Facilitates measuring of results
- Enables setting of priorities

Specific to quality, an ABM system facilitates quality implementation by:

- Identifying activity costs
- Increasing the visibility of associated costs of quality
- Providing quality cost measures that can be easily incorporated in cost-of-quality reports

Because traditional accounting systems focus on functions (e.g., research and design, production, sales and marketing, etc.), collecting data about the costs of quality is more problematic. With ABM, activity costs resulting from poor quality are more readily identifiable.

Advantages and Disadvantages of ABM

ABM has six advantages over traditional cost management techniques:

1. It uses continuous improvement to maintain the firm's competitive advantage.
2. It allocates more resources to activities, products, and customers that add more value, strategically redirecting management focus.
3. It eliminates non-value-added activities.
4. It measures process effectiveness and identifies areas to reduce costs or increase customer value.
5. It works well with just-in-time processes.
6. It ties performance measurement to ABC to provide consistent incentives for using ABC.

ABM has three disadvantages when compared to traditional cost management:

1. Changing to ABC/ABM will result in different pricing, process design, manufacturing technology, and product design decisions. The company must be prepared to support managers who embrace these methods and discourage managers who continue to use the older methods.
2. ABC/ABM is not used for external financial reporting. The need to prepare reports using traditional methods may influence management decision making enough to dilute the impact of ABC/ABM.
3. Implementing ABC/ABM is expensive and time-consuming, so a cost-benefit analysis should be done to identify all hidden costs and benefits.

Continuous Improvement (Kaizen) Concepts

Kaizen is a Japanese term used to describe continuous improvement at all levels in an organization. The premise is that as every process, beginning with the most important, is examined, worked on, and improved, the total enterprise improves. Kaizen acknowledges that innovation is valuable, but it also maintains that innovations do not collectively contribute as much as continuous incremental improvements.

The kaizen process is often described as a staircase of improvement. Moving from step to step, an organization uses a continuous process of following an improvement, maintaining an improvement, following an improvement, maintaining an improvement, and so on. Although the steps may be small, each step moves the organization upward toward sustained improvements.

Continuous improvements often are based on standards, which become organizational performance expectations and goals. Standards allow an enterprise to identify the cost to manufacture and sell a product or a service and to determine the causes of cost overruns.

Organizations can develop standards based on:

- Activity analysis
- Historical data
- Benchmarking
- Market expectations
- Strategic decisions

Company benchmarking, for example, could be used to compare a firm's current cost structure to that of similar businesses and to develop appropriate standards. Once standards are determined, a series of continuous improvements could be implemented to increase efficiency and effectiveness and minimize variances.

Best Practice Analysis

The term **best practice** generally refers to a process or technique that has produced outstanding results in one situation and that can be applied and/or adapted to improve effectiveness, efficiency, quality, safety, innovativeness, and/or some other performance measure in another situation. Best practice analysis refers to the collective steps in a gap analysis. A gap analysis is generally described as the difference between the current state and a desired state, or the space between what is and what an organization hopes to be. The current state is defined by current practices, and the desired state is defined by best practices.

Best practice analysis involves assessing how a firm's given performance level measures up to a best practice and then defining the logical next steps in transitioning to the desired performance level.

Typical activities are:

- Defining the gap (through a comparison to internal operational data)
- Determining the reasons for the gap
- Examining the factors that contribute to the existence of the best practice(s)
- Developing recommendations and an approach to implement the best practice(s)

Techniques and tools for conducting a best practice analysis vary. Qualitative and quantitative tools are used, but most of the tools are common to TQM and kaizen.

It may be said that best practice analysis tools—such as VCA, process analysis, BPR, benchmarking, TQM, and kaizen—are the clout behind business process improvement initiatives. Best practice analysis enables firms to identify and undertake performance improvements.

Costs of Quality Analysis

Process improvement teams need to know the specific costs for each part of the production process in order to determine how changes in a quality design affect profitability. The costs of quality (COQ) are broken down into four categories:

1. **Prevention costs** are the costs of quality system design, implementation, and maintenance, including audits of the quality system itself. Examples include quality planning, review of new products, surveys of supplier capabilities, team meetings for quality, and training for quality, as well as those related to ensuring the quality or quality improvement of the product: market research, product testing, and product design.

2. **Appraisal costs** are the costs of auditing processes for quality, including formal and informal measurements and evaluations of quality levels and setting quality standards and performance requirements. Examples include inspection and testing of raw materials, work-in-process and finished goods testing, calibration of equipment, and audits or operations or services. In addition, they address more externally focused costs, such as monitoring market reaction and competitors' products.

3. **Internal failure costs** include the costs involved with defective products and components that are caught before shipping them to the customer. Examples include scrap, rework, spoilage, retesting, and reinspection. They also include systemic problems, such as the inability to meet the design, manufacturing, and service standards identified for the product.

4. **External failure costs** are the costs involved with shipping a defective product to a customer. Examples include customer complaints, returns, product recalls, and warranty claims. Overall, these costs relate to an inability to meet customer perceptions for product quality and service.

A quality-oriented approach can achieve gains in productivity and profit, but only if the company makes a long-term commitment to implement and sustain the effort.

Business Process Improvement in Accounting Operations

The concept of business process improvement goes beyond simply creating efficiencies, improvements, and enhancing quality in the production process. In fact, internal services provided within an organization by "back office" departments and/or "cost centers," such as the accounting and finance department, provide key opportunities for creating efficiencies by focusing on continuous improvement and cost reduction in the activities performed by these departments, particularly routine activities. Through this process of creating efficiencies, organizations can work to identify the root causes for errors in the work flow and eliminate waste and overcapacity. Some ways in which organizations can do this is by conducting process walk-throughs, process training, reducing the accounting close cycle so as to effect a "fast close," and implementing shared services, where applicable.

Process walk-throughs involve meeting with process owners and gaining an understanding of how their work gets done in order to uncover opportunities for improvement. Through this process, every step performed, every piece of paper created, every input, and every output should be scrutinized. Questions need to be asked, such as, "Is this step or process necessary?" "Does it add value?" "Can it be automated?" "Does it take excessive time to complete?" "Is there duplication of effort?" After completing the process walkthroughs, an evaluation of staff training should be made. Most organizations send employees to professional development seminars and provide systems training; however, rarely do organizations provide training on how to properly accomplish day-to-day activities. Significant productivity can be achieved through appropriate training.

Organizations can also create efficiencies by identifying ways to reduce the accounting cycle and realize a fast close. While there are a host of ways to do so, organizations should focus on improving and eliminating the time and effort it takes to perform key close activities. Just a few examples are standardizing the chart of accounts and creating templates for journal entries and accounting policies and procedures, particularly for organizations that have multiple locations, or even consolidating local accounting close operations into one centralized location. In addition, using period-close checklists and conducting process analyses can also prevent omitting a step in the close process and/or error oversights.

Finally, organizations can look to implement shared services among routine and often lower-level accounting tasks and activities, such as billing, collections, accounts payable, and payroll processing. This involves grouping employees performing these tasks and activities by business function rather than by business unit. This results in a reduction of costs that would otherwise result from overcapacity (i.e., multiple employees performing the same function), and it also helps to mitigate errors.

Knowledge Check: Business Process Improvement

The next questions are intended to help you check your understanding and recall of the material presented in this topic. They do not represent the type of questions that appear on the CMA exam.

Directions: Answer each question in the space provided. Correct answers and section references appear after the knowledge check questions.

1. Which of the following statements best characterizes value chain analysis?
    - ☐ a. It emphasizes a firm's functional structure.
    - ☐ b. It examines a firm's hierarchal structure.
    - ☐ c. It examines distinct strategic activities.
    - ☐ d. It promotes product/service differentiation.

For questions 2 through 4, match the following business process concepts to the appropriate application.

   a. Noncompetitive firms exchanging information about similar manufacturing processes
   b. An airline removing seats in a plane to give coach passengers more leg room
   c. An internal system examining past, current, and future performance

2. __b__ Value chain analysis
3. __a__ Benchmarking
4. __c__ Activity-based management

5. Which of the following statements accurately differentiates activity-based costing (ABC) and activity-based management (ABM)?
    - ☐ a. ABC provides information on process, product, and market performance; ABM finds ways to improve them.
    - ☐ b. ABC provides actionable information; ABM is a source of explanatory data.
    - ☐ c. ABC seeks to change costs and their drivers; ABM focuses on understanding them.
    - ☐ d. ABC is predominately forward-looking; ABM is primarily historical.

6. The four categories used for cost of quality analysis are:
    - a. _____
    - b. _____
    - c. _____
    - d. _____

Knowledge Check Answers: Business Process Improvement

1. Which of the following statements best characterizes value chain analysis? [See *Steps in Value Chain Analysis*.]
   - ☐ a. It emphasizes a firm's functional structure.
   - ☐ b. It examines a firm's hierarchal structure.
   - ☒ c. It examines distinct strategic activities.
   - ☐ d. It promotes product/service differentiation.

For questions 2 through 4, match the following business process concepts to the appropriate application. [See *Value Chain Analysis, Benchmarking,* and *Activity-Based Management*.]

   a. Noncompetitive firms exchanging information about similar manufacturing processes

   b. An airline removing seats in a plane to give coach passengers more leg room

   c. An internal system examining past, current, and future performance

2. __b__ Value chain analysis

3. __a__ Benchmarking

4. __c__ Activity-based management

5. Which of the following statements accurately differentiates activity-based costing (ABC) and activity-based management (ABM)? [See *Activity-Based Management*.]
   - ☒ a. ABC provides information on process, product, and market performance; ABM finds ways to improve them.
   - ☐ b. ABC provides actionable information; ABM is a source of explanatory data.
   - ☐ c. ABC seeks to change costs and their drivers; ABM focuses on understanding them.
   - ☐ d. ABC is predominately forward-looking; ABM is primarily historical.

6. The four categories used for cost of quality analysis are: [See *Costs of Quality Analysis*.]
   - a. prevention costs
   - b. appraisal costs
   - c. internal failure costs
   - d. external failure costs

Practice Questions: Cost Management

Directions: This sampling of questions is designed to emulate actual exam questions. Read each question and write your response on another sheet of paper. See the "Answers to Section Practice Questions" section at the end of this book to assess your response. Validate or improve the answer you wrote. For a more robust selection of practice questions, access the **Online Test Bank** at www.wileycma.com.

Question 1D1-CQ02
Topic: Measurement Concepts

A company employs a just-in-time (JIT) production system and utilizes backflush accounting. All acquisitions of raw materials are recorded in a raw materials control account when purchased. All conversion costs are recorded in a control account as incurred, while the assignment of conversion costs are from an allocated conversion cost account. Company practice is to record the cost of goods manufactured at the time the units are completed using the estimated budgeted cost of the goods manufactured.

The budgeted cost per unit for one of the company's products is as shown:

Direct materials	$15.00
Conversion costs	35.00
Total budgeted unit cost	$50.00

During the current accounting period, 80,000 units of product were completed, and 75,000 units were sold. The entry to record the cost of the completed units for the period would be which of the following?

a. Work-in-Process—Control	4,000,000	
Raw Material—Control		1,200,000
Conversion Cost Allocated		2,800,000
b. Finished Goods—Control	4,000,000	
Raw Material—Control		1,200,000
Conversion Cost Allocated		2,800,000
c. Finished Goods—Control	3,750,000	
Raw Material Control		1,125,000
Conversion Cost Allocated		2,625,000
d. Cost of Goods Sold	3,750,000	
Raw Material—Control		1,125,000
Conversion Cost Allocated		2,625,000

Question 1D1-CQ03

Topic: Measurement Concepts

From the budgeted data shown, calculate the budgeted indirect cost rate that would be used in a normal costing system.

Total direct labor hours	250,000
Direct costs	$10,000,000
Total indirect labor hours	50,000
Total indirect labor-related costs	$5,000,000
Total indirect non-labor-related costs	$7,000,000

- a. $20
- b. $28
- c. $40
- d. $48

Question 1D1-CQ06

Topic: Measurement Concepts

Chassen Company, a cracker and cookie manufacturer, has these unit costs for the month of June.

Variable Manufacturing Cost	Variable Marketing Cost	Fixed Manufacturing Cost	Fixed Marketing Cost
$5.00	$3.50	$2.00	$4.00

A total of 100,000 units were manufactured during June, of which 10,000 remain in ending inventory. Chassen uses the first-in, first-out (FIFO) inventory method, and the 10,000 units are the only finished goods inventory at month-end. Using the full absorption costing method, Chassen's finished goods inventory value would be

- a. $50,000
- b. $70,000
- c. $85,000
- d. $145,000

Question 1D1-CQ12

Topic: Measurement Concepts

During the month of May, Robinson Corporation sold 1,000 units. The cost per unit for May was as shown:

	Cost per Unit
Direct materials	$5.50
Direct labor	3.00
Variable manufacturing overhead	1.00
Fixed manufacturing overhead	1.50
Variable administrative costs	0.50
Fixed administrative costs	3.50
Total	$15.00

May's income using absorption costing was $9,500. The income for May, if variable costing had been used, would have been $9,125. The number of units Robinson produced during May was

- a. 750 units
- b. 925 units
- c. 1,075 units
- d. 1,250 units

Question 1D1-CQ13

Topic: Measurement Concepts

Tucariz Company processes Duo into two joint products, Big and Mini. Duo is purchased in 1,000 gallon drums for $2,000. Processing costs are $3,000 to process the 1,000 gallons of Duo into 800 gallons of Big and 200 gallons of Mini. The selling price is $9 per gallon for Big and $4 per gallon for Mini.

The 800 gallons of Big can be processed further into 600 gallons of Giant if $1,000 of additional processing costs are incurred. Giant can be sold for $17 per gallon. If the net-realizable-value (NRV) method were used to allocate costs to the joint products, the total cost of producing Giant would be:

- a. $5,600
- b. $5,564
- c. $5,520
- d. $4,600

Question 1D1-CQ14

Topic: Measurement Concepts

Tucariz Company processes Duo into two joint products, Big and Mini. Duo is purchased in 1,000 gallon drums for $2,000. Processing costs are $3,000 to process the 1,000 gallons of Duo into 800 gallons of Big and 200 gallons of Mini. The selling price is $9 per gallon for Big and $4 per gallon for Mini.

If the sales value at split-off method is used to allocate joint costs to the final products, the per gallon cost (rounded to the nearest cent) of producing Big is:

- ☐ a. $5.63 per gallon
- ☐ b. $5.00 per gallon
- ☐ c. $4.50 per gallon
- ☐ d. $3.38 per gallon

Question 1D1-CQ15

Topic: Measurement Concepts

Tempo Company produces three products from a joint process. The three products are sold after further processing as there is no market for any of the products at the split-off point. Joint costs per batch are $315,000. Other product information is shown next.

	Product A	Product B	Product C
Units produced per batch	20,000	30,000	50,000
Further processing and marketing cost per unit	$0.70	$3.00	$1.72
Final sales value per unit	$5.00	$6.00	$7.00

If Tempo uses the net realizable value method of allocating joint costs, how much of the joint costs will be allocated to each unit of Product C?

- ☐ a. $2.10
- ☐ b. $2.65
- ☐ c. $3.15
- ☐ d. $3.78

Question 1D1-CQ16

Topic: Measurement Concepts

Fitzpatrick Corporation uses a joint manufacturing process in the production of two products, Gummo and Xylo. Each batch in the joint manufacturing process yields 5,000 pounds of an intermediate material, Valdene, at a cost of $20,000.

Each batch of Gummo uses 60% of the Valdene and incurs $10,000 of separate costs. The resulting 3,000 pounds of Gummo sells for $10 per pound.

The remaining Valdene is used in the production of Xylo, which incurs $12,000 of separable costs per batch. Each batch of Xylo yields 2,000 pounds and sells for $12 per pound.

Fitzpatrick uses the net realizable value method to allocate the joint material costs. The company is debating whether to process Xylo further into a new product, Zinten, which would incur an additional $4,000 in costs and sell for $15 per pound. If Zinten is produced, income would increase by:

- ☐ a. $2,000
- ☐ b. $5,760
- ☐ c. $14,000
- ☐ d. $26,000

Question 1D2-CQ03
Topic: Costing Systems

Loyal Co. produces three types of men's undershirts: T-shirts, V-neck shirts, and athletic shirts. In the Folding and Packaging Department, operations costing is used to apply costs to individual units, based on the standard time allowed to fold and package each type of undershirt. The standard time to fold and package each type of undershirt is shown next.

T-shirt	40 seconds per shirt
V-neck shirt	40 seconds per shirt
Athletic shirt	20 seconds per shirt

During the month of April, Loyal produced and sold 50,000 T-shirts, 30,000 V-neck shirts, and 20,000 athletic shirts. If costs in the Folding and Packaging Department were $78,200 during April, how much folding and packaging cost should be applied to each T-shirt?

- ☐ a. $0.5213
- ☐ b. $0.6256
- ☐ c. $0.7820
- ☐ d. $0.8689

Question 1D2-CQ04
Topic: Costing Systems

During December, Krause Chemical Company had these selected data concerning the manufacture of Xyzine, an industrial cleaner.

Production Flow	Physical Units
Completed and transferred to the next department	100
Add: Ending work-in-process inventory	10 (40% complete as to conversion)
Total units to account for	110
Less: Beginning work-in-process inventory	20 (60% complete as to conversion)
Units started during December	**90**

All material is added at the beginning of processing in this department, and conversion costs are added uniformly during the process. The beginning work-in-process inventory had $120 of raw material and $180 of conversion costs incurred. Material added during December was $540, and conversion costs of $1,484 were incurred. Krause uses the weighted-average process-costing method. The total raw material costs in the ending work-in-process inventory for December are:

- ☐ a. $120
- ☐ b. $72
- ☐ c. $60
- ☐ d. $36

Question 1D2-CQ08
Topic: Costing Systems

Oster Manufacturing uses a weighted-average process costing system and has these costs and activity during October:

Materials	$40,000
Conversion cost	32,500
Total beginning work-in-process inventory	$72,500
Materials	$700,000
Conversion cost	617,500
Total production costs—October	$1,317,500
Production completed	60,000 units
Work-in-process, October 31	20,000 units

All materials are introduced at the start of the manufacturing process, and conversion cost is incurred uniformly throughout production. Conversations with plant personnel reveal that, on average, month-end in-process inventory is 25% complete. Assuming no spoilage, how should Oster's October manufacturing cost be assigned?

	Production Completed	**Work in Process**
☐ a.	$1,042,500	$347,500
☐ b.	$1,095,000	$222,500
☐ c.	$1,155,000	$235,000
☐ d.	$1,283,077	$106,923

Question 1D2-CQ10
Topic: Costing Systems

During December, Krause Chemical Company had these selected data concerning the manufacture of Xyzine, an industrial cleaner:

Production Flow	Physical Units
Completed and transferred to the next department	100
Add: Ending work-in-process inventory	10 (40% complete as to conversion)
Total units to account for	110
Less: Beginning work-in-process inventory	20 (60% complete as to conversion)
Units started during December	**90**

All material is added at the beginning of processing in this department, and conversion costs are added uniformly during the process. The beginning work-in-process inventory had $120 of raw material and $180 of conversion costs incurred. Material added during December was $540, and conversion costs of $1,484 were incurred. Krause uses the weighted-average process-costing method. The total conversion cost assigned to units transferred to the next department in December was

- a. $1,664
- b. $1,600
- c. $1,513
- d. $1,484

Question 1D2-CQ12
Topic: Costing Systems

Waller Co. uses a weighted-average process-costing system. Material B is added at two different points in the production of shirts; 40% is added when the units are 20% completed, and the remaining 60% of Material B is added when the units are 80% completed. At the end of the quarter, there are 22,000 shirts in process, all of which are 50% completed. With respect to Material B, the ending shirts in process represent how many equivalent units?

- a. 4,400 units
- b. 8,800 units
- c. 11,000 units
- d. 22,000 units

Question 1D2-CQ14
Topic: Costing Systems

The Chocolate Baker specializes in chocolate baked goods. The firm has long assessed the profitability of a product line by comparing revenues to the cost of goods sold. However, Barry White, the firm's new accountant, wants to use an activity-based costing system that takes into consideration the cost of the delivery person. Listed are activity and cost information relating to two of Chocolate Baker's major products.

	Muffins	Cheesecake
Revenue	$53,000	$46,000
Cost of goods sold	$26,000	$21,000
Delivery Activity		
Number of deliveries	150	85
Average length of delivery	10 minutes	15 minutes
Cost per hour for delivery	$20.00	$20.00

Using activity-based costing, which one of the following statements is correct?

- a. The muffins are $2,000 more profitable.
- b. The cheesecakes are $75 more profitable.
- c. The muffins are $1,925 more profitable.
- d. The muffins have a higher profitability as a percentage of sales and, therefore, are more advantageous.

Question 1D2-CQ16

Topic: Costing Systems

Baldwin Printing Company uses a job order costing system and applies overhead based on machine hours. A total of 150,000 machine hours have been budgeted for the year. During the year, an order for 1,000 units was completed and incurred:

Direct material costs	$1,000
Direct labor costs	$1,500
Actual overhead	$1,980
Machine hours	450

The accountant calculated the inventory cost of this order to be $4.30 per unit. The annual budgeted overhead in dollars was:

- a. $577,500
- b. $600,000
- c. $645,000
- d. $660,000

Question 1D3-CQ01

Topic: Overhead Costs

During December, Krause Chemical Company had these selected data concerning the manufacture of Xyzine, an industrial cleaner.

Production Flow	Physical Units
Completed and transferred to the next department	100
Add: Ending work-in-process inventory	10 (40% complete as to conversion)
Total units to account for	110
Less: Beginning work-in-process inventory	20 (60% complete as to conversion)
Units started during December	90

All material is added at the beginning of processing in this department, and conversion costs are added uniformly during the process. The beginning work-in-process inventory had $120 of raw material and $180 of conversion costs incurred. Material added during December was $540, and conversion costs of $1,484 were incurred. Krause uses the first-in, first-out (FIFO) process-costing method. The equivalent units of production used to calculate conversion costs for December was:

- a. 110 units
- b. 104 units
- c. 100 units
- d. 92 units

Question 1D3-CQ03
Topic: Overhead Costs

Cynthia Rogers, the cost accountant for Sanford Manufacturing, is preparing a management report that must include an allocation of overhead. The budgeted overhead for each department and the data for one job are shown next.

	Department	
	Tooling	**Fabricating**
Supplies	$ 690	$ 80
Supervisor's salaries	1,400	1,800
Indirect labor	1,000	4,000
Depreciation	1,200	5,200
Repairs	4,400	3,000
Total budgeted overhead	$8,690	$14,080
Total direct labor hours	440	640
Direct labor hours on Job #231	10	2

Using the departmental overhead application rates and allocating overhead on the basis of direct labor hours, overhead applied to Job #231 in the Tooling Department would be:

- a. $44.00
- b. $197.50
- c. $241.50
- d. $501.00

Question 1D3-CQ05
Topic: Overhead Costs

Atmel Inc. manufactures and sells two products. Data with regard to these products are given next.

	Product A	Product B
Units produced and sold	30,000	12,000
Machine hours required per unit	2	3
Receiving orders per product line	50	150
Production orders per product line	12	18
Production runs	8	12
Inspections	20	30

Total budgeted machine hours are 100,000. The budgeted overhead costs are shown next.

Receiving costs	$450,000
Engineering costs	300,000
Machine setup costs	25,000
Inspection costs	200,000
Total budgeted overhead	$975,000

The cost driver for engineering costs is the number of production orders per product line. Using activity-based costing, what would the engineering cost per unit for Product B be?

- ☐ a. $4.00
- ☐ b. $10.00
- ☐ c. $15.00
- ☐ d. $29.25

Question 1D3-CQ08
Topic: Overhead Costs

Logo Inc. has two data services departments (the Systems Department and the Facilities Department) that provide support to the company's three production departments (Machining Department, Assembly Department, and Finishing Department). The overhead costs of the Systems Department are allocated to other departments on the basis of computer usage hours. The overhead costs of the Facilities Department are allocated based on square feet occupied (in thousands). Other information pertaining to Logo is as shown next.

Department	Overhead	Computer Usage Hours	Square Feet Occupied
Systems	$200,000	300	1,000
Facilities	100,000	900	600
Machining	400,000	3,600	2,000
Assembly	550,000	1,800	3,000
Finishing	620,000	2,700	5,000
		9,300	11,600

Logo employs the step-down method of allocating service department costs and begins with the Systems Department. Which one of the following correctly denotes the amount of the Systems Department's overhead that would be allocated to the Facilities Department and the Facilities Department's overhead charges that would be allocated to the Machining Department?

	Systems to Facilities	Facilities to Machining
☐ a.	$0	$20,000
☐ b.	$19,355	$20,578
☐ c.	$20,000	$20,000
☐ d.	$20,000	$24,000

Question 1D3-CQ09
Topic: Overhead Costs

Adam Corporation manufactures computer tables and has this budgeted indirect manufacturing cost information for next year:

	Support Departments		Operating Departments		
	Maintenance	Systems	Machining	Fabrication	Total
Budgeted Overhead	$360,000	$95,000	$200,000	$300,000	$955,000
Support work furnished					
From Maintenance		10%	50%	40%	100%
From Systems	5%		45%	50%	100%

If Adam uses the direct method to allocate support department costs to production departments, the total overhead (rounded to the nearest dollar) for the Machining Department to allocate to its products would be which of the following?

- a. $418,000
- b. $422,750
- c. $442,053
- d. $445,000

To further assess your understanding of the concepts and calculations covered in Part 1, Section D: Cost Management, practice with the **Online Test Bank** for this section. REMINDER: See the "Answers to Section Practice Questions" section at the end of this book.

SECTION E

Internal Controls

Internal controls are designed to ensure that the goals and objectives of a business are achieved efficiently. As a business grows, management becomes removed from the firm's operations and increasingly depends on reports to evaluate the business's performance. Management must have assurance that the reports are accurate and that subordinates carry out management's directives. An internal control system provides a higher level of confidence in these matters. This system of controls starts at the top of the organization with the establishment of an effective corporate governance structure. This structure "governs" the way in which a corporation is directed and controlled. It provides a "structure" within which corporations establish and pursue their objectives, and is a mechanism for monitoring an organization's actions, policies, and decisions.

This section looks at the creation of an effective corporate governance structure and the manner in which that structure provides oversight and monitoring of an organization's actions, policies, and decisions; several interrelated approaches to establishing control: the assessment and management of risk; the process of internal auditing and responsibilities of auditors; and measures taken to ensure the security and reliability of systems and the information they provide.

An emphasis on controls has grown from several policy and legislative initiatives. The Sarbanes-Oxley Act of 2002 (SOX) created the Public Company Accounting Oversight Board (PCAOB) as a part of the Securities and Exchange Commission. The PCAOB is responsible for the setting of standards for audits of publicly held corporations. The PCAOB has adopted the Committee of Sponsoring Organizations (COSO) internal control model as its guide. The COSO model (which was updated in 2013), was originally put into effect in 1992 and is called the *Internal Control—Integrated Framework*. It contains five primary integrated components of internal control, defines internal control, and establishes the criteria for determining the effectiveness of an internal control system. The five integrated internal control components of the original 1992 COSO model (as updated in 2013) are:

1. Control environment
2. Risk assessment
3. Control activities

4. Information and communication
5. Monitoring

In an effort to further address risk management, the original COSO model was expanded in 2004 to incorporate three additional risk-related components. The expanded risk-driven framework (which remains unchanged with the 2013 COSO Framework update) is called the *Enterprise Risk Management—Integrated Framework*. It serves as a guide for successful enterprise risk management implementation. The 1992 COSO model (as updated in 2013) is covered in this section of the CMA body of knowledge. The 2004 *Enterprise Risk Management-Integrated Framework* is discussed in Part 2, Section D, which covers risk management topics.

Sections 302 and 404 of SOX instituted specific requirements for chief executive officers and chief financial officers of publicly held corporations relative to the financial reports and internal controls of the organization. The result of this legislation is that greater responsibility is placed on high-level management for establishing and maintaining adequate internal control policies. The external auditor must also provide input on the internal control structure.

PCAOB Auditing Standard No. 5 requires auditors to follow a risk-based approach to the development of auditing procedures. Auditors are also required to scale the audit to the size of the organization and to follow other prescribed approaches to perform the audit.

Learning Outcome Statements Overview: Internal Controls

Section E.1. Governance, Risk, and Compliance

A. Demonstrate an understanding of internal control risk and the management of internal control risk.
   a. Risk—Exposure to circumstances that may increase the likelihood of loss. From an internal control perspective, it can be defined as the probability of a threat multiplied by the probability that the control to prevent or detect the threat fails, multiplied by the amount of the loss from the threat. Management seeks to minimize risks by preventing threats from occurring, increasing systems controls, and insuring or otherwise reducing possible losses.

B. Identify and describe internal control objectives.
   a. Internal controls are designed to provide reasonable assurance regarding achievement of an entity's objectives in five areas, which can be remembered by the acronym SCARE:

   Safeguarding of assets

   Compliance with applicable laws and regulations

   Accomplishment of organizational goals and objectives

   Reliability of financial reporting records

   Efficiency of operations

C. Explain how a company's organizational structure, policies, objectives, and goals, as well as its management philosophy and style, influence the scope and effectiveness of the control environment.
   a. The organizational structure defines lines of responsibility and authority. Formal communication about these lines of responsibility, as well as about control procedures, plays an important role in the organization's overall adherence to internal controls. Management's philosophy and operating style send signals to employees about the importance of internal controls. Management behavior—for example, whether it is prone to taking risks

or conservative—sends signals to employees, as well as the auditor, about management's attitude toward internal control.
- D. Identify the Board of Directors' responsibilities with respect to ensuring that the company is operated in the best interest of shareholders.
  - a. The primary responsibility of the board of directors is to ensure that the company operates in the best interest of shareholders. The board of directors is elected by the shareholders and is charged with establishing corporate policies and hiring the major officers (such as the chief executive officer) to set the tone of the organization and to manage day-to-day affairs.
- E. Identify the hierarchy of corporate governance (i.e., articles of incorporation, bylaws, policies, and procedures).
  - a. The articles of incorporation is the document prepared by the persons establishing a corporation and filed with the state in which the corporation is formed. The articles become the corporate charter enabling the corporation to function. They include: corporate name and address; names of the incorporators; nature of the property acquired by the corporation; business to be carried on; corporate powers; and character and amount of capital stock authorized and issued. The corporate bylaws are the rules adopted by the stockholders that define the method by which the corporate functions are to be carried on. The bylaws cover such things as: stockholder and director meetings; appointment and duties of officers; issue and transfer of stock; fiscal year; appointment of auditors; and how the bylaws are amended. The bylaws follow from the articles of incorporation. Corporate policies and procedures cover the day-to-day operation of the corporation and follow from the bylaws.
- F. Demonstrate an understanding of corporate governance, including rights and responsibilities of the CEO, the board of directors, managers, and other stakeholders; and the procedures for making corporate decisions.
  - a. The shareholders elect the board of directors while the board appoints the management of the corporation. The primary purpose of the board of directors is to direct the corporation. The board is also responsible for monitoring and oversight. The CEO is the board's agent responsible for managing the corporation on a day-to-day basis. The procedures for making corporate decisions are spelled out in the corporate bylaws.
- G. Describe how internal controls are designed to provide reasonable (but not absolute) assurance regarding achievement of an entity's objectives involving (i) effectiveness and efficiency of operations, (ii) reliability of financial reporting, and (iii) compliance with applicable laws and regulations.
  - a. Internal controls are designed with costs versus benefits in mind. It would be extremely costly for an organization to attempt to ensure that 100% of errors or fraud would be prevented, detected, or corrected. Even if it tried, employee collusion or management override is difficult to control. As such, internal controls are designed to provide reasonable, but not absolute, assurance regarding achievement of an entity's objectives. Auditors assess the inherent risk, control risk, and planned detection risk in order to gain

a basis for what the acceptable audit risk is for a particular area and design their testing procedures accordingly. These tests provide reasonable assurance that there are no material weaknesses in the internal control structure.

H. Explain why personnel policies and procedures are integral to an efficient control environment.

    a. Hiring and other human resource policies affect adherence to internal controls. Competent and trustworthy employees, combined with timely and effective training, minimize the corrective need of internal control. Part of the firm's control procedures may relate to methods used for hiring, evaluating, and training employees.

I. Define and give examples of segregation of duties.

    a. Segregation of duties—The concept of having more than one person required to complete a single task. The basic idea is that no employee or group of employees should be in a position to perpetrate and conceal errors or fraud. For example, one individual should not be assigned to record deposits, take the deposits to the bank, and reconcile the bank. This individual would be able to misappropriate funds and conceal it because there isn't another individual to verify transactions.

J. Explain why the following four types of functional responsibilities should be performed by different departments or different people within the same function: (i) authority to execute transactions, (ii) recording transactions, (iii) custody of assets involved in the transactions, and (iv) periodic reconciliations of the existing assets to recorded amounts.

    a. The four types of functional responsibilities that should be segregated include authority to execute transactions, the recording of transactions, the custody of assets involved in the transactions, and the reconciliations for those transactions. These should be separated in order to prevent an individual or group from perpetrating a fraud or error and being able to conceal it as well.

K. Demonstrate an understanding of the importance of independent checks and verification.

    a. Independent checks and verifications are important in order to provide additional assurance that control procedures have not been violated or circumvented in some manner. An independent third-party check, such as that provided by an internal audit staff or external CPA firm, can test controls tested and check them for compliance and can confirm the assets or financial reporting information in question.

L. Identify examples of safeguarding controls.

    a. Some safeguarding controls include: door locks, security systems, computer passwords, and requirements for dual control of valuable assets.

M. Explain how the use of pre-numbered forms, as well as specific policies and procedures detailing who is authorized to receive specific documents, is a means of control.

    a. Prenumbered forms are a control mechanism to help ensure that invoices, receiving reports, checks, and the like don't go missing. If documents are prenumbered, it is easy to identify when a document is not in sequence. Lack of sequence can mean that someone is using a document to misappropriate assets in some way. All prenumbered documents should be accounted for and maintained as prescribed by law.

N. Define inherent risk, control risk, and detection risk.
   a. Inherent risk—The susceptibility of financial statements to material misstatement when there are no internal controls.
   b. Control risk—The likelihood that misstatements exceeding an acceptable level will not be prevented or detected by the firm's internal controls.
   c. Detection risk—A measure of the risk that audit evidence will fail to detect misstatements exceeding an acceptable audit risk. It is the risk the auditor is willing to take that an error or fraud goes undetected by audit procedures.

O. Define and distinguish between preventive controls and detective controls.
   a. Preventive controls are those internal controls designed and implemented to prevent errors or irregularities (fraud) from occurring. Detective controls are those designed and implemented to discover errors or irregularities before they cause damage that requires correction.

P. Describe the major internal control provisions of the Sarbanes-Oxley Act (Sections 201, 203, 302, and 404).
   a. The Sarbanes-Oxley Act contains numerous internal control provisions that are tested on the CMA examination. Here is a highlight of the listed sections:
      i. Section 201—Prohibits external auditors from performing nonaudit services, such as bookkeeping, internal audit functions, consulting, systems design, and so on.
      ii. Section 203—Requires audit partners to rotate at least every five years from an audit they have been responsible for.
      iii. Section 302—Requires a public company's principal officers (e.g. the CEO and CFO) to certify as to the accuracy and completeness (including full disclosures) of the company's financial report(s) and, thus, the integrity of the report(s).
      iv. Section 404—Each annual report must contain an assessment of internal controls and state management's responsibility for establishing and maintaining an adequate internal control structure.

Q. Identify the role of the PCAOB in providing guidance on the auditing of internal controls.
   a. The passage of the Sarbanes-Oxley Act increased the cost of compliance for the external audit function tremendously. The PCAOB approved PCAOB Auditing Standard No. 5 in order to provide guidance to management and the external auditor in complying with Section 404 requirements. The standard requires auditors to perform their internal control assessment using a top-down, risk assessment (TDRA) approach. TDRA is a hierarchical approach that applies specific risk factors to determine the scope of work and evidence required in the assessment of internal controls.

R. Differentiate between a top-down (risk-based) approach and a bottom-up approach to auditing internal controls.
   a. The TDRA approach to auditing internal controls starts by identifying significant accounts or disclosures and the misstatement risks associated with those accounts or disclosures. Management and auditors then identify which controls address those risks and which controls compensate for control failures. After that analysis, they can determine the nature, extent, and timing of evidence to be gathered to complete the assessment of internal controls. This method is much more effective than a bottom-up approach that treats every risk equally and applies the same level of detailed examination to the processes required to control those risks.

S. Identify the PCAOB preferred approach to auditing internal controls as outlined in Auditing Standard No. 55.
   a. PCAOB Auditing Standard No. 5 was approved to provide guidance to management and the external auditor in complying with Section 404 requirements. The standard requires auditors to perform their internal control assessment using a top-down, risk assessment (TDRA) approach as described above.

T. Identify and describe the major internal control provisions of the Foreign Corrupt Practices Act.
   a. The FCPA mandated that public companies make and keep books, records, and accounts that, in reasonable detail, accurately and fairly reflect the transactions and disposition of the assets of the company. In addition, the company must devise and maintain a system of internal accounting controls sufficient to provide reasonable assurances that:
   - Transactions are executed in accordance with management's general or specific authorization.
   - Transactions are recorded as necessary to permit preparation of financial statements in conformity with generally accepted accounting principles or any other criteria applicable to such statements and to maintain accountability for assets.
   - Access to assets is permitted only in accordance with management's general or specific authorization.
   - The recorded accountability for assets is compared with the existing assets at reasonable intervals, and appropriate action is taken with respect to any differences.

U. Identify and describe the five major interrelated components of COSO's *Internal Control Framework* (as updated in 2013).
   a. Control environment—Refers to the set of standards, processes, and structures that provide the basis for carrying out internal control across the organization. It reflects the tone at the top of the organization regarding the importance of internal control including expected standards of conduct. The updated 2013 COSO Framework sets forth five principles that

are fundamental to establishing an effective control environment. Those principles include:

1. The organization demonstrates a commitment to integrity and ethical values.
2. The board of directors demonstrates independence from management and exercises oversight responsibility.
3. Management establishes structures, reporting lines, and appropriate authorities and responsibilities throughout the organization in pursuing organizational objectives.
4. The organization demonstrates a commitment to attracting, developing, and retaining competent Individuals in aligning with organizational objectives.
5. The organization enforces accountability for internal control responsibilities.

b. Risk assessment—The risk assessment component of the COSO Framework (as updated in 2013) involves a dynamic and iterative process for identifying and assessing risks to the achievement of objectives. A precondition to risk assessment is the establishment of objectives, linked at different levels of an entity. Four fundamental principles are associated with the risk assessment component of the 2013 updated COSO Framework. They include:

1. The organization must specify objectives with sufficient clarity to enable the identification and assessment of risks relating to objectives.
2. The organization must identify risks to the achievement of its objectives across the entity and analyze risks as a basis for determining how risks should be managed.
3. The organization must consider the potential for fraud in assessing risks to the achievement of objectives.
4. The organization must identify and assess changes that could significantly impact the internal control system.

c. Control activities—Control activities include the policies and procedures that help ensure management's directives to mitigate risks are carried out effectively. These activities are performed at all levels of an organization, at various stages with business processes, and over the technology environment. There are three fundamental principles associated with the Control Activities component of the 2013 updated COSO Framework. They are as follows:

1. The organization needs to select and develop control activities that contribute to the mitigation of risks to acceptable levels.
2. The organization needs to select and develop general control activities over technology.
3. The organization needs to deploy control activities through policies that set forth what is expected and procedures that put policies into action.

d. Information and communication—The information and communication component of the COSO Framework (as updated in 2013) focuses on providing, sharing, and obtaining necessary information through continual communication. Communication is both internal and external. Internal communication is that which is disseminated throughout the organization and enables personnel to receive a clear message from senior management that control responsibilities must be taken seriously. External communication enables inbound communication of relevant external information and provides information to external parties in response to requirements and expectations. Three fundamental principles are outlined in the 2013 updated COSO Framework as it relates to information and communication:

1. The organization obtains and uses relevant, quality information to support the functioning of internal control.
2. The organization internally communicates information regarding internal control.
3. The organization communicates with external parties regarding matters affecting the functioning of internal control.

    e. Monitoring activities—Monitoring activities address the ongoing evaluations, separate evaluations, or some combination of the two to assess whether an organization's internal controls are present and functioning. In this regard, the 2013 updated COSO Framework sets forth two key principles:

1. The organization conducts ongoing and/or separate evaluations to assess whether internal controls are present and functioning evaluations.
2. The organization evaluates and communicates internal control deficiencies in a timely manner to parties responsible for taking corrective action.

V. Assess the level of internal control risk within an organization and recommend risk mitigation strategies.

    a. Risk is the exposure to circumstances that may increase the likelihood of loss. From an internal control perspective, risk can be defined in this way:

$$\text{Risk} = P(t) \times P(f) \times (\text{Amount of Loss})$$

where:
P = probability
t = threat
f = failure of a control

The level of risk is a combination of the dollar value of assets exposed to loss and the probability that such a loss will occur.

    b. Management attempts to minimize risks by preventing threats from occurring, increasing system controls, and insuring or reducing possible losses. The design of controls should be driven by risk assessments. Controls should be established to limit the risk of a potential loss of assets or misstatements of material information. The greater the risks, the more control is needed. The level of risk may be impacted by the frequency of

independent checks on performance, consistency of enforcement of controls, and adequacy of systems controls that limit access to physical control of assets, records, software, or data, among other risk factors.
  c. When considering risk, regular monitoring of control policies and procedures as well as independent audits to monitor compliance with internal controls is needed.
W. Demonstrate an understanding of external auditors' responsibilities, including the types of audit opinions the external auditors issue.
  a. The external auditors' responsibility is to plan and perform the audit with an attitude of professional skepticism in order to obtain reasonable assurance as to whether the financial statements (of the entity under audit) are free from material error or misstatement. The auditors' findings are communicated in the form of an opinion via an audit report. The types of audit opinions an auditor may issue are:
   i. Unmodified.
   ii. Unmodified with emphasis-of-matter or other-matter paragraph.
   iii. Modified, which may include a qualified, adverse, or disclaimer of opinion.
  b. An unmodified opinion is issued when these conditions have been met:
   - A complete set of general-purpose financial statements (e.g., balance sheet, income statement, statement of cash flows) is included.
   - The three general standards have been followed in all aspects of the audit engagement. Those standards include:
     - The audit is to be performed by a person or persons having adequate technical training and proficiency as an auditor.
     - Independence in mental attitude is to be maintained by the auditor or auditors in all matters relating to the audit engagement.
     - Due professional care is to be exercised in the planning and performance of the audit and the preparation of the audit report.
   - Sufficient, competent evidence to support the opinion has been obtained.
   - The financial statements are prepared, in all material respects, in accordance with the applicable reporting framework (most frequently generally accepted auditing principles [GAAP] in the United States). This implies that adequate financial statement disclosures have been made.
   - There are no conditions requiring the addition of an emphasis-of-matter or other-matter paragraph in the audit report.
  c. An unmodified opinion with emphasis-of-matter or other-matter paragraph meets the criteria of a complete audit with satisfactory results and the financial statements are fairly presented, but professional standards require that, when material, the matter be brought to the attention of the financial statement users and, when the auditor believes it is important to "emphasize" the matter and provide additional information about the matter, in the audit report. Some more common situations that would warrant

the inclusion of emphasis-of-matter or other-matter paragraphs in the audit report include:
- Inconsistency in the application of accounting principles (e.g., GAAP).
- Going-concern doubts.
- Uncertainties, such as where conclusive audit evidence concerning the ultimate outcome of a situation (e.g., a lawsuit) does not exist at the time of the audit but instead will occur at some time in the future.
- A change in opinion for a prior period when reporting on current statements in comparative form.
- Predecessor auditor's report for a prior period is not presented when reporting on current financial statements in comparative form.
- Other discretionary circumstances, which might include a major catastrophe that affects the audited company's financial position, significant transactions with related parties, or unusually important subsequent events.

d. A qualified opinion is issued when the auditor concludes that either the financial statements are materially (but not pervasively) misstated (e.g., a departure from GAAP) or there is a scope limitation due to the auditor's inability to obtain sufficient appropriate audit evidence, which is not pervasive.

e. An adverse opinion is issued when the auditor concludes that financial statements are materially misstated (due to major GAAP violation or departure) and the effects of the misstatements are both material and pervasive.

f. A disclaimer opinion is issued when the auditor is unable to obtain sufficient appropriate audit evidence and the possible effects of this are both material and pervasive. A disclaimer states that the auditor does not express an opinion on the financial statements.

Section E.2. Internal Auditing

A. Define the internal audit function and identify its functions and scope.
   a. The primary purpose of an internal audit is to appraise the design of, effectiveness of, and adherence to internal control policies and procedures and to assess the firm's quality of performance. The internal auditor ensures that any risk to the business is addressed and verifies that the firm's goals and objectives are met efficiently and effectively. The scope of internal auditing is broad and may include: the efficacy of operations; the reliability of financial reporting; deterring, detecting, and investigating fraud; safeguarding assets; and compliance with laws and regulations.

B. Identify how internal auditors can test compliance with controls and evaluate the effectiveness of controls.
   a. Establishing and maintaining internal controls are the responsibility of management. After the controls and operational benchmarks have been

established, internal auditors are charged to assess the adherence to those controls and identify any weaknesses that may exist. An engagement plan should be developed, much like that of an external audit, to assess the control risks associated with particular areas and design tests to gather evidence to support the performance of particular controls. When planning an engagement, the internal auditor should consider the objectives and performance controls of the activity, any significant risks to the activity, the adequacy and effectiveness of the activity's risk management and control systems compared with a relevant model and should indicate opportunities for improvement.

C. Explain how internal auditors determine what controls to audit, when to audit, and why.
   a. Internal auditors determine what controls to audit by assessing the risks associated with control breakdowns, the inherent risks associated with particular accounts or disclosures, and the mitigating factors that address those risks. Major risks should be the primary focus and typically are audited more frequently than minor risks.

D. Identify and describe control breakdowns and related risks that internal auditors should report to management or to the Board of Directors.
   a. An internal auditor may report a number of findings to management. General findings may include such items as: inadequate control procedures, lack of adherence to control procedures (e.g., disorganized records), inadequate safeguarding of assets, inefficient allocation of resources, and so on. The auditor can provide a service by prioritizing the various risks in terms of their potential costs.

E. Define and identify the objectives of a compliance audit and an operational audit.
   a. Compliance audit—The auditor determines whether the firm has complied with applicable laws and regulations as well as professional or industry standards or contractual responsibilities.
   b. Operational audit—A nonfinancial audit that is intended to evaluate the effectiveness and efficiency of the organization or one of its divisions, departments, or processes.

Section E.3. Systems Controls and Security Measures

A. Describe how the segregation of accounting duties can enhance system security.
   a. There should be a separation of systems development, operations, and technical support duties within the information technology function to ensure that someone is not able to perpetrate and conceal fraud or errors. Controls for segregation of duties should include separation of responsibilities within the information processing department. For example, employees involved in the design, development, and maintenance of the information system should not be involved in day-to-day processing of transactions.

B. Identify threats to information systems, including input manipulation, program alteration, direct file alteration, data theft, sabotage, viruses, Trojan horses, theft, and phishing.
   a. Input manipulation—Occurs where false or misleading data are input into a computer to achieve a specific criminal purpose. A common input manipulation is a data processing clerk altering supporting documents to cover a theft.
   b. Program alteration—Program alterations can occur by using trapdoors to enter a computer program while bypassing its normal security systems. For example, a programmer could make unauthorized program changes to divert monies to accounts that he or she created.
   c. Direct file alteration—Inputting data into a computer system while bypassing the normal process. For example, an employee uses special software tools to modify files or databases directly.
   d. Data theft—Involves unauthorized individuals stealing sensitive company information.
   e. Sabotage—Deliberate action aimed at weakening an organization through subversion, obstruction, disruption, or destruction.
   f. Viruses—A type of malware that, when executed, replicates by inserting copies of itself into other computer programs, data files, or the boot sector of the hard drive.
   g. Trojan horse—A program in which malicious or harmful code is contained inside apparently harmless programming or data in such a way that it can get control and do its chosen form of damage.
   h. Phishing—The act of attempting to acquire user identity information such as username, password, credit card details, or social security number by masquerading or impersonating a trustworthy entity in an electronic communication, commonly an e-mail.

C. Demonstrate an understanding of how systems development controls are used to enhance the accuracy, validity, safety, security, and adaptability of systems input, processing, output, and storage functions.
   a. Creating or implementing new systems presents risks as a result of malicious or careless developers who create trapdoors, buffer-overflow vulnerabilities, or other weaknesses that can leave a system open to exploitation by malicious individuals. To protect against these vulnerabilities, it's vital to introduce controls into the entire systems development life cycle to enhance the accuracy, validity, safety, security, and adaptability of the systems input, processing, output, and storage functions.

D. Identify procedures to limit access to physical hardware.
   a. Limiting access to physical hardware can be done by locating the hardware away from public places and requiring key codes or biometrics to control entrance to hardware. Cameras and security systems also should be used to prevent or detect access to hardware.

E. Identify means by which management can protect programs and databases from unauthorized use.

a. Companies must use a variety of controls to protect their systems including passwords, data encryption, routing verification, firewalls, and intrusion detection systems.
F. Identify input controls, processing controls, and output controls and describe why each of these controls is necessary.
   a. Input controls—Controls that are designed to prevent or detect errors in the time data are entered into the computer system. These controls help ensure accuracy and reliability of reporting data. Examples of input controls include: batch controls, approval mechanisms, dual observation, supervisory procedures, well-designed source documents, redundant data checks, unfound records test, preformatted screens, and check digits.
   b. Processing controls—Controls that address the system's manipulation of the data after they are input. These controls ensure that once data have been entered into the system, they remain reliable and accurate for final output. Examples of processing controls include: mechanization, standardization, default option, batch balancing, run-to-run totals, balancing, matching, clearing accounts, tickler files, redundant processing, trailer labels, and automated error corrections.
   c. Output controls—Controls that are designed to check that input and processing result in accurate and valid output. These controls help ensure the accuracy and validity of information and regulate the distribution of output. Examples of output controls include: reconciliation, aging, suspense files, suspense accounts, periodic audits, and discrepancy reports.
G. Identify and describe the types of storage controls and demonstrate an understanding of when and why they are used.
   a. After data have been input, processed, and distributed, they must be stored in secure places to ensure their safety and confidentiality. Physical output can be stored with locks and safes. Electronic documents can be stored with data encryption technologies and should be password protected to prevent unauthorized access.
H. Identify and describe the inherent risks of using the internet as compared to data transmissions over secured transmission lines.
   a. The Internet has introduced risks to computer systems that do not exist on private networks. Among the threats is a greatly increased risk of unauthorized access, as hackers have grown both more numerous and more sophisticated in their attacks. Internet presence also exposes systems to malware, including virus, worms, spyware, spam, and Trojan horses.
I. Define data encryption, and describe why there is a much greater need for data encryption methods when using the internet.
   a. Data encryption—Converts data from an easily read local language into a code that can be read only by those with the correct decryption key. The data are encoded during the input or transmission stage, then decrypted at output by the person authorized to receive them. Data encryption is important when transmitting information over the Internet since there is greater risk of unauthorized access.

J. Identify a firewall and its uses.
   a. A firewall is used to help prevent unauthorized access from the Internet. Within the company network, firewalls may be used to prevent unauthorized access to specific systems, such as payroll or personnel. Multiple firewalls are recommended in order to improve security.

K. Demonstrate an understanding of how flowcharts of activities are used to assess controls.
   a. A flowchart visually depicts the flow of transactions through the process from initiation to storage of data to its final destination. Diagramming the process can help understand the process as well as identify gaps or flaws in the controls. Flowcharts can be useful not only for summarizing the internal auditor's information about processes but also to aid in design, development, and implementation of new accounting information systems or new control procedures.

L. Explain the importance of backing up all program and data files regularly, and storing the backups at a secure remote site.
   a. Backup policies and procedures are instituted to ensure that data that are lost due to malware, natural disasters, hardware failures, theft, deletions, and software malfunctions can be recovered. Off-site storage should be considered mandatory, because data can be recovered in the event of a disaster that affects the data center.

M. Define business continuity planning.
   a. Business continuity planning (BCP) is a strategy that looks to identify an organization's exposure to internal and external threats and bring together its critical resources and assets in order to protect those resources and ensure continuing operations and effective recovery, in the event of some significant adverse event or disaster.

N. Define the objective of a disaster recovery plan and identify the components of such a plan.
   a. Disaster recovery policies and procedures—also referred to as business continuance plans—are designed to enable the firm to carry on business in the event that an emergency, such as a natural disaster, disrupts normal functioning of the business. The plan should define the roles of all members of the business continuance team and specify backup sites for alternate computer processing and procedures for restoring data to full functionality.

TOPIC 1

Governance, Risk, and Compliance

THE PRIMARY OBJECTIVE OF A system of internal controls is to reduce risk to an acceptable level. The internal control system is designed to provide reasonable (but not absolute) assurance regarding the achievement of an entity's objectives. Specifically, the control activities are a set of policies and procedures established and implemented to assign authority for the day-to-day operations, provide a system of authorizations and documentations, protect company assets, require independent verifications, and accomplish effective separation of duties. The board of directors is charged with the hiring of managers who will create, implement, and monitor these activities in order to promote the effectiveness and efficiency of operations, the reliability of financial reporting, the safeguarding of assets, and the firm's compliance with applicable laws and regulations. When determining internal control policies and procedures, management must weigh the cost of suggested controls against the risks that the policies and procedures are intended to reduce. The controls should be cost beneficial.

This topic begins by defining risk and the types of risks auditors must assess. It looks at design controls to address risk and the role of management philosophy and internal control structure on its risk control efforts. It also addresses the controls imposed by the U.S. government through the Sarbanes-Oxley Act and the Foreign Corrupt Practices Act and discusses types of internal controls and methods of control.

> **READ** the Learning Outcome Statements (LOS) for this topic as found in Appendix A and then study the concepts and calculations presented here to be sure you understand the content you could be tested on in the CMA exam.

Risk

Risk is defined as exposure to circumstances that may increase the likelihood of loss. From an internal control perspective, it can be defined as the probability of a threat multiplied by the probability that the control to prevent or detect the threat fails, multiplied by the amount of the loss from the threat.

> Risk = P(*t*) × P(*f*) × (Amount of Loss)

where:
P = probability
t = threat
f = failure of a control

The level of risk is a combination of both the total dollar value of assets that are exposed to loss and the probability that such a loss will occur. Management seeks to minimize risks by:

- Preventing threats from occurring
- Increasing systems controls
- Insuring or otherwise reducing possible losses

The design of controls should be driven by risk assessments. Controls should be established to limit risk of a potential loss of assets or misstatements of material information. Greater risks warrant more extensive control.

Factors affecting risk include:

- Frequency of independent checks on performance
- Adequacy of organizational control methods
- Adequacy of communication of authority and responsibility
- Consistency of enforcement of controls
- Adequacy of systems controls that limit access to or physical control of assets, records, software, or data

When considering risk, there is need for regular monitoring of control policies and procedures as well as regular independent audits to monitor compliance with internal controls.

Types of Risk

Auditors assess risk as part of an audit. Auditors divide risk into three types:

1. **Inherent risk (IR)** is the susceptibility of financial statements to material misstatement when there are no internal controls. It is the probability of an error or irregularity (fraud). Errors are unintentional and relate to the competence of the organization's personnel. Fraud is intentional and relates to the integrity of the organization's personnel. Competence and integrity of personnel are the cornerstones of effective internal control.
2. **Control risk (CR)** is the likelihood that misstatements exceeding an acceptable level will not be prevented or detected by the firm's internal controls. It is the probability of a control failure.
3. **Detection risk (DR)**, or planned detection risk, is a measure of the risk that audit evidence will fail to detect misstatements exceeding an acceptable audit

risk. It is the risk the auditor is willing to take that an error or fraud goes undetected by audit procedures.

Acceptable Audit Risk

Acceptable audit risk (AAR) is the probability of an audit failure and is a function of the three types of risk that were just defined. It is the probability that the auditor will conclude that the financial statements "fairly present" and issues an unmodified opinion when, in fact, the statements are materially misleading. It represents the risk the auditor is willing to take that the audit will fail.

AAR is a function of three things:

1. Management integrity
2. The number of financial statement users
3. The auditee's financial condition

If auditors want to have greater certainty that the financial statements are not materially misstated, they will lower the acceptable audit risk. The lower the management integrity, the lower the AAR. The more financial statement users, the lower the AAR. The worse the auditee's financial condition, the lower the AAR.

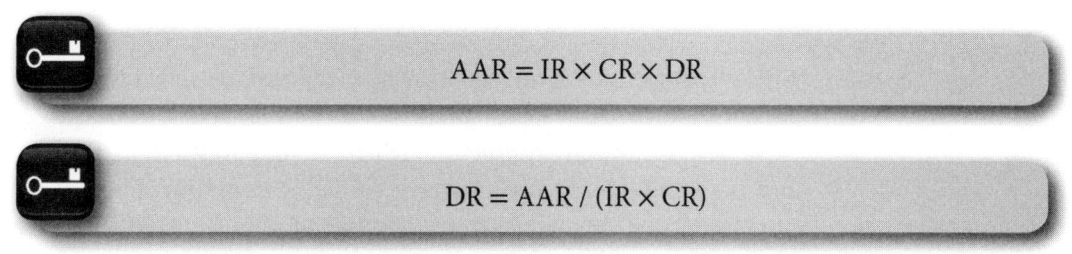

$$AAR = IR \times CR \times DR$$

$$DR = AAR / (IR \times CR)$$

where:
AAR = acceptable audit risk
IR = inherent risk
CR = control risk
DR = detection risk

The auditor sets the AAR based on factors noted earlier, and assesses the IR and CR. The combination of IR and CR is normally either high or low, because lack of integrity and/or competence normally results in weaker controls. The lower the calculated DR, the more evidence the auditor would require to support the audit.

Design Controls to Address Risks

The most broadly accepted model for designing and assessing internal control is the *Internal Control—Integrated Framework*, which was established in 1992 by the Committee of Sponsoring Organizations (COSO) of the Treadway Commission (the National Committee on Fraudulent Financial Reporting). The framework also is recognized by both the Public Company Accounting Oversight Board (PCAOB) and the American Institute of Certified Public Accountants (AICPA) as one within which an organization's internal controls can be tested, assessed, and opined on. In 2004, COSO incorporated this model into a more expansive risk management framework—the *Enterprise Risk Management (ERM)—Integrated Framework*—which, as the name implies, goes beyond internal controls to provide guidelines for managing risk across an organization.

The original COSO framework comprises five mutually reinforcing components. They are meant to be integrated with an organization's management processes and applied in successive iterations to adapt to changing conditions. Each component may have an impact on any or all of the others. In 2013, the COSO released revisions and updates to the original 1992 Framework. The new framework, known as the 2013 *Internal Control—Integrated Framework*, retains the core definition of internal control and the original five integrated internal control components, but it clarifies the application of the Framework in the current environment with various business models, technology, and related risks; codifies criteria (through 17 explicit principles and attributes) that can be used in developing an internal control structure and evaluating its effectiveness; and expands reporting objectives to support both internal and external and financial and nonfinancial reporting and operational and compliance objectives. The next list summarizes the five internal control components of the COSO *Internal Control—Integrated Framework*:

1. **Control environment.** The control environment refers to the organization's management philosophy and appetite for risk and includes integrity, ethical values, and the environment in which an organization operates.
2. **Risk assessment.** The model included a component for assessing risk—determining its probability and degree of importance. Risks are classified as either inherent or residual. Inherent risks are those that the organization will face unless management takes action to avoid or mitigate them. They are the first to be assessed. Residual risks are those that remain after any actions management might take with regard to inherent risks.
3. **Control activities.** Policies and procedures are established and implemented to help ensure that the risk responses are effectively carried out. The COSO model lists the following control activities:
    a. The assignment of authority and responsibility (job descriptions), which requires the board of directors to hire the chief executive officer [CEO] and other managers who will hire, train, and appropriately compensate competent, reliable, ethical employees to accomplish the day-to-day operations of the company.
    b. A system of transaction authorizations, which helps to avoid duplicate and fictitious payments, safeguard assets, and generate reliable accounting information. These controls include signatures of approval, reconciliations, and the forms that document those actions.
    c. Adequate documentation and records, which are necessary because documents provide the details of the company's operations. Documents, such as invoices and orders, may be paper or electronic.

The prenumbering of documents, such as invoices, purchase orders, and checks, helps to prevent theft and inefficiencies by drawing attention to gaps in sequences.

d. Security of assets is enabled by a good system of authorizations and segregation of duties in order to reduce the opportunities for fraud and theft. Production activities and sales activities should not be performed by accounting personnel.

e. Independent verifications may be internal (such as the internal audit staff) or external (such as an independent certified public accountant who audits financial statements or a regulator who audits regulatory issues).

f. Adequate separation of duties requires the separation of the authorization for a transaction from the execution of the transaction, from the recording of the transaction, and from the custody of the assets resulting from the transaction.

For example: A purchase is authorized by a purchase requisition originating in inventory control. The purchase is executed by the purchasing agent and is recorded by the information technology department. The raw materials are received by the receiving department. Receiving validates the receipt to the purchase order by counting, inspecting, and preparing the receiving report. The materials are then released to inventory control.

4. **Information and communication.** The COSO model recognizes that relevant information must be identified, captured, and communicated in a form and time frame that enables people to do their jobs successfully. This assumes that the data communicated are secure and accurate.

5. **Monitoring activities.** All aspects of internal controls are monitored, and modifications made as necessary. Monitoring is accomplished through ongoing management activities, separate evaluations, or both. Internal auditors, the audit committee, and the disclosure committee, as well as management, may all be involved in monitoring controls.

The COSO model encompasses internal control and emphasizes the role of managing risk in order to achieve success. It includes the internal environment in which risks are evaluated and managed, objective setting to allow the assessment of risks that may hinder success, identification of risks (as well as positive events), and methods of responding to risks once they have been assessed.

When management encounters situations in which controls might add to the efficiency of operations, it must weigh the risk of loss or inefficiency against the cost of the controls.

Effective Control Principles

Controls are designed to prevent unintentional errors due to carelessness or lack of knowledge. Fraud, however, is intentional, and it is difficult to prevent collusion and management override. No matter how well internal controls are designed, they cannot provide complete assurance against intentional fraud. Moreover, human error, carelessness in executing control procedures, fatigue or stress, and the tendency to let familiarity supersede control procedures can result in errors or even fraud. In addition, even a well-designed control system is subject to obsolescence over time if not adjusted to changes in operations. There is a twofold risk in designing controls. On one hand, they may be too lax, thus failing to ensure compliance or to provide reliable information to help management achieve the goals of the organization. On the other hand, they may be so complex and detailed as to increase the difficulty of processing transactions, reducing productivity without adding value.

The four principles of accounting system design apply to the creation of effective controls:

1. **Control principle.** Requires that an accounting system provide internal control features in order to protect a firm's assets and ensure that data is reliable.
2. **Compatibility principle.** Holds that the design of an accounting system must be in harmony with the organizational and human factors of the business.
3. **Flexibility principle.** Holds that an accounting system must be flexible enough to allow the volume of transactions to grow and organizational changes to be made.
4. **Cost-benefit principle.** Holds that the benefits derived from an accounting system and the information it generates must be equal to or greater than the system's costs, both tangible and intangible. Tangible costs include personnel, forms, and equipment. Intangible costs include the cost of wrong decisions.

Governance, Internal Control Aspects of Organizational Structure, and Management Philosophy

Corporate governance refers to the system by which a corporation is directed and controlled. The governance structure specifies the distribution of rights and responsibilities among a number of participants within a corporation, such as the board of directors and managers, and parties external to the corporation, such as shareholders, creditors, regulators, and the company's external auditors. The governance structure further specifies the rules and procedures for making decisions in corporate affairs. Governance provides the structure through which corporations establish and pursue their objectives while considering the social, regulatory, and market environments in which they operate. Governance is a mechanism for monitoring an organization's actions, policies, and decisions.

A corporation's governance structure must comply with a number of federal and state laws. Each state in the United States has its own set of laws regulating a corporation's governance. The basic framework of a company's corporate governance structure is designed to meet the laws of its home state and nation. Before the corporation is formed, it must submit several documents to its state. Two important documents are the company's corporate charter and articles of incorporation. These documents provide a detailed outline of a corporation's planned governance structure and define the hierarchy within the corporation—the means by which authority is communicated and the processes that will be used to maintain the governance structure.

Corporate governance begins with the company's shareholders. The shareholders elect the board of directors, who then appoint the senior management of the corporation (such as the CEO and the chief financial officer [CFO]). The primary purpose of the board of directors is to direct the operation of the corporation. The board is also responsible for monitoring and oversight. The CEO is the board's agent responsible for managing the corporation on a day-to-day basis. The procedures for making corporate decisions are spelled out in the corporate bylaws.

A company's organizational structure, policies, objectives, and goals, as well as its management philosophy and style, influence the scope and effectiveness of the control environment. The organizational structure defines lines of responsibility and authority. Formal communication about these lines of responsibility, as well as about control procedures, plays an important role in the organization's overall adherence to internal controls.

Management organizes resources into various functions, such as financial management, production, and so on. Separation of responsibility establishes a structure within which the goals of the business may be accomplished. An organization's structure identifies individual components and the operational and informational interrelationships among the various components. The most common method of documenting organizational structure is through the organizational chart.

The next level of organizational structure outlines the key decisions for which each organizational component is responsible. For example, the controller will determine the financial controls and accounting principles the firm will employ. The production manager will be responsible for determining the best means of fulfilling production commitments.

The internal control aspects of a company's organizational structure are discussed in the context of these three components:

1. Control environment
2. Information systems (accounting system)
3. Control procedures

Control Environment

Management and the board of directors of a company set the environment for the business, including its control environment. Management's philosophy and operating style send signals to employees about the importance of internal controls. Management behavior—for example, whether it is prone to taking risks or conservative—sends signals to employees, as well as the auditor, about management's attitude toward internal control.

If management and the board project an attitude that controls are not important, others in the business will act accordingly and management's control objectives are unlikely to be met. If management and the board of directors send a message that internal control is important to them, employees will respond by carefully observing the established controls.

The same holds true for the firm's overall integrity and ethical values. Management's actions to remove or reduce temptation that might prompt personnel to engage in dishonest, illegal, or unethical acts set the tone for the firm's integrity. Management also communicates the entity's values and behavioral standards to personnel through policy statements and codes of conduct, and also by example.

The sum of the components of a firm's control procedures can provide an external auditor a picture of management's attitude toward internal control. As this topic progresses, the control environment will continue to be mentioned in relation to the components of the firm's control procedures, such as hiring and training policies covered under control policies.

Board of Directors and Audit Committee Responsibilities

The board of directors bears final responsibility for business practices and results; it sets broad purposes of operations that guide how control systems should be designed and monitored. The primary responsibility of the board of directors is to ensure that the company operates in the best interest of shareholders. The board of directors is charged with establishing corporate policies and hiring the major officers of the organization who set the organizational tone and to manage day-to-day affairs.

For firms that have an internal audit function, the internal auditor provides that assurance to the board of directors by verifying that control procedures are adequate and being followed. The organizational chart should show the audit director reporting directly to the audit committee of the board of directors.

Audit committees have not always been effective. Investors have blamed such committees for lacking the independence or financial expertise to uncover financial reporting failures. Audit committees have also fallen short in cases where a CEO has picked members willing to "go with the flow."

Audit committees need independent directors with sophisticated financial backgrounds. The Sarbanes-Oxley Act of 2002 (SOX) requires that the audit committee consist entirely of directors who are independent of the organization, meaning that they cannot accept any consulting, advisory, or other compensatory fee from the organization or be affiliated with the organization or any of its subsidiaries. At least one of the audit committee members must qualify as a "financial expert" within the meaning and rules of the Securities and Exchange Commission (SEC).

Management Responsibility Under Sarbanes-Oxley Act of 2002

Section 404 of SOX requires that public companies establish and maintain a system of internal controls, which is then audited by external auditors. The act requires that corporate officers (namely the CEO and CFO) annually certify that management is responsible for establishing and maintaining adequate internal control over financial reporting and that those internal controls have been tested and assessed as to their effectiveness. This certification is explicitly stated in a report that must accompany financial statements filed with the SEC and must also include notations of significant defects or material noncompliance found internal control testing. Additionally, the report must provide a statement regarding the external auditor's attestation on management's assessment of the company's internal control over financial reporting.

External Auditor's Responsibilities: Financial Statement Audit

The primary responsibility of the external auditor is to plan and perform the audit with an attitude of professional skepticism in order to obtain reasonable assurance as to whether the financial statements (of the organization under audit) are free from material error or misstatement. The types of audit opinions an auditor may issue include the following:

- An unmodified opinion
- An unmodified opinion with emphasis-of-matter or other-matter paragraph
- A modified opinion, which may include: a qualified opinion, an adverse opinion, and a disclaimer of opinion

An unmodified opinion is issued when the next conditions have been met:

- A complete set of general purpose-financial statements (i.e., balance sheet, income statement, statement of cash flows) is included.
- The three general standards (adequate technical training and proficiency, independence is mental attitude, and due professional care) have been followed in all aspects of the engagement.
- Sufficient, competent evidence to support the opinion has been obtained.
- The financial statements are prepared, in all material respects, in accordance with the applicable reporting framework (most frequently generally accepted accounting principles (GAAP)in the United States). This implies that adequate financial statement disclosures have been made.
- There are no conditions requiring the addition of an emphasis-of-matter or other-matter paragraph in the audit report.

An unmodified opinion with emphasis-of-matter or other-matter paragraph meets the criteria of a complete audit with satisfactory results and the financial statements fairly presented, but professional standards require that, when material, the matter be brought to the attention of the financial statement users, and when the auditor believes it is important to "emphasize" the matter and provide additional information about the matter, in the audit report. Some more common situations that would warrant the inclusion of emphasis-of-matter or other-matter paragraphs in the audit report are listed next:

- Inconsistency in the application of accounting principles (i.e., GAAP)
- Going-concern doubts

- Uncertainties, such as where conclusive audit evidence concerning the ultimate outcome of a situation (i.e., a lawsuit) does not exist at the time of the audit but instead will occur at some time in the future
- A change in opinion for a prior period when reporting on current statements in comparative form
- Predecessor auditor's report for a prior period is not presented when reporting on current financial statements in comparative form
- Other discretionary circumstances, which might include: a major catastrophe that affects the audited company's financial position, significant transactions with related parties, or unusually important subsequent events

A qualified opinion is issued when the auditor concludes that either the financial statements are materially (but not pervasively) misstated (i.e., a departure from GAAP), or there is a scope limitation due to the auditor's inability to obtain sufficient appropriate audit evidence, which is not pervasive.

An adverse opinion is issued when the auditor concludes that financial statements are materially misstated (due to a major GAAP violation or departure) and the effects of the misstatements are both material and pervasive.

A disclaimer of opinion is issued when the auditor is unable to obtain sufficient appropriate audit evidence and the possible effects of this are both material and pervasive. A disclaimer states that the auditor does not express an opinion on the financial statements.

External Auditor's Responsibilities: Reporting on Internal Controls

As mentioned previously, Section 404 of SOX also requires the external auditor to attest to and report on the adequacy of an organization's financial reporting internal controls.

In 2007, the PCAOB issued PCAOB Auditing Standard No. 5, which provides guidance for the external auditor in complying with Section 404 requirements. PCAOB Auditing Standard No. 5 requires auditors to perform their internal control assessment using a top-down, risk assessment (TDRA) approach. TDRA is a hierarchical approach that applies specific risk factors to determine the scope of work (i.e., the controls to test) and evidence required in the assessment of internal controls.

TDRA begins at the financial statement level and with the auditor's understanding of the overall risks to internal control over financial reporting. The steps in TDRA include:

1. Identifying and evaluating entity-level controls. Entity-level controls are those internal controls that help ensure that management directives pertaining to the entire entity are carried out (e.g., a policies and procedures manual, a whistle-blower hotline, a code of conduct).
2. Identifying significant accounts or disclosures (e.g., cash, inventory).
3. Identifying material misstatement risks within these accounts or disclosures (e.g., theft risk for cash, risk of obsolescence for inventory). Doing this requires the determination as to whether an account/disclosure is significant and, if

significant, rating the misstatement risk as low, medium, or high. Management is charged with developing a list of assertion-level control objectives for each significant account/disclosure and from those objectives developing the risks that have a reasonably possible likelihood to cause material misstatement risk (MMR) in the financial statements.

4. Determining which entity-level controls sufficiently address the risk.
5. Determining which transaction-based controls compensate for possibly entity-level control failures. For each MMR, controls (either entity-level controls or transaction-based controls) are identified that will sufficiently mitigate the risk, which is defined as reducing the risk to a low level.
6. Determining the nature, extent, and timing of evidence gathering tests needed to complete the assessment of the internal controls. This is the final step based on the assessments in Steps 4 and 5.

The TDRA is a principle-based approach and provides the auditor flexibility in designing the scope of the controls to test and the nature, timing, and extent of testing procedures to be performed.

Information System (Accounting System)

Information systems typically are divided into two functions: the accounting information system and the operating information system. The accounting information system contains data used to produce the company's financial statements and other financial reports. The operating information system accepts and stores data from various operations of the company and provides reports on activities and functions.

The objective of internal control to maintain reliability and integrity of the information system is important to the management decision-making process. Compromising integrity of the information system could have the effect of producing unreliable and inaccurate information. Because management uses information produced by the information system to make important decisions, data that is unreliable and/or inaccurate could negatively impact those decisions by leading management to take action in a particular direction that diverts resources from more profitable activities.

Control Procedures

General controls relating to the control environment are different from specific controls directed at detailed procedures and activities. Examples of specific controls include requiring competitive bids on projects and requiring use of only authorized vendors. Examples of general controls include procedures such as segregating purchasing responsibilities from responsibility for custody of assets. The general control environment can offset or render ineffective the potential effectiveness of such controls.

Each general control has at least one corresponding specific control. For example, a general control regarding purchases requires authorization by a specified officer and corresponding specific controls for accuracy. Design of control policies and procedures must consider potential risk, stated risk, and actual risk exposure when selecting which specific controls to employ.

Internal controls are designed to provide reasonable assurance regarding achievement of an entity's objectives involving five areas, which can be remembered by the acronym SCARE:

Safeguarding of assets

Compliance with applicable laws and regulations

Accomplishment of organizational goals and objectives

Reliability of financial reporting records

Efficiency of operations

Safeguarding of Assets

Internal controls designed to protect the firm's assets are often the most visible safeguarding controls. Such controls include door locks, security systems, computer passwords, and requirements for dual control of valuable assets. Assets can be stolen, misused, or accidentally destroyed unless protected by adequate controls. Controls for safeguarding of assets include segregation of functions in processing transactions. For example, the person who writes up an order should not have access to the assets for fulfillment of the order.

Multiple levels of access controls should be built into an organization's operations and information systems. For example, users with authority to arrange shipments are able to update the inventory system, but sales staff is given read-only access to the data.

Compliance with Applicable Laws and Regulations

To comply with externally imposed laws and regulations, the firm establishes internal controls in the form of policies, plans, and procedures. Failure to comply with such controls jeopardizes the firm's compliance with the associated laws and regulations.

Accomplishment of Organizational Goals and Objectives

The focus of controls and organizational activities is on the accomplishment of the business's goals and objectives. Effectiveness is the accomplishment of goals and objectives.

If an organization fails in this area, how well it does anything else is irrelevant.

Reliability of Financial Reporting

Management has legal and professional responsibility to ensure that information in financial statements is fairly represented and prepared in accordance with GAAP. Examples of controls for reliability of financial reporting include control procedures for budgeting, internal performance reports, accounting groups to which transactions are posted, and control over account balances. These controls have importance not only for financial reporting but also for ensuring that management decisions are based on accurate information.

Efficiency of Operations

Internal controls are designed to promote efficient use of resources. The economic principle of scarcity of resources applies to the firm's desire to produce with as little waste as possible. If facilities are underutilized, if work is nonproductive, if procedures are not cost-justified, or if the company is overstaffed or understaffed, the organization will not realize maximum profits.

Operating standards provide a basis for measuring economy and efficiency that will ultimately be reflected in the financial statements. Internal auditors as well as others in the firm, including production workers, should continue to watch for opportunities for improvements in efficiency.

Foreign Corrupt Practices Act

The U. S. Congress passed the **Foreign Corrupt Practices Act** (FCPA) in 1977 as a result of SEC investigations in the mid-1970s revealing that hundreds of companies admitted to making questionable or illegal payments to foreign government officials to secure favorable action. The act forbids an American company doing business overseas to pay bribes to a foreign government for obtaining contracts or business.

Firms and/or any officer or director of a firm that violate provisions of the FCPA are subject to criminal and civil penalties. Criminal penalties allow for fines of up to $2 million and imprisonment for up to five years.

Every issuer of securities subject to the FCPA is required to make and keep books, records, and accounts that, in reasonable detail, accurately and fairly reflect the transactions and dispositions of the assets of the issuer. In addition, the issuer must devise and maintain a system of internal accounting controls sufficient to provide reasonable assurances that:

- Transactions are executed in accordance with management's general or specific authorization.
- Transactions are recorded as necessary to permit preparation of financial statements in conformity with GAAP or any other criteria applicable to such statements and to maintain accountability for assets.
- Access to assets is permitted only in accordance with management's general or specific authorization.
- The recorded accountability for assets is compared with the existing assets at reasonable intervals, and appropriate action is taken with respect to any differences.

These objectives should be related to specific internal control procedures in order to evaluate control effectively. Such procedures may include requirements for completion and supervision of expense reports, defining who is authorized to approve expense reports, and obtaining cash and documenting its use. Internal control procedures should include a routine accounting for agreement between totals on expense reports and cash advances.

The SEC is responsible for monitoring compliance with the internal controls provisions of the FCPA.

Types of Internal Controls

Internal controls can be classified as preventive, detective, corrective, directive, or compensating.

Preventive Controls

Preventive controls are intended to prevent errors and misappropriation of assets. For example, a control may create an obstacle that prevents the processing of a particular type of transaction. Credit checks on potential clients (intended to prevent sales to clients with poor credit risk) or guards at exit points (intended to prevent employee theft) are other types of preventive controls.

Transactional controls are a specific type of preventive control designed to ensure that every transaction is documented, that false transactions are not entered into the system, and that all valid exchanges are accurately recorded. The types of controls selected in large part will depend on the quantity and the nature of the transactions the firm completes.

Preventive controls that depend on functions or people performing their roles effectively may include:

- Separation of duties.
- Supervisory review, such as a supervisor approving a purchase transaction.
- Dual control, such as two authorizations for every transaction above a certain threshold.
- Edit and accuracy checks, such as reconciling of invoice amounts against original warehouse receipt records before an invoice is paid.
- Reasonableness checks, such as verifying the total of a transaction against a customer's credit limit. (Reasonableness checks are often built into software systems.)
- Completeness checks, such as a computer form that will not allow the operator to continue until required fields are completed. (If during data entry a data entry screen insists on complete fields before it permits processing, the screen itself operates as a preventive control to ensure completeness.)

As with internal controls in general, no preventive control can be expected to be foolproof. Thus, it is important for a firm to recognize the dependence of preventive controls upon detective controls.

Detective Controls

Detective controls are intended to back up preventive controls by detecting errors after they have occurred. Reconciliation of bank statements is an example of a detective control over cash assets. Detective controls complement preventive controls and are essential components of a well-designed control system. In some cases, detective controls may be less costly than preventive controls because random transactions, rather than every transaction, can be examined.

Corrective Controls

Corrective controls correct problems identified using detective controls. For example, an ordering system's routine edit function may detect an inaccurate account number on a sales order, read the client's name, search the database for the correct account number, and correct the original record. In some cases, if a record cannot be found on the database matching the customer name, the computer may generate an error report, which an employee can use to follow up on and resolve the discrepancy.

Directive Controls

In contrast to controls that prevent, detect, and correct negative results, directive controls are designed to produce positive results. For example, a firm may have a policy to use local vendors as often as possible. Directive controls may be intended to create a favorable image for the company in the community.

Compensating Controls

Compensating controls, also called mitigating controls, are designed to compensate for shortcomings elsewhere in the control structure. For example, a bank reconciliation process performed by a party independent of accounting and cash handling can compensate for a number of flaws in the controls over cash transactions. Similarly, a hands-on owner-manager's supervision of operations might compensate for a lack of segregation of duties in a small business.

Compensating controls are an approach to limiting risk exposure. Risk exposure must be analyzed in the context of what could happen, given particular system weaknesses. Compensating controls may include redundancy. Data entry verification often has been achieved by having two entry points, reconciliation of resulting records, and generation of exceptions reports on any detected differences.

Methods of Internal Control

Internal control methods can be placed into five categories: organizational controls, operational controls, controls for personnel management, review controls or monitoring controls, and controls for facilities and equipment.

Organizational Controls

Organizational controls establish statements of purpose, authority, and responsibility for each division in the company. These statements include such controls as authorized range of activities and reporting responsibilities. A firm's organizational structure—such as separate departments for financial management, production, marketing, engineering, and so on—identifies the operational and informational relationships and decision authority among components. The primary organizational control is the adequate separation of duties.

Operational Controls

Operational controls include activities such as planning, budgeting, documentation, and controls for the accounting and information systems. Transaction controls are critical. An organization should have a transaction control system that provides reasonable assurance that all transactions are authorized, complete, accurate, and timely.

Controls for Personnel Management

Hiring and other human resource policies affect adherence to internal controls. Competent and trustworthy employees, combined with timely and effective training, minimize the corrective need of internal control. Part of the firm's control procedures may relate to methods used for hiring, evaluating, and training employees.

Recruitment and Selection of Suitable Personnel

Businesses generally define qualifications for personnel in various positions. Staff is recruited, screened, and hired based on these qualifications, such as educational requirements, work experience, and professional certifications. Hiring practices may include reference and credit checks, security checks, and drug testing. Employers should also screen for conflicts of interest. Organizational structure, lines of authority, and job descriptions, while important, do not substitute for good employees. Personnel who are unsuitable to perform their assigned tasks can threaten even the best-designed internal control policies and procedures.

Orientation, Training, and Development

Even the most qualified and skilled employees require an orientation to the business's goals, objectives, policies, and procedures. Job orientation should be given immediately at the start of employment. Ongoing training and development is usually desirable, and, in some fields, is required by law or certification requirements. Most organizations recognize the importance of training and development to the overall success of the enterprise, and many provide or compensate employees for attending training sessions.

Supervision

Most employees require some degree of supervision. Supervisory responsibilities include observation of the work process and examination of the work product. The amount of supervision each employee or position requires varies depending on the abilities and experience of the employee and the complexity of the work.

Bonding and Personnel Practices

Personnel controls often include the bonding of those having custody of money and other assets. Rotation of duties and rotation of shifts can be an important control, especially for personnel with financial responsibilities. Requiring that each employee takes occasional vacation time is another means of helping ensure that one individual has not compromised the controls. Having another employee handle the same tasks during an employee's vacation provides a check on the processes.

Review Controls or Monitoring Controls

Periodic reviews help firms assess the performance of individual employees and the achievement of corporate goals and objectives. In fact, monitoring (or reviewing) controls is one of the components of COSO's *Enterprise Risk Management—Integrated Framework*. Monitoring can be carried out on a formal, continuous basis in addition to periodic reviews and audits.

Most firms provide for regularly scheduled reviews for individual employees, usually conducted by the employee's supervisor. Employee reviews examine the employee's performance in relation to his or her goals and identify skills or functions in which the employee could improve. The employee review often sets goals and identifies methods for achieving them.

Most firms also provide for regular review of operations and projects. These review (or monitoring) controls might include any or all of the following:

- Internal audits carried out by employees working independently of accounting and other departments and charged with responsibility to assess financial, operational, and other aspects of the organization.
- Management reviews carried out by company managers in formal meetings.
- Audit committee reviews performed by a committee appointed by the board of directors to oversee audit operations. The audit committee prepares SEC-mandated reports for the proxy statement issued to investors, provides a point of contact between the board and independent auditors, and is generally responsible for the integrity of the company's financial statements and its compliance with laws and regulations.
- Activities of a disclosure committee chartered to ensure that the organization's reporting standards are in compliance with SOX and that all information released to shareholders and investors is complete and accurate. Disclosure committees may design controls relating to investment reporting, monitor the disclosure controls, review financial reports, and perform other related duties.

Any firm that issues public securities is required to have an external audit, which is an external review by an independent party. Many firms that do not issue public securities also provide for annual external audits.

Controls for Facilities and Equipment

Facilities and equipment represent the fixed assets of the corporation. Controls for maintaining suitable equipment and facility standards include such things as design, cleanliness, and repair and maintenance schedules. Controls for protecting fixed assets from theft or damage include security systems, fire and smoke alarms, locked doors, and affixing permanent identification tags on equipment to facilitate inventory and identify assets in the case of theft.

Inherent Limitations on Internal Controls

Certain human factors or exceptions may present inherent limitations to otherwise well-designed and well-supported control policies and procedures. The major ones are management override of controls and collusion between employees and between employees and outsiders. Other inherent weaknesses are errors, misunderstandings, mistakes in judgment, and the cost-benefit nature of controls.

Management Override

Management override can be a threat to any control system. If a well-designed control structure can be overridden at management's discretion, the resulting risk exposure can be the same as having no controls in place. Circumstances sometimes justify management override. However, the control environment can be maintained only if management overrides are monitored and limited. For example, a control may be set in place to automatically trigger an exception report any time there is a management override of a control procedure.

Conflicts of Interest

Employees' conflicts of interest pose a threat to any business. For example, a purchasing agent for a clothing retailer who has a financial interest in a clothing design and manufacturing company has a conflict of interest when deciding which supplier to use.

Documenting Control Policies and Procedures

Internal control policies and procedures need to be documented. Documentation serves a number of purposes, including use in training and for audits. At the most detailed level, written job descriptions outline the specific requirements of each job in the firm, including job qualifications, specific responsibilities, and reporting relationships.

The most common methods used to document control policies and procedures include written narratives accompanied by flowcharts that graphically depict a step-by-step process. Section 404 of SOX requires that publicly held companies document their internal controls.

Knowledge Check: Governance, Risk, and Compliance

The next questions are intended to help you check your understanding and recall of the material presented in this topic. They do not represent the type of questions that appear on the CMA exam.

Directions: Answer each question in the space provided. Correct answers and section references appear after the knowledge check questions.

1. Which of the following is **not** a type of risk?
   - a. Inherent risk
   - b. Detection risk
   - c. Safeguarding risk
   - d. Control risk

2. Which of the following is true of control risk?
   - a. Control risk is an assessment of the likelihood that misstatements exceeding an acceptable level will not be detected by internal controls.
   - b. Control risk is an assessment of the likelihood that misstatements exceeding an acceptable level will not be detected by an internal audit.
   - c. Control risk is dependent on detection risk.
   - d. Control risk is measured in combination with safeguarding risk to determine overall risk.

3. The primary authority over the internal audit is:
   - a. departmental managers.
   - b. senior management.
   - c. the external auditor.
   - d. the audit committee.

4. Internal controls are designed to provide reasonable assurance regarding which of the following?
   - I. Efficiency of operations
   - II. Reliability of financial reporting
   - III. Compliance with applicable laws and regulations
   - IV. Feasibility of project completion
   - a. I
   - b. II and III
   - c. I, II, and III
   - d. I, II, III, and IV

5. The audit committee can contain all of the following **except**:
   - a. the company president.
   - b. the chair of the board of directors.
   - c. a member of the board of directors who owns a separate business not related to the business of the company.
   - d. the president of the local chamber of commerce.

6. Which of the following are types of internal controls?
   I. Preventive
   II. Detective
   III. Corrective
   IV. Compensating
   - a. I
   - b. II and III
   - c. I, II, and III
   - d. I, II, III, and IV

7. Detective controls
   - a. serve as a backup for corrective controls.
   - b. are the procedures the internal auditor follows to detect flaws in the control process.
   - c. serve as a backup for preventive controls.
   - d. are the procedures the external auditor follows if fraud is suspected

8. Directive controls
   - a. serve as a backup for corrective controls.
   - b. relate to the override of controls by management.
   - c. serve as a backup for preventive controls.
   - d. are designed to create positive results.

9. Name the five components of the *Internal Control—Integrated Framework* established by COSO:
   - a. _____
   - b. _____
   - c. _____
   - d. _____
   - e. _____

10. Which of the following are required under the Foreign Corrupt Practices Act?
    I. A firm must design internal control procedures.
    II. A firm must have an internal audit department.

III. Transactions must be executed with management's authorization.

IV. Access to assets must be authorized.

- ☐ **a.** I and II
- ☐ **b.** III
- ☐ **c.** I, III, and IV
- ☐ **d.** I, II, III, and IV

Knowledge Check Answers: Governance, Risk, and Compliance

1. Which of the following is **not** a type of risk? [See *Types of Risk*.]
   - ☐ a. Inherent risk
   - ☐ b. Detection risk
   - ☒ c. Safeguarding risk
   - ☐ d. Control risk

2. Which of the following is true of control risk? [See *Types of Risk*.]
   - ☒ a. Control risk is an assessment of the likelihood that misstatements exceeding an acceptable level will not be detected by internal controls.
   - ☐ b. Control risk is an assessment of the likelihood that misstatements exceeding an acceptable level will not be detected by an internal audit.
   - ☐ c. Control risk is dependent on detection risk.
   - ☐ d. Control risk is measured in combination with safeguarding risk to determine overall risk.

3. The primary authority over the internal audit is: [See *Board of Directors and Audit Committee Responsibilities*.]
   - ☐ a. departmental managers.
   - ☐ b. senior management.
   - ☐ c. the external auditor.
   - ☒ d. the audit committee.

4. Internal controls are designed to provide reasonable assurance regarding which of the following? [See *Control Procedures*.]
   I. Efficiency of operations
   II. Reliability of financial reporting
   III. Compliance with applicable laws and regulations
   IV. Feasibility of project completion
   - ☐ a. I
   - ☐ b. II and III
   - ☒ c. I, II, and III
   - ☐ d. I, II, III, and IV

Section E, Topic 1—Governance, Risk, and Compliance

5. The audio committee can contain all of the following **except**: [See *Board of Directors and Audit Committee Responsibilities*.]
    - ☑ **a.** the company president.
    - ☐ **b.** the chair of the board of directors.
    - ☐ **c.** a member of the board of directors who owns a separate business not related to the business of the company.
    - ☐ **d.** the president of the local chamber of commerce.

6. Which of the following are types of internal controls? [See *Types of Internal Controls*.]
    I. Preventive
    II. Detective
    III. Corrective
    IV. Compensating
    - ☐ **a.** I
    - ☐ **b.** II and III
    - ☐ **c.** I, II, and III
    - ☑ **d.** I, II, III, and IV

7. Detective controls [See *Detective Controls*.]
    - ☐ **a.** serve as a backup for corrective controls.
    - ☐ **b.** are the procedures the internal auditor follows to detect flaws in the control process.
    - ☑ **c.** serve as a backup for preventive controls.
    - ☐ **d.** are the procedures the external auditor follows if fraud is suspected

8. Directive controls [See *Directive Controls*.]
    - ☐ **a.** serve as a backup for corrective controls.
    - ☐ **b.** relate to the override of controls by management.
    - ☐ **c.** serve as a backup for preventive controls.
    - ☑ **d.** are designed to create positive results.

9. Name the five components of the *Internal Control–Integrated Framework* established by COSO: [See *Design Controls to Address Risks*.]
    a. **Control environment**
    b. **Risk assessment**
    c. **Control activities**
    d. **Information and communication**
    e. **Monitoring**

10. Which of the following are required under the Foreign Corrupt Practices Act? [See *Foreign Corrupt Practices Act.*]

   I. A firm must design internal control procedures.

   II. A firm must have an internal audit department.

   III. Transactions must be executed with management's authorization.

   IV. Access to assets must be authorized.

   ☐ a. I and II
   ☐ b. III
   ☒ c. I, III, and IV
   ☐ d. I, II, III, and IV

TOPIC 2

Internal Auditing

THE PRIMARY PURPOSE OF AN internal audit is to appraise the design of, effectiveness of, and adherence to internal control policies and procedures and to assess the firm's quality of performance. The internal auditor ensures that any risk to the business is addressed and verifies that the firm's goals and objectives are met efficiently and effectively. The scope of internal auditing is broad and may include: the efficacy of operations; the reliability of financial reporting; deterring, detecting, and investigating fraud; safeguarding assets; and compliance with laws and regulations.

This topic discusses standards that apply to the internal audit function, management of the internal audit department, reporting and recommendations, and audit evidence. It also looks at the types of audits conducted by internal auditors.

> **READ** the Learning Outcome Statements (LOS) for this topic as found in Appendix A and then study the concepts and calculations presented here to be sure you understand the content you could be tested on in the CMA exam.

Responsibility and Authority of the Internal Audit Function

The internal audit function receives professional guidance from the Institute of Internal Auditors (IIA). Like the American Institute of Certified Public Accountants, the IIA has established standards for internal auditors. The IIA's standards fall into three categories: attribute standards, performance standards, and implementation standards. According to the organization's Web site (www.theiia.org), "The attribute standards address the characteristics of organizations and parties performing internal audit activities. The performance standards describe the nature of internal audit activities and provide quality criteria against which the performance of these services can be evaluated." The implementation standards provide more specific guidance on how particular attribute or performance standards should be applied within different types of engagements or activities. The implementation standards have been established for assurance and consulting activities.

Attribute Standards

The attribute standards provide guidance in these areas:

- Purpose, authority, and responsibility
- Independence and objectivity
- Proficiency and due professional care
- Quality assurance and improvement programs

Purpose, Authority, and Responsibility

The purpose, authority, and responsibility of the internal audit function should be defined in a formal charter consistent with IIA standards and signed by the board of directors.

Independence and Objectivity

To maintain organizational independence, the chief audit executive (CAE) should report to a level within the organization that allows the internal audit activity to fulfill its responsibilities without feeling biased toward one area or function of the organization. The internal audit activity should be free from interference in determining the scope of internal auditing, performing work, and communicating results. To ensure individual objectivity, internal auditors should maintain an impartial, unbiased attitude and avoid conflicts of interest. Internal auditors should not assess operations for which they had any responsibility during the past year. A person outside the internal audit activity should oversee any assurance engagements in functions over which the CAE has responsibility. Any impairments of independence or objectivity affecting internal auditors should be reported to appropriate parties.

Proficiency and Due Professional Care

Each internal auditor should possess the knowledge, skills, and other competencies necessary to his or her individual responsibilities. Collectively, the internal audit function should possess all the proficiencies required by its responsibilities. The internal auditor should be able to identify the indicators of fraud but need not have the same level of expertise of someone whose primary responsibility is detecting and investigating fraud. All internal auditors need some knowledge of information technology, but not all need to have the same expertise as an auditor who specializes in information technology.

Internal auditors need not be infallible, but they should exercise the care and skill of a "reasonably prudent and competent internal auditor." This includes considering the use of computers and data analysis when performing audits.

Internal auditors should enhance proficiency through continuing professional development.

Quality Assurance and Improvement Programs

A quality assurance and improvement program should cover all aspects of the internal audit activity and should be subject to continuous internal monitoring as well as periodic internal and external quality assessments. The program should help the internal auditing activity add value and improve the organization's operations in conformity with the IIA's standards and the code of ethics. The CAE should be responsible for developing and maintaining the program and for communicating results of external assessments of the program to the board.

Performance Standards

The IIA performance standards provide descriptions of activities that internal auditing should perform and indicate appropriate levels of quality. The next summary touches on the main points in the performance standards.

Managing the Internal Audit Activity

The CAE's role is to manage the internal audit activity effectively, ensuring that it adds value to the organization. The responsibilities of this role include:

- Establishing risk-based plans
- Communicating plans to senior management and the board
- Ensuring that sufficient resources are available to carry out the plans
- Establishing policies and procedures to guide audit activity
- Coordinating activities and sharing information
- Reporting relevant information periodically to senior management and the board
- Defining the nature of work

The internal audit should evaluate and contribute to the improvement of risk management, control, and governance using a systematic and disciplined approach. Assessing governance and recommending improvements involves promoting ethics and values within the organization as well as ensuring performance management, communicating risk and control information throughout the organization, and coordinating and sharing information among stakeholders. The objectives of the engagement should be consistent with the overall goals of the organization.

Engagement Planning

When planning an engagement, the internal auditor should consider:

- The objectives and performance controls of the activity.
- Significant risks to the activity and means of keeping the risk level acceptable.
- Adequacy and effectiveness of the activity's risk management and control systems compared with a relevant model.
- Opportunities to improve the activity's risk management and controls.

Objectives should be developed for each engagement, and the scope should be sufficient to satisfy the objectives. Consultant engagements that develop during an assurance engagement should be based on a written understanding of objectives, scope, and so on, and the results should be communicated in accordance with consulting standards. Engagement with parties outside the organization should also be based on a written understanding.

Performing the Engagement

Internal auditors should identify, analyze, evaluate, and record sufficient information to achieve the objectives of the engagement. The CAE should control access to the records and develop retention requirements and policies to govern custody.

Communicating Results

Internal auditors should communicate the results of the engagement, including objectives and scope, as well as conclusions, recommendations, and action plans.

Monitoring Progress

The senior audit executive should develop a follow-up process to ensure that management implements the recommendations of the audit report or accepts the risks of not taking actions.

Resolution of Management's Acceptance of Risks

Assurance engagements conclude with the development of a residual risk profile for the organization. If the CAE believes that senior management has accepted an unacceptably high level of risk for the organization's risk appetite, then the CAE and senior management should report the matter to the board.

Management of the Internal Auditing Department

The director of internal auditing should manage the auditing department, including establishing the next controls:

- Statement of purpose, authority, and responsibility for the internal auditing department
- Plans to carry out the department's responsibilities
- Written policies and procedures to guide the audit staff
- Program for selecting and developing the human resources of the audit department
- Coordination of internal and external audit efforts
- A quality assurance program to evaluate the operation of the internal auditing department

Reporting Audit Results

Potential audiences for the audit report include divisional and operational managers as well as top management and the board of directors. The internal auditor should inform management of all problems. Because of the possible use of the internal audit report by external auditors, legal counsel may need to be consulted before highly sensitive information is included in a written audit report. According to IIA Standard 2440.A2:

> If not otherwise mandated by legal, statutory, or regulatory requirements, prior to releasing results to parties outside the organization, the chief audit executive should:
> - assess the potential risk to the organization,
> - consult with senior management and/or legal counsel as appropriate, and
> - control dissemination by restricting the use of the results.

Such discussions minimize misunderstandings.

The auditor's report identifies conditions as findings, or issues to address or recognize. One audit report may include several specific findings, and each finding, which may be positive or negative, should be documented on a separate summary findings sheet. Negative findings are called exceptions. Findings are performance or actions as measured against the firm's policies, procedures, standards, or external laws and regulations and against risks such as inadequate safeguarding of company assets.

Each summary findings sheet should report the condition and the policy, legal criteria, or expectation regarding the finding. The auditor's report should include conclusions regarding the effect of the condition and the cause of the condition. The auditor should also provide recommendations that offer alternatives relative to the specific control objective for each finding. A recommendation does not necessarily represent a solution for the condition.

Recommendations should:

- Identify the internal control breakdown and the associated risks involved.
- Identify what needs to be achieved by the change and leave the details of strategy and tactics to management.
- Be stated clearly and succinctly but should be detailed enough to require no further explanation.
- Be fully supported by evidence.
- Be action-oriented and achievable, with reasonable expenditures, deadlines, staffing, and so on, in relation to the problem addressed.

Types of Recommendations

The auditor can make four types of recommendations:

1. **Make no changes.** If the audit determines that the activities investigated do not represent any significant problems—such as noncompliance with regulations, failure to safeguard assets, insufficient control of transactions, and so on—the auditor will recommend no change. It is also possible that recommending change is not the most effective way to achieve a desired result in the organization. In such cases, the auditor may seek an exception to the standard and instead submit an analysis to management.

2. **Modify internal control policies and/or procedures** If the auditor does uncover problems, the audit report should recommend changes in the areas of risk or poor performance.
3. **Add insurance for potential risks discovered during the audit.** Rather than suggesting new policies or procedures to address a potential risk, the auditor may suggest insuring against the liability involved. The auditor must be certain that insurance is an appropriate as well as cost-effective measure. Whether to eliminate a potential liability or insure against its occurrence may involve ethical as well as practical considerations, depending on the nature of the risk.
4. **Adjust the required rate of return on an activity to match the associated risk.** In assessing the nature of potential risks in light of the organization's attitudes and risk appetite, the auditor may report that one of the organization's activities involves more potential risk than is justified by its current projected return.

General and Specific Findings

An internal auditor may report a number of findings to management. General findings may include such items as inadequate control procedures, lack of adherence to control procedures (e.g., disorganized records), inadequate safeguarding of assets, inefficient allocation of resources, and so on. The auditor can provide a service by prioritizing the various risks in terms of their potential costs.

Each general finding should be supported by specific findings and backed up by solid evidence. For example, an internal auditor conducting a compliance audit might provide managers with a report indicating which employees failed to have their time cards up to date. An internal auditor conducting an audit of the physical security of assets might report anyone whose sensitive files were found unlocked during an after-hours check. A software audit might result in a report of computers on which unlicensed software had been loaded.

Audit Evidence

Audit evidence can take a number of forms. Evidence gathered by auditors is called **primary evidence** and might be gathered by observation, surveys, interviews, inspection of documents (canceled checks to verify disbursements, time cards to verify hours worked, etc.), or other means. Primary evidence is the least open to question from the viewpoint of the auditor who gathered it. Evidence gathered and submitted by the subject of the audit, or by third parties, constitutes **secondary evidence**. Auditors will assign credibility to this evidence according to their assessment of the internal controls relevant to it. The weaker the controls, the more corroborating evidence the auditors will require.

Evidence can also be considered according to legal categories. Primary evidence is direct; secondary evidence from the subject of the audit is hearsay. Checks, stock certificates, time cards, and the like are documentary evidence, useful in corroborating direct testimony or hearsay. Expert opinion can be used in audits as in courtrooms. An internal auditor is not expected to be an ultimate expert in all relevant matters. Computer programmers may, for example, be useful in reviewing computer systems controls. **Circumstantial evidence** is not direct, hearsay, or opinion. Rather, it is a set of conditions—circumstances—that make one suspect the existence of a particular problem. The suspected problem must be verified by harder evidence.

Analytical evidence includes such things as financial ratios and vertical and horizontal financial statement analysis. This type of evidence can be useful in testing the success of financial operations in supporting corporate objectives. Analysis can include period-to-period comparisons of results (this quarter against last quarter or the same quarter of one or more previous years). Budgets can be compared to forecasts. The organization's performance—in terms of profits, revenues, sales, margins, and so on—can be compared to industry averages. Financial ratios are used by analysts and investors, as well as financial auditors, to assess a company's performance and prospects.

Types of Audits Conducted by Internal Auditors

Internal audits are conducted for a number of reasons, including financial control, assurance of compliance with regulations, and assessment of internal control policies and procedures. An internal auditor could conduct one or more of several types of audits: financial, operational, performance, electronic data processing, contract, compliance, and special investigations (such as fraud). A data processing audit might include running special mapping software that scans computer systems searching for malicious, hidden code designed to steal data, crash the computer, or provide access to outsiders. Internal auditors have concentrated less on financial audits and more on operational audits. Over half of the average internal auditor's time is spent on operational audits. The compliance audit is another key type of audit.

Financial Audit

A **financial audit** is an audit of the firm's financial statements. The objective is to determine whether the overall financial statements fairly represent the firm's operations and financial condition. The internal auditor may conduct an audit of financial reports for a department or a segment of a department. The audience for a financial audit is the board of directors and senior management. The direction of a financial audit conducted by an internal auditor is forward-looking, in contrast to the external audit, which is backward-looking.

When designing a financial audit, the auditor assesses the adequacy of internal controls as they relate to financial activities. The nature, timing, and extent of substantive testing will depend on the auditor's assessment of the amount of control risk and the credibility of assertions regarding the company's transactions. Substantive tests in the financial audit might focus on the details of account balances, analytical procedures, transactions, and the physical security of assets, among other matters.

Operational Audit

An **operational audit** is a nonfinancial audit that is intended to evaluate the effectiveness and efficiency of the organization or one of its divisions, departments, or processes. Businesses often combine financial and operational audits.

The operational audit is an organized search for improvements in efficiency and effectiveness of operations and often takes on the form of constructive criticism. It is a tool for regularly and systematically appraising the effectiveness of the firm against organizational and industry standards, organizational goals and objectives, and applicable laws and regulations. The objectives of this type of audit are to ensure the board of directors and senior management that the organization's goals and objectives are being met and to identify conditions that can be improved. In an operational audit, the auditor has the responsibility of discovering operating problems, informing the board of directors and management of the problems, and recommending realistic courses of action for resolving the problems.

Compliance Audit

During a **compliance audit**, the auditor determines whether the firm has complied with applicable laws and regulations as well as professional or industry standards or contractual responsibilities. A compliance audit can be part of a financial or operational audit or undertaken separately. Compliance audits can be initiated by management or may be required by law or regulation.

The auditor first needs to determine whether management has a system in place for identifying applicable policies, procedures, standards, laws, and regulations. Then the auditor evaluates whether controls are being applied and followed properly. This testing should lead to conclusions as to whether the firm is in compliance.

Internal Audit Assistance Provided to Management

To assist management, the internal audit function provides analyses, appraisals, recommendations, counsel, and information concerning activities reviewed.

The organization's operating management, such as department heads or supervisors, is accountable for the effectiveness and efficiency of operations. Audit reports support operating management in this regard by identifying areas needing improvement and stimulating action in the appropriate direction. In addition, the results of an internal audit may provide objective support to the operations manager for issues that will require the support of upper management to address and improve. An audit may bring to a manager's attention activities or practices of which he or she was not aware—for example, the shipping manager needing to recheck all the sales orders because of repeated inaccuracies by sales staff. Expectations of the internal audit, as well as lessons learned from previous internal audits, ultimately may serve to promote more disciplined operations.

Audit reports serve to identify for the board of directors and senior management the changing level and types of risks that management needs to address. Due to the nature or scope of the audit or the independence and objectivity of the internal auditor, an internal audit report can provide senior management with details about operations as well as controls that are not included in other reports.

Knowledge Check: Internal Auditing

The next questions are intended to help you check your understanding and recall of the material presented in this topic. They do not represent the type of questions that appear on the CMA exam.

Directions: Answer each question in the space provided. Correct answers and section references appear after the knowledge check questions.

1. Which of the following are categories of standards for internal auditing?
    - I. Attribute
    - II. Characteristic
    - III. Performance
    - IV. Implementation
    - ☐ a. I and III
    - ☐ b. II and IV
    - ☐ c. I, III, and IV
    - ☐ d. I, II, III, and IV

2. A compliance audit in a manufacturing firm could verify which of the following?
    - ☐ a. Compliance with GAAP
    - ☐ b. Compliance with employment laws
    - ☐ c. Compliance with worker safety and health laws
    - ☐ d. All of the above

3. Which of the following would **not** be a type of recommendation an internal auditor would make?
    - ☐ a. Add a procedure for ensuring that transactions cannot be placed by unauthorized personnel.
    - ☐ b. Controls should be implemented to ensure that unauthorized personnel cannot access payroll files.
    - ☐ c. Controls should be implemented that ensure increasing compensation for production managers.
    - ☐ d. Add a procedure for ensuring that key files cannot be accidentally deleted from the computer system.

4. The auditor can make four types of recommendations. Complete the next list.
    - a. Make no changes.
    - b. Modify internal control policies and/or procedures.

c. _____.
d. _____.

5. Which of the following is **not** something that would be done by the chief audit executive prior to releasing results about an audit?

    ☐ a. Provide a summary report to the external auditors.
    ☐ b. Assess the potential risk to the organization.
    ☐ c. Control dissemination by restricting the use of the results.
    ☐ d. Consult with senior management and/or legal counsel as appropriate.

Knowledge Check Answers: Internal Auditing

1. Which of the following are categories of standards for internal auditing? [See *Responsibility and Authority of the Internal Audit Function*.]
   I. Attribute
   II. Characteristic
   III. Performance
   IV. Implementation
   - ☐ a. I and III
   - ☐ b. II and IV
   - ☑ c. I, III, and IV
   - ☐ d. I, II, III, and IV

2. A compliance audit in a manufacturing firm could verify which of the following? [See *Compliance Audit*.]
   - ☐ a. Compliance with GAAP
   - ☐ b. Compliance with employment laws
   - ☐ c. Compliance with worker safety and health laws
   - ☑ d. All of the above

3. Which of the following would **not** be a type of recommendation an internal auditor would make? [See *Types of Recommendations*.]
   - ☐ a. Add a procedure for ensuring that transactions cannot be placed by unauthorized personnel.
   - ☐ b. Controls should be implemented to ensure that unauthorized personnel cannot access payroll files.
   - ☑ c. Controls should be implemented that ensure increasing compensation for production managers.
   - ☐ d. Add a procedure for ensuring that key files cannot be accidentally deleted from the computer system.

4. The auditor can make four types of recommendations. Complete the next list. [See *Types of Recommendations*.]
   a. Make no changes.
   b. Modify internal control policies and/or procedures.
   c. Add insurance for potential risks discovered during the audit.
   d. Adjust the required rate of return on an activity to match the associated risk.

5. Which of the following is **not** something that would be done by the chief audit executive prior to releasing results about an audit? [**See *Reporting Audit Results.***]
   - ☑ a. Provide a summary report to the external auditors.
   - ☐ b. Assess the potential risk to the organization.
   - ☐ c. Control dissemination by restricting the use of the results.
   - ☐ d. Consult with senior management and/or legal counsel as appropriate.

TOPIC 3

Systems Controls and Security Measures

INFORMATION IS A KEY ASSET of any company, and internal controls are imperative for the protection of this asset. Information stored on a computer system is subject to loss or inaccuracy resulting from:

- Computer or network crashes
- Natural disaster or theft
- Human error in input or application
- Manipulation of input data
- Intentional alteration of records or programs
- Sabotage
- Software bugs
- Computer viruses and worms
- Trojan horse programs and other computer system threats

A company must consider all of these very real risks in establishing internal controls to prevent or minimize losses of sensitive information assets. Systems controls enhance the accuracy, validity, safety, security, and adaptability of systems input, processing, output, and storage functions.

This topic deals with the risks associated with information systems and the controls that companies can put in place to reduce these risks, including organizational controls, personnel policies, and systems development controls. It describes some of the network, hardware, and facility controls organizations put in place, strategies used to help prevent loss of business information and ensure operations in case of a system failure, and accounting controls that are incorporated into computer systems and manual processes. Finally, the topic looks at the use of flowcharting to assess controls and identify gaps.

> **READ** the Learning Outcome Statements (LOS) for this topic as found in Appendix A and then study the concepts and calculations presented here to be sure you understand the content you could be tested on in the CMA exam.

General Information Systems Controls

Information systems are usually divided into two functions: financial accounting and operating information systems.

1. **Financial accounting information systems** generate an organization's financial statements, budgets, and cost reports for managers.
2. **Operating information systems** gather information relating to various operational activities and generate reports for managers.

Having internal controls to maintain the reliability and integrity of the information system is critical to management's decision-making processes. Protecting the information system and the information in its databases is essential for accurate and reliable financial reports as well as for the operating reports that management uses to make decisions.

Information system controls consist of general and application controls. **General controls**, sometimes called pervasive controls, are controls related to the computer, technology, or information technology (IT) function. They include:

- Organizational, personnel, and operations controls
- Systems development controls
- Network, hardware, and facility controls
- Backup and disaster recovery controls
- Accounting control

General systems controls include a plan for the organization of the information system and the methods and procedures that apply to the systems operations in a business. General controls, as a basis for effective application controls, are vital in the protection of information systems.

Application controls consist of input, process, and output controls. These controls are covered in greater detail in the discussion of accounting controls, later in this topic. As with other controls, the control environment plays a vital role in the effectiveness of information systems controls. The actions that management and the board of directors take regarding oversight of systems controls and involvement with key decisions regarding the information systems provide clear signals to the rest of the company.

Risks Associated with Information Systems

Computers and networks present risks that are specific to their nature within the company's operations:

- There is less visibility of the audit trail, with the reduction or elimination of source documents and records that auditors can use to trace accounting information. Other controls must be put into place to replace the traditional ability to compare output information with hard copy data.
- Hardware or software may malfunction.
- Human involvement is reduced and, along with it, the possibility that human intervention could identify mistakes that the software may not be designed to catch.

- Systematic errors may occur because of flaws in the program design.
- Unauthorized users may accidentally alter or delete data.
- Data can be lost or stolen, which could result in costly business interruptions or errors. Stolen personal information can create substantial public relations and financial risks for a company.
- Systems may be damaged by malicious code.
- Segregation of duties may be reduced, so that functions that traditionally were separated as a control are made more accessible.
- There may be a lack of traditional authorization when transactions are initiated automatically.
- The risk of information loss and fraud should be of great concern to organizations. Threats to an information system can occur both internally and externally. Internal threats to an information system can come from systems personnel including computer maintenance persons, programmers, computer operators, computer and information systems administrative personnel, and data control clerks. External threats to an information system can come from intruders. Losses can occur from input manipulation, program alteration, direct file alteration, data theft, and sabotage.
- Input manipulation requires the least amount of technical skill and is the most common threat in practice. Common input manipulation examples are hacking into a Web site to steal credit card numbers or data processing clerks altering supporting documents and entering inaccurate information into the computer system.
- Program alteration requires programming skills and knowledge and may be the least common method used to commit computer fraud. Program alterations can occur by using trapdoors to enter a computer program while bypassing its normal security systems. For example, a programmer could make unauthorized program changes to divert monies to accounts that he or she created. Companies with good internal control systems can prevent this type of fraud by carefully reviewing, testing, approving, and logging all program changes before they are implemented.
- In some cases, individuals find ways to bypass the normal process for inputting data into computer programs. An example of direct file alteration is when an employee uses special software tools to modify files or databases directly. Direct file alteration is easily prevented by limiting access and encrypting the files and databases.
- Data theft fraud is difficult to detect because it is often performed by trusted employees who have routine access to data. Further, in highly competitive industries, quantitative and qualitative information about competitors is constantly being sought.
- Sabotage is a deliberate action aimed at weakening an organization through subversion, obstruction, disruption, or destruction. Sabotage often is carried out by disgruntled or recently fired employees to interrupt operations and destroy software and electronic files.
- Phishing communications may be received and acted on, which can cause damage to the company (and/or its employees) ranging from denial of access to e-mail to substantial financial loss. Phishing is the act of attempting to acquire sensitive information such as user names, passwords, credit card details,

and/or money by pretending to be a trustworthy entity in an electronic communication. Communications purporting to be from popular social Web sites, banks, the government (i.e., the Internal Revenue Service), or even the company's IT administrators are common ways phishers lure recipients with their communications. Phishing communications often direct users to enter details at a fake Web site whose look and feel is almost identical to the legitimate one and that contains links to Web sites that are infected with malware (software that is used to disrupt computer operations or gain access to the computer system).

Organization Controls and Personnel Policies

Some general information systems controls include personnel policies that apply to the structuring of duties and use of systems.

Segregation of Duties and Functions

Segregation of duties and functions in IT begins with the separation of the IT function from the rest of the organization. The head of IT or chief information officer should report to the firm's chief executive officer. IT belongs to the entire organization, not to any one function.

There should also be a separation of systems development, operations, and technical support within the IT function. Systems development covers the application programmers and analysts—those responsible for application software development or selection. IT operations include computer operators, the input/output function, and the library function. Technical support includes the network administrator, the database administrator, the security administrator, and the systems programmers. Systems programmers are responsible for the systems programs. Systems programs include the operating system, the library system, and systems utilities. Systems utilities are housekeeping programs for common functions, such as sorts, merges, compilers, and translators.

Controls for information systems should clearly define the responsibilities associated with the accounting and operating subsystems and ensure that these responsibilities are appropriately segregated. Authorizations for all transactions should be outside IT. IT's role is the processing, storage, and dissemination of information and data. The information and data belong to the users only. For example, authorization for issuance of paychecks should be initiated within the accounting or payroll department, not by data processing personnel.

Any changes made to the master file or transaction files should be authorized by the appropriate accounting person before they are implemented. Many firms implement control policies that require change request forms that document information about the origin of the change, including the date and a supervisor's approval. Some systems may provide a log of file request changes.

Controls for segregation of duties should include separation of responsibilities within the information processing department. For example, employees involved in the design, development, and maintenance of the information system should not be involved in day-to-day processing of transactions. Conversely, employees doing data entry should not be provided with access to program documentation or source code. The database is the responsibility of the database administrator. The network administrator is responsible for all data communication hardware and software and usage. The security administrator is responsible for the assignment and control of user access.

Each application should include functions for tracking program changes and for controlling access to the production version of the application. The controls should also include a supervisory review of program maintenance and revisions.

Vacation Rule

Many fraud schemes require constant action by the perpetrator, who juggles (or laps) accounts to keep the fraud from being detected. For this reason, many firms require personnel in certain positions to take vacation for a certain length of time to help detect this or similar types of fraudulent activity.

Computer Access Controls

Only approved users should be allowed to access systems. Administrators can control the rights of individual users as well as their access to information within the system. System usage can be tracked by time of day, duration of access, and location of access. This tracking provides administrators with information regarding unusual access or usage of the system.

Systems Development Controls

Systems development controls begin with an appropriate set of systems development standards that cover the various stages of the systems development life cycle, which include analysis, design, implementation, and maintenance.

Analysis

The purpose of analysis is twofold: to understand the system and to develop appropriate design specifications. Design consists of general design (gross or conceptual design) and detailed design (physical design). Detailed design can involve either software selection or software development. Software selection involves purchasing off-the-shelf software and using it as is or modifying it to suit the needs of the organization. Software development consists of design specifications, prototyping, and programming. Implementation consists of quality assurance, pilot (beta) and parallel testing, conversion, and user acceptance.

A firm planning to purchase or develop a large computer system usually assembles a team that oversees the design, development (or selection), and implementation of the new system. This team should be made up of employees from the information systems department as well as others, including managers and end users of the system.

In support of segregation of duties, an auditor assigned to direct the development, installation, and testing of a new information system should be excluded from the team that audits the accounting system and related functional areas.

Design

The system specifications must be documented in detail before development begins. Team members should study the functionality of the current system, identify needs not met by the current system, and identify other features the new system must or should have. Having personnel from different areas of the company on the team helps ensure that the new system design incorporates usability, appropriate reporting capabilities, and internal controls.

Prototype

Making changes to a system or program that is near completion is costly. Therefore, most development projects include the creation of a prototype that shows the interface design and general features. Changes usually are expected during the prototype stage.

Programming/Development

In the development phase, control policies should ensure that no individual programmer or systems analyst is responsible for the design or development of the complete information system. The design, development, and implementation of a new computer system program should be subject to strict controls that will ensure system reliability and data integrity.

Quality Assurance

A quality assurance program must test the new system with realistic data to ensure that it functions as expected and is compatible with existing programs and hardware.

Prior to testing the entire system, modular testing is performed. **Modular testing** is the testing of individual modules of the system to see that they are functioning properly.

End user testing of the system often includes both pilot testing and parallel testing. **Pilot testing**, also called beta testing, is the initial testing of the system by a select group while most of the company continues to use the old software. Pilot testing is conducted at the stage at which the programming is completed and the system is largely is ready for production. Testing by end users is aimed at identifying both system bugs and usability issues. **Parallel testing** involves inputting and processing identical information on both the old and new systems and comparing the output.

After successful testing, user acceptance should be documented by appropriate user management sign-offs.

Implementation

Once the system has been tested, accepted, and approved for release, the programming staff will provide the system files and documentation to the system administrator for release (with data converted from the old system).

Maintenance

System maintenance involves monitoring the system over time to make sure performance is maintained at the desired level. Version control software tracks all changes and maintenance to the program. System maintenance and upgrades usually are scheduled for off-peak hours.

Network, Hardware, and Facility Controls

To protect the information on a system, controls must be in place to protect the hardware and the facility that houses it.

Facility and Hardware Controls

Protecting systems and information assets begins with controlling access to the building. Within the building, the data center should be in a location away from public spaces. Access should be granted only to specifically authorized personnel. Many data centers use individual keycodes or biometrics to control entrance to the facility. In addition to protection from unauthorized entry, computer equipment must also be protected from environmental threats, such as fire and floods, and from human sabotage or attack. Environmental controls, including air conditioning and humidity control, are also required.

Computer equipment must be protected from power surges and outages through the use of surge protectors and backup power supplies. The system and its supporting network should be designed to handle periods of peak volume. Additional protection with redundant components should be put in place so the system can switch to a backup unit in the event of hardware failure.

Finally, the controls must extend to the individual users. Software controls can be implemented to require users to have strong passwords and change them frequently. However, users must take responsibility for securing their equipment and the information on it. This is especially important with the growing use of laptops, tablets, and smart phones.

Network Controls

The objective of a network is to enable authorized employees to access and work with the firm's data and programs. However, without well-designed and strictly enforced control policies and procedures, unauthorized people both within and outside the company may access and alter critical information.

Even the smallest organizations are likely to use **local area networks** (LANs), either wired or wireless, to share data, applications, and other network resources.

Larger organizations may implement a **wide area network** (WAN), a private network connecting multiple LANs over a broad geographic area. Many organizations also use virtual private networks (VPNs) that permit secure communications over public or shared network facilities, including the Internet.

The Internet has introduced risks to computer systems that do not exist on private networks. Among the threats is a greatly increased risk of unauthorized access, as the number of hacks has grown and hackers have become more sophisticated in their attacks. Internet presence also exposes systems to "malware"—including virus, worms, spyware, spam, and Trojan horses.

Companies must use a variety of controls to protect their systems and data, beginning, at the most basic, with passwords. Software-based access controls allow the system administrators to manage access privileges. An additional step many firms take is to encrypt data so that unauthorized users who have been able to bypass first-level controls are not able to read, change, add to, or remove the data.

Data Encryption and Transmission

Data Encryption

Data encryption converts data from an easily read local language into a code that can be read only by those with the correct decryption key. The data are encoded during the input or transmission stage, then decrypted at output by the person authorized to receive them. Other controls designed to reduce the risk of interception and to detect errors or alterations in data transmissions include routing verification and message acknowledgment.

Routing Verification

Routing verification procedures add assurance that transactions are routed to the correct computer address. A transaction transmitted over a network contains a header label identifying its destination. When the transaction is received, the sending system verifies that the identity of the receiving computer matches the transaction's destination code. Routing verification is assisted by dual transmissions and echo checks. An echo check is a verification by the receiving node that what the sending node sent is in fact what was received.

Message Acknowledgment

Message acknowledgment procedures require a trailer message that the receiving computer can use to verify that the entire transmission was received. The receiving computer signals the sending computer regarding the successful completion of the transmission. If the receiving computer detects an error, data are retransmitted.

Virus Protection and Firewalls

Network information needs to be protected from both corruption and intruders. Antivirus software scans files to detect viruses and other malicious code. Many companies have policies that prohibit employees from installing any programs not approved by the information systems department.

A **firewall**—a combination of hardware and software—is used to help prevent unauthorized access from the Internet. Within the company network, firewalls may be used to prevent unauthorized access to specific systems, such as the payroll or personnel. Multiple firewalls are recommended in order to improve security.

A number of different controls or control alerts can be contained within a firewall system. The firewall may include an automated disconnect if a user enters a specified number of wrong passwords. Change control software provides an audit trail showing the sources of all changes made to files. And the network or firewall software may produce a network control log that lists all transmissions to or from a computer. This log can be useful for identifying the source of errors or attempts at unauthorized access.

Intrusion Detection System

If someone gains unauthorized access to a company's network, intrusion detection systems analyze network activity for aberrant or unauthorized activity and keep a centralized security event log that includes event logs from servers and workstations and provides alerts to security breaches. Event logs also can be used to detect misuse from internal sources.

Business Continuity Planning

Business continuity planning (BCP) is a strategy that looks to identify an organization's exposure to internal and external threats and bring together its critical resources and assets in order to protect those resources, and ensure continuing operations and effective recovery, in the event of some significant adverse event or disaster.

As part of the BCP process and the development of a **business continuity plan**, organizations implement certain control policies and procedures that are essential to the prevention of loss of critical business information and that enable the organization to continue operations in typical fashion in the face of a major system failure or facility destruction. Two levels of policies and procedures must be established to protect against these eventualities: data backup policies and procedures and disaster recovery policies and procedures.

Data Backup Policies and Procedures

Backup policies and procedures are instituted to ensure that data that are lost due to malware, natural disasters, hardware failures, theft, deletions, and software malfunctions can be recovered. Most firms institute procedures for backing up all files on the network daily, during slow processing times. Backup is normally achieved by copying files to tape or other offline media that may be kept in the data processing center or stored off-site. Off-site storage should be considered mandatory, because data can be recovered in the event of a disaster that affects the data center. Backup files also can be electronically transferred to off-site locations. This is called electronic vaulting.

Many firms institute a procedure called the grandfather-father-son (GFS) method. With this method, the most recent three generations (e. g., days) of backup files are secured at all times. If data are lost or altered, they may be retrieved from the most recent "clean" backup file.

Some firms that employ a master file and transaction files institute the checkpoint procedure, which runs at intervals throughout the day and facilitates recovery from a system failure. Using this procedure, the network system temporarily does not accept new transactions while it finishes updating procedures for transactions entered since the last checkpoint and then generates a backup copy of all data values and other information. Should a system failure occur, the system can be restarted by reading in the last checkpoint from the backup.

The control policies also should provide for backup of system configurations. Significant time may be lost before backup files can be recovered from storage tapes if a network first must be reformatted and reconfigured to its previous status.

Disaster Recovery Policies and Procedures

Disaster recovery policies and procedures—also often referred to as business continuance plans—are designed to enable the firm to carry on business in the event that an emergency, such as a natural disaster, disrupts normal business functioning. A company's business continuance or disaster recovery plan should define the roles of all members of the business continuance team, appointing both a primary leader and an alternate leader for the process.

The plan should specify backup sites for alternate computer processing. This site may be another location owned by the firm or may be owned by another organization.

A "hot site" is a location that includes a system configured like the firm's production system. Hot sites are often called duplex systems. Duplex systems run simultaneously with the regular system, and a failure in the main system can trigger an automatic switchover to the backup. A "warm site" is a backup site that has hardware and software available and can be made operational within a short timeframe. A "cold site" provides a location where the company can install equipment and personnel on fairly short notice and begin operations using backup files. If a cold site is the designated recovery site, additional arrangements must be in place for obtaining computer equipment matching the lost system's configuration requirements.

The business continuance/disaster recovery plan should be tested, documented, reviewed regularly, and updated as required. All relevant personnel must be thoroughly trained in the procedures.

Accounting Controls

The accounting system should contain controls that readily confirm or question the reliability of recorded data. Types of controls that can be implemented in an accounting system include those listed next.

Batch totals. The input preparer reports the total amount in the batch; this amount is also listed on the cover sheet of the group of transaction documents. This number can be the total number of records or the total dollar value of all the transactions being entered.

Control accounts. This type of control allows only authorized personnel into particular accounts on the system. For example, a payroll professional may not have access to accounts that do not involve payroll.

Voiding/cancellation. This type of control involves proper voiding or cancellation of invoices and supporting documents after payment.

Feedback controls. Feedback controls provide information about system performance, especially information selected to see that the system, or model, is performing as intended. Feedback can be delivered in different ways depending on the nature of the organization and the system; it may consist of written or oral reports or it may be automated. To allow effective corrective action, feedback information must be delivered quickly (depending on the problem's size, severity, and difficulty of correction). It is essentially diagnostic, and any amelioration occurs after problems arise and then are discovered, reported, and analyzed. In a sense, all monitoring controls are feedback controls, because they are designed to collect, analyze, and report data that can be used to determine the success of all other controls.

Feedforward and preventive controls. Feedforward controls are based on predictions about future events. They are less common and more complicated to manage than feedback controls. Feedforward controls based on current actions are predictions of future events with some degree of probability. Because feedforward controls are based on predictions of future occurrences, they may be designed to prevent anticipated problems. Setting up an off-site location ready for use in an emergency is an example of feedforward, preventive controls.

Application and Transaction Controls

Application and transaction controls are designed to prevent, detect, and correct errors and irregularities in transactions that are processed by accounting systems. Application controls can be divided into three categories: input controls, processing controls, and output controls. The purpose of application controls is to provide reasonable assurance that all processing is authorized, complete, and timely.

Input Controls

Input controls are designed to provide a system of checks and balances over the input of data or transactions into the system. Input controls are designed to prevent or detect errors in the time information is data entered into the computer system. Often this involves conversion of transaction data into a machine-readable format. The capability of these control procedures to correct errors early helps ensure accuracy and reliability of reporting data.

Among the manual methods used to increase the accuracy of input are:

- Batch controls, which include a batch number, record count, control totals, and a hash total. (A hash total is a total of nonsignificant numbers, such as customer numbers and part numbers, that is used to detect deletions or insertions in a batch.)
- Approval mechanisms.
- Dual observation, to review data before input.
- Supervisory procedure to confirm accuracy of data gathered by the employee before input.

Well-designed source documents are an important input control. Data should be organized on the input form in a way that facilitates accurate input. Many accounting systems contain built-in edit tests, such as an accounting input control that requires that debits equal credits before the system will accept a journal entry. A full edit check should be performed on all transactions before they are entered as updates to the master file.

Other input control procedures include redundant data checks, unfound records tests, anticipation checks, preformatted screens, interactive edits, and check digits.

- **Redundant data checks** encode repetitious data on a transaction record, enabling a later processing test to compare the two data items for compatibility. For example, a grocery store system may compare the bar code on the product and an alpha description of the item. If they do not match, an exceptions report is produced.
- **Unfound records tests** (also called validity tests or master file checks) are run as data are input. Any transaction with no master file will be rejected. Note, however, that computers process data on two different time schedules: real time and batch processing. With real-time processing, data in master files are updated as each transaction is entered. Batch processing systems collect data throughout a time period, such as a day, and then process the group of transactions together. An operator inputting to a batch system must wait until the new information appears in the master file. With a real-time system, the new account information appears as soon as it is entered, after which the transaction can be input.
- **Anticipation checks** are dependence or consistency checks and look for a relationship between two items or conditions. An example of this type of check could be that sales tax is not included when a sale is made to a nonprofit or governmental organization.

- **Preformatted screens** with logical content groupings and "forced choices" when only certain options are available improve the efficiency and accuracy of input entry.
- **Interactive edits** are performed as the data are entered to check that the data in a particular field meet specified requirements, such as:
  - Character checks. A character in a particular field has to be alphabetic, numeric, or some particular symbol.
  - Completeness checks. All fields requiring characters are filled.
  - Limit, range, or reasonable checks. Values in a field are neither too large nor too small and are reasonable. Examples would be not allowing a paycheck above a certain amount or not allowing a purchase or shipment quantity greater than a certain amount.

  A transaction should not be entered until it passes ("clears") all of the edit checks.
- **Check digit** is derived from an operation on all the digits in a number (e.g., a sum). The sum of digits in the account number 5678, for example, would be 26 (5 + 6 + 7 + 8); the check digit would be the last digit of the sum, or 6.

Processing Controls

Processing controls address the system's manipulation of the data after they are input. Processing controls often are interdependent with input controls and output controls, as in the example of check digits. They involve the reediting of data and the resulting error correction and reentry routines. Processing controls include run-to-run totals. Such totals help ensure that the output from one application agrees to the input to an application it feeds. An example is the output of cash disbursements equaling the input to the vouchers payable system. The sum is meaningless except for the computer's batch control in processing checks. Typical processing controls include the next items:

Mechanization. Consistency is provided by machine processing. An example of mechanization is when cash deposits are totaled by adding machine or calculator.

Standardization. Consistent procedures are developed for all processing. An example of standardization is the use of a chart of accounts to identify the normal debits and credits for each account.

Default option. The automatic use of a predefined value for input transactions that are left blank. An example of default option is automatically paying salaried employees for 40 hours each week.

Batch balancing. A comparison of the items or documents actually processed against a predetermined control totals. An example of batch balancing is when a cashier balances deposit tickets to control totals of cash remittances.

Run-to-run totals. The use of output control totals resulting from one process as input control totals over subsequent processing. The control totals are used as links in a chain to tie one process to another in a sequence of processes over a period of time. An example of run-to-run totals are when beginning accounts receivable balance less payments plus new purchases should equal ending accounts receivable.

Balancing. A test for equality between the values of two equivalent sets of items or one set of items and a control total. An example of balancing is confirming that the balance of the accounts payable subsidiary ledger equals the balance of the general ledger control account.

Matching. Matching items with other items received from independent sources to control the processing of transactions. An example of matching occurs when an accounts payable clerk matches vendor invoices to receiving reports and purchase orders.

Clearing account. An amount that results from the processing of independent items of equivalent value. After all items are processed, the net control value should equal zero. An example is imprest checking, which should have a zero balance after all paychecks have been cashed by employees for the week.

Tickler file. A control file consisting of items sequenced by date for processing or follow-up purposes. An example of a tickler file is invoices received and filed by due date.

Redundant processing. Duplicate processing and comparison of individual results for equality. An example of redundant processing is when two clerks compute the gross and net pay of each employee for comparison purposes.

Trailer label. A record providing a control total for comparison with accumulated counts or values of records processed. An example of a trailer label is the last record of a receivable file containing a record count of the number of records in the file.

Automated error correction. Automatic error correction of transactions or records that violate a detective control. An example of an automated error correction is the automatic initiation of a credit memo when customers overpay their account balances.

Output Controls

Output controls are designed to check that input and processing resulted in accurate and valid output. Output includes data files and reports produced after computer processing is completed. Two types of output controls are required to ensure accuracy and validity of information: controls for validating processing results and controls regulating the distribution and disposal of the output.

Controls for Validating Processing Results. The validity, accuracy, and completeness of output from accounting systems can be verified by activity reports that provide detailed information about all changes to the master files. File changes can be tracked to the events or documents that initiated the changes, and the accuracy can be verified. Where the volume of transactions makes verification using activity reports impractical, exception reports showing material changes to files can be used.

Controls Regulating Distribution of Output. There are a number of concerns regarding controls for output from computers, printed or electronic. Forms controls can be used for printed output along with precautions on how and by whom the materials are distributed, stored, and disposed of. Appropriate controls also need to be put in place for electronic distribution, including password protection of the document, encryption, controlled distribution lists, and access restrictions.

Additionally, specific output controls include:

Reconciliation. An identification and analysis of differences between the values contained in a detail file and a control total. Reconciliation is completed to identify errors rather than the existence of a difference between the balances. An example of reconciliation is completing a monthly reconciliation of a checking account.

Aging. Identification of unprocessed or retained items in files according to their date, usually the transaction date. The aging classifies items according to various date ranges. An example of aging is to complete a report to identify delinquent accounts within 30 days, 60 days, 90 days or more.

Suspense file. A file containing unprocessed or partially processed items that need further action. An example of a suspense file is a file of back-ordered raw materials awaiting receipt.

Suspense account. A control total for items that need further processing. An example of a suspense account is when the total of the accounts payable subsidiary ledger should equal the general ledger control account.

Periodic audit. Periodic verification of a file or process to detect control problems. An example of a periodic audit is sending confirmations to customers and vendors to verify account balance.

Discrepancy reports. A listing of items that have violated some control and require further investigation. An example of a discrepancy report is a list of employees who have exceeded overtime limits.

Flowcharting to Assess Controls

Documenting an organization's information system and related control procedures often can be done most effectively through flowcharting. A flowchart visually depicts the flow of transactions through the process from initiation to storage of data. Diagramming the process can help identify gaps or flaws in the controls.

Flowcharts can be useful not only for summarizing the internal auditor's information about processes but also to aid in design, development, and implementation of new accounting information systems or new control procedures.

Standard flowcharting symbols are recognized by the American National Standards Institute and the International Organization for Standardization. A few of the basic symbols are shown in Figure 1E-1.

Figure 1E-1 Flowchart Symbols

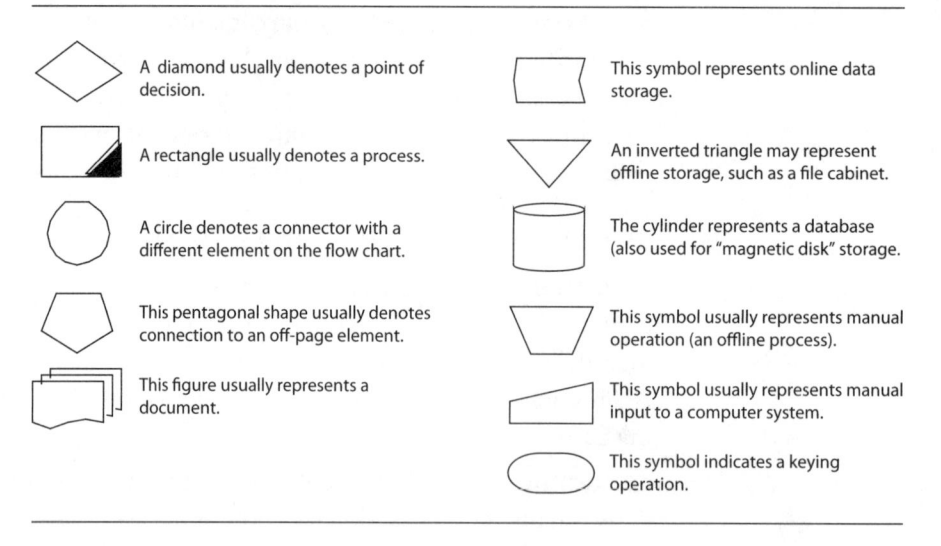

Symbol	Description
Diamond	A diamond usually denotes a point of decision.
Rectangle	A rectangle usually denotes a process.
Circle	A circle denotes a connector with a different element on the flow chart.
Pentagon	This pentagonal shape usually denotes connection to an off-page element.
Document	This figure usually represents a document.
Online storage	This symbol represents online data storage.
Inverted triangle	An inverted triangle may represent offline storage, such as a file cabinet.
Cylinder	The cylinder represents a database (also used for "magnetic disk" storage).
Trapezoid	This symbol usually represents manual operation (an offline process).
Manual input	This symbol usually represents manual input to a computer system.
Oval	This symbol indicates a keying operation.

Thus, an internal auditor's flowchart of a transaction process may look something like that shown in Figure 1E-2.

Some computer programs have the ability to create an automated flowchart of a program's functionality and processes.

Figure 1E-2 Flowchart of Transaction Process

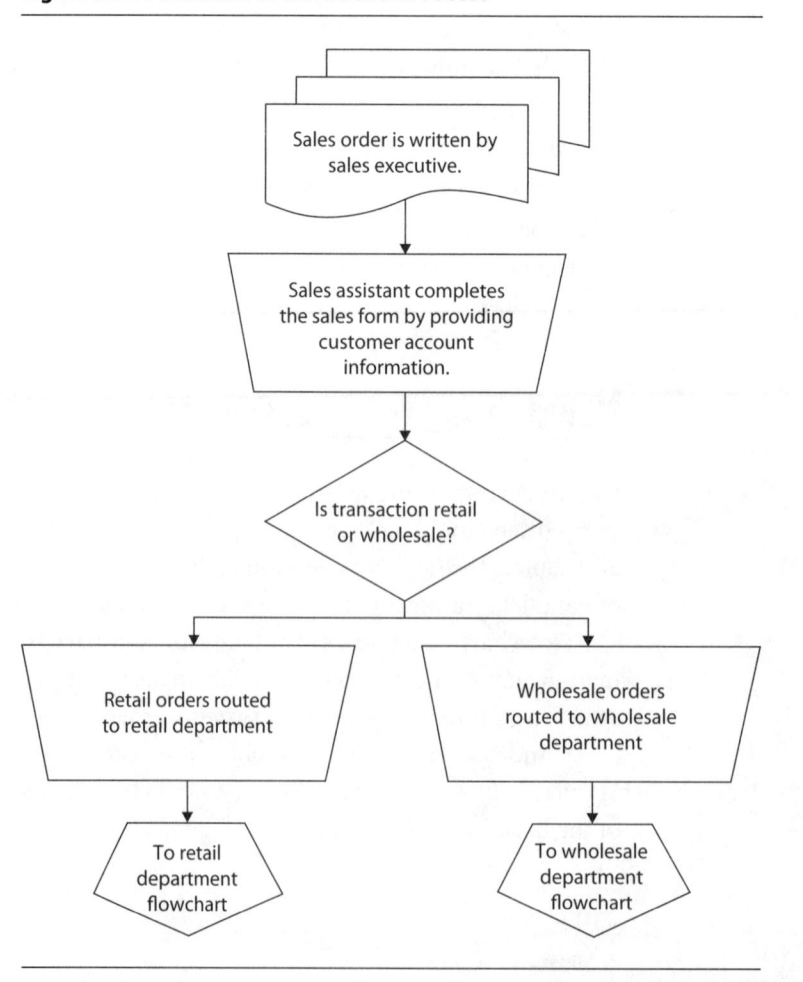

```
   Sales order is written by
        sales executive.
                │
                ▼
   Sales assistant completes
   the sales form by providing
      customer account
         information.
                │
                ▼
       Is transaction retail
         or wholesale?
          /           \
         ▼             ▼
  Retail orders routed    Wholesale orders
  to retail department    routed to wholesale
                             department
         │                      │
         ▼                      ▼
     To retail             To wholesale
     department            department
     flowchart             flowchart
```

Flowcharts can help the auditor and management analyze a set of internal controls to find both strengths and weaknesses and to develop recommended corrections. Analysis might begin by matching a flowchart submitted as data to see if it corresponds to the reality of the system it purports to describe. Are retail orders actually routed as the flowchart claims, or are there perhaps unnecessary intervening procedures that are not identified on the chart? At each control point, the auditor might ask, "Is there sufficient oversight by a qualified person?" For example, in Figure 1E-2, management may see inefficiency in the fact that input of transaction orders is done by two different input operators. Management may want to examine whether it can be more efficient by routing all orders to the same input area and subsequently providing the retail and wholesale departments with reports regarding their transactions.

Flowcharts ultimately can be used to depict any process or other relationships in the firm, to illustrate relationships between different data elements, or to depict the movement of a single document throughout the process.

Knowledge Check: Systems Controls and Security Measures

The next questions are intended to help you check your understanding and recall of the material presented in this topic. They do not represent the type of questions that appear on the CMA exam.

Directions: Answer each question in the space provided. Correct answers and section references appear after the knowledge check questions.

1. Which of the following is a risk specifically associated with computer systems?
    - a. Risk of information assets being stolen
    - b. Risk of errors caused by careless input
    - c. Risk of limited visibility of the audit trail
    - d. Risk of break-in to the facility

2. Which of the following control procedures can be used to uncover a fraud scheme?
    - a. Prototype
    - b. Vacation rule
    - c. Disaster recovery procedures or business continuance plans
    - d. Backup procedures

3. Which of the following are effective systems development controls?
    - I. Designate a team involving end users and representatives from various departments to create a thorough design.
    - II. Develop a prototype for the design team and end users to test and approve before full production.
    - III. Conduct thorough pilot and parallel testing.
    - IV. Each programmer should be responsible for placing the final version of his or her program into the final version of the system.

    - a. I
    - b. II and III
    - c. I, II, and III
    - d. I, II, III, and IV

4. Which of the following is (are) true regarding accounting controls?
    - I. Batch totals are calculated when the transaction is output.
    - II. Control accounts should be accessed only by authorized personnel.
    - III. Invoices and supporting documents should be subject to controls for appropriate voiding after payment is received.
    - IV. Input should be processed only by management accountants.

- [ ] a. I
- [ ] b. II and III
- [ ] c. II and IV
- [ ] d. I, II, III, and IV

5. Which of the following is an example of computerized input control procedures?
   - [ ] a. Unfound records test
   - [ ] b. Dual observation
   - [ ] c. Processing controls
   - [ ] d. Backup procedures

6. Which of the following is (are) true regarding network controls?
   I. Data encryption helps protect information from unauthorized access.
   II. Routing verification procedures ensure that transmissions are routed to the correct address.
   III. Electronic funds transfer transmissions require strict control procedures to protect from unauthorized funds transfers.
   IV. Firewalls are designed principally to detect unauthorized access from the Internet.
   - [ ] a. I
   - [ ] b. II and III
   - [ ] c. I, II, and III
   - [ ] d. I, II, III, and IV

7. Which of the following statements about backup and disaster recovery procedures (or business continuance plans) is true?
   - [ ] a. Disaster recovery procedures are recommended in the situation where backups are run only on a weekly basis.
   - [ ] b. Disaster recovery procedures ensure the uninterrupted operation of the business.
   - [ ] c. Backup procedures protect the company from complete loss of data.
   - [ ] d. Backup procedures ensure the uninterrupted operation of the business in the event of a natural disaster that destroys the computer system.

8. Which of the following statements about flowcharting is **not** correct?
   - [ ] a. Flowcharts can help the auditor and management analyze a set of internal controls.
   - [ ] b. Flowcharts can be useful for summarizing the internal auditor's information about processes.
   - [ ] c. Flowcharts can be used to depict the movement of a single document through a process.
   - [ ] d. All of the above are correct.

Knowledge Check Answers: Systems Controls and Security Measures

1. Which of the following is a risk specifically associated with computer systems? [See *Risks Associated with Information Systems*.]
   - ☐ a. Risk of information assets being stolen
   - ☐ b. Risk of errors caused by careless input
   - ☒ c. Risk of limited visibility of the audit trail
   - ☐ d. Risk of break-in to the facility

2. Which of the following control procedures can be used to uncover a fraud scheme? [See *Vacation Rule*.]
   - ☐ a. Prototype
   - ☒ b. Vacation rule
   - ☐ c. Disaster recovery procedures or business continuance plans
   - ☐ d. Backup procedures

3. Which of the following are effective systems development controls? [See *Systems Development Controls*.]
   - I. Designate a team involving end users and representatives from various departments to create a thorough design.
   - II. Develop a prototype for the design team and end users to test and approve before full production.
   - III. Conduct thorough pilot and parallel testing.
   - IV. Each programmer should be responsible for placing the final version of his or her program into the final version of the system.
   - ☐ a. I
   - ☐ b. II and III
   - ☒ c. I, II, and III
   - ☐ d. I, II, III, and IV

4. Which of the following is (are) true regarding accounting controls? [See *Accounting Controls*.]
   - I. Batch totals are calculated when the transaction is output.
   - II. Control accounts should be accessed only by authorized personnel.
   - III. Invoices and supporting documents should be subject to controls for appropriate voiding after payment is received.
   - IV. Input should be processed only by management accountants.
   - ☐ a. I
   - ☒ b. II and III

Section E, Topic 3—Systems Controls and Security Measures   695

- [ ] **c.** II and IV
- [ ] **d.** I, II, III, and IV

5. Which of the following is an example of computerized input control procedures? [See *Input Controls*.]
   - [x] **a.** Unfound records test
   - [ ] **b.** Dual observation
   - [ ] **c.** Processing controls
   - [ ] **d.** Backup procedures

6. Which of the following is (are) true regarding network controls? [See *Network Controls*.]

   I. Data encryption helps protect information from unauthorized access.

   II. Routing verification procedures check that data is delivered to the correct address.

   III. Electronic funds transfer transmissions require strict control procedures to protect from unauthorized funds transfers.

   IV. Firewalls are designed principally to detect unauthorized access from the Internet.

   - [ ] **a.** I
   - [ ] **b.** II and III
   - [x] **c.** I, II, and III
   - [ ] **d.** I, II, III, and IV

7. Which of the following statements about backup and disaster recovery procedures (or business continuance plans) is true? [See *Disaster Recovery Policies and Procedures*.]
   - [ ] **a.** Disaster recovery procedures are recommended in the situation where backups are run only on a weekly basis.
   - [ ] **b.** Disaster recovery procedures ensure the uninterrupted operation of the business.
   - [x] **c.** Backup procedures protect the company from complete loss of data.
   - [ ] **d.** Backup procedures ensure the uninterrupted operation of the business in the event of a natural disaster that destroys the computer system.

8. Which of the following statements about flowcharting is **not** correct? [See *Flowcharting to Assess Controls*.]
   - [ ] **a.** Flowcharts can help the auditor and management analyze a set of internal controls.
   - [ ] **b.** Flowcharts can be useful for summarizing the internal auditor's information about processes.
   - [ ] **c.** Flowcharts can be used to depict the movement of a single document through a process.
   - [x] **d.** All of the above are correct.

Practice Questions: Internal Controls

Directions: This sampling of questions is designed to emulate actual exam questions. Read each question and write your response on another sheet of paper. See the "Answers to Section Practice Questions" section at the end of this book to assess your response. Validate or improve the answer you wrote. For a more robust selection of practice questions, access the **Online Test Bank** at www.wileycma.com

Question 1E1-CQ01

Topic: Governance, Risk, and Compliance

A firm is constructing a risk analysis to quantify the exposure of its data center to various types of threats. Which one of the following situations would represent the highest annual loss exposure after adjustment for insurance proceeds?

	Frequency of Occurrence (years)	Loss Amount	Insurance (% coverage)
☐ a.	1	$15,000	85
☐ b.	8	$75,000	80
☐ c.	20	$200,000	80
☐ d.	100	$400,000	50

Question 1E1-AT12

Topic: Governance, Risk, and Compliance

When management of the sales department has the opportunity to override the system of internal controls of the accounting department, a weakness exists in which of the following?

- ☐ a. Risk management
- ☐ b. Information and communication
- ☐ c. Monitoring
- ☐ d. Control environment

Question 1E1-AT04

Topic: Governance, Risk, and Compliance

Segregation of duties is a fundamental concept in an effective system of internal control. Nevertheless, the internal auditor must be aware that this safeguard can be compromised through

- ☐ a. lack of training of employees.
- ☐ b. collusion among employees.

☐ c. irregular employee reviews.

☐ d. absence of internal auditing.

Question 1E1-AT05

Topic: Governance, Risk, and Compliance

A company's management is concerned about computer data eavesdropping and wants to maintain the confidentiality of its information as it is transmitted. The company should utilize:

☐ a. data encryption.

☐ b. dial-back systems.

☐ c. message acknowledgment procedures.

☐ d. password codes.

Question 1E1-AT08

Topic: Governance, Risk, and Compliance

Preventive controls are:

☐ a. usually more cost beneficial than detective controls.

☐ b. usually more costly to use than detective controls.

☐ c. found only in general accounting controls.

☐ d. found only in accounting transaction controls.

Question 1E1-AT10

Topic: Governance, Risk, and Compliance

Which of the following is **not** a requirement regarding a company's system of internal control under the Foreign Corrupt Practices Act of 1977?

☐ a. Management must annually assess the effectiveness of its system of internal control.

☐ b. Transactions are executed in accordance with management's general or specific authorization.

☐ c. Transactions are recorded as necessary (1) to permit preparation of financial statements in conformity with GAAP or any other criteria applicable to such statements, and (2) to maintain accountability for assets.

☐ d. The recorded accountability for assets is compared with the existing assets at reasonable intervals, and appropriate action is taken with respect to any differences.

Question 1E2-AT09

Topic: Internal Auditing

There are three components of audit risk: inherent risk, control risk, and detection risk. Inherent risk is described as:

- [ ] **a.** the risk that the auditor may unknowingly fail to appropriately modify his or her opinion on financial statements that are materially misstated.
- [ ] **b.** the susceptibility of an assertion to a material misstatement, assuming that there are no related internal control structure policies or procedures.
- [ ] **c.** the risk that a material misstatement that could occur in an assertion will not be prevented or detected on a timely basis by the entity's internal control structure policies or procedures.
- [ ] **d.** the risk that the auditor will not detect a material misstatement that exists in an assertion.

Question 1E3-AT11

Topic: Systems Controls and Security Measures

Which one of the following would **most** compromise the use of the grandfather-father-son principle of file retention as protection against loss or damage of master files?

- [ ] **a.** Use of magnetic tape
- [ ] **b.** Inadequate ventilation
- [ ] **c.** Storing of all files in one location
- [ ] **d.** Failure to encrypt data

Question 1E3-AT12

Topic: Systems Controls and Security Measures

In entering the billing address for a new client in Emil Company's computerized database, a clerk erroneously entered a nonexistent zip code. As a result, the first month's bill mailed to the new client was returned to Emil Company. Which one of the following would **most** likely have led to discovery of the error at the time of entry into Emil Company's computerized database?

- [ ] **a.** Limit test
- [ ] **b.** Validity test
- [ ] **c.** Parity test
- [ ] **d.** Record count test

Question 1E3-AT07

Topic: Systems Controls and Security Measures

In the organization of the information systems function, the **most** important separation of duties is:

- [ ] **a.** assuring that those responsible for programming the system do not have access to data processing operations.
- [ ] **b.** not allowing the data librarian to assist in data processing operations.
- [ ] **c.** using different programming personnel to maintain utility programs from those who maintain the application programs.

    ☐ **d.** having a separate department that prepares the transactions for processing and verifies the correct entry of the transactions.

Question 1E3-AT01
Topic: Systems Controls and Security Measures

Accounting controls are concerned with the safeguarding of assets and the reliability of financial records. Consequently, these controls are designed to provide reasonable assurance that all of the following take place **except**:

    ☐ **a.** executing transactions in accordance with management's general or specific authorization.

    ☐ **b.** comparing recorded assets with existing assets at periodic intervals and taking appropriate action with respect to differences.

    ☐ **c.** recording transactions as necessary to permit preparation of financial statements in conformity with generally accepted accounting principles and maintaining accountability for assets.

    ☐ **d.** compliance with methods and procedures ensuring operational efficiency and adherence to managerial policies.

Question 1E2-AT02
Topic: Internal Auditing

In planning an audit, the auditor considers audit risk. Audit risk is the

    ☐ **a.** susceptibility of an account balance to material error assuming the client does not have any related internal control.

    ☐ **b.** risk that a material error in an account will not be prevented or detected on a timely basis by the client's internal control system.

    ☐ **c.** risk that the auditor may unknowingly fail to appropriately modify his or her opinion on financial statements that are materially misstated.

    ☐ **d.** risk that the auditor's procedures for verifying account balances will not detect a material error when in fact such error exists.

Question 1E2-AT03
Topic: Internal Auditing

Control risk is the risk that a material error in an account will not be prevented or detected on a timely basis by the client's internal control system. The **best** control procedure to prevent or detect fictitious payroll transactions is

    ☐ **a.** to use and account for prenumbered payroll checks.

    ☐ **b.** personnel department authorization for hiring, pay rate, job status, and termination.

☐ c. internal verification of authorized pay rates, computations, and agreement with the payroll register.

☐ d. storage of unclaimed wages in a vault with restricted access.

Question 1E2-AT10

Topic: Internal Auditing

Of the following, the **primary** objective of compliance testing is to determine whether

☐ a. procedures are regularly updated.

☐ b. controls are functioning as planned.

☐ c. financial statement line items are properly stated.

☐ d. collusion is taking place.

Question 1E3-AT05

Topic: Systems Controls and Security Measures

A critical aspect of a disaster recovery plan or business continuance is to be able to regain operational capability as soon as possible. In order to accomplish this, an organization can have an arrangement with its computer hardware vendor to have a fully operational facility available that is configured to the user's specific needs. This is **best** known as a(n)

☐ a. uninterruptible power system.

☐ b. parallel system.

☐ c. cold site.

☐ d. hot site.

> To further assess your understanding of the concepts and calculations covered in Part 1, Section E: Internal Controls, practice with the **Online Test Bank** questions for this section. REMINDER: See the "Answers to Section Practice Questions" section at the end of this book.

Essay Exam Support Materials

Writing an effective essay exam is a special challenge. It tests your written communication skills in addition to your knowledge of the content. Essay questions also test your understanding of how specific pieces of information relate to one another, and your ability to apply your knowledge to real-life situations. The next information is included to help you learn more about how to respond to the exam part content in written essay form.

Preparing for the Essay Portion of the Exam

The essay portion of the CMA exam can draw from any of the LOS and content from Part 1: Financial Reporting, Planning, Performance, and Control. It requires understanding the content and being prepared to evaluate the issues presented as well as making recommendations for the resolution of specific situations.

Your study plan should help you learn the content, learn how to respond to the content in multiple-choice questions, and learn to respond to essay questions presented on the content. This is a significant part of the challenge of the CMA exams. One way to meet this challenge is to break it down into smaller challenges—learn the content first, then practice multiple-choice exam-type questions, then learn how to respond to essay questions.

How to Write Essay Answers

The CMA exam essay questions require you to discuss the main points of a specific topic and then examine their implications. When developing your responses, you must support your answers with evidence of your thinking in order to demonstrate your knowledge and comprehension of a topic and your ability to apply that knowledge via thoughtful analysis.

You will be expected to present written answers that:

- Directly respond to the questions asked.
- Are presented in a logical manner.
- Demonstrate an appropriate understanding of the subject matter.

Clues within the questions can be used to help you formulate and organize your responses. Verbs such as *analyze, apply, explore, interpret,* and *examine* can help delineate the requirements of the question. Using the same verbs within your answer will help ensure that you are responding directly and completely to the specific questions being asked.

Candidates are expected to have a working knowledge of using word processing and electronic spreadsheets. They are also expected to have an understanding of basic financial statements, time value of money concepts, and elementary statistics. The essay portion of the exam is computer driven. Answers are entered using a text editor similar to Microsoft Notepad. Some questions may require a spreadsheet similar to, but not exactly the same as, Microsoft Excel.

Writing Skills

The essay section of the CMA exam is a way to assess your ability to analyze, evaluate, and effectively communicate about business situations. Written communication is an important skill required in today's business environment.

The Institute of Certified Management Accountants (ICMA) assesses your writing skills in the essay portion of the CMA exam. The assessment is based on these criteria:

- Use of standard English
- Organization
- Clarity

Use of Standard English

The use of standard English is an integral part of expressing ideas in a business environment. Assessment of the use of clear and concise terminology as is standard to the English language will be administered on the essay portion of the exam.

Organization

When answering essay questions, organizing your answers in a logical manner is important to effective business writing skills. As you read through the question, order your thoughts in a manner that exercises your process of thinking. Make sure that your answer has a clear beginning, outlining what you will be answering, followed by the answer, backed up by CMA content-specific facts, and a summary of what you just described.

Clarity

Being clear in your response is as important as the use of standard English and organization of your response on the CMA exam. Assessors of the essay portion of the CMA exam will look at the answer and critique based on whether the answer is clearly expressed and that the answer is supported by CMA content-specific rationale. When answering, make sure that you read your answer thoroughly to make sure that your response is clear and that the reader will understand how you are attempting to answer the questions.

Using Standard English, Organization, and Clarity in Your Responses to the Essays

When reading through the essay examples, work through the problems as if you were actually answering the questions on the actual CMA exam. When working through the essays, pay close attention to the key words in the question, organize your response, and start writing the answer to the question. When answering, make sure that you are answering the question in a clear and concise manner and make sure that you use standard English. Once complete, compare your answer to the answer provided in the textbook. Pay close attention to the way the answer is organized, the key words that are used, and way the answer is presented. Compare the textbook answer to your answer to see how you did.

Essay Exam Study Tips

On the actual four-hour CMA exam, the essay portion of the exam will begin once you complete the multiple-choice section or after three hours, whichever comes first. This means you will have at least one hour to complete the two essay questions presented.

To make the best use of your time to complete the essay portion:
- Prior to taking the exam, take the online tutorial to become familiar with the testing screens. The tutorial is not part of your testing time and may be repeated. However, total tutorial time is limited to 20 minutes.
- Briefly skim through both essay questions and get an idea what each question is asking you to do (i.e., describe, analyze, calculate, etc.)
- You have one hour to complete the full essay exam (more if you have finished the multiple-choice section earlier than the three-hour limit). Determine how much time you will dedicate to each essay question.
- Start with the question you know best. Begin by writing key words, thoughts, facts, figures, and anything else that can be used to answer the question.
- As you answer one question, issues related to the other may occur to you. Write that information next to the appropriate question. This will build your confidence and give you a starting place when you begin the second question.

To answer each question:
- Read the entire question for requirements.
- Be aware of the verb clues that delineate what is being asked. This will help you formulate and organize your answer. Note that you may have more than one task—for example, define abc and interpret its applicability to xyz.
- Write the basic requirements in the answer space so that you are sure to address them.
- Begin your answer with one or two sentences that directly answer the question. If possible, rephrase the question's essential terms in a statement that directly answers the question.

- Use bullet points to show main ideas, and support each point with sufficient detail to show that you understand all the issues relevant to the question.
- Make it as easy as possible for graders to give you points. The goal in grading is to award you points, so show your thinking clearly and effectively. Do not write too little or too much.
- Finish your essay with one or two sentences that summarize your main point(s).
- Proofread your answer for logic, thoroughness, and clarity.
- Keep track of time. Do not spend too much time on one question.
- If you do not have enough time to write a full essay, write an outline of your main points to show what you know in order to get partial credit.

Examples of Essay Question Answers

EACH ESSAY QUESTION ACTUALLY CONSISTS of several related questions based on one scenario. The question as a whole is worth a set number of points and is graded against a scorecard to ensure consistent grading. The scorecard lists appropriate terms, topics, and ideas that address the answer. Presented here are two essay questions drawn from previous exams. The first essay question is followed by an example of an answer that would be awarded maximum points—a "best" answer. How these points are awarded is shown on a scorecard similar to ones used by the Institute of Certified Management Accountants (ICMA).

Following the second essay question are two answers that were awarded fewer points because they do not address all the issues. The "good" answer meets some but not all of the criteria. The "better" answer covers more of the requested information, as shown on the scorecard, and receives more points.

As you will see, the goal of the graders is to give test takers points rather than take them away. If test takers earn more credits than the maximum allowable points, they can be awarded only the maximum allowable number of points.

There are two types of essay questions: questions that ask for a **written response** and questions that ask for a **series of calculations, tables, or charts for a response**.

Note: The questions, answers, and scorecards used in these examples were provided by the ICMA and are used with their permission.

Example Question 1: Amur Company

Amur Company manufactures three lawn care component parts: fuel systems, transmission assemblies, and electrical systems. For the past five years, manufacturing overhead has been applied to products on standard direct labor hours for the units actually produced. The standard cost information is shown next.

Exhibit A shows standard cost information.

Exhibit A Standard Cost Information

	Fuel Systems	Transmission Assemblies	Electrical Systems
Units produced and sold	10,000	20,000	30,000
Standard labor hours	2.0	1.5	1.0
Standard direct material cost per unit	$25.00	$36.00	$30.00
Budgeted and actual manufacturing overhead		$3,920,000	

The current direct labor rate is $10 per hour. New machinery that highly automates the production process was installed two years ago and greatly reduced the direct labor time to produce the three products. The selling price for each of the three products is 125% of the manufacturing cost.

Amur's segment of the lawn care component industry has become very competitive, and the company's profits have been decreasing. Eric West, Amur's controller, has been asked by the president of the company to analyze the overhead allocations and pricing structure. West thinks that future allocations should be based on machine hours and direct labor hours rather than the current allocation method, which is based on direct labor hours only. West has determined the additional product information shown in Exhibit B.

Exhibit B Additional Product Information

	Fuel Systems	Transmission Assemblies	Electrical Systems
Standard machine hours	2.0	4.0	6.0
Manufacturing overhead:			
Direct labor cost		$ 560,000	
Machine cost		$3,360,000	

Questions

1. By allocating all of the budgeted overhead based on direct labor hours, calculate the unit manufacturing cost and unit sales price for each of the three products manufactured at Amur Company.
2. Prepare an analysis for Amur Company using the appropriate cost driver(s) determined by Eric West for manufacturing overhead. Calculate the unit manufacturing cost and unit sales price for each of the three products.
3. Based on your calculations in Questions 1 and 2, prepare a recommendation for the president at Amur Company to increase the firm's profitability.

Sample "Best" Answer for Amur Business Scenario

Question 1

The allocation of all of Amur Company's budgeted manufacturing overhead based on direct labor hours results in the unit manufacturing costs and unit sales prices for its three products is calculated as follows:

Fuel systems

Units: 10,000
Standard labor hour/unit: 2.0

Total standard labor hours: 20,000

Direct material: $25.00
Direct labor at $10/hour: $20.00
Overhead at $49/DLH[1]: $98.00

Total cost: $143.00

Sales price (125% of cost): $178.75

Transmission Assemblies

Units: 20,000
Standard labor hour/unit: 1.5

Total standard labor hours: 30,000

Machine hours per unit: 4.0

Total machine hours: 80,000

Direct material: $36.00
Direct labor at $10/hour: $15.00
Overhead at $49/DLH[1]: $73.50

Total cost: $124.50

Sales price (125% of cost): $155.63

Electrical Systems

Units: 30,000
Standard labor hour/unit: 1.0

Total standard labor hours: 30,000

Direct material: $30.00
Direct labor at $10/hour: $10.00
Overhead at $49/DLH[1]: $49.00

Total cost: $89.00

Sales price (125% of cost): $111.25

Note:

[1] Total manufacturing overhead of $3,920,000 / 80,000 total direct labor hours = $49.00 per direct labor hour.

Question 2

When the cost drivers identified by Eric West are used to allocate manufacturing overhead, the unit manufacturing costs and unit sales prices for the three products manufactured at Amur Company are calculated as follows:

Fuel systems

Units: 10,000
Standard labor hour/unit: 2.0

Total standard labor hours: 20,000

Machine hours per unit: 2.0

Total machine hours: 20,000

Direct material: $25.00
Direct labor at $10/hour: $20.00
Overhead (DLH at $7/hr[1]): $14.00
Overhead (Machine hrs at $12/hr[2]): $24.00

Total cost: $83.00

Sales price (125% of cost): $103.75

Transmission Assemblies

Units: 20,000
Standard labor hour/unit: 1.5

Total standard labor hours: 30,000

Machine hours per unit: 4.0

Total machine hours: 80,000

Direct material: $36.00
Direct labor at $10/hour: $15.00
Overhead (DLH at $7/hr[1]): $10.50
Overhead (Machine hrs at $12/hr[2]): $48.00

Total cost: $109.50

Sales price (125% of cost): $136.88

Electrical Systems

Units: 30,000
Standard labor hour/unit: 1.0

Total standard labor hours: 30,000

Machine hours per unit: 6.0

Total machine hours: 180,000

Direct material: $30.00
Direct labor at $10/hour: $10.00
Overhead (DLH at $7/hr[1]): $7.00
Overhead (Machine hrs at $12/hr[2]): $72.00

Total cost: $119.00

Sales price (125% of cost): $148.75

Notes:

[1] Direct labor overhead of $560,000 / 80,000 total direct labor hours = $7.00 per direct labor hour.

[2] Machine overhead of $3,360,000 / 280,000 total machine hours = $12.00 per machine hour.

Question 3

The summary of the revised margins for each of Amur Company's three products, assuming the sales prices developed in Question 1 (allocation of all manufacturing overhead based on direct labor hours) is compared to revised costs developed in Question 2 (allocation of manufacturing overhead based on cost drivers), is as follows:

Fuel Systems

Current price: $178.75

Revised cost: $83.00

Gross profit (loss): $95.75

Margin: 54%

Transmission Assemblies

Current price: $155.63

Revised cost: $109.50

Gross profit (loss): $46.13

Margin: 30%

Electrical Systems

Current price: $111.25

Revised cost: $119.00

Gross profit (loss): ($7.75)

Margin: NA

Based on this analysis, fuel systems and transmission assemblies are producing a higher return than Amur Company previously thought. Fuel systems are the most profitable (54% gross margin) followed by transmission assemblies; however, electrical systems are losing money on a full-cost basis.

Recommendations for improving profitability include:

- Focus on fuel systems, through actions such as increasing marketing expenditures and reducing the price to increase sales.
- Improve profitability of electrical systems through changes to the manufacturing process to reduce the machine hours required.
- Decrease marketing of this electrical system, and increase the selling price if possible.

Scoring of "Best" Answer for Amur Business Scenario

The Amur question would be graded against a scorecard similar to the one shown next. Note that:

- The scorecard addresses more issues than is required by the question. This is done to accommodate variations between test takers and to provide the greatest opportunity for a maximum score. The goal of the graders is to give test takers points rather than taking them away. If test takers earn more credits than the maximum allowable points, they will be awarded only the maximum allowable points.
- At times, the process is more important than the numeric answers. Test takers should show all work/calculations to earn the maximum allowable points.
- Explanations add points.
- Formatting is not judged. You will be using simple text editing, such as Microsoft Notepad, so you may not be able to make charts and should use dashes for bullets.

Amur Scorecard

Amur—Total allowable points 17

Question 1: Maximum allowable points = 5
Issues to address
Unit manufacturing cost and price (DLH allocation) =
Total labor hrs = Standard Hr/Unit × Units for each product
Totals all product labor hrs/ (80,000)
Overhead of $3,920,000/ 80,000 DLH = Overhead rate
Includes unit direct materials cost in product cost
Direct labor = $10 × Standard DLH per unit
OH/Unit for each product = OH rate × standard DLH/Unit
DM + DL + OH = Product cost/ ($143($89)) / ($124.5)
Sales price = 125% × Product cost

Question 2: Maximum allowable points = 5
Unit manufacturing cost and price (Cost driver allocation) =
Total machine hours = (Standard hour / Unit) × Units for each product
Totals all product machine hours / (280.000)
Machine OH = $3,360,000 / 280,000)
DL OH = $560,000 / 80,000 hours / ($7 per DHL)
OH / unit for each product = OH rate × standard MH / unit
OH / unit for each product = OH rate × standard DLH / unit
Includes DM and DLH for each product
Totals all costs / ($83) / ($109.50) / ($119)
Sales price = 125% × Product cost

Question 3: Maximum allowable points = 7
Issues to address
Recommendation

Increase emphasis on fuel systems
    Margin/Profit highest

Increase emphasis on Transmission
    Margin/Profit is high

Increase marketing to generate sales

Decrease price to stimulate sales

Other recommendations to leverage profitability

Decrease emphasis on electrical systems
    Margin is lower/losing money

Improve manufacturing process

Raise price if market will bear it

Other recommendations to deal with electrical systems

Example Question 2: Zylon Corporation

Business Scenario

Jeff Frankie is the chief financial officer of Zylon Corporation, a manufacturer and distributor of electronic security devices primarily suited for residential applications. Frankie is currently in the process of preparing the Y2 annual budget and implementing an incentive plan to reward the performance of key personnel. The final operating plans will then be presented to the board of directors for approval.

Frankie is aware that next year may be very difficult due to announced price increases to major customers. Zylon's president has put pressure on management to achieve the current year's earnings per share amounts. Frankie is, therefore, considering introducing zero-based budgeting in order to bring costs into line with revenue expectations.

Duke Edwards, Zylon's manufacturing director, is attempting to convince Frankie to build budgetary slack into the operating budget. Edwards contends that productivity is burdened by an abnormal amount of product design changes and small lot size production orders that incur costly setup times.

Questions

1. Explain at least three advantages and at least three disadvantages of budgetary slack from the point of view of Zylon Corporation's management group as a whole.
2. Describe how zero-based budgeting could be advantageous to Zylon Corporation's overall budget process.

Sample "Better" Answer for Zylon Business Scenario

Question 1

At least three advantages and three disadvantages of budgetary slack from the point of view of Zylon Corporation's management group as a whole include the following:

Advantages

1. It provides flexibility for operating under unknown circumstances, such as an extra margin for discretionary expenses in case budget assumptions on inflation are incorrect or adverse circumstances arise.
2. Additional slack may be included to offset the costly setups from design changes and/or small lot size orders.
3. The increased pressure to meet Y1 earnings per share targets may result in postponing expenditures into Y2 or aggressively pulling sales into Y1. Budgetary slack in Y2 may compensate for shifting those earnings from Y2 into Y1.

Disadvantages

1. It decreases the ability to highlight weaknesses and take timely corrective actions on problem areas.
2. It decreases the overall effectiveness of corporate planning. Actions such as pricing changes or reduced promotional spending may be taken from a perceived need to improve earnings, when eliminating the budgetary slack could accomplish the same objective without marketplace changes.
3. It limits the objective evaluation of departmental managers and performance of subordinates by using budgetary information.

Question 2

Zero-based budgeting (ZBB) could be advantageous to Zylon Corporation's overall budget process for the following reasons:

- The ZBB process evaluates all proposed operating and administrative expenses as if they were being initiated for the first time. Each expenditure is justified, ranked, and prioritized according to its order of importance to the overall corporation, not just its role in one department.
- The focus is on evaluation of all activities rather than just incremental changes from the prior year. This allows addressing activities that have been ongoing to determine if they are still useful in the current environment. The objectives, operations, and costs of all activities are evaluated, and alternative means of accomplishing the objectives are more likely to be identified.

Scoring of "Better" Answer for Zylon Business Scenario

The Zylon question would be graded against a scorecard similar to the one shown following. Note that:

- The scorecard addresses more issues than is required by the question. This is done to accommodate variations between test takers and to provide the greatest opportunity for a maximum score. The goal of the graders is to give test

takers points rather than taking them away. If test takers earn more credits than the maximum allowable points, they can be awarded only the maximum allowable points.
- At times, the process is more important than the numeric answers. Test takers should show all work/calculations to earn the maximum allowable points.
- Explanations add points.
- Formatting is not judged. You will be using simple text editing such as Microsoft Notepad, so you may not be able to make charts and should use dashes for bullets.

Zylon Scorecard

Zylon Total allowable points 12

Question 1: Maximum allowable points = 6
Issues to address

Advantages

Provides flexibility under uncertainty

Extra margin for discretionary expenses

If assumptions wrong or adverse circumstances

Offsets unexpected setup costs
   Design changes
   Small lot sizes

Can compensate for earnings timing shifts
   Pressure to meet EPS
   Postponing expenses or accelerating sales

Other
   Explanation

Disadvantages

Decreases ability to ID weakness and take action
   Expenses are overstated in budget

Decreases effectiveness of overall planning process

Unnecessary actions taken such as
   Price changes or promotional spending cuts
   When eliminating slack would have solved problem

Limits objective evaluation of employees
   Measured against inflated budget

Other

Explanation

Question 2: Maximum allowable points = 6
Issues to address

Advantages

Each expense is justified and ranked
   Each exp is evaluated as it were first time

Unnecessary activities can be eliminated
   All activities are evaluated
   Ongoing activities must be justified

(Continued)

> (Continued)
>   Slack can be reduced
>   Expenses must be grounded in realistic assumptions
>   Alternative means can be identified
>   Are forced to evaluate processes
>   Other
>   With explanation

Sample "Good" Answer for Zylon Business Scenario

A good answer would address enough of the identified three issues on the Zylon scorecard to earn a sore of 70% or 80% of the maximum allowable points. A good answer for the Zylon scenario is shown next. It addresses the issues but does not go beyond the question to provide explanations and clarification.

Question 1

At least three advantages and three disadvantages of budgetary slack from the point of view of Zylon Corporation's management group as a whole include the following:

Advantages

- It provides operating flexibility.
- Additional slack may be included to offset costs.
- Zylon will need to postpone expenditures.

Disadvantages

- It decreases the ability to highlight weaknesses and take timely corrective actions on problem areas.
- It decreases the overall effectiveness of corporate planning.
- It limits the objective evaluation of departmental managers and performance of subordinates.

Question 2

Zero-based budgeting (ZBB) could be advantageous to Zylon Corporation's overall budget process for these reasons:

- The ZBB process evaluates all proposed operating and administrative expenses as if they were being initiated for the first time.
- The focus is on evaluation of all activities.

Practice Essay Questions and Answers

The next essay questions, and the answers that appear beginning at page 751, were adapted from the *Revised CMA Exam, Questions and Answers: Part 4* (2005 and 2008) books supplied by the Institute of Certified Management Accountants and are used with their permission (unless otherwise indicated).

The focus of the questions will be on the test taker's ability to apply concepts presented in the part being tested to a business scenario.

The answers supplied are meant to serve as samples of answers that address 80% or more of the points listed on the question grading guide. There are generally more points on the grading guide than points that can be awarded (i.e., there may be 110 possible points but only 100 that can be awarded in total), so answers scoring 80% may vary among test takers. Thus, the answers presented here represent one possible answer, not a definitive correct answer.

Part 1 Section A Questions*

Question 1A-ES01

It is almost midnight on December 31, 20XX, and the bookkeeping program at Crank-M-Up, Inc. is malfunctioning. Instead of producing an income statement, it keeps printing an alphabetical list of accounts:

Administrative expenses	$215,000
Cost of goods sold	408,500
Extraordinary casualty loss	70,000
Income taxes	54,900
Loss on inventory write-down (nonrecurring)	13,000
Gain on foreign currency translation	19,500
Loss from discontinued operations	30,000
Sales	945,000
Selling expenses	145,000

---

*The practice essay questions for Section A are original questions and are not released ICMA questions.

Questions

A. As the new accountant for Crank-M-Up, your first job is to prepare the firm's multiple-step income statement for 20XX with EPS disclosures in accordance with GAAP. Crank-M-Up has 50,000 shares of common stock outstanding and has a 30% federal income tax rate.

B. Mark M. Down, the CEO of Crank-M-Up, is confused about the accounting treatment for irregular items on the income statement and wants you to explain: (1) Why GAAP requires special treatment for irregular items; (2) How to determine whether an item is unusual or extraordinary.

Question 1A-ES02

The accountant at Dark Daze, Inc. suddenly quit on December 31, 2015, leaving behind a mess. You managed to find the following information:

Accum. Depr.—Building	$15,000	Interest Payable	600
Accum. Depr.—Equipment	10,000	Inventory	$102,000
Accounts Receivable	2,000	Land	137,320
Allowance for Bad Debt	140	Notes Payable (due 7/1/16)	14,400
Bonds Payable (due 12/31/20)	78,000	Prepaid Advertising	5,000
Buildings	80,400	Retained Earnings	?
Cash	30,000	Salaries Payable	900
Common Stock	60,000	Taxes Payable	3,000
Equipment	40,000		

Questions

A. Prepare the firm's classified balance sheet for 2015.

B. Ebony Dark, the CEO of Dark Daze, is concerned about the types of disclosures that the firm needs for its balance sheet items. Discuss the disclosures that the firm needs to make for: (1) Inventories; (2) Accounts Receivable; (3) Property, Plant, and Equipment; (4) Bonds Payable; and (5) Common Stock.

Question 1A-ES03

Information for Cash-N-Carry is shown below:

Cash-N-Carry
Comparative Balance Sheet
As of December 31

	2015	2014
Cash	$ 21,500	$120,000
Accounts receivable	195,000	105,000
Inventories	180,000	225,000
Long-term investments	0	60,000
Total assets	$396,500	$510,000

Accounts payable	$ 75,000	$120,000
Operating expenses payable	24,000	15,000
Bonds payable	70,000	100,000
Common stock	125,000	125,000
Retained earnings	102,500	150,000
Total liabilities and stockholders' equities	$396,500	$510,000

Cash-N-Carry
Income Statement
For the year ended December 31, 2015

Sales	$560,000
Cost of goods sold	375,000
Gross profit	185,000
Operating expenses	180,000
Operating income	5,000
Loss on sale of investment	(7,500)
Net loss	$ (2,500)

Other Information

- Accounts payable relate to the purchase of inventory.
- $60,000 of long-term investments were sold for $52,500.
- Cash dividends of $45,000 were declared and paid in 2015.

Questions

A. Prepare the statement of cash flows using the indirect method.
B. Prepare the operating section of the statement of cash flows using the direct method.
C. Buck Spender, the CEO of Cash-N-Carry, is confused about how to classify various types of cash flows. Explain to him which cash flows are classified as operating, investing, and financing.

Question 1A-ES04

On January 1, 2015, Lotsa Loot, Inc. purchased $500,000 of 8%, 5-year bonds for $520,790 for an effective interest rate of 7%. The bonds pay interest on July 1 and January 1, and Lotsa Loot uses the effective-interest method to account for these available-for-sale securities.

Present Value of an Ordinary Annuity

Period	1%	2%	3%	4%	5%	6%	7%	8%	9%	10%
1	0.990	0.980	0.971	0.962	0.952	0.943	0.935	0.926	0.917	0.909
2	1.970	1.942	1.913	1.886	1.859	1.833	1.808	1.783	1.759	1.736
3	2.941	2.884	2.829	2.775	2.723	2.673	2.624	2.577	2.531	2.487

(*Continued*)

Present Value of an Ordinary Annuity (Continued)

Period	1%	2%	3%	4%	5%	6%	7%	8%	9%	10%
4	3.902	3.808	3.717	3.630	3.546	3.465	3.387	3.312	3.240	3.170
5	4.853	4.713	4.580	4.452	4.329	4.212	4.100	3.993	3.890	3.791
6	5.795	5.601	5.417	5.242	5.076	4.917	4.767	4.623	4.486	4.355
7	6.728	6.472	6.230	6.002	5.786	5.582	5.389	5.206	5.033	4.868
8	7.652	7.325	7.020	6.733	6.463	6.210	5.971	5.747	5.535	5.335
9	8.566	8.162	7.786	7.435	7.108	6.802	6.515	6.247	5.995	5.759
10	9.471	8.983	8.530	8.111	7.722	7.360	7.024	6.710	6.418	6.145

Questions

A. Record the journal entry for the purchase of the bonds.
B. Record the journal entry for the receipt of interest on July 1, 2015.
C. Record the journal entry to accrue interest on December 31, 2015.
D. Write the entry to recognize the $530,000 fair value of the bonds on December 31, 2015.
E. On January 1, 2016, Lotsa Loot received a check for the interest on the bonds. Immediately after receiving the check, the firm sold the bonds for $530,000. Write the entries for these events.
F. Record the journal entries for the sale of AAA and the purchase of CCC.
G. On December 31, 2017, Lotsa Loot's Trading portfolio of equity securities had the following values:

	Cost	Fair Value at 12/31/17
10,000 shares of BBB Corp. common stock	$182,000	$195,500
600 shares of CCC Corp. common stock	27,550	25,500
	$209,550	$221,000

Record the fair value adjusting entry on December 31, 2017.

H. On January 1, 2018, Lotsa-Loot purchased a 25% interest in the common stock of Gobbled Up Company for $500,000. At that time, Gobbled Up had 1,000,000 shares of its $1 par common stock issued and outstanding.
Lotsa Loot has significant influence over Gobbled Up, and uses the equity method to account for this available-for-sale investment. Record the journal entries for the following events on the books of Lotsa Loot:
  1. Purchase of Gobbled Up common stock on January 1, 2018:
  2. Gobbled Up paid a total $160,000 cash dividend on July 1, 2018:
  3. Net income for Gobbled Up was $360,000 in 2018:
  4. What is the balance of Lotsa Loot's investment in Gobbled Up at the end of 2018 before any market fair value adjustment?
     Balance = _____
  5. What would these entries have been if Lotsa Loot had been a passive investor that did not have significant influence over Gobbled Up and used the cost method to account for this investment?

6. Gobbled Up paid a $160,000 cash dividend on July 1, 2018.
7. Net income for Gobbled Up was $360,000 in 2018.
8. What would the balance of Lotsa Loot's investment in Gobbled Up have been at the end of 2018 before any market fair value adjustment?
Balance = _____

Question 1A-ES05

On January 1, 2015, Equi-Tee, Inc. was granted a charter that authorizes issuance of 50,000 shares of 8%, $100 par value, cumulative preferred stock and 150,000 shares of $5 par value common stock.

Questions

Journalize the following transactions for 2015:
   A. On January 2, the firm exchanged 8,000 shares of common stock for land valued at $300,000.
   B. On January 5, the firm issued 12,000 shares of common stock to the public at $60 per share. The firm also issued 100 shares of common stock to its lawyer for costs associated with the formation of the firm.
   C. On February 3, 2015, the firm issued 1,000 bundles of preferred and common stock for $720 each. Each bundle contained 10 shares of common stock and 1 share of 8%, $100 par value preferred stock. On that date, the common stock had a market value of $60 per share, but the preferred stock had no determinable market value.
   D. The firm had $200,000 in retained earnings as of June 30, 2015, and the market price for common stock was $60 per share. On that day, the firm declared a 10% stock dividend on common stock.
   E. On July 31, the firm issued the shares to fulfill the stock dividend.
   F. On August 1, the firm paid $60,000 to reacquire 2,000 shares of its common stock for treasury stock. Equi-Tee uses the cost method to account for treasury stock transactions.
   G. On September 1, the firm declared a $20,000 total cash dividend to be paid to preferred and common stockholders on September 30.
   Total preferred stock dividend = _____
   Dividend per share for preferred stockholders = _____
   Total common stock dividend = _____
   Dividend per share for common stockholders = _____
   Journal entry to record the declaration of the dividend:
   H. On September 30, the firm paid the cash dividend.
   I. On October 1, the firm reissued the treasury stock at $58 per share.

Question 1A-ES06

Hot Stuff, Inc. makes a boutique line of espresso machines that it sells with attached warranties.

Questions

Write the journal entries for the following events:

A. In 2015, Hot Stuff sold 700 espresso machines with attached warranties to restaurants on account for $1,500 each.
B. Hot Stuff estimated that 50% of the machines would need repair during the life of the warranty at a cost of $90 per machine for parts and labor. In 2015, Hot Stuff did warranty repairs on 100 espresso machines.
C. On December 31, 2015, Hot Stuff accrued the liability for future warranty work:
D. If Hot Stuff had sold those 700 espresso machines to restaurants on account for $1,500 each, plus extended warranties for $100 each:
E. Hot Stuff estimated that 50% of the machines would need repair during the life of the warranty at a cost of $90 per machine for parts and labor. In 2015, Pop-Up did warranty repairs on 100 espresso machines.
F. During December 2015, employees at Hot Stuff earned wages of $70,000. Withholdings for these wages included $2,250 for the employees' share of social security (FICA), $7,500 for federal income tax, $2,200 for state income tax, and $500 for union dues. The firm also incurred payroll tax expenses that included $2,250 for its share of FICA, $200 for federal unemployment tax (FUTA), and $700 for state unemployment tax (SUTA).
Write the journal entry to record the firm's wage expense for December.
G. Write the journal entry to record the firm's payroll tax expense for December.
H. On December 15, 2015, Pop-Up borrowed $12,000 from the bank on a 7%, 4-month note. Write the following journal entries:
To record the issuance of the note.
I. To accrue interest on the note as of December 31, 2015.
J. To record repayment of the note and interest on April 15, 2016.

Question 1A-ES07

On January 1, 2015, Done-Right Manufacturing issued $10,000,000 of 6%, 5-year bonds when the market interest rate for similar debt is 5%. The bonds pay interest semiannually on July 1 and January 1 and Done-Right uses the effective-interest method to account for long-term debt.

Present Value	2.5%	3.0%	5.0%	6.0%
Single sum for 5 periods	0.88385	0.86261	0.78353	0.74726
Single sum for 10 periods	0.78120	0.74409	0.61391	0.55839
Annuity for 5 periods	4.64583	4.57971	4.32948	4.21236
Annuity for 10 periods	8.75206	8.53020	7.72173	7.36009

Questions

A. Are the bonds issued at a discount or a premium? _____
B. How much cash did the firm get for the bonds? _____
C. Issuance of the bonds on January 1, 2015.

D. Payment of interest on July 1, 2015.
E. Accrual of interest on December 31, 2015.
F. Payment of interest on January 1, 2016.
G. After paying interest on 1/1/16, the firm redeemed the bonds at 98.
H. R. U. Sure, the CEO of Done-Right, has asked you to explain why bonds are sometimes issued at a premium, but sometimes issued at a discount. What would you tell him?

Question 1A-ES08

In 2015, We-Got-Stuff, Inc. purchased some land that it used to build a factory. Expenditures during the year included:

- $100,000 to buy the land
- $5,000 in Realtor fees
- $3,000 in accrued property tax
- $10,000 to demolish an old building on the property
- $2,000 salvage value from the demolished building
- $16,000 for architectural fees
- $54,000 for construction costs
- $7,000 for supervision during construction
- $1,500 for 6 months of insurance during construction
- Construction was completed in 5 months
- $4,400 for shrubs and fences
- $8,000 for office furniture

Questions

A. Cost of the land = _____
B. Cost of the factory = _____
C. We-Got-Stuff is disposing of a truck that originally cost $50,000 and has $40,000 in accumulated depreciation.

   Journal entry if We-Got-Stuff sells the truck for $11,000

D. Journal entry if We-Got-Stuff XYZ sells the truck for $6,000
E. Journal entry if We-Got-Stuff scraps the truck
F. Journal entry if the truck had been fully depreciated (accumulated depreciation = acquisition cost) when it was scrapped
G. In 2015, We-Got-Stuff exchanged equipment with Mercury Manufacturing:

	We-Got-Stuff	Mercury Manufacturing
Equipment (cost)	$100,000	$80,000
Accumulated depreciation	50,000	25,000
Fair value (FV)	60,000	50,000
Cash given up		10,000

Value of asset(s) that We-Got-Stuff gives up = _____

H. Value of asset(s) that We-Got-Stuff receives = _____
I. Gain or loss on the exchange for We-Got-Stuff = _____
J. Value of asset(s) that Mercury Manufacturing gives up = _____
K. Value of asset(s) that Mercury Manufacturing receives = _____
L. Gain or loss on the exchange for Mercury Manufacturing = _____
M. Journal entries if the transaction has commercial substance:
    i. On the books of We-Got-Stuff
    ii. On the books of Mercury Manufacturing
N. Journal entries if the transaction lacks commercial substance
    i. On the books of We-Got-Stuff
    ii. On the books of Mercury Manufacturing

Part 1 Section B Questions

Question 1B-ES01

Rein Company, a compressor manufacturer, is developing a budgeted income statement for the calendar year 2006. The president is generally satisfied with the projected net income for 2005 of $700,000 resulting in an earnings per share figure of $2.80. However, next year he would like earnings per share to increase to at least $3. Rein Company employs a standard absorption cost system. Inflation necessitates an annual revision in the standards as evidenced by an increase in production costs expected in 2006. The total standard manufacturing cost for 2005 is $72 per unit produced.

Rein expects to sell 100,000 compressors at $110 each in the current year (2005). Forecasts from the sales department are favorable, and Rein Company is projecting an annual increase of 10% in unit sales in 2006 and 2007. This increase in sales will occur even though a $15 increase in unit selling price will be implemented in 2006. The selling price increase was absolutely essential to compensate for the increased production costs and operating expenses. However, management is concerned that any additional sales price increase would curtail the desired growth in volume.

Standard production costs are developed for the two primary metals used in the compressor (brass and a steel alloy), the direct labor, and manufacturing overhead. The following schedule represents the 2006 standard quantities and rates for material and labor to produce one compressor.

Brass	4 pounds	@	$5.35/pound	$21.40
Steel alloy	5 pounds	@	$3.16/w	15.80
Direct labor	4 hours	@	$7.00/hour	28.00
			Total prime costs	$65.20

The material content of the compressor has been reduced slightly, hopefully without a noticeable decrease in the quality of the finished product. Improved labor productivity and some increase in automation have resulted in a decrease in labor hours per unit from 4.4 to 4.0. However, the significant increases in material prices and hourly labor rates more than offset any savings from reduced input quantities. The manufacturing overhead cost per unit schedule has yet to be completed. Preliminary data is as follows:

	Activity Level (units)		
	100,000	110,000	120,000
Overhead items			
Supplies	$475,000	$522,000	$570,000
Indirect labor	530,000	583,000	636,000
Utilities	170,000	187,000	204,000
Maintenance	363,000	378,000	392,000
Taxes and insurance	87,000	87,000	87,000
Depreciation	421,000	421,000	421,000
Total overhead	$2,046,000	$2,178,000	$2,310,000

The standard overhead rate is based on direct labor hours and is developed by using the total overhead costs from the above schedule for the activity level closest to planned production. In developing the standards for the manufacturing costs, the following two assumptions were made.

- Brass is currently selling at $5.65/pound. However, this price is historically high, and the purchasing manager expects the price to drop to the predetermined standard early in 2006.
- Several new employees will be hired for the production line in 2006. The employees will be generally unskilled. If basic training programs are not effective and improved labor productivity is not experienced, then the production time per unit of product will increase by 15 minutes over the 2006 standards.

Rein employs a LIFO inventory system for its finished goods. Rein's inventory policy for finished goods is to have 15% of the expected annual unit sales for the coming year in finished goods inventory at the end of the prior year. The finished goods inventory at December 31, 2005, is expected to consist of 16,500 units at a total carrying cost of $1,006,500.

Operating expenses are classified as selling, which are variable, and administrative, which are all fixed. The budgeted selling expenses are expected to average 12% of sales revenue in 2006, which is consistent with the performance in 2005. The administrative expenses in 2006 are expected to be 20% higher than the predicted 2005 amount of $907,850.

Management accepts the cost standards developed by the production and accounting department. However, it is concerned about the possible effect on net income if the price of brass does not decrease, and/or the labor efficiency does not improve as expected. Therefore, management wants the budgeted income statement to be prepared using the standards as developed but to consider the worst possible situation for 2006. Each resulting manufacturing variance should be separately identified and added to or subtracted from budgeted cost of goods sold at standard. Rein is subject to a 45% income tax rate.

Questions

A. Prepare the budgeted income statement for 2006 for Rein Company as specified by management. Round all calculations to the nearest dollar.
B. Review the 2006 budgeted income statement prepared for Rein Company and discuss whether the president's objectives can be achieved.

Question 1B-ES02

Gleason Company, a manufacturer of children's toys and furniture, is beginning budget preparation for next year. Jack Tiger, a recent addition to the accounting staff at Gleason, is questioning Leslie Robbins and James Crowe, sales and production managers, to learn about Gleason's budget process.

Crowe says that he incorporates Robbins's sales projections when estimating closing inventories but that the resulting numbers aren't completely reliable because Robbins makes some "adjustments" to her projections. Robbins admits that she does indeed lower initial sales projections by 5% to 10% to give her department some breathing room. Crowe admits that his department makes adjustments not unlike Robbins's; specifically, production adds about 10% to its estimates. "I think everyone here does something similar," he says, and Robbins nods assent.

Questions

A. What benefits do Robbins and Crowe expect to realize from their budgetary practices?
B. What are possible adverse effects of introducing budgetary slack for Robbins and Crowe?

Question 1B-ES03

Matchpoint Racquet Club (MRC) is a sports facility that offers tennis, racquetball, and other physical fitness facilities to its members. MRC owns and operates a large club with 2,000 members in a metropolitan area. The club has experienced cash flow problems over the last five years, especially during the summer months when both court use and new membership sales are low. Temporary bank loans have been obtained to cover the summer shortages.

The owners have decided to take action to improve MRC's net cash flow position. They have asked the club's financial manager to prepare a projected cash budget based on a proposed revised fee structure. The proposal would increase membership fees and replace the hourly tennis and racquetball court fees with a quarterly charge that would allow unlimited usage of the courts. The new rates would remain competitive when compared to the rates of other clubs in the area. Although there will be some members who do not renew because of the increase in price, management believes that the offer of unlimited court time will increase membership by 10%.

The proposed fee structure is shown next, along with the current membership distribution. The membership distribution is assumed to remain unchanged. All members would be required to pay the quarterly court charges.

Proposed Fee Structure

Membership Category	Annual Membership Fees	Quarterly Court Charges
Individual	$300	$50
Student	$180	$40
Family	$600	$90

Membership Distribution	
Individual	60%
Student	10%
Family	30%

Projected Membership Payment Activity

			Court Time in Hours	
Quarter	New	Renewed	Prime	Regular
1	100	700	5,000	7,000
2	70	330	2,000	4,000
3	50	150	1,000	2,000
4	200	600	5,000	7,000

The average membership during the third quarter is projected to be 2,200 people. Fixed costs are $157,500 per quarter, including a quarterly depreciation charge of $24,500. Variable costs are estimated at $15 per hour of total court usage time.

Questions

A. Prepare MRC's cash budget for the third quarter. Assume the opening cash balance is $186,000, that membership at the beginning of the quarter is 2,000, and that the change to the new pricing structure will be implemented. Include supporting calculations where appropriate.
B. How would sensitivity analysis help MRC management in the decision-making process?
C. Identify at least four factors that MRC should consider before implementing this decision.

Question 1B-ES04

Coe Company is a manufacturer of semicustom motorcycles. The company used 500 labor hours to produce a prototype of a new motorcycle for one of its key customers. The customer then ordered three additional motorcycles to be produced over the next six months. Coe estimates that the manufacturing process for these additional motorcycles is subject to a 90% learning curve. Although the production manager was aware of the learning curve projections, he decided to ignore the learning curve when compiling his budget in order to provide a cushion to prevent exceeding the budgeted amount for labor.

Questions

1. By using the cumulative average-time learning curve, estimate the total number of labor hours that are required to manufacture the first four units of product. Show your calculations.
2. Assume the 90% learning curve is realized. Calculate Coe's cost savings in producing the three additional units if the cost of direct labor is $25 per hour. Show your calculations.
3. a. Define *budgetary slack*.
   b. Identify and explain two negative effects that budgetary slack can have on the budgeting process.
4. Assume that Coe actually used 1,740 labor hours to produce the four units at a total cost of $44,805.
   a. If the company ignored the learning curve when creating the budget, for the four units produced, compute Coe's
      1. direct labor rate (price) variance.
      2. direct labor efficiency variance.
   b. How would the above two variances differ if the learning curve had been considered when creating the budget? Show your calculations.
5. Assume that the price variance is unfavorable and the efficiency variance is favorable. Identify and discuss one reason that explains both of these variances.
6. Explain the effect on the direct labor efficiency variance if the manufacturing process was subject to an 80% learning curve.
7. Identify and explain one limitation of learning curve analysis.

Question 1B-ES05

Law Services Inc. provides a variety of legal services to its clients. The firm's attorneys each have the authority to negotiate billing rates with their clients. Law Services wants to manage its operations more effectively, and established a budget at the beginning of last year. The budget included total hours billed, amount billed per hour, and variable expense per hour. Unfortunately, the firm failed to meet its budgeted goals for last year. The results are shown next.

	Actual	Budget
Total hours billed	5,700	6,000
Amount billed/hour	$275	$325

The budgeted variable expense per hour is $50, and the actual total variable expense was $285,000. There is disagreement among the attorneys over the reasons that the firm failed to meet its budgeted goals.

Questions

1. What is the advantage of using a flexible budget as opposed to a static budget to evaluate Law Services' results for last year? Explain your answer.
2. Explain the process of creating a flexible budget for Law Services.
3. Calculate the total static budget revenue variance, the flexible budget revenue variance, and the sales-volume revenue variance. Show your calculations.
4. a. Calculate the variable expense variance. Show your calculations.
   b. Was the variable expense variance a flexible budget variance or a sales volume variance? Explain your answer.

Part 1 Section C Questions

Question 1C-ES01

Handler Company distributes two power tools to hardware stores—a heavy-duty ½-inch hand drill and a table saw. The tools are purchased from a manufacturer where the Handler private label is attached. The wholesale selling prices to the hardware stores are $60 each for the drill and $120 each for the table saw. The 2005 budget and actual results are presented next. The budget was adopted in late 2004 and was based on Handler's estimated share of the market for the two tools.

Handler Company Income Statement for the Year Ended December 31, 2005
(000s omitted)

	Hand Drill		Table Saw		Total		
	Budget	Actual	Budget	Actual	Budget	Actual	Variance
Sales in units	120	86	80	74	200	160	40
Revenue	$7,200	$5,074	$9,600	$8,510	$16,800	$13,584	$(3,216)
Cost of goods sold	6,000	4,300	6,400	6,068	12,400	10,368	2,032
Gross margin	$1,200	$774	$3,200	$2,442	4,400	3,216	(1,184)
Unallocated costs							
Selling					1,000	1,000	—
Advertising					1,000	1,060	(60)
Administration					400	406	(6)
Income taxes (45%)					900	338	562
Total unallocated costs					3,300	2,804	496
Net income					$1,100	$412	$(688)

During the first quarter of 2005, Handler's management estimated that the total market for these tools actually would be 10% below its original estimates. In an attempt to prevent Handler's unit sales from declining as much as industry projections, management developed and implemented a marketing program. Included in the program were dealer discounts and increased direct advertising. The table saw line was emphasized in this program.

Questions

A. Analyze the unfavorable gross margin variance of $1,184,000 in terms of:
   1. Sales price variance
   2. Cost variance
   3. Volume variance
B. Discuss the apparent effect of Handler Company's special marketing program (i.e., dealer discounts and additional advertising) on 2005 operating results. Support your comments with numerical data where appropriate.

Question 1C-ES02

The Jackson Corporation is a large manufacturing company where each division is viewed as an investment center and has virtually complete autonomy for product development, marketing, and production. Performance of division managers is evaluated periodically by senior corporate management. Divisional return on investment is the sole criterion used in performance evaluation under current corporate policy. Corporate management believes return on investment is an adequate measure because it incorporates quantitative information from the divisional income statement and balance sheet in the analysis.

Some division managers complained that a single criterion for performance evaluation is insufficient and ineffective. These managers have compiled a list of criteria that they believe should be used in evaluating division managers' performance. The criteria include profitability, market position, productivity, product leadership, employee development, employee attitudes, public responsibility, and balance between short-range and long-range goals.

Questions

A. Jackson management believes that return on investment is an adequate criterion to evaluate division management performance. Discuss the shortcomings or possible inconsistencies of using return on investment as the sole criterion to evaluate divisional management performance.
B. Discuss the advantages of using multiple criteria versus a single criterion to evaluate divisional management performance.
C. Describe the problems or disadvantages which can be associated with the implementation of the multiple performance criteria measurement system suggested to Jackson Corporation by its division managers.

Question 1C-ES03

George Nickles has recently been appointed vice president of operations for Merriam Corporation. The company's business segments include manufacture of heavy equipment, food processing, and financial services. Nickles has suggested to Merriam's chief financial officer, Karen Schilling, that segment managers should be evaluated on segment data contained in the company's annual report, which presents revenues, earnings, identifiable assets, and depreciation for each segment for a five-year period. Nickles reasons that segment managers may be appropriately evaluated by the same criteria used to evaluate top management. Schilling has doubts about using information from the annual report for that purpose and suggests that Nickles consider other ways of evaluating the segment managers.

Questions

A. What legitimate concerns might Karen Schilling have regarding the evaluation of segment managers using segment information prepared for public reporting?

B. What could the possible behavioral impact be on Merriam Corporation's segment managers if their performance evaluations are based on information published in the annual report?

C. What types of financial information would be more appropriate for George Nickles to use in evaluating the performance of segment managers?

Question 1C-ES04

ARQ Enterprises was formed by the merger of Andersen, Rolvaag, and Quie Corporations. Its three divisions retain the names of the former companies and operate with complete autonomy. Corporate management evaluates the divisions and division management according to return on investment.

The Rolvaag and Quie divisions are currently negotiating a transfer price for a component that Quie manufactures and Rolvaag needs. Quie, which sells the component already into a market that it expects to grow rapidly, currently has excess capacity. Rolvaag could buy the component from other suppliers.

Three transfer prices are under consideration:

1. Rolvaag has bid $3.84 for the component, which is Quie's standard variable manufacturing cost plus a 20% markup.
2. Quie has offered the component to Rolvaag at $5.90, which is its regular selling price in the marketplace ($6.50) minus variable selling and distribution expenses.
3. ARQ management, which has no established policy on transfer pricing, has offered the compromise price of $5.06, which is the standard full manufacturing cost plus 15%.

Both the Quie and Rolvaag divisions have rejected the compromise price. Refer to the pricing chart for a summary of this information.

Pricing Chart	
Regular selling price	$6.50
Standard variable manufacturing cost	$3.20
Standard full manufacturing cost	$4.40
Variable selling and distribution expenses	$0.60
Standard variable manufacturing cost plus 20% ($3.20 × 1.20)	$3.84
Regular selling price less variable selling and distribution expenses ($6.50−$0.6)	$5.90
Standard full manufacturing cost plus 15% ($4.40 × 1.15)	$5.06

Questions

A. What effect might each of the three proposed prices have on the Quie division management's attitude toward intracompany business?

B. Would a negotiation of a price between Quie and Rolvaag be a satisfactory method to establish a transfer price in this situation? Explain your decision.

C. Should ARQ corporate management become involved in resolving this transfer price controversy? Explain your decision.

Question 1C-ES05

Within Sparta Enterprises, the extraction division transfers 100% of its total output of 500,000 units of a particular type of clay to the pet products division, which treats the clay and sells it as cat litter for $42 a unit. The pet products division currently pays a transfer price for the clay of cost plus $1, or $22 a unit. The clay has many other uses and could be sold in the marketplace for $26 in virtually unlimited quantities. If the extraction division did sell the clay into the wider market, it would incur a variable selling cost of $1.50 per unit.

The extraction division recently hired a new manager, Keith Richardson, who immediately complained to top management about the disparity between the transfer price and the market price. For the most recent year, the pet products division's contribution margin on the sale of 500,000 units of cat litter was $5,775,000. The extraction unit's contribution margin on the transfer of an equal number of units of clay to the pet products division was $1,625,000.

Refer to the Unit Cost Structure chart for more information.

Unit Cost Structure

	Extraction Division	Pet Products Division
Transfer price for clay	—	$22.00
Material cost	$4.00	2.00
Labor cost	6.00	4.00
Overhead	11.00*	7.00†
Total cost per unit	$21.00	$35.00

*Overhead in the extraction division is 25% fixed and 75% variable.
†Overhead in the pet products division is 65% fixed and 35% variable.

Questions

A. Why don't cost-based transfer prices provide an appropriate measure of divisional performance?

B. Using the market price for the clay, what is the contribution margin for the two divisions for the most recent year?

C. What price range for the clay would be acceptable to both divisions if Sparta instituted negotiated transfer pricing and allowed the divisions to buy and sell clay on the open market? Explain your answer.

D. Why should a negotiated transfer price result in desirable behavior from the management of the two divisions?

Question 1C-ES06

4-Cycle, Inc., manufactures small engines for recreational vehicles, motorcycles, boats, and stationary equipment. Each line has its own product manager. The company chief financial officer, Stan Downs, prepares divisional budgets on a per-month basis using a standard cost system. Each product line occupies its own space, with square footage varying considerably among lines. Fixed production costs are allocated on the basis of square feet using a factory-wide rate. Variable factory overhead is based on machine hours. Other costs are based on revenue.

At the company's quarterly meeting, Laura Fleur, the new product manager for marine engines, received an unpleasant surprise. When distributing the performance report (shown next) to each manager, Stan Downs remarked aloud that Fleur would need to see him after the meeting to discuss ways to improve her line's lackluster performance. Since she thought her first quarter's performance was impressive, she was taken aback by Downs's comments. The performance report provided her with no clue to what had gone wrong.

4-Cycle, Inc. Marine Engine Quarterly Performance Report

	Actual	Budget	Variance
Units	10,500	8,500	2,000 F
Revenue	$17,500,000	$14,700,000	$2,800,000 F
Variable production costs			
Direct materials	2,500,000	2,164,750	335,250 U
Direct labor	2,193,000	1,790,000	403,000 U
Machine time	2,300,000	1,950,000	350,000 U
Factory overhead	4,500,000	3,825,000	675,500 U
Fixed production costs			
Indirect labor	925,000	580,250	344,750 U
Depreciation	500,000	500,000	—
Taxes	232,500	220,000	12,500 U
Insurance	437,000	437,000	—
Administrative expense	1,226,000	919,500	306,500 U
Marketing expense	848,000	540,000	308,000 U
Research and development	613,000	460,000	153,000 U
Operating profit	$1,225,000	$1,313,500	$88,500 U

Questions

A. What are at least three weaknesses in 4-Cycle's quarterly performance report? Explain your answer.

B. What are some ways in which 4-Cycle can eliminate the weaknesses in the way it reports quarterly performance to its managers? Revise the quarterly report accordingly.

Question 1C-ES07

SieCo is a sheet metal manufacturer whose customers are mainly in the automobile industry. The company's chief engineer, Steve Simpson, has recently presented a proposal for automating the Drilling Department. The proposal recommended that SieCo purchase from Service Corp. two robots that would have the capability of replacing the eight direct labor workers in the department. The cost savings in the proposal included the elimination of the direct labor costs plus the elimination of manufacturing overhead cost in the Drilling Department as SieCo charges manufacturing overhead on the basis of direct labor costs using a plant-wide rate.

SieCo's controller, Keith Hunter, gathered the information shown in Exhibit 1 to discuss the issue of overhead application at the management meeting at which the proposal was approved.

Exhibit 1

Date	Average Annual Direct Labor Cost	Average Annual Manufacturing Overhead Cost	Average Manufacturing Overhead Rate
Current Year	$4,000,000	$20,000,000	500%

Category	Cutting Department	Grinding Department	Drilling Department
Average Annual Direct Labor	$2,000,000	$1,750,000	$250,000
Average Annual Overhead Cost	11,000,000	7,000,000	2,000,000

Simpson met the chief accountant, Leslie Altman, in the lunchroom and inquired about the status of the proposal. Altman told Simpson that the project had been approved. Simpson said, "That's great. Be sure to make the payment as soon as possible as my brother-in-law owns Service Corp."

Altman was puzzled by the fact that there had been no competitive bidding and spoke to his supervisor, Keith Hunter. Hunter told Altman not to worry; Service Corp will do a great job.

Questions

A. Using the information from Exhibit 1, describe the shortcomings of the system for applying overhead that is currently used by SieCo.

B. Recommend two ways to improve SieCo's method for applying overhead in the Cutting and Grinding Departments.

C. Recommend two ways to improve SieCo's method for applying overhead to accommodate the automation of the Drilling Department.
D. Explain the misconceptions underlying the statement that the manufacturing overhead cost in the Drilling Department would be reduced to zero if the automation proposal were implemented.
E. Referring to the specific standards outlined in IMA's *Statement of Ethical Professional Practice,* identify and discuss the ethical conflicts that Altman needs to resolve.
F. According to IMA's *Statement of Ethical Professional Practice,* identify the steps that Altman should take to resolve this situation

Question 1C-ES08

For many years, Lawton Industries has manufactured prefabricated houses where the houses are constructed in sections to be assembled on customers' lots. The company expanded into the precut housing market in 2006 when it acquired Presser Company, one of its suppliers. In this market, various types of lumber are precut into the appropriate lengths, banded into packages, and shipped to customers' lots for assembly. Lawton decided to maintain Presser's separate identity and, thus, established the Presser Division as an investment center of Lawton.

Lawton uses return on average investment (ROI) as a performance measure the investment defined as operating assets employed. Management bonuses are based in part on ROI. All investments in operating assets are expected to earn a minimum return of 15% before income taxes. Presser's ROI has ranged from 19.3% to 22.1% since it was acquired in 2006. The division had an investment opportunity in the year just ended that had an estimated ROI of 18%, but Presser's management decided against the investment because it believed the investment would decrease the division's overall ROI.

Presser's operating statement for the year just ended is presented next. The division's operating assets employed were $12,600,000 at the end of the year, a 5% increase over the balance at the end of the previous year.

Presser Division Operating Statement for the Year Ended December 31 ($000 omitted)		
Sales revenue		$24,000
Cost of goods sold		15,800
Gross profit		$8,200
Operating expenses		
Administrative	$2,140	
Selling	3,600	5,740
Income from operations before income taxes		$2,460

Questions

A. Calculate these performance measures for the year just ended for the Presser Division of Lawton Industries:
  1. Return on average investment in operating assets employed (ROI).
  2. Residual income calculated on the basis of average operating assets employed.

B. Would the management of Presser Division have been more likely to accept the investment opportunity it had during the year if residual income were used as a performance measure instead of ROI? Explain you answer.

C. The Presser Division is a separate investment center with Lawton Industries. Identify and describe the items Presser must control if it is to be evaluated fairly by either the ROI or residual income performance measures.

Question 1C-ES09

Klein, Thompson Corporation's CFO, has determined that the Motor Division has purchased switches for its motors from an outside supplier during the current year rather than buying them from the Switch Division. The Switch Division is operating at full capacity and demanded that the Motor Division pay the price charged to outside customers rather than the actual full manufacturing costs, as it has done in the past. The Motor Division refused to meet the price demanded by the Switch Division. The Switch Division contracted with an outside customer to sell its remaining switches, and the Motor Division was forced to purchase the switches from an outside supplier at an even higher price.

Klein is reviewing Thompson Corporation's transfer pricing policy because she believes that suboptimization has occurred. While Klein believes the Switch Division made the correct decision to maximize its divisional profit by not transferring the switches at actual full manufacturing cost, this decision was not necessarily in the best interest of Thompson Corporation.

Klein has requested that the corporate Accounting Department study alternative transfer pricing methods that would promote overall goal congruence, motivate divisional management performance, and optimize overall company performance. The three transfer pricing methods being considered are listed next. One of these methods will be selected and will be applied uniformly across all divisions.

1. Standard full manufacturing costs plus markup
2. Market selling price of the products being transferred
3. Outlay (out-of-pocket) costs incurred to the point of transfer plus opportunity cost per unit

Questions

1. Identify and explain two positive and two negative behavioral implications that can arise from employing a negotiated transfer price system for goods that are exchanged between divisions.
2. Identify and explain two behavioral problems that can arise from using actual full (absorption) manufacturing costs as a transfer price.

3. Identify and explain two behavioral problems **most** likely to arise if Thompson Corporation changes from its current transfer pricing policy to a revised transfer pricing policy that it applies uniformly to all divisions.
4. Discuss the likely behavior of both "buying" and "selling" divisional managers for each of the next transfer pricing methods being considered by Thompson Corporation:
   a. Standard full manufacturing costs plus markup
   b. Market selling price of the products being transferred
   c. Outlay (out-of-pocket) costs incurred to the point of transfer plus opportunity cost per unit

Part 1 Section D Questions

Question 1D-ES01

Many companies recognize that their cost systems are inadequate for today's powerful global competition. Managers in companies selling multiple products are making important product decisions based on distorted cost information, as most cost systems designed in the past focused on inventory valuation. In order to elevate the level of management information, it has been suggested that companies should have as many as three cost systems for (1) inventory valuation, (2) management control of operations, and (3) an activity-based costing system for decision making.

Questions

A. Discuss why the traditional cost system, developed to value inventory, distorts product cost information.
B. 1. Describe the benefits that management can expect from activity-based costing.
   2. List the steps that a company, using a traditional cost system, would take to implement activity-based costing.

Question 1D-ES02

TruJeans, a new start-up company, plans to produce blue jean pants, customized with the buyer's first name stitched across the back pocket. The product will be marketed exclusively via an Internet Web site. For the coming year, sales have been projected at three different levels: optimistic, neutral, and pessimistic. TruJeans does keep inventory on hand but prefers to minimize this investment.

The controller is preparing to assemble the budget for the coming year and is unsure about a number of issues, including:

- The level of sales to enter into the budget
- How to allocate the significant fixed costs to individual units
- Whether to use job order costing or process costing

In addition, the controller has heard of kaizen budgeting and is wondering if such an approach could be used by TruJeans.

Questions

A. How could the use of variable (direct) costing mitigate the problem of how to allocate the fixed costs to individual units?

B. Which cost system seems to make more sense for TruJeans, job order costing or process costing? Explain your answer.

Question 1D-ES03

Sonimad Sawmill Inc. (SSI) purchases logs from independent timber contractors and processes the logs into three types of lumber products:

1. Studs for residential building (e.g., walls, ceilings)
2. Decorative pieces (e.g., fireplace mantels, beams for cathedral ceilings)
3. Posts used as support braces (e.g., mine support braces, braces for exterior fences around ranch properties)

These products are the result of a joint sawmill process that involves removal of bark from the logs, cutting the logs into a workable size (ranging from 8 to 16 feet in length), and then cutting the individual products from the logs, depending on the type of wood (pine, oak, walnut, or maple) and the size (diameter) of the log. The joint process results in the following costs and output of products for a typical month.

Joint production costs	
Materials (rough timber logs)	$500,000
Debarking (labor and overhead)	50,000
Sizing (labor and overhead)	200,000
Product cutting (labor and overhead)	250,000
Total joint costs	$1,000,000

Product yield and average sales value on a per unit basis from the joint process are shown next.

Product	Monthly Output	Fully Processed Sales Price
Studs	75,000	$8
Decorative pieces	5,000	100
Posts	20,000	20

The studs are sold as rough-cut lumber after emerging from the sawmill operation without further processing by SSI. Also, the posts require no further processing. The decorative pieces must be planed and further sized after emerging from the SSI sawmill. This additional processing costs SSI $100,000 per month and normally results in a loss of 10% of the units entering the process. Without this planning and sizing process, there is still an active intermediate market for the unfinished decorative pieces where the sales price averages $60 per unit.

Questions

A. Based on the information given for Sonimad Sawmill Inc., allocate the joint processing costs of $1,000,000 to each of the three product lines using the
1. Relative sales value method at split-off
2. Physical output (volume) method at split-off
3. Estimated net realizable value method

B. Prepare an analysis for Sonimad Sawmill Inc. to compare processing the decorative pieces further, as the company currently does, with selling the rough-cut product immediately at split-off, and recommend which action the company should take. Be sure to provide all calculations.

Question 1D-ES04

Alyssa Manufacturing produces two items in its Trumbull plant: Tuff Stuff and Ruff Stuff. Since inception, Alyssa has used only one manufacturing overhead pool to accumulate costs. Overhead has been allocated to products based on direct labor hours.

Until recently, Alyssa was the sole producer of Ruff Stuff and was able to dictate the selling price. However, last year Marvella Products began marketing a comparable product at a price below the standard costs developed by Alyssa. Market share has declined rapidly, and Alyssa must now decide whether to meet the competitive price or to discontinue the product line. Recognizing that discontinuing the product line would place additional burden on its remaining product, Tuff Stuff, Alyssa is using activity-based costing to determine if it would show a different cost structure for the two products.

The two major indirect costs for manufacturing the products are power usage and setup costs. Most of the power usage is used in fabricating, while most of the setup costs are required in assembly. The setup costs are predominantly for the Tuff Stuff product line. A decision was made to separate the Manufacturing Department costs into two activity centers: (1) fabricating using machine hours as the cost driver (activity base) and (2) assembly using the number of setups as the cost driver (activity base).

Manufacturing Department

Annual Budget Before Separation of Overhead

	Total	Product Line	
		Tuff Stuff	Ruff Stuff
Number of units		20,000	20,000
Direct labor*		2 hrs./unit	3 hrs./unit
Total direct labor	$800,000		
Direct material		$5.00/unit	$3.00/unit

(Continued)

(Continued)

Budgeted overhead:	
Indirect labor	$24,000
Fringe benefits	5,000
Indirect material	31,000
Power	180,000
Setup	75,000
Quality assurance	10,000
Other utilities	10,000
Depreciation	15,000

*Direct labor hourly rate is the same in both departments.

Manufacturing Department

Cost Structure after Separation of Overhead into Activity Pools

	Fabrication	Assembly
Direct labor	75%	25%
Direct material	100%	0%
Indirect labor	75%	25%
Fringe benefits	80%	20%
Indirect material	$20,000	$11,000
Power	$160,000	$20,000
Setup	$5,000	$70,000
Quality assurance	80%	20%
Other utilities	50%	50%
Depreciation	80%	20%

Activity Base	Tuff Stuff	Ruff Stuff
Machine hours per unit	4.4	6.0
Number of setups	1,000	272

Questions

A. By allocating overhead based on direct labor hours, calculate the
1. Total budgeted cost of the Manufacturing Department
2. Unit standard cost of Tuff Stuff
3. Unit standard cost of Ruff Stuff

B. After separation of overhead into activity pools, compute the total budgeted cost of the
1. Fabricating Department
2. Assembly Department

C. Using activity-based costing, calculate the unit standard costs for
1. Tuff Stuff
2. Ruff Stuff

D. Discuss how a decision by Alyssa Manufacturing regarding the continued production of Ruff Stuff will be affected by the results of your calculations in Requirement C.

Question 1D-ES05

Inman Inc. is a manufacturer of a single product and is starting to develop a budget for the coming year. Because cost of goods manufactured is the biggest item, Inman's senior management is reviewing how costs are calculated. In addition, senior management wants to develop a budgeting system that motivates managers and other workers to work toward the corporate goals. Inman has incurred the following costs to make 100,000 units during the month of September:

Materials	$400,000
Direct labor	100,000
Variable manufacturing overhead	20,000
Variable selling and administrative costs	80,000
Fixed manufacturing overhead	200,000
Fixed selling and administrative costs	300,000

Inman Inc.'s September 1 inventory consisted of 10,000 units valued at $72,000 using absorption costing. Total fixed costs and variable costs per unit have not changed during the past few months. In September, Inman sold 106,000 units at $12 per unit.

Questions

1. Using absorption costing, calculate:
   a. Inman's September manufacturing cost per unit.
   b. Inman's September 30 inventory value.
   c. Inman's September net income.
2. Using variable costing, calculate:
   a. Inman's September manufacturing cost per unit.
   b. Inman's September 30 inventory value.
   c. Inman's September net income.
3. Identify and explain one reason why the income calculated in the previous two questions might differ.
4. Identify and discuss one advantage of using each of the following:
   a. Absorption costing
   b. Variable costing
5. a. Identify one strength and one weakness each of authoritative budgeting and participative budgeting.
   b. Which of these budgeting methods will work best for Inman Inc.? Explain your answer.
   c. Identify and explain one method the top managers can take to restrict the production manager from taking advantage of budgetary slack.

Question 1D-ES06

Smart Electronics manufactures two types of gaming consoles, Models M-11 and R-24. Currently, the company allocates overhead costs based on direct labor hours; the total overhead cost for the past year was €80,000. Additional cost information for the past year is presented next.

Product Name	Total Direct Labor Hours Used	Units Sold	Direct Costs per Unit	Selling Price per Unit
M-11	650	1,300	€10	€90
R-24	150	1,500	€30	€60

Recently the company lost bids on a contract to sell Model M-11 to a local wholesaler and was informed that a competitor offered a much lower price. Smart's controller believes that the cost reports do not accurately reflect the actual manufacturing costs and product profitability for these gaming consoles. He also believes that there is enough variation in the production process for Models M-11 and R-24 to warrant a better cost allocation system. Given the nature of the electronic gaming market, setting competitive prices is extremely crucial. The controller has decided to try activity-based costing and has gathered the next information:

	Number of Setups	Number of Components	Number of Material Movements
M-11	3	17	15
R-24	7	33	35
Total activity cost	€20,000	€50,000	€10,000

The number of setups, number of components, and number of material movements have been identified as activity-cost drivers for overhead.

Questions

1. Using Smart's current costing system, calculate the gross margin per unit for Model M-11 and for Model R-24. Assume no beginning or ending inventory. Show your calculations.
2. Using activity-based costing, calculate the gross margin for Model M-11 and for Model R-24. Assume no beginning or ending inventory. Show your calculations.
3. Describe how Smart Electronics can use the activity-based costing information to formulate a more competitive pricing strategy. Be sure to include specific examples to justify the recommended strategy.
4. Identify and explain two advantages and two limitations of activity-based costing.

Part 1 Section E Questions

Question 1E-ES01

Superior Co. manufactures automobile parts for sale to major automakers. Superior's internal audit staff is reviewing the internal controls over machinery and equipment and making recommendations for improvements where appropriate.

The internal auditors obtained the information presented next during this review.

- Purchase requests for machinery and equipment normally are initiated by the supervisor in need of the asset. The supervisor discusses the proposed acquisition with the plant manager. A purchase requisition is submitted to the purchasing department when the plant manager determines that the request is reasonable and that there is a remaining balance in the plant's share of the total corporate budget for capital acquisitions.
- Upon receiving a purchase requisition for machinery or equipment, the purchasing department manager looks through the records for an appropriate supplier. A formal purchase order is then completed and mailed. When the machine or equipment is received, it is immediately sent to the user department for installation. This allows the economic benefits from the acquisition to be realized at the earliest possible date.
- The property, plant, and equipment ledger control accounts are supported by lapsing schedules organized by year of acquisition. These lapsing schedules are used to compute depreciation as a unit for all assets of a given type that are acquired in the same year. Standard rates, depreciation methods, and salvage values are used for each major type of fixed asset. These rates, methods, and salvage values were set ten years ago during the company's initial year of operation.
- When machinery or equipment is retired, the plant manager notifies the accounting department so that the appropriate entries can be made in the accounting records.
- There has been no reconciliation since the company began operations between the accounting records and the machinery and equipment on hand.

Question

Identify the internal control weaknesses and recommend improvements that the internal audit staff of Superior Co. should include in its report regarding the internal controls employed for fixed assets. Use the following format in preparing your answer.

Weaknesses	Recommendations
1.	1.

Question 1E-ES02

The board of directors of a large corporation recently learned that some members of the senior management team had circumvented the company's internal controls for personal gain. The board appointed a special task force of external auditors and outside legal counsel to investigate the situation.

After extensive review, the task force has concluded that for a period of several years the expenses of the company's chief executive officer, president, and vice president-public relations were charged to an account called the Limited Expenditure Account (LEA). The account was established five years ago and was not subject to the company's normal approval authorization process. Approximately $2,000,000 of requests for reimbursement were routinely processed and charged to LEA.

Accounting personnel were advised by the controller to process such requests based on the individual approval of any of the three executives, even when the requests were not adequately documented.

The vice president-public relations and his department were in charge of political fundraising activities. The task force determined, however, that only a small portion of the $1,000,000 raised last year was actually used for political purposes. In addition, departmental resources were used for personal projects of the three identified executives. The task force also uncovered an additional $4,000,000 of expenditures that were poorly documented so that even the amounts for proper business purposes could not be identified.

The task force noted that these payment practices, as well as LEA, were never disclosed in the Internal Audit Department's audit reports even though company disbursements were tested annually. References to these practices and LEA were included on two occasions in recent year's work papers. The director of internal audit, who reports to the controller, advised that she reviewed these findings with the controller who, in turn, advised that he mentioned these findings to the president. The president recommended that they not be included in the internal audit reports. Furthermore, the external auditors, who reviewed the internal audit work papers, did not mention LEA or these payment practices in their recommendations for improved internal control procedures to management or in their external audit reports. The task force also noted that the company did not have a formal, published ethics policy.

Questions

A. Identify at least three internal control weaknesses in the company's internal control system.

B. Identify at least three illegal or improper practices uncovered at the company.

C. Identify at least four important steps the company should take, both procedurally and organizationally, to correct the problems that were uncovered in order to prevent a similar situation in the future.

Question 1E-ES03

Brawn Technology, Inc. is a manufacturer of large wind energy systems. The company has its corporate headquarters in Buenos Aires and a central manufacturing facility about 200 miles away. Since the manufacturing facility is so remote, it does not receive the attention or the support from the staff that the other units do. The president of Brawn is concerned about whether proper permits have been issued for new construction work being done to handle industrial waste at the facility. In addition, he wants to be sure that all occupational safety laws and environmental issues are being properly addressed. He has asked the company's internal auditor to conduct an audit focusing on these areas of concern.

Questions

A. Identify the seven types of internal audits and describe the two most common types of internal audits. Using examples, describe two situations where each type of common audit would be applicable.

B. Referring to Brawn Technology:
1. Identify the type of audit that would best address the concerns of the president.
2. Identify the objective of this audit.
3. Give two reasons why this type of audit would best address the concerns of the president.

C. Recommend two procedures that could be implemented at Brawn's manufacturing plant that would lessen the president's concerns. Explain each of your recommendations.

Question 1E-ES04

Ted Crosby owns Standard Lock Inc., a small business that manufactures metal door handles and door locks. When he first started the company, Crosby managed the business by himself, overseeing purchasing and production as well as maintaining the financial records. The only employees he hired were production workers.

As the business expanded, Crosby decided to hire John Smith as the company's financial manager. Smith had an MBA and ten years of experience in the finance department of a large company. During the interview, Smith mentioned that he was considering an offer from another company and needed to know of Crosby's decision within the next couple of days. Since Crosby was extremely impressed with Smith's credentials, he offered him the job without conducting background checks. Smith seemed to be a dedicated and hard-working employee. His apparent integrity quickly earned him a reputation as an outstanding and trusted manager.

Later in the year, Crosby hired another manager, Joe Fletcher, to oversee the production department. Crosby continued to take care of purchasing and authorized all payments.

Fletcher was highly qualified for the position and seemed to be reliable and conscientious. After observing Fletcher's work for one year, Crosby concluded that he was performing his duties efficiently. Crosby believed that Fletcher and Smith were both good managers whom he could trust and gave them expanded responsibilities. Fletcher's additional responsibilities included purchasing and receiving; Smith paid all the bills, prepared and signed all checks, maintained records, and reconciled the bank statements.

Soon Crosby began taking a hands-off approach to managing his business. He frequently took long vacations with his family and was not often at the office to check on the business. He was pleased that the company was profitable and expected that it would continue to be profitable in the future under the supervision of two qualified and trusted managers. One year after Crosby left the management of the company to Smith and Fletcher, business began to experience a decline in profits. Crosby assumed that it was due to a cyclical downturn in the economy. When Standard continued to decline even as the economy improved, Crosby began to investigate. He noticed that revenues were increasing but profits were declining. He also discovered that purchases from one vendor had increased significantly as compared to the other five vendors. Crosby is concerned that fraud may be occurring in the company.

Questions

A. Identify and describe four internal control deficiencies within Standard Lock Inc.
B. For each of the internal control deficiencies identified, recommend an improvement in procedures that would mitigate these deficiencies.
C. If the company were to implement an ideal internal control system, can it guarantee that fraud would not occur in future? Explain your answer.

Question 1E-ES05

Sam Pierce is a division controller with Med Direct, Inc., a publicly traded multinational corporation that manufactures large-scale medical equipment and also provides financing services to its customers. Pierce has seen many news stories recently of competitors having severe financial difficulty, including bankruptcy. He has also seen other corporations suffer from regulatory indictments and fines. Pierce not only wants to avoid such problems, but he also wants his company to report stable earnings and a rising stock price. Pierce's goal is to integrate enterprise risk management into the culture and operations of his division, and throughout the whole corporation. He also wants to make sure the company is in compliance with the requirements of the Sarbanes-Oxley Act of 2002.

Questions

A. Identify and explain two risks that a multinational firm such as Med Direct may encounter in each of these three areas:
  1. Buying raw materials from other countries
  2. Selling on credit terms to customers in foreign countries
  3. Developing and manufacturing high-tech equipment
B. Identify two reasons why each of the next three elements is important for a risk assessment and control program to be effective. Provide one example of each element.
  1. Understanding your business
  2. Implementing checks and balances
  3. Developing procedures that set limits or establish standards
C. Explain how a company's organizational policies and management style impact the effectiveness of the control environment and its management of risk.
D. Identify and explain the compliance requirements with respect to internal controls in the Sarbanes-Oxley Act of 2002 (SOX 404).

Question 1E-ES06

Ace Contractors is a large regional general contractor. As the company grew, Eddie Li was hired as the controller and tasked with analyzing the monthly income statements and reconciling all of the accounts formerly handled by Susan Zhao, the sole accounting associate. Li noticed a large amount of demolition expense for February, even though no new projects had started over the past few months. Since Li did not expect such a large amount of demolition expense, nor was any of this type of expense budgeted, Li dug a little deeper. He found that all of those expenses were bank transfers into another bank account. After additional research, it became evident that Zhao had been transferring funds out of the company bank account and into her own and recording fake expenses to make the bank account reconciliation work. While the president kept the prenumbered checks locked up until check run time and signed all of the outgoing checks, he was unaware of the ability to initiate transfers via the Internet. Li had also reviewed the bank reconciliations, which were completed by the office manager, and this fraud was not evident since the ending balance was reasonable.

Questions

1. a. Identify and explain the four types of functional responsibilities that should be segregated properly.
   b. Identify and explain two incompatible duties that Zhao had that allowed her to take company funds.
2. Identify and explain two ways that the company had attempted to safeguard its assets, and suggest two ways to strengthen controls in this area.
3. Refer to COSO's *Internal Control Framework* to answer the next questions.
   a. Identify and describe the three objectives of internal control.
   b. Identify and describe five components of internal controls.
4. Identify and explain three ways internal controls provide reasonable assurance.

Question 1E-ES07

SmallParts is a manufacturer of metal washers, screws, and other parts required in the manufacture of various handmade craft and novelty items. The firm has the ability to custom make virtually any small part, provided the client is able to provide SmallParts with the dimensions and tolerance required of the product. Because of its niche in the market, SmallParts has over 1,000 clients. Unfortunately, many of its small business clients eventually merge or cease operations. One of the company's biggest challenges is the return of shipped product. Usually this is because the small business client has ceased operations. Although most of the product is custom made, SmallParts has found that much of it can be sold to other clients for adapted use. The company's accountant is reviewing the company's internal controls and financial accounting procedures, in particular, with respect to inventory.

Currently, SmallParts has one salesperson responsible for marketing returned product. This salesperson has exclusive and total control over the returned product, including arranging of sales terms, billing, and collection. The salesperson receives the returned product and attempts to find a client who may be able to adapt the product for his or her use. The inventory of returned product is not entered in the accounting records, under the logic that the cost is sunk. Revenue generated from its sale is classified as other revenue on the SmallParts income statement.

Questions

1. Identify and describe the three objectives of a system of internal control.
2. Identify and explain three ways that the procedure for handling returned product violates the internal control system of segregation of duties.

3. Identify four functional responsibilities within an organization that should be separated. Explain why these responsibilities should be separated.
4. Identify and describe three ways that SmallParts can provide for better internal control over its inventory of returned product.
5. The company accountant is concerned about SmallParts' current procedure for accounting for returned product and has turned to the IMA *Statement of Ethical Professional Practice* for guidance.
   a. Identify the ethical principles that should guide the work of a management accountant.
   b. Assume the company's accountant identifies a possible conflict of interest on the part of the salesperson responsible for the returned product.
      (1) Identify and describe the standards that relate to this situation, and explain how they apply.
      (2) Identify the steps the company accountant should take to resolve this situation.

Question 1E-ES08

Michael Hanson is an internal auditor who has been asked to evaluate the internal controls and risks of his company, Consolidated Enterprises Inc. He has been asked to present recommendations to senior management with respect to Consolidated's general operations with particular attention to the company's database procedures. With regard to database procedures, he was specifically directed to focus attention on (1) transaction processing, (2) virus protection, (3) backup controls, and (4) disaster recovery controls.

Questions

1. Define the objectives of
   a. a compliance audit.
   b. an operational audit.
2. For each of the areas shown next, identify two controls that Hanson should review, and explain why.
   a. Transaction processing
   b. Virus protection
   c. Backup controls
3. Identify four components of a sound business continuance plan.
4. During his evaluation of general operations, Hanson found the following conditions:
   a. Daily bank deposits do not always correspond with cash receipts.
   b. Physical inventory counts sometimes differ from perpetual inventory records, and there have been alterations to physical counts and perpetual records.
   c. An unexplained and unexpected decrease in gross profit percentage has occurred.

   For each of these conditions, (1) describe a possible cause of the condition and (2) recommend actions to be taken and/or controls to be implemented that would correct the condition.

Part 1 Section A Answers

Answer to Question 1A-ES01

Answer A:

Crank-M-Up
INCOME STATEMENT
For the Year Ended December 31, 20XX

Sales		$945,000
Cost of goods sold		408,500
Gross profit		536,500
Operating expenses		
Selling expenses	$145,000	
Administrative expenses	215,000	360,000
Income from operations		176,500
Other revenue and gains:		
Gain on foreign currency translation		19,500
		196,000
Other expenses and losses:		
Loss on inventory write-down		13,000
Income from continuing operations before taxes		183,000
Income taxes		54,900
Income from continuing operations		128,100
Loss from discontinued operations, net of $9,000 tax[1]		21,000
Income before extraordinary item		107,100
Extraordinary casualty loss, net of $21,000 tax[2]		49,000
Net income		$ 58,100
Earnings per share of common stock—		
Income from continuing operations[3]		$2.56
Discontinued operations loss, net of tax[4]		(0.42)
Income before extraordinary item		2.14
Extraordinary item, net of tax[5]		(0.98)
Net income		$1.16

Supporting Calculations:

1. Loss from discontinued operations = $30,000
   $30,000 loss × 30% tax rate = $9,000 tax shield
   $30,000 loss − $9,000 tax shield = $21,000 loss net of tax
2. Extraordinary casualty loss = $70,000
   $70,000 loss × 30% tax rate = $21,000 tax shield
   $70,000 loss − $21,000 tax shield = $49,000 loss net of tax
3. EPS: Income from continuing operations = $128,100
   $128,100/50,000 shares = $2.56 per share

4. EPS: Discontinued operations loss, net of tax = $21,000
   $21,000/÷ 50,000 shares = $0.42 per share
5. EPS: Extraordinary casualty loss, net of tax = $49,000
   $49,000/50,000 shares = $0.98 per share

Answer B:

External users of financial statements are interested in the income statement because current income is considered to be a predictor of future income. However, not all items on the income statement have the same predictive value. Irregular items (discontinued operations, casualty losses from extraordinary events, or expropriation by a foreign government) have little predictive value because they are unrelated to continuing operations and are unlikely to reoccur. Thus, they are separated from income from continuing operations, which is considered to be the most predictive part of net income.

Extraordinary items must be both unusual in nature and infrequent in occurrence. These items are shown net of tax after income from continuing operations. Unusual items may be either unusual or infrequent but not both. They are shown in a separate section labeled "Other revenues and gains" or "Other expenses and losses" after income from operations.

Answer to Question 1A-ES02

Answer A:

Dark Daze, Inc.
BALANCE SHEET
December 31, 2015

Assets

Current assets
Cash		$ 30,000	
Accounts receivable, net of $140 allowance		1,860	
Inventory		102,000	
Prepaid advertising		5,000	
Total current assets			$ 138,860

Property, plant, and equipment
Land		137,320	
Building	$ 80,400		
Accumulated depreciation—Building	(15,000)	65,400	
Equipment	40,000		
Accumulated depreciation—Equipment	(10,000)	30,000	232,720
Total assets			$ 371,580

Liabilities and Stockholders' Equity

Current liabilities
Notes payable	$ 14,400	
Taxes payable	3,000	
Salaries payable	900	
Interest payable	600	
Total current liabilities		$ 18,900

Long-term liabilities		
Bond payable		78,000
Total liabilities		96,900
Stockholders' equities		
Common stock	60,000	
Retained earnings*	214,680	
Total stockholders' equity*		274,680
Total liabilities and stockholders' equity		$ 371,580

Supporting Calculations:

Assets = Liabilities + Stockholders' Equities

Assets = $371,580

Liabilities = $96,900

Therefore, Stockholders' Equities = $371,580 − $96,900 = $274,680

Within Stockholders' Equities, Common stock = $60,000

Therefore, Retained Earnings = $274,680 − $60,000 = $214,680

Answer B:

1. For inventories, the firm must disclose the cost flow assumption that it used to value its inventory (FIFO, LIFO, weighted average, or specific identification) and the FIFO equivalent if the firm uses LIFO. In addition, the firm must disclose its valuation basis (net realizable value or lower of cost or market) and any product financing arrangements. Finally, the firm must disclose significant inventory categories:

Service firms	Supplies
Merchandising firms	Supplies
	Purchases
Manufacturing firms	Supplies
	Raw materials
	Work in process
	Finished goods

2. For accounts receivable, the firm must disclose its collection policy, the way that it determined expected future bad debt, and the net realizable value of the receivables.
3. For property, plant, and equipment, the firm must describe the major classifications as well as the valuation basis, depreciation method(s) used, and the accumulated depreciation for each class.
4. For bonds payable, the firm must disclose the face (par) value, the stated and effective interest rates, the maturity date, and any special provisions, such as call provisions or convertibility.
5. For common stock, the firm must disclose the par or stated value of the stock as well as any changes in the number of shares authorized, issued, and outstanding during the period.

Answer to Question 1A-ES03

Answer A:

Cash-N-Carry
Statement of Cash Flows
For the year ended December 31, 2015

Cash flows from operating activities		
Net loss		$ (2,500)
Adjustments to reconcile net income to net cash flows from operating activities		
Loss on sale of investments ($60,000 − $52,500)	$ 7,500	
Increase in accounts receivable	(90,000)	
Decrease in inventories	45,000	
Decrease in accounts payable	(45,000)	
Increase in operating expenses payable	9,000	(73,500)

Cash-N-Carry
Comparative Balance Sheet
As of December 31

	2015	2014	
Cash	$ 21,500	$120,000	$98,500 ↓
Accounts receivable	195,000	105,000	90,000 ↑
Inventories	180,000	225,000	45,000 ↓
Long-term investments	0	60,000	60,000 ↓
Total assets	$396,500	$510,000	
Accounts payable	$ 75,000	$120,000	$45,000 ↓
Operating expenses payable	24,000	15,000	9,000 ↑
Bonds payable	70,000	100,000	30,000 ↓
Common stock	125,000	125,000	
Retained earnings	102,500	150,000	47,500 ↓
Total liabilities and stockholders' equities	$396,500	$510,000	

Net cash flows from operating activities	$(76,000)
Cash flows from investing activities	
Sale of long-term investments	52,500
Cash flows from financing activities	
Redemption of bonds	(30,000)
Payment of cash dividend	(45,000)
Net cash flows from financing activities	(75,000)
Net decrease in cash	(98,500)
Cash balance, January 1	120,000
Cash balance, December 31	$ 21,500

Answer B:

Cash flows from operating activities		
Cash inflows from customers[1]		$470,000
Cash outflows		
To suppliers for goods[2]	$(375,000)	
For operating expenses[3]	(171,000)	546,000
Net cash flows from operating activities		$(76,000)

(1) Sales Revenue	$560,000	
Less: Increase in Accounts Receivable	− 90,000	
Cash inflow from customers	$470,000	
(2) Cost of Goods Sold	$375,000	
Add: Decrease in Accounts Payable	+ 45,000	
Less: Decrease in Inventories	− 45,000	
Cash outflow to suppliers for goods	$375,000	
(3) Operating Expenses	$180,000	
Less: Increase in operating expenses payable	− 9,000	
Cash outflow for operating expenses	$171,000	

Answer C:

Operating cash flows relate to ordinary firm operations. Operating cash inflows come primarily from customers but may also include cash rent, interest, or dividends received from investments. Operating cash outflows include payments for inventory, operating expenses, or interest on any borrowing.

Investing cash flows come from transactions in long-term assets. Thus, investing cash outflows include cash paid to buy land, buildings, equipment, or to buy patents, trademarks, copyrights, or the stocks and bonds of other firms. Similarly, investing cash inflows come from selling any of these long-term assets.

Financing cash flows come from transactions in long-term liabilities or stockholders' equities. Thus, borrowing money and issuing new bonds or shares of the firm's own stock would be classified as cash inflows from financing activities. By contrast, repaying loans, redeeming bonds, or reacquiring the firm's own stock for treasury stock would be classified as cash outflows from financing activities. In addition, paying cash dividends to shareholders would be classified as a financing cash outflow since it is a transaction with the owners of the firm.

Answer to Question 1A-ES04

Answer A:

1/1/15	Dr. Available-for-sale securities	520,790	
	Cr. Cash		520,790

Answer B:

7/1/15	Dr. Cash[1]	20,000	
	Cr. Interest revenue[2]		18,228
	Cr. Available-for-sale securities[3]		1,772

1. Cash interest = Face value × Stated rate × Fraction of year = $500,000 × 0.08 × ½ year = $20,000
2. Carrying value from 1/1/15 = $520,790
   Interest revenue = Carrying value × Effective rate Fraction of year = $520,790 × 0.07 × ½ = $18,228
3. Premium amortization = Cash interest − Interest revenue = $20,000 − $18,228 = $1,772

New carrying value as of 7/1/15 = Old carrying value − Premium amortized = $520,790 − $1,772 = $519,018

Answer C:

12/31/15	Dr. Interest receivable[1]	20,000	
	Cr. Interest revenue[2]		18,166
	Cr. Available-for-sale securities[3]		1,834

1. Cash interest = Face value × Stated rate × Fraction of year = $500,000 × 0.08 × ½ year = $20,000
   Note: Cash interest is due to be received on 1/1/16.
2. Carrying value from 7/1/15 = $519,018
   Interest revenue = Carrying value × Effective rate × Fraction of year = $519,018 × 0.07 × ½ = $18,166
3. Premium amortization = Cash interest − Interest revenue = $20,000 − $18,166 = $1,834

New carrying value as of 12/31/15 = Old carrying value − Premium amortized = $519,018 − $1,834 = $517,184

Answer D:

12/31/15	Dr. Market FV Adj. − AFS[1]	12,816	
	Cr. Unrealized Holding Gain − Equity		12,816

1. Market fair value adjustment = Fair value − Carrying value = $530,000 − $517,184 = $12,816

Answer E:

1/1/16	Dr. Cash	20,000	
	Cr. Interest receivable		20,000
	Dr. Cash	530,000	
	Cr. Available-for-sale securities		517,184
	Cr. Gain on sale of securities		12,816

Answer F:

2/1/17	Dr. Cash [(5,000 × $31) − $1,500 fees]	153,500	
	Dr. Loss on Sale of Securities	1,500	
	Cr. Trading Securities		155,000
10/1/17	Dr. Trading Securities	27,550	
	Cr. Cash [(600 × $45) + $550 fees]		27,550

Answer G:

| 12/31/17 | Dr. Securities FV Adj. (Trading) | 19,450 | |
| | Cr. Unrealized Holding Gain – Income | | 19,450 |

$$\begin{aligned} \text{Fair Value} &\quad \$221,000 \\ \text{Cost} &\quad -209,550 \\ \text{Increase in value} &\quad \$\ 11,450 \end{aligned}$$

This means that the Securities FV Adj. (Trading) account should have an ending debit balance of $11,450. It currently has an $8,000 credit balance from 12/31/15, so we need to add ($11,450 + $8,000) = $19,450.

Securities FV Adj. (Trading)		**Trading Securities**	
	8,000	209,550	
19,450			
11,450			

$$\begin{aligned} \text{Fair value} &= \text{Cost} + \text{Securities FV Adj. (Trading)} \\ &= \$209,550 + \$11,450 = \$221,000 \end{aligned}$$

Answer H:

1.
| 1/1/18 | Dr. Investment in Gobbled-Up | 500,000 | |
| | Cr. Cash | | 500,000 |

2.
| 7/1/18 | Dr. Cash ($160,000 × 25%) | 40,000 | |
| | Cr. Investment in Gobbled-Up | | 40,000 |

3.
| 12/31/18 | Dr. Investment in Gobbled-Up | 90,000 | |
| | Cr. Investment revenue ($360,000 × 25%) | | 90,000 |

4. $500,000 + $90,000 − $40,000 = $550,000

5. 1/1/18	Dr. Available-for-sale securities		500,000	
	Cr. Cash			500,000

6. 7/1/18	Dr. Cash ($160K × 0.25)		40,000	
	Cr. Dividend revenue			40,000

7. 12/31/18   No entry

8. As a passive investor under the cost method, Lotsa Loot does not recognize a portion income earned by Gobbled-Up, so the balance of Lotsa Loot's investment in Gobbled-Up at the end of 2018 before any market fair value adjustment = $500,000.

Answer to Question 1A-ES05

Answer A:

1/2/15	Dr. Land[1]		300,000	
	Cr. Common stock[2]			40,000
	Cr. Additional paid-in capital—common stock[3]			260,000

1. Given
2. Par value of common stock = 8,000 shares × $5/share = $40,000
3. APIC = Difference between market value and par value

Answer B:

1/5/15	Dr. Cash[1]		720,000	
	Cr. Common stock[2]			60,000
	Cr. Additional paid-in capital—common stock[3]			660,000
	Dr. Org. expense[4]		6,000	
	Cr. Common stock[5]			500
	Cr. Additional paid-in capital—common stock[6]			5,500

1. Cash received for shares issued to the public = 12,000 shares × $60/share = $720,000
2. Par value of common stock = 12,000 shares × $5/share = $60,000
3. APIC = Difference between market value and par value
4. Implied value of shares issued to lawyer for organizational work = 100 shares × $60/share = $6,000
5. Par value of shares = 100 shares × $5/share = $500
6. APIC = Difference between market value and par value

Answer C:

2/3/15	Dr. Cash[1]	720,000	
	Cr. Common stock[2]		50,000
	Cr. Additional paid-in capital—common stock[3]		550,000
	Cr. Preferred stock[4]		100,000
	Cr. Additional paid-in capital—preferred stock[5]		20,000

1. 1,000 bundles × $720/bundle = $720,000
2. 1,000 bundles × 10 common shares/bundle = 10,000 shares
   Par value of common stock = 10,000 shares × $5/share = $50,000
3. Market value of preferred stock is unknown, but market value of common stock = 10,000 shares × $60/share = $600,000
   APIC for common stock = Market value of common stock – Par value of common stock = $600,000 – $50,000 = $550,000
4. 1,000 bundles × 1 preferred share/bundle = 1,000 shares
   Par value of preferred stock = 1,000 shares × $100/share = $100,000
5. APIC for preferred stock = Residual value = $720,000 – $50,000 – $550,000 – $100,000 = $20,000

Answer D:

6/30/15	Dr. Retained earnings	180,600	
	Cr. Common stock dividends distributable[2]		15,050
	Cr. Additional paid-in capital—common stock[3]		165,550

1. Dividends always reduce retained earnings. A 10% stock dividend is a small dividend, which is accounted for at market price. Thus, retained earnings is reduced by the number of shares to be issued times the market price per share on the declaration date:

Shares issued and outstanding as of June 30, 2015:

8,000 shares	1/2/15 for land
12,000 shares	1/5/15 for cash
100 shares	1/5/15 to lawyer
10,000 shares	2/3/15 in bundles
30,100 shares	

30,100 shares × 10% stock dividend = 3,010 shares for dividend
Market value = 3,010 shares × $60/share = $180,600

2. The amount credited to common stock dividends distributable on the declaration date is:

3,010 shares × $5 par value/share = $15,050

3, APIC for common stock = Market value – Par value = $180,600 – $15,050 = $165,550

Answer E:

7/30/15	Dr. Common stock dividends distributable	15,050	
	Cr. Common stock		15,050

Answer F:

8/1/15	Dr. Treasury stock	60,000	
	Cr. Cash		60,000

Answer G:

Total preferred stock dividend = 1,000 shares × $100 par × 8% = $8,000
Preferred stock dividend/share = $8,000/1,000 shares = $8.00/share
Total common stock dividend = $20,000 − $8,000 = $12,000
Common shares outstanding = 30,100 + 3,010 − 2,000 = 31,110 shares
Note: No dividend is paid on treasury stock.
Common stock dividend/share = $12,000/31,110 shares = $0.386/share

9/1/15	Dr. Retained earnings	20,000	
	Cr. Dividends payable—common stock		8,000
	Cr. Dividends payable—preferred stock		12,000

Answer H:

9/30/15	Dr. Dividends payable—preferred stock	8,000	
	Dr. Dividends payable—common stock	12,000	
	Cr. Cash		20,000

Answer I:

10/1/15	Dr. Cash[1]	116,000	
	Cr. Treasury stock[2]		60,000
	Cr. Additional paid-in capital—treasury stock[3]		56,000

1. Cash received = $58/share × 2,000 shares = $116,000
2. In the cost method, the treasury stock account is credited for the same amount that it cost the firm when it acquired those shares.

APIC for treasury stock is the difference between the cash received when the shares are reissued and the cash that was paid when the shares were originally acquired.

Answer to Question 1A-ES06

Answer A:

2015	Dr. Accounts receivable	1,050,000	
	Cr. Sales (700 × $1,500)		1,050,000

Answer B:

2015	Dr. Warranty expense (100 × $90)	9,000	
	Cr. Repair parts, labor, etc.		9,000

Answer C:

12/31/15	Dr. Warranty expense (250 × $90)	22,500	
	Cr. Est. liability under Warranties		22,500

Answer D:

2015	Dr. Accounts receivable	1,120,000	
	Cr. Sales (700 × $1,500)		1,050,000
	Cr. Unearned warranty revenue		70,000

Answer E:

2015	Dr. Warranty expense (100 × $90)	9,000	
	Cr. Repair parts, labor, etc.		9,000
	Dr. Unearned warranty revenue	20,000	
	Cr. Warranty revenue		20,000
	($70,000 × 100/350)		

Answer F:

12/31/2015	Dr. Wage expense	70,000	
	Cr. FICA payable		2,250
	Cr. Federal income tax payable		7,500
	Cr. State income tax payable		2,200
	Cr. Union dues payable		500
	Cr. Wages payable or Cash		57,550

Answer G:

12/31/2015	Dr. Payroll tax expense	3,150	
	Cr. FICA payable		2,250
	Cr. FUTA payable		200
	Cr. SUTA payable		700

Answer H:

12/1/15	Dr. Cash	12,000	
	Cr. Notes payable		12,000

Answer I:

12/31/15	Dr. Interest expense	35	
	($12K \times 0.7 \times 0.5/_{12}$)		
	Cr. Interest payable		35

Answer J:

4/15/16	Dr. Interest expense ($12K \times 0.7 \times 3.5/_{12}$)	245	
	Dr. Interest payable ($12K \times 0.7 \times 0.5/_{12}$)	35	
	Dr. Notes payable	12,000	
	Cr. Cash		12,280

Answer to Question 1A-ES07

Answer A:

The bonds are issued at a premium because the 6% stated rate on the bonds is greater than the current market rate of 5% for similar debt.

Answer B:

Interest payments = $10,000,000 × 3% per period = $300,000/payment

PV – OA (i = 2.5%, n = 10) = 8.75206 × $300,000 = $2,625,618

Principal = $10,000,000

PV (i = 2.5%, n = 10) = 0.78120 × $10,000,000 = $7,812,000

Cash value of the bonds = $2,625,618 + $7,812,000 = $10,437,618

Note: $10,437,618 is the amount of cash that the firm receives when the bonds are issued. It also is the initial carrying value of the bonds. The difference between the cash received and the $10,000,000 face value of the bonds is the premium on the bonds payable. In this case, the premium = ($10,437,618 – $10,000,000) = $437,618. At the end of each interest period, a portion of that premium is amortized away:

Bond interest expense = Carrying value × Market rate × Fraction of a year

Cash interest = Face value × Stated rate × Fraction of a year

Premium amortized = Cash interest – Bond interest expense

New carrying value = Old carrying value – Premium amortized

At the end of 5 years, the premium will be completely amortized, the carrying value will equal the face value, and the bonds will be redeemed for $10,000,000.

Answer C:

1/1/15	Dr. Cash[1]	10,437,618	
	Cr. Bonds payable[2]		10,000,000
	Cr. Premium on bonds payable[3]		437,618

1. See computation above.
2. Face value (given).
3. Premium = Cash value − Face value

Answer D:

7/1/15	Dr. Bond interest expense[1]	260,940	
	Dr. Premium on bonds payable[2]	39,060	
	Cr. Cash[3]		300,000

1. Bond interest expense = Carrying value × Market rate × Fraction of a year = $10,437,618 × 0.05 × ½ = $260,940
2. Premium amortized = Cash interest − Bond interest expense = $300,000 − $260,940 = $39,060
   Remaining premium = Old premium balance − Premium amortized = $437,618 − $39,060 = $398,558
   New carrying value = Old carrying value − Premium amortized = $10,437,618 − $39,060 = $10,398,558
3. Cash interest = Face value × Stated rate × Fraction of a year = $10,000,000 × 0.05 × ½ = $300,000

Answer E:

12/31/15	Dr. Bond interest expense[1]	259,964	
	Dr. Premium on bonds payable[2]	40,036	
	Cr. Bond interest payable[3]		300,000

1. Bond interest expense = Carrying value × Market rate × Fraction of a year = $10,398,558 × 0.05 × ½ = $259,964
2. Premium amortized = Cash interest − Bond interest expense = $300,000 − $259,964 = $40,036
   Remaining premium = Old premium balance − Premium amortized = $398,558 − $40,036 = $358,522
   New carrying value = Old carrying value − Premium amortized = $10,437,618 − $40,036 = $10,358,522
3. Cash interest (to be paid on 1/1/16) = Face value × Stated rate × Fraction of a year = $10,000,000 × 0.05 × ½ = $300,000

Answer F:

1/1/16	Dr. Bond interest payable	300,000	
	Cr. Cash		300,000

Answer G:

The price of bonds is usually expressed as a percentage of their face value. Therefore, when "the firm redeemed the bonds at 98," it means that the firm paid 98% of the face value to buy the bonds back from the public. $10,000,000 face value × 98% = $9,800,000 cash paid by the firm to reacquire the bonds.

1/1/16	Dr. Bonds payable[1]	10,000,000	
	Dr. Premium on bonds payable[2]	358,522	
	Cr. Gain on redemption of bonds payable[3]		558,522
	Cr. Cash[4]		9,800,000

1. Face value of the bonds redeemed.
2. Remaining unamortized premium: See solution to part E) above.
3. Since the book value of the bonds is greater than the cash paid to redeem them, the firm recognizes a gain for the difference.

Bonds payable	$10,000,000
Unamortized premium	+ 358,522
Book value	$10,358,522
Cash paid	−9,800,000
Gain on redemption	$ 558,522

4. See discussion above.

Answer H:

The stated (face) rate on bonds is determined before the bonds are issued. It represents the contractual interest that the firm must pay annually to bondholders, but it often differs from the market interest rate that investors demand on the issue date.

If the stated rate is lower than the current market interest rate, investors will not buy the bonds at their face value, but they will buy the bonds for less. The resulting discount represents the present value of the difference between the stated rate and the market rate over the life of the bonds. Thus, the effective rate that investors receive is equal to the market rate.

By contrast, if the stated rate is lower than the current market interest rate, the firm will not issue the bonds at their face value, but they will issue the bonds for more. The resulting premium represents the present value of the difference between the stated rate and the market rate over the life of the bonds. Thus, the effective rate that the firm pays is equal to the market rate.

Answer to Question 1A-ES08

Answer A:

$100,000	Purchase of land
+ 5,000	Realtor fees
+ 3,000	Accrued property tax
+ 10,000	Demolishing old building on the property
− 2,000	Salvage from demolished building
$116,000	

Answer B:

	$ 16,000	Architectural fees
+	54,000	Construction costs
+	7,000	Supervision during construction
+	1,500	6 months of insurance policy
−	250	1 month of insurance expensed, not capitalized
	$ 78,250	

Answer C:

Dr. Cash	11,000	
Dr. Accumulated depreciation	40,000	
Cr. Trucks		50,000
Cr. Gain on disposal		1,000

Answer D:

Dr. Cash	6,000	
Dr. Accumulated depreciation	40,000	
Dr. Loss on disposal	4,000	
Cr. Trucks		50,000

Answer E:

Dr. Accumulated depreciation	40,000	
Dr. Loss on disposal	10,000	
Cr. Trucks		50,000

Answer F:

Dr. Accumulated depreciation	50,000	
Cr. Trucks		50,000

Note: We-Got-Stuff can still use the truck, even if it is fully depreciated, but the firm cannot recognize any additional depreciation expense.

Answer G:

Cost	$100,000
Accumulated depreciation	− 50,000
Book value of asset given up	$ 50,000

Answer H:

FV of new equipment	$ 50,000
Cash received	+ 10,000
FV received	$ 60,000

Answer I:

FV received	$ 60,000
Book value of asset given up	− 50,000
Gain on exchange	$ 10,000

Answer J:

Cost	$ 80,000
Accumulated depreciation	− 25,000
Book value given up	$ 55,000
Cash given up	+ 10,000
Total given up	$ 65,000

Answer K:

Fair value of new equipment	$ 60,000

Answer L:

FV of asset received	$ 60,000
Total given up	− 65,000
Loss on exchange	$ (5,000)

Answer M:

i.

Dr. Equipment (new)	50,000	
Dr. Cash	10,000	
Dr. Accumulated depreciation (old)	50,000	
Cr. Equipment (old)		100,000
Cr. Gain in exchange		10,000

ii.

Dr. Equipment (new)	60,000	
Dr. Accumulated depreciation (old)	25,000	
Dr. Loss on exchange	5,000	
Cr. Equipment		80,000
Cr. Cash		10,000

Answer N:

i.

Dr. Equipment (new)[2]	41,667	
Dr. Cash	10,000	
Dr. Accumulated Depreciation (old)	50,000	
Cr. Equipment (old)		100,000
Cr. Gain in exchange[1]		1,667

1. $10,000/($10,000 + $50,000) = 0.1667
   $10,000 × 0.1667 = $1,667 gain recognized
   $10,000 − $1,667 gain recognized = $8,333 gain deferred
2. $50,000 (FV) − $8,333 gain deferred = $41,667 recorded value

ii.

Dr. Equipment (new)	60,000	
Dr. Accumulated depreciation (old)	25,000	
Dr. Loss on exchange	5,000	
Cr. Equipment		80,000
Cr. Cash		10,000

Note: The journal entry for Mercury Manufacturing is the same regardless of whether the transaction has commercial substance because losses always are recognized when incurred.

Part 1 Section B Answers

Answer to Question 1B-ES01

Answer A:

Rein Company
Budgeted Income Statement
for the Year Ended December 31, 2006

Sales [100,000 × 1.1 × ($110 + 15)]		$13,750,000
Cost of goods sold at standard [110,000 × (65.20 + 19.80)[1]]		9,350,000
Gross margin at standard		$4,400,000
Variances		
Material—brass—unfavorable [(111,650 compressors[2]) × (4 lbs/compressor) × ($.30/lb)]	$(133,980)	
Labor efficiency—unfavorable [(111,650 compressors) × (0.25 hours/compressor) × ($7/hr)]	(195,388)	
Variable overhead efficiency—unfavorable [(111,650 compressors) × (0.25 hrs/compressor) × ($3.30/hour[3])]	(92,111)	
Fixed overhead volume—favorable [(111,650 − 110,000 compressors) × $6.60/compressor[4]]	10,890	(410,589)
Gross margin at actual		$3,989,411
Operating expenses		
Selling expense ($13,750,000 × .12)	$1,650,000	
Administrative expense ($907,850 × 1.2)	1,089,420	2,739,420
Income before taxes		$1,249,991
Income tax expense (45%)		562,496
Net income		$687,495
Earnings per share (250,000 shares)		$2.75

Supporting Calculations

1 Standard cost of compressor

Brass 4 lbs. @ $5.35/lb.	$21.40
Steel alloy 5 lbs. @ $3.16/lb.	15.80
Direct labor 4 hrs. @ $7.00/hr.	28.00
Overhead (2,178,000 ÷ 110,000)	19.80
Total cost per compressor	$85.00

2 Production schedule

2006 sales	110,000
Desired ending inventory 12/31/06 (110,000 × 1.1 × .15)	18,150
Required inventory	128,150
Beginning inventory 1/1/06 (110,000 × .15)	16,500
2006 production	111,650

3 Determination of the variable overhead rate and total fixed overhead

$$\text{Variable overhead rate per compressor} = \frac{\text{Change in Overhead}}{\text{Change in Activity}}$$

$$= \frac{(\$2{,}178{,}000 - \$2{,}046{,}000)}{110{,}000 - 100{,}000} = \frac{\$132{,}000}{10{,}000}$$

$$= \$13.20/\text{compressor}$$

$$\text{Variable overhead rate/direct labor hour} = \frac{\$13.20/\text{compressor}}{4 \text{ hrs./compressor}}$$

$$= \$3.30/\text{direct labor hour}$$

Total overhead at 110,000 compressors	$2,178,000
Total variable overhead at 110,000 compressors (110,000 × $13.20)	−1,452,000
Total budgeted fixed overhead	$726,000

4 Normal activity level and fixed overhead rate

$$\text{Fixed overhead rate} = \frac{\text{Budgeted fixed overhead (See note 3)}}{\text{Normal production activity level}}$$

$$= \frac{\$726{,}000}{110{,}000}$$

$$= \$6.60/\text{compressor}$$

Answer B:

Based on the results of the 2006 budgeted income statement, the president's objective cannot be achieved. A review of the statement highlights these circumstances:

- A 2006 income statement prepared using the worst situation gives a net income of $687,495 and earnings per share of $2.75, which is a decrease from the 2005 income of $700,000 and earnings per share of $2.80. These budgeted figures are also considerably below the president's objective of $750,000 net income and $3 earnings per share.
- If the unfavorable variances do not occur, net income will increase by $231,813 after taxes ($421,479 × .55), resulting in an increase in earnings per share of $.927, giving a total earnings per share of $3.677 which is well above the president's objective.

- Manufacturing costs are 65. 5% of the selling price ($72 / $110) in 2005, and 68% of the selling price in 2006. Administrative expenses increased 20% in 2006. Therefore, the 13. 6% sales price increase in 2006 was not sufficient to cover the increases in manufacturing cost and increases in administrative expense.

Answer to Question 1B-ES02

Answer A:

Robbins and Crowe introduce slack into their budgets for these reasons:

- To hedge against uncertainties that might cause actual results to differ markedly from their projections.
- To allow their employees to exceed expectations, show consistent performance, or both. This becomes especially significant if their performance is evaluated by comparing actual results to budget projections.
- To bring the organization's goals into alignment with their own goals by using budgetary slack to improve the organization's assessment of their performance, thus earning higher salaries, better bonuses, or promotions.

Answer B:

Slack might adversely affect Robbins and Crowe in these ways:

- By limiting the usefulness of the budget to motivate top performance from their employees
- By affecting their ability to identify trouble spots and take appropriate corrective action
- By reducing their credibility in the eyes of management

The use of budgetary slack also may affect management decisions, since the budgets will show lower contribution margins (fewer sales, higher expenses). Decisions regarding profitability of product lines, staffing levels, incentives, and other matters could adversely affect Robbins's and Crowe's departments.

Answer to Question 1B-ES03

Answer A:

MRC Cash Budget Proposed	
Third Quarter (only)	
Beginning cash balance (given)	$186,000
Add: Third-quarter cash receipts[1]	200,650
Less: Third-quarter cash expenditures[2]	178,000
Ending cash balance	$208,650
Supporting Calculations	

[1] Third-quarter cash receipts.

[2] Cash expenditures.

Fee			Distribution	
Memberships				
Individual	$300	60%	$36,000	[(50 new + 150 renew)×0.60×$300]
Student	180	10%	3,600	[(50 + 150)×0.10×$180]
Family	600	30%	36,000	[(50 + 150)×0.30×$600]
Total			$75,600	
Court Fees				
Individual	$50	60%	$61,500	[(50 new + 2,000 reg.)×0.60×$50]
Student	40	10%	8,200	[2,050×0.10×$40]
Family	90	30%	55,350	[2,050×0.30×$90]
Total			125,050	
Total Third-Quarter Cash Receipts:			$200,650	

Fixed costs	$157,500	
Less: Depreciation	24,500	
Add: Variable costs	45,000	[(1000 hours + 2000 hours) × $15]
Total Costs:	$178,000	

Answer B:

Sensitivity analysis would help MRC management by testing the assumed projections and seeing how sensitive the cash flows are to changes in the number of members or the distribution of members.

Answer C:

Other factors that MRC should consider include:

- Communication strategy to current members
- Market acceptance of the new pricing strategy
- Cost associated with the change
- Timing of the change
- Effect on the mix of membership class
- Anticipated rate of return for excess cash and the costs of borrowing funds
- Reliability of the projections
- Capacity of the tennis and racquetball courts
- Price elasticity for memberships in similar clubs
- Reaction of the competition
- Quality of its facilities and staff
- Cost of advertising/communicating this price change

Answer to Question 1B-ES04

Answer 1:

Cumulative Number of Units	Cumulative Average Time/Unit	Cumulative of Total Time
1	500	500
2	500 × .9 = 450	450 × 2 = 900
4	450 × .9 = 405	405 × 4 = 1620

Answer 2:

$25 × 500 hours × 4 units = $50,000 with no learning curve

$25 × 405 × 4 units = $40,500 with 90% learning curve

$50,000 − $40,500 = $9,500 savings

Answer 3:

a. Budgetary slack is the practice of underestimating budgeted revenues, or overestimating budgeted costs, to make budgeted targets more easily achievable.

b. Budgetary slack misleads top management about the true profit potential of the company, which leads to inefficient resource planning and allocation as well as poor coordination of activities across different parts of the company.

Answer 4:

a.1. 1. 1,740 × (25.00 − [44,805/1,740]) = 1,305 U

a.2. 2. 25.00 × (1,740 − [4 × 500]) = 6,500 F

b. Direct labor rate variance remains the same, but direct labor efficiency variance will become $3000 negative, because actual hours (1740) is more than expected from 90% learning curve (1620).

Answer 5:

A factor that could cause an unfavorable price variance and a favorable efficiency variance is using a higher-skilled labor force that would be paid more per hour but would work more quickly.

Answer 6:

Direct labor efficiency variance would be even more unfavorable if an 80% learning curve were used. The lower number implies more benefit from learning.

Answer 7:

For a new product, the company may have no way of forecasting the amount of improvement (if any) from savings. The company may set up a production method that is more efficient than prototype but will not gain further efficiencies.

Answer to Question 1B-ES05

Answer 1:

A flexible budget allows the attorneys to tell how much of their unfavorable variance is due to lower-than-planned billing hours and how much is due to performance issues, such as the negotiated billed amount or variable expenses. A master budget is static, and any variance must be analyzed further to determine its cause.

Answer 2:

The flexible budget revenues are calculated by multiplying the actual billed hours by the budgeted amount per billed hour. Then the budgeted variable expense per billed hour is multiplied by the actual billed hours. The flexible budget variable expense is subtracted from the flexible budget revenue. The results are compared to the actual results from last year.

Answer 3:

6,000 × 325 = $1,950,000 static budget revenue

5,700 × 275 = $1,567,500 actual revenue

1,950,000 − 1,567,500 = $382,500 unfavorable static budget revenue variance

5,700 × 325 = $1,852,500 flexible budget revenue

1,852,500 − 1,567,500 = $285,000 flexible budget variance

6,000 × 5,700 = 300 hours unfavorable sales volume

300 × 325 = $97,500 unfavorable sales volume variance

Answer 4:

6,000 × 50 = $300,000 static budget variable expense

300,000 − 285,000 = $15,000 favorable variable expense variance

5,700 × 50 = $285,000 flexible budget variable expense

285,000 − 285,000 = $0, so the variance is a sales volume variance

Part 1 Section C Answers

Answer to Question 1C-ES01

Answer A:

Sales Price Variance	Budget Sales Price	Actual Sales Price	Unit Variance	Actual Unit Sales	Sales Price Variance	Total
Hand Drills	$60	$59	$1 U	86,000	$86,000	
Table Saws	$120	$115	$5 U	74,000	$370,000	$456,000 U

Cost Price Variance	Budgeted Cost	Actual Cost	Unit Variance	Actual Unit Purchases	Cost Price Variance
Hand Drills	$50	$50	$0	86,000	None
Table Saws	$80	$82	$2 U	74,000	$148,000	$148,000 U

Volume Variance	Budgeted Volume in Units	Actual Volume in Units	Unit Variance	Budgeted[1] Contribution Margin/Unit	Volume Variance	
Hand Drills	120,000	86,000	34,000 U	$10	$340,000	
Table Saws	80,000	74,000	6,000 U	$40	240,000	$580,000 U
Total Gross Margin Variance						$1,184,000 U

[1]Budgeted total margin ÷ Budget unit sales

	Hand Drills	Table Saws
	$1,200,000	$3,200,000
	120,000	80,000
	$10/unit	$40/unit

Answer B:

The effectiveness of Handler's marketing program is difficult to judge in the absence of actual industry-wide performance data. If the industry estimate of a 10% decline in the market for these tools is used as a basis for comparison, then Handler's gross margin should have fallen to $3,960,000 ($4,400,000 × .9) as summarized next ($000 omitted).

	Hand Drill	Table Saw	Total
Budgeted gross margin	$1,200	$3,200	$4,400
Budget adjusted for 10% industry decline	$1,080	$2,880	$3,960
Less: Actual gross margin	774	2,442	3,216
Shortage	$ 306	$ 438	$ 744

Handler's gross margin actually fell to $3,216,000, which is $744,000 lower than might have been expected. To have been considered a success, the marketing program should have generated a gross margin above $4,020,000 (the original budget minus the projected industry decline plus the incremental cost of the marketing program, i.e., $4,400 − 440 + 60).

Handler hoped to do better than the industry average by giving dealer discounts and increasing direct advertising. However, to be successful, the discounts and advertising must be offset by an increase in volume. Handler was not successful in this regard in total; sales volume dropped 7.5% in the table saw line as compared to a 28.3% decline in hand drill volume. Note that the table saw price was dropped by 4.2% as against a price decline of only 1.7% on hand drilled. Apparently the discounts and advertising did not generate enough unit sales volume to offset and compensate for the promotion.

Answer to Question 1C-ES02

Answer A:

The shortcomings or possible inconsistencies of using return on investment (ROI) as the sole criterion to evaluate divisional management performance include:

- ROI tends to emphasize short-run performance at the possible expense of long-run profitability.
- ROI is not consistent with cash flow models used for capital expenditure analysis.
- ROI frequently is not controllable by the division manager because many components included in the computation are committed in amount or are the responsibility of others.
- Reliance on ROI as the only measurement indicator could lead to an inaccurate decision or investment at either the divisional or corporate level.

Answer B:

The advantages of using multiple criteria to evaluate divisional management performance include:

- Multiple performance measures provide a more comprehensive picture of performance by considering a wider range of responsibilities.
- Multiple performance measures emphasize both the short-term and long-term results, thereby emphasizing the total performance of the division.
- Multiple performance measures may highlight nonquantitative as well as quantitative-oriented aspects.
- Multiple performance criteria will enhance goal congruence and reduce the importance of the dysfunctional short-run goal of profit maximization.

Answer C:

The problems or disadvantages of implementing a multiple performance criteria measurement system include:

- The measurement criteria are not all equally quantifiable.
- Management may have difficulty applying the criteria on a consistent basis, some criteria may be subjectively more heavily weighted than other criteria, and some criteria may be in conflict with each other.
- A multiple performance measurement system may be confusing to division management.
- Overemphasis on multiple evaluation criteria may lead to diffusion of effort and the failure to perform as well as expected in any one area.

Answer to Question 1C-ES03

Answer A:

Segment information prepared for public reporting may be inappropriate for evaluation of segment managers for these reasons:

- An allocation of common costs incurred for the benefit of more than one segment must be included for public reporting purposes.
- Common costs generally are allocated on an arbitrary basis.
- Segments identified for public reporting may not coincide with actual management responsibilities.
- Information in the annual report does not distinguish between a segment that is a poor investment and one in which the manager has done well despite adverse circumstances.

Answer B:

Segment managers may become frustrated and dissatisfied if their performance is evaluated on the basis of information in the annual financial report. Using that information may lead to their being held responsible for earnings figures that include the arbitrary allocation of common costs and costs that are traceable to them but are not under their control. Such evaluations reduce motivation and may even cause managers to seek other employment.

Answer C:

Merriam Corporation should define responsibility centers that coincide with managers' actual responsibilities rather than using segment rules developed for public reporting. All reports should be prepared using the contribution approach, which separates costs by behavior and assigns costs only to segments that control them. The report should disclose contribution margin, contributions controllable by segment managers, and contribution by each segment after the allocation of common costs.

Answer to Question 1C-ES04

Answer A:

Because Quie's management apparently has excess capacity, it should be positive toward each suggested price in decreasing order. Each price exceeds variable costs and thus will increase Quie's ROI, which is the basis of its evaluation by corporate management.

Answer B:

Negotiating a price between the two divisions is the best method to resolve the controversy in this situation. ARQ is highly decentralized and exhibits all four conditions required for negotiating a transfer price:

1. Outside markets exist to give both parties alternatives to dealing with each other.
2. Both parties have access to market price information.
3. Both parties are free to buy and sell outside the corporation.
4. Top management supports the continuation of the decentralized arrangement.

Answer C:

ARQ management should not become involved in resolving the controversy. This would violate the autonomous relationship of the divisions, which ARQ intends to maintain. Imposing conditions on the pricing will adversely affect the current ROI-based evaluation system, since the two divisions will no longer be in control of their profits. Finally, division management would most likely respond negatively to a loss of the autonomy it is used to exercising.

Answer to Question 1C-ES05

Answer A:

Transfer prices based on cost are not appropriate measures of divisional performance for several reasons, including these:

- The selling division has little incentive to control costs if all costs will be recovered in the transfer price.
- The company as a whole often makes poor decisions when one division is covering another's full costs.

Answer B:

The next table shows the results for both the extraction and pet products divisions of using the market price as the transfer price.

Results of Using Market-Based Transfer Pricing

	Extraction Division	Pet Products Division
Selling price	$26.00	$42.00
Less variable costs		
Material cost	$4.00	$2.00
Labor cost	$6.00	$4.00
Overhead (variable)	$8.25 *	$2.45†
Transfer price	–	$26.00
Unit contribution margin	$7.75	$7.55
Volume	× 500,000	× 500,000
Total contribution margin	$3,875,000.00	$3,775,000.00

*Variable overhead = $11 × 75% = $8.25.
†Variable overhead = $7 × 35% = $2.45.

Answer C:

If Sparta Enterprises lets its divisions buy and sell in the open market and also allows them to negotiate an acceptable transfer price, the result would be as shown:

- Any price between $24. 50 and $26 will result in an overall benefit to the company.

- The extraction division would prefer to sell its clay to the pet products division at the same price it receives in the market: $26 per unit. But it would be willing to sell at $24. 50, because it saves $1. 50 in selling costs per unit by selling within the company.
- Similarly, the pet products division would like to continue paying $22 per unit for the clay, but if it cannot purchase the clay within the company, it will have to pay the full $26 market price. Therefore, it will be willing to pay the $24.50 transfer price it can negotiate with the extraction division.

Answer D:

Using a negotiated transfer price should result in desirable management behavior because it will:

- Encourage the management of the extraction division to control costs.
- Benefit the pet products division by providing the clay at a below-market price.
- Provide a more realistic measure of divisional performance.

Answer to Question 1C-ES06

Answer A:

The quarterly performance report that 4-Cycle provides to its managers includes at least these three weaknesses:

1. It is based on a static budget. The company should switch to a flexible budget that compares the same levels of activity and shows variances between the actual budget and the flexible budget.
2. The report includes costs that supervisors cannot control, such as fixed production costs and overhead.
3. The report allocates fixed production costs using a single rate for all lines. Since the amount of space occupied by production may not, in fact, determine fixed production costs, the company should select an appropriate base to determine the rate for each product line.

Answer B:

To remove the weaknesses in the performance report, you could recommend that the CFO at 4-Cycle, Inc. :

- Use flexible rather than static budgeting.
- Stop holding product managers responsible for costs they cannot control.
- Include footnotes to make the report easier to understand.

A revised quarterly report that incorporates these suggested changes is shown next.

4-Cycle, Inc.
Marine Engine Quarterly Performance Report

	Actual	Flexible Budget	Flexible Budget Variance
Units	10,500	10,500	
Revenue	17,500,000	$18,158,805[1]	$658,805 U
Variable production costs			
Direct material	2,500,000	2,674,140[2]	174,140 F
Direct labor	2,193,000	2,211,195[3]	18,195 F
Machine time	2,300,000	2,408,805[4]	108,805 F
Factory overhead	4,500,500	4,725,000[5]	224,500 F
Total variable costs	11,493,500	12,019,140	525,640 F
Contribution margin	$6,006,500	$6,139,665	$133,165 U

(1) ($14,700,000 budget ÷ 8,500 budgeted units) × 10,500 actual units
(2) ($2,164,750 budget ÷ 8,500 budgeted units) × 10,500 actual units
(3) ($1,790,000 budget ÷ 8,500 budgeted units) × 10,500 actual units
(4) ($1,950,000 budget ÷ 8,500 budgeted units) × 10,500 actual units
(5) ($3,825,000 budget ÷ 8,500 budgeted units) × 10,500 actual units

Note: All calculations rounded amounts to two decimal places.

Answer to Question 1C-ES07

A. SieCo is currently using a plant-wide overhead rate that is applied on the basis of direct labor costs. In general, a plant-wide manufacturing overhead rate is acceptable only if a similar relationship between overhead and direct labor exists in all departments or the company manufactures products that receive proportional services from each department.

In most cases, departmental overhead rates are preferable to plant-wide overhead rates because plant-wide overhead rates do not provide:

- A framework for reviewing overhead costs on a departmental basis, identifying departmental cost overruns, or taking corrective action to improve departmental cost control
- Sufficient information about product profitability, thus increasing the difficulties associated with management decision making

B. In order to improve the allocation of overhead costs in the Cutting and Grinding Departments, SieCo should:

- Establish separate overhead accounts and rates for each of these departments.
- Select an application basis for each of these departments that best reflects the relationship of the departmental activity to the overhead costs incurred (i.e., machine hours, direct labor hours, etc.).
- Identify, if possible, fixed and variable overhead costs and establish fixed and variable overhead rates for each department.

C. In order to accommodate the automation of the Drilling Department in its overhead accounting system, SieCo should:

- Establish separate overhead accounts and rates for the Drilling Department.
- Identify, if possible, fixed and variable overhead costs and establish fixed and variable overhead rates.
- Apply overhead costs to the Drilling Department on the basis of robot or machine hours.

D. Because SieCo uses a plant-wide overhead rate applied on the basis of direct labor costs, the elimination of direct labor in the Drilling Department through the introduction of robots may appear to reduce the overhead cost of the Drilling Department to zero. However, this change will not reduce fixed manufacturing expenses, such as depreciation, plant supervision, and the like. In reality, the use of robots is likely to increase fixed expenses because of increased depreciation expense. Under SieCo's current method of allocating overhead costs, these costs merely will be absorbed by the remaining departments.

E. Under competence, Altman has a responsibility to "provide decision support information and recommendations that are accurate, clear, concise and timely." It is possible that the decision was made with less than optimal decision support.

Under confidentiality, he must keep information confidential except when disclosure is authorized or legally required, and he must inform his subordinates of the same requirement.

No information is presented that indicates that this standard has been or may be violated.

Under integrity, Altman must "avoid actual or apparent conflicts of interest and advise all appropriate parties of any potential conflict." He must also "refrain from engaging in any activity that would prejudice his ability to carry out his duties ethically." He should also "refrain from engaging in any activity that would discredit the profession." There appears to be a conflict of interest here when Simpson's brother-in-law has won the contract.

Finally, under credibility, Altman must "communicate information both fairly and objectively." He should "disclose fully all relevant information that could reasonably be expected to influence an intended user's understanding of the reports and recommendations presented." The ownership by Simpson's brother-in-law should be disclosed to Hunter.

F. According to the IMA *Statement of Ethical Professional Practice,* Altman should first follow the established policies of the organization he is employed by in an effort to resolve the ethical dilemma. If such policies do not exist or are not effective, he should follow the steps as outlined in "Resolution of Ethical Conflict."

First, he should discuss the problems with his immediate superior. except when it appears the superior is involved. In this case, it is not clear if Hunter is involved. If this step is not successful in solving the dilemma, he should proceed up the chain of command, which in this case would appear to be the president and then the board of directors.

However, he should note that except where legally prescribed, communication of such internal problems should not be discussed with authorities or individuals not employed or engaged by the organization.

Spencer should clarify relevant ethical issues by confidential discussion with an objective advisor (e.g., an IMA ethics counselor) to obtain a better understanding of possible courses of action. He should consult his own attorney as to his legal obligations and rights concerning the ethical conflict.

Answer to Question 1C-ES08

A. 1. Average investment in operating assets employed:

Balance end of current year	$12,600,000
Balance end of previous year*	12,000,000
Total	$24,600,000
Average operating assets employed†	$12,300,000

*$12,600,000 ÷ 1.05
†$24,600,000 ÷ 2

ROI = Income from operations ÷ Average operating assets employed
= $2,460,000 ÷ $12,300,000
= .20 or 20%

2. Residual Income:

Income from operations	$2,460,000
Minimum return on assets employed*	1,845,000
Residual income	$615,000

*$12,300,000 × .15

B. Yes, Presser's management probably would have accepted the investment if residual income were used. The investment opportunity would have lowered Presser's ROI because the expected return (18%) was lower than the division's historical returns as well as its actual ROI (20%) for the year just ended. Management rejected the investment because bonuses are based in part on the performance measure of ROI. If residual income was used as a performance measure (and as a basis for bonuses), management would accept any and all investments that would increase residual, including the investment opportunity rejected in the year just ended.

C. Presser must control all items related to profit (revenues and expenses) and investment if it is to be evaluated fairly as an investment center by either the ROI or residual income performance measures. Presser must control all elements of the business except the cost of invested capital, that being controlled by Lawton Industries.

Answer to Question 1C-ES09

Answer 1:

The positive and negative behavioral implications arising from employing a negotiated transfer price system for goods exchanged between divisions include the following:

Positive

- Both the buying and selling divisions have participated in the negotiations and are likely to believe they have agreed on the best deal possible.
- Negotiating and determining transfer prices will enhance the autonomy/ independence of both divisions.

Negative

- The result of a negotiated transfer price between divisions may not be optimal for the firm as a whole and therefore will not be goal congruent.
- The negotiating process may cause harsh feelings and conflicts between divisions.

Answer 2:

The behavioral problems that can arise from using actual full (absorption) manufacturing costs as a transfer price include these:

a. Full-cost transfer pricing is not suitable for a decentralized structure when the autonomous divisions are measured on profitability as the selling unit is unable to realize a profit.
b. This method can lead to decisions that are not goal congruent if the buying unit decides to buy outside at a price less than the full cost of the selling unit. If the selling unit is not operating at full capacity, it should reduce the transfer price to the market price if this would allow the recovery of variable costs plus a portion of the fixed costs. This price reduction would optimize overall company performance.

Answer 3:

The behavioral problems that could arise if Thompson Corporation decides to change its transfer pricing policy to one that would apply uniformly to all divisions including these:

- A change in policy may be interpreted by the divisional managers as an attempt to decrease their freedom to make decisions and reduce their autonomy. This perception could lead to reduced motivation.
- If managers lose control of transfer prices and thus some control over profitability, they will be unwilling to accept the change to uniform prices.
- Selling divisions will be motivated to sell outside if the transfer price is lower than market as this behavior is likely to increase profitability and bonuses.

Answer 4:

The likely behavior of both "buying" and "selling" divisional managers for each of the listed transfer pricing methods being considered by Thompson Corporation include the following:

a. Standard full manufacturing costs plus a markup
   The selling division will be motivated to control costs because any costs over standard cannot be passed on to the buying division and will reduce the profit of the selling division.

   The buying division may be pleased with this transfer price if the market price is higher. However, if the market price is lower and the buying divisions are forced to take the transfer price, the managers of the buying division will be unhappy.

b. Market selling price of the product being transferred
   This creates a fair and equal chance for the buying and selling divisions to make the most profit they can. It should promote cost control, motivate divisional management, and optimize overall company performance. Since both parties are aware of the market price, there will be no distrust between the parties, and both should be willing to enter into the transaction.

c. Outlay (out-of-pocket) costs incurred to the point of transfer, plus opportunity costs per unit.

   This method is the same as market price when there is an established market price and the seller is at full capacity. At any level below full capacity, the transfer price is the outlay cost only (as there is no opportunity cost), which would approximate the variable costs of the goods being transferred.

   Both buyers and sellers should be willing to transfer under this method because the price is the best either party should be able to realize for the product under the circumstances. This method should promote overall goal congruence, motivate managers, and optimize overall company profits.

Part 1 Section D Answers

Answer to Question 1D-ES01

Answer A:

The traditional cost system, developed to value inventory, distorts product cost information because the cost system:

- Was designed to value inventory in the aggregate and not relate to product cost information.
- Uses a common departmental or factory-wide measure of activity, such as direct labor hours or dollars (now a small portion of overall production costs) to distribute manufacturing overhead to products.
- Deemphasizes long-term product analysis (when fixed costs become variable costs).

- Causes managers, who are aware of distortions in the traditional system, to make intuitive, imprecise adjustments to the traditional cost information without understanding the complete impact.

Answer B:

1. The benefits that management can expect from activity-based costing include:

    - It leads to a more competitive position by evaluating cost drivers (e.g., costs associated with the complexity of the transaction rather that the production volume).
    - It streamlines production processes by reducing non-value-adding activities (e.g., reduced setup times, optimal plant layout, and improved quality).
    - It provides management with a more thorough understanding of product costs and product profitability for strategies and pricing decisions.

2. The steps that a company, using a traditional cost system, would take to implement activity-based costing include these:

    - Evaluation of the existing system to assess how well the system supports the objective of an activity-based cost system
    - Identification of the activities for which cost information is needed with differentiation between value-adding and non-value-adding activities.

Answer to Question 1D-ES02

Answer A:

Under direct costing, fixed manufacturing costs are expensed rather than being added to the inventoriable cost of each unit. Thus, it is not necessary to determine the allocation of fixed costs to individual units.

Answer B:

At first glance, job order costing appears to make more sense, as each pair of jeans is literally unique, given that the buyer's name is stitched on the back pocket. However, in reality, process costing should be used, because jeans will be produced continually and for cost purposes, will be same for each pair.

Answer to Question 1D-ES03

A. 1. Relative sales value method at split-off:

Product	Monthly Output	Sales Price	Split-Off Value	% of Sales	Allocated Costs
Studs	75,000	$8	$600,000	46.15%	$461,539
Decorative Pieces	5,000	60	300,000	23.08%	230,769
Posts	20,000	20	400,000	30.77%	307,692
Totals			**$1,350,000**	**100%**	**$1,000,000**

A. 2. Physical output (volume) method at split-off:

Product	Monthly Output	% of Output	Allocated Costs
Studs	75,000	75.00%	$ 750,000
Decorative pieces	5,000	5.00%	50,000
Posts	20,000	20.00%	200,000
Totals	100,000	100.00%	$1,000,000

A. 3. Estimated net realizable value method:

Product	Monthly Output	Sales Price	Split-Off Value	% of Sales	Allocated Costs
Studs	75,000	$ 8	$600,000	46.15%	$461,539
Decorative Pieces	4,500[1]	100	350,000[2]	23.08%	230,769
Posts	20,000	20	400,000	30.77%	307,692
Totals			$1,300,000	100%	$1,000,000

(1) 5,000 monthly units of output − 10% normal spoilage = 4,500 good units
(2) 4,500 good units × $100 = $450,000 − further processing costs of $100,000 = $350,000

B. Presented next is an analysis for Sonimad Sawmill comparing the processing of decorative pieces further versus selling the rough-cut product immediately at split-off. Based on this analysis, it is recommended that Sonimad further process the decorative pieces as this action results in an additional contribution of $50,000.

	Units	Dollars
Monthly unit output	5,000	
Less: Further normal processing shrinkage	500	
Units available for sale	4,500	
Final sales value (4,500 units × $100 each)		$450,000
Less: Sales value at split-off		300,000
Differential revenue		$150,000
Less: Further processing costs		100,000
Additional contribution from further processing		$50,000

Answer to Question 1D-ES04

Answer A:

A. 1. The total budgeted costs for the Manufacturing Department at Alyssa Manufacturing are presented next.

Direct material
  Tuff Stuff ($5.00/unit × 20,000 units) $100,000
  Ruff Stuff ($3.00/unit × 20,000 units)   60,000

Total direct material		$160,000
Direct labor		800,000
Overhead		
Indirect labor	$ 24,000	
Fringe benefits	5,000	
Indirect material	31,000	
Power	180,000	
Setup	75,000	
Quality assurance	10,000	
Other utilities	10,000	
Depreciation	15,000	
Total overhead		350,000
Total budgeted cost		$1,310,000

A. 2 & 3. The unit standard costs of Tuff Stuff and Ruff Stuff, with overhead allocated based on direct labor hours, are calculated as shown.

Tuff Stuff

Direct material	$5.00
Direct labor ($8.00/hour × 2 hours)*	16.00
Overhead ($3.50hour × 2 hours)*	7.00
Tuff Stuff unit standard cost	$28.00

Ruff Stuff

Direct material	$3.00
Direct labor ($8.00/hour × 3 hours)*	24.00
Overhead ($3.50/hour × 3 hours)*	10.50
Ruff Stuff unit standard cost	$37.50

*Budgeted direct labor hours

Tuff Stuff (20,000 units × 2 hours)	40,000
Ruff Stuff (20,000 units × 3 hours)	60,000
Total budgeted direct labor hours	100,000

Direct labor rate: $800,000 ÷ 100,000 hours = $8.00/hour
Overhead rate: $350,000 ÷ 100,000 hours = $3.50/hour

Answer B:

B. 1 & 2. The total budgeted cost of the Fabricating and Assembly Departments, after separation of overhead into the activity pools, is calculated as shown.

		Fabricating		Assembly	
	Total	Percent	Dollars	Percent	Dollars
Direct material	$160,000	100%	$160,000		
Direct labor	800,000	75%	600,000	25%	$200,000
Overhead					
Indirect labor	24,000	75%	18,000	25%	6,000
Fringe benefits	5,000	80%	4,000	20%	1,000
Indirect material	31,000		20,000		11,000
Power	180,000		160,000		20,000
Setup	75,000		5,000		70,000
Quality assurance	10,000	80%	8,000	20%	2,000
Other utilities	10,000	50%	5,000	50%	5,000
Depreciation	15,000	80%	12,000	20%	3,000
Total overhead	350,000		232,000		118,000
Total budget	$1,310,000		$992,000		$318,000

Answer C:

C. 1 & 2. The unit standard costs of the products using activity-based costing are calculated next.

Fabricating Department	
Total cost	$992,000
Less: Direct material	160,000
Less: Direct labor	600,000
Pool overhead cost for allocation	$232,000
Hours: Tuff Stuff (4.4 hours × 20,000 units)	88,000
Ruff Stuff (6.0 hours × 20,000 units)	120,000
Total machine hours	208,000

Overhead cost/machine hour: $232,000 ÷ 208,000 = $1.1154/hour

Fabrication cost per unit: Tuff Stuff $1.1154 × 4.4 hours = $4.91 per unit
Ruff Stuff $1.1154 × 6.0 hours = $6.69 per unit

<u>Assembly Department</u>

Total cost − Direct labor = Pool overhead cost for allocation
    $318,000 − $200,000 = $118,000

Setups = 1,000 (Tuff Stuff) + 272 (Ruff Stuff) = 1,272
Cost per setup: $118,000 ÷ 1,272 = $92.77 per setup

Setup cost per unit:

Tuff Stuff: ($92.77 × 1,000) ÷ 20,000 units = $4.64 per unit
Ruff Stuff: ($92.77 × 272) ÷ 20,000 units = $1.26 per unit

Tuff Stuff Standard Activity-Based Cost

Direct material	$ 5.00
Direct labor	16.00
Fabrication Department overhead allocation	4.91
Assembly Department overhead allocation	4.64
Total cost	$30.55

Ruff Stuff Standard Activity-Based Cost

Direct material	$ 3.00
Direct labor	24.00
Fabrication Department overhead allocation	4.91
Assembly Department overhead allocation	6.69
Total cost	$34.95

Answer D:

When compared to the old standard cost ($37.50), the new activity-based standard cost for Ruff Stuff ($34.95) should lead the company to decide to lower the price for Ruff Stuff in order to be more competitive in the market and continue production of the product. Using ABC for allocating overhead costs generally leads to a more accurate estimate of the costs incurred to produce a product, and Alyssa should be able to make better informed decisions regarding pricing and production.

Answer to Question 1D-ES05

Answer 1:

a.

Materials	$400,000
Direct labor	100,000
Variable manufacturing overhead	20,000
Fixed manufacturing overhead	200,000
	$720,000/100,000 = $7.20

b. 10,000 beginning inventory + 100,000 manufactured − 106,000 sold = 4,000 units in ending inventory; 4,000 × $7.20 = $28,800.

c. Sales (106,000 × $12)		$1,272,000
Cost of Goods Sold:		
Beginning inventory	$ 72,000	
Cost of goods manufactured (100,000 × $7.20)	720,000	
− Ending inventory	(28,800)	763,200
Gross profit		508,800
Less selling and administrative		
Variable costs	80,000	
Fixed costs	300,000	380,000
Income		$ 128,800

Answer 2:

a.

Materials	$400,000
Direct labor	100,000
Variable manufacturing overhead	20,000
	$520,000/100,000 = $5.20

b. 4,000 units × $5.20 = $20,800

c.

Sales		$1,272,000
Less variable costs:		
Manufacturing = $5.20 × 106,000	$551,200	
Selling and administrative	80,000	631,200
Contribution margin		640,800
Less fixed costs:		
Manufacturing	200,000	
Selling and administrative	300,000	500,000
Income		$ 140,800

Answer 3:

The difference in incomes is caused by the treatment of fixed manufacturing overhead. Absorption costing treats this cost as a product cost that is held in inventory until the goods are sold; variable costing treats fixed manufacturing overhead as a period cost, showing it as an expense immediately. Because inventory decreased, absorption costing would expense all of the current month's fixed manufacturing overhead as well as some of the costs that were previously deferred in the prior period's inventory; variable costing would expense only the current month's amount, resulting in a higher income.

Answer 4:

a. The advantages of using absorption costing are:
   - It is required for external reporting.
   - It matches all manufacturing costs with revenues.
b. The advantages of using variable costing are:
   - Data required for cost-volume-profit analysis can be taken directly from the statement.
   - The profit for a period is not affected by changes in inventories.
   - Unit product costs do not contain fixed costs that are often unitized, a practice that could result in poor decision making.
   - The impact of fixed costs on profits is emphasized.
   - It is easier to estimate a product's profitability.
   - It ties in with cost control measures such as flexible budgets.

Answer 5:

a. Top-down advantage: speed, control top down; disadvantage: little buy-in, top has less information
   Bottom-up advantage: more likely to commit; disadvantage: may set easier targets
b. Best: top-down, cost of products most important, want to focus on control
c. Benchmark with outside examples, mutual learning about problems, balanced scorecard methods of evaluation

Answer to Question 1D-ES06

Answer 1:

Model M-11:

Overhead cost allocated (per unit): [€80,000 / (650 + 150)] × 650 = €65,000

65000 / 1300 = 50

Gross margin per unit: €90 – €10 – €50 = €30

Model R-24:

Overhead cost allocated (per unit): [€80,000 / (650 + 150)] × 150 = €15,000

15,000 / 1500 = 10

Gross margin per unit: €60 – €30 – €10 = €20

Answer 2:

Setups: €20,000 / (3 + 7) = €2,000

Components: €50,000 / (17 + 33) = €1,000

Material Movements: €10,000 / (15 + 35) = €200

Model M-11:

(€2,000 × 3) + (€1,000 × 170) + (€200 15) = €26,000

Overhead cost allocated by ABC (per unit): €26,600 / 1300 = €20.00

Gross margin per unit: €90 – €10 – €20.00 = €60.00

Model R-24:

(€2,000 × 7) + (€1000 × 33) + (€200 × 35) = €54,000

Overhead cost allocated by ABC (per unit): €54,000 / 1,500 = €36.00

Gross margin per unit: €60 – €30 – €36 = –€6.00

Answer 3:

Because the products do not all require the same proportionate shares of the overhead resources of setup hours and components, the ABC system provides different results than the traditional system. The traditional method use volume base allocation base, which allocates overhead costs on the basis of direct labor hours. The ABC system considers important differences in overhead resource requirements by using multiple cost drivers and thus provides a better picture of the costs of each product model, provided that the activity measures are fairly estimated.

In the case of Smart Electronics, Model R-24 uses more setups, components, and material movements, which might not be reflected in the labor hours. The following table shows the overhead allocated per unit and profit margin per unit under the current conventional costing system and ABC. As indicated, Model R-24 was previously under-costed and Model M-11 was over-costed.

Overhead Allocated per unit under the current costing system and ABC:

	Current costing system	ABC
Model M-11	€50	€20.00
Model R-24	€10	€36.00

Gross Margin per unit under the current costing system and ABC

	Current costing system	ABC
Model M-11	€30	€60.00
Model R-24	€20	-€6.00

Smart Electronics' management can use the information from the ABC system to make better pricing decisions. After allocating overhead by ABC, it gives a clear cost picture that Model R-24 costs more to manufacture because it uses more setups, components, and material movements. The current price of $60 is inadequate to cover the total cost and results in negative gross margin. Therefore, the company might decide to increase the price of the Model R-24. For Model M-11, the previous overhead was overestimated, given that it was allocated by labor hours. Under ABC, only €60.00 of the overhead was allocated to every unit of Model M-11. Management might reduce the price of Model M-11 to make it more competitive.

Answer 4:

Advantages

The ABC system better captures the resources needed for Model M-11 and Model R-24. It identifies all of the various activities undertaken when producing the products and recognizes that different products consume different amounts of activities. Hence, the ABC system generates more accurate product costs.

Limitations

ABC requires continuously estimating cost drivers and updating and maintaining the system, which make the system relatively costly.

A complicated system is sometimes confusing to top management.

Estimation of cost of activities and selection of cost drivers sometimes may cause estimation errors, which could result in misleading cost information.

Part 1 Section E Answers

Answer to Question 1E-ES01

	Weaknesses	Recommendations
1.	An authorization document that describes the item to be acquired, indicates the benefits to be derived, and estimates its cost is not prepared and reviewed with management.	To obtain approval for the purchase of machinery and equipment, an appropriations request should be prepared, describing the item, indicating why it is needed, and estimating its expected costs and benefits. The document also could include the item's accounting classification, expected useful life, depreciation method and rate, and name the approving company executives.
2.	There is no control over authorized acquisitions. The purchase requisitions and purchase orders for fixed assets are interspersed with other requisitions and purchase orders and handled through normal purchasing procedures.	Authorized acquisitions should be processed using special procedures and purchase orders. These purchase orders should be subjected to numerical control. Copies of purchase orders should be distributed to all appropriate departments so that the acquisition can be monitored.
3.	Plant engineering does not appear to be inspecting machinery and equipment upon receipt.	Purchases of machinery and equipment should be subject to normal receiving inspection routines. In the case of machinery and equipment, plant engineering is usually responsible for reviewing the receipt to make certain the correct item was delivered and that it was not damaged in transit. All new machinery and equipment would be assigned a control number and tagged at the time of receipt.
4.	The lapsing schedules are not reconciled periodically to general ledger control accounts to verify agreement.	At least once each year, machinery and equipment lapsing schedules, which provide information on asset cost and accumulated depreciation, should be reconciled to general ledger control accounts. Furthermore, an actual physical inventory of existing fixed assets should be taken periodically and reconciled to the lapsing schedules and general ledger control account to assure accuracy.
5.	Machinery and equipment accounting policies, including depreciation, have not been updated to make certain that the most desirable methods are being used.	Machinery and equipment accounting procedures, including depreciation, must be updated periodically to reflect actual experience, and changes in accounting pronouncements and income tax legislation.

Answer to Question 1E-ES02

Answer A:

At least three weaknesses in the company's internal control system include:

1. The Limited Expenditure Account (LEA) not being subject to normal accounting controls.

2. The lack of adequate supporting documentation for personal and other expenditures. There is an improper or inadequate identification of the use of these resources, which makes proper accounting classification difficult or impossible. This increases the possibility of illegal use and material misstatements.
3. The Internal Audit Department not reporting its findings in connection with the payment practices and the LEA.

Answer B:

At least three illegal or improper practices uncovered at the company include:

1. Funds raised for political purposes were diverted to other uses. This misappropriation of funds included Public Relations Department resources being used for personal projects and the authorizing of payments to vendors for personal services and goods.
2. Management fraud. Senior management advised the Internal Audit Department to conceal findings; this act is detrimental to the company. There also appears to be a senior management conspiracy.
3. The external auditors not reporting these practices in their recommendations for improved internal control procedures.

Answer C:

At least four important steps that the company should take, both procedurally and organizationally, to correct the problems that were uncovered in order to prevent a similar situation in the future include:

1. Terminating the employment of the chief executive officer, president, vice president-public relations, as well as the controller and director of the Internal Audit Department.
2. Strengthening the company's internal controls, including:
   - The establishment of a company policy that all payments and reimbursements must be supported by appropriate documentation and, also, approved by at least one higher level of authority.
   - Establishing dollar limits that can be approved at each level of authority.
3. Issuing a strong formal company-wide code of ethics.
4. Restructuring the organization so that the Internal Audit Department reports to the audit committee of the board of directors.

Answer to Question 1E-ES03

Answer A:

The seven types of internal audits are financial, operational, performance, information systems, contract, compliance, and special investigation (e.g., fraud). The two most common types of internal audits are operational audits and compliance audits.

An operational audit is a comprehensive review of the varied functions within an enterprise to appraise the efficiency and economy of operations and the effectiveness with which those functions achieve their objective. An example would be an audit to assess productivity. Other examples could include an evaluation of processes to reduce rework, or reduce the time required to process paperwork or goods.

A compliance audit is the review of both financial and operating controls to see how they conform to established laws, standards, regulations, and procedures. An environmental audit would be an example of a compliance audit. Other examples of compliance audits could include the review of controls over industrial wastes or the review of procedures ensuring that proper disclosure is made regarding hazardous materials on site.

Answer B:

1. A compliance audit would best fit the requirements of the president of Brawn.
2. The objective of this compliance audit is to assure the president that the manufacturing facility has appropriate policies and procedures in place for obtaining the needed permits, has obtained all the required permits in accordance with the law, and that environmental and safety issues are being properly addressed.
3. The assignment specifically is to address the proper use of permits, compliance with safety regulations, and compliance with environmental standards. These issues can be properly addressed only by conducting a compliance audit. Although financial and operational areas might be involved, they would be secondary to the compliance issues. For example, a financial impact could result from the evaluation of compliance with safety regulations. The findings might result in additional expenditures for safety precautions or a reduction in the company's risk of being fined for lack of compliance.

Answer C:

To mitigate the president's concern, these activities and procedures could be implemented.

- Set the tone at the top. The president should communicate to all employees that the company expects appropriate business practices on the part of all employees in all divisions.
- Ensure that all employees have the necessary information to perform their duties. Keep the lines of communication open. For example, involve senior mangers from the manufacturing facility in monthly operational meetings for the whole company.
- Conduct regularly scheduled audits of compliance with applicable laws, regulations, and standards.
- Periodically review and update policies, rules, and procedures to ensure that internal controls prevent or help to detect material risks. Make sure all employees have access to the relevant policies and procedures. For example, post the policies and procedures on the company's intranet.

Answer to Question 1E-ES04

Answer A:

1. Crosby, the owner is taking a hands-off approach. He is hardly around to check on the business.
2. The two managers, Smith and Fletcher, have too much control without any independent checks on them.
3. Hiring policies to hire the right kind of employees are lacking; Crosby does not screen the job applicants; he did not check any background references for Smith and Fletcher.
4. Proper internal controls such as segregation of duties, authorizations, independent checks are not in place. Fletcher places purchase orders, and also receives materials. Crosby is in charge of collecting the payments, maintaining records, reconciling the bank accounts, preparing and signing checks, and approving payments. Lack of basic internal controls seems to have opened the door for employees to commit fraud.

Answer B:

Proper internal controls must be in place so that opportunities to commit, and/or conceal fraud are eliminated. In this case, the internal controls needed are: (1) segregation of duties; (2) system of authorizations; (3) independent checks; and (4) proper documentation. No one department or individual should handle all aspects of a transaction from beginning to end. No one person should perform more than one function recording transactions, and reconciling bank accounts (as done by Crosby in this case). In a similar manner, Fletcher should not authorize purchases, receive inventory, and issue materials for production. The company also should separate the duties of preparing and signing checks, especially because the same person has the authority to approve payment.

There is a failure to enforce authorization controls. Crosby should authorize purchases and approve payments. He might consider hiring another person so that the two tasks, record keeping and bank reconciliation, can be separated.

In addition to that, the company must have better hiring policies in place, may require vacations, conduct internal audits, and have good oversight over employees.

Require vacations, conduct internal audits, owner/board oversight.

Answer C:

Even the best internal controls do not guarantee that fraud will be eliminated. These controls provide reasonable, not absolute, assurance against fraud. Internal controls are not fraud-proof, internal controls never provide absolute insurance that fraud will be prevented. Effectiveness depends on competency and dependability of people enforcing the controls.

Answer to Question 1E-ES05

Answer A:

1. Buying raw materials from other countries will expose the company to market risk, including the exposure to potential loss that would result from changes in market prices or rates. Examples include foreign exchange valuation, interest rate changes, and the volatility of crude oil prices. If a company has a contract to purchase products in a foreign currency, the cost of those products may increase drastically due to depreciation of the home currency. Foreign products may increase in price, or become unavailable, due to political events, such as expropriation or inflation.
2. Credit risk is the economic lost suffered due to the default of a borrower or counterparty. Default can be legal bankruptcy or failure to fulfill contractual obligations in a timely manner, due to inability or unwillingness. Credit risk includes loan default, failure to pay accounts receivable, or the inability of a business partner to fulfill agreed-on actions or payments. These conditions may be worsened when dealing with international counterparties, due to differences in legal systems, accounting systems, and credit reporting services.
3. International companies may have additional operational risk, defined as the risk of direct or indirect loss resulting from inadequate or failed internal processes, people, and systems or from external events. An example is failure to follow quality standards resulting in the shipment of deficient products, customer dissatisfaction, and reputation damage. Other examples include failure to properly monitor financial transactions, the hacking of computer files, and failure to follow loan approval controls.

Answer B:

1. Without a thorough understanding of your business, it is not possible to (1) identify the risks associated with daily operations, (2) understand the external risks associated with elements such as competitors or changes in technology, or (3) to assign individual accountability for risk management. If you do not understand your business position, decisions can be made that would undermine that position. For example, if your customers buy your service or good because of its quality and they don't care about price, you need to know this to mitigate the risk of damaging this relationship.
2. A system of checks and balances (1) prevents any individual or group from gaining the power to take unplanned risks on behalf of an organization, and (2) safeguards assets, and (3) prevents fraudulent activities. Examples include the segregation of duties to safeguard financial transactions and the use of passwords to limit access to records and programs.
3. Procedures that set limits and set standards can (1) prevent inappropriate behavior, and (2) tell a business when to stop. Examples might include standards for sales practices and product disclosures, standards for hiring practices regarding background checks on prospective employees, or termination policies for violation of company policy.

Answer C:

Management should be involved with:

- Setting the tone from the top and building awareness through demonstration of senior management commitment
- Establishing the principles that will guide the company's risk culture and values
- Facilitating open communication for discussing risk issues, escalating exposures, and sharing lessons learned and best practices
- Providing training and development programs
- Selecting appropriate performance measures to promote desired behavior
- Setting compensation policies that reward desired behavior

Answer D:

Management should be involved with:

- Section 404 of the Sarbanes-Oxley Act of 2002 (SOX 404) requires management to "take ownership" of internal controls over financial reporting by assessing and publicly reporting on their effectiveness.
- Each annual report of an issuer (of public securities) will contain an "internal control report." This report contains a statement that management is responsible for maintaining adequate internal controls. The report also contains an assessment of the effectiveness of the internal control structure.
- Each issuer is required to disclose the content of its code of ethics for senior financial officers.
- The auditor's report will evaluate management's assessment of the internal controls and issue an opinion as to the effectiveness of the internal controls.

Answer to Question 1E-ES06

Answer 1:

a. Four types of functional responsibilities that should be performed by different people:
   - Authority to execute transactions
   - Recording transactions
   - Custody of assets and
   - Periodic reconciliations
b. Which incompatible duties did Zhao have?

Zhao could execute transactions by initiating a transfer and could record transactions by entering the joint venture that was erroneous.

Answer 2:

Attempted controls:

- The company had physical controls over its checks.
- The president authorized and signed all checks.

- The company maintained prenumbered check stock.
- The company had a prepared budget to compare to actuals to identify variances.

Ways to strengthen:

- Restrict fund online transferability.
- Randomly select audit expense transactions on a periodic basis.
- Separate the incompatible duties.

Answer 3:

a. Three internal control objectives
   1. Effectiveness and efficiency of operations—operations should be as efficient as possible
   2. Compliance with applicable laws and regulations—care should be taken to follow and be in compliance with all applicable laws and regulations
   3. Reliability of financial reporting—financial data should be reliable and timely so that it can be useful for management decisions or outside users
b. Five components of internal control.
   1. Control environment—sets the tone of an organization, influencing the control consciousness of its people
   2. Risk assessment—identify and analyze relevant risks as a basis for management
   3. Control activities—the policies and procedures that help ensure that management directives are carried out.
   4. Information and communication
      - Information. Systems support the identification, capture, and exchange of information in a form and time frame that enable people to carry out their responsibilities.
      - Communication. Providing an understanding to employees about their roles and responsibilities.
   5. Monitoring—assesses the quality of internal control performance over time

Answer 4:

Three ways internal controls are designed to provide reasonable assurance.

1. Segregation of duties—assigning different employees to perform functions
2. Reconciliation of recorded accountability with assets
3. Safeguarding controls—limit access to an organization's assets to authorized personnel

Answer to Question 1E-ES07

Answer 1:

A good system of internal control is designed to provide reasonable assurance regarding achievement of an entity's objectives involving effectiveness and efficiency of operations, reliability of financial reporting, and compliance with applicable laws and regulations.

Answer 2:

Segregation of duties requires that no one person have control over the physical custody of an asset and the accounting for it. There is no evidence to suggest Smallparts makes any effort to account for the value of returned product, which may indeed be significant. The one salesperson seems to be in charge of all aspects related to returned product, including authorizing returns, crediting customers, receiving returns, handling physical custody, finding new customers, concluding sales, shipping, billing, and collecting. Most of these duties should be separated.

Answer 3:

A good system of internal control suggests that four functional responsibilities be separated and handled by different individuals: (1) authority to execute transactions, (2) recording transactions, (3) custody of assets involved in the transactions, and (4) periodic reconciliations of the existing assets to recorded amounts. Smallparts might improve its control over the inventory of returned product by separating these responsibilities among four different individuals.

Answer 4:

Separate responsibilities and duties. While the salesman may be assigned to work with customers who return products and find other customers for these products, other staff should post credits to customer accounts following written policy. The products should be received, inventoried, booked, and shipped just like regular products.

Answer 5:

- **a.** The *IMA Statement of Ethical Professional Practice* lists the following four ethical principles: Honesty, Fairness, Objectivity, Responsibility.
- **b.1.** Several standards from the *Statement* apply.
  - Credibility: "Each practitioner has a responsibility to disclose deficiencies in internal controls."
  - Competence: Duty to maintain an appropriate level of professional expertise relative to standard procedure commonly used in the accounting of firms dealing with returned product.
  - Confidentiality: Refrain from using this confidential information for unethical advantage, by not informing firms of the lax controls and availability of steep discounts on returned product.
  - Integrity: Mitigating any conflict of interest.
- **b.2.** Steps are outlined in the IMA *Statement of Ethical Professional Practice*.

Answer to Question 1E-ES08

Answer 1:

a. The objective of a compliance audit is to see how financial controls and operating controls conform with established laws, standards, and procedures.

b. The objective of an operational audit is to appraise the efficiency and economy of operations and the effectiveness with which those functions achieve their objectives.

Answer 2:

a. Transaction processing controls include: passwords to limit access to input or change data, segregation of duties to safeguard assets, control totals to ensure data accuracy.

b. Virus protection controls include: ensuring that the latest edition of antivirus software is installed and updated, firewalls are set up to deter incoming risks, Internet access is limited to business-related purposes to reduce chances of viruses.

c. Backup controls include identification of vital systems to be backed up regularly, development of disaster recovery plan, testing of backup communications and resources.

Answer 3:

A sound business continuances plan contains the following components:

- Establish priorities for recovery process.
- Identify software and hardware needed for critical processes.
- Identify all data files and program files required for recovery.
- Store files in off-site storage.
- Identify who has responsibility for various activities, which activities are needed first.
- Set up and check arrangements for backup facilities.
- Test and review recovery plan.

Answer 4:

a. Bank deposits do not always correspond with cash receipts. Cause: Cash received after bank deposits are made. Action: Have a separate individual reconcile incoming cash receipts to bank deposits.

b. Physical inventory counts sometimes differ from perpetual inventory record, and sometimes there have been alterations to physical counts and perpetual records. Cause: Timing differences. Actions: Limit access to physical inventory, require and document specific approvals for adjustments to records,

c. Unexpected and unexplained decrease in gross profit percentage. Causes: Unauthorized discounts or credits provided to customers. Actions: Establish policies for discounts credits, document approvals.

Answers to Section Practice Questions

Section A: External Financial Reporting Decisions Answers and Explanations

Question 1A1-W001
Topic: Financial Statements

The multistep income statement, with additional income statement items, for Harrington Technologies Inc. is given below.

Net sales		$2,000,000
Less:	Cost of goods sold	890,000
Gross profit		1,110,000
Less:	Transportation and travel	45,000
	Depreciation	68,000
	Pension contributions	21,000
Operating income		976,000
Less:	Discontinued operations	76,000
Income before taxes		900,000
Less:	Tax expense @ 30%	270,000
Net Income		$630,000

Glen Hamilton, a financial analyst, analyzed the company's financial statements and concluded that the real net income should be $683,200 instead of $630,000. Which of the following arguments is **most** likely to support his conclusion?

- ☐ **a.** $53,200 due from a client was written off as irrecoverable after the finalization of accounts for the current period.

- ☐ **b.** The company valued its inventory using the specific identification method, whereas the financial analyst used the LIFO method for the current period.

801

- c. The company might have liquidated its LIFO reserve.
- d. The company has included expenses in relation to discontinued operations as part of income from continued operations.

Explanation: The correct answer is **d**. The company has included expenses in relation to discontinued operations as part of income from continued operations.

Revenue and expenses from discontinued operations do not form part of income from continued operations. In this case, the analyst has excluded discontinued operations since it is a nonrecurring item.

Question 1A1-W002
Topic: Financial Statements

The current ratio for Garrett Inc. for the previous five years is as follows.

	Year 1	Year 2	Year 3	Year 4	Year 5
Current Ratio	5	4.5	4.9	1.2	4.2

Which of the following factor is the **most** likely reason for the low current ratio in Year 4?

- a. Materials were purchased on credit in Year 4 for which payment is due.
- b. Long-term debts were due for repayment in Year 4.
- c. The company reduced its credit period in Year 4.
- d. Working capital in Year 4 decreased due to an increase in accounts payable.

Explanation: The correct answer is **b**. Long-term debts were due for repayment in Year 4.

The current portion of long-term debt is included in current liabilities in the year of repayment. Hence, the principal amount for long-term debts might have been due in Year 4 and classified as current liabilities.

Question 1A1-W003
Topic: Financial Statements

The cash flows and net income from four business segments for Taylor Laboratories Inc. have been provided.

	Segment 1	Segment 2	Segment 3	Segment 4
Cash flow from operations	$3,000	$(250)	$(3,000)	$2,000
Cash flow from investing activities	(4,000)	6,000	8,000	(3,000)
Cash flow from financing activities	1,080	(1,000)	(1,000)	1,080
Net income	1,500	1,750	2,375	1,500

Based on the information, which segment should be discontinued by the company?

- ☐ **a.** Segment 3, because cash used in operations is high and cash inflow is predominantly from investing activities.
- ☐ **b.** Segment 1, because net income is lowest and requires high investments.
- ☐ **c.** Segment 4, because net income and cash inflow from operations are low.
- ☐ **d.** Segment 2, because cash used in operations is low and cash flow from investing activities is not properly utilized.

Explanation: The correct answer is **a**. Segment 3, because cash used in operations is high and cash inflow is predominantly from investing activities.

Segment 3 should be discontinued because the major portion of income of the segment could be from the sale of its assets.

Question 1A1-W004
Topic: Financial Statements

The cash flow from operations for Charlene Energy Inc. is $25,000 for the current year. If the amortization expense increases by $5,000 and other factors remain same, under which of the following assumptions will the cash flow from operations remain unaffected?

- ☐ **a.** A change in amortization method will not have a retrospective effect.
- ☐ **b.** The company has an infinite life.
- ☐ **c.** The company is operating in a tax-free environment.
- ☐ **d.** The company can change the depreciation method in between a financial year.

Explanation: The correct answer is **c**. The company is operating in a tax-free environment.

Cash inflow from amortization arises because of the tax shield. In a tax-free environment, change in amortization will not affect the cash flows from operations.

Question 1A1-W005
Topic: Financial Statements

The following information is extracted from the latest financial information of Hines Materials Inc.

Tax rate	30%
Net Income	$15,000
Cash flow from operations	$45,000

Additional information:

1. The tax rate for the coming year is expected to increase by 2%.
2. The company is planning to purchase equipment worth $500,000 in the first quarter of next year.
3. A 15% increase in capacity is expected with the use of new equipment.

Considering the given factors, which of the following would be an ideal strategy to decrease the tax liability for the next year?

- ☐ a. Defer the purchase of equipment to next year to take advantage of tax loss carryforward.
- ☐ b. Depreciate the asset using the double-declining balance method to show higher cash flows from operations in initial years.
- ☐ c. Prepare the cash flow statement using direct method to show lower cash from operations and lower net income.
- ☐ d. Defer the purchase of equipment to next year if there is a deferred tax liability can be reasonably estimated.

Explanation: The correct answer is **b**. Depreciate the asset using the double-declining balance method to show higher cash flows from operations in initial years.

Depreciating the equipment using double-declining balance method will result in higher depreciation in the initial years and lower net income. Therefore, net tax liability of the company will decrease.

Question 1A1-W006
Topic: Financial Statements

The financial accountant of Eva Wolfe Corp. has ascertained the cash flows from operations as follows:

Net Income	$15,000
Depreciation on equipment	2,500
Dividend income	2,500
Interest income	5,000
Increases in current assets	8,000
Increases in current liabilities	6,500
Cash flow from operations	$16,000

The management accountant of the company argues that the cash flow from operations should be $8,500. Which of the following statements, if true, will support the management accountant's calculation?

- ☐ a. The company operates in a tax-free environment.
- ☐ b. The company uses IFRS to ascertain cash flow from operations.
- ☐ c. Cash flow from operations is ascertained using direct method.
- ☐ d. Depreciation on equipment should not be added back to net income for calculating cash flows from operations.

Explanation: The correct answer is **b**. The company uses IFRS to ascertain cash flow from operations.

The management accountant has followed IFRS for ascertaining cash flows from operations. He has not included dividend income and interest income as part of cash flows from operations. IFRS gives the flexibility of inclusion of dividend income and interest income as part of either operating activities or financing activities. Hence, CFO = $15,000 + $2,500 − ($8,000 − $6,500) − ($2,500 + $5,000) = $8,500.

Question 1A1-W007
Topic: Financial Statements

The management of Arthur Energy recognized a contingent liability of $50,000 in the current year. However, before the annual report was issued, the company resolved the issue making a lump-sum payment of $42,000. The board of directors has decided to incorporate the transaction in the subsequent year's financial statements. Which of the following provisions of US GAAP, if applicable, is likely to prove the management decision wrong?

- ☐ **a.** Loss contingencies must be recognized when it is both probable that a loss has been incurred and the amount of the loss is reasonably estimable.
- ☐ **b.** Whenever GAAP or industry-specific regulations allow a choice between two or more accounting methods, the method selected should be disclosed.
- ☐ **c.** If an event alters the estimates used in preparing the financial statements, then the financial statements should be adjusted.
- ☐ **d.** If an event provides additional evidence about conditions that existed as of the balance sheet date and alters the estimates used, then the financial statements should be adjusted.

Explanation: The correct answer is **d**. If an event provides additional evidence about conditions that existed as of the balance sheet date and alters the estimates used, then the financial statements should be adjusted.

In this case, the amount of contingent liability needs to be revised, as the estimate of the amount of liability had changed. The subsequent event provides evidence regarding conditions present on the balance sheet date. Therefore, the financial statements need to be adjusted.

Question 1A1-W008
Topic: Financial Statements

Shelton Devin Corp. has two subsidiaries, of which 30% of ownership in each subsidiary lies with Shelton Devin. The CEO of the company is not in favor of presenting consolidated financial statements. Based on the information, which of the following is **most** likely true?

- ☐ **a.** The decision of the CEO is correct as companies are required to issue consolidated statements only when the ownership exceeds 50%.
- ☐ **b.** The decision of the CEO is wrong as companies are required to issue consolidated statements when the ownership exceeds 20%.
- ☐ **c.** The decision of the CEO is wrong as companies are required to issue consolidated statements only if it holds more than ten subsidiaries.
- ☐ **d.** The decision of the CEO is correct as companies are required to issue consolidated statements when a company has three or more subsidiaries.

Explanation: The correct answer is **a**. The decision of the CEO is correct as companies are required to issue consolidated statements only when the ownership exceeds 50%.

As required by SFAS No. 94, *Consolidation of All Majority-Owned Subsidiaries*, all companies with subsidiaries are required to issue consolidated statements including each subsidiary they control, usually meaning 50% or more ownership.

Question 1A2-W001

Topic: Recognition, Measurement, Valuation, and Disclosure

An extract of the footnotes of McGee Systems Inc., with ten subsidiaries across five countries, reads as follows:

> The company uses the temporal method for translation of subsidiary accounts. All nonmonetary balances and the expenses associated with them have been translated using historical exchange rates. Monetary assets and liabilities and other assets and liabilities measured at current values have been translated at the current exchange rate on the balance sheet date. Income statement accounts, other than nonmonetary accounts, have been translated using the historical exchange rate.

The company's CFO did not approve the financial statements, stating that the accounting policies followed are not in line with US GAAP. Which of the following statements support the CEO's decision?

- ☐ **a.** Income statement accounts should be translated based on the current exchange rate on the balance sheet date.
- ☐ **b.** Income statement accounts, other than nonmonetary accounts, should be translated based on the average rate for the current year.
- ☐ **c.** All assets and liabilities should be translated using the average rate for the current year.
- ☐ **d.** All assets and liabilities should be translated based on the spot rate for the current year.

Explanation: The correct answer is **b**. Income statement accounts, other than nonmonetary accounts, should be translated based on the average rate for the current year.

Under the temporal method, nonmonetary balances (all balance sheet items other than cash, claims to cash, and cash obligations) are translated using historical exchange rates, and the expenses associated with them should be translated at the historical exchange rate in effect when the item was originally recorded. Monetary assets and liabilities (cash, receivables, and payables) and other assets and liabilities measured at current values (market values or discounted cash flows) are translated at the current exchange rate on the balance sheet date. Income statement accounts other than nonmonetary accounts are translated using the average exchange rate for the current year (quarter or month) for simplicity.

Question 1A2-W002
Topic: Recognition, Measurement, Valuation, and Disclosure

Claire Enterprises has $150,000 in accounts receivable at the end of Year 1, and it estimates its bad debts to be 5% of the receivables. Hence, the accountant reports $7,500 as bad debts and the net realizable value as $142,500. Under which of the following circumstances will the amount of bad debts reported **most** likely reduce?

- ☐ a. If the company shortens the credit period allowed
- ☐ b. If the company lengthens the credit period allowed
- ☐ c. If the allowance for doubtful accounts has a credit balance of $1,500
- ☐ d. If the allowance for doubtful accounts has a debit balance of $1,500

Explanation: The correct answer is **c**. If the allowance for doubtful accounts has a credit balance of $1,500.

If there is an existing credit balance in the allowance for doubtful accounts, then the bad debt expense should be adjusted downward, as it is necessary to adjust the balance only to the desired level. Therefore, the correct balance will be $7,500 − $1,500 = $6,000.

Question 1A2-W003
Topic: Recognition, Measurement, Valuation, and Disclosure

The latest financial statements of Darlene Properties show 140,000 outstanding shares, par value $10. The current market value per share is $25. At the beginning of current year, the company reacquired 10,000 shares at $4 per share. The company follows the cost method for the accounting of treasury stock. The current year's books of accounts show the value of outstanding shares as follows:

Common stock, $10 par	$1,400,000
Less: Treasury stock	100,000
Net common stock, $10 par	$1,300,000

The company's CFO did not approve the financial statements. The **most** likely reason for CFO's disapproval is that:

- ☐ **a.** The treasury stock is incorrectly valued based on par value, instead of valuing at the acquisition price.
- ☐ **b.** The treasury stock is incorrectly valued based on par value, instead of valuing at the current market rate.
- ☐ **c.** The par value of the treasury stock should be presented as a deduction from par value of issued shares of the same class
- ☐ **d.** The treasury stock should be reported as an asset.

Explanation: The correct answer is **a**. The treasury stock is incorrectly valued based on par value, instead of valuing at the acquisition price.

In the cost method, the treasury stock account is debited for the cost of the shares reacquired. Therefore, the value of treasury stocks should be $40,000 (10,000 shares × $4), acquired at the acquisition price.

Question 1A2-W004

Topic: Recognition, Measurement, Valuation, and Disclosure

Rogers Electronics is planning to make a market in the company's stock. The company's CFO suggests the reacquisition of shares. Which of the following is **most** likely to happen if the CFO's suggestion is implemented?

- ☐ **a.** The risk of takeovers by competitors will increase.
- ☐ **b.** This will hinder exercise of employee stock options.
- ☐ **c.** The stock price will increase.
- ☐ **d.** This could serve as an indication of the company's negative outlook about its future performance.

Explanation: The correct answer is **c**. The stock price will increase.

Reacquisition of shares reduces the number of shares a company has outstanding without altering the value of the company. Therefore, the stock price of the company will increase.

Question 1A2-W005

Topic: Recognition, Measurement, Valuation, and Disclosure

AWS Inc. is engaged in the construction of rail tracks. The CEO suggests allocating insurance, property taxes, and supervisory factory labor to construction. But the management accountant opines that a proportional amount of such indirect costs should be allocated to the rail tracks. Which of the following, if true, will support the management accountant's argument?

- ☐ **a.** The indirect costs were allocated to the extent of the difference between net realizable value and carrying value.
- ☐ **b.** The indirect costs were allocated to the extent of proportionate completion.

☐ **c.** The costs incurred on the rail tracks were in excess of their market value.

☐ **d.** The indirect costs were not capitalized to the rail tracks.

Explanation: The correct answer is **c**. The costs incurred on the rail tracks were in excess of their market value.

Any costs incurred in excess of the asset's market value should not be capitalized but would be recorded as a loss.

Question 1A2-W006

Topic: Recognition, Measurement, Valuation, and Disclosure

Calvin Software has invested in the equity stock of BioTech Corp. Its holdings consisted of 35% of the voting stock. The CFO suggests acquiring more stock of BioTech. Based on the information, which of the following will be **true**?

☐ **a.** Additional acquisitions beyond 15% will require Calvin Software to issue consolidated financial statements.

☐ **b.** Calvin's total value will decrease as incidental costs of acquisition must be subtracted when holding exceeds 35%.

☐ **c.** The circumstances leading to the decision to acquire additional shares shall be disclosed in the notes to the financial statements.

☐ **d.** Any additional acquisition of assets up to 20% should be classified as held to maturity.

Explanation: The correct answer is **a**. Additional acquisitions beyond 15% will require Calvin Software to issue consolidated financial statements.

Feedback: When an investor acquires an interest in the investee, the acquired percentage of voting stock determines the method of accounting. If the holdings are greater than 50%, the investor company needs to issue consolidated financial statements.

Question 1A2-W007

Topic: Recognition, Measurement, Valuation, and Disclosure

Warner Machines missed recording purchases worth $10,000 in the current year's income statement. While finalizing the financial statements, the company's accountant detected the error and partially corrected it. Under which of the following situations will the company report lower than actual net income?

☐ **a.** If the accountant has reduced cash by $10,000

☐ **b.** If the accountant has only added the missing purchases worth $10,000 to the cost of goods sold

☐ **c.** If the accountant has only increased accounts payable by $10,000

☐ **d.** If the accountant has reduced inventory by $10,000

Explanation: The correct answer is **b**. If the accountant has only added the missing purchases worth $10,000 to the cost of goods sold.

When the company misses recording a purchase but includes the purchases as part of cost of goods sold (COGS) in income statement, COGS will be understated and the net income will be overstated. The missing $10,000 should have been in included both in purchases and in ending inventory, which will result in the COGS being unaffected.

Question 1A2-W008
Topic: Recognition, Measurement, Valuation, and Disclosure

Sandra Bellucci, a financial analyst, is analyzing inventory of companies from four different industries: consumer goods, sports goods manufacturers, electronics, and aircraft manufacturers. Assuming the inventory valuation methods reflect the actual flow of inventory and the inventory only includes finished goods, which of the following industries will **most** likely have zero LIFO reserve?

- ☐ a. Consumer goods
- ☐ b. Sports goods manufacturers
- ☐ c. Electronics
- ☐ d. Aircraft manufacturers

Explanation: The correct answer is **d**. Aircraft manufacturers.

Since this industry deals with high value and customized orders, the production usually starts after receiving the order. Since there will not be any equipment in inventory, the inventory balance will be zero, irrespective of the method of valuation used. Therefore, the balance in LIFO reserve will **most** likely be zero.

Section B: Planning, Budgeting, and Forecasting Answers and Explanations

Question 1B5-CQ02
Topic: Annual Profit Plan and Supporting Schedules

Troughton Company manufactures radio-controlled toy dogs. Summary budget financial data for Troughton for the current year are shown next.

Sales (5,000 units at $150 each)	$750,000
Variable manufacturing cost	400,000
Fixed manufacturing cost	100,000
Variable selling and administrative cost	80,000
Fixed selling and administrative cost	150,000

Troughton uses an absorption costing system with overhead applied based on the number of units produced, with a denominator level of activity of 5,000 units.

Underapplied or overapplied manufacturing overhead is written off to cost of goods sold in the year incurred.

The $20,000 budgeted operating income from producing and selling 5,000 toy dogs planned for this year is of concern to Trudy George, Troughton's president. She believes she could increase operating income to $50,000 (her bonus threshold) if Troughton produces more units than it sells, thus building up the finished goods inventory.

How much of an increase in the number of units in the finished goods inventory would be needed to generate the $50,000 budgeted operating income?

- ☐ a. 556 units
- ☐ b. 600 units
- ☐ c. 1,500 units
- ☐ d. 7,500 units

Explanation: The correct answer is: **a.** 1,500 units.

Increasing production over sales allows the company to bury fixed overhead costs in the ending inventory, resulting in an increase in net income. The increase in net income from the extra production can be calculated as shown:

Increase in Net Income = (Fixed Overhead Rate) (Excess of Production over Sales)
= $30,000

Fixed Overhead Rate = (Fixed Manufacturing Costs) / (Denominator Activity Level)

Fixed Overhead Rate = $100,000 / 5,000 Units = $20 per Unit

Therefore, the increase in production over sales = $30,000 / $20 per unit = 1,500 units.

Question 1B5-CQ04

Topic: Annual Profit Plan and Supporting Schedules

Hannon Retailing Company prices its products by adding 30% to its cost. Hannon anticipates sales of $715,000 in July, $728,000 in August, and $624,000 in September. Hannon's policy is to have on hand enough inventory at the end of the month to cover 25% of the next month's sales. What will be the cost of the inventory that Hannon should budget for purchase in August?

- ☐ a. $509,600
- ☐ b. $540,000
- ☐ c. $560,000
- ☐ d. $680,000

Explanation: The correct answer is: **b.** $540,000.

Sales = 1.3 (Cost of Sales), which can also be stated as:

Cost of Sales = (Sales) / 1.3

Expected Ending Inventory for Each Month = 0.25 (Next Month's Sales)

The purchases in a given month can be computed as shown:

Inventory Purchased for a Month = (Sales for the Month / 1.3)
  + (Expected Ending Inventory / 1.3)
  − (Expected Beginning Inventory / 1.3)

Inventory Purchased for August = [($728,000) / 1.3] + [(0.25) ($624,000) / 1.3]
  − [(0.25) ($728,000) / 1.3]

Inventory Purchased for August = $560,000 + $120,000 − $140,000 = $540,000

Question 1B5-CQ06

Topic: Annual Profit Plan and Supporting Schedules

Tyler Company produces one product and budgeted 220,000 units for the month of August with these budgeted manufacturing costs:

	Total Costs	Cost per Unit
Variable costs	$1,408,000	$6.40
Batch setup cost	880,000	4.00
Fixed costs	1,210,000	5.50
Total	$3,498,000	$15.90

The variable cost per unit and the total fixed costs are unchanged within a production range of 200,000 to 300,000 units per month. The total for the batch setup cost in any month depends on the number of production batches that Tyler runs. A normal batch consists of 50,000 units unless production requires less volume. In the prior year, Tyler experienced a mixture of monthly batch sizes of 42,000 units, 45,000 units, and 50,000 units. Tyler consistently plans production each month in order to minimize the number of batches. For the month of September, Tyler plans to manufacture 260,000 units. What will be Tyler's total budgeted production costs for September?

- ☐ a. $3,754,000
- ☐ b. $3,930,000
- ☐ c. $3,974,000
- ☐ d. $4,134,000

Explanation: The correct answer is: **b.** $3,930,000.

September Budgeted Production Costs = (Fixed Costs) + (Variable Costs) + (Batch Setup Costs)

Variable Costs = (260,000 Units) ($6.40 per Unit) = $1,664,000

Batch setup costs: 260,000 units require a minimum of 6 batches.

In August, 220,000 units were produced in 5 batches for a total of $880,000. The cost per batch was $880,000 / 5 = $176,000.

6 Batches at $176,000 per Batch = $1,056,000

September Budgeted Production Costs = ($1,210,000) + ($1,664,000) + ($1,056,000) = $3,930,000

Question 1B5-CQ08

Topic: Annual Profit Plan and Supporting Schedules

Savior Corporation assembles backup tape drive systems for home microcomputers. For the first quarter, the budget for sales is 67,500 units. Savior will finish the fourth quarter of last year with an inventory of 3,500 units, of which 200 are obsolete. The target ending inventory is 10 days of sales (based on 90 days in a quarter). What is the budgeted production for the first quarter?

- a. 75,000
- b. 71,700
- c. 71,500
- d. 64,350

Explanation: The correct answer is: **b.** 71,700.

The expected beginning inventory is calculated as shown:

Expected Beginning Inventory = (3,500 Units − 200 Obsolete Units) = 3,300 Units

The expected ending inventory is 10 days' sales, which is calculated as shown:

Expected Ending Inventory = [(67,500 Units) / 90] (10) = 7,500 Units

Therefore, budgeted production = 67,500 Units + 7,500 Units − 3,300 Units = 71,700 Units.

Question 1B5-CQ09

Topic: Annual Profit Plan and Supporting Schedules

Streeter Company produces plastic microwave turntables. Sales for the next year are expected to be 65,000 units in the first quarter, 72,000 units in the second quarter, 84,000 units in the third quarter, and 66,000 units in the fourth quarter.

Streeter usually maintains a finished goods inventory at the end of each quarter equal to one half of the units expected to be sold in the next quarter. However, due to a work stoppage, the finished goods inventory at the end of the first quarter is 8,000 units less than it should be.

How many units should Streeter produce in the second quarter?

- ☐ a.   75,000 units
- ☐ b.   78,000 units
- ☐ c.   80,000 units
- ☐ d.   86,000 units

Explanation: The correct answer is: **d.** 86,000 units.

Budgeted production is calculated as shown:

Budgeted Production = (Expected Sales) + (Expected Ending Inventory) − (Expected Beginning Inventory)

The expected ending inventory for each quarter equals 50% of the next quarter's expected sales. Since the finished goods inventory at the end of the first quarter is 8,000 less than it should be, the budgeted production for the second quarter is calculated as shown:

Budgeted Production, Second Quarter = 72,000 Units + 0.5(84,000 Units) − [0.5(72,000 Units) − 8,000 Units]

Budgeted Production, Second Quarter = 72,000 Units + 42,000 Units − [36,000 Units − 8,000 Units]

Budgeted Production, Second Quarter = 114,000 Units − 28,000 Units = 86,000 Units

Question 1B5-CQ10

Topic: Annual Profit Plan and Supporting Schedules

Data regarding Rombus Company's budget are shown next.

Planned sales	4,000 units
Material cost	$2.50 per pound
Direct labor	3 hours per unit
Direct labor rate	$7 per hour

Finished goods beginning inventory 900 units
Finished goods ending inventory 600 units
Direct materials beginning inventory 4,300 units
Direct materials ending inventory 4,500 units
Materials used per unit 6 pounds

Rombus Company's production budget will show total units to be produced of:

- ☐ **a.** 3,700
- ☐ **b.** 4,000
- ☐ **c.** 4,300
- ☐ **d.** 4,600

Explanation: The correct answer is: **a.** 3,700.

Budgeted production is calculated as shown:

Budgeted Production = (Expected Sales) + (Expected Ending Inventory) − (Expected Beginning Inventory)

Budgeted Production = 4,000 Units + 600 Units − 900 Units = 3,700 Units

Question 1B5-CQ11

Topic: Annual Profit Plan and Supporting Schedules

Krouse Company is in the process of developing its operating budget for the coming year. Given next are selected data regarding the company's two products, laminated putter heads and forged putter heads, sold through specialty golf shops.

	Putter Heads	
	Forged	**Laminated**
Raw materials		
Steel	2 pounds @ $5/pound	1 pound @ $5/pound
Copper	None	1 pound @ $15/pound
Direct labor	1/4 hour @ $20/hour	1 hour @ $22/hour
Expected sales	8,200 units	2,000 units
Selling price per unit	$30	$80
Ending inventory target	100 units	60 units
Beginning inventory	300 units	60 units
Beginning inventory (cost)	$5,250	$3,120

Manufacturing overhead is applied to units produced on the basis of direct labor hours. Variable manufacturing overhead is projected to be $25,000, and fixed manufacturing overhead is expected to be $15,000.

The estimated cost to produce one unit of the laminated putter head (PH) is:

- ☐ a. $42
- ☐ b. $46
- ☐ c. $52
- ☐ d. $62

Explanation: The correct answer is: **c.** $52.

Production Costs = Direct Materials + Direct Labor + Manufacturing Overhead

Direct Materials = (1 Pound Steel) ($5/Pound) + (1 Pound Copper) ($15/Pound)
= $5 + $15 = $20

Direct Labor = (1 Hour) ($22/Hour) = $22

Manufacturing overhead is calculated as shown:

Manufacturing Overhead = (Total Expected Overhead) / (Total Expected Direct Labor Hours)

Manufacturing Overhead = ($25,000 Variable Overhead + $15,000 Fixed Overhead) / 4,000 Direct Labor Hours
= $10

Use the next calculation to determine direct labor hours for the overhead calculation:

Direct Labor Hours = (# Laminated PHs Produced) (# Hours/Laminated PH) + (# Forged PHs Produced) (# Hours/Forged PH)

Production of PHs = (Expected Sales) + (Expected Ending Inventory) − (Expected Beginning Inventory)

Production of Laminated PHs = 2,000 + 60 − 60 = 2,000 Units

Production of Forged PHs = 8,200 + 100 − 300 = 8,000 Units

Direct Labor Hours = (2,000 Units) (1 Hour/Unit) + (8,000 Units) (0.25 Hours/Unit)

Direct Labor Hours = 2,000 Hours + 2,000 Hours = 4,000 Hours

Question 1B5-CQ12

Topic: Annual Profit Plan and Supporting Schedules

Tidwell Corporation sells a single product for $20 per unit. All sales are on account, with 60% collected in the month of sale and 40% collected in the following month. A partial schedule of cash collections for January through March of the coming year reveals these receipts for the period:

	Cash Receipts		
	January	February	March
December receivables	$32,000		
From January sales	$54,000	$36,000	
From February sales		$66,000	$44,000

Other information includes:

- Inventories are maintained at 30% of the following month's sales.
- Assume that March sales total $150,000.

The number of units to be purchased in February is

- ☐ a. 3,850 units
- ☐ b. 4,900 units
- ☐ c. 6,100 units
- ☐ d. 7,750 units

Explanation: The correct answer is: **c.** 6,100 units.

The expected unit purchases for any month are calculated as shown:

Expected Purchases = (Expected Sales in Units) + (Expected Ending Inventory) − (Expected Beginning Inventory)

The expected ending inventory for a month is 30% of the next month's expected sales.

Expected sales are calculated as shown:

Expected Sales = (Sales in $) / ($20 Selling Price per Unit)

Number of Units to Be Purchased in February = ($110,000 / $20 per Unit) + [0.3($150,000 / $20 per Unit)] − [0.3($110,000 / $20 per Unit)]

Number of Units to Be Purchased in February = 5,500 Units + [0.3 (7,500 Units)] − [0.3 (5,500 Units)]

Number of Units to Be Purchased in February = 5,500 Units + 2,250 Units − 1,650 Units
= 6,100 Units

Question 1B5-CQ13

Topic: Annual Profit Plan and Supporting Schedules

Stevens Company manufactures electronic components used in automobile manufacturing. Each component uses two raw materials, Geo and Clio. Standard usage of the two materials required to produce one finished electronic component, as well as the current inventory, are shown next.

Material	Standard Usage per Unit	Price	Current Inventory
Geo	2.0 pounds	$15/pound	5,000 pounds
Clio	1.5 pounds	$10/pound	7,500 pounds

Stevens forecasts sales of 20,000 components for each of the next two production periods. Company policy dictates that 25% of the raw materials needed to produce the next period's projected sales be maintained in ending direct materials inventory.

Based on this information, what would the budgeted direct material purchases for the coming period be?

	Geo	Clio
☐ a.	$450,000	$450,000
☐ b.	$675,000	$300,000
☐ c.	$675,000	$400,000
☐ d.	$825,000	$450,000

Explanation: The correct answer is: **b.** $675,000 and $300,000.

The expected material purchases in units for any month can be calculated as shown:

Expected Material Purchases = (Production Needs for the Month)
+ (Expected Ending Inventory) − (Expected Beginning Inventory)

The expected ending inventory for any month is 25% of the next month's expected sales.

Since 2 pounds of Geo are used per unit, the expected purchase of Geo can be calculated as shown:

Expected Purchases of Geo = (2 Pounds) (20,000) + (0.25) (2 Pounds) (20,000)
− 5,000 Pounds

Expected Purchases of Geo = 40,000 Pounds + 10,000 Pounds − 5,000 Pounds
= 45,000 Pounds

Total Cost of Geo = (45,000 Pounds) ($15/Pound) = $675,000

Since 1.5 pounds of Clio are used per unit, the expected purchase of Clio can be calculated as shown:

Expected Purchase of Clio = (1.5 Pounds) (20,000) + (0.25) (1.5 Pounds) (20,000) −7,500 Pounds

Expected Purchase of Clio = 30,000 Pounds + 7,500 Pounds − 7,500 Pounds = 30,000 Pounds

Total Cost of Clio = (30,000 Pounds) ($10/Pound) = $300,000

Question 1B5-CQ14
Topic: Annual Profit Plan and Supporting Schedules

Petersons Planters Inc. budgeted these amounts for the coming year:

Beginning inventory, finished goods	$ 10,000
Cost of goods sold	400,000
Direct material used in production	100,000
Ending inventory, finished goods	25,000
Beginning and ending work-in-process inventory	Zero

Overhead is estimated to be two times the amount of direct labor dollars. The amount that should be budgeted for direct labor for the coming year is:

- ☐ a. $315,000
- ☐ b. $210,000
- ☐ c. $157,500
- ☐ d. $105,000

Explanation: The correct answer is: **d.** $105,000.

Since there was no change in work-in-process inventory, cost of goods manufactured equals total manufacturing costs.

Cost of goods manufactured is calculated as shown:

Cost of Goods Manufactured = (Ending Finished Goods) + (Cost of Goods Sold) − (Beginning Finished Goods)

Cost of Goods Manufactured = $25,000 + $400,000 − $10,000 = $415,000

Since cost of goods manufactured is equal to total manufacturing costs, use the next formula to solve for direct labor costs:

Total Manufacturing Costs = (Direct Material) + (Direct Labor) + (Manufacturing Overhead)

$415,000 = $100,000 + Direct Labor + 2 (Direct Labor)

$415,000 = $100,000 + 3 \text{ (Direct Labor)}$

$315,000 = 3 \text{ (Direct Labor)}$

Direct Labor = $105,000

Question 1B5-CQ15

Topic: Annual Profit Plan and Supporting Schedules

Over the past several years, McFadden Industries has experienced the costs shown regarding the company's shipping expenses:

Fixed costs	$16,000
Average shipment	15 pounds
Cost per pound	$0.50

Shown next are McFadden's budget data for the coming year.

Number of units shipped	8,000
Number of sales orders	800
Number of shipments	800
Total sales	$1,200,000
Total pounds shipped	9,600

McFadden's expected shipping costs for the coming year are:
- a. $4,800.
- b. $16,000.
- c. $20,000.
- d. $20,800.

Explanation: The correct answer is: **d.** $20,800.

Total shipping costs include both fixed and variable shipping costs.

Total Shipping Costs = Fixed Shipping Cost + Variable Shipping Cost

Total Shipping Costs = $16,000 + ($0.50) (Number of Pounds Shipped)

Total Shipping Costs = $16,000 + ($0.50) (9,600 Pounds)

Total Shipping Costs = $16,000 + $4,800 = $20,800

Question 1B5-CQ18

Topic: Annual Profit Plan and Supporting Schedules

In preparing the direct material purchases budget for next quarter, the plant controller has this information available:

Budgeted unit sales	2,000
Pounds of materials per unit	4
Cost of materials per pound	$3
Pounds of materials on hand	400
Finished units on hand	250
Target ending units inventory	325
Target ending inventory of pounds of materials	800

How many pounds of materials must be purchased?

- ☐ a. 2,475
- ☐ b. 7,900
- ☐ c. 8,700
- ☐ d. 9,300

Explanation: The correct answer is: **c.** 8,700.

The direct material purchases budget is calculated as shown:

Direct Materials Purchases = (Production Requirement) + (Expected Ending Inventory in Pounds) − (Expected Beginning Inventory in Pounds)

Direct Materials Purchases = 8,300 Pounds + 800 Pounds − 400 Pounds = 8,700 Pounds

Production Requirement = (4 Pounds per Unit) (Expected Production)

Production Requirement = (4 Pounds per Unit) (2,075 Units) = 8,300 Pounds

Expected Production = (Sales) + (Expected Ending Finished Goods Inventory) − (Expected Beginning Finished Goods Inventory)

Expected Production = 2,000 Units + 325 Units − 250 Units = 2,075 Units

Question 1B5-CQ22

Topic: Annual Profit Plan and Supporting Schedules

Given the next data for Scurry Company, what is the cost of goods sold?

Beginning inventory of finished goods	$100,000
Cost of goods manufactured	700,000
Ending inventory of finished goods	200,000
Beginning work-in-process inventory	300,000
Ending work-in-process inventory	50,000

- ☐ a. $500,000
- ☐ b. $600,000

☐ c. $800,000
☐ d. $950,000

Explanation: The correct answer is: **b.** $600,000.

Cost of goods sold is calculated as shown:

Cost of Goods Sold = (Cost of Goods Manufactured) + (Beginning Finished Goods Inventory) − (Ending Finished Goods Inventory)

Cost of Goods Sold = $700,000 + $100,000 − $200,000

Cost of Goods Sold = $600,000

Question 1B5-CQ23

Topic: Annual Profit Plan and Supporting Schedules

Tut Company's selling and administrative costs for the month of August, when it sold 20,000 units, were:

	Cost per Unit	Total Cost
Variable costs	$18.60	$372,000
Step costs	4.25	85,000
Fixed costs	8.80	176,000
Total selling and administrative costs	$31.65	$633,000

The variable costs represent sales commissions paid at the rate of 6.2% of sales.

The step costs depend on the number of salespersons employed by the company. In August there were 17 persons on the sales force. However, 2 members have taken early retirement effective August 31. It is anticipated that these positions will remain vacant for several months.

Total fixed costs are unchanged within a relevant range of 15,000 to 30,000 units per month.

Tut is planning a sales price cut of 10%, which it expects will increase sales volume to 24,000 units per month. If Tut implements the sales price reduction, the total budgeted selling and administrative costs for the month of September would be:

☐ a. $652,760
☐ b. $679,760
☐ c. $714,960
☐ d. $759,600

Explanation: The correct answer is: **a.** $652,760.

Total budgeted selling and administrative costs in this problem can be calculated as shown:

Total Budgeted Selling and Administrative Costs = (Variable Costs)
 + (Step Costs) + (Fixed Costs)

Total Budgeted Selling and Administrative Costs = $401,760 + $75,000
 + $176,000

Total Budgeted Selling and Administrative Costs = $652,760

Rearrange the next formula to determine sales for August, then sales price per unit.

Variable Costs = (6.2%) (Sales)

Sales = (Variable Costs) / (0.062) = $372,000 / 0.062 = $6,000,000

Sales Price per Unit = (Sales) / (# Units Sold) = $6,000,000 / 20,000 = $300

Expected Sales in September = (90%) (August Sales Price per Unit)
 (September Sales Volume)
 = (0.9) (($300) (24,000) = $6,480,000

Budgeted Variable Costs = (0.062) ($6,480,000) = $401,760

Step Costs per Salesperson = $85,000 / 17 Salespeople = $5,000

Due to the retirement of two salespeople, the budgeted step costs are reduced and are calculated as shown:

Budgeted Step Costs = (15 Salespeople) ($5,000 Cost per Salesperson)
 = $75,000

Total Budgeted Selling and Administrative Costs = $401,760 + $75,000
 + $176,000

Total Budgeted Selling and Administrative Costs = $652,760

Question 1B5-CQ36

Topic: Annual Profit Plan and Supporting Schedules

Data regarding Johnsen Inc.'s forecasted dollar sales for the last seven months of the year and Johnsen's projected collection patterns are shown next.

Forecasted Sales

June	$700,000
July	600,000
August	650,000
September	800,000

October	850,000
November	900,000
December	840,000

Types of Sales

Cash sales	30%
Credit sales	70%

Collection pattern on credit sales (5% determined to be uncollectible)

During the month of sale	20%
During the first month following the sale	50%
During the second month following the sale	25%

Johnsen's budgeted cash receipts from sales and collections on account for September are:

- a. $635,000
- b. $684,500
- c. $807,000
- d. $827,000

Explanation: The correct answer is: **b.** $684,500.

The budgeted cash receipts from sales and collections on account for September are calculated as shown:

Budgeted Cash Receipts from Sales and Collections on Account, September
= (September Cash Sales) + (Collections from September Credit Sales)
+ (Collections from August Sales) + (Collections from July Sales)

September Cash Sales = (30%) (September Sales)
= (0.3) ($800,000) = $240,000

Collections from September Credit Sales = (20%) (70%) (September Sales)

Collections from September Credit Sales = (0.2) (0.7) ($800,000) = $112,000

Collections from August Sales = (50%) (70%) (August Sales)

Collections from August Sales = (0.5) (0.7) ($650,000) = $227,500

Collections from July Sales = (25%) (70%) (July Sales)

Collections from July Sales = (0.25) (0.7) ($600,000) = $105,000

Budgeted Cash Receipts from Sales and Collections on Account, September
= $240,000 + $112,000 + $227,500 + $105,000
= $684,500

Question 1B5-CQ37

Topic: Annual Profit Plan and Supporting Schedules

The Mountain Mule Glove Company is in its first year of business. Mountain Mule had a beginning cash balance of $85,000 for the quarter. The company has a $50,000 short-term line of credit. The budgeted information for the first quarter is shown next.

	January	February	March
Sales	$60,000	$40,000	$50,000
Purchases	$35,000	$40,000	$75,000
Operating costs	$25,000	$25,000	$25,000

All sales are made on credit and are collected in the second month following the sale. Purchases are paid in the month following the purchase while operating costs are paid in the month that they are incurred. How much will Mountain Mule need to borrow at the end of the quarter if the company needs to maintain a minimum cash balance of $5,000 as required by a loan covenant agreement?

- ☐ a. $0
- ☐ b. $5,000
- ☐ c. $10,000
- ☐ d. $45,000

Explanation: The correct answer is: **c.** $10,000.

The projected cash balance, without borrowing, at the end of the quarter is calculated as shown:

Projected Cash Balance, Without Borrowing, End of Quarter
= (Beginning Cash Balance) + (Projected Cash Receipts)
 − (Projected Cash Disbursements)

Beginning Cash Balance for the Quarter = $85,000

Projected cash receipts for the quarter are equal to the January sales amount, because all sales are made on credit and are collected in the second month following business.

Projected Cash Receipts for the Quarter = $60,000

Projected cash disbursements for the quarter will include the purchases from January and February (March purchases are not included, because they will be paid for in April), plus the operating costs for the months of January, February, and March.

Projected Cash Disbursements = $35,000 + $40,000 + $25,000
$$+ \$25{,}000 + \$25{,}000$$
$$= \$150{,}000$$

The projected cash balance, without borrowing, for the end of the quarter can be calculated as shown:

Projected Cash Balance, Without Borrowing, End of Quarter
= $85,000 + $60,000 − $150,000
= −$5,000

Therefore, $10,000 will have to be borrowed to maintain a minimum cash balance of $5,000.

Question 1B3-CQ05
Topic: Forecasting Techniques

Aerosub, Inc. has developed a new product for spacecraft that includes the manufacture of a complex part. The manufacturing of this part requires a high degree of technical skill. Management believes there is a good opportunity for its technical force to learn and improve as it becomes accustomed to the production process. The production of the first unit requires 10,000 direct labor hours. If an 80% learning curve is used, the cumulative direct labor hours required for producing a total of eight units would be:

- ☐ a. 29,520 hours
- ☐ b. 40,960 hours
- ☐ c. 64,000 hours
- ☐ d. 80,000 hours

Explanation: The correct answer is: **b.** 40,960 hours.

Using a cumulative average time learning curve, as the cumulative output doubles, the cumulative average direct labor hours per unit becomes the learning curve percentage times the previous cumulative average direct labor hours per unit. So, if the direct labor hours for the first unit are 10,000 and an 80% learning curve is used, the cumulative average direct labor hours for 2 units would be calculated as shown:

Cumulative Average Direct Labor Hours for 2 Units
= 0.8 (10,000 Direct Labor Hours)
= 8,000 Direct Labor Hours

When output doubles to 4 units, the cumulative average direct labor hours would be calculated as shown:

Cumulative Average Direct Labor Hours for 4 Units = 0.8 (8,000 Direct Labor Hours)
= 6,400 Direct Labor Hours

When output doubles again, this time to 8 units, the cumulative average direct labor hours would be calculated as shown:

Cumulative Average Direct Labor Hours for 8 Units = 0.8 (6,400 Direct Labor Hours)
= 5,120 Direct Labor Hours

Therefore, the cumulative direct labor hours for 8 units = (5,120 direct labor hours) (8 units) = 40,960 direct labor hours.

Question 1B3-CQ18
Topic: Forecasting Techniques

Scarf Corporation's controller has decided to use a decision model to cope with uncertainty. With a particular proposal, currently under consideration, Scarf has two possible actions: invest or not invest in a joint venture with an international firm. The controller has determined this information:

Action 1: Invest in the Joint Venture

> Events and Probabilities:
> Probability of success = 60%
>   Cost of investment = $9.5 million
> Cash flow if investment is successful = $15.0 million
> Cash flow if investment is unsuccessful = $2.0 million
> Additional costs to be paid = $0
> Costs incurred up to this point = $650,000

Action 2: Do Not Invest in the Joint Venture

> Events:
> Costs incurred up to this point = $650,000
> Additional costs to be paid = $100,000

Which one of the next alternatives correctly reflects the respective expected values of investing versus not investing?

- a. $300,000 and ($750,000)
- b. ($350,000) and ($100,000)
- c. $300,000 and ($100,000)
- d. ($350,000) and ($750,000)

Explanation: The correct answer is: **c.** $300,000 and ($100,000).

The expected value of not investing is ($100,000), since this is the additional cost that would be incurred if no investment is made.

The expected value of investing can be calculated by adding together the expected value of when the investment is successful and adding to it the expected value of when the investment is unsuccessful and then subtracting the initial investment cost.

Expected Value of Investing = (Expected Value When Successful) + (Expected Value When Unsuccessful) − (Initial Investment Cost)

Expected Value of Investing = (0.6) ($15,000,000) + (0.4) ($2,000,000) − $9,500,000

Expected Value of Investing = $9,000,000 + $800,000 − $9,500,000

Expected Value of Investing = $300,000

Note that the $650,000 in costs incurred up to this point are sunk costs and are irrelevant to the analysis.

Section C: Performance Management Answers and Explanations

Question 1C1-CQ22

Topic: Cost and Variance Measures

The following performance report was prepared for Dale Manufacturing for the month of April.

	Actual Results	Static Budget	Variance
Sales units	100,000	80,000	20,000 F
Sales dollars	$190,000	$160,000	$30,000 F
Variable costs	125,000	96,000	29,000 U
Fixed costs	45,000	40,000	5,000 U
Operating income	$20,000	$24,000	$4,000 U

Using a flexible budget, Dale's total sales-volume variance is:
- a. $4,000 unfavorable.
- b. $6,000 favorable.
- c. $16,000 favorable.
- d. $20,000 unfavorable.

Explanation: The correct answer is: **c.** $16,000 favorable.

The sales-volume variance is the difference between the static budget profit of $24,000 and the flexible budget profit at the actual volume of 100,000 sales units.

Flexible Budget Profit at 100,000 Units = Budgeted Sales − Budgeted Variable Costs − Budgeted Fixed Costs all at 100,000 Units.

Budgeted Sales = (Budgeted Price) (Actual Sales in Units)

Budgeted Sales = ($160,000 / 80,000 Units) (100,000 Units)

Budgeted Sales = $200,000

Budgeted Variable Costs = (Unit Variable Cost) (Actual Sales in Units)

Budgeted Variable Costs = ($96,000 / 80,000 Units) (100,000 Units)

Budgeted Variable Costs = $120,000

Budgeted Fixed Costs = $40,000 at Any Volume in the Relevant Range.

Flexible Budget Profit = $200,000 − $120,000 − $40,000
= $40,000

Total Sales-Volume Variance = $24,000 − $40,000
= $(16,000), or $16,000 Favorable

Question 1C1-CQ17
Topic: Cost and Variance Measures

MinnOil performs oil changes and other minor maintenance services (e. g. , tire pressure checks) for cars. The company advertises that all services are completed within 15 minutes for each service.

On a recent Saturday, 160 cars were serviced resulting in the following labor variances: rate, $19 unfavorable; efficiency, $14 favorable. If MinnOil's standard labor rate is $7 per hour, determine the actual wage rate per hour and the actual hours worked.

	Wage Rate	Hours Worked
☐ a.	$6.55	42.00
☐ b.	$6.67	42.71
☐ c.	$7.45	42.00
☐ d.	$7.50	38.00

Explanation: The correct answer is: **d.** $7.50 and 38.00.

The labor efficiency variance of $(14), or $14 favorable, is used in the next formula to determine the actual hours (AH):

Labor Efficiency Variance = (Standard Rate) (Actual Hours − Standard Hours)

$$-\$14 = (\$7) [AH - (160 \text{ Units}) (1/4 \text{ Hour per Unit})]$$
$$-\$14 = \$7(AH - 40)$$
$$-\$14 = \$7AH - \$280$$
$$-\$14 = \$7AH - \$280$$
$$\$266 = \$7AH$$
$$AH = 38$$

The labor rate variance of $19, or $19 unfavorable, is used in the next formula to determine the actual wage rate (AR):

Labor Rate Variance = (Actual Hours) (Actual Wage Rate − Standard Wage Rate)

$$\$19 = (38 \text{ Hours})(AR - \$7)$$
$$\$19 = (38 \text{ Hours})(AR - \$7)$$
$$\$19 = 38AR - \$266$$
$$\$285 = 38AR$$
$$AR = \$7.50$$

Question 1C1-CQ24

Topic: Cost and Variance Measures

Frisco Company recently purchased 108,000 units of raw material for $583,200. Three units of raw materials are budgeted for use in each finished good manufactured, with the raw material standard set at $16.50 for each completed product.

Frisco manufactured 32,700 finished units during the period just ended and used 99,200 units of raw material. If management is concerned about the timely reporting of variances in an effort to improve cost control and bottom-line performance, the materials purchase price variance should be reported as

- ☐ **a.** $6,050 unfavorable.
- ☐ **b.** $9,920 favorable.

☐ c. $10,800 unfavorable.

☐ d. $10,800 favorable.

Explanation: The correct answer is: **d.** $10,800 favorable.

The material purchase price variance is calculated as shown:

Material Purchase Price Variance = (Actual Quantity Purchased) (Actual Price)
   − (Actual Quantity Purchased) (Standard Price)

Material Purchase Price Variance = ($583,200) − (108,000 Units) ($16.50 / 3 Units)

Material Purchase Price Variance = $583,200 − $594,000
   = $(10,800) Favorable

Question 1C1-CQ18

Topic: Cost and Variance Measures

Christopher Akers is the chief executive officer of SBL Inc., a masonry contractor. The financial statements have just arrived showing a $3,000 loss on the new stadium job that was budgeted to show a $6,000 profit. Actual and budget information relating to the materials for the job are shown next.

	Actual	Budget
Bricks – number of bundles	3,000	2,850
Bricks – cost per bundle	$7.90	$8.00

Which one of the following is a **correct** statement regarding the stadium job for SBL?

☐ a. The price variance was favorable by $285.

☐ b. The price variance was favorable by $300.

☐ c. The efficiency variance was unfavorable by $1,185.

☐ d. The flexible budget variance was unfavorable by $900.

Explanation: The correct answer is: **b.** The price variance was favorable by $300.

The material price variance is calculated as shown:

Material Price Variance = (Actual Quantity Purchased)
   (Actual Price − Standard Price)

Material Price Variance = (3,000) ($7.90 − $8.00) = $(300) favorable.

The other available answer choices are incorrect. Note that the flexible budget variance includes all variable cost variances (material, direct labor, and variable overhead) as well as the fixed overhead budget variance.

Question 1C1-CQ19

Topic: Cost and Variance Measures

A company isolates its raw material price variance in order to provide the earliest possible information to the manager responsible for the variance. The budgeted amount of material usage for the year was computed as shown:

150,000 Units of Finished Goods × 3 Pounds/Unit × $2.00/Pound = $900,000

Actual results for the year were the following:

Finished goods produced	160,000 units
Raw materials purchased	500,000 pounds
Raw materials used	490,000 pounds
Cost per pound	$2.02

The raw material price variance for the year was

- ☐ a. $9,600 unfavorable.
- ☐ b. $9,800 unfavorable.
- ☐ c. $10,000 unfavorable.
- ☐ d. $20,000 unfavorable.

Explanation: The correct answer is: **c.** $10,000 unfavorable.

The raw material price variance is calculated as shown:

Raw Material Price Variance = (Actual Quantity Purchased) (Actual Price − Standard Price)

Raw Material Price Variance = (500,000) ($2.02 − $2.00)
 = $10,000 Unfavorable.

Question 1C1-CQ20

Topic: Cost and Variance Measures

At the beginning of the year, Douglas Company prepared this monthly budget for direct materials.

Units produced and sold	10,000	15,000
Direct material cost	$15,000	$22,500

At the end of the month, the company's records showed that 12,000 units were produced and sold and $20,000 was spent for direct materials. The variance for direct materials is:

- a. $2,000 favorable.
- b. $2,000 unfavorable.
- c. $5,000 favorable.
- d. $5,000 unfavorable.

Explanation: The correct answer is: **b.** $2,000 unfavorable.

The variance for direct materials is calculated as shown:

Variance for Direct Materials = (Actual Direct Material Cost) − (Budgeted Direct Material Cost at Actual Level of Production)

Variance for Direct Materials = ($20,000) − (12,000 Units) ($15,000 / 10,000 Units)

Variance for Direct Materials = $20,000 − $18,000
= $2,000 unfavorable

Question 1C1-CQ21

Topic: Cost and Variance Measures

Cordell Company uses a standard cost system. On January 1 of the current year, Cordell budgeted fixed manufacturing overhead cost of $600,000 and production at 200,000 units. During the year, the firm produced 190,000 units and incurred fixed manufacturing overhead of $595,000. The production volume variance for the year was:

- a. $5,000 unfavorable.
- b. $10,000 unfavorable.
- c. $25,000 unfavorable.
- d. $30,000 unfavorable.

Explanation: The correct answer is: **d.** $30,000 unfavorable.

The fixed overhead volume variance is calculated as shown:

Fixed Overhead Volume Variance (FOVV) = (Fixed Overhead Rate) (Normal Base Level of Production − Actual Production Level)

Fixed Overhead Rate = SRF

FOVV = (SRF) (200,000 Units − 190,000 Units)

FOVV = 10,000 SRF

The fixed overhead rate (SRF) is equal to the budgeted fixed overhead of $600,000, divided by the normal (budgeted) base of 200,000 units, which comes to $3.00 per unit.

Therefore, the FOVV = (10,000) ($3) = $30,000 unfavorable.

Question 1C1-CQ22

Topic: Cost and Variance Measures

Harper Company's performance report indicated this information for the past month:

Actual total overhead	$1,600,000
Budgeted fixed overhead	$1,500,000
Applied fixed overhead at $3 per labor hour	$1,200,000
Applied variable overhead at $0.50 per labor hour	$200,000
Actual labor hours	430,000

Harper's total overhead spending variance for the month was:

- ☐ a. $100,000 favorable.
- ☐ b. $115,000 favorable.
- ☐ c. $185,000 unfavorable.
- ☐ d. $200,000 unfavorable.

Explanation: The correct answer is: **b.** $115,000 favorable.

The overhead spending variance is calculated as shown:

Overhead Spending Variance (OSV) = (Actual Overhead) − (Budgeted Overhead at Actual Direct Labor Hours Used)

OSV = ($1,600,000) − (Budgeted Overhead at Actual Direct Labor Hours Used)

Budgeted Overhead at the Actual Direct Labor Hours Used = (Fixed Overhead) + (Actual Direct Labor Hours) (Rate of Labor Hours Used to Apply Variable Overhead)

Budgeted Overhead at the Actual Direct Labor Hours Used
= $1,500,000 + (430,000 Hours × $0.50 per Direct Labor Hour)

Budgeted Overhead at the Actual Direct Labor Hours Used
= $1,500,000 + $215,000 = $1,715,000

OSV = $1,600,000 − $1,715,000 = $(115,000) Favorable

Question 1C1-CQ23
Topic: Cost and Variance Measures

The JoyT Company manufactures Maxi Dolls for sale in toy stores. In planning for this year, JoyT estimated variable factory overhead of $600,000 and fixed factory overhead of $400,000. JoyT uses a standard costing system, and factory overhead is allocated to units produced on the basis of standard direct labor hours. The denominator level of activity budgeted for this year was 10,000 direct labor hours, and JoyT used 10,300 actual direct labor hours.

Based on the output accomplished during this year, 9,900 standard direct labor hours should have been used. Actual variable factory overhead was $596,000, and actual fixed factory overhead was $410,000 for the year. Based on this information, the variable overhead spending variance for JoyT for this year was:

- ☐ a. $24,000 unfavorable.
- ☐ b. $2,000 unfavorable.
- ☐ c. $4,000 favorable.
- ☐ d. $22,000 favorable.

Explanation: The correct answer is: **d.** $22,000 favorable.

The variable overhead spending variance is calculated as shown:

Variable Overhead Spending Variance (VOSV) = (Actual Variable Overhead) − (Budgeted Variable Overhead at the Actual Level of Direct Labor Hours Used)

VOSV = ($596,000) − (Budgeted Variable Overhead at the Actual Level of Direct Labor Hours Used)

The budgeted variable overhead at the actual level of direct labor hours used is calculated as shown:

Budgeted Variable Overhead at the Actual Level of Direct Labor Hours Used = (Variable Overhead Rate, or SRV) (Actual Direct Labor Hours Used)

Budgeted Variable Overhead at the Actual Level of Direct Labor Hours Used = (SRV) (10,300 Direct Labor Hours)

SRV = (Estimated Variable Overhead) / (Budgeted Direct Labor Hours)

SRV = ($600,000) (10,000 Budgeted Direct Labor Hours)
= $60 per Direct Labor Hour

Budgeted Variable Overhead at the Actual Level of Direct Labor Hours
= $60 (10,300 Hours)

Budgeted Variable Overhead at the Actual Level of Direct Labor Hours = $618,000

VOSV = $596,000 − $618,000 = −$22,000, or $22,000 Favorable

Question 1C1-CQ24

Topic: Cost and Variance Measures

Johnson Inc. has established per unit standards for material and labor for its production department based on 900 units normal production capacity as shown.

3 pounds of direct materials @ $4 per pound	$12
1 direct labor hour @ $15 per hour	15
Standard cost per unit	$27

During the year, 1,000 units were produced. The accounting department has charged the production department supervisor with the next unfavorable variances.

Material Quantity Variance		Material Price Variance	
Actual usage	3,300 pounds	Actual cost	$4,200
Standard usage	3,000 pounds	Standard cost	4,000
Unfavorable	300 pounds	Unfavorable	$200

Bob Sterling, the production supervisor, has received a memorandum from his boss stating that he did not meet the established standards for material prices and quantity and corrective action should be taken. Sterling is very unhappy about the situation and is preparing to reply to the memorandum explaining the reasons for his dissatisfaction.

All of the following are valid reasons for Sterling's dissatisfaction **except** that the:

- ☐ a. material price variance is the responsibility of the purchasing department.
- ☐ b. cause of the unfavorable material usage variance was the acquisition of substandard material.
- ☐ c. standards have not been adjusted to the engineering changes.
- ☐ d. variance calculations fail to properly reflect that actual production exceeded normal production capacity.

Explanation: The correct answer is: **d.** variance calculations fail to properly reflect that actual production exceeded normal production capacity.

Production variances (cost, spending, and efficiency variances) are based on *actual production volumes*. They are not based on normal production, capacity production, budgeted production, estimated production, projected production, expected production, or any other measure of production. Therefore, the difference between actual production and any other measure of production is irrelevant.

Question 1C3-AT35

Topic: Cost and Variance Measures

Teaneck Inc. sells two products, Product E and Product F, and had these data for last month:

	Product E		Product F	
	Budget	Actual	Budget	Actual
Unit sales	5,500	6,000	4,500	6,000
Unit contribution margin (CM)	$4.50	$4.80	$10.00	$10.50

The company's sales mix variance is:

- ☐ a. $3,300 favorable.
- ☐ b. $3,420 favorable.
- ☐ c. $17,250 favorable.
- ☐ d. $18,150 favorable.

Explanation: The correct answer is: **a.** $3,300 favorable.

CM = Contribution Margin

Budgeted mix:
55% E × $4.50 CM	$2.475
45% F × $10.00 CM	4.500
Per unit CM	$6.975

Actual mix:
50% E × $4.50 CM	$2.250
50% F 3 $10.00 CM	5.000
Per unit CM	$7.250

Increase in CM 0.275 × Actual Units of 12,000 = $3,300 favorable

Question 1C2-CQ17

Topic: Responsibility Centers and Reporting Segments

Manhattan Corporation has several divisions that operate as decentralized profit centers. At the present time, the Fabrication Division has excess capacity of 5,000 units with respect to the UT-371 circuit board, a popular item in many digital applications. Information about the circuit board is presented next.

Market price	$48
Variable selling/distribution costs on external sales	$5
Variable manufacturing cost	$21
Fixed manufacturing cost	$10

Manhattan's Electronic Assembly Division wants to purchase 4,500 circuit boards either internally or else use a similar board in the marketplace that sells for $46. The Electronic Assembly Division's management feels that if the first alternative is pursued, a price concession is justified, given that both divisions are part of the same firm. To optimize the overall goals of Manhattan, the minimum price to be charged for the board from the Fabrication Division to the Electronic Assembly Division should be:

- ☐ a. $21.
- ☐ b. $26.
- ☐ c. $31.
- ☐ d. $46.

Explanation: The correct answer is: **a.** $21.

The optimal transfer price is calculated as shown:

Optimal Transfer Price, T(o) = (Manufacturing Division's Opportunity Cost of Production) + (Any Avoidable Fixed Costs) + (Any Forgone Contribution from Manufacturing the Product)

The Manufacturing Division's opportunity cost of production is equal to its relevant unit variable cost per unit, or $21 in this case.

Since the Fabrication Division has excess capacity, the forgone contribution is $0.

There is no mention of avoidable fixed costs.

T(o) = $21 + $0 + $0 = $21

Question 1C3-CQ12

Topic: Performance Measures

Performance results for four geographic divisions of a manufacturing company are shown next.

Division	Target Return on Investment	Actual Return on Investment	Return on Sales
A	18%	18.1%	8%
B	16%	20.0%	8%
C	14%	15.8%	6%
D	12%	11.0%	9%

The division with the **best** performance is:

- ☐ a. Division A.
- ☐ b. Division B.

☐ **c.** Division C.

☐ **d.** Division D.

Explanation: The correct answer is: **b.** Division B.

Division B exceeded its target return on investment (ROI) by 25%, which is calculated as shown:

Percent of ROI Achieved = (Actual ROI − Target ROI) / (Actual ROI)

Percent of ROI Achieved = (20 − 16) / 16
= 25%

Divisions A and C exceeded their targets by much less. Division D's actual ROI was lower than its target ROI.

Question 1C3-CQ13

Topic: Performance Measures

KHD Industries is a multidivisional firm that evaluates its managers based on the return on investment (ROI) earned by its divisions. The evaluation and compensation plans use a targeted ROI of 15% (equal to the cost of capital), and managers receive a bonus of 5% of basic compensation for every one percentage point that the division's ROI exceeds 15%.

Dale Evans, manager of the Consumer Products Division, has made a forecast of the division's operations and finances for next year that indicates the ROI would be 24%. In addition, new short-term programs were identified by the Consumer Products Division and evaluated by the finance staff as shown.

Program	Projected ROI
A	13%
B	19%
C	22%
D	31%

Assuming no restrictions on expenditures, what is the optimal mix of new programs that would add value to KHD Industries?

☐ **a.** A, B, C, and D

☐ **b.** B, C, and D only

☐ **c.** C and D only

☐ **d.** D only

Explanation: The correct answer is: **b.** B, C, and D only.

KHD would want to invest in any project whose ROI exceeds the corporate target of 15%. Programs B, C, and D all have ROI's that exceed 15%.

Question 1C1-AT03

Topic: Cost and Variance Measures

Franklin Products has an estimated practical capacity of 90,000 machine hours, and each unit requires two machine hours. The next data apply to a recent accounting period.

Actual variable overhead	$240,000
Actual fixed overhead	$442,000
Actual machine **hours** worked	88,000
Actual finished **units** produced	42,000
Budgeted variable overhead at 90,000 machine hours	$200,000
Budgeted fixed overhead	$450,000

Of the following factors, the production volume variance is **most** likely to have been caused by:

- ☐ a. acceptance of an unexpected sales order.
- ☐ b. a wage hike granted to a production supervisor.
- ☐ c. a newly imposed initiative to reduce finished goods inventory levels.
- ☐ d. temporary employment of workers with lower skill levels than originally anticipated.

Explanation: The correct answer is: **c.** a newly imposed initiative to reduce finished goods inventory levels.

Volume variances are caused by a difference in the budgeted fixed overhead and the amount allocated on the basis of actual output. A newly imposed initiative to reduce finished goods inventory levels is consistent with the change in production compared to budget.

A wage hike would affect the spending variance, not the volume variance.

Since the volume variance in this case is unfavorable (amount allocated less than budget), acceptance of an unexpected sales order would not be correct because an unexpected sales order would increase the amount allocated.

Question 1C3-AT19

Topic: Performance Measures

Which one of the following **best** identifies a profit center?

- ☐ a. A new car sales division for a large local auto agency
- ☐ b. The Information Technology Department of a large consumer products company

- **c.** A large toy company
- **d.** The Production Operations Department of a small job-order machine shop company

Explanation: The correct answer is: **a.** A new car sales division for a large local auto agency.

A profit center is a responsibility center whose manager is responsible for revenues as well as costs. Profit is used to measure performance of a new car sales division of a local auto agency, which best identifies a profit center as it has its own costs and revenues.

Question 1C3-AT21
Topic: Performance Measures

The balanced scorecard provides an action plan for achieving competitive success by focusing management attention on key performance indicators. Which one of the following is **not** one of the key performance indicators commonly focused on in the balanced scorecard?

- **a.** Financial performance measures
- **b.** Internal business processes
- **c.** Competitor business strategies
- **d.** Employee innovation and learning

Explanation: The correct answer is: **c.** Competitor business strategies.

The critical success factors used in the balanced scorecard are:

- Financial performance
- Customer satisfaction
- Internal business processes
- Innovation and learning

Section D: Cost Management Answers and Explanations

Question 1D1-CQ02
Topic: Measurement Concepts

A company employs a just-in-time (JIT) production system and utilizes backflush accounting. All acquisitions of raw materials are recorded in a raw materials control account when purchased. All conversion costs are recorded in a control account as incurred, while the assignment of conversion costs are from an allocated conversion cost account. Company practice is to record the cost of goods manufactured at the time the units are completed using the estimated budgeted cost of the goods manufactured.

The budgeted cost per unit for one of the company's products is as shown:

Direct materials	$15.00
Conversion costs	35.00
Total budgeted unit cost	$50.00

During the current accounting period, 80,000 units of product were completed, and 75,000 units were sold. The entry to record the cost of the completed units for the period would be which of the following?

a. Work-In-Process—Control	4,000,000	
Raw Material—Control		1,200,000
Conversion Cost Allocated		2,800,000
b. Finished Goods—Control	4,000,000	
Raw Material—Control		1,200,000
Conversion Cost Allocated		2,800,000
c. Finished Goods—Control	3,750,000	
Raw Material Control		1,125,000
Conversion Cost Allocated		2,625,000
d. Cost of Goods Sold	3,750,000	
Raw Material—Control		1,125,000
Conversion Cost Allocated		2,625,000

Explanation: The correct answer is:

b. Finished Goods—Control	4,000,000	
Raw Material—Control		1,200,000
Conversion Cost Allocated		2,800,000

With JIT, there is no work-in-process inventory. To record the cost of the completed units during the period, the next entries would be made:

Credit the Raw Material—Control account for $1,200,000 (80,000 units @ $15 direct materials each) to show the transfer of raw materials to finished goods. The offsetting debit would go to the Finished Goods—Control account.

Credit the Conversion Cost Allocated account for $2,800,000 (80,000 units @ $35 conversion costs each) to show the transfer of conversion costs to finished goods. The offsetting debit would go to the Finished Goods—Control account.

In total, the Finished Goods—Control account would receive a debit in the amount of $4,000,000, which is made up of $1,200,000 of raw materials and $2,800,000 of conversion costs.

Question 1D1-CQ03

Topic: Measurement Concepts

From the budgeted data shown, calculate the budgeted indirect cost rate that would be used in a normal costing system.

Total direct labor hours	250,000
Direct costs	$10,000,000
Total indirect labor hours	50,000
Total indirect labor-related costs	$ 5,000,000
Total indirect non-labor-related costs	$ 7,000,000

- ☐ a. $20
- ☐ b. $28
- ☐ c. $40
- ☐ d. $48

Explanation: The correct answer is: **d.** $48.

The budgeted indirect cost rate per direct labor hour is calculated as shown.

Budgeted Indirect Labor Cost Rate per Direct Labor Hour
= (Budgeted Indirect Costs) / (Budgeted Direct Labor Hours)

Budgeted Indirect Labor Cost Rate per Direct Labor Hour
= ($5,000,000 + $7,000,000) / $250,000

Budgeted Indirect Labor Cost Rate per Direct Labor Hour
= $12,000,000 / $250,000

Budgeted Indirect Labor Cost Rate per Direct Labor Hour
= $48 per Direct Labor Hour

Question 1D1-CQ06

Topic: Measurement Concepts

Chassen Company, a cracker and cookie manufacturer, has these unit costs for the month of June.

Variable Manufacturing Cost	Variable Marketing Cost	Fixed Manufacturing Cost	Fixed Marketing Cost
$5.00	$3.50	$2.00	$4.00

A total of 100,000 units were manufactured during June, of which 10,000 remain in ending inventory. Chassen uses the first-in, first-out (FIFO) inventory method, and the 10,000 units are the only finished goods inventory at month-end. Using the full absorption costing method, Chassen's finished goods inventory value would be

- ☐ a. $50,000
- ☐ b. $70,000
- ☐ c. $85,000
- ☐ d. $145,000

Explanation: The correct answer is: **b.** $70,000.

The full absorption cost inventory consists of variable and fixed manufacturing costs per unit multiplied by the number of units in the inventory.

Full Absorption Cost Inventory = ($5 + $2) (10,000 Units)
= $7(10,000 Units) = $70,000

Question 1D1-CQ12

Topic: Measurement Concepts

During the month of May, Robinson Corporation sold 1,000 units. The cost per unit for May was as shown:

	Cost per Unit
Direct materials	$ 5.50
Direct labor	3.00
Variable manufacturing overhead	1.00
Fixed manufacturing overhead	1.50
Variable administrative costs	0.50
Fixed administrative costs	3.50
Total	$15.00

May's income using absorption costing was $9,500. The income for May, if variable costing had been used, would have been $9,125. The number of units Robinson produced during May was

- ☐ a. 750 units
- ☐ b. 925 units
- ☐ c. 1,075 units
- ☐ d. 1,250 units

Explanation: The correct answer is: **d.** 1,250 units.

Use the next formula to solve for the production units:

Full Absorption Cost Operating Income = (Variable Cost Operating Income) + (Fixed Manufacturing Cost per Unit) (Production Units − Sales Units)

Full absorption cost operating income is given as $9,500.

Variable cost operating income is given as $9,125.

$9,500 = $9,125 + ($1.50) (Production Units − 1,000 Units)

$9,500 = $9,125 + $1.50 (Production Units) − $1,500

$9,500 = $7,625 + $1.50 (Production Units)

$1,875 = $1.50 (Production Units)

1,250 = Production Units

Question 1D1-CQ13

Topic: Measurement Concepts

Tucariz Company processes Duo into two joint products, Big and Mini. Duo is purchased in 1,000 gallon drums for $2,000. Processing costs are $3,000 to process the 1,000 gallons of Duo into 800 gallons of Big and 200 gallons of Mini. The selling price is $9 per gallon for Big and $4 per gallon for Mini.

The 800 gallons of Big can be processed further into 600 gallons of Giant if $1,000 of additional processing costs are incurred. Giant can be sold for $17 per gallon. If the net-realizable-value (NRV) method was used to allocate costs to the joint products, the total cost of producing Giant would be:

- ☐ a. $5,600
- ☐ b. $5,564
- ☐ c. $5,520
- ☐ d. $4,600

Explanation: The correct answer is: **a.** $5,600.

The NRV of a product at split-off is its market value less the costs to complete and dispose of the product.

The NRV of Giant at split-off is calculated as shown:

NRV of Giant at Split-Off = (Market Value) − (Separable Processing Costs)

Market Value of Giant = (600 Gallons) ($17 Each) = $10,200

NRV of Giant at Split-Off = $10,200 − $1,000 = $9,200

The NRV of Mini at split-off is calculated as shown:

NRV of Mini at Split-Off = (Market Value) − (Separable Processing Costs)

NRV of Mini at Split-Off = (200 Gallons) ($4 Each) = $800

NRV of Giant and Mini = $9,200 + $800 = $10,000

Therefore, Giant's share of the joint costs is ($9,200 / $10,000) ($5,000) = $4,600.

Cost of Using NRV at Split-Off, Giant = (Separable Costs)
  + (Share of Joint Processing Costs)

Cost of Using NRV at Split-Off, Giant = $1,000 + $4,600 = $5,600

Question 1D1-CQ14
Topic: Measurement Concepts

Tucariz Company processes Duo into two joint products, Big and Mini. Duo is purchased in 1,000 gallon drums for $2,000. Processing costs are $3,000 to process the 1,000 gallons of Duo into 800 gallons of Big and 200 gallons of Mini. The selling price is $9 per gallon for Big and $4 per gallon for Mini.

If the sales value at split-off method is used to allocate joint costs to the final products, the per gallon cost (rounded to the nearest cent) of producing Big is:

- ☐ a. $5.63 per gallon
- ☐ b. $5.00 per gallon
- ☐ c. $4.50 per gallon
- ☐ d. $3.38 per gallon

Explanation: The correct answer is: **a.** $5.63 per gallon.

The per gallon cost of Big, using the relative sales value at split-off method, is calculated by finding Big's share of the joint costs and dividing it by the 800 gallons produced.

Sales Value of Big at Split-Off = (800 Gallons) ($9) = $7,200

Sales Value of Mini at Split-Off = (200 Gallons) ($4) = $800

Total Sales Value (Big + Mini) at Split-Off = $7,200 + $800 = $8,000

Big's Share of the Joint Costs = ($7,200/$8,000) ($5,000) = $4,500

Big's Cost per Gallon = $4,500 / 800 Gallons = $5.625, or $5.63 rounded

Question 1D1-CQ15
Topic: Measurement Concepts

Tempo Company produces three products from a joint process. The three products are sold after further processing as there is no market for any of the products at the split-off point. Joint costs per batch are $315,000. Other product information is shown next.

	Product A	Product B	Product C
Units produced per batch	20,000	30,000	50,000
Further processing and marketing cost per unit	$0.70	$3.00	$1.72
Final sales value per unit	$5.00	$6.00	$7.00

If Tempo uses the net realizable value method of allocating joint costs, how much of the joint costs will be allocated to each unit of Product C?

- ☐ a. $2.10
- ☐ b. $2.65
- ☐ c. $3.15
- ☐ d. $3.78

Explanation: The correct answer is: **d. $3.78.**

The joint cost per unit assigned to Product C using the net realizable value (NRV) at split-off method is calculated by taking the product's share of the joint costs of $315,000 and dividing it by the 50,000 units produced.

NRV at Split-Off for Product A = (Product A Market Value) − (Separable Costs)

NRV at Split-Off for Product A = (20,000 Units) ($5 per Unit)
 − (20,000) ($0.70 per Unit)

NRV at Split-Off for Product A = $100,000 − $14,000 = $86,000

NRV at Split-Off for Product B = (Product B Market Value) − (Separable Costs)

NRV at Split-Off for Product B = (30,000 Units) ($6 per Unit) − (30,000 Units) ($3.00 per Unit)

NRV at Split-Off for Product B = $180,000 − $90,000 = $90,000

NRV at Split-Off for Product C = (Product C Market Value) − (Separable Costs)

NRV at Split-Off for Product C = (50,000 Units) ($7 per Unit) − (50,000 Units) ($1.72 per Unit)

NRV at Split-Off for Product C = $350,000 − $86,000
 = $264,000

Sum of the Three NRVs = $86,000 + $90,000 + $264,000 = $440,000

Product C's Share of Total Costs = ($264,000 / $440,000) ($315,000) = $189,000

Product C's Cost per Unit Using NRV at Split-Off Method = $189,000/50,000 Units

Product C's Cost per Unit Using NRV at Split-Off Method = $3.78

Question 1D1-CQ16

Topic: Measurement Concepts

Fitzpatrick Corporation uses a joint manufacturing process in the production of two products, Gummo and Xylo. Each batch in the joint manufacturing process yields 5,000 pounds of an intermediate material, Valdene, at a cost of $20,000.

Each batch of Gummo uses 60% of the Valdene and incurs $10,000 of separate costs. The resulting 3,000 pounds of Gummo sells for $10 per pound.

The remaining Valdene is used in the production of Xylo, which incurs $12,000 of separable costs per batch. Each batch of Xylo yields 2,000 pounds and sells for $12 per pound.

Fitzpatrick uses the net realizable value method to allocate the joint material costs. The company is debating whether to process Xylo further into a new product, Zinten, which would incur an additional $4,000 in costs and sell for $15 per pound. If Zinten is produced, income would increase by:

- ☐ a. $2,000
- ☐ b. $5,760
- ☐ c. $14,000
- ☐ d. $26,000

Explanation: The correct answer is: **a.** $2,000.

The increase in income from producing Zinten is calculated by taking the $30,000 market value of Zinten (2,000 pounds at $15 per pound) and subtracting both the $24,000 market value of Xylo (2,000 pounds at $12 per pound) and the $4,000 in additional processing costs.

Increase in Income = $30,000 − $24,000 − $4,000 = $2,000

The joint costs and their allocation are sunk and are therefore irrelevant.

Question 1D2-CQ03

Topic: Costing Systems

Loyal Co. produces three types of men's undershirts: T-shirts, V-neck shirts, and athletic shirts. In the Folding and Packaging Department, operations costing is used to apply costs to individual units, based on the standard time allowed to fold and package each type of undershirt. The standard time to fold and package each type of undershirt is shown next.

T-shirt	40 seconds per shirt
V-neck shirt	40 seconds per shirt
Athletic shirt	20 seconds per shirt

During the month of April, Loyal produced and sold 50,000 T-shirts, 30,000 V-neck shirts, and 20,000 athletic shirts. If costs in the Folding and Packaging Department were $78,200 during April, how much folding and packaging cost should be applied to each T-shirt?

- ☐ a. $0.5213
- ☐ b. $0.6256
- ☐ c. $0.7820
- ☐ d. $0.8689

Explanation: The correct answer is: **d.** $0.8689.

The folding and packaging cost applied to each T-shirt can be calculated as shown.

Folding and Packaging Cost Applied = (40 Seconds) (Cost Rate per Second)

Cost Rate per Second = ($78,200) / (Total Seconds)

Cost Rate per Second = ($78,200) / [(50,000 T-Shirts) (40 Seconds per Shirt) + (30,000 V-Neck Shirts) (40 Seconds per Shirt) + (20,000 Athletic Shirts) (20 Seconds per Shirt)]

Cost Rate per Second = ($78,200) / (2,000,000 Seconds + 1,200,000 Seconds + 400,000 Seconds)

Cost Rate per Second = $78,200 / 3,600,000 Seconds

Cost Rate per Second = $0.0217222 per Second

Cost Applied to Each T-Shirt = (40 Seconds) (0.0217222 per Second) = $0.8689

Question 1D2-CQ04

Topic: Costing Systems

During December, Krause Chemical Company had these selected data concerning the manufacture of Xyzine, an industrial cleaner.

Production Flow	Physical Units
Completed and transferred to the next department	100
Add: Ending work-in-process inventory	10 (40% complete as to conversion)
Total units to account for	110
Less: Beginning work-in-process inventory	20 (60% complete as to conversion)
Units started during December	**90**

All material is added at the beginning of processing in this department, and conversion costs are added uniformly during the process. The beginning work-in-process inventory had $120 of raw material and $180 of conversion costs incurred. Material added during December was $540, and conversion costs of $1,484 were incurred. Krause uses the weighted-average process-costing method. The total raw material costs in the ending work-in-process inventory for December are:

- ☐ a. $120
- ☐ b. $72
- ☐ c. $60
- ☐ d. $36

Explanation: The correct answer is: **c.** $60.

The total raw material cost in the ending inventory is calculated by taking the equivalent units of raw material in the ending inventory and multiplying it by the raw material costs per equivalent unit.

Total Raw Material Cost, Ending Inventory = (Equivalent Units, Raw Material Ending Inventory) (Raw Material Costs per Equivalent Unit)

The weighted-average method assumes that all units and costs are current (i.e., there is no beginning inventory). Therefore, 110 equivalent units of raw material are required to yield a transfer-out of 100 units and 10 units in the ending inventory.

Raw Material Cost per Equivalent Unit = (Total Material Cost) / (Equivalent Units)

Raw Material Cost per Equivalent Unit = ($120 + $540) / (110 Equivalent Units)

Raw Material Cost per Equivalent Unit = $660 / 110 Units
= $6 per Unit

Therefore, the total raw material cost, ending inventory = (10 equivalent units) ($6 per unit) = $60.

Question 1D2-CQ08

Topic: Costing Systems

Oster Manufacturing uses a weighted-average process costing system and has these costs and activity during October:

Materials	$40,000
Conversion cost	32,500
Total beginning work-in-process inventory	$72,500
Materials	$700,000
Conversion cost	617,500
Total production costs—October	$1,317,500

Production completed	60,000 units
Work-in-process, October 31	20,000 units

All materials are introduced at the start of the manufacturing process, and conversion cost is incurred uniformly throughout production. Conversations with plant personnel reveal that, on average, month-end in-process inventory is 25% complete. Assuming no spoilage, how should Oster's October manufacturing cost be assigned?

	Production Completed	**Work in Process**
☐ a.	$1,042,500	$347,500
☐ b.	$1,095,000	$222,500
☐ c.	$1,155,000	$235,000
☐ d.	$1,283,077	$106,923

Explanation: The correct answer is: **c.** $1,155,000 and $235,000.

The cost of the units completed is calculated as shown:

Cost of Units Completed = (Number of Units) (Total Cost per Equivalent Unit)

Cost of Units Completed = (60,000 Units) (Total Cost per Equivalent Unit)

Because all materials are introduced at the start of the manufacturing process, the equivalent units of material for October consist of the completed units and the work-in-process units.

Equivalent Units of Material for October = (Completed Production Units)
   + (Work-in-Process Units)
   = 60,000 + 20,000 = 80,000.

The Equivalent Units for Conversion are calculated by adding together the units that were started and finished to the equivalent units that were in work-in-process inventory.

Equivalent Units for Conversion = (Units Started and Finished)
   + (% Complete for Conversion) (Ending Work-in-Process Inventory)

Equivalent Units for Conversion = (60,000) + (0.25) (20,000)
   = 65,000 Equivalent Units for Conversion

Cost per Equivalent Unit for Materials = ($40,000 + $700,000) / 80,000 Equivalent Units

Cost per Equivalent Unit for Materials = $740,000 / 80,000 Equivalent Units
   = $9.25

Cost per Equivalent Unit for Conversion = ($32,500 + $617,500) / 65,000 Equivalent Units

Cost per Equivalent Unit for Conversion = $650,000 / 65,000 Equivalent Units
= $10

Total Cost per Equivalent Unit = ($9.25 + $10) = $19.25

The cost of the 60,000 units completed would be calculated as shown:

Cost of Units Completed = (60,000 Units) ($19.25) = $1,155,000

Cost of the Ending Inventory = (Equivalent Units for Materials)
(Materials Cost per Equivalent Unit) +
(Equivalent Units for Conversion
Costs) (Conversion Cost per Equivalent Unit)

Cost of the Ending Inventory = (20,000 Equivalent Units for Materials)
($9.25 per Unit) + (5,000 Equivalent Units for
Conversion) ($10 per Unit)
= $235,000

Question 1D2-CQ10

Topic: Costing Systems

During December, Krause Chemical Company had these selected data concerning the manufacture of Xyzine, an industrial cleaner:

Production Flow	Physical Units
Completed and transferred to the next department	100
Add: Ending work-in-process inventory	10 (40% complete as to conversion)
Total units to account for	110
Less: Beginning work-in-process inventory	20 (60% complete as to conversion)
Units started during December	**90**

All material is added at the beginning of processing in this department, and conversion costs are added uniformly during the process. The beginning work-in-process inventory had $120 of raw material and $180 of conversion costs incurred. Material added during December was $540, and conversion costs of $1,484 were incurred. Krause uses the weighted-average process-costing method. The total conversion cost assigned to units transferred to the next department in December was

- ☐ a. $1,664
- ☐ b. $1,600
- ☐ c. $1,513
- ☐ d. $1,484

Explanation: The correct answer is: **b.** $1,600.

The total conversion cost assigned to the units transferred to the next department can be calculated as shown:

Total Conversion Cost Assigned to Units Transferred to Next Department
= (Number of Units Transferred) (Conversion Cost per Equivalent Unit)

Number of Units Transferred = 100

The weighted-average method assumes that all units and costs are current (i.e., there is no beginning inventory).

Therefore, the Equivalent Units for Conversion Cost
= (Units Completed) + (Units in Ending Inventory) (% Complete).

Equivalent Units for Conversion Cost = (100) + (10) (40%) = 104

Conversion Cost per Equivalent Unit = ($180 + $1,484) / 104 Equivalent Units

Conversion Cost per Equivalent Unit = $1,664 / 104 = $16 per Equivalent Unit

Total Conversion Cost Assigned to the Units Transferred to the Next Department
= (100 Units) ($16) = $1,600

Question 1D2-CQ12

Topic: Costing Systems

Waller Co. uses a weighted-average process-costing system. Material B is added at two different points in the production of shirts; 40% is added when the units are 20% completed, and the remaining 60% of Material B is added when the units are 80% completed. At the end of the quarter, there are 22,000 shirts in process, all of which are 50% completed. With respect to Material B, the ending shirts in process represent how many equivalent units?

- a. 4,400 units
- b. 8,800 units
- c. 11,000 units
- d. 22,000 units

Explanation: The correct answer is: **b.** 8,800 units.

The ending inventory of 22,000 shirts is only 50% complete. Therefore, the inventory units have only 40% of the Material B.

This equates to 8,800 equivalent units, which is calculated by multiplying the number of units in ending inventory (22,000) by the percent of Material B (40%).

Equivalent Units, Shirts = (22,000 Units) (0.4) = 8,800 Units

Question 1D2-CQ14

Topic: Costing Systems

The Chocolate Baker specializes in chocolate baked goods. The firm has long assessed the profitability of a product line by comparing revenues to the cost of goods sold. However, Barry White, the firm's new accountant, wants to use an activity-based costing system that takes into consideration the cost of the delivery person. Listed are activity and cost information relating to two of Chocolate Baker's major products.

	Muffins	Cheesecake
Revenue	$53,000	$46,000
Cost of goods sold	$26,000	$21,000
Delivery Activity		
Number of deliveries	150	85
Average length of delivery	10 minutes	15 minutes
Cost per hour for delivery	$20.00	$20.00

Using activity-based costing, which one of the following statements is correct?

- ☐ a. The muffins are $2,000 more profitable.
- ☐ b. The cheesecakes are $75 more profitable.
- ☐ c. The muffins are $1,925 more profitable.
- ☐ d. The muffins have a higher profitability as a percentage of sales and, therefore, are more advantageous.

Explanation: The correct answer is: **c.** The muffins are $1,925 more profitable.

The gross profit for muffins after assigning delivery costs would be calculated as shown:

Gross Profit, Muffins = Revenue − Cost of Goods Sold − Assigned Delivery Costs

Gross Profit, Muffins = $53,000 − $26,000 − Assigned Delivery Costs

Gross Profit, Muffins = $27,000 − Assigned Delivery Costs

The assigned delivery costs are calculated as shown:

Assigned Delivery Costs, Muffins = (Number of Deliveries) (Cost per Delivery)

Assigned Delivery Costs, Muffins = (150 Deliveries) (10 Minutes / 60 Minutes) ($20 per Hour)
= $500

Gross Profit for Muffins = $27,000 − $500 = $26,500.

The gross profit for cheesecake after assigning delivery costs would be calculated as shown:

Gross Profit, Cheesecake = Revenue − Cost of Goods Sold − Assigned Delivery Costs

Gross Profit, Cheesecake = $46,000 − $21,000 − Assigned Delivery Costs

Gross Profit, Cheesecake = $25,000 − Assigned Delivery Costs

The assigned delivery costs are calculated as shown:

Assigned Delivery Costs, Cheesecake = (Number of Deliveries) (Cost per Delivery)

Assigned Delivery Costs, Cheesecake = (85 Deliveries) (15 Minutes/ 60 Minutes) ($20 per Hour)
= $425

Gross Profit for Cheesecake = $25,000 − $425 = $24,575

The gross profit for cheesecake is $1,925 less than the gross profit for muffins.

$26,500 − $24,575 = $1,925

Question 1D2-CQ16

Topic: Costing Systems

Baldwin Printing Company uses a job order costing system and applies overhead based on machine hours. A total of 150,000 machine hours have been budgeted for the year. During the year, an order for 1,000 units was completed and incurred:

Direct material costs	$1,000
Direct labor costs	$1,500
Actual overhead	$1,980
Machine hours	450

The accountant calculated the inventory cost of this order to be $4.30 per unit. The annual budgeted overhead in dollars was:

- ☐ **a.** $577,500
- ☐ **b.** $600,000
- ☐ **c.** $645,000
- ☐ **d.** $660,000

Explanation: The correct answer is: **b.** $600,000.

The total inventory cost, or total manufacturing cost, per unit of $4.30, is made up of direct materials cost, direct labor cost, and manufacturing overhead cost.

Total Manufacturing Cost = Direct Materials Cost + Direct Labor Cost + Manufacturing Overhead Cost

Direct Materials Cost per Unit = $1,000 / 1,000 Units = $1.00 per Unit

Direct Labor Cost per Unit = $1,500 / 1,000 Units = $1.50 per Unit

Therefore,

$4.30 = $1.00 + $1.50 + Manufacturing Overhead Cost

Manufacturing Overhead Cost = $1.80 per Unit

Use the next formula to calculate the overhead rate, which you will then use to calculate the budgeted overhead cost:

Manufacturing Overhead Cost per Unit = (Machine Hours) (Overhead Rate) / (# Units)

$1.80 = (450 Machine Hours) (Overhead Rate) / (1,000 Units)

($1.80) (1,000 Units) = (450 Machine Hours) (Overhead Rate)

1,800 = (450 Machine Hours) (Overhead Rate)

Overhead Rate = 1,800 / 450 = $4

Now calculate the budgeted overhead cost:

Overhead Rate = (Budgeted Overhead Cost) / (Total Budgeted Machine Hours)

$4 = (Budgeted Overhead Cost) / (150,000 Machine Hours)

Budgeted Overhead Cost = $4 × 150,000 = $600,000

Question 1D3-CQ01

Topic: Overhead Costs

During December, Krause Chemical Company had these selected data concerning the manufacture of Xyzine, an industrial cleaner.

Production Flow	Physical Units
Completed and transferred to the next department	100
Add: Ending work-in-process inventory	10 (40% complete as to conversion)
Total units to account for	110
Less: Beginning work-in-process inventory	20 (60% complete as to conversion)
Units started during December	**90**

All material is added at the beginning of processing in this department, and conversion costs are added uniformly during the process. The beginning work-in-process inventory had $120 of raw material and $180 of conversion costs incurred. Material added during December was $540, and conversion costs of $1,484 were incurred. Krause uses the first-in, first-out (FIFO) process-costing method. The equivalent units of production used to calculate conversion costs for December was:

- ☐ a. 110 units
- ☐ b. 104 units
- ☐ c. 100 units
- ☐ d. 92 units

Explanation: The correct answer is: **d.** 92 units.

FIFO follows the actual flow of the units through the process. Therefore, the equivalent units of production used to calculate conversion costs for December can be calculated as shown:

Equivalent Units, Conversion Costs = (Units in Beginning Inventory)
(1 − Completion Rate at the Beginning of the Period) + (Units Started and Finished) + (Units in Ending Inventory) (Completion %)

Equivalent Units, Conversion Costs = (20 Units) (1 − 0.6) + (80 Units) + (10 Units) (0.4)

Equivalent Units, Conversion Costs = 8 Units + 80 Units + 4 Units = 92 Units

Question 1D3-CQ03

Topic: Overhead Costs

Cynthia Rogers, the cost accountant for Sanford Manufacturing, is preparing a management report that must include an allocation of overhead. The budgeted overhead for each department and the data for one job are shown next.

	Department	
	Tooling	**Fabricating**
Supplies	$ 690	$ 80
Supervisor's salaries	1,400	1,800
Indirect labor	1,000	4,000
Depreciation	1,200	5,200
Repairs	4,400	3,000
Total budgeted overhead	$8,690	$14,080
Total direct labor hours	440	640
Direct labor hours on Job #231	10	2

Using the departmental overhead application rates and allocating overhead on the basis of direct labor hours, overhead applied to Job #231 in the Tooling Department would be:

- ☐ a. $44.00
- ☐ b. $197.50
- ☐ c. $241.50
- ☐ d. $501.00

Explanation: The correct answer is: **b.** $197.50.

The overhead applied to Job #231 in the Tooling Department is calculated as shown:

Tooling Overhead Applied, Job #231 = (Tooling Overhead Rate) (Number of Direct Labor Hours Used by Job #231)

Tooling Overhead Rate = (Total Tooling Overhead Costs) / (Total Direct Labor Hours Used in Tooling Department)

Tooling Overhead Rate = ($8,690) / (440 Direct Labor Hours)
= $19.75 per Direct Labor Hour

Tooling Overhead Applied, Job #231 = ($19.75) (10 Direct Labor Hours) = $197.50

Question 1D3-CQ05

Topic: Overhead Costs

Atmel Inc. manufactures and sells two products. Data with regard to these products are given next.

	Product A	Product B
Units produced and sold	30,000	12,000
Machine hours required per unit	2	3
Receiving orders per product line	50	150
Production orders per product line	12	18
Production runs	8	12
Inspections	20	30

Total budgeted machine hours are 100,000. The budgeted overhead costs are shown next.

Receiving costs	$450,000
Engineering costs	300,000
Machine setup costs	25,000
Inspection costs	200,000
Total budgeted overhead	$975,000

The cost driver for engineering costs is the number of production orders per product line. Using activity-based costing, what would the engineering cost per unit for Product B be?

- ☐ a. $4.00
- ☐ b. $10.00
- ☐ c. $15.00
- ☐ d. $29.25

Explanation: The correct answer is: **c.** $15.00.

The engineering cost per unit for Product B is calculated as shown:

Engineering Cost per Unit, Product B
= [(Engineering Cost per Production Order) (Number of Production Orders for Product B)] / (Number of Units of Product B)

Engineering Cost per Production Order = ($300,000) / 30 Total Production Orders

Engineering Cost per Production Order = $10,000 per Production Order

Engineering Cost per Unit, Product B = [($10,000) (18)] / (12,000 Units)
= $15 per Unit

Question 1D3-CQ08

Topic: Overhead Costs

Logo Inc. has two data services departments (the Systems Department and the Facilities Department) that provide support to the company's three production departments (Machining Department, Assembly Department, and Finishing Department). The overhead costs of the Systems Department are allocated to other departments on the basis of computer usage hours. The overhead costs of the Facilities Department are allocated based on square feet occupied (in thousands). Other information pertaining to Logo is as shown next.

Department	Overhead	Computer Usage Hours	Square Feet Occupied
Systems	$200,000	300	1,000
Facilities	100,000	900	600
Machining	400,000	3,600	2,000
Assembly	550,000	1,800	3,000
Finishing	620,000	2,700	5,000
		9,300	11,600

Logo employs the step-down method of allocating service department costs and begins with the Systems Department. Which one of the following correctly denotes the amount of the Systems Department's overhead that would be allocated to the Facilities Department and the Facilities Department's overhead charges that would be allocated to the Machining Department?

	Systems to Facilities	Facilities to Machining
☐ a.	$0	$20,000
☐ b.	$19,355	$20,578
☐ c.	$20,000	$20,000
☐ d.	$20,000	$24,000

Explanation: The correct answer is: **d.** $20,000 and $24,000.

The amount of the Systems Department's overhead that would be allocated to the Facilities Department is calculated as follows:

Systems Department Overhead Allocated to Facilities Department
= [(Number of Facilities Computer Usage Hours) (Systems Department Overhead Cost)] / (Number of Computer Usage Hours Used by All Departments Except System)

System's Department Overhead Allocated to Facilities Department
= [(900 Hours) ($200,000)] / (9,000 Hours) = $20,000

The Facilities Department now has $120,000 to allocate to the three production departments.

The Facilities Department's overhead charges that would be allocated to the Machining Department are:

Facilities Department Overhead to Be Allocated to Machining Department
= ($120,000) (2,000 Square Feet Occupied by Machining) / (10,000 Square Feet Occupied by the Three Production Departments)

Facilities Department Overhead to Be Allocated to Machining Department
= $24,000

Question 1D3-CQ09
Topic: Overhead Costs

Adam Corporation manufactures computer tables and has this budgeted indirect manufacturing cost information for next year:

	Support Departments		Operating Departments		
	Maintenance	Systems	Machining	Fabrication	Total
Budgeted Overhead	$360,000	$95,000	$200,000	$300,000	$955,000
Support work furnished					
From Maintenance		10%	50%	40%	100%
From Systems	5%		45%	50%	100%

If Adam uses the direct method to allocate support department costs to production departments, the total overhead (rounded to the nearest dollar) for the Machining Department to allocate to its products would be which of the following?

- ☐ a. $418,000
- ☐ b. $422,750
- ☐ c. $442,053
- ☐ d. $445,000

Explanation: The correct answer is: **d.** $445,000.

The direct method of cost allocation assumes service departments serve production only. There are no interservice department services. Therefore, the total overhead for the Machining Department to allocate to its products is calculated as:

Total Overhead, Machining Department
= (Machining Department Overhead) + (Machining Department Share of Maintenance Overhead) + (Machining Department Share of Systems' Overhead)

Total Overhead, Machining Department
= ($200,000) + [(0.50) / (0.50 + 0.40)] ($360,000) + [(0.45) / (0.45 + 0.50)] ($95,000)

Total Overhead, Machining Department = $200,000 + $200,000 + $45,000
= $445,000

Section E: Internal Controls Answers and Explanations

Question 1E1-CQ01

Topic: Governance, Risk, and Compliance

A firm is constructing a risk analysis to quantify the exposure of its data center to various types of threats. Which one of the following situations would represent the highest annual loss exposure after adjustment for insurance proceeds?

	Frequency of Occurrence (years)	Loss Amount	Insurance (% coverage)
☐ a.	1	$15,000	85
☐ b.	8	$75,000	80
☐ c.	20	$200,000	80
☐ d.	100	$400,000	50

Explanation: The correct answer is: **a.** 1, $15,000, 85.

The exposure is the same as the expected loss, which is calculated by dividing 1 by the "Frequency of Occurrence," multiplying it by the loss amount, and then multiplying that by 1 minus the "Insurance % coverage" rate.

Expected Loss = (Frequency of Occurrence) (Loss Amount) (1 – % Insurance Coverage)

For answer a, the Expected Loss = (1/1) ($15,000) (1– 0.85) = $2,250.

For answer b, the Expected Loss = (1/8) ($75,000) (1– 0.8) = $1,875.

For answer c, the Expected Loss = (1/20) ($200,000) (1– 0.8) = $2,000.

For answer d, the Expected Loss = (1/100) ($400,000) (1– 0.5) = $2,000.

Answer a represents the highest annual loss exposure after adjusting for insurance proceeds.

Question 1E1-AT12

Topic: Governance, Risk, and Compliance

When management of the sales department has the opportunity to override the system of internal controls of the accounting department, a weakness exists in which of the following?

☐ a. Risk management

☐ b. Information and communication

☐ c. Monitoring

☐ d. Control environment

Explanation: The correct answer is: **d.** Control environment. The control environment includes attitude of management toward the concept of controls.

Question 1E1-AT04

Topic: Governance, Risk, and Compliance

Segregation of duties is a fundamental concept in an effective system of internal control. Nevertheless, the internal auditor must be aware that this safeguard can be compromised through

☐ a. lack of training of employees.

☐ b. collusion among employees.

☐ c. irregular employee reviews.

☐ d. absence of internal auditing.

Explanation: The correct answer is: **b.** collusion among employees.

Effective segregation of duties means that no single employee has control over authorization, recording, and custody. If two or more employees are in collusion, these controls can be overridden.

Question 1E1-AT05

Topic: Governance, Risk, and Compliance

A company's management is concerned about computer data eavesdropping and wants to maintain the confidentiality of its information as it is transmitted. The company should utilize:

☐ a. data encryption.

☐ b. dial-back systems.

☐ c. message acknowledgment procedures.

☐ d. password codes.

Explanation: The correct answer is: **a.** data encryption.

Data encryption, which uses secret codes, ensures that data transmissions are protected from unauthorized tampering or electronic eavesdropping.

Question 1E1-AT08

Topic: Governance, Risk, and Compliance

Preventive controls are:

☐ a. usually more cost beneficial than detective controls.

☐ b. usually more costly to use than detective controls.

- ☐ **c.** found only in general accounting controls.
- ☐ **d.** found only in accounting transaction controls.

Explanation: The correct answer is: **a.** usually more cost beneficial than detective controls.

The three types of controls designed into information systems are preventive, detective, and corrective. Preventive controls are designed to prevent threats, errors, and irregularities from occurring. They are more cost beneficial than detecting and correcting the problems that threats, errors, and irregularities can cause.

Question 1E1-AT10

Topic: Governance, Risk, and Compliance

Which of the following is **not** a requirement regarding a company's system of internal control under the Foreign Corrupt Practices Act of 1977?

- ☐ **a.** Management must annually assess the effectiveness of its system of internal control.
- ☐ **b.** Transactions are executed in accordance with management's general or specific authorization.
- ☐ **c.** Transactions are recorded as necessary (1) to permit preparation of financial statements in conformity with GAAP or any other criteria applicable to such statements, and (2) to maintain accountability for assets.
- ☐ **d.** The recorded accountability for assets is compared with the existing assets at reasonable intervals, and appropriate action is taken with respect to any differences.

Explanation: The correct answer is: **a.** Management must annually assess the effectiveness of its system of internal control.

Management's annual assessment of internal control is not a requirement of the Foreign Corrupt Practices Act. It became a requirement with the passage of the 2002 Sarbanes-Oxley Act.

Question 1E2-AT09

Topic: Internal Auditing

There are three components of audit risk: inherent risk, control risk, and detection risk. Inherent risk is described as:

- ☐ **a.** the risk that the auditor may unknowingly fail to appropriately modify his or her opinion on financial statements that are materially misstated.
- ☐ **b.** the susceptibility of an assertion to a material misstatement, assuming that there are no related internal control structure policies or procedures.

☐ c. the risk that a material misstatement that could occur in an assertion will not be prevented or detected on a timely basis by the entity's internal control structure policies or procedures.

☐ d. the risk that the auditor will not detect a material misstatement that exists in an assertion.

Explanation: The correct answer is: **b.** the susceptibility of an assertion to a material misstatement, assuming that there are no related internal control structure policies or procedures.

Inherent risk is the probability of an error or irregularity causing a material misstatement in an assertion. This is also referred to as the probability that a threat to the system will occur.

Question 1E3-AT11

Topic: Systems Controls and Security Measures

Which one of the following would **most** compromise the use of the grandfather-father-son principle of file retention as protection against loss or damage of master files?

☐ a. Use of magnetic tape
☐ b. Inadequate ventilation
☐ c. Storing of all files in one location
☐ d. Failure to encrypt data

Explanation: The correct answer is: **c.** Storing of all files in one location.

Storing all files in one location undermines the concept of multiple backups inherent in the grandfather-father-son principle.

Question 1E3-AT12

Topic: Systems Controls and Security Measures

In entering the billing address for a new client in Emil Company's computerized database, a clerk erroneously entered a nonexistent zip code. As a result, the first month's bill mailed to the new client was returned to Emil Company. Which one of the following would **most** likely have led to discovery of the error at the time of entry into Emil Company's computerized database?

☐ a. Limit test
☐ b. Validity test
☐ c. Parity test
☐ d. Record count test

Explanation: The correct answer is: **b.** Validity test.

A validity test compares data against a master file for accuracy. Data that cannot possibly be correct (e. g. , a nonexistent zip code) would be discovered at that time.

Question 1E3-AT07

Topic: Systems Controls and Security Measures

In the organization of the information systems function, the **most** important separation of duties is:

- ☐ a. assuring that those responsible for programming the system do not have access to data processing operations.
- ☐ b. not allowing the data librarian to assist in data processing operations.
- ☐ c. using different programming personnel to maintain utility programs from those who maintain the application programs.
- ☐ d. having a separate department that prepares the transactions for processing and verifies the correct entry of the transactions.

Explanation: The correct answer is: **a.** assuring that those responsible for programming the system do not have access to data processing operations.

The information technology (IT) function should be separate from the other functional areas in the organization. In addition, within IT, there should be a separation between programmers/analysts, operations, and technical support.

Question 1E3-AT01

Topic: Systems Controls and Security Measures

Accounting controls are concerned with the safeguarding of assets and the reliability of financial records. Consequently, these controls are designed to provide reasonable assurance that all of the following take place **except**:

- ☐ a. executing transactions in accordance with management's general or specific authorization.
- ☐ b. comparing recorded assets with existing assets at periodic intervals and taking appropriate action with respect to differences.
- ☐ c. recording transactions as necessary to permit preparation of financial statements in conformity with generally accepted accounting principles and maintaining accountability for assets.
- ☐ d. compliance with methods and procedures ensuring operational efficiency and adherence to managerial policies.

Explanation: The correct answer is: **d.** compliance with methods and procedures ensuring operational efficiency and adherence to managerial policies.

An internal control system is concerned with safeguarding assets, accuracy and reliability of records, operational efficiency, adherence to policy, and compliance with laws and regulations. The first two are called accounting controls. The latter three are referred to as administrative controls.

Question 1E2-AT02

Topic: Internal Auditing

In planning an audit, the auditor considers audit risk. Audit risk is the

- ☐ a. susceptibility of an account balance to material error assuming the client does not have any related internal control.
- ☐ b. risk that a material error in an account will not be prevented or detected on a timely basis by the client's internal control system.
- ☐ c. risk that the auditor may unknowingly fail to appropriately modify his or her opinion on financial statements that are materially misstated.
- ☐ d. risk that the auditor's procedures for verifying account balances will not detect a material error when in fact such error exists.

Explanation: The correct answer is: **c.** risk that the auditor may unknowingly fail to appropriately modify his or her opinion on financial statements that are materially misstated.

Audit risk is the probability of an audit failure. An audit failure occurs when the auditor's opinion states that the financial statements "fairly present, in all material respects, in accordance with GAAP (generally accepted accounting principles)" when, in fact, they are materially misstated.

Question 1E2-AT03

Topic: Internal Auditing

Control risk is the risk that a material error in an account will not be prevented or detected on a timely basis by the client's internal control system. The **best** control procedure to prevent or detect fictitious payroll transactions is

- ☐ a. to use and account for prenumbered payroll checks.
- ☐ b. personnel department authorization for hiring, pay rate, job status, and termination.
- ☐ c. internal verification of authorized pay rates, computations, and agreement with the payroll register.
- ☐ d. storage of unclaimed wages in a vault with restricted access.

Explanation: The correct answer is: **b.** personnel department authorization for hiring, pay rate, job status, and termination.

An independent personnel department responsible for hiring personnel, maintaining personnel records, and processing and documenting personnel terminations is a key control needed to prevent or detect fictitious personnel.

Question 1E2-AT10

Topic: Internal Auditing

Of the following, the **primary** objective of compliance testing is to determine whether

- ☐ **a.** procedures are regularly updated.
- ☐ **b.** controls are functioning as planned.
- ☐ **c.** financial statement line items are properly stated.
- ☐ **d.** collusion is taking place.

Explanation: The correct answer is: **b.** controls are functioning as planned.

A compliance audit is a review of controls to see how they conform to established laws, standards, and procedures.

Question 1E3-AT05

Topic: Systems Controls and Security Measures

A critical aspect of a disaster recovery plan is to be able to regain operational capability as soon as possible. In order to accomplish this, an organization can have an arrangement with its computer hardware vendor to have a fully operational facility available that is configured to the user's specific needs. This is **best** known as a(n)

- ☐ **a.** uninterruptible power system.
- ☐ **b.** parallel system.
- ☐ **c.** cold site.
- ☐ **d.** hot site.

Explanation: The correct answer is: **d.** hot site.

A hot site is a backup site in another location that has the company's hardware and software and is ready to run on a moment's notice.

APPENDIX A

ICMA Learning Outcome Statements—Part 1

(Revised January 2015)
Source: Institute of Certified Management Accountants

Section A. External Financial Reporting Decisions (15%—Levels A, B, and C)

Part 1—Section A.1. Financial statements

For the balance sheet, income statement, statement of changes in equity, and the statement of cash flows, the candidate should be able to:

a. identify the users of these financial statements and their needs
b. demonstrate an understanding of the purposes and uses of each statement
c. identify the major components and classifications of each statement
d. identify the limitations of each financial statement
e. identify how various financial transactions affect the elements of each of the financial statements and determine the proper classification of the transaction
f. identify the basic disclosures related to each of the statements (footnotes, supplementary schedules, etc.)
g. demonstrate an understanding of the relationship among the financial statements
h. prepare a balance sheet, an income statement, a statement of changes in equity, and a statement of cash flows (indirect method)

Part 1—Section A.2. Recognition, measurement, valuation, and disclosure

Asset valuation

The candidate must be able to:

a. identify issues related to the valuation of accounts receivable, including timing of recognition and estimation of uncollectible accounts
b. determine the financial statement effect of using the percentage-of-sales (income statement) approach as opposed to the percentage-of-receivables (balance sheet) approach in calculating the allowance for uncollectible accounts

c. distinguish between receivables sold (factoring) on a with-recourse basis and those sold on a without-recourse basis, and determine the effect on the balance sheet
d. identify issues in inventory valuation, including which goods to include, what costs to include, and which cost assumption to use
e. identify and compare cost flow assumptions used in accounting for inventories
f. demonstrate an understanding of the lower of cost or market rule for inventories
g. calculate the effect on income and on assets of using different inventory methods
h. analyze the effects of inventory errors
i. identify advantages and disadvantages of the different inventory methods
j. recommend the inventory method and cost flow assumption that should be used for a firm given a set of facts
k. demonstrate an understanding of the following security types: trading, available-for-sale, and held-to-maturity
l. demonstrate an understanding of the fair value method, equity method, and consolidated method for equity securities
m. determine the effect on the financial statements of using different depreciation methods
n. recommend a depreciation method for a given set of data
o. demonstrate an understanding of the accounting for impairment of long-term assets
p. demonstrate an understanding of the accounting for impairment of intangible assets, including goodwill

Valuation of liabilities

The candidate must be able to:

q. identify the classification issues of short-term debt expected to be refinanced
r. compare the effect on financial statements when using either the expense warranty approach or the sales warranty approach for accounting for warranties
s. define off-balance sheet financing and identify different forms of this type of borrowing

Income taxes (applies to Assets and Liabilities subtopics)

The candidate must be able to:

t. demonstrate an understanding of interperiod tax allocation/deferred income taxes
u. define and analyze temporary differences, operating loss carrybacks, and operating loss carryforwards
v. distinguish between deferred tax liabilities and deferred tax assets
w. differentiate between temporary differences and permanent differences and identify examples of each
x. indicate the proper income statement and balance sheet presentation of income tax expense and deferred taxes
y. explain the issues involved in determining the amount and classification of tax assets and liabilities

Leases (applies to Assets and Liabilities subtopics)

The candidate must be able to:

- **z.** distinguish between an operating lease and a capital lease
- **aa.** explain why an operating lease is a form of off-balance sheet financing
- **bb.** demonstrate an understanding of why lessees may prefer the accounting for a lease as an operating lease as opposed to a capital lease
- **cc.** recognize the correct financial statement presentation of operating and capital lease

Equity transactions

The candidate must be able to:

- **dd.** identify transactions that affect paid-in capital and those that affect retained earnings
- **ee.** determine the effect on shareholders' equity of large and small stock dividends, and stock splits
- **ff.** identify reasons for the appropriation of retained earnings

Revenue recognition

The candidate should be able to:

- **gg.** apply revenue recognition principles to various types of transactions
- **hh.** identify issues involved with revenue recognition at point of sale, including sales with buyback agreements, sales when right of return exists, and trade loading (or channel stuffing)
- **ii.** identify instances where revenue is recognized before delivery and when it is recognized after delivery
- **jj.** distinguish between percentage-of-completion and completed-contract methods for recognizing revenue
- **kk.** compare and contrast the recognition of costs of construction, progress billings, collections, and gross profit under the two long-term contract accounting methods
- **ll.** identify the situations in which each of the following revenue recognition methods would be used: installment sales method, cost recovery method, and deposit method
- **mm.** discuss the issues and concerns that have been identified with respect to revenue recognition practices
- **nn.** demonstrate an understanding of the matching principle with respect to revenues and expenses and be able to apply it to a specific situation

Income measurement

The candidate should be able to:

- **oo.** define gains and losses and indicate the proper financial statement presentation
- **pp.** demonstrate an understanding of the proper accounting for losses on long-term contracts

- **qq.** demonstrate an understanding of the treatment of gain or loss on the disposal of fixed assets
- **rr.** demonstrate an understanding of expense recognition practices
- **ss.** define and calculate comprehensive income
- **tt.** identify correct treatment of extraordinary items and discontinued operations

GAAP—IFRS differences

The candidate should be able to recognize major differences in reported financial results when using GAAP vs. IFRS and the impact on analysis

- **uu.** identify and describe the following differences between U.S. GAAP and IFRS: (i) revenue recognition, with respect to the sale of goods, services, deferred receipts and construction contracts; (ii) expense recognition, with respect to share-based payments and employee benefits; (iii) intangible assets, with respect to development costs and revaluation; (iv) inventories, with respect to costing methods, valuation and write-downs (e.g., LIFO); (v) leases, with respect to leases of land and buildings; (vi) long-lived assets, with respect to revaluation, depreciation, and capitalization of borrowing costs; (vii) impairment of assets, with respect to determination, calculation, and reversal of loss; and (viii) financial statement presentation, with respect to extraordinary items and changes in equity

Section B. Planning, Budgeting and Forecasting (30%—Levels A, B, and C)

Part 1—Section B.1. Strategic planning

The candidate should be able to:

- **a.** discuss how strategic planning determines the path an organization chooses for attaining its long-term goals and mission
- **b.** identify the time frame appropriate for a strategic plan
- **c.** identify the external factors that should be analyzed during the strategic planning process and understand how this analysis leads to recognition of organizational opportunities, limitations, and threats
- **d.** identify the internal factors that should be analyzed during the strategic planning process and explain how this analysis leads to recognition of organizational strengths, weaknesses, and competitive advantages
- **e.** demonstrate an understanding of how mission leads to the formulation of long-term business objectives such as business diversification, the addition or deletion of product lines, or the penetration of new markets
- **f.** explain why short-term objectives, tactics for achieving these objectives, and operational planning (master budget) must be congruent with the strategic plan and contribute to the achievement of long-term strategic goals
- **g.** identify the characteristics of successful strategic plans
- **h.** describe Porter's generic strategies, including cost leadership, differentiation, and focus

i. demonstrate an understanding of the following planning tools and techniques: SWOT analysis, Porter's 5 Forces, situational analysis, PEST analysis, scenario planning, competitive analysis, contingency planning, and the BCG Growth-Share Matrix

Part 1—Section B.2. Budgeting concepts

The candidate should be able to:

a. describe the role that budgeting plays in the overall planning and performance evaluation process of an organization
b. explain the interrelationships between economic conditions, industry situation, and a firm's plans and budgets
c. identify the role that budgeting plays in formulating short-term objectives and planning and controlling operations to meet those objectives
d. demonstrate an understanding of the role that budgets play in measuring performance against established goals
e. identify the characteristics that define successful budgeting processes
f. explain how the budgeting process facilitates communication among organizational units and enhances coordination of organizational activities
g. describe the concept of a controllable cost as it relates to both budgeting and performance evaluation
h. explain how the efficient allocation of organizational resources are planned during the budgeting process
i. identify the appropriate time frame for various types of budgets
j. identify who should participate in the budgeting process for optimum success
k. describe the role of top management in successful budgeting
l. identify best practice guidelines for the budget process
m. demonstrate an understanding of the use of cost standards in budgeting
n. differentiate between ideal (theoretical) standards and currently attainable (practical) standards
o. differentiate between authoritative standards and participative standards
p. identify the steps to be taken in developing standards for both direct material and direct labor
q. demonstrate an understanding of the techniques that are used to develop standards such as activity analysis and the use of historical data
r. discuss the importance of a policy that allows budget revisions that accommodate the impact of significant changes in budget assumptions
s. explain the role of budgets in monitoring and controlling expenditures to meet strategic objectives
t. define budgetary slack and discuss its impact on goal congruence

Part 1—Section B.3. Forecasting techniques

The candidate should be able to:

a. demonstrate an understanding of a simple regression equation
b. define a multiple regression equation and recognize when multiple regression is an appropriate tool to use for forecasting

c. calculate the result of a simple regression equation
d. demonstrate an understanding of learning curve analysis
e. calculate the results under a cumulative average-time learning model
f. list the benefits and shortcomings of regression analysis and learning curve analysis
g. calculate the expected value of random variables
h. identify the benefits and shortcomings of expected value techniques
i. use probability values to estimate future cash flows

Part 1—Section B.4. Budget methodologies

For each of the budget systems identified (annual/master budgets, project budgeting, activity-based budgeting, zero-based budgeting, continuous (rolling) budgets, and flexible budgeting), the candidate should be able to:

a. define its purpose, appropriate use, and time frame
b. identify the budget components and explain the interrelationships among the components
c. demonstrate an understanding of how the budget is developed
d. compare and contrast the benefits and limitations of the budget system
e. evaluate a business situation and recommend the appropriate budget solution
f. prepare budgets on the basis of information presented
g. calculate the impact of incremental changes to budgets

Part 1—Section B.5. Annual profit plan and supporting schedules

The candidate should be able to:

a. explain the role of the sales budget in the development of an annual profit plan
b. identify the factors that should be considered when preparing a sales forecast
c. identify the components of a sales budget and prepare a sales budget
d. explain the relationship between the sales budget and the production budget
e. identify the role that inventory levels play in the preparation of a production budget and define other factors that should be considered when preparing a production budget
f. prepare a production budget
g. demonstrate an understanding of the relationship between the direct materials budget, the direct labor budget, and the production budget
h. explain how inventory levels and procurement policies affect the direct materials budget
i. prepare direct materials and direct labor budgets based on relevant information and evaluate the feasibility of achieving production goals on the basis of these budgets
j. demonstrate an understanding of the relationship between the overhead budget and the production budget
k. separate costs into their fixed and variable components

l. prepare an overhead budget
m. identify the components of the cost of goods sold budget and prepare a cost of goods sold budget
n. demonstrate an understanding of contribution margin per unit and total contribution margin, identify the appropriate use of these concepts, and calculate both unit and total contribution margin
o. identify the components of the selling and administrative expense budget
p. explain how specific components of the selling and administrative expense budget may affect the contribution margin
q. prepare an operational (operating) budget
r. prepare a capital expenditure budget
s. demonstrate an understanding of the relationship between the capital expenditure budget, the cash budget, and the pro forma financial statements
t. define the purposes of the cash budget and describe the relationship between the cash budget and all other budgets
u. demonstrate an understanding of the relationship between credit policies and purchasing (payables) policies and the cash budget
v. prepare a cash budget

Part 1—Section B.6. Top-level planning and analysis

The candidate should be able to:

a. define the purpose of a pro forma income statement, a pro forma balance sheet, and a pro forma statement of cash flows; and demonstrate an understanding of the relationship among these statements and all other budgets
b. prepare pro forma income statements based on several revenue and cost assumptions
c. evaluate whether a company has achieved strategic objectives based on pro forma income statements
d. use financial projections to prepare a pro forma balance sheet and a pro forma statement of cash flows
e. identify the factors required to prepare medium- and long-term cash forecasts
f. use financial projections to determine required outside financing and dividend policy

Section C. Performance Management (20%—Levels A, B, and C)

Part 1—Section C.1. Cost and variance measures

The candidate should be able to:
a. analyze performance against operational goals using measures based on revenue, manufacturing costs, non-manufacturing costs, and profit depending on the type of center or unit being measured

b. explain the reasons for variances within a performance monitoring system
c. prepare a performance analysis by comparing actual results to the master budget, calculate favorable and unfavorable variances from budget, and provide explanations for variances
d. identify and describe the benefits and limitations of measuring performance by comparing actual results to the master budget
e. prepare a flexible budget based on actual sales (output) volume
f. calculate the sales-volume variance and the sales-price variance by comparing the flexible budget to the master (static) budget
g. calculate the flexible-budget variance by comparing actual results to the flexible budget
h. investigate the flexible-budget variance to determine individual differences between actual and budgeted input prices and input quantities
i. explain how budget variance reporting is utilized in a management by exception environment
j. define a standard cost system and identify the reasons for adopting a standard cost system
k. demonstrate an understanding of price (rate) variances and calculate the price variances related to direct material and direct labor inputs
l. demonstrate an understanding of efficiency (usage) variances and calculate the efficiency variances related to direct material and direct labor inputs
m. demonstrate an understanding of spending and efficiency variances as they relate to fixed and variable overhead
n. calculate a sales-mix variance and explain its impact on revenue and contribution margin
o. calculate and explain a mix variance
p. calculate and explain a yield variance
q. demonstrate how price, efficiency, spending, and mix variances can be applied in service companies as well as manufacturing companies
r. analyze factory overhead variances by calculating variable overhead spending variance, variable overhead efficiency variance, fixed overhead spending variance, and production volume variance
s. analyze variances, identify causes, and recommend corrective actions

Part 1—Section C.2. Responsibility centers and reporting segments

The candidate should be able to:

a. identify and explain the different types of responsibility centers
b. recommend appropriate responsibility centers given a business scenario
c. calculate a contribution margin
d. analyze a contribution margin report and evaluate performance
e. identify segments that organizations evaluate, including product lines, geographical areas, or other meaningful segments

f. explain why the allocation of common costs among segments can be an issue in performance evaluation
g. identify methods for allocating common costs such as stand-alone cost allocation and incremental cost allocation
h. define transfer pricing and identify the objectives of transfer pricing
i. identify the methods for determining transfer prices and list and explain the advantages and disadvantages of each method
j. identify and calculate transfer prices using variable cost, full cost, market price, negotiated price, and dual-rate pricing
k. explain how transfer pricing is affected by business issues such as the presence of outside suppliers and the opportunity costs associated with capacity usage
l. describe how special issues such as tariffs, exchange rates, taxes, currency restrictions, expropriation risk, and the availability of materials and skills affect performance evaluation in multinational companies

Part 1—Section C.3. Performance measures

The candidate should be able to:

a. explain why performance evaluation measures should be directly related to strategic and operational goals and objectives; why timely feedback is critical; and why performance measures should be related to the factors that drive the element being measured, e.g., cost drivers and revenue drivers
b. explain the issues involved in determining product profitability, business unit profitability, and customer profitability, including cost measurement, cost allocation, investment measurement, and valuation
c. calculate product-line profitability, business unit profitability, and customer profitability
d. evaluate customers and products on the basis of profitability and recommend ways to improve profitability and/or drop unprofitable customers and products
e. define and calculate return on investment (ROI)
f. analyze and interpret ROI calculations
g. define and calculate residual income (RI)
h. analyze and interpret RI calculations
i. compare and contrast the benefits and limitations of ROI and RI as measures of performance
j. explain how revenue and expense recognition policies may affect the measurement of income and reduce comparability among business units
k. explain how inventory measurement policies, joint asset sharing, and overall asset measurement policies may affect the measurement of investment and reduce comparability among business units
l. define key performance indicators (KPIs) and discuss the importance of these indicators in evaluating a firm

m. define the concept of a balanced scorecard and identify its components

n. identify and describe the perspectives of a balanced scorecard, including financial measures, customer satisfaction measures, internal business process measures, and innovation and learning measures

o. identify and describe the characteristics of successful implementation and use of a balanced scorecard

p. analyze and interpret a balanced scorecard and evaluate performance on the basis of the analysis

q. recommend performance measures and a periodic reporting methodology given operational goals and actual results

Section D. Cost Management (20%—Levels A, B, and C)

Part 1—Section D.1. Measurement concepts

The candidate should be able to:

a. demonstrate an understanding of the behavior of fixed and variable costs in the long and short terms and how a change in assumptions regarding cost type or relevant range affects these costs

b. identify cost objects and cost pools and assign costs to appropriate activities

c. demonstrate an understanding of the nature and types of cost drivers and the causal relationship that exists between cost drivers and costs incurred

d. demonstrate an understanding of the various methods for measuring costs and accumulating work-in-process and finished goods inventories

e. identify and define cost measurement techniques such as actual costing, normal costing, and standard costing; calculate costs using each of these techniques; identify the appropriate use of each technique; and describe the benefits and limitations of each technique

f. demonstrate an understanding of variable (direct) costing and absorption (full) costing and the benefits and limitations of these measurement concepts

g. calculate inventory costs, cost of goods sold, and operating profit using both variable costing and absorption costing

h. demonstrate an understanding of how the use of variable costing or absorption costing affects the value of inventory, cost of goods sold, and operating income

i. prepare summary income statements using variable costing and absorption costing

j. determine the appropriate use of joint product and by-product costing

k. demonstrate an understanding of concepts such as split-off point and separable costs

l. determine the allocation of joint product and by-product costs using the physical measure method, the sales value at split-off method, constant gross profit (gross margin) method, and the net realizable value method; and describe the benefits and limitations of each method

Part 1—Section D.2. Costing systems

For each cost accumulation system identified (job order costing, process costing, activity-based costing, life-cycle costing), the candidate should be able to:

a. define the nature of the system, understand the cost flows of the system, and identify its appropriate use
b. calculate inventory values and cost of goods sold
c. demonstrate an understanding of the proper accounting for normal and abnormal spoilage
d. discuss the strategic value of cost information regarding products and services, pricing, overhead allocations, and other issues
e. identify and describe the benefits and limitations of each cost accumulation system
f. demonstrate an understanding of the concept of equivalent units in process costing and calculate the value of equivalent units
g. define the elements of activity-based costing such as cost pool, cost driver, resource driver, activity driver, and value-added activity
h. calculate product cost using an activity-based system and compare and analyze the results with costs calculated using a traditional system
i. explain how activity-based costing can be utilized in service firms
j. demonstrate an understanding of the concept of life-cycle costing and the strategic value of including upstream costs, manufacturing costs, and downstream costs

Part 1—Section D.3. Overhead costs

The candidate should be able to:

a. distinguish between fixed and variable overhead expenses
b. determine the appropriate time frame for classifying both variable and fixed overhead expenses
c. demonstrate an understanding of the different methods of determining overhead rates, e.g., plant-wide rates, departmental rates, and individual cost driver rates
d. describe the benefits and limitations of each of the methods used to determine overhead rates
e. identify the components of variable overhead expense
f. determine the appropriate allocation base for variable overhead expenses
g. calculate the per unit variable overhead expense
h. identify the components of fixed overhead expense
i. identify the appropriate allocation base for fixed overhead expense
j. calculate the fixed overhead application rate
k. describe how fixed overhead can be over or under applied and how this difference should be accounted for in the cost of goods sold, work-in-process, and finished goods accounts

l. compare and contrast traditional overhead allocation with activity-based overhead allocation
m. calculate overhead expense in an activity-based costing setting
n. identify and describe the benefits derived from activity-based overhead allocation
o. explain why companies allocate the cost of service departments such as Human Resources or Information Technology to divisions, departments, or activities
p. calculate service or support department cost allocations using the direct method, the reciprocal method, the step-down method, and the dual allocation method
q. estimate fixed costs using the high-low method and demonstrate an understanding of how regression can be used to estimate fixed costs

Part 1—Section D.4. Supply chain management

The candidate should be able to:

a. explain supply chain management
b. define lean manufacturing and describe its central purpose
c. identify and describe the operational benefits of implementing lean manufacturing
d. define materials requirements planning (MRP)
e. identify and describe the operational benefits of implementing a just-in-time (JIT) system
f. identify and describe the operational benefits of enterprise resource planning (ERP)
g. explain the concept of outsourcing and identify the benefits and limitations of choosing this option
h. demonstrate a general understanding of the theory of constraints
i. identify the five steps involved in theory of constraints analysis
j. define throughput costing (super-variable costing) and calculate inventory costs using throughput costing
k. define and calculate throughput contribution
l. describe how capacity level affects product costing, capacity management, pricing decisions and financial statements
m. explain how using practical capacity as denominator for fixed costs rate enhances capacity management
n. calculate the financial impact of implementing the above mentioned methods

Part 1—Section D.5. Business process improvement

The candidate should be able to:

a. define value chain analysis
b. identify the steps in value chain analysis
c. explain how value chain analysis is used to better understand a firm's competitive advantage

- d. define, identify and provide examples of a value-added activity and explain how the value-added concept is related to improving performance
- e. demonstrate an understanding of process analysis and business process reengineering
- f. define best practice analysis and discuss how it can be used by an organization to improve performance
- g. demonstrate an understanding of benchmarking process performance
- h. identify the benefits of benchmarking in creating a competitive advantage
- i. apply activity-based management principles to recommend process performance improvements
- j. explain the relationship among continuous improvement techniques, activity-based management, and quality performance
- k. explain the concept of continuous improvement and how it relates to implementing ideal standards and quality improvements
- l. describe and identify the components of the costs of quality, commonly referred to as prevention costs, appraisal costs, internal failure costs, and external failure costs
- m. calculate the financial impact of implementing the above mentioned processes
- n. identify and discuss ways to make accounting operations more efficient, including process walk-throughs, process training, identification of waste and over capacity, identifying the root cause of errors, reducing the accounting close cycle (fast close), and shared services

Section E. Internal Controls (15%—Levels A, B, and C)

Part 1—Section E.1 Governance, risk, and compliance

The candidate should be able to:

- a. demonstrate an understanding of internal control risk and the management of internal control risk
- b. identify and describe internal control objectives
- c. explain how a company's organizational structure, policies, objectives, and goals, as well as its management philosophy and style, influence the scope and effectiveness of the control environment
- d. identify the Board of Directors' responsibilities with respect to ensuring that the company is operated in the best interest of shareholders
- e. identify the hierarchy of corporate governance; i.e. articles of incorporation, bylaws, polices, and procedures
- f. demonstrate an understanding of corporate governance, including rights and responsibilities of the CEO, the Board of Directors, managers and other stakeholders; and the procedures for making corporate decisions
- g. describe how internal controls are designed to provide reasonable (but not absolute) assurance regarding achievement of an entity's objectives involving (i) effectiveness and efficiency of operations, (ii) reliability of financial reporting, and (iii) compliance with applicable laws and regulations

h. explain why personnel policies and procedures are integral to an efficient control environment
i. define and give examples of segregation of duties
j. explain why the following four types of functional responsibilities should be performed by different departments or different people within the same function: (i) authority to execute transactions, (ii) recording transactions, (iii) custody of assets involved in the transactions, and (iv) periodic reconciliations of the existing assets to recorded amounts
k. demonstrate an understanding of the importance of independent checks and verification
l. identify examples of safeguarding controls
m. explain how the use of pre-numbered forms, as well as specific policies and procedures detailing who is authorized to receive specific documents, is a means of control
n. define inherent risk, control risk, and detection risk
o. define and distinguish between preventive controls and detective controls
p. describe the major internal control provisions of the Sarbanes-Oxley Act (Sections 201, 203, 302 and 404)
q. identify the role of the PCAOB in providing guidance on the auditing of internal controls
r. differentiate between a top-down (risk-based) approach and a bottom-up approach to auditing internal controls
s. identify the PCAOB preferred approach to auditing internal controls as outlined in Auditing Standard No. 5
t. identify and describe the major internal control provisions of the Foreign Corrupt Practices Act
u. identify and describe the five major components of COSO's Internal Control Framework (2013 update)
v. assess the level of internal control risk within an organization and recommend risk mitigation strategies
w. demonstrate an understanding of external auditors responsibilities, including the types of audit opinions the external auditors issue

Part 1—Section E.2 Internal auditing

The candidate should be able to:

a. define the internal audit function and identify its functions and scope
b. identify how internal auditors can test compliance with controls and evaluate the effectiveness of controls
c. explain how internal auditors determine what controls to audit, when to audit, and why
d. identify and describe control breakdowns and related risks that internal auditors should report to management or to the Board of Directors
e. define and identify the objectives of a compliance audit and an operational audit

Part 1—Section E.3 Systems controls and security measures

The candidate should be able to:

    a. describe how the segregation of accounting duties can enhance systems security

    b. identify threats to information systems, including input manipulation, program alteration, direct file alteration, data theft, sabotage, viruses, Trojan horses, theft, and phishing

    c. demonstrate an understanding of how systems development controls are used to enhance the accuracy, validity, safety, security, and adaptability of systems input, processing, output, and storage functions

    d. identify procedures to limit access to physical hardware

    e. identify means by which management can protect programs and databases from unauthorized use

    f. identify input controls, processing controls, and output controls and describe why each of these controls is necessary

    g. identify and describe the types of storage controls and demonstrate an understanding of when and why they are used

    h. identify and describe the inherent risks of using the internet as compared to data transmissions over secured transmission lines

    i. define data encryption and describe why there is a much greater need for data encryption methods when using the internet

    j. identify a firewall and its uses

    k. demonstrate an understanding of how flowcharts of activities are used to assess controls

    l. explain the importance of backing up all program and data files regularly, and storing the backups at a secure remote site

    m. define business continuity planning

    n. define the objective of a disaster recovery plan and identify the components of such a plan

Bibliography and References

American Institute of Certified Public Accountants, www.aicpa.org.

Anderson, David R., Dennis J. Sweeney, Thomas A. Williams, Jeff Camm, and R. Kipp Martin. *Quantitative Methods for Business*, 11th ed. Mason, OH: South-Western, 2010.

Arens, Alvin A., Randal J. Elder, and Mark S. Beasley. *Auditing and Assurance Services: An Integrated Approach*, 13th ed. Upper Saddle River, NJ: Prentice-Hall, 2009.

Bergeron, Pierre G. *Finance: Essentials for the Successful Professional*. Independence, KY: Thomson Learning, 2002.

Bernstein, Leopold A., and John J. West. *Financial Statement Analysis: Theory, Application, and Interpretation*, 6th ed. Homewood, IL: Irwin, 1997.

Blocher, Edward J., David E. Stout, Paul E. Juras, and Gary Cokins. *Cost Management: A Strategic Emphasis,* 6th ed. New York: McGraw-Hill, 2013.

Bodnar, George H., and William S. Hopwood. *Accounting Information Systems*, 10th ed. Upper Saddle River, NJ: Prentice-Hall, 2010.

Brealey, Richard A., Stewart C. Myers, and Franklin Allen. *Principles of Corporate Finance*, 10th ed. New York: McGraw-Hill, 2011.

Brigham, Eugene F., and Michael C. Ehrhardt. *Financial Management: Theory and Practice*, 14th ed. Mason, OH: Cengage, 2013.

Campanella, Jack, ed. *Principles of Quality Costs: Principles, Implementation, and Use,* 3rd ed. Milwaukee: ASQ Quality Press, 1999.

Committee of Sponsoring Organizations of the Treadway Commission (COSO), www.coso.org

Committee of Sponsoring Organizations of the Treadway Commission (COSO). Enterprise Risk Management—Integrated Framework, 2004.

Daniels, John D., Lee H. Radebaugh, and Daniel Sullivan. *International Business: Environments and Operations*, 14th ed. Upper Saddle River, NJ: Prentice-Hall, 2012.

Evans, Matt H. Course 11: The Balanced Scorecard, www.exinfm.com/training/pdfiles/course11r.pdf

Flesher, Dale. *Internal Auditing: Standards and Practices*. Altamonte Springs, FL: Institute of Internal Auditors, 1996.

Financial Accounting Standards Board, www.fasb.org

Financial Accounting Standards Board. *Statements of Financial Accounting Concepts*. Norwalk, CT: Author.

Forex Directory. "U. S. Dollar Charts," www.forexdirectory.net/chartsfx.html

Garrison, Ray H., Eric W. Noreen, and Peter Brewer. *Managerial Accounting,* 14th ed. Boston: McGraw-Hill/Irwin, 2011.

Gelinas, Ulric J. Jr., Richard B. Dull, and Patrick Wheeler. *Accounting Information Systems,* 9th ed. Cincinnati: South-Western College Publishing, 2011.

Gibson, Charles H. *Financial Reporting and Analysis*, 13th ed. Mason, OH: South-Western Cengage Learning, 2013.

Goldratt, Elihayu M., and Jeff Cox. *The Goal: A Process of Ongoing Improvement*, 25th anniversary revised ed. Great Barrington, MA: North River Press, 2011.

Grant Thorton, LLP, www.grantthornton.ca

Greenstein, Marilyn, and Todd M. Feinman. *Electronic Commerce: Security, Risk Management, and Control.* Boston: McGraw-Hill Higher Education, 2000.

Hildebrand, David K., R. Lyman Ott, and J. Brian Gray. *Basic Statistical Ideas for Managers*, 2nd ed. Belmont, CA: Thomson Learning, 2005.

Hilton, Ronald W., Michael W. Maher, and Frank H. Selto. *Cost Management: Strategies for Business Decisions,* 4th ed. Boston: McGraw-Hill Irwin, 2007.

Horngren, Charles T., Srikant M. Datar, and Madhav Rajan. *Cost Accounting: A Managerial Emphasis*, 14th ed. Upper Saddle River, NJ: Prentice-Hall, 2012.

Hoyle, Joe B., Thomas F. Schaefer, and Timothy S. Doupnik. *Advanced Accounting,* 10th ed. Boston: McGraw-Hill Irwin, 2010.

Institute of Internal Auditors. *International Standards for the Professional Practice of Internal Auditing,* https://na.theiia.org/standards-guidance/mandatory-guidance/Pages/Standards.aspx

Institute of Management Accountants, www.imanet.org

Institute of Management Accountants. *Enterprise Risk Management: Frameworks, Elements, and Integration.* Montvale, NJ: Author, 2006.

Institute of Management Accountants. *Enterprise Risk Management: Tools and Techniques for Effective Implementation.* Montvale, NJ: Author, 2007.

Institute of Management Accountants. *IMA Statement of Ethical Professional Practice.* Montvale, NJ: Author, 2005.

Institute of Management Accountants. *Managing Quality Improvements.* Montvale, NJ: Author, 1993.

Institute of Management Accountants. *Value and Ethics: From Inception to Practice.* Montvale, NJ: Author, 2008.

International Accounting Standards Board, www.ifrs.org

Investopedia.com, *www.investopedia.com*

Kaplan, Robert S., and David P. Norton. *The Balanced Scorecard: Translating Strategy into Action.* Boston: Harvard Business School Press, 1996.

Kaplan, Robert S., and David P. Norton. *The Strategy-Focused Organization: How Balanced Scorecard Companies Thrive in the New Business Environment.* Boston: Harvard Business School Press, 2001.

Kaplan, Robert S., and David P. Norton. "Using the Balanced Scorecard as a Strategic Management System." *Harvard Business Review* (January–February 1996).

Kieso, Donald E., Jerry J. Weygandt, and Terry D. Warfield. *Intermediate Accounting*, 14th ed. Hoboken, NJ: John Wiley & Sons, 2012.

Larsen, E. John. *Modern Advanced Accounting*, 10th ed. New York: McGraw-Hill, 2006.

Laudon, Kenneth C., and Jane P. Laudon. *Management Information Systems,* 11th ed. Upper Saddle River, NJ: Pearson Prentice Hall, 2010.

Mackenzie, Bruce, Danie Coetsee, Tapiwa Njikizana, Raymond Chamboko, Blaise Colyvas, and Brandon Hanekom. *Interpretation and Application of International Financial Reporting Standards.* Hoboken, NJ: John Wiley & Sons, 2012.

McMillan, Edward J. *Not-for-Profit Budgeting and Financial Management.* Hoboken, NJ: John Wiley & Sons, 2010.

Moeller, Robert R., *COSO Enterprise Risk Management,* 2nd ed. Hoboken, NJ: John Wiley & Sons, 2011.

Moyer, R. Charles, James R. McGuigan, and Ramesh P. Rao. *Contemporary Financial Management*, 13th ed. Mason, OH: Cengage, 2014.

MSN Money, "Currency Exchange Rates," http://investing.money.msn.com/investments/exchange-rates/

Nicolai, Loren A., John D. Bazley, and Jefferson P. Jones. *Intermediate Accounting*, 11th ed. Mason, OH: Cengage, 2010.

Olve, Nils-Göran, and Anna Sjöstrand. *The Balanced Scorecard*, 2nd ed. Oxford, UK: Capstone, 2006.

Hartgraves, Al L., and Wayne J. Morse. *Managerial Accounting*, 6th ed. Lombard, IL: Cambridge Business, 2012.

Rosenberg, Jerry M. *The Essential Dictionary of International Trade*. New York: Barnes & Noble, 2004.

Sarbanes-Oxley, www.sarbanesoxleysimplified.com/sarbox/compact/htmlact/sec406.html

Sawyer, Lawrence B., Mortimer A. Dittenhofer, and Anne Graham, eds. 2003. *Sawyer's Internal Auditing: The Practice of Modern Internal Auditing*, 5th ed. Altamonte Springs, FL: Institute of Internal Auditors, 2003.

Securities and Exchange Commission, www.sec.gov/rules/final/33-8177.htm

Shim, Jae K., and Joel G. Siegel. *Schaum's Outlines: Managerial Accounting*, 2nd ed. New York: McGraw-Hill, 2011.

Siegel, Joel G., Jae K. Shim, and Stephen W. Hartman. *Schaum's Quick Guide to Business Formulas: 201 Decision-Making Tools for Business, Finance, and Accounting Students*. New York: McGraw-Hill, 1998.

Simkin, Mark G., Jacob M. Rose, and Carolyn S. Norman. *Core Concepts of Accounting Information Systems*, 12th ed. Hoboken, NJ: John Wiley & Sons, 2012.

Stiglitz, Joseph E. *Globalization and Its Discontents*. New York: Norton, 2002.

Subramanyam, K. R., and John L. Wild, *Financial Statement Analysis,* 10th ed. New York: McGraw-Hill, 2009.

U.S. Department of Justice. Foreign Corrupt Practices Act, Antibribery Provisions, www.usdoj.gov/criminal/fraud/fcpa/guide.pdf

U.S. Securities and Exchange Commission, www.sec.gov

Van Horne, James C., and John M. Wachowicz Jr. *Fundamentals of Financial Management*, 13th ed. Harlow, UK: Pearson Education, 2008.

Warren, Carl S., James M. Reeve, and Jonathan Duchac. *Financial and Managerial Accounting*, 12th ed. Mason, OH: Cengage, 2013.

Wessels, Walter J. *Economics*, 5th ed. New York: Barron's, 2012.

XE.com, www.xe.com

Index

This index identifies the page on which a key term or concept is introduced in context. It is not meant as a comprehensive index of all references to that term or concept.

A

AAR (acceptable audit risk), 639
ABB (activity-based budgeting), 309
ABC (activity-based costing), 541, 558, 600
ABM (activity-based management), 600
Absorption costing, 506
Accelerated depreciation methods, 100
Acceptable audit risk (AAR), 639
Accounting:
   financial accounting information systems, 676
   responsibility, 425
   variable overhead, 405
Accounting changes, 186
Accounting Changes and Error Corrections (ASC Topic 250), 186
Accounting controls (IT systems), 685
Accounting system, 647
Accounts payable, 115
Accounts receivable (A/R), 48, 330
Account share, 450
Accrual basis (warranties), 119
Accumulated benefit obligation, 169
Activity analysis, 285
Activity-based budgeting (ABB), 309
Activity-based cost drivers, 500
Activity-based costing (ABC), 541, 558, 600
Activity-based management (ABM), 600
Activity cost driver, 541
Activity method, 99

Actual costing, 503
Actual fixed overhead, 406
Actual variable overhead, 403
Alliances, 251
Allowance method, 51
Amortization, 111
Analytical evidence (audits), 667
Anticipation checks, 686
Application controls, 676, 685
Applied fixed overhead, 406
Applied variable overhead, 403
A/R (accounts receivable), 48, 330
Artistic intangibles, 110
Attribute standards, 662
Audit committee, 644
Audit evidence, 666
Authoritative budget, 279
Authoritative standards, 283
Available-for-sale securities, 81
Average cost method, 66

B

Backflush costing, 546
Balanced scorecard (BSC), 263, 446
Balance pattern, 330
Balance sheet:
   in financial statements, 30
   pro forma, 334, 350
Balance sheet approach (allowance method), 51
BAR (business process reengineering), 597
Bargaining leverage, 241

Base technologies, 246
Basic earnings per share (EPS), 148
Batch balancing, 687
Batch controls, 686
Batch-level activities, 542
Batch totals, 685
BCG Growth-Share matrix, 269
BCP (Business continuity planning), 683
Beginning inventory, 526
Bench marking, 285, 598
Best practices, 603
Best practice analysis, 603
Bonds, 124
Bonus obligations, 118
Bottom-up budget, 279
BSC (balanced scorecard), 263, 446
Budget, 273
   activity-based, 309
   authoritative, 279
   capital, 288, 328
   cash, 329
   continuous, 311
   cost of goods manufactured and sold, 325
   cost of goods sold, 325
   direct labor, 323
   direct materials, 322
   financial, 288, 320, 327
   flexible, 394
   incremental, 310
   master, 286, 287, 307, 319
   non-manufacturing costs, 326
   operating, 288, 320
   overhead, 324
   participative, 279
   production, 321
   and pro forma statement, 347
   project, 308
   rolling, 311
   sales, 320
   selling and administrative expense, 326
   static, 392, 394
   and strategic plans, 261
   zero-based, 310
Budgetary control, 273
Budget cycle, 274
Budgeted fixed overhead, 406

Budgeting, 273
   activity-based, 309
   flexible, 312
   zero-based, 310
Business combinations, 187
Business Combinations (ASC Topic 805), 111, 187
Business continuity planning (BCP), 683
Business process improvement, 605
Business process reengineering (BPR), 597
Business unit profitability analysis, 438
By-products, 509, 514

C
Callable bonds, 125
Capacity, 498, 583
   practical, 498
   theoretical, 498
Capacity utilization:
   master budget, 499
   normal, 499
Capital:
   corporate, 135
   paid-in, 140
Capital budget, 288, 328
Capital lease obligation, 163
Capital leases, 162
Capital stock, 137
Cash, 46
Cash basis (warranties), 118
Cash budget, 329
Cash disbursements, 329
Cash discounts, 49, 65
Cash equivalents, 46
Cash excess or deficiency, 329
Cash flow hedge, 191
Cash receipts, 329
Cause-and-effect relationships, 448
Centers:
   cost, 426
   investment, 426
   profit, 426
   revenue, 426
Channel crowding, 240
Channel stuffing, 154
Check digit, 687
Circumstantial evidence (audits), 667
Clearing account, 688

Combined financial statements, 188
Combined statement of income, 161
Committed cost, 496
Common cost, 429
Common cost allocation, 429
Compatibility principle, 642
Compensated absences, 118
Compensating balance, 47
Compensating controls, 651
Compensation–Retirement Benefits (ASC Topic 715), 169
Compensation—Stock Compensation (ASC Topic 718), 142, 181
Competitive analysis, 268
Completed-contact method, 158
Compliance audit, 668
Composite methods (depreciation), 102
Comprehensive income, 161
Comprehensive Income (ASC Topic 220), 26
Computer access controls, 679
Conflicts of interest, 654
Consigned goods, 64
Consolidated financial statements, 188
Consolidation (ASC Topic 810), 188
Contingencies, 37
Contingencies for Gain and Loss (ASC Topic 450), 120
Contingency planning, 265
Contingent liabilities, 120
Continuous budget, 311
Continuous improvement, 603
Contract intangibles, 110
Contractual situations, 38
Contribution margin, 427, 439
Contribution margin cost allocation method, 562
Contribution reporting, 427
Controls, information system, 676
Control activities, 640
Control environment, 640, 643
Control principle, 642
Control procedures, 647
Control risk (CR), 638
Conversion costs, 527
Convertible bonds, 125
Corporate capital, 135
Corporate governance, 642
Corrective controls, 651

Cost(s), 495
  committed, 496
  discretionary, 496
  fixed, 496
  step, 497
  total (mixed), 498
  variable, 496
Cost approach (fair value), 46
Cost-benefit principle, 642
Cost center, 426
Cost driver(s), 399, 499, 592
  activity-based, 500
  executional, 502
  structural, 501
  volume-based, 500
Cost flow assumptions, 65
Costing systems, 521
Cost method, 139
Cost of goods available for sale or use, 63
Cost of goods manufactured and sold budget, 325
Cost of goods sold, 63
Cost of goods sold budget, 325
Cost of quality analysis, 604
Cost recovery method, 155
Cost standards, 283
CR (control risk), 638
Cumulative average-time learning model, 298
Current liabilities, 114
Customer intangibles, 110
Customer-level activities, 543
Customer profitability analysis, 440

D

Data analysis, 291
Data backup (IT systems), 683
Data encryption, 682
DBR (drum-buffer-rope) system, 579
Debt securities, 79, 88
Decision theory, 292
Declining balance method, 101
Deductible amount, 174
Deep-discount bonds, 125
Deferred tax assets, 174
Deferred tax liabilities, 174
Departmental overhead rate, 558
Depletion accounting, 107

Deposit method, 156
Depreciation, 98
Derivatives, 191
Derivatives and Hedging (ASC Topic 815), 191
Detection risk (DR), 638
Detective controls, 650
Differentiation, of products/services, 240
Diluted earnings per share (EPS), 150
Direct costing, 506
Directive controls, 651
Direct labor budget, 323
Direct materials budget, 322
Direct materials usage budget, 322
Direct method, 34, 562
Direct profit, 439
Direct write-off method, 51
Disaster recovery policies and procedures (IT systems), 684
Disclosures, to financial statements, 35, 37, 172
Discontinued operations, 29, 183
Discretionary cost, 496
Distinguishing Liabilities from Equity (ASC Topic 480), 138
Dividends, 144
Dollar-value LIFO, 70
DR (detection risk), 638
Drum-buffer-rope (DBR) system, 579

E

Earnings per share (EPS), 148
Effective interest rate method (bond valuation), 128
Effectiveness, 392
Efficiency, 391, 649
Efficiency variance, 401
Elements of Financial Statements (SFAC No. 6), 114
Employee stock ownership plans (ESOPs), 141
Enterprise Resource Planning (ERP), 576
EPS (earnings per share), 148
Equity securities, 82, 88
Equity share options, 142
Equivalent unit (EU), 526
Equivalent unit (EU) costing, 529
ERP (Enterprise Resource Planning), 576

Error corrections, 186
ESOPs (employee stock ownership plans), 141
EU (Equivalent unit), 526
Executional cost drivers, 502
Exercise price (stock), 181
Expected value, 300
Expense recognition, 160
Expense warranty approach (warranties), 119
External auditor responsibility, under SOX, 645
External customers, 595
External users, of financial statements, 40
Extraordinary items, 29, 185

F

Facility controls (IT systems), 681
Facility-sustaining activities, 542
Factory overhead budget, 324
Fair value, 45
Fair-value hedge, 191
Fair Value Measurement (IFRS no. 13), 46
Fair Value Measurements and Disclosures (ASC Topic 820), 45
Favorable variance, 392
FCPA (Foreign Corrupt Practices Act), 649
Feedback controls, 685
Feedforward controls, 685
FIFO (first-in, first-out), 67, 528
Financial accounting information systems, 676
Financial audit, 667
Financial budget, 288, 320, 327
Financial reporting, reliability of, 648
Financial statements, 25
 limitations of, 36
 users of, 40
Financing, 329
Financing activity, 35, 335
Firewalls, 683
First-in, first-out (FIFO), 67, 528
Fixed cost, 496
Fixed overhead, 406, 553
Fixed overhead costs, 553
Flexibility principle, 642
Flexible budgeting, 312, 394
Flexible budget variance, 396

Flowcharting, 689
Footnotes, to financial statements, 37
Forecasts, 278
Forecasting, 291
Foreign Corrupt Practices Act (FCPA), 649
Foreign currency hedge, 192
Full costing, 506
Full cost (absorption) model, 431

G

Gain contingencies, 120
Globalization, 250
Global organization, 251
Goods in transit, 64
Goodwill, 110, 111
Governance, corporate, 642
Grandfather-father-son (GFS) method, 684
Grant date (stock), 181
Gross method, 49
Gross profit method, 77, 511
Group methods (depreciation), 102

H

Hardware controls (IT systems), 681
High-low method, 556
Historical cost, 36, 91
Historical data, 285

I

Ideal standard, 283
If-converted method, 150
Impairment:
    goodwill tested for, 112
    of intangibles, 113
    of PP&E, 104
    of value, 88
Impairment of Assets (IAS No. 36), 198
Imputed interest, 123
Income:
    comprehensive, 161
    net, 440
Income approach (fair value), 46
Income before taxes, 439
Income statement:
    in financial statements, 26
    pro forma, 327, 348
Income statement approach (allowance method), 52

Income Taxes (ASC Topic 740), 174
Income taxes payable, 117
Incremental budget, 310
Incremental cost allocation method, 429
Incremental method, 143
Incremental unit-time learning model, 297
Independence and objectivity standard, 662
Indirect method (cash flows), 34
Information and communication (in COSO model), 641
Information system, 647
Information system controls/security, 676
Inherent risk (IR), 638
Input controls, 686
Installment sales method, 155
Intangible assets, 109, 196
Intangible Assets (IAS No. 38), 196
Intangibles—Goodwill and Other (ASC Topic 350), 111
Interactive edits, 687
Interest (ASC Topic 835), 50
Interest-bearing notes, 115
Interest expense, 170
Intermediate product, 430
Internal audit function, 644
Internal auditing, 661
Internal business process measures, 451
Internal capability analysis, 252
Internal control(s):
    inherent limitations on, 654
    methods of, 651
    types of, 650
Internal Control–Integrated Framework, 639
Internal control structure, 642
Internal customers, 594
Internal users, of financial statements, 40
Intrusion detection system, 683
Inventories (IAS No. 2), 196
Inventory, 61
Inventory levels, in process costing, 538
Investing activity, 34, 335
Investment center, 426
Investments: Debt and Equity Securities (ASC Topic 320), 79
Investments—Equity Method and Joint Ventures (ASC Topic 323), 84
IR (inherent risk), 638

J

JIT (just-in-time) system, 546, 574
Job order costing, 522
Joint costs, allocated to joint products, 510
Joint products, 509
   accounting treatment of, 514
   allocating joint costs to, 510
Joint ventures, 251
Just-in-time (JIT) system, 546, 574

K

Kaizen, 603
Kanban, 575
Key technologies, 246

L

LANs (local area networks), 681
Last-in, first-out (LIFO), 68
LCM (lower of cost or market) rule, 75
Lean manufacturing, 572
Learning curve analysis, 297
Leases, 162
Leases (ASC Topic 840), 162
Leases (IAS No. 17), 197
Legal factors, and strategic planning, 237
Liabilities:
   contingent, 120
   current, 114
   long-term, 122
Life-cycle costing, 545
LIFO (last-in, first-out), 68
LIFO liquidation, 69
LIFO reserve, 70
Linear regression analysis, 292
Local area networks (LANs), 681
Long-term liabilities, 122
Long-term planning, 286
Loss contingencies, 120
Lower of cost or market (LCM) rule, 75

M

Maintenance (IT systems), 681
Malware, 682
Management by exception method, 398
Management override, 654
Management responsibility, under SOX, 644
Manufacturing, lean, 572
Manufacturing overhead costs, 64
Marketable securities, 47
Market approach (fair value), 46
Market expectations and strategic decisions, 285
Market forces, 239
Marketing intangibles, 109
Market price model, 430
Market share, 450
Market value, 48
Master budget, 286, 287, 307, 319
Master budget capacity utilization, 499
Materials requirements planning (MRP), 572
Measurement, 495
Message acknowledgment, 682
Mission statement, 259
Misstated ending inventory, 74
Misstated purchases and inventory, 74
Mixed costs, 498
Mix ratio, 413
Mix variance, 413
MNC (Multinational corporation), 251
Model building, 291
Modular testing, 680
Monitoring (in COSO model), 641
Mortgage notes payable, 123
MRP (materials requirements planning), 572
Multinational companies, 433
Multinational corporation (MNC), 251
Multiple regression analysis, 292, 295

N

Negotiated price model, 430
Net income, 440
Net method (cash discounts), 49
Net realizable value (NRV), 51, 75
Net realizable value (NRV) method, 512
Network controls (IT systems), 681
Noncash transactions, 37
Non-manufacturing costs budget, 326
Nontrade receivables, 48
Normal capacity utilization, 499
Normal costing, 503
Notes issued at face value, 123
Notes issued for property, goods, and services, 123
Notes not issued at face value, 123

Notes payable, 115, 122
Notes receivable, 48, 53
Notes to Financial Statements (ASC Topic 235), 38
NRV (Net realizable value), 51, 75
NRV (net realizable value) method, 512

O

Objectives, 260
Off-balance-sheet financing, 124
Off-balance-sheet information, 37
Operating activity, 33, 335
Operating budget, 288, 320
Operating income variance, 392
Operating information systems, 676
Operational audit, 668
Operational controls, 652
Operational plan, 261
Operation costing, 545
Organizational controls, 651, 678
Outcome measures, 448
Output controls, 688
Outsourcing, 577
Overhead budget, 324
Overhead costs, 553

P

Pacing technologies, 246
Paid-in capital, 140
Parallel testing, 680
Participative budget, 279
Participative standards, 283
Partnerships, 251
Par value method, 139
Payroll deductions, 117
Pension plans, 168
Percentage-of-completion method, 157, 160
Percentage-of-sales method, 348
Performance drivers, 448
Performance measures, 437
Performance measurement reports, 432
Performance standards, 663
Period costs, 65
Permanent differences, 177
Personnel management, controls for, 652
Personnel policies, for information systems, 678
PEST analysis, 268

Physical measure method, 513
Pilot testing, 680
Plant-wide overhead rate, 558
Point-of-sale recognition, 154
PP&E (property, plant, and equipment), 90
Practical capacity, 498, 583
Predicted variable overhead, 403
Preferred stock, 138
Preformatted screens, 687
Presentation of Financial Statements (ASC Topic 205), 183
Pretax financial income, 173
Preventive controls, 650, 685
Price sensitivity, 241
Price (rate) variance, 400
Primary evidence (audits), 666
Process, 596
Process analysis, 596
Process costing, 522, 525, 538
Processing controls, 687
Process reengineering, 596
Product costs, 65
Production budget, 321
Production Cost Report, 527
Product profitability analysis, 437
Product-sustaining activities, 542
Proficiency and due professional care standard, 662
Profitability analysis:
    business unit, 438
    customer, 440
    product, 437
Profit centers, 426
Pro forma statements, 274
    assessing anticipated performance with, 353
    balance sheet, 334, 350
    and budgets, 347
    cash disbursements schedule, 330
    cash receipts schedule, 330
    income statement, 327, 348
    sensitivity analysis, 355
    statement of cash flows, 335, 352
Project budgets, 308
Projected benefit obligation, 169
Promissory notes, 53
Property, Plant, and Equipment (ASC Topic 360), 104

Property, Plant, and Equipment (IAS No. 16), 197
Property, plant, and equipment (PP&E), 90
Proportional method, 143
Prototypes (IT system), 680
Purchased intangibles, 110
Purpose, authority, and responsibility standard, 662

Q
Quality assurance (IT systems), 680
Quality assurance and improvement programs standard, 662

R
Rate variance, 400
R&D (research and development), 113
Reasonably attainable standard, 284
Reciprocal method, 565
Recommendations, of internal audits, 665
Redundant data checks, 686
Regression analysis, 292
Regression coefficient, 294
Regulatory factors, and strategic planning, 237
Relative sales value method, 76
Relevant range, 495
Research and Development (ASC Topic 730), 113
Research and development (R&D), 113
Residual income (RI), 443
Resource allocation, 286
Responsibility accounting, 425
Restricted cash, 47
Retail inventory method, 78
Return on assets (ROA), 442
Return on equity (ROE), 442
Return on investment (ROI), 441
Revenue centers, 426
Revenue recognition, 153
Revenue Recognition (ASC Topic 605), 106, 156
Rework, 525
RI (residual income), 443
Risk, 637
  definition of, 637
  with information systems, 676
  types of, 638

Risk assessment, 640
ROA (return on assets), 442
ROE (return on equity), 442
ROI (return on investment), 441
Rolling budget, 311
Routing verification procedures, 682
R-squared, 294
Run-to-run totals, 687

S
Safeguarding of assets, 648
Sale agreements, 64
Sale budget, 320
Sales forecast, 320
Sales taxes payable, 117
Sales value at split-off method, 510
Sales volume variance, 396, 410
Sales warranty approach (warranties), 119
Sales with buyback agreements, 64, 154
Sarbanes-Oxley Act of 2002 (SOX), 644
SBU (strategic business unit), 438
SCARE (acronym), 648
Scenario planning, 268
Scrap, 525
SE (standard error of estimate), 295
Secondary evidence (audits), 666
Secured bonds, 125
Security, information system, 676
Segment margin, 428
Segment reporting, 192, 428
Segment Reporting (ASC Topic 280), 192, 193
Segregation of duties/functions (in IT), 678
Self-imposed budget, 279
Selling and administrative expense budget, 326
Sensitivity analysis, 355
Service costs, 170
Service department cost allocation, 560
Service period (stock), 181
Short-term objectives, 287
Simple regression analysis, 292
Single-rate cost allocation method, 561
Situational analysis, 267
Social responsibility, 248
SOX (Sarbanes-Oxley Act of 2002), 644
Specific goods pooled LIFO approach, 70

Specific identification method, 66
Spoilage, 524, 541
Stakeholder analysis, 249
Stakeholders, 247
Stand-alone cost allocation, 429
Standards, 283
Standard costing, 283, 398, 506
Standard error of estimate (SE), 295
Standard input, 399
Statement of cash flows, 33
Statement of cash flows, pro forma, 335, 352
Static budget, 392, 394
Static budget variance, 396
Step cost, 497
Step-down method, 563
Stock options, 181
Stock rights, 143
Stocks:
    capital, 137
    issuance of, 135
    as payment for PP&E, 95
    preferred, 138
    treasury, 138
Straight-line method, 99
Strategic business unit (SBU), 438
Strategic goals, 260
Strategic planning, 233
Strategic plans, 278
Structural cost drivers, 501
Subsequent events, 38
Substitution method, 96
Sum-of-the-years'-digits method, 100
Supply chain, 592
Supply chain management, 571
Suspense file, 689
Switching costs, 240
SWOT analysis, 254, 447
Systems development controls (IT), 679

T

Tactical goals, 260
Taxable amount, 174
Taxable income, 173
Technological changes, 244
Technological intangibles, 110
Temporary differences, 173
Theoretical capacity, 498, 583

Theory of constraints (TOC), 578
Tickler file, 688
Top-down budget, 279
Total cost (mixed cost), 498
Total quantity variance, 412
T.O.W.S matrix, 256
Trade discounts, 49
Trade loading, 154
Trade receivables, 48
Trading securities, 80
Trailer label, 688
Transaction controls, 685
Transfer pricing, 430
Transfer pricing models, 430
Transferred-in costs, 534
Transfers and Servicing (ASC Topic 860), 60
Treasury stock, 138
Treasury stock method, 151
T-value, 295

U

Unfavorable variance, 392
Unfound records tests (validity tests), 686
Unit-level activities, 542
Units-of-production method, 513
Unsecured bonds, 125

V

Vacation rule, 679
Value, 591
Value activities, 592
Value added, 595
Value chain, 592
Value chain analysis (VCA), 591
Value propositions, 449
Variable costing, 496, 506
Variable cost model, 430
Variable overhead accounting, 405
Variable overhead costs, 554
Variable overhead efficiency variance, 404
Variable overhead spending variance, 403
Variance, 391
Variance analysis in nonmanufacturing organizations, 419
Variances for fixed overhead, 406
VCA (value chain analysis), 591
Vested benefit obligation, 169

Vesting date (stock), 181
Virtual private networks (VPNs), 682
Virus protection, 682
Vision statement, 258
Voiding/cancellation controls, 685
Volume-based cost drivers, 500
VPNs (virtual private networks), 682

W
WAN (wide area network), 681
Warranties, 118

Warrants, 142
Weighted-average method, 530
Wide area network (WAN), 681

Y
Yield variance, 413
Y intercept, 294

Z
Zero-based budgeting, 310
Zero-interest-bearing notes, 115